Alban and Sergius

Alban *and* Sergius

The Story of a Journal

Aidan Nichols OP

GRACEWING

First published in England in 2018
by
Gracewing
2 Southern Avenue
Leominster
Herefordshire HR6 0QF
United Kingdom
www.gracewing.co.uk

No part of this publication may be reproduced, stored in a retrieval system, or transmitted in any form or by any means, electronic, mechanical, photocopying, recording or otherwise, without the written permission of the publisher.

The right of The Trustees of the English Province of the Order of Preachers
to be identified as the author of this work
has been asserted in accordance with
the Copyright, Designs and Patents Act 1988.

© 2018 The Trustees of the English Province of the Order of Preachers

ISBN 978 085244 937 0

Typeset by Word and Page, Chester, UK

Cover design by Bernardita Peña Hurtado

We are not in exile; we are on a mission
Dmitri Sergeevich Merezhkovsky

In commemoration

of the ninetieth anniversary of

The Fellowship of St Alban and St Sergius

1928–2018

CONTENTS

Preface ix

PART I: THE ENCOUNTER OF EAST AND WEST: THE FIRST FORTY YEARS OF THE JOURNAL SOBORNOST

1. The Beginnings 3
2. The Story 25
3. Discovering the Russians 55
4. Assessing Anglicanism 73
5. Forming a Spirituality 93
6. An Interest in Art 119
7. The Sophia Affair 133
8. Writing Theology 145
9. Ecumenical Prospects 189

PART II: A VOICE FOR ORTHODOXY: THE LAST FIFTY YEARS OF THE JOURNAL SOBORNOST

1. The Continuing Story 235
2. The Wider East 289
3. Anglicans and Latins, and their Critics 323
4. The Dialogues 361
5. Commending the Liturgy 399
6. The Icon Again 411
7. The Rise of Green Orthodoxy 425
8. Looking Ahead 431

Notes 445

Bibliography 511

Icon on front cover:

St Alban, Protomartyr of Britain

and

St Sergius, Abbot of Radonezh

PREFACE

Of the Fellowship of St Alban and St Sergius there might be said on a smaller English scale what one eminent student of the Russian Diaspora has claimed for the 'Paris School', so many of whose teachers crossed the Channel to participate in Fellowship events. 'It was an opportunity for Russian Orthodoxy to speak with a voice never heard as powerfully before in the western world. Russian Orthodoxy was also offered a chance to break out of its nationalist isolation and provincialism in a sustained encounter with the Christian West.'[1] From the date of its foundation in 1928 the *Journal of the Fellowship of St Alban and St Sergius*, later *Sobornost*, sought to strike a good balance between Western and Eastern contributions to Christian thought. If, in significant part, this had changed by 1968 (when, despite the occasional meander into 1969, Part One of *Alban and Sergius* terminates) that was because enough members or at any rate office-holders in the Fellowship had been persuaded by writers such as Vladimir Lossky, Olivier Clément and Christos Yannaras that the Western tradition had taken too many wrong turnings to be a reliable guide for Christian theology at large. The marriage, in 1979, of *Sobornost* with the *Eastern Churches Review*, which in principle reinforced the Anglican element in the Fellowship's publication with a Roman Catholic one, did not reverse this direction.

On my reading, the 1970s would open a second principal stage in the history of the journal where the meeting of East and West would be increasingly on the East's terms—and, in another striking development, this meant the Greek East rather than the Russian. Hence my Part Two, 'A Voice for Orthodoxy. The Last Fifty Years of the Journal *Sobornost*'. By the start of the twenty-first century, *Sobornost* was fast becoming, especially through its mediation of modern Greek philosophy, theology and spirituality, as well as the more traditional discipline of Byzantine studies, a largely monophonic voice for Orthodoxy in the West. This was a far cry from its origins, even if that voice was also much needed in an often disoriented English, European and North American Christianity.

If the likelihood of organic union between the Anglican Communion and Orthodoxy has, at the present time, receded to vanishing-point, it is all the more important to rehearse the lively hopes of an earlier epoch. Insofar as at that epoch the Church of England (and other episcopally ordered Western ecclesial communities) stood, in the annals of the Fellowship, for the Church of the West at large, the same is more or less true for the Roman Catholic Communion, whose current dialogue with the Orthodox is beset with difficulties, which, if different in character, are no less than those in the Orthodox dialogue with Anglicans. In any case, the contents of *Sobornost* for those first four decades (1928–68) provide an intellectual and spiritual feast to which I have sought to do justice in these pages. Yet I am conscious that, with so many riches spread before me, I could hardly represent them all.

The aim of Part One, 'The Encounter between East and West. The First Forty Years of *Sobornost*', then, is to show how the *Journal of the Fellowship of St Alban and St Sergius*—*Sobornost*'s original name—came into existence and flourished. 'Encounter' between Eastern and Western Christians was sealed in a compact. As with all successful compacts, both partners—the 'East' and the 'West'—were looking for something they needed. The exiled Orthodox intelligentsia of the Russian Diaspora, and their Russian-speaking students, needed a sympathetic audience and friends. They found a receptive audience in England (and, through the Paris Group, in France), impressed not only by the tale of their vicissitudes in Revolution and Civil War, but also, and more importantly, by their theological, philosophical, historical and social ideas. English Anglicans, faced with a lively Free Church movement and a renascent Roman Catholicism, needed like-minded ecumenical partners in the global Church. They found in the Russians a traditional Church, with a national-ethnic tradition, a powerful liturgy, and a rich spirituality that drew on ancient sources. The Russian Church seemed if not always to mirror then at any rate to complement the qualities of Catholic-minded Anglicanism at home.

True, the non-Orthodox membership of the Fellowship was never limited to Anglo-Catholics—or, since some High Church Anglicans eschewed that label—to 'Anglican Catholics'. There were always a few Church of England clergy or laity of other 'parties', including, in the early years, some strict (but, evidently, open-minded) Evangelicals. There were occasional Presbyterians, Methodists and other Protestants—indeed, on the evidence of Nicolas Zernov's reminiscences, the whole

Preface

idea of the Fellowship was initially suggested by a Presbyterian with the uncompromisingly Reformation surname of 'Tyndal'. The Fellowship had offshoots in the Scandinavian Lutheran State Churches as well, and a sister organization north of the Border in largely Presbyterian Scotland. But while one strand of thinking in the Fellowship insisted that the Orthodox should not be corralled into meeting only Catholic Anglicans, but must be exposed to the full range of Church of England opinion, the strength of the Fellowship lay nonetheless in the affinities between the Orthodox and the Catholic party in the English Church. From the side of official Orthodoxy, the only way that 'Reunion', the organic integration of the Russian and English Churches, could possibly be feasible, was for the Catholic view of Anglican origins and identity to spread and leaven the whole lump. That—assuming the resultant 'Catholicism' was expressed in a way consonant with Orthodox and not just (or even rather than) Roman doctrine—would have made possible the unconditional recognition of Anglican orders and full sacramental communion. In the late 1920s and 1930s, the time of the great Anglo-Catholic congresses, that would not have seemed an unrealistic hope.

By the end of the 1960s and the beginning of the 1970s, the decline of the Anglo-Catholic movement in the Church of England had rendered this hope forlorn. The Neo-Liberal theology of the 1960s 'both undermined and unsettled many Anglican Catholics, and also found a home in some quarters. It was a disturbing phenomenon for churchmen who in any case were struggling with their own problems of identity and purpose, and were beginning to have a collective sense of insecurity and uncertainty about their distinctive beliefs and their special role and function within the Church of England.'[2] The reforms of the Second Vatican Council (1962–5) had a disorienting effect not only on the Church of Rome but also on Anglo-Catholics, who had looked to the Counter-Reformation for much of their liturgical, intellectual and spiritual inspiration. In 1968 the Lambeth Conference resolved that the theological arguments concerning the ordination of women were inconclusive, and by 1978 the Anglican Churches of Canada, the United States and New Zealand had admitted women to the priesthood, thereby abandoning what had been in matters sacramental (or, at least, ministerial) a shared patrimony of Anglicans and Orthodox. The traditional sexual ethics was also in retreat in much of Anglicanism, and in the (supposedly anonymous) Preface to *Crockford's Clerical Directory* for 1987–8, the Anglo-Catholic Gareth Bennett (prior to taking his own life) deplored the way Anglican theologians were distancing themselves from Scripture and the Fathers as prescriptive sources for doctrine. In 1990 the formation of the movement 'Affirming Catholicism' ratified these trends by re-defining Tradition in remarkably flexible terms.

This is why the succeeding history of *Sobornost*—the next five decades (1968–2018)—was inevitably to be the story of its transformation. It moved from being a journal where Western and Eastern (above all, Anglican and Russian Orthodox) interests were at parity to a publication that was reinventing itself as a 'voice for Orthodoxy' for an English-speaking public attracted to, or otherwise interested in, the Orthodox Church for its own sake. This transformation was only gradual. It was slowed by the emergence of the official bilateral dialogues between the Orthodox and the Anglican Communion and, rather later, between the Orthodox and Rome. But by the end of the period covered by this book the metamorphosis was pretty complete. Hence the title I have given to Part Two, 'A Voice for Orthodoxy. The Last Fifty Years of the Journal *Sobornost*'. This did not invalidate the history of the journal or of the Fellowship. It had always been the case that obtaining information about the Western Churches was, for obvious reasons, easier for Western readers and members. The provision of information about the Eastern Churches, and especially the Byzantine or Chalcedonian Orthodox, was always the more important part of both Fellowship and journal. It continued to carry out that task admirably, and no doubt will do so for many years to come.

I would not have been able to carry out this work without the help of Archpriest Stephen Platt of the Moscow Patriarchal parish of St Nicholas in Oxford, who kindly supplied me with the wherewithal so to do, in the form of an electronic version of the *Journal* and *Sobornost*, and access to the Fellowship archives. It has been a work of love, conscious as I am of how much I gained in my undergraduate years and while a student-friar in the Dominican Order from attendance at the Liturgy at 1 Canterbury Road, meetings of the Oxford branch of the Fellowship there, and a Fellowship conference at High Leigh. I retain the warmest memories of Nicolas and Militza Zernov, and of my tutor in monastic and patristic theology (and examiner, many moons ago, of my doctoral thesis), Metropolitan Kallistos of Diokleia, who also appears in these pages.

Blackfriars, Cambridge
Feast of Saints Cyril and Methodius, 2018

PART I

THE ENCOUNTER OF EAST AND WEST:

THE FIRST FORTY YEARS OF THE JOURNAL *SOBORNOST*

→ 1 ←

The Beginnings

In the beginning was a redoubtable couple. Nicolas Zernov was a Muscovite, the son of a physician, an émigré of the early Bolshevik period, and the first Spalding Lecturer in Eastern Christian Studies in the University of Oxford, into which post he had been ushered thanks to his winning gifts as a lecturer on the Orthodox Church—and, in France, energetic organizer of the Russian Student Christian Union in exile.[1] His wife Militza, née Lavrova, was a Civil War emigrant from Tiflis to Paris, a university-trained physician and later consultant in oral surgery to the London hospitals.[2] In a shared memoir of the Fellowship of St Alban and St Sergius in its earliest years, looking back from the vantage-point of 1979, Nicolas and Militza ascribed its origins—'paradoxically', as they admitted—to the work of Vladimir Ilyich Lenin. It 'would not have been founded without the catastrophe of the Leninist victory in 1917 and the ensuing massive exodus of Russian emigrants'.[3]

A pertinent memoir

Exiled Russian Christians, among whom the Orthodox were naturally predominant and Orthodox thinkers and scholars disproportionately represented, sought out willing hearers for a message which concerned not only the perils of Bolshevism for any Christian culture or Church. Their message was also about the spiritual and theological riches available to the West from a Russia that, in the years immediately preceding the Revolutions of 1917, had experienced a remarkable 'religious renaissance'.[4] And, for some (it must be said, rather atypical) Orthodox, among whom Nicolas Zernov was outstanding, the encounter with the West meant the possibility of learning from separated Western Christians. When Western Christians, above all, as it turned out, Anglicans, seemed suitably disposed, there might even be the possibility of working towards some form of sacramental union, at any rate of a partial and provisional kind.

Although the Fellowship attracted a small number of Anglican Evangelicals and Free Churchmen, it was in its first decades above all a love-affair between High Anglicans and the Russian Orthodox, whether in England, or, where the numerical strength of the Russian Diaspora lay—namely, in France and more specifically at Paris, which circling round St George's, the embassy church, had a substantial English 'expatriate' colony of its own. The days had yet to come when Roman Catholics—and especially Eastern-rite Roman Catholics—could be considered in this connexion, for the coldness of Rome was proverbial as it looked with displeasure at the nascent ecumenical movement, by its origin a Protestant and Anglican affair to which various Orthodox Churches gradually acceded. And indeed the dislike of Roman Catholicism on the part of many High Anglicans—less so of Anglo-Catholics like T. S. Eliot practising liturgically the 'Western Use'—was more than equalled by the longstanding animosities (not all, by any manner of means, without foundation), which steeled the Orthodox against any temptation to resume relations with Rome, a see which had regularly called for their 'return' and a resumption of 'obedience'.

The Anglican–Orthodox background

Quite rightly, the Zernovs emphasized the episodic yet far from nugatory pre-history of relations between the Church of England and the 'Chalcedonian' Orthodox Churches of the East. In particular they emphasized two moments.

The first of these was the interest in the Eastern Orthodox Church shown by a number of the seventeenth-century English divines. Appeal to the 'old authors' or, less vaguely, the 'most ancient Doctors of the Church', seen as useful corroborators of biblical teaching, had not been unknown even among the English Reformers, notably Thomas Cranmer and John Jewel.[5] A Church of England canon of 1571 forbad preaching anything 'save what is agreeable to the teaching of the Old or New Testament, and what the catholic fathers and ancient bishops have collected from this same doctrine'.[6] But this was combined with acceptance of influence from the Continental (and especially the Swiss) Reformers. Not that the Orthodox were necessarily aware of such Anglican interest in the Fathers—or that any sympathy between early Protestants and the East was reciprocated. During the reign of King James I and VI, a short-lived English scholarship programme for the Greeks would scarcely have been possible unless a semi-Calvinist had been occupying the see of Constantinople.[7]

The later Jacobean and Caroline divines went considerably further than their Anglican predecessors in reverent exploration of the writings of the Greek Fathers and the texts of the Oriental liturgies. Some of this was in the new editions that had been arriving from the Continent since the sixteenth century. The Civil War, which itself was essentially a war of religion, concentrated minds. Among Royalist Anglicans exiled during the Interregnum, and then at the Restoration when both king and Churchmen returned, this generated some interest in encountering the Eastern Church on the ground. That was not easy, except for consular officials.[8] Overall, in Michael Ramsey's words, 'The study of the Fathers created the desire to reach out to Eastern Christendom'.[9] Yet such contacts as took place, whether clerical or lay,[10] were strictly limited, and, truth to tell, they were sometimes unamiable and unadmiring—unless, that is, they could furnish the enquirers with arguments against Rome.

The sympathy shown to the Orthodox by Anglican authorities in England also had its limits.[11] As with the short-lived Greek College in Oxford (1699–1705), the offer of higher education to Orthodox students was sometimes fuelled by the hope they would return to their homes bearing with them the sober piety of the English Church.[12] These sporadic encounters would culminate in the abortive union negotiations between the 'Non-Jurors'—Church of England bishops ejected from their sees for refusal to take the Oath of Allegiance to the Dutch Calvinist William III—and various Orthodox hierarchs or authorities in the Ottoman and Russian empires in the years 1716 to 1725.[13] So much for the first 'moment'.

The second 'moment' the Zernovs underlined was the impetus given by Tractarianism.[14] Tractarianism was the catholicizing Anglicanism of the Oxford Movement (named after the polemical re-call to patristic origins of the 'Tracts for the Times'), hugely influential as this became in the Church of England—often under its sobriquet of 'Puseyism', since, after John Henry Newman's secession to Rome, Edward Bouverie Pusey, Professor of Hebrew at Oxford, became its chief champion. That influence reached its high water mark in the 1920s and 1930s, thanks especially to Tractarianism's successor movement, Anglican Ritualism or 'Anglo-Catholicism'.

The contacts made in Russia in the early 1840s by a major Tractarian figure, William Palmer of Magdalen College, Oxford;[15] the unfinished project of writing a history of the Eastern patriarchates by the hymnographer and founder of religious life for women, John Mason Neale; the 1867 visit to Russia of Henry Parry Liddon, Pusey's successor as effective leader of the Oxford Movement, who travelled there accompanied by Charles Dodgson of *Alice in Wonderland* fame:[16] such straws in the wind anticipated the Anglo-Catholic founding of an 'Eastern Church Association' in 1863–4 and the creation in 1906 of an 'Anglican and Eastern Orthodox Churches Union'. On the eve of the First World War these two bodies merged as the 'Anglican and Eastern Churches Association'. In due course their expertise would prove useful to the Fellowship.

An article in the June 1945 issue of *Sobornost* by Henry Brandreth sketched out the history of such 'Anglican Eastern Associations'. The 'movers' in the founding of the first of these, the Eastern Church Association, were all younger-generation Tractarians. There was Liddon himself, about to become a residentiary canon of St Paul's Cathedral and Dean Ireland Professor of Exegesis at Oxford; John Wordsworth, Oriel Professor of the Interpretation of Scripture at Oxford and later bishop of Salisbury; Thomas Thelluson Carter, the founder of the Community of St John the Baptist at Clewer, one of the earliest Tractarian sisterhoods; George Williams, sometime Anglican chaplain at St Petersburg, who edited the correspondence between the Eastern patriarchs and the Nonjurors.[17]

And, almost at the end of his life as he was, there was Neale, whose *History of the Eastern Church* Brandreth rightly calls 'the first large and sympathetic work on the subject to be published in English'.[18] Neale's biographer Michael Chandler, citing a comment by Williams in the introductory material to the posthumous volume of the *History*, eloquently described Neale's 'sacred cause'. It was 'the gradual approximation and ultimate reconciliation of the long-estranged families of Catholic Christendom, on the basis of a better mutual understanding'.[19] And, looking ahead to the creation of the Fellowship of St Alban and St Sergius, though without explicit mention of its name, Chandler went on, 'In the event, it was not until the dispersion of many Russian Orthodox after the First World War that contacts between the East and Anglicanism became sufficiently commonplace for ecumenical contacts to be developed on a meaningful scale; notable in this respect were the arrivals in the west of exiled Russian Orthodox thinkers such as Nicholas Berdyaev and Serge

Bulgakov. However, in the nineteenth century Neale's studies of the Eastern church brought to the knowledge of English readers an awareness of a branch of Catholicism about which they could not elsewhere have gained adequate information.'[20]

The ignorance was mutual. Hitherto Orthodox churchmen had been somewhat suspicious of Anglicans owing to the strongly Protestant and indeed proselytizing mindset of such bodies as the Church Missionary Society and the Bible Society in their various outposts in the Near East. But a change in attitude was coming, thanks to the advent not only of a more emphatically Catholic-minded Anglicanism but also to the sheer accumulation of reliable information about the Orthodox world. In the latter regard, the Occasional Papers produced by the Eastern Church Association were helpful. But Williams's death in 1878 caused a hiatus.

In 1893 the Association was revived, chiefly through the efforts of Wordsworth, now bishop of Salisbury, and Arthur Cayley Headlam, later bishop of Gloucester and a major figure in early- and mid-twentieth-century ecumenism. The survivors of the Eastern Church Association in effect joined forces with another organization, the 'Committee for the Defence of Church Principles in Palestine'. Headlam acted as secretary to a revived body, whose refreshed leadership included such luminaries as W. J. Birkbeck, dubbed the 'English Slavophile' for his Russophilia,[21] William Bright, who was Regius Professor of Ecclesiastical History at Oxford, Canon T. A. Lacey, a robust apologist for Anglican claims, and Athelstan Riley, a wealthy and active Anglo-Catholic layman with fingers in many pies.

In this group, Headlam was a key figure for the future, at any rate so far as Church officialdom was concerned. Brought up in a Tractarian household, he had become a disciple of the leading luminary of 'Liberal Catholicism'. This was Charles Gore, the founder of the Community of the Resurrection, and bishop of Birmingham (from which see he was later translated to Oxford). Headlam must count as an academic heavyweight. A Fellow of All Souls, he had specialized in Coptic variants of the New Testament, and other early Christian Egyptian material. He sought to mediate between the 'old Catholic school', i.e. Tractarianism, and 'the modern critical school', i.e. Liberal Catholicism.[22] His real initiation into the Christian East came in the years 1890–1, when he accompanied the Roman historian Sir William Ramsay on a very demanding field trip to Asia Minor, followed by a journey of his own to Greece (including Mount

Athos), and Egypt (where he interviewed Coptic clergy and visited the surviving monastic settlements). The tour generated a written report for the archbishop of Canterbury on Church conditions in the countries he had visited. Part of Headlam's material derived from information from American missionaries, Congregationalist in Asia Minor, Presbyterian in Egypt. Their methods, which could galvanize the ancient Churches but also split them, attracted both his admiration and his dismay. He recommended a different approach: inviting Eastern Church students to come to England for theological training and sending select Anglican teachers to the Middle East. Headlam's 1894 report as secretary of the Eastern Church Association defined the 'ultimate object' of the Association as 'Church reunion'—a daring step—while also cautioning against any attempt to move too quickly. The building up of friendship and the dissemination of knowledge were crucial, while the Association's agents must remain in any location only 'so long as they can commend themselves to and work harmoniously with the English Bishop there'.[23] There were elements here that foreshadowed the Fellowship of St Alban and St Sergius—but the emphasis on official status was not among them.

With the revival of the Association, the publication of relevant material resumed. In 1894 there appeared A. J. Maclean's *The East Syrian Daily Offices*, a pioneering venture in making known that particular liturgical tradition through the medium of English.[24] It was followed in 1895 by Birkbeck's *Russia and the English Church during the Last Fifty Years*.[25] In the mid-1890s the Association sent the Reverend H. T. F. Duckworth to Cyprus, where over a period of years he made a study of the Cypriot Church; his 1901 *Greek Manuals of Church Doctrine* would be an important source for Western students of contemporary Orthodoxy.[26] Headlam's 1897 pamphlet *The Teaching of the Russian Church*, for whose writing he learned Russian, and the article on 'The Church of England and the Eastern Churches', which he contributed in 1900 to a collection of essays on 'Church Problems', were reprinted in 1909 in his own *History, Authority and Theology*.[27] His biographer, Ronald Jasper, describes Headlam's position as follows. 'The theological position of the two Churches [i.e. Anglican and Orthodox] was in many ways strikingly similar'—in regard especially to the appeal to Scripture and Tradition, teaching on the sacraments, the use of the Nicene Creed (leaving aside the *Filioque* issue where, Headlam thought, the West was wrong to have added a clause unilaterally, but the East was also wrong in stigmatizing its content as heretical).[28] Headlam noted how it served the interests of the Church of England that the East 'bore vigorous witness against the uncatholic and unhistorical claims of the Roman Catholic Church', and represented like the Church of England the 'National Church' idea.[29]

It was not surprising, therefore, that 'when... the Lambeth Conference of 1908 requested the Archbishop of Canterbury to appoint a permanent Committee "to take cognizance of all that concerns our relations with the Churches of the Orthodox East", Headlam was one of those from whom Dr Davidson sought advice as to the best way of implementing the resolution.'[30] But before that conference opened, there was, as of 1906, another body in the field. In that year Henry Joy Fynes-Clinton, better known as an 'Anglican Papalist' (and creator of the Ionian splendour, thus hailed in Eliot's *The Waste Land*, of St Magnus the Martyr, London Bridge), had founded the Anglican and Eastern Orthodox Churches Union.[31] Unlike the Eastern Church Association, the Union restricted its interest to ecclesial bodies in communion with Constantinople. Also unlike the Association, it understood its Anglican aspect internationally. The Union encouraged the holding of worship services in which Anglicans and Orthodox might take part. Such worship would become a regular and essential feature of the Fellowship's life and apostolate.

In 1914, as the Zernovs noted, the two organizations—the Eastern Church Association and the Anglican and Eastern Orthodox Churches Union—came together as the 'Anglican and Eastern Churches Association', with the younger body effectively absorbing the older. In due course the new entity established a journal of its own, *The Christian East*, though its publication was somewhat erratic (1920 to 1928 and 1950 to 1954).

The First World War saw some significant advance in Anglican–Orthodox relations. After the fall of Serbia in December 1915, Headlam, by then Regius Professor of Divinity at Oxford, arranged for Serbian Orthodox ordinands to study at theological colleges at Cuddesdon and Dorchester-on-Thames, both situated in Oxfordshire villages. Some went on to read for a degree, living at St Stephen's House in the city of Oxford, where they were looked after by Walter Frere, Gore's successor as superior of the Community of the Resurrection and the Fellowship's first Anglican president. Serbian Orthodox, in the shape of four monks, a priest and some laymen, were taken in by the Community of the Resurrection at its mother house at Mirfield in Yorkshire and others in the Community's London house.[32]

Headlam's immediately post-War study *The Doctrine of the Church and Christian Reunion* outlined the basic ecumenical principles from which he personally never deviated and which might reasonably be called 'classically Anglican' in character.³³ Reunion with the Orthodox (or with any other non-Anglican body) should be built on the 'Lambeth Quadrilateral': its four pillars were Scripture, the historic Creeds, Baptism and Eucharist, the historic episcopate. So far as the Orthodox were concerned, the notion that, beyond these, no further confessional tests ought to be required fell at the first fence. In 1918 negotiations began with the somewhat controversial figure, in contemporary and later Orthodox circles, of Metropolitan Meletios Metaxakis of Athens. Later ecumenical patriarch, from 1921 to 1923, and, after his resignation, patriarch of Alexandria from 1926 to 1935, Metaxakis had been a strong supporter of the Allied Powers in the Great War. He now visited America and England in the hope of forging closer collaboration with the Anglican Communion—a hope not unconnected with the position of strength the United States and the British Empire enjoyed as victorious powers. Casting aside his customary caution, Randall Davidson had agreed to help his attempt to secure Hagia Sophia for the Orthodox after the defeat of Ottoman Turkey—but only by writing a private letter to Arthur Balfour, then Foreign Secretary, whose reply was not encouraging. But various meetings arranged for the Greek bishop in New York, Oxford and London moved Davidson to set up under Gore's chairmanship an 'Eastern Churches Committee', the first official Anglican entity of its kind. It would fulfil, however belatedly, the wish of the 1908 Lambeth Conference. In this context, Headlam and the liturgical historian Frank Edward Brightman, a Fellow of Magdalen College, Oxford, and the editor of the *Journal of Theological Studies*, received a joint mandate to draw up terms of possible 'intercommunion' with the Orthodox. Only lightly modified by the Eastern Churches Committee, the 'Suggested Terms of Intercommunion', reflecting Headlam's ecumenical doctrine, appeared in 1921. They were immediately challenged by the most knowledgeable of contemporary Anglicanism's ecclesiastical bureaucrats. This was Canon J. A. Douglas, later the first general secretary of the Archbishop's Council for Foreign Relations. 'Douglas was most emphatic that both reunion and intercommunion were impossible without full dogmatic union', and the official report of the Orthodox delegation from the patriarchate of Constantinople to the 1920 Lambeth Conference (it appeared in English in *The Christian East* for March 1922) 'undoubtedly gave support to Douglas' point of view'.³⁴

The Beginnings

In 1921 the patriarchal election in Constantinople was disputed, and both sides appealed to Davidson, who explained his inability to intervene—but pressed Lord Curzon (Balfour's successor as Foreign Secretary) not to accede to the Turkish demand at the Lausanne Peace Conference that the patriarchate should be removed from Constantinople altogether. The price to be paid for that concession was the abdication of Meletios IV, a Venizelist who had supported the Greek invasion of Anatolia after the war ended. This was a setback to Anglican hopes, for in May 1922 he had nominated an *apokrisarios*, or permanent official representative, to Canterbury. In Douglas's opinion—and, thanks to his increasing influence at Lambeth, his view came to prevail—the first step toward Anglican-Orthodox union would have to be what was termed 'economic' (broadly speaking, conditional) recognition of Anglican orders. This, Douglas thought, might be forthcoming if a large body of Anglican clergy signed a statement indicating they considered themselves priests in the same sense as the Orthodox clergy.[35] The resultant Declaration, made in the name of the 'Catholic Societies' in the Church of England, appeared in the British Press on 26 May 1922. It differed from the suggested terms by its more 'Catholic' (and thus for the most part Orthodox) character on a range of issues. But, with most unfortunate timing, a report of the Anglican-Free Church Conferences on Church Unity, with a very different message for its readers, had appeared just four days before. As Jasper comments, 'it must have seemed incredible to many people—not least to the Orthodox church—that both could come from the Church of England at the same time.'[36] Headlam was especially incensed at seeing Gore's name heading the list of the Declaration's signatories (which included three other members of Archbishop Davidson's committee), and he threatened the primate with resignation. The Declaration, he objected, was inconsistent with Anglican teaching, 'a travesty of the English Church dressed up in the clothes of the Eastern Church.'[37] He was dissuaded with some difficulty; Gore removed his name from the head of the list, but not from the list as such. But in any case, as George Bell (during the Second World War a celebrated bishop of Chichester but at this time Davidson's private secretary), wrote to Headlam, 'Communications have just been received from Constantinople to the effect that as the Orthodox authorities have heard of the controversy in England with regard to the declaration, they can no longer treat it as having significance for the purpose of what is described as "Economic Intercommunion".'[38]

Yet owing, it seems, to the work of Greek-speaking Orthodox theologians behind the scenes, 'economic' recognition of Anglican Orders *was* in fact granted by the Ecumenical Throne in July 1922 and acceded to by the patriarchate of Jerusalem and the autocephalous Church of Cyprus in the early months of 1923. Evidently these bodies did not represent a pan-Orthodox consensus, but Headlam now felt emboldened to seek from Davidson agreement to the use of the 'Suggested Terms' as a basis for inter-Church discussion. Accordingly, they were sent to Constantinople, where they were noted but not acted upon.

In 1933 Headlam would become the chairman of a new 'Commission on Relations with Foreign Churches', with four sections, concerning respectively the Roman Catholic, Orthodox, Lesser Eastern, and 'Continental' Churches. The division concerned with the Orthodox then took over the work of the Eastern Churches Committee.[39] In time it would produce two 'surveys' of Orthodoxy, one (1934) rather short, on recent events in the various Orthodox Churches, the other (1937) much fuller, notably in its report on the Athens congress of Orthodox theological professors in 1936. Evidently, the early years of the Fellowship of St Alban and St Sergius did not find either Anglican or Orthodox Church leaders entirely uninformed. But the time has come to turn to the origins of the Fellowship itself.

The founding

The existence of student organizations bringing together highly committed Christians—among the Russian Orthodox exiles in Europe these would have the general title 'study circles'—was an essential preliminary to the foundation of the Fellowship. The American incarnation of the Young Men's Christian Association, the 'YMCA', played an especially crucial role. Ralph Hollinger, one of its secretaries, made a successful overture to the Russian study circle at Belgrade, where initial coolness, in consequence of Orthodox suspicions of Protestant Evangelicalism, turned to warm admiration for Hollinger the man—as well as confidence that his offer of help to Orthodox students struggling to find their feet in the West came without ideological strings attached. This was a surprising development, both in retrospect and at the time—for it might have been expected that the same Anglo-Saxon Protestant animus as was customarily directed against Roman Catholics would affect its attitude to the Orthodox. 'Our image of the YMCA is influenced by its later developments. Where it flourished, in North America, England and Germany, it was already shifting towards providing sports facilities and cheap lodgings by the 1890s. Elsewhere, as in mainland Europe, it was a youth movement of the Protestant churches, eagerly trying to convert Catholics.'[40] Typically, at least in England, the YMCA targeted young adults from the lower middle class (especially those working as clerks in offices), rather than students. But Hollinger encouraged Orthodox participation, without fear of proselytism, at the inter-confessional student conferences which had been such a feature of Church life in the decades immediately preceding the First World War.

One historian even goes so far as to say, 'As is well known, the ecumenical movement very largely grew out of the Student Christian Movement.'[41] This may be an exaggeration but it was certainly true of the Fellowship. It was how Nicolas Zernov, and an unnamed colleague, came to attend the (British) 'Student Christian Movement' conference at Swanwick in Derbyshire at one of its extremely well attended sessions in 1923. In 1905 the 'British College Christian Union' had become the 'Student Christian Movement' with, initially, the strictly Evangelical local unions on board. In time these would secede—and later still largely displace the Student Christian Movement in the British Universities generally. (The Cambridge Inter-Collegiate Christian Union had withdrawn as early as 1910, but this was not on the same grounds as with others later, for 'CICCU' of that time wanted to be a purely Anglican affair—which the wider Union was not.) But for the moment the movement found itself under a relatively wide umbrella.

As to Zernov himself, he had left Russia as a twenty-three-year-old graduate, together with his family, in 1921. Militza Zernov in her preface to his autobiography and looking ahead to the life that would follow described him thus. 'His experience of revolutionary terror, and the family's miraculous escape from the Bolsheviks, had a profound effect on Nicolas' attitude to life. From this time he dedicated himself to the service of God and His Church. His life was that of a Russian emigrant full of continuous struggle, first for mere survival, then for higher education, and later to create new movements, ecumenical journals and centres.'[42] Like many Russian exiles of the first generation, the Balkans (via the Crimea, Georgia and Istanbul) were the initial port of call. In 1925 Nicolas gained a theology degree in Belgrade and became a co-founder of the Russian

Student Christian Movement in the Diaspora. Once settled in Paris he became its secretary and edited its journal, *Vestnik*, throughout the latter part of the 1920s. *Vestnik* quadrupled its circulation to two thousand copies during his editorship from 1925 to 1929, an early sign of his talents as organizer and communicator. His editorial policy was equally distanced from the monarchist 'Right', who hoped to restore the tsardom, and the liberal 'Left', whose inspiration was the constitutional revolution of February 1917. Russia, he believed, had not simply taken a wrong political turning, she was spiritually ill. In Christianity lay 'the sole force which could renew and cleanse the Russian people.'[43] But Zernov did not intend to live in a Russian ghetto. He wanted to seek out the common Christian roots of Western and Russian culture at their best. By 1929 his sights were set on England, and the preparation of a dossier that would take him to Keble College, Oxford, to write a doctoral thesis on his principal theme, 'The Unity of the Church and the Reunion of the Churches'. It was accepted by the University of Oxford in 1932. In the thesis he restricted his focus to the 'problem of Church unity' in the first four centuries. But he was far from doing so in his wide-ranging ecumenical concern for the reintegration of Christendom during all the years that would follow. 'Work for Christian unity became the mission of his life.'[44]

On his first visit to England Zernov was struck by what he called 'the affinity I discovered between the Anglican tradition and my own.'[45] It was a conviction he never lost though it was sometimes sorely tried. Zernov sought to persuade Zoe Fairfield, one of the British Student Christian Movement's officials, that a conference devoted to the commonalities joining together English Anglicanism and Russian Orthodoxy might be a good idea. But at the time the World Christian Student Federation (of which the British Student Christian Movement was an affiliate) was unsympathetic to gatherings held along confessional or national lines. In the light of the low profile of Orthodoxy in the West it can hardly have seemed a priority.

Yet the seismic plates of world Christianity were shifting. The same year, 1923, a 'Russian Student Movement in Exile' appeared on the international conference circuit, in the newly formed Czecho-Slovak republic, where it brought together the surviving leaders of the 'Russian Religious Renaissance' and the cream of the Church of Russia's youth.[46] In 1925 a number of the philosophers, theologians and historians from that 'Renaissance' who, whether through flight or deportation, found themselves in Western exile came together at Paris to establish, under the auspices of the Orthodox hierarchy, the 'Theological Academy of Saint Sergius'—eventually to be well known under its French name, 'Saint-Serge'.[47] The General Secretary of the YMCA, a founder of the World Student Christian Movement, the American Presbyterian John Mott, played a major part in financing not only the Institut Saint-Serge but also the Russian language YMCA Press in Paris. There was, then, a special interest in the Russian exiles on the part of these global, overwhelmingly Protestant, organizations.[48]

That interest went back as long as 1911, as one of the movers and shakers, Paul Anderson, noted in a contribution to *Sobornost* for 1978 entitled 'The Fellowship's Origins: A Charter Member's Notes'. At the urging of Mott, who in the early years of the twentieth century had lectured at St Petersburg and Dorpat, and been greatly struck by the worship and piety of Russian Orthodoxy, the Federation held its 1911 conference at Prinkipo on the Sea of Marmara, in the vicinity, deliberately chosen, of Constantinople. There were few Orthodox students in the countries where the Federation worked, but a 1911 delegation from the Student Christian Movement of St Petersburg made a great impact, led as it was by a State official who was a Finnish Lutheran but a 'man of great comprehension and deep appreciation of Orthodoxy'.[49] This laid the foundation for an understanding of Orthodoxy when the great wave of exiles, many of them youthful, began arriving in the West in the wake of the Bolshevik Revolution and the Russian Civil War. In particular, John Mott appears to have grasped the notion that Episcopalianism could be a form of *entrée* to the world of Orthodoxy. 'Mott hoped to persuade American Episcopalians to work with the YMCA in the American Universities. He had a much wider goal than this, to set up youth movements in the countries of Orthodox Eastern Europe, where Episcopalianism might open doors where a simply Protestant YMCA had no chance. It was not simply a matter of finding Episcopalian stalking-horses: Mott did think that Protestantism had something to learn from the Catholic teaching on church and sacraments.'[50] Mott's attempt to woo American Episcopalians did not, it seems, have much success—but his tendency to cluster together Episcopalians and the Orthodox as 'Catholic' foreshadowed the predominant approach of the Fellowship during the twentieth century.

In the summer of 1926, a meeting of the General Committee of the World Student Federation on Danish soil (at Nyborg Strand) proved sympathetic to the notion that Orthodoxy must be allowed to be represented in its own distinctive totality—which was what the delegates of the nascent 'Russian Student Christian Movement Abroad' were asking. That in turn produced the decision, by the British Student Christian Movement leaders together with the Russians, to hold an 'Anglo-Russian conference' along the lines Zernov had indicated. He himself ascribed the outcome principally to the efforts of a Dutch-born Swiss, Dr Gustave Kullmann, in later years a convert to Orthodoxy (as of 1929), who acted as the liaison between the American YMCA with its considerable financial resources and the distinctly impoverished Russian Student Movement. Zernov wrote an obituary in *Sobornost*, which revealed Kullmann's leading part in acquiring for the Russian intellectuals expelled from their country in 1922 the American funds that enabled them to set up a 'Religio-Philosophical Academy' in Berlin—the predecessor of the Parisian re-gathering of this intellectual élite.[51] In the course of the later 1920s, from his headquarters in the Boulevard Montparnasse, Kullmann 'became the trusted adviser of all major Russian religious institutions centred in Paris'.[52] That included taking the initiative in establishing ecumenical discussions with Catholics and the Reformed. Zernov ascribed to the lecture tours Kullmann made in Britain a significant role in gaining acceptance for the Fellowship. Kullmann's gifts were recognized by his becoming Deputy High Commissioner for refugees of the League of Nations (and later of the United Nations Organization), in which capacity he secured international protection and legal status for thousands of the displaced. Zernov, who should perhaps have declared an interest since he was his brother-in-law (Kullmann had married Nicolas's sister Maria Zernova) found him 'a living example of a creative synthesis between the East and the West'.[53] He would return to the subject in 1965, when he shared with readers of *Sobornost* Kullmann's pamphlet-length essay on 'The Religious Situation among Intellectuals in Orthodox Lands', which had been distributed to the 1928 World Student Christian Federation gathering at Mysore.[54]

Kullmann had concentrated on the Russian Diaspora, emphasizing the deeply liturgical nature of the Russian student movement in the West but also its determination to confront the social problem and build a better 'Holy Russia' for tomorrow.[55] Zernov commented that, thirty-six years later, many hopes had been frustrated and new problems had arisen, but the resumption of a dialogue between East and West, another of Kullmann's themes, had proved its worth.

The Beginnings

Zernov downplayed his own role, but in his autobiography he explained the change of sensibility which made it possible. 'When I left Russia I was convinced that the only true Church was the Orthodox Church, and that all Christians in the West were the victims of error. When I met the heterodox face to face I gradually changed my convictions. It was not that I began to doubt the truth of Orthodoxy—on the contrary the Orthodox Church was then revealed to me in all the richness of its spiritual gifts—but I learnt that it is not given to us to know the frontiers of the Church, and from my experience I became convinced that the Holy Spirit has not denied His gifts to Western Christians or deprived them of the grace which transforms the lives of such very different people and nations, overcoming their errors, sins and divisions.'[56]

The combination of (mainly) teachers and students from Saint-Serge, for the Orthodox, and, for the Anglicans, clergy and ordinands at the universities of Oxford and Cambridge (together with a number of Anglican theological colleges which Zernov had identified during a visit to England in the autumn of 1926) made possible the first of the proposed conferences, which was held in the Hertfordshire cathedral city of St Albans, conveniently close to London as it was, in January, 1927. Fairfield, originally sceptical, had been converted to the idea when Zernov met her again in Denmark at the time of the general committee meeting of the World Student Confederation in August 1926. As he recalled in her obituary in *Sobornost*, 'It was she who chose St Albans as the place where the conference was to be held. It was she who asked Canon Tatlow to take her and Miss Braikevitch to see the Bishop of St Albans and who persuaded him to give his support to the whole project. Under her supervision my first tour in England was organized.'[57] The names of 'Tatlow' and 'Braikevitch' will recur in my narrative.

Zernov singled out Charles Gore, by then bishop of Oxford, for mention on the Anglican side. It may not be irrelevant to note that the official historian of the Community of the Resurrection called the 1889 manifesto of Liberal Catholicism, *Lux Mundi*, which in large part had been Gore's brain-child, 'a dynamic fusion between aspects of Tractarianism, Greek patristic thought, Broad Church liberalism and biblical criticism.'[58] In various ways all of these elements were of interest to some, if not all, the early Russian Diaspora scholars and intellectuals. Among the Orthodox delegation, Zernov drew attention to the presence of the Russian New Testament scholar Sergius Bezobrazov (later Bishop Cassian) and the philosophical theologian Lev Zander, who would become the principal interpreter of the classic corpus of Russian Sophiology, the writings of Father Sergius Bulgakov. Gore seems to have had misgivings about the delegation's make-up. At any rate Georges Florovsky, later a severe critic of the Bulgakov school, was under the impression Gore had used the opportunity formally to propose him for attendance at future events: 'for the Anglicans further encounters would be beneficial only if there were included among the Orthodox speakers someone more identified with the traditional Orthodox position than had been the case to date'.[59] That might have been wishful thinking on Florovsky's part, retrojecting into the 1920s his later quarrels with Saint-Serge. Florovsky's American biographer, Andrew Blane, while admitting that, for the Anglican members of the future Fellowship, 'Bulgakov remained unquestionably the central Orthodox figure', held that 'in theological exchanges the two "were regarded on the same level"'.[60]

Aside from the language difficulties at the first informal encounters where none of the English had any Russian, and the Russians' English was poor, Zernov noted from the proceedings two main difficulties and one great advantage. The difficulties were that while the Russians—in the wake of the Revolution—were cultural pessimists, the English—with a very different modern history in Church and State behind them—were cultural optimists, and whereas the Orthodox were interested in 'meta-history and the mystery of the Church', the Anglicans were concerned above all with how to optimize the findings of biblical criticism. One need only think of the case of Bishop Gore. Zernov implies that, had the meeting remained on the level of intellectual discussion, it might well have been the last of its kind. But it did not remain there, and this was thanks to the 'one great advantage' just mentioned: '[a] realization of their brotherhood in Christ came in the Chapel, where every morning Orthodox and Anglicans together worshipped the same Saviour. There the linguistic, theological and ideological barriers were removed and the gift of their oneness was experienced.'[61] Liturgical worship, mutually attended though with careful respect for the particularity of each tradition and its canons, would be, along with friendship, the mainstay of the Fellowship's intellectual life.

The success of the first Anglo-Russian conference decided participants to hold a second, which met, again at St Albans, at New Year 1928. It was now that the Fellowship was born—according to Zernov at the suggestion of a Scottish Presbyterian, William Tyndal, who was at the time secretary of the (British) Student Christian Movement.[62] The Fellowship was initially restricted to past attendees of the conferences, but its aim was wider. In Zernov's words, 'This informal conference was an experiment in Reunion work which discovered a new road towards that inspiring goal. The conference had its centre neither in the animated debates nor in the learned addresses, but in the worship in the chapel, where, on alternate days, the Anglican and the Eastern Orthodox Eucharist was celebrated. Such a participation in the prayer-life of another tradition was a revolutionary experience for both Anglicans and Orthodox. Many misunderstandings and even deep-rooted prejudices were removed in this way, and a genuine sense of unity was achieved which led to the formation of the Fellowship. Bishop Frere [Walter Frere, Gore's successor as superior of the Community of the Resurrection, had become bishop of Truro in 1923] impressed every member of the conference so much that he was unanimously invited to become the President of the newly formed Society. He willingly consented, and this started the second period of his relations with the Russian Church, lasting until his death in 1938, and reaching its culminating point in 1936, when, during his visit to Paris, Bishop Frere sang in the Russian cathedral an Anglican Litany for the Russian Congregation.'[63]

Frere was the first monk-bishop in the Reformed Church of England (rather resisted, accordingly, by King George V). He was an excellent and indeed the obvious choice, thanks to his knowledge of Russia and Russian. After his death Zernov would lay out the story of Frere's credentials. 'His early contacts with the Russian Church took place in the years immediately preceding the outbreak of the First World War. Frere paid at that time three visits to Russia. He went there first with his sister in May–June 1909, when, as representative of Cambridge University, he attended the celebrations in commemoration of the Russian writer Nikolay Gogol at the unveiling of his monument in Moscow. In August 1910 Frere again spent a month in Russia, mostly in Finland and the Baltic Provinces, by way of holiday. His last and most important visit took place in the winter of 1914. He was away from England from January until March, and in the course of these months he delivered a number of addresses on the life of the Anglican Church in Riga, Polotsk, St Petersburg, Moscow, and in the Monastery of the Holy Trinity founded by St Sergius of Radonezh at Zagorsk. This lecture tour had been organized by a Russian society for promoting rapprochement between the Anglican and Eastern Orthodox Churches, founded as this had been in 1912, at a time of Anglo-Russian political reconciliation, as a parallel body to the Anglican and Eastern Orthodox Church Union. Frere made careful preparation for this journey, and learned enough Russian to be able to read and to understand that language. While in Russia he spent several weeks in a convent near Riga, living with the family of a deacon and 'thus becoming familiar with the mentality of ordinary members of the Russian Church ... His lectures addressed to the St Petersburg audience were also published in English and in Russian, and they help their readers to understand the main reasons for his interest in reunion with the East.'[64] Zernov represented Frere's overall view well enough when he wrote, 'Bishop Frere represented the Anglican position as a legitimate protest against the one-sidedness of Western medieval tradition, and he considered the reunion with the Orthodox Church as a part of a general move towards the restoration of the fullness of Catholic life'.[65] In a more recent biographical sketch by Alan Wilkinson the attraction to Orthodoxy is differently expressed. 'Though he remained a Western Catholic, he warmed to Orthodoxy because of its "timelessness" and "its wonderful sense of fellowship with the departed".'[66]

Introducing the journal

This, then, was the immediate background to the first issue of the *Journal of the Fellowship of St Alban and St Sergius*, later *Sobornost*, in June 1928. Its first editor was Francis Jarvis, a member of the Society of the Sacred Mission, alongside the Community of the Resurrection and the Society of St John the Evangelist (the 'Cowley Fathers') the premier men's religious order in the Church of England. Ill-health forced Jarvis's retirement after editing the initial number. His assistant, a Russian laywoman based in London, Zenia (or Xenia) Braikevitch, whose name has already been mentioned in connexion with the first St Albans conference, took care of the second issue. By the time of the third issue the torch had been handed on to another Anglican priest, Ambrose Reeves, a newly ordained product of the theological college run by the Community of the Resurrection at Mirfield. Reeves was later rector of Liverpool parish church and, under apartheid, a controversial bishop of Johannesburg. He was a theologically gifted High Churchman, one of the authors of the influential 1947 multi-authored report *Catholicity*. In the way it looked behind the Reformation divide to the Tradition of the undivided Church, that report, submitted to the then archbishop of Canterbury, Geoffrey Fisher, would have been congenial to many in the Fellowship.[67]

The journal's first issue, thanks to the choice of genres for its component parts, already established some continuing features of the mature product. Naturally enough, there was an editorial, short on mission statement, perhaps, but full enough on description of the new buds of the Fellowship opening in some major centres. What would later be termed 'Fellowship Notes' covered meetings of the London, Oxford and Paris groups. The body of the issue consisted of a saint's life (that of Vitalius the Monk, a desert father who on attaining perfect love of God gave himself to practical love of neighbour by a ministry to fallen women in Alexandria); an essay in Orthodox doctrine (on the Transfiguration, a favourite Byzantine feast day); an Anglican survey article, by the premier theologian of the Society of the Sacred Mission, Gabriel Hebert, assessing the pros and cons of that essentially Western concern, the 'Higher Criticism';[68] an Orthodox homily (from no less a figure than Father Pavel Florensky, the polymath executed by the Soviets in 1937), and two reports on contemporary religious affairs. One was an exploration of 'Christianity and Atheism in Russia', giving heartening indications of recent resistance to the anti-Church campaign. The other was a simpler affair where Reeves described his experiences at a conference that year of various Christian student movements, representing in all sixteen nationalities, at Luhacovice in Czecho-Slovakia (though in his own conversations, mindful, no doubt, of his Fellowship commitments, he concentrated on Russian participants). The magazine was typed, not immaculately, rather than printed. It ended with a moving testimony from the confessing Church in the form of a letter from an unnamed Orthodox prisoner in Moscow to an equally anonymous relative at Paris, who was connected with the Russian Student Christian Movement there.

In the same initial issue of the *Journal of the Fellowship of St Alban and St Sergius*, the name of 'Mr E. Mascall' appears as a speaker to the London Group. In his autobiography, Eric Mascall, that unique Anglican Thomist, later Professor of Historical Theology at King's College, London, explains the background to his participation, which took him back in memory to his student days as a mathematician at Pembroke College, Cambridge. 'An event which turned out to be of lasting importance to me in a number of ways took place in the Christmas vacation of 1927, when I was invited to attend the Second Anglo-Russian Student Conference organized by the Student Christian Movement. Like many Anglicans I had acquired an interest, not unmixed with a certain romantic curiosity, in the Eastern Orthodox Church as the great non-papal Christian communion which antedated our Western schisms and prided itself on its immutability.'[69] After describing his presence in Westminster Abbey (as a nineteen-year-old) at the sixteenth centenary celebrations of the Council of Nicaea (in 1925) with Davidson presiding, and two patriarchs and two exiled Russian metropolitans in attendance, Mascall commented: 'it was, in these post-First-World-War years, easy to convince oneself that Anglican–Orthodox union would soon be achieved and that Rome was both incorrigible and unimportant'.[70] It was true enough that a growing amity between the Church of England and the Orthodox Churches in his time found expression on that day, 29 June 1925, with the patriarchs of Jerusalem and Alexandria attending, as well as Metropolitan Evlogy Georgievsky, Russian exarch of the Ecumenical Patriarchate in Western Europe and the presiding bishop of the Synodal Church (later the 'Russian Church outside Russia') Antony Khrapovitsky, formerly archbishop of Kiev, along with representatives of the Rumanian and Greek Churches.[71]

The conference experience marked the young Eric Mascall for life. 'It is no exaggeration to say that this conference opened up for me a new world of Christian thought, worship and spirituality which subsequent experience over a great many years has deepened, enriched and, since it was inevitably in some respects partial and unbalanced, has corrected, but of which nothing has dimmed the impression that I then received . . . Both for the personal friendships to which they led and for the realm of theological understanding and spiritual experience which they disclosed, I have since come to reckon those few days at the end of 1927 as one of the turning-points of my life.'[72] From 1929 to 1936 Mascall would act as chairman of the Fellowship's executive committee (a signal honour, since from 1928 to 1931 he remained a layman and, by his own account, a very unsuccessful mathematics master at Bablake School in Coventry),[73] while his ordination training at Ely Theological College, when he finally got round to it, lasted only a year, from 1931 to 1932. But in 1934, while a curate at St Andrew's, Stockwell, in the Southwark diocese, he had already edited the first book of essays ever published by the Fellowship's members, and between the years 1937 (when he left Westminster to become sub-warden of Lincoln Theological College in succession to Michael Ramsey[74]) and 1946 he acted as editor of the Fellowship's journal. Mascall would oversee the emergence of the Fellowship as a major source of theological writing.[75] After 1962, when he left Oxford, where, since 1945, he had been a Student (i.e. Fellow) of Christ Church, his participation gradually decreased—owing not just to other activities but also to the feeling that he had 'seen too many cases of vigorous organizations gradually turning into gerontocracies and finally into necrocracies to wish ever to hold on to power myself'.[76]

The journal's first issue reported that at the 'invitation of Mr Spalding', a distinguished Russian scholar had visited the Fellowship's Oxford equivalent of the 'London Group' where Mr Mascall had spoken. Henry Norman Spalding, a north Oxford-based philanthropist with broad religious interests, would finance the Oxford Lectureship in Eastern Christian Studies that provided an academic platform for Nicolas Zernov, and, later, for Timothy Ware (in religion, Father Kallistos, and subsequently, under that name, Archimandrite, then Bishop and finally Metropolitan), so this was a development of some importance. 'Spalding was fascinated by Eastern philosophy, and the family fortune—derived from guano mined from a remote Pacific island by Mrs Spalding's father—enabled the couple to establish posts in Oriental Religions at several universities.'[77]

It was, however, the 'Paris Group' that had by far the most to report in terms of Anglican–Orthodox exchange, reflecting the far greater availability of Orthodox speakers in the French capital. That Nicolas Zernov, with his gifts of enthusing and organizing, was the Paris Group's chairman, must have been crucial. As late as 1935, Paul Anderson, the purse-holder of the Russian section of the global Student Christian Movement, a major player in all funding, was writing to Zernov in terms which asserted both the Englishness and the importance of the Paris branch. Zernov had been concerned how exactly to formulate invitations to its meetings. Anderson responded to his queries. 'The Fellowship must be considered as an organization and movement embracing both English and Russians so far as membership is concerned. In the way of organization, the Fellowship divides itself into two natural sections, namely, those who reside in England and those who reside in France.' Each was to have a directing body, whether the 'Paris Council' or the 'London Executive'.[78] The Paris Group's report that 'in the fundamental principles the Orthodox and the Anglicans do not differ' was counterposed by the acknowledgement of 'many differences in practice'. More worryingly for the future, a 'lively discussion' exhibited not only the 'difference of emphasis' but also the 'diverse opinions which exist in the Anglican Church'.[79]

A letter appended to the editorial was prescient for the future. The expression of faith and experience of our two communions was the 'central reality', yet liturgical worship, which is already an 'affirmation of faith in the doctrines of Incarnation and Atonement' does not deny the need for the 'discipline of thought and study by which we make explicit to ourselves, and for others, what this redemption means, how it operates, what are the conditions of its acceptance.'[80] The *Journal*, and later and more fully *Sobornost*, would seek to combine these two features—worship and theological enquiry—as did the conferences of the Fellowship itself from which the majority of the published material emerged.

→ 2 ←

The Long Story

In the last chapter, an account has been given, against the foil of the relevant background, of the emergence of the *Journal of the Fellowship of St Alban and St Sergius*. A long story lay ahead of it, whether under its own name or the successor style of *Sobornost*.

The 1930s

A major part of the editorial charge lay in helping to define the aims of the Fellowship and therefore of the *Journal*—though one might also reverse these terms, for certainly the *Journal* contributed to forming the mind of the Fellowship. For obvious reasons this was especially true of members who were above all subscribers rather than attenders at conferences or participants in Groups. In June 1931 the editorial took the opportunity of reminding readers that 'from the first our conference and Fellowship personnel has consisted almost entirely of Anglicans of the Catholic school of thought', adding, 'We have never disguised this fact nor pretended that there are not other schools of thought in the Anglican Church'. It is 'for the Fellowship and the Student Christian Movement under whose aegis it lives to decide whether an attempt shall be made to make the Anglican side representative of the whole of the Anglican Church—a sort of microcosm of Lambeth—or to continue as heretofore'.[1]

Despite its rather 'party' character, thus acknowledged, the Fellowship was obliged to make some use of what might be termed 'Establishment' Anglicans, especially bureaucrats who knew the ropes at Lambeth Palace, in the Church Assembly, and with regard to ecumenical contacts already made. Canon Tissington Tatlow, who had mediated with the bishop of St Albans to make possible the first residential meeting of the proto-Fellowship, was a case in point. He now stepped forward as a contributor to the Fellowship's journal, in the hope of acquainting readers with the history of the Russian

Student Christian Movement from the last years of the tsardom to the present. Tatlow painted an impressive picture of its geographical spread in the emigration, from the Baltic Republics to Brussels, and the work it did in organizing Sunday schools, religious circles, discussion groups, social meetings, clubs, conference and summer camps for the young.[2]

Later that year (1931), yet another editor, Father O. F. ('Bernard') Clarke, who had returned from missionary work in India, drew members' attention to the freshly published report from the 1930 Lambeth Conference, to which he ascribed a 'newer and wider vision of the mission of the Anglican Communion', commenting, 'If that new Anglicanism is to find its soul it needs Orthodoxy tremendously—not that Anglicanism may just become Orthodoxy, but that it may learn from Orthodoxy a Catholicity that is free from the legalism of Rome and an Evangelicalism that has never been distorted by the Protestant Reformation.'[3] This was rather a good formulation.

But there fell an almost immediate blow; the first founder member to die was an invaluable one, Bishop Gore. The editor noted, 'We Anglicans often venture the belief, we hope with all humility, that we have a special contribution to make in Christendom in helping the Church to assimilate new truth. In this work Bishop Gore was pioneer and ardent labourer'— the context of such 'assimilation' was notably evolutionary theory and historical-critical exegesis of the Bible, and the special target of these remarks was Gore's essay in *Lux Mundi* on biblical inspiration, his *The Reconstruction of Belief*, and his editorial work on *A New Commentary on Holy Scripture*.[4] Gore's social involvement in labour issues had helped to bring it about that unlike in Continental Europe, the 'assumption ... that Christianity and Socialism are incompatible, has never been accepted in England'.[5] Most Orthodox members of the Fellowship, one suspects, were never really to be enthused by the prospect of learning from Anglican exegesis of the Bible, for the historical-critical study of Scripture largely passed them by. And above all in the Paris Group, where the Orthodox were potentially numerous and certainly influential, thanks to the proximity of the Institut Saint-Serge, they were utterly divided over the political and social questions to which, in connexion with Gore, the *Journal* had referred.

In the year of Gore's death, 1932, Zernov directed an open letter to the editor, analysing his impressions of a wide ranging lecture tour. He would be indefatigable as a lecturer to British audiences, and the emergence of local branches of the Fellowship in widely dispersed parts of England, often transient though these growths might be, was the result of his labours and those of colleagues, especially professors from the Institut Saint-Serge, whom he went to some lengths to rope in. At this time Zernov was himself actively planning a 'St Basil's House' in Oxford where Eastern and Western Christian students might live together in one community. From his address at Keble he wrote to Meletios Metaxakis, then patriarch of Alexandria, seeking moral and financial support, and laying out his stall.[6]

The year 1933 saw an important statement of the 'aims and basis' of the Fellowship.

> The Fellowship is not an official body, nor is it representative of either the Anglican or of the Orthodox Church as a whole, and therefore has only an indirect relation to negotiations for reunion, although both the Conferences and the life of the Fellowship itself evoke and deepen the desire for the restoration of the unity of the Body of Christ ... The nature of the Fellowship and the work of the Conferences derive from the conviction that the realization of any fuller measure of Christian unity depends on the fostering of mutual respect and understanding, and that in this task the most creative moment is that of common worship.[7]

In 1935 the *Journal* changed its name to *Sobornost*, by which henceforth—even when united with the *Eastern Churches Review*—it would be known. As the editor (still Bernard Clarke) explained, the old title had been 'long and cumbersome', and, moreover, a 'more imaginative title' would be better if it could 'express more clearly the spirit and aims of our work'.[8] A 'New Series' began, commencing, as was professionally correct, with a new numbering (1935 was, therefore, Year One). Vladimir Illyin, a Saint-Serge polymath who taught courses on, among other things, liturgy, psychology and mediaeval philosophy, presented the new title at more length in an opening essay on 'The Nature and the Meaning of the Term "Sobornost"'. Illyin explained that the unity of the universal Church, if that idea is neither to be mere sentiment nor an invitation to 'sectarian individualism', requires a hierarchical-canonical structure for its expression. Yet if the Church only had unity in that sense it would be at the mercy of an opposite danger: namely, repressive collectivism. Fortunately, by a 'marvellous activity of the Spirit of Love, who is the Holy Ghost', there is created a 'free mystical-ontological union of those who, though they differ in personal qualities and in individual being, are nevertheless one in the Spirit of Love'.[9] And this is *sobornost*. It makes possible a 'Church symphony' in which all the faithful can contribute.[10] This was, then, the distinctive pitch of the *Journal*, on the Fellowship's behalf.

The secretary's diary for the early summer of the following year, 1936, gave some idea of the proliferation of groups. The city of Leeds had been 'attacked' by a trio consisting of Georges Florovsky, Leo Zander and Vladimir Weidlé—three of the most notable members of the Paris Orthodox intelligentsia—as well as involving Zernov himself. Between them, with the encouragement of the bishop of Ripon, they had given as many as ten addresses. Florovsky, increasingly estranged from Saint-Serge over the Sophiological dispute (discussed below), was especially active as a travelling lecturer for the Fellowship, more than earning his appointment as a vice-president in 1937. As to Zernov, in the course of a three-month period he had spoken not only at Leeds but at Wakefield, Aldershot, Kidderminster, Matlock, Lincoln, Scunthorpe, Boston, Grantham, Stamford and Bedford as well as at London, where one of his presentations (on Russian iconography) had been made in the Royal School of Art.

The visits to the Lincoln diocese were orchestrated with the help of Michael Ramsey, a future president and, later, archbishop of Canterbury, but then a lecturer at Lincoln Theological College. Zernov used his visit to the College to devise with Ramsey a plan of theological study for the Fellowship's use.[11] This might be regarded as a *quid pro quo*. Ramsey was already indebted to the Fellowship's inspiration. Looking back, Rowan Williams, another Fellowship member and Ramsey's successor as Anglican primate at three removes, saw the mark of the Fellowship's influence in the book that made Ramsey's name. This was *The Gospel and the Catholic Church*, dating from 1936. The work suggested 'a perspective that was beginning to appear in continental Catholicism and was being introduced into the ecumenical scene largely by émigré Russian writers. It is essentially the vision of the Church as "epiphany": what matters about the Church is not a system of ideas as such (though doctrine and dogma have their place) nor the structure of an organization competent to deliver authoritative judgments and to require obedience (though order is important in its proper context), but what the bare fact of the Church shows. *The Gospel and the Catholic Church* sets out first to determine the shape of divine action (gift, sacrifice, the creation of a qualitatively new human fellowship) and then to demonstrate how doctrine and discipline in the Catholic tradition make present and tangible the pattern of divine action'.[12] The debt to Orthodoxy was the more surprising given Ramsey's Barthianism at this epoch, and his own Congregationalist roots. Ramsey's biographer, Owen Chadwick, cited Ramsey as calling the period initiated by collaboration with Zernov his 'Orthodox honeymoon'; it lasted until the end of his Cambridge professorship in 1952. 'More than once, later, Ramsey said that while he was a professor he was more an eastern Christian thinker than a western; or once, that he was more an Orthodox thinker than an Anglican.' This changed when he became a bishop and 'carried the responsibility for a Church in good part Protestant'.[13]

As to Zernov, his willingness to go beyond the more predictable High Church circles was demonstrated in his attendance at the Cromer Convention of the 'Anglican Evangelical Group Movement', where he felt he had been well received. Abroad, he attended the (fourth) diocesan conference of the Russian Church in Western Europe, where he represented the Russian Church Aid Fund, a Church of England initiative which also provided the Fellowship with office-space for Zernov as secretary. Evidently, since the vote was described as unanimous, he must have supported the decision of Metropolitan Evlogy's diocese to reject the appeal of the Karlovci Synod to abandon the direct canonical link with Constantinople—not least because acceptance of the Synod's authority would have involved 'the exclusion of clergy and laity from the administration of Church affairs, which would reverse the decisions of the All-Russian Church Council of 1917–1918'.[14]

In 1937 Zernov and Mascall (that is, the Fellowship's then secretary and outgoing chairman as well as incoming editor of *Sobornost*) wrote a joint account of 'The Theological Task of the Fellowship'. The paper actually given under that title at the Fellowship conference was Mascall's; it must be assumed that Zernov's role lay in honing the shortened version produced for *Sobornost*. It was Mascall's last act as chairman, which position he had occupied since 1929, for he was moving to Lincoln as sub-warden of the theological college there. (It was also, more or less, his first act as editor.) It defined the task at hand as, in the first place, to 'deepen the understanding of the common life of the Anglican and Eastern Churches and so, by studying agreements rather than differences' to (a) 'produce a common body of thought and life' and (b) 'forward the establishment of a united Catholic Front against present day secularist movements'.[15] This mission statement then suggested an agenda for five distinct areas. These were: the

God-world relation and the problem of creation (are the Sophiological and Thomist approaches really contradictory?); ecclesiology (the question of authority: catholicity or *sobornost*?); ascetic theology (asceticism or humanism?; the imitation of Christ or transformation by the indwelling Spirit?; can these be reconciled in a theocentric manner?); liturgiology (the issue of frequent communion; the priesthood of the laity; relation to the Liturgical Movement in the Church of Rome); sociology (English freedom over against Russian experience, and the possibility of a common front against the secular enemies of both communions). Overall, the Fellowship aimed to elicit a common attitude to the 'world-situation facing the Church today'.[16]

In 1938 Zernov's secretary's report stressed the youthfulness of the Fellowship's membership. Its 650 members were chiefly Anglicans. Of thirty-one Church of England dioceses where it was present, in seven the Fellowship was well organized, in fifteen promising, in nine stagnant. Sixteen out of twenty-six theological colleges had accepted a scheme of lectures on the Orthodox Church. King's College, London, had a seminar. Rumania (the then spelling of the country's name) had study-circles, Estonia (about to disappear from the map, though it would re-emerge) had members. Continuing anxiety was expressed about the future of the Institut Saint-Serge without whose lecturers and students the Fellowship would never have started.

In the last issue of the 1930s Zernov again attempted an overview of the Fellowship's place. He saw it as sufficiently distinct from the older Anglican and Eastern Churches Association on the ground that: *a.* all its activities were set around the Liturgy—the 'eucharistic method'; *b.* its preferred vehicle was the conference, general or local; *c.* it was oriented towards the young, especially students; *d.* it placed union between the Anglican and Orthodox Churches in the context of reunion all round; *e.* it treated East and West as at parity. After listing its many events over the twelve-year period since its foundation, Zernov regretted that its success was so limited—but what could be expected with an annual income of, at best, £350? Nothing more was possible until the Churches put the same effort of manpower and money into ecumenical work as into missionary work. Zernov believed the Roman Catholic Church had done that, noting its work with the Russian Orthodox in China, Manchukuo, Finland, Estonia, Lithuania, France, and Belgium. Anglicans and Orthodox should also have a proper, permanent centre for their encounter. This was the notion behind the hypothetical 'St Basil's House', which had not come to fruition, though the 'St Macrina House' proposed for Anglicans and Orthodox at Birmingham by Mme Gorodetzky, a professional teacher of Russian and later a university lecturer at Oxford (and subsequently holder of a chair at Liverpool), came close to the concept, despite its restriction of residents to women.

In the *Historical Memoir* he co-authored with Militza, Nicolas Zernov had this to say about the year 1939.

> The outbreak of hostilities in 1939 made doubtful the survival of the Fellowship; but the 'phoney' war of the winter of 1939–40 encouraged the Fellowship committee to try to continue its activities, though the only assets were £100 in the bank and my readiness to carry on the work until I was called up for military service. A letter was sent to all our members asking whether they were prepared to support the work during the war, and 243 responded by sending £206. The Russian Church Aid Fund closed down so I moved the office of the Fellowship to our two-roomed flat, and Rachel Hotham volunteered to act as my honorary secretary. To everyone's surprise the invitations to speak in churches, colleges and various societies poured in. Never before had there been such a demand. Interest in Russia and her Church was, in particular, shown by the public schools.[17]

In an 'open letter' to the Fellowship for the start of hostilities Bulgakov struck a graver note. He told them that the Book of the Apocalypse was becoming newly pertinent (he had just been writing a commentary on it.) Not that he thought the End had arrived, but, still within history as they were, the present conflict might turn out to be one of those wars which in the Apocalyptic Discourse in St Matthew's Gospel (24:6) portend the proximity of the End. At any rate it would be a moment of judgment to which men must respond since even in wartime they retain their humanity, their spiritual personality, their creativity—three crucial notions in Bulgakov's anthropology. He asked for a 'new mobilization ... for the spiritual conflict'.[18] Part of the novelty involved was a fresh openness to Roman Catholics.

> [W]hatever other conquest a soul may pray for at this time, it also desires victory in the further widening and deepening of the links between our several churches, and especially with those members of the Roman Catholic Church that are friendly towards us.

He also added:

We are well aware in what degree this depends neither upon us nor upon them, and with what difficulty the conception of unity which is still dominant in that church will yield the ascendancy.[19]

Meanwhile the opening of St Macrina's House in Birmingham was put on hold, since the times were hardly propitious for encouraging Orthodox students from abroad to come to Britain.

The 1940s

The high hopes entertained by the Zernovs in the 'phoney war' proved justified only in part. As they reported:

> The first winter of the war was so deceptively calm that there was even a scheme to have a small conference in the summer of 1940 with Russian delegates from Paris. All these hopes were shattered by the German invasion of France in May 1940. At this critical moment Mercy Collinson made a vital contribution by offering to organize a 'camp' to help farmers at harvest time as a substitute for our conferences. Some sixty people attended for six weeks at Haynes in Bedfordshire. An entirely new experience, this 'Camp' combined liturgical worship, theological discussion, domestic chores and work in the fields. Most of the members sleep in the local school, others in farmhouses. The school was not only dormitory but also kitchen, dining room and lecture hall. Each morning began with the celebration of the Eucharist in a neighbouring church, Anglican and Orthodox on alternate days. Most of the day we were harvesting; in the evening there were lectures, concerts and debates. This venture proved a great success and incidentally earned us some money.[20]

The camps, attracting increasing numbers, were held annually during the war. The Zernovs singled out for praise the contribution to these gatherings where 'senior theologians and young people met on a truly family footing' of Father Alexis van der Mensbrugghe and the Armenian Father Tiran Nersoyan, both of whom later became bishops in their respective communions.[21]

What about the journal? For understandable reasons (there was a paper shortage) the issues of *Sobornost* halved in the first years of the War. The editorial of the first number from 1940 wondered whether it was also a consequence of War that so little of a purely theological nature had come the editor's way, rather than simply news and views. There was no shortage of news, at any rate. In December 1940 *Sobornost* devoted its editorial to the travails of the Orthodox as a consequence of the Stalinist gains. With the takeover of the Baltic Republics and Finnish Karelia the two ancient monasteries of Petseri and Valamo, 'almost the sole surviving representatives of Russian monasticism', had fallen under Soviet rule and Orthodoxy had ceased to be an authorized religion in these areas. The same was true of Bessarabia and the northern Bukovina, forcibly ceded to Russia by Rumania, while the quasi-annexation of much of Transylvania to Hungary, 'under the instructions of Germany', had 'crippled the largest Orthodox nation in Europe since the bolshevization of Russia'.[22] Rumania was the only country outside England and France where the pre-War Fellowship had circles. Meanwhile, the other Balkan nations were threatened by Fascist advance. The editor feared that the German occupation of northern France must mean the end of the Institut Saint-Serge. It was naught for one's comfort, quoting lines from G. K. Chesterton's *The Ballad of the White Horse*, which had gained a new piquancy at this point of the Axis advance. Putting on a brave face, Nadejda Gorodetzky, in a piece on 'War and Reunion', recalled how the Great War had not in fact been a disaster for Reunionist aspirations. Zernov imagined that the result of the War would be to throw Orthodox and Anglicans much more together, so the 'ground' must be prepared.[23]

In 1941 Mascall wrote an upbeat editorial. The War was a just one, if not a holy one. Conceivably, the Church of Russia would emerge with new strength and wisdom from a chastened Soviet Union. He prophesied that if so 'it will have acquired an understanding of its own inner nature that will not separate it from the Christian West, but will draw West and East together'.[24]

In the June 1942 issue, Alexis van der Mensbrugghe as Orthodox assistant editor (Florovsky, who had held that largely nominal post from 1936, was incommunicado in German-occupied Yugoslavia and would subsequently emigrate to the United States), wrote of 'The Need for an Orthodox Centre in England'. Such a centre would serve, he thought, no fewer than six purposes. The first three were stated plainly. It would help overcome ethnophyletism, for Orthodoxy's Achilles' heel is 'exaggerated nationalism'.[25] It would be a meeting place for bodies like the Anglican and Eastern Churches Association and the Fellowship and indeed 'all interested individuals'. It could act as an information centre with a reading and circulating library and relevant publications on display. The fourth started a hare. Furnished with a Chapel, such an establishment would be a centre of liturgical life—and, hopefully, of liturgical reform. Van der Mensbrugghe was clearly an enthusiast for the latter. Forgetting the (at this stage) purely hypothetical character of the 'Orthodox Centre' he began to list his general liturgical desiderata. 'It is not so much a question of returning to the Tradition, as to prevent the excess of later development smothering the magnificence of the older treasures.'[26] There were too many repetitive small icons on church walls—and 'Orthodoxy, too [like Latin Catholicism, he meant], needs a call away from the "bondieuseries" of the Eastern "Saint-Sulpices"'.[27] There had to be some shortening of services but it was usually done in such a way that the more important elements were omitted and the less important preserved. The formalistic 'anticipation' of Hours, driven by an excessive regard for fasting, which was given greater weight than the meaning of the Liturgy, had to stop, and such anomalies as morning Vespers abolished. Van der Mensbrugghe then remembered he was supposed to be commending the need for a Centre, so reverted to his list of six reasons. The fifth was to be a place for the holding of retreats (a borrowing from Anglican practice[28]). The sixth and last rationale was that Orthodox students needed somewhere to foregather—which suggested a location in London, Oxford or Cambridge.

In 1943 John Findlow became Anglican secretary of the Fellowship. Formerly a student at Lincoln Theological College (with Ramsey and Mascall among his teachers), he had been ordained at St Albans, the original 'home' of the Fellowship, in 1939. Subsequently a curate at Little St Mary's, Cambridge, he had wanted to go to the Institut Saint-Serge to deepen his knowledge of Orthodoxy but the outbreak of the Second World War prevented this.[29] With his Orthodox interests and his Russian wife, he was well suited for the post. Unfortunately his tenure was short-lived. In 1946 he became assistant secretary to the Archbishop of Canterbury's Council on Foreign Relations at Lambeth, and at the end of the decade the Findlows would move abroad, where John was successively chaplain of the English church in Rome, then English chaplain at Montreux and subsequently Athens, and from 1964 until 1969 the representative of the archbishop of Canterbury to the Holy See and first director of the Anglican Centre in Rome.[30] (His widow would retire to Oxford and play a lively part in the Fellowship there.)

Along with Nicolas Zernov, Findlow was the first warden of 'St Basil's House', not, as Zernov had originally hoped, in Oxford, but in London. In the last issue of *Sobornost* for 1943 a 'stop press' leaflet was inserted announcing that the Fellowship had acquired a home of its own, hopefully of a permanent kind, at 52 Ladbroke Grove. This is how the Zernovs remembered it in their *Memoir* (calling Militza Zernov the first warden—which she may perhaps have been in practical terms though her actual title was 'Bursar').

> Despite the war, the St Basil's House project was finally realized in 1943. The freehold of 52 Ladbroke Grove was bought for £2544. In the face of desperate odds it was repainted and equipped with secondhand furniture. Militza Zernov, its first Warden, inaugurated the 'At Homes' in spite of the black-outs and with meals improvised from meagre rations.[31]

The decision to make London the base was not really an option for downplaying Oxford. Oxford would become extremely important for the Fellowship. Eric Mascall was ensconced at Christ Church from 1939, with his assistant editor, Patrick Thompson, at Magdalen. In 1946 Thompson would succeed him in the editorial chair. Moreover, in 1947 Nicolas Zernov was at last to take up the lectureship in the Theology School planned for him by Spalding. There would soon be a scheme for starting a Fellowship House at Oxford dedicated to St Gregory and St Macrina.

In the first issue for 1946 the Fellowship announced its plans for the post-War period: an ambitious summer school, open again, now that peace had arrived, to foreigners; the renewal of summer visits to England by Russian students in France; and the setting up of a memorial fund for Bulgakov, who had died in 1944, including the expenses of a fitting monument at his grave, a Saint-Serge scholarship and a subsidy towards the costs of his last book (presumably his commentary on the Apocalypse,[32] though his Christology was also posthumously published). The second and final issue of 1946 brought news of Metropolitan Evlogy's death—with which the second great figure among the Paris exiles (after Bulgakov, that is) departed from the scene. The editor lamented the passing of one who 'for so many years guided the life of that section of the Russian church in Western Europe from which the Orthodox membership of the Fellowship has been mainly drawn, and to whose never-failing support the Fellowship itself is deeply indebted'.[33] Father Lev Gillet gave the memorial address at the church lent to Russians in London's Holland Park, outlining his life story and stressing his ecumenical work, his defence of Saint-Serge (but also the blessing he gave to 'the new Theological Institute of St Denis, also in Paris'[34]), his pastoral care for the Russian Student Christian Movement, his support of the charitable outreach of Action Orthodoxe, and, above all, his help to so many individual people. The recognition of St Denis belonged with Evlogy's renewal of canonical contact with Moscow in his last years, though Gillet was too sanguine in the optimistic conclusion that the effect of this was to bring about happy relations all round—with Constantinople as well as with Moscow. A note following recorded that not all Evlogy's parishes had accepted the exarch appointed by Patriarch Alexei, Metropolitan Seraphim (a returnee to Moscow from the Karlovci Synod), rather than Metropolitan Vladimir of Nice, who had been put in place as his successor by Evlogy himself. Constantinople had not released the Evlogian parishes from its jurisdiction—though in the eyes of Moscow they had never canonically belonged there in the first place.

When in 1946 John Findlow relinquished his office as Anglican secretary to the Fellowship his post remained officially unfilled. In effect he was replaced by a Greek laywoman, Helle Giorgiadis, then still an Orthodox, but, so Mascall assured readers, with a good knowledge of Anglicanism besides. In the next issue it was explained that from the official standpoint she was actually succeeding Van der Mensbrugghe, who had gone to Paris to teach in the new Institut Saint-Denis, the Moscow Patriarchate's answer to Saint-Serge. She and Thompson would find no dearth of talented writers, despite the passing of Bulgakov, soon to be followed by Berdyaev. Mascall noted some of them who would be prominent in the post-War years. There was Lionel Thornton, priest of the Community of the Resurrection, a devotee of biblical typology,[35] H. A. Hodges, professor of philosophy at Reading and a former Methodist, now Anglican,[36] and, above all Vladimir Lossky, on whom there will be much more to say.[37]

The 1947 conference at Abingdon was Zernov's last stand as general secretary. Its most startling event was what Giorgiadis described as a 'provocative address' by an Anglican clerical member of the Fellowship, Derwas Chitty, on 'Orthodoxy and the Conversion of England'.[38] Probably for diplomatic reasons, Chitty's lecture did not appear in *Sobornost* but, in somewhat revised form, it was brought out by the speaker as a freestanding pamphlet. *Orthodoxy and the Conversion of England* cannot have gone down well with many Anglican members of the Fellowship. Speaking of such members he wrote:

> [I]t has been too commonly assumed that all we have to gain from Russian or Greek, apart from support for our determination to be Catholic without being Papist, was in the nature of caviare or rose-petal jam—a spiritual luxury delightful in its place, but not to be indulged in to excess—for 'we must remain Western'—and not indispensable.[39]

Chitty, who had almost become Orthodox in Jerusalem in 1927 when attending the French Dominicans' school of biblical and archeological studies there, believed that, to the contrary, the proper vocation of the Fellowship within the Church of England was to return that Church to its lost Orthodox identity—lost, that is to say, in the clerical revolution in the Latin West of the Gregorian reform. Chitty held that, in the eleventh-century crisis between West and East, the East was quite simply right and the West straightforwardly wrong, while, so far as the sixteenth-century Reformation was concerned, on every point where the Reformers disagreed with Roman teaching, that teaching was itself 'deeply if subtilly [sic] different from the Greek.'[40] '[B]oth then and subsequently, all the divisions of Western Christendom have been rooted in the search for some elements of the Christian life which would have been found in Orthodoxy.'[41] Hence (he believed) the way Free Churchmen can sometimes grasp Orthodoxy better than Anglicans do. He urged his hearers/readers to 'get back behind the division.'[42]

> I put it to you—were Jerome and Augustine themselves, Patrick and Columba, Gregory of Rome and Benedict, Wilfrid and Chad, to return to earth today, may it not be that they would all alike find in modern Eastern Orthodoxy something more recognizably identical with the Church they had known in their own countries than anything they would find now in the Western Churches?[43]

This going back beyond the Schism, would it mean for the Orthodox divesting themselves of what came afterwards—which includes, for instance, the fourteenth-century St Gregory Palamas and the nineteenth-century St Seraphim? Chitty answered, in a sense, Yes, but in another sense, No, since these saints, like 'the heart of accepted Orthodox Theology, have always called us to such a divesting, saying, "Not I, but Christ living in me"'.[44] They were travelling on a way of humility, obedient to a primacy to which the 'Western Church of the last nine centuries has not dared to submit herself.'[45]

But if from the early Middle Ages onwards the Latin Church was such a hopeless case, what then becomes of the Christian patrimony the Church of England inherited from mediaeval Christendom in the Tudor age?

> I, as an Anglican, must believe that the one Spirit did and does continue, however imprisoned, in the Roman Church, if I am to believe that the same Spirit has been handed down through History to us. Only, may it be that in some sense the Faith has remained in the West like the Sleeping Beauty, needing the kiss of Orthodoxy to bring it back to full life: And remember, that kiss might come too late.[46]

Though conceding that, on most points, the 'official Roman dogma does not really shut the door on Orthodox interpretation,'[47] Chitty distanced himself from a number of beliefs and practices advanced Anglo-Catholics would hold dear—as well as common beliefs of Anglicanism, such as the procession of the Spirit from Father and Son.

> Perhaps I should remind Anglo-Catholics of the fact that, very often, Orthodox people actually seem to find themselves more at home in 'Evangelical' English churches—just as also 'Evangelicals' and other Anglicans have been known to find themselves more at home in the Orthodox Liturgy than in some of our Masses. This cannot be treated as insignificant.[48]

Chitty's manifesto was a distinctly disturbing document.

By 1948 Patrick Thompson (now with an Orthodox wife and child) and Helle Giorgiadis were the joint editors of *Sobornost*. Nicolas Berdyaev had just died and they decided to devote their opening editorial to him. Essays by Berdyaev, extracts from his books, and reviews of his books, had been prominent, after all, in the first issues of the journal. Their comments were nothing if not frank.

> He was not interested in the 're-union of the Church' or the 'oecumenical movement'. He could not be, for he did not believe in the Church (as a social institution), and he did not believe in the world (as a centre of 'being') ... [Yet] his heart, his loves and hatreds, his pity and his hope, were Orthodox and Russian.[49]

In England academic philosophers did not recognize Berdyaev. If he was noticed at all it was a social commentator. The editors recommended his little book on Dostoevsky as replete with the themes of his life and work: spirit, man, freedom, evil, love, revolution, socialism, Russia, Christ, Anti-

Christ.⁵⁰ Some attempt was made to help readers work this out. George Every offered 'Background for Berdyaev', stressing how much he belongs to 'a line of unorthodox Orthodox laymen, whose religious philosophy is derived from a mixture in varying proportions, of Russian and Greek theology with German philosophy',⁵¹ and he added that the speculative audacity of these men is partly conditioned by the conservatism of the religious tradition together with their own detachment from all authority, secular or ecclesiastical.

> It is to the credit of Berdyaev that he knows how much modern German philosophy he is carrying. But it would be as well if his Christian readers, Anglican and Russian, could remain aware of his illuminism, and his radical readers aware of his Orthodoxy.⁵²

In 1949 the winter issue described the dedication of the chapel of St Basil's House by Germanos of Thyateira, the exarch of the Ecumenical Patriarchate in western Europe. His address was carefully crafted. The chapel was for the Orthodox liturgy but with Anglicans also praying (and singing, since they frequently directed or indeed made up the choir). Anglican worship could be catered for on a separate Holy Table. Germanos recalled the ancient canons which prohibited prayer with heretics, adding:

> But present-day practice, although it does not cancel this canonical prohibition, has moderated its sternness and thus the Orthodox Church permits her children to pray in company with people professing other doctrines, whenever she sees that these people have no tendency to proselytism but, on the contrary have a living desire for the fulfilment of the prayer of our Lord to His Father, 'That they may all be one.'⁵³

The bishop explained his policy of encouraging Orthodox without access to their own churches to go to Anglican rites, though not to Holy Communion. In his pro-ecumenical attitude he was following the throne of Constantinople in its policy of the last thirty years and he did not think 'the great Orthodox Church of Russia' was differently minded—although there are some 'sombre and stiff-necked individuals who insist on the exact observation of the letter, but not of the spirit, of the sacred canons'.⁵⁴ A description followed of the ceremony, which also gave an opportunity to describe Sister Joanna's Reitlinger's iconography.

Meanwhile the Fellowship had gone on pilgrimage to Walsingham (14–15 May, 1949) and Lev Gillet, then chaplain at St Basil's House, wrote an encomium of the place. His former Latin Catholicism emerging and not for the first time, Gillet compared Walsingham with La Salette, Lourdes, and Fatima. Unlike those shrines, it has no specific message, none aimed (more or less) at contemporary circumstances. Instead, 'Walsingham takes us into the mystery of Mary's very personality, as revealed in the hidden life of Nazareth and above all in the moment of acquiescence to the Divine Will concerning the Incarnation of the Son in Mary's womb.'[55] He found an excellent citation from the Roman Catholic layman E. I. Watkin to illustrate his meaning. It was an interpretation of the historic image of our Lady of Walsingham, which is known to have survived on mediaeval seals. 'The expressionless countenance expresses what is beyond expression. It is the countenance of one whose spirit dwells in a region beyond emotion and thought... Mary is beyond joy and sorrow. For her spirit is in God, and she knows as He knows, receiving His knowledge. No longer the Mother of Sorrows nor yet of the human joy of the crib, she understands the secret counsel of God to whose accomplishment Calvary and Bethlehem alike ministered. Therefore her peace, the central peace of God, is beyond the changes of earthly experience.'[56] The Holy House within the Shrine Church at Walsingham is an analogy for the 'inner centre', the Word made flesh, carried in Mary.[57] And Gillet promised that

> An amazing simplification and integration comes when we 'centre down', when our life is lived with singleness from a holy centre and wholly yielded to it.[58]

The 1950s

In 1951 Zernov sought to state again the aims of the Fellowship—with, admittedly, the ever-present financial worries in mind, but also for their own sake. Zernov held that the 'sin of division' explains the contemporary paradox that 'whereas the standard of Christian integrity, morality and learning is widely accepted, yet the authority and power of the Church in the world has noticeably declined.'[59] Christianity is becoming, he wrote, the 'spare time interest of a few devout people'.[60] He was exaggerating, but he was also donning a prophetic mantle. In the words of a present-day writer:

> In the 1950s the great majority of people living in Western countries were nominally Christian; the majority of the younger generation

were still being socialized into membership of a Christian society; links between religious and secular elites were often close. Yet the foundations on which the edifice of Christendom was built were far from solid. A small but influential section of the population had broken away entirely from Christianity, including many intellectuals, writers, and popular radicals. There was a much larger section of the population, including a large part of the working class, whose involvement in the church was limited to participation in rites of passage. There was a growing tension between the sexual ethics taught by the churches and the messages which had been coming over several decades from literature and films and from the writings of psychologists; there was also a wide, and probably increasing, divergence, between church teaching and what people, including church-goers, were actually doing. The ground was already well prepared for the crisis of Christendom in the 1960s. The most important of the immediate precipitants of the crisis was the wide-ranging impact of the unprecedented affluence enjoyed by most Western countries from the later 1950s ... [I]t favoured a trend towards greater individualism and weakened the collective identities which had been central to the processes of social emancipation in the nineteenth century and the first half of the twentieth.[61]

On Zernov's analysis, though Christians are 'no longer inflamed by denominational rivalries' (though of course this was hardly true of much of the Orthodox world, or of, say, Northern Ireland or the American South in the period in question), they are not willing to take the 'frank and energetic action of reparation, which alone could heal the wound inflicted upon the Body of Christ and enable the fullness of the power of the Holy Spirit to be manifested in the Church'.[62] Without further explanation, Zernov argued that the healing of the schism between East and West is a precondition for healing internal Western schisms (from the Anglican side the 1947 report *Catholicity* had also made this claim, but with reasons adduced[63]). It is Anglicans and the Orthodox who bear a special responsibility here since they are the people best placed to carry out this great task. The Fellowship exists, quite simply, so as to promote it. The Fellowship as such has no blueprint for reunion, but it seeks to 'awaken Christians to the possibility of Unity, and to stir their imagination by making possible for them personal contacts with the representatives of other traditions'.[64]

Helle Giorgiadis struck a note of realism, perhaps salutary, in her own report on the context of the Fellowship's activities.

The 'ecumenical movement', so-called, is still young; but, as its supporters coalesce into like-minded groups, differences of approach, of background, of immediate local needs, and even of outstanding personalities, must be expected to generate the same tensions within the movement as were responsible for those divisions in Christendom which we seek to heal.[65]

There was in this decade much soul-searching and some discontent. The editorial of the winter 1953 issue felt obliged to ask again, Why does the Fellowship exist? Its answer was more confined than Zernov's though it was also more strictly in line with the Fellowship's beginnings. It existed in order to try to

> learn and obey the will of God in regard to... one schism in particular, that which consists in the breach of communion between the dioceses of Christendom, East and West; and, more particularly still, that schism as it affects the national churches of Eastern Christendom (the 'Orthodox') and, on the other hand, the provinces of Canterbury and York, and those in communion with these.[66]

And the editors went on:

> If Protestant, Dissenting or Romanist fellow-travellers care to take part in its doings—and some of them have—they are welcome, no questions asked: but their presence cannot modify the purpose of the Fellowship, which is dictated by its nature as surely as it is true that *operatio sequitur esse*. These are 'first principles' to which we will always do well to return.[67]

Some criticisms had been heard. The Western members were not keeping up with recent significant theological or liturgical trends, and were insufficiently representative of Anglicanism. The editors wondered how lasting or valuable the trends in question might be ('a significant trend' is, they said, acidly enough, a 'statistician's expression'[68]). Among Anglicans it is High Churchmen alone who value union with the Orthodox. Low Churchmen prefer union with English Dissenters, Scots Presbyterians, or Continental or American Protestants. Meanwhile, the objective the Fellowship was founded to achieve was looking further off than ever. The Church of England had not changed enough in an Orthodox direction, while the Orthodox, for instance at their 1948 Moscow conference, had if anything changed for the worse, so far as ecumenical attitudes were concerned. The roads still remain, to Jerusalem, Moscow, Constantinople.

The Long Story

The travelling, however, is rougher. So be it. The editorial team advised positive resignation to circumstance. We are in the world and of our times and must make the best of it.

The death of Archbishop Germanos triggered discussion of a delicate question, that of the Fellowship's presidents, both Orthodox and Anglican. Some Anglo-Catholics did not want Bishop John Rawlinson of Derby to continue as the Anglican president. From the Anglican Catholic fastness of Mirfield, the Superior of the Community of the Resurrection and nine other priest-members (some, such as Lionel Thornton, Mark Tweedy, and Geoffrey Curtis, extremely active in Fellowship events) wrote to the Fellowship secretary pleading for a replacement. They admitted that Rawlinson had been Walter Frere's candidate. Initially this had been with good reason, but not later.

> Bishop Rawlinson had shown himself not only a theologian of great distinction but a strong witness to and supporter of the catholic tradition of our own Church. Since those days the balance of his sympathies has changed, and he has lost no opportunity of showing that he has espoused an ideal of a different character and of advocating a programme of action in the cause of Christian unity which is opposed to that of Bishop Frere, Bishop Gore, Bishop Seaton and other great Anglican churchmen, who took a leading part amongst those Anglicans who helped to initiate the Fellowship. The Fellowship has always been glad to include on its English side, beside Anglo-Catholics, some who belong to other traditions within the Church of England. But its inspiring force amongst ourselves was that of men who, desiring ardently 'the restoration of unity between unity between the East and the West', considered the reunion with the Orthodox Church as a part of the general move towards the restoration of 'the fullness of Catholic life' amongst us.[69]

The words quoted towards the end of the letter were, tellingly, from Zernov's chapter on 'Walter Frere and the Russian Church' in the memorial collection of essays about Frere's life and work.[70] Yet Rawlinson, arguing in his own defence that officers like ordinary members must always follow their conscience, was re-elected. Gillet reviewed C. B. Moss's critique of Rawlinson's *Problems of Reunion* in a more gentle style than was usual with him, aware no doubt of Rawlinson's high standing and Moss's harshness of temper.[71] Claude Beaufort Moss was the leading Anglican expert on the Old Catholics, a sometime joint assistant secretary of the Archbishop's Council for Foreign Relations, and a fervent anti-Papist. In *What Do We*

Mean by Reunion? he banged his usual drums, now at the expense of the bishop of Derby.

> Dr Rawlinson had taken a somewhat middle position between Catholics and Protestants. Dr Moss is strongly opposed both to the Roman and the reformed religion. His 'Catholicism' rejects Calvin, but detests Rome and has no sympathy with romanizing Anglo-Catholicism. He violently objects to the doctrine of the invisible Church, insists on episcopacy and priesthood, appeals to the ancient tradition represented by the Orthodox Church as the true 'standard' of reunion, and entertains friendly feelings for the Old Catholic and the Lutheran Episcopal Churches.[72]

A non-Anglican should keep out of this, thought Gillet, though he pointed out distinguished Orthodox of the mediaeval and later periods who had no problem with the notion of an invisible Church.

In 1953 it fell to Helle Giorgiadis to celebrate editorially the silver jubilee of the Fellowship. She felt that, while early optimism had given way to realism, the will to unity was if anything stronger than a quarter century earlier.

> The old inter-confessional tensions are gradually being superseded by the familiar 'progressive' versus 'reactionary' tension within the different confessions themselves.[73]

To these tensions the Fellowship, she reported, was not immune, while the intercommunion based on Orthodox recognition of the Churches of the Anglican Communion has been 'courteously replaced... in the archives of history'.[74] She explained that the Fellowship was now incorporated as a company at law, enabling it to hold its own property. The opportunity was taken to increase the number of vice presidents from two to seven so Bishop Michael Ramsey of Durham was included, and the Earl of Halifax, famously associated with Anglo-Roman détente via the 'Malines Conversations'. Presumably these appointments were intended as a counter-balance to Rawlinson.

1954 proved a controversial year for the Fellowship. In a meeting of its consultative council in May, Bishop Rawlinson, in his capacity as president, had called for a discussion of how the Fellowship was achieving its aims. Since reunion was clearly not about to happen in the near future, what should count as the purpose of the Fellowship's work? At this juncture Mascall stepped in to renew the criticisms made by the Mirfield objectors to Rawlinson's election two years earlier. The president's support for reunion schemes with Free Church bodies and other Protestants would, thought Mascall, inevitably hamper rapprochement between Anglicans and the Orthodox. Rawlinson wanted to know—and this was pertinent to Mascall's remarks—whether the Fellowship aimed to introduce the Orthodox to the entire Church of England or only to one section of it. The question was linked both to Anglican Evangelicals' preference for 'Home Reunion' and to the liturgical style of the Anglican Eucharist as celebrated at Fellowship conferences. The president was of the mind that on such occasions the Book of Common Prayer should be in exclusive use (in all likelihood, Western Rite, i.e. Roman, and/or English Use, i.e. Sarum Missals, in vernacular translation, rather than the 1928 'Deposited Book', which many bishops tolerated, were the order of the day). Another pointed question concerned the lack of Orthodox attendance at events. Was the Fellowship a club for Anglicans interested in Orthodox matters— or was it a genuine meeting-place? Finally, Rawlinson had been asked to raise the question of the Fellowship's attitude to 'individual conversions'. Presumably this meant of Anglicans to Orthodoxy since joined with it was the issue of attitudes to a 'possible future English-speaking Orthodox Church', which, it was said, Father Anthony Bloom was keen to promote.[75]

In June 1954 a sub-committee was appointed to consider these matters and met seven times before producing its report, which it did in March 1955. It was radical in tone. The Fellowship should set out to arouse interest in all Church of England traditions, and indeed those of Christians belonging to non-Anglican traditions too. It should also seek to address present-day theological concerns. It must drum up more Orthodox support—and interpret Anglicanism to the Orthodox, not just Orthodoxy to Anglicans. A new council should be elected to reflect these wider concerns. The Fellowship and the Anglican and Eastern Churches Association should be merged. The council should meet regularly, for the overall direction of a policy, and appoint a small executive committee for day-to-day affairs. The Fellowship needed at St Basil's House a male general secretary who was theologically competent, and understood both communions, and a female warden, the two to be appointed, ideally, for three years. The finance necessary to pay proper salaries must be raised.

The latter provisions were timely since there were at this time doubts as to whether Helle Giorgiadis and her colleague Joan Ford, who in practice were running both House and Fellowship, would want to continue.

Mascall as chairman had written to council members two months earlier with the news that the two women had announced their departure for the coming summer—unless, that is, the Fellowship could guarantee salaries and tenure for a future five year period. That, explained Mascall, would leave the Fellowship without an administrator for correspondence, for the organization of the conference, of meetings, services, the business side of *Sobornost* and part of the journal's editing and sub-editing, as well as a manager for the running of St Basil's House. Mascall clearly wanted to keep at any rate Giorgiadis, whose efficiency he admired, against the wishes of Zernov, who in a letter of April 1955 complained about her 'dictatorial manners'.[76] Zernov also disputed her memory of a council minute, taking the line she had deliberately distorted his words in order to 'deepen the gulf that is rapidly growing between Paris and London'.

Placing such a negative construction on conflicting memories of a discussion was evidence of a somewhat dire state of inter-personal relations—or the lack of them. It justified some words of Mascall in a letter of the previous month, which identified the underlying issue as disagreement about 'perfectly good different lines along which the Fellowship might develop'. The trouble was that 'very few of us are prepared to follow other lines than our own, if we find ourselves in a minority'.[77] Rawlinson's request for a fuller definition of both goals and means was, after all, right. Mascall now resigned his post as well as membership of the council, pleading the difficulty of getting to meetings from Oxford. Yet the better definition of aims and methods was not settled by the end of the 1950s, as will be seen.

The increasingly full and professional reports on the running of St Basil's House showed the quality of its manager, Joan Ford, who by now was in her eighth year. 1955 described advances in the library, as well as chapel matters and the outreach in hospitality, which was growing in its internationalism thanks a tour by the Zernovs of India and Ceylon. The report of that year ended with a thoughtful reflection on the significance of the dedication to St Basil the Great. Ford, incidentally, was not a glorified housekeeper: she had a double first in English from Cambridge. It was not surprising to find in the list of officers and council of the Fellowship that she had become, alongside Giorgiadis, its secretary. In the listing of officers, Thompson began to be described as 'honorary' editor of *Sobornost*, while both his name and that of Giorgiadis or 'the Secretaries' (i.e. Ford and Giorgiadis) continued to appear in the opening pages of each issue as the 'Editors' in an unqualified sense. Mascall had evidently succeeded in his aim of marginalizing (to a degree) Rawlinson, for by the end of the year Michael Ramsey was president while Rawlinson, like the new exarch of the ecumenical patriarch, Athenagoras of Thyateira, continued as an 'honorary' co-president.

In the later 1950s agonizing resumed. In the last issue of 1959 Nicolas Zernov wrote a pessimistic account of 'The Ways of the Fellowship, 1928–1958'.

> It seems to me that our main weakness today is the lack of direction. We have no clear object either for study or action. Our Fellowship promotes goodwill, spreads information and provides opportunities for personal contacts between Eastern and Western Christians. Useful though these activities are, they are insufficient. We have lost the sense of the urgency of reintegration and also the feeling of the pain of division. We discuss the theological points of agreement and disagreement without attempting to arrive at any practical conclusions. We remain a small body with little material resources at our disposal and therefore all that we do is on a restricted scale. The Western and Eastern reconciliation is a major task of our time, and we have not been able to present it in the right way either to Eastern or to Western Christians. We have also been losing touch with the younger generation and our annual conferences have a decreasing number of students.[78]

Meanwhile, the Russians in exile—the original Orthodox members of the Fellowship on whom it had largely depended for new ideas—were playing a very reduced role. Indeed they were dying off, and were unlikely to be replaced: after the Second World War a variety of their institutions did not re-open and, for a younger generation, Diaspora consciousness had diminished. What could not have been foreseen was a post-Soviet world in Russia itself, where a new generation would take up with alacrity the writings of the exiled Orthodox intelligentsia and give them new life.

Zernov's lament received an editorial footnote disclaiming responsibility for either the accuracy of the factual statements or the justice of the opinions. The matter proved serious. The Anglican Franciscan Barnabas Lindars, a biblical scholar who was acting chairman, wrote to Zernov to explain the setting up of yet another working party to 'consider the policy and staffing in the best interests of the explicit aims of the Fellowship', recommendations to be forthcoming in time for decision-making by the end of the year. Zernov was not only invited to answer the question, 'Is the Fellowship at present fulfilling the purposes for which it exists?'[79] He was also asked to comment on the viability or otherwise of the multi-tasking roles of the two Secretaries. By now Giorgiadis and Ford had withdrawn, to be replaced by an Australian Anglican clergyman, Eric Hampson, assisted by a laywoman, Rae Phillips. Hampson was already complaining how an unrealistic workload left him no time to read up on Orthodoxy or attend the liturgies of the Orthodox Church so as to deepen his knowledge. He was also frustrated by the difficulties of correspondence with hierarchs. As John Lawrence (see below) wrote to a correspondent (with copies to Zernov, Gillet and a new name among the major players, A. M. Allchin), 'he does not realize that Greek Bishops do not answer letters'.[80] Neither Hampson nor Phillips would last much over a year. When Hampson finally resigned, taking himself off, as he put it, to the 'bush' of North Queensland, he used the occasion to deplore Zernov's 1959 article as 'damaging'. Evidently the wound had remained open.[81]

By the spring of 1959, though Thompson was still regarded as Editor, assisted by the Secretaries, the opening article on current affairs—which might have been thought an editorial preserve—had been signed 'J. W. L.' and 'A. M. A.' The latter was evidently Donald Allchin, a future counsellor to archbishops of Canterbury on Eastern Church affairs, and a towering figure in the Fellowship in the coming generation; the former was Sir John Lawrence, former British diplomat in wartime Moscow, writer on matters Russian, and founder in 1957 of the ecumenical quarterly *Frontier*. In 1960 Lawrence and Allchin chose to explain that the Fellowship had never been 'anti-anyone'. The membership was never exclusively Orthodox and Anglican. By chance, Dom Bede Winslow, monk of St Augustine's Abbey, Ramsgate, and founder of the journal's Catholic counterpart, the *Eastern Churches Quarterly*, had just died, and they took the opportunity to stress the 'value which we attach to our contacts with Roman Catholic friends and fellow-workers, as well as with members of the Free Churches'.[82] There must have been those who wanted to see a clearer alignment in the Fellowship of Orthodox and Catholic-minded Anglicans so as to recreate the Reunionist hopes of an earlier period. But the ecumenical scene was becoming more open and more complicated. Moreover, the question would soon arise of how interested the Orthodox—and especially, perhaps, converts to Orthodoxy—still were in what the Christian West had to offer. 1960 would, by happenstance, air both concerns.

The 1960s

In the opening year of the decade, Mr Gerald Bonner of the University of Durham, a patrologist specializing in the Latin tradition, produced a scathing review of a book by the lay convert to Orthodoxy, Philip Sherrard.[83] Sherrard's *The Greek East and the Latin West* bristled with historical mistakes and lacunae but, more importantly, it belonged to a bad tradition of authors 'marked by a strong prejudice against what they regard as the Latin mind, and none of them even begins to do it justice'.[84] Bonner's attempted demolition would not go unanswered. Correspondence included robust defences of Sherrard from Geoffrey Curtis and Benedict Green, both of the Community of the Resurrection (Bonner was not reviewing for *The Journal of Theological Studies* and did not take seriously the book's positive expositions of Orthodox teaching), and also from Timothy Ware (who defended the book's Palamism and its decision to treat doctrinal concerns, rather than non-theological factors, as the real key to the schism). Bonner was allowed a reply, and repeated his accusations of 'slapdash'. He felt Sherrard had done his Church a disservice, by giving scope for others to say lack of scruple about historical fact is not a problem for Orthodoxy. Sherrard would remain a favourite of *Sobornost* in later decades, and his systematically anti-Western tone, unerringly echoed by a majority of modern Greek theologians, would somewhat tarnish the ecumenical credentials of the journal.

Meanwhile the Fellowship's president, Michael Ramsey, still at this time archbishop of York, had addressed the 1960 conference at Broadstairs that September. He stressed the way concern for unity could not be sundered from concern for holiness and truth—it was a threefold cord based on chapter 17 of St John's Gospel, the farewell discourse to the disciples by the departing Lord. The ecumenical movement cannot be in its essence the mere 'reduction of the number of ecclesiastical bodies as such'.[85] Joining up, say, three denominations might harden division with others, rather than contributing to the Great Church of the future. Actually, Ramsey believed that Orthodoxy alone has a 'wholeness in which these elements of unity, truth and sanctification are never allowed to be separated', and it is from this that Anglicans must learn.[86] This was not what some in the Fellowship wanted, a privileging of Anglican–Orthodox reunion as such. Ramsey was not the antidote to Rawlinson not a few had hoped.

In retrospect, Ramsey thought the attempt to secure Orthodox recognition of Anglican Orders had been a 'false track', a consequence of seeing the matter 'through the spectacles of relations with Pope Leo XIII'.[87] It had also been a mistake to play down the 39 Articles, which in the 1920s and 1930s the combination of liberalism and Anglican Catholicism conspired to put low on the list of priorities. And finally, optimism about how many dogmas both sides could agree on missed the point that Orthodoxy is a theoretical-practical whole, which must be taken altogether or not at all. Exploratory Anglo-Russian conversations in 1956 had put paid to these illusions, though Ramsey repeated his earlier comments that the Orthodox have not given sufficient attention to the way Reformation-period Anglicans had to struggle free from the poor performance of the late mediaeval Latin Church. Faith is mediated in historical circumstance and by verbal formulations: these modifying factors must be taken into account to do justice to Anglicans.

Such nuanced words could not, however, stabilize all shifting ground. As Hampson remarked in his last full year as secretary, there had been a significant shift in the structure of the Fellowship as a whole.

> We have grown from a small gathering of the theologically alert who could meet and discuss and write and pray, to a large fellowship which thinks and cares and prays, but which is very unlikely to meet as a group and which is becoming more difficult to co-ordinate in theological output.[88]

It was once the mark of a member that he or she had attended a conference, 'partaken, so to speak, of the excitement of physical ecumenical experience'.[89] But now things are different, so 'the most we can say is that the Fellowship is like an *eikon* of what the Abbé Couturier used to describe as his "invisible monastery"'.[90] But perhaps, Hampson concluded, the mere fact of continuing existence with some experience of the past and a readiness to adapt in the future should count as a vocation of some sort. Whatever else this 'thinking aloud' might be called, it was not a ringing manifesto. Hampson, announcing his resignation as secretary in a move to Australia, and the advent of his successor Basil Minchin, gave out, not for the first time, curiously mixed signals. The pre-War camaraderie ws dead. The Fellowship had become an Orthodox information-bureau plus a 'pentecostal' community which is inter-confessional but without, alas, the Orthodox Russian-Parisian element formerly so vital.[91] To demonstrate its distance from the conservative and moribund, perhaps, he fantastically suggested, the Fellowship should move its HQ to America.

What actually transpired was rather more modest. Margaret Minchin, Basil's wife, became the new *responsable* of the reassuringly actual St Basil's House. But their ideas were not restricted to the creation of a cosy *ménage*. Basil and Margaret Minchin gave a new lease of life to the Fellowship owing to a deliberate policy of foreign travel in Orthodox lands. These were not disguised holidays, as Nicolas Zernov explained with reference to the period 1958–68:

> The main problem which confronted the Conference organizers was the decrease in the number of Orthodox participants. The Russian colony in Paris was shrinking and was no longer able to provide new recruits. The Minchins tried to compensate for this by regular visits to the Balkans in the hope of enlisting for the Fellowship conferences theologians from Eastern Europe. Political conditions were unfavourable and only a few were able to come.[92]

The Minchins were indefatigable on what must sometimes have been uncomfortable journeys. No one individual (or couple) could be expected to master all the tongues needed for converse on these tours. Instead, Basil Minchin devised a way of lecturing at theological academies and monasteries 'using a technique that combined the use of slides with taped commentaries in a number of languages'.[93] And so, as Zernov explains, their travels brought the Fellowship's message to those who, through limitations of politics or finance, were unable to come to the West.

The editorial for winter 1966 noted the awarding to Zernov by the University of Oxford of a doctorate of divinity and the news that Timothy (Kallistos) Ware had succeeded him as Spalding Lecturer. In retrospect, it was a momentous occasion in the development of the Fellowship. Ware would become the first native Englishman to be an Orthodox bishop and the best-known theological and spiritual voice of Orthodoxy in the English-speaking world.[94] Here is what Zernov had to say about him in his *Memoir*.

> Archimandrite Kallistos, lecturer in Eastern Studies at Oxford University, though a convert from Anglicanism has never attacked Western Christianity. His objective and friendly attitude to both the Roman and Anglican churches has secured wide recognition of his authority among Western theologians. His book *The Orthodox Church* has had a greater success as an introduction to Orthodoxy

than any other book. He has exemplified the positive role which a Western Orthodox can play in the efforts to reconcile the Christian East and West.[95]

Zernov went on to reflect on the phenomenon of the influential Western Orthodox convert, taking it to be (not necessarily correctly, but the new immigration from both Russia and the European Union was still over the horizon) the pattern of the future.

> The passing of the Orthodox leadership into the hands of Western converts could seem to undermine the very foundations of a society which had been conceived as a meeting-place between Eastern and Western Christians. In reality, however, they, just as the Orthodox from the East, include both ecumenically minded Christians and those who are either indifferent or even hostile to reunion. It has become more and more evident that the Orthodox of Western background have a mission in the work of reintegration of the Church.

Zernov explained these remarks under three headings. Western converts are 'better able to expound the spirit of Orthodoxy in terms and language familiar to the West'; hitherto 'Orthodoxy has been seen as a specific form of Christianity restricted to the eastern nations', whereas the 'presence of western Orthodoxy emphasizes the universality of Orthodoxy'; and 'western Orthodox are called to create new expressions of Orthodoxy congenial to their own national character'.[96]

Donald Allchin, now editor, would never become Orthodox. He was careful not to commit himself wholly to the thesis of some younger Orthodox theologians that new trends in the world-Church of the 1960s had exposed the wrong turnings of Western theology as a whole. But the shaking of the foundations of Western Christianity, so painfully visible in the discussions of 'the death of God' and 'Christian atheism', gave new relevance, he thought, to theology of the Christian East, not least its apophaticism. Vladimir Lossky's master-idea seemed, thought Allchin, 'more and more evidently applicable to our situation'.[97] Lossky's French disciple Olivier Clément was speaking at this time about 'purification by atheism', not least in an essay reproduced in the journal.[98]

Also in 1966, Derek Allen, principal of Oxford's St Stephen's House, the 'Palm Court' of English Anglo-Catholicism, had come to the conclusion (or something strongly resembling it) that only the East could now save the West. He drew up a list of the desiderata of radical discontents and compared them with 'Great Tradition' solutions. First, critics wanted a 'holy worldliness', Christian involvement in or identification with the world. Well, creation is a major theme of the Great Tradition, and the East has drawn a less sharp distinction than the West between nature and grace.[99] Secondly, the critics wanted more lay theologians. The Great Tradition could offer them such—not least Nicolas Zernov! Thirdly, they do not care for Church institutions. The Great Tradition, as manifested East of Ravenna, concentrates on the 'supernatural organism' instead—and here 'eucharistic ecclesiology', in the contemporary Orthodox mode of Nikolai Afanasiev and Alexander Schmemann was recommended.[100] Fourthly, critics stressed as essential the spirit of service to the 'gracious neighbour'. The 'Eastern understanding of the ontological unity of humanity' was surely pertinent to this, and perhaps in particular the Russian tradition of imitating the 'humiliated Christ' (no doubt Allen was thinking of Gorodetzky's study of this theme[101]). Fifthly, the Western radicals expect a minority Church to be a remnant that leavens. Historic Orthodoxy under the *Tourkrateia* and Bolshevism has certainly been a remnant—though Allen abstained from claiming it had always leavened, pausing instead to strike a note of wonder at a Western oscillation between a fortress approach and a 'woolly' conception that barely distinguished between the Church and total humanity. Sixthly, and most crucially, the critics reject transcendence in the name of a secular Christianity. The Great Tradition would tell them that the God beyond words and images is to be sought mystically not intellectually, for the transcendence in question is not simply linguistic but a property of divine Being. 'Secularity' is not a problem if by it is meant that contemplative prayer on the mystical way can be practised anywhere, in any state of life.

This shift in the balance of the scales between Eastern and Western Christianity was instructive. Over the next fifty years, as the 'long story' continued, more theological weight would attach to East than to West. But that remains for Part Two of this history to relate.

→ 3 ←

Discovering the Russians

Discovering Eastern Christianity has meant very different things in the long life of the Fellowship and its journal. But for the most part, until Greece (and up to a point Rumania) came to enter the picture more fully, it meant discovering the Russians, even if this was for the most part via 'Russia Abroad', among the scattered of the Diaspora. In time, the Fellowship also remembered the Oriental Orthodox, for unlike at least one of its Anglican forerunners, it had no constitutional reason to exclude them from the meeting of East and West. But given the origins of the Fellowship, permanently recorded in its choosing of the premier Russian saint, Sergius of Radonezh, as co-patron, along with the Romano-British St Alban, it could be expected that Russian affairs might have the lion's share of its attention. And in any case, Russia was by far the largest historically Orthodox nation. Certainly in the first forty years of the Fellowship's existence, its eye was principally drawn to Russia and Russians abroad.

Discovering Russian Church history

At one level, discovering the Russians meant finding out about their history. The first issue of the re-baptized *Sobornost*, in 1935, contained the initial instalment of a compendium of Russian Church history by George Fedotov. Fedotov had been professor of history at the newly created University of Saratov and fled Russia in 1925. In the obituary by Zernov in the winter 1951 *Sobornost* we learn how he was among the leaders of the movement called *Novy Grad*, which 'advocated the social reconstruction of Russia on the basis of the Christian doctrine of man.'[1] He was, wrote Zernov, 'the first to discern behind the Orthodox tradition of Russian Christianity those peculiar features of Russian spirituality which distinguished it from the Byzantine pattern, and which escaped the notice of the old generation of Russian scholars.'[2]

Alban and Sergius

Fedotov provided a highly positive assessment of the pre-Mongol period (987–1237), especially in what concerned the relations of Church and prince. 'In the history of the relationships between the Church and the State in Russia these first centuries will for ever remain as an ideal epoch, a time of the greatest freedom for the Church and the greatest purity of its influence.'[3] He explained that the Russian polity 'originated in the ninth and tenth centuries from an association of Mongolian, Eastern Slav, and Finnish tribes, under the rule of the "Rurikovichi", a Norman [i.e. Norse] dynasty which reigned at Kiev.'[4] The baptism of Vladimir of Kiev in or around the year 988 did not make this prince the first Christian in the Russian land but it greatly accelerated a process of conversion from the top down, establishing Kiev and Novgorod as the chief centres of Orthodoxy. Kiev was the seat of a metropolitanate of the patriarchate of Constantinople, and Novgorod a republic comparable to the civic communes of mediaeval Italy, ruled in the name of St Sophia, its principal church, with its bishop as its senior office-holder. From the point of view of the encounter of East and West, Fedotov's comments on the relations of early mediaeval Russians with the Latin Church are worth citing.

> The theological polemics of the Greeks with the Latins are to a certain extent imitated in Russia only at the beginning of the twelfth century. Even in the twelfth century at Novgorod we still hear of women taking their children to be baptized in the Norse (Roman-Catholic) churches, for the practice has to be condemned by the bishop. The princes of Kiev, if expelled from their domain, had the right to appeal to the Roman pope for justice, and we see that they still do this at the end of the eleventh century. But notwithstanding all this the split in the Church became gradually a fact for Russia also, and Russians began to appropriate Greek ideas on Latin 'heresies' (mostly interpreting them as differences in ritual).[5]

Fedotov stressed the role played by coenobitic monasteries, more or less on the Studite model, situated close to towns with accessibility to non-monastics. Beginning with the Kievan abbot St Theodosius, a distinctive ethos became the typical profile of a Russian saint: the imitation of Christ in his kenosis or self-humiliation. Fedotov thought this 'cult of the "kenotic" Christ of the Gospels' was 'strange to Byzantium of that time' and anticipated by a hundred years the spirit of St Francis of Assisi. He drew attention to another characteristic type of Russian holiness, likewise based on the imitation of Christ: the 'passion-bearers', who were, as he says, 'not martyrs for the faith, but people who have suffered death because of non-resistance for Christ's sake'.[6] The first of these were also the first canonized Russian saints, the princes Boris and Gleb, sons of St Vladimir.

The visual art of mediaeval Russia, the worth of which was rediscovered only towards the end of the tsardom, excels its literature, restricted as this is to homiletic material and chronicles. The lack of either dogmatic theology or early scientific speculation misled nineteenth-century Westernizers into denying to this epoch any high culture. Its art gainsays them. They failed to take into account the way the heritage of antiquity was unavailable in ancient Russia, for only through the mediation of Old Slavonic (i.e. mediaeval Bulgarian) did texts arrive from outside.

Two issues later, a second instalment of Fedotov's short history took a dimmer view of the Mongol era (dated by him as 1237–1480) than had become fashionable with 'Eurasian' theorists among the exiles.

> In our time the so-called 'Eurasian' movement in the Russian emigration regards the Mongolian domination as a fortunate episode in Russian history, since it laid the foundations of a strong monarchy. Undoubtedly the Oriental character of serfdom in the Muscovite state—which forms such a contrast to the free institutions of ancient Russia—is closely associated with this period of Mongolian domination. The fact of a moral and cultural decline, which resulted from this yoke, is even more indisputable. Northern Russia, in medieval times, in contrast to the ancient Russia of the South-West, strikes us as a poor, rural, country, with badly developed trade and weak town life, as a country lost in immense forests.[7]

Some will concede it was an historic catastrophe but ascribe to it the revival of religious life. 'The history of the Mongolian Yoke in Russia refutes this wide-spread opinion.'[8] Only in the fourteenth century did monasticism recover, and then it was on a new basis, sylvan and eremitical, not urban and corporate—though Sergius of Radonezh, who 'continues to be an ideal of spiritual completeness and harmony in the Russian Church',[9] inspired both sorts of community through his own monastic foundation fifty miles north of Moscow. The fifteenth century would be the golden age of Holy Russia, in terms of monastic life, the flowering of sanctity and art.

The emergence of the Grand Principality at Moscow was supported by the Church, allowing the local bishop to be metropolitan of Russia (still a Constantinople nominee at this point). The metropolitans did not hesitate to support the Muscovite Grand Prince against the other princes and the free cities, whereas, Fedotov implies, the hierarchy ought really to have stood 'above the party struggle'.[10] "Thus the Metropolitans in Russia are already tending towards the Byzantine conception of monarchy, and it is here that we must look for the origin of Russian Byzantinism in the relationships between the Church and the State.'[11] The sixteenth and seventeenth centuries, described by Fedotov as the epoch of 'Orthodox Moscovite tsardom', were in his judgment lacking in the spiritual content that might have corresponded to their outward splendour. The Sergian stream emphasizing poverty and contemplation, the 'monks beyond the Volga' led by Nil Sorsky, was stifled, while their opponents, the 'Possessors', put in place a 'national-social monasticism' linked to the name of abbot Joseph of the Volotsky monastery, whose 'personal devotion ... quite foreign to mysticism, was based on liturgical prayer, the practice of asceticism, and a strict observance of the rule'.[12]

> [A]s time went on, Joseph's teaching concerning resistance to tyranny and his social conception of monasticism were forgotten. Only a ritualistic tendency in devotion, Church nationalism, and a justification of the power of the sword in the struggle with heretics remained.[13]

Perhaps the rise of 'fools for Christ's sake' was a Providential consequence, keeping the flame of holy humility alight.

Meanwhile the loss of ties with the Greeks led to a turning to the Latins for ecclesiastical knowledge, which coincided with the opening to Western science under Peter the Great. In the south-west the need to answer Counter-Reformation apologetics in their own terms added to the attraction of a Latin learned culture; Peter Mogila's academy in Kiev was modelled on the lines of a Jesuit college. 'Thus in their fight for the Orthodox Church the learned inhabitants of Kiev applied the method and sometimes even the spirit of Rome.'[14]

In the last issue of 1935, Fedotov's third instalment dealt with the 'synodical' period of the eighteenth and nineteenth centuries (though the system continued until early 1917). Fedotov painted a bleak picture of a theological scene whose main features were, first, the attempt to present a 'golden mean' between Roman Catholicism and Protestantism as the proper way to describe Orthodox theology and, second, the influence of Protestant mysticism on the higher clergy, saving them from

Enlightenment rationalism but at the cost of Pietistic overlay. Yet from these difficulties the disciplines of archaeology and history at least were exempt and the study of 'Russo-Byzantine Orthodox antiquity' became well advanced.[15] Even so, academic theologians of merit emerged, of whom Fedotov promised to speak in his concluding part. What remained of the ancient Russian Christian culture of his opening gambit was the monastery and its liturgy, though Fedotov was harsh on the spiritual life lived in more than a few of these. The phenomenon of the *starets*, which opened monastic spirituality to the laity, partly redeemed the situation, but this was recent, dating only from the second half of the nineteenth century. All in all, he concluded, it was 'on the broad backs of the peasants and the lowest classes of townsfolk, not of the upper classes, nor even of the clergy, that the Church was brought through these centuries'.[16]

The fourth instalment of Fedotov's sketch of Russian Church history reached 'The Two Revolutions and the Great War'. In the last decades of the tsardom the supporters of radical reform were chiefly among the 'white' or married clergy and the liberal wing of the professoriate in the theological Academies. They supported the admission of married priests to the episcopate and a role for lay election of parish clergy. There was no dogmatic liberalism, or interest in 'higher criticism' of the Bible (textual or 'lower' criticism was a different matter.) Reformers wanted the use of the vernacular in the liturgy and a mode of preaching that stressed ethical and social concerns. The lay theologian Alexis Khomiakov was important to them. This was their only link, however, to the theological movement of contemporary Russian Orthodoxy, of whom Vladimir Soloviev was the fountain head. The renaissance of Russian religious thought, not least through the religious-philosophical societies in the three great cities of St Petersburg, Moscow and Kiev, drew for its personnel, so to say, on former Marxists such as Berdyaev, Bulgakov and Semyon Frank, who brought with them a continuing interest in society (and eschatology), and likewise on former adherents of the aesthetic movement, which had acquired something of a mystical character via its theory of symbol. Here Pavel Florensky was the obvious case to cite. The reform looked for by the time the year was reached which saw the advent of a semi-constitutional monarchy (1905) might be described as both 'mystical' and 'eschatological' in character. It certainly 'had nothing in common with a Protestant reformation'.[17] Its Achilles' heel was the lack of contact with the common people. The popular element in the 1905 disturbances was, like the intelligentsia element, predominantly socialist and atheist. It led the tsardom in its last years of life to lean by reaction more and more on the Church for support, and found sometimes extreme partisans for its position in a minority of bishops and priests, including among the former the metropolitan of Kiev, Antony Khrapovitsky, who had been a leading theologian and counted among the 'liberals' in the past. Fedotov comments bitterly:

> These reactionary exploits of representatives of the Church in 1905 and in the years that followed, compromised the entire Church in the eyes of the masses more than anything ever done in the past, and had a grave bearing on the 1917 Revolution.[18]

There were also left-wing priests, even sitting in the Duma, but characteristically they either left the priesthood or were removed from it. But by March 1917, in Fedotov's constitutionalist view, the tsardom had no defenders left, and churchmen were ready to throw off the procuratorial system, even though the historian shows a degree of embarrassment at the Provisional Government's removal—despite its professed sympathy for the notion of Church independence—of a number of bishops regarded as protégés of Rasputin, the discredited erstwhile favourite of Nicholas and Alexandra. Nicholas II's 1906 promise of a *sobor* (council) had not been honoured, and now the time was both ripe—and too late. The *Sobor* opened just in time for the Bolshevik Revolution. Fedotov admits that its elected majority was conservative, with the 'group of liberal professors and democratic priests . . . left in the minority'.[19] The option of returning to the patriarchal system did not please all the delegates, but opposition was reduced by the decision that a regularly assembled *sobor* should govern with him.

Meanwhile Zernov was reflecting on 'The Russian Church Thirty Years Ago',[20] i.e. roughly in 1905. He was keen to dispel the belief that the adventurous theologians of the Russian emigration (Bulgakov must have been chiefly in mind) represent a total rupture with the traditional Orthodoxy of the late tsardom. When after the mini-revolution of 1905, Russian churchmen, from bishops down, were free to speak their mind,[21] and once, in early 1917, an All-Church *Sobor* was at least conceded and public debate could ensue, it became plain that the desire of senior ecclesiastics for Church reform extended not only to governance but also to what at Saint-Serge might be called 'ecumenical openness' vis-à-vis at any rate Anglicans and the Old Catholics.[22] So the Parisian institute, a creation of the exiles from this generation, should not be thought so innovatory as all that.

Contemporary Russia

The contemporary Russian scene was patently of more concern than the remote or even near background, however educative the historian's contribution might be. The opening editorial of the 1930s (March 1930) had described the deteriorating Church situation in Russia, as signalled by the public prayers for Russian Christians for which the convocations of Canterbury and York had asked some weeks before. Though detailed information from inside Russia was hard to get, Ambrose Reeves thought that, at the least, members of the Fellowship could be made aware of the economic hardships endured by the Orthodox exiles in Western Europe.[23]

In 1931 the *Journal* reprinted an article from *Vestnik*, the review of the Russian Student Christian Movement, which was, by contrast, exceptionally street-wise. Ivan Lagovsky, who had succeeded Zernov as *Vestnik*'s editor, argued that Russian Communism had proved a catalysing agent for anti-Christian forces, altering spiritual dynamics on a global scale. A condition of 'a-religiousness, of a complete inner indifference to religious requirements' is turning into a 'state of deliberate, conscious, God-fighting anti-religiousness'.[24] The 'Union of the Militant Godless' in the Soviet Union did not confine itself to Russia, but sought to work in Europe and Asia too. In Germany the Internationale Proletarische Freidenker, commanded by German Social Democrats, and the Belgian International of Freethinkers, linked to Freemasonry and numbering some hundred thousand members, chiefly from the professional classes, united various national organizations in Europe and America—including in England the National Secular Society. The article provided a rich store of detailed information about the activities of these bodies. Lagovsky had been teaching at Saint-Serge but he made the mistake of moving to Estonia. In the Soviet invasion of the Baltic Republics he was executed by Stalin's secret police.

Fedotov now brought down his history to contemporary times, describing the ferocious and systematic steps taken against the Church both during the Red Terror of the Civil War and after the stabilization of the Bolshevik regime—notwithstanding the clause in the Soviet constitution, which, up to 1929, enshrined liberty of conscience and freedom of religious propaganda. The closure (and often demolition) of churches and the sending of priests to concentration camps reached its height during the years of Stalin's Five Year Plan, from 1928 to 1932. Though both these actions and the atheistic propaganda carried out by all possible means had, undoubtedly, a huge effect (Fedotov reported the claim of the League of the Militant Godless that a third of the population was now entirely emancipated from religion), there had also been, by way of reaction, a 'growth of spiritual power within the persecuted Church'.[25] This manifested itself in the entry of intellectuals into the Church, in young adults taking monastic vows in the world, in new monks appearing in remote areas like the Caucasus and the northern forests, and in such public manifestations as well-attended Church processions in Moscow and Petrograd.

A weak spot was located in the lack of unity in the Church organization, which enabled the Bolsheviks to divide and rule. Members of the minority in the *sobor* of 1917–18 had accused the patriarch and the general run of Church members of counter-revolution. By 1922 the 'Living' or 'Renovationist' Church had managed to secure a majority of the church buildings still open. Reformist demands already heard towards the end of the tsardom—for a married episcopate, for instance—re-emerged but now in 'the context of a revolutionary-modernistic ideology'.[26] But with the execution of its ecclesiastical opponents the 'Living Church' guaranteed its own death so far as the faithful were concerned. Fedotov regretted that the 'healthy seed of reform ... represented by the Slavophil tradition' was so damaged by this history. In the patriarchal Church conservative tendencies could only be strengthened.

The acting substitute for the *locum tenens* of the patriarchal throne, Metropolitan Sergei Stragorodsky (formerly archbishop of Nizhny-Novgorod), had paid a heavy price for the legalization of his status. Fedotov was severe.

> Metropolitan Sergius limited the activities of his Church to the cult, and voluntarily deprived himself and his supporters of any freedom of moral judgment. He not only abandoned all resistance to the anti-Christian policy of the governing party, but went further than the members of the 'Living Church' in his deferential attitude to those in authority... It would be true to say that at present, in actual practice, there is no difference between the ideology and the tactics of the Patriarchal and of the 'Living Church'. The only thing that

distinguishes them is the canonical conservatism of Metropolitan Sergius and the undoubted legal succession of his authority.[27]

And Fedotov made it plain that Sergius's single greatest offence was to sign a declaration to the effect that the martyrs of the Russian Church had been executed for counter-revolutionary crimes.

The divisions in the Russian Church in exile were, Fedotov claimed, entirely political in character. They concern whether the Church should ally itself with monarchical restoration (the Synodal Church, with its centre at Sremsky Karlovci in Yugoslavia), or whether it should make its peace with the Soviet State (the patriarchal parishes under the jurisdiction of Metropolitan Eleutherius of Latvia), or whether, again, it should be independent (the parishes, but also the Institut Saint-Serge, under the jurisdiction of Metropolitan Evlogy of Paris, who was originally appointed to be responsible for the entire Church in exile by Patriarch Tikhon). Fedotov described the process which led Evlogy to break with Sergius over the question of loyalty oaths to the Bolshevik State and Sergius's condemnation of Evlogy's role in offering public prayers for the persecuted in Russia (which actually happened, though Fedotov does not mention this, on English soil). Fedotov saw the reform movement as partly discredited, even liquidated, by the Living Church fiasco, but he also thought some of its task would be pursued in the future. He was convinced of the Russian Church's superabundant energies.

One point which might have been made by Russians present at this lecture by Fedotov to the Fellowship's 'Paris Group' was that English Christians had not yet been required to show their steadfastness under conditions of extreme trial, as Russian Christians had. Bulgakov's philosophical admirer Leo Zander, in a piece entitled 'Light of Suffering', offered a short meditation on the sufferings of the contemporary Church in Russia, with its 'multitudes of new martyrs'.[28] Who would have thought it of the well-organized and State-directed Church of the tsardom? Yet, it turns out, 'The life of the Church ... is mysterious not only in the unfathomableness of her sacraments, but also in the unexpectedness of her surprising action'.[29] It was an extraordinary rejuvenation, as the old woman, imagined by the early Roman author Hermas in his curious tractate *The Shepherd*, 'in the days of persecution ... decks herself in her bridal robe and lives in the expectation of the Divine Bridegroom, knowing that he is "very nigh, even at the doors" (Mark 13:24)'.[30]

That the anti-religious campaign showed no sign of lessening, despite the apparently more generous provision for freedom of religion in the 1937 Constitution of the USSR was made plain in an account of 'new Soviet anti-religious legislation' by Paul Anderson, though his title was somewhat misleading. The point was that henceforth anti-religious propaganda was to be undertaken by the Party and not just by the Union of Militant Godless. This in turn meant that the judiciary could interpret the Constitution in terms of 'revolutionary legality', treating Party norms as in practice equally authoritative as State law.[31]

After the British declaration of War on Germany in 1939 and the making of the Ribbentrop-Molotov pact to dismember Poland, there was some understandable speculation as to whether the Allied effort might extend eastwards to the armed overthrow of the Soviet regime. A letter from Zernov to Archbishop William Temple (then archbishop of York), along with Temple's reply, shows how the Nazi-Soviet compact had suggested to some Russian exiles that war might be pursued not only against Germany but also against the USSR, with the prospect of overturning the Bolshevik regime. In his response to Zernov Temple was canny. The experience of the French Revolution had taught a lesson. Giving regicides the opportunity to present their enemies as anti-patriotic (as when Austria declared war on France, with émigré support), might play into the hands of Revolutionary leaders, strengthening their position at home.[32] Perhaps it was to diffuse a whiff of bellicosity that *Sobornost* published in the same number a letter to Stalin by Metropolitan Visarion of the (Rumanian) Bukovina arguing that, were it allowed not only to exist but to flourish, the Russian Orthodox Church could help consolidate the social solidarity the Soviet State wished to see on its territory, as well as win the USSR new sympathy abroad.[33] This was prophetic of the Stalinist future, though the alliance (if that is the word) of Party and Church swiftly evaporated under Stalin's successor Nikita Krushchev.

Meanwhile an anonymous reviewer sought to establish 'The Truth about Religion in Russia' on the basis of an official but highly diplomatic—not to say propagandistic—multi-authored study published by the Moscow Patriarchate in 1942 (and in English translation by the London publishing house of Hutchinson in 1944): the 'first public pronouncement made by the Orthodox Church in Russia after long years of complete silence.'[34]

> The tone of the articles, the luxurious production, and the absence of copies in Russian bookshops, all indicate that the book was printed for foreign consumption. This does not mean, however, that it is simply a fake, engineered by the agents of the NKDV (Soviet Secret Police); all the authors are genuine members of the Church, and the articles are undoubtedly written by them, but on subjects and in a style prescribed by the State and not chosen by the Christians themselves.[35]

The majority of the articles were not on religious subjects but on patriotic ones. The authors were allowed to assert that the faith and hope of Orthodoxy was sustaining the Russian war effort—but they were not permitted to ascribe any militant anti-Church attitudes to State or Party. Metropolitan Sergius, the only writer to touch on the issue, claimed that clergy and laity who suffered at the hands of the authorities did so on account of their politics, not religion. The reviewer suggested that when Sergius spoke of a bishop as necessarily prepared to undergo any form of humiliation to serve his flock he was including his own consent to the making of such mendacious statements. This was charitable of the reviewer in question. The December 1943 issue of *Sobornost* was able to announce the election of the new patriarch of Moscow (the said Sergius), which did indeed signal a change in Stalin's attitude to the Orthodox Church, now sorely needed as she was to shore up patriotic feeling in the war against Germany. In a considerable *volte-face*, Zernov even called it a turning-point in the evolution of Russia. In the struggle with organized atheism the State 'has been obliged to recognize the fact that it cannot defeat the believers and that the Church must be allowed to have a place in the life of the nation.'[36] The Anglican president of the Fellowship, at the time Rawlinson of Derby, had written to Zernov on the subject that September.

> The recently reported election of a Patriarch in Russia and the visit to that country of the Archbishop of York suggests that this might be in general a very favourable moment at which to enlist interest and sympathy for the ideals of our Fellowship.

But Rawlinson also went on to express a doubt. 'Are most of us too "White" Russian or at least too anti-Soviet in our sympathies to make it easy to buy this opportunity?'[37]

The secretary's diary registered Zernov's belief—based on reports of the attitudes of Russians liberated by the Allied armies—that Orthodoxy remained profoundly influential in Soviet life. In December 1945 *Sobornost* recorded the visit of the Metropolitan Nicholas of Krutitsky to Paris, where he concelebrated with representatives of the exarchate and the Synodal Church, the first such event since the Revolution and the breakup of juridical unity.

Russian Protestants might be included in the Fellowship's sights, if only *per modum exceptionis*. An unusual article for *Sobornost* was an outstanding study by Walter Kolarz on Russian Protestants under the Soviet regime. The title was somewhat misleading since the Old Believers were at least touched on. A better overall label might have been 'Russian Nonconformity'. The author noted how, from sources of various kinds, it could be inferred that groups exist, sometimes sizeable in particular regions, that are not under the umbrella of the Government sponsored All Union Council of Evangelical Christians and Baptists ('anarchic religious congregations'[38]). But even events taking place with the participation of that council could be the occasion for introducing, despite verbal echoes of State policy, specifically Christian tenets and attitudes. Protestant bodies found biblical grounds for urging 'Stakhanovite' efforts to outdo ordinary Soviet workers on a variety of State projects—to the combined admiration and annoyance of the authorities. In contrast to the period before the October Revolution, Protestants were often sympathetic to the Moscow Patriarchate on account of its witness in suffering. Such sympathy was not by any means fully reciprocated for statements by individual hierarchs about the need to combat growth in non-Orthodox religiosity could still be found. Radical sectarians existed who chose to identify the USSR with the 'dragon' of the Johannine Apocalypse. They avoided contact with Soviet institutions, and even with unbelievers, and constituted a form of interior emigration much deplored by the State media.

In the course of 1960 both Bishop Anthony Bloom and Nicolas Zernov had spent time in Russia—a comparatively rare experience for well-known Orthodox figures from the West in the Cold War years. Bloom had been born abroad, so it was his first sight of his parental motherland. His account of the trip was notable for his frank exchanges with State officials (he did not conceal his tsarist loyalties), and they, while justifying the ban on religious teaching (without it they would only have propaganda, whereas the Church would have propaganda plus cult, which would be unfair), did not hide the feebleness by this date of atheistic activism. Zernov, in a lay party (with one deacon) from the exarchate in Western Europe, took especial interest in parish structure and attendance, pointing out how the closure of so many churches had hugely invigorated those that remained.

Five years later Philippe Sabant wrote about the 'Intellectual Life of the Russian Church' in the USSR, basing himself on conversations with clergy in Moscow and Leningrad, and issues of the *Journal of the Moscow Patriarchate*. On the one hand, people do not want philosophy when they come to church: they have more than enough ideology outside. Rather, they want to hear of the great theological realities mediated by the liturgy. That the academic formation of the clergy is based on the Fathers of the Church is not, in this context, inappropriate. On the other hand, professors are aware of the need to keep abreast of secular knowledge and contemporary problems, and the supplementation of the syllabus texts by intensive reading on the part of their students is encouraged in the academies and seminaries. But given the nature of the Soviet regime it is unrealistic to expect that contemporary affairs would be addressed in the patriarchate's journal. The names of the great Russian Christian intellectuals, past and present, were known, though officially disapproved of. The official Soviet periodical *Voprosy filosofii* for 1962 spoke of 'such reactionaries and mystics as A. Khomyakov, V. Solovyev, V. Lossky and others' as enjoying moral authority among present-day Orthodox in Russia.[39] More positively, or at least neutrally, the *Journal of the Moscow Patriarchate* had mentioned Bulgakov, Pavel Florensky, Sergei and Evgeny Trubetskoy, Cyprian Kern, Jean Meyendorff. One name never mentioned was Berdyaev, though Sabant had heard him spoken of as a possible influence for the future.

Two vignettes of Russia abroad

In the last decades of the tsardom, the Russian Orthodox Church had been active in foreign missions. In the late 1950s there was a reminder of this from a well-connected member of the Fellowship. Richard Rutt was an Anglican missionary bishop in Korea. (In due course he would marry Joan Ford, the warden of St Basil's House, who for some time had served with Helle Giorgiadis as co-secretary of the Fellowship.) The growth of Korean Christianity, said Rutt, had been a remarkable feature of the global Church in the first half of the twentieth century though in the wake of the Korean War, for obvious reasons, it was largely restricted to the southern portion of the peninsula. The Catholic Church had appeared in Korea in the late eighteenth century, the Anglicans in 1890, the Russian Orthodox in 1900—though, as Rutt explained, many Koreans living in Russian Manchuria had already received Orthodox baptism. The Orthodox church of St Nicholas at Seoul, close by the Russian Legation there, was dedicated in 1903, and included a mission house and school. Despite the setback of the Russo-Japanese war ending Russian political influence in Korea, by the year 1912—by which date Japan had annexed Korea—there were some three hundred Korean Orthodox, and a start had been made on translating the Liturgy into their language. In 1923, so Rutt reported, the infant Church was placed by patriarchal decree under the authority of the diocese of Tokyo—with the Koreans steadfastly refusing to recognize the canonical change, though its aim was entirely benign: namely, to protect this tender shoot from icy air blowing from the Kremlin. After liberation from the Japanese at the end of the Second World War, a Soviet delegation duly arrived to take possession. The Seoul church fell, as Rutt puts it, 'under the shadow of communism', being endowed with a red flag and a prominently displayed picture of Stalin.[40] During the Communist invasion of the South in the Korean War the mission-house was gutted but the church itself survived, and in 1954 Orthodox services resumed, this time with a Korean priest ordained by Tokyo but functioning under the *omophorion* of Archbishop Michael of all the Americas, and hence of the Ecumenical Throne. At the time of writing, so Rutt reckoned, there were some four hundred Korean Orthodox, with regular adult baptisms in progress.

My other 'vignette' is a little diptych of travelogues by Nicolas Zernov's sister Maria, Mme Kullmann, which took as their subject the fate of Russian nuns in Serbia. The first introduced readers of *Sobornost* to the exiled Russian nuns of Khopovo, in the Frushka mountains. The former abbess of the community, Katarina Countess Efimovskaya, had presided in pre-Revolutionary times over a community of four hundred nuns, with seven hundred children in the attached orphanage. She is described as the foundress of the 'active religious life' for women in Russia.[41] Maria Kullmann's account included striking descriptions of both austerities and preternatural powers, the latter especially associated with a former itinerant, Lydia, who herself became a nun. The story resumed the following year in 'Meetings in Serbia: Mother Diodora's Convent', where Kullmann explained how Lydia (whom she had met in Belgrade as

'Mother Diodora') was now in the disputed Serb-Bulgarian borderlands, serving as an abbess herself. Under her rule were thirty Russian nuns from Bessarabia. The customs at their forest convent were Athonite of the severest sort. Diodora predicted that their way of life would not last much longer, since in the modern world few nuns have the ardent faith required. An encounter in the woods below the monastery with Kseniushka, a Siberian woman pilgrim, told of extraordinary faith. Soon before the First World War her husband, Roman, heard a voice proclaiming the imminent reign of Anti-Christ in Russia, and calling him to be a preacher. The couple sold everything and entered upon the life of wandering pilgrims, visiting monasteries, venerating relics, and meeting many people, both good and bad. After the October Revolution Roman developed an extraordinary gift of touching hearts, including Red Army soldiers who converted to Christ. She herself, asked what she thought of war, replied it began as war in heaven. We—human beings—did not start it, we cannot stop it. We can only decide to be 'on the side of the angels of light or on the side of the angels of darkness'.[42]

This was the eschatological note which, often enough in the encounter with Diaspora Russians, struck Anglican members of the Fellowship so forcibly. It seemed to be the message sent by Russian history, and echoed in the Diaspora in thought and art.

And the rest

In the period covered by this study, editors of *Sobornost* were beginning to dip their toes into the waters of other peoples and other lands. It would be false to convey the impression that they had no interest in Orthodoxy outside the Russian-speaking sphere.

Rumania (after the Second World War, more commonly, 'Romania') was a subsidiary focus of the journal's outreach and a target for the travels of its more peripatetic readers—including office-holders. Moreover, especially after Nicolas Zernov's time spent teaching in India in 1953–4, *Sobornost* had showed concern for the 'Lesser' Eastern Churches. Armenia had in any case been an early interest, via clerical contacts such as Nersoyan, whom I mentioned in the last chapter. In later years, beginning in 1965, there would also be highly informed reports from an Anglican layman living in Ethiopia. In time, *Sobornost* would also follow the fortunes of the Syrian Orthodox minority in Turkey and adjacent areas, stimulated not least by the fine translations from ancient Syriac poetry owed, above all, to Sebastian Brock. In 1961 Paul Verghese of the Syrian Orthodox Church in India—he called it 'The Catholicate of India', for other Indians belonged to the Jacobite Patriarchate of Antioch—was allowed to write in defence of the 'The Christology of the Non-Chalcedonian Churches'.[43] In the following issue, he would be challenged, though, by the formidable duo of Ware and Chitty, who pointed out flaws in his piece.

And above all, among the 'rest', there was Greece. First attempts to come to terms with the Orthodoxy of the Greeks were impressionistic, if in high literary style. Peter Hammond summoned up 'A Greek Festival': a description of the Assumption as celebrated in a village on the Bulgarian border. It was a foretaste of his award-winning *The Waters of Marah*, a study of the life of the contemporary Greek Church from the standpoint of an immensely percipient English expatriate.[44] The travelogue contained some barbs directed at Anglo-Catholics. 'As in our own Anglican tradition prior to the liturgical chaos initiated by the Ritualists, Mattins is invariably sung in its entirety before the Holy Liturgy begins.'[45] Describing how the presiding bishop sent him the portion of unconsecrated bread bearing the initials of Christ, he commented: 'How many a holy custom have we lost in exchanging the artos of Scripture and primitive tradition for the azymes which bear no evident relation to the work of simple men and women.'[46] Hammond also noted that

> Practice in regard to the use of the sacrament of penance in the country districts of Greece is by no means as rigid as is commonly supposed; or as might be inferred from that of the Russians of the diaspora—among whom sacramental confession has tended to become a sort of invariable preparation for Holy Communion.[47]

In 'A Thessalian Thebaid' Hammond was, as always, a delight to read, but the situation at that time of the cliff-top monasteries of the Meteora (only three still open) was pathetic in the extreme. That followed on not only a general history of post-mediaeval decline—in 1834 Robert Curzon, author of *Visits to Monasteries in the Levant,* found just seven out of twenty-four foundations functioning—but, and more especially, the combined effects of the Italian invasion and the Communist insurgency, neither of which had spared the monks (or their property). The desolation Hammond describes is hard to imagine when, by the early twenty-first century, a number of the monasteries have undergone a revival, though the climatic harshness he described—and the physical debility it can bring—is still of course a reality. The fidelity of the few monks who remained to the demanding timetable of the Offices was deeply impressive, and he saluted it in a peroration of great literary beauty.[48] It was an article which presaged the interest in Greek Church life, and above all monastic life, especially on Athos, in the Fellowship's later decades.

That began in the early 1960s. In 1962 Timothy Ware (not yet 'Kallistos') wrote on contemporary Greek monasticism. It is good to record a prophecy of doom that did not come true. Judging by the seemingly inexorable decline in the number of monks in Greece and the high average age of those that were left, Ware prophesied, wrongly, a gloomy future for Athos as it entered its millennial year. The position was much the same, he said, throughout the Greek Church, including in its outposts in Jerusalem and Mount Sinai. The only bright spots he could see were the revival of interest in 'classic works of monastic and ascetic spirituality' (a topic he covered in some detail), and the renaissance in monastic life for women.[49]

The reprinted works included a new edition of the complete *Philokalia*, the first since 1900, with illustrations by Ralles Kopsides, a pupil of the leading Greek iconographer Photios Kontoglous. The introduction spoke of the part-translations into English and French as a sign of growing interest in philokalic spirituality on the part of Westerners, and mentioned the rallying to the specifically Hesychast texts in the collection on the part of the Jesuit patrologist Irenée Hausherr, who had once been, like most earlier Roman Catholic scholars, sceptical of their value. Ware noted wryly how educated Greeks were surprised to find Westerners taking Athonite spirituality seriously. Ware included a contemporary apologia for the monastic way, which had given his essay its title. This was *Metaxu Ouranou kai Ges* ('Between Heaven and Earth'), subtitled 'Hagioritic Monasticism', by Father Theoklitos, a monk of Dionysiou, an Athonite monastery, and the author of the foreword to the new *Gerontikon* or compilation of the 'Sayings of the [Desert] Fathers'. Ware found Theoklitos excessively anti-intellectual. His claim that the scholar-monk has no place in Orthodoxy did not fit with Ware's own future as a monk-academic.

There was less to say about the women, but Ware noted how many of the most flourishing communities were new, and was impressed especially by the Old Calendarist convent of the Mother of God at Keratea in Attica, which, from a starting-date in 1925, had achieved a total of almost three hundred nuns. Its strictness put even Athos to shame, though the austerity was easier to bear given that most of the nuns had come from peasant backgrounds. Not all, however, as an essay by one highly literate nun, Theodora Hambaki, followed Ware's survey.[50] She mentioned that some bishops had begun to found apostolic sisterhoods for such purposes as helping women prisoners, educating orphans, running homes for the elderly. There was a precedent in the sixteenth-century Athenian nun St Philothei. It was too soon to evaluate their success.

Greek monasticism was a subject to which, in the second half of its period of existence, the journal would return.

4

Assessing Anglicanism

From the beginning, Anglicans had to explain the nature of their Church to their Orthodox counterparts in the Fellowship. It was to be a journey of mutual exploration. The most important problem for the Orthodox in assessing Anglicanism lay in the famed Anglican 'comprehensiveness'. How could they get a clear view of this chameleon-like ecclesiastical creature?

'Our Domestic Difficulties'

Certainly Anglicans did not seek to hide their difficulties from the Orthodox. The problems were not simply a matter of managing the internal complexity caused by comprehensiveness. There was also the question of whether and how the Church of England could maintain itself as the soul of the nation in the changed circumstances of modernity. G. W. O. Addleshaw's provocative essay 'Our Domestic Difficulties' arranged the problems facing the Church of England under the three heads of theological, pastoral and administrative.

Under 'theological', he wrote of the overall difficulty for sustaining the Christianity of the English in terms of a prevailing contemporary mindset which made man the measure, took a subjective view of knowledge, and was intoxicated by the fruits of applied science. Appealing to the Italo-German Catholic philosopher of religion Romano Guardini, that mind-set 'exalts ethos above logos, prefers action to thought, morality to faith', while its accompanying morality stresses friendship and pleasure, and these are not enough to guide life.[1] We are beginning to realize, wrote Addleshaw, that the difficulty will not be overcome by reinterpreting the faith in either a Modernist or a Liberal Catholic direction, since

> it is not modern science or philosophy in themselves which make it hard for us to gain a hearing for the gospel, but the mental attitude

and presuppositions of the modern man which lie behind modern science and philosophy.[2]

He considered that the Church of England had few pertinent theological resources. Its strength lay in biblical scholarship. Otherwise there were only isolated individuals at work, not a true tradition of thought. A body of religious philosophy is needed to meet the challenge. 'Until we can find a philosophy of religion which will make the mind of the modern man capable of receiving the Christian faith, all our recalls to religion will fall on deaf ears.'[3] Hence, Addleshaw thought, the interest that was beginning to be shown in Continental Thomism, notably as represented by Jacques Maritain and Étienne Gilson. 'The widespread interest shown by thoughtful Anglicans in Thomism as a possible solution to our philosophical difficulties makes re-union with Rome much nearer than we imagine.'[4] Hence too the interest in the modern Russian Orthodox philosophy of religion:

> It is the Russian Church which can help us out of its theological and philosophical treasures to learn anew the meaning of creation, to find a theory of knowledge in sympathy with our faith, and so lead us out of the waste land into which we have been led by a misplaced emphasis on biblical study.[5]

As to 'pastoral': the author found a number of serious gaps behind the impressive façade of Anglicanism. He identified the lack of training in religious philosophy, moral theology, ascetical theology, as disabling the clergy from being more helpful to people than they might. Perhaps it was only by increasing the presence of religious Orders in the Church of England that the vast mass of the unchurched could be reached (probably a reference to the sisterhoods that were such a feature of the Catholic Revival in the English Church). Somehow Anglican churches generally have not succeeded in persuading people to use them devotionally outside of service times, while at the official services many clergy have developed a bad habit of substituting texts of their own choosing for the liturgical prayers. Active Church members have not acquired any other idea of prayer than petitionary prayer. So we 'want our Russian friends not only to pray for us in our pastoral difficulties, but to teach us the meaning of prayer and worship.'[6]

The 'administrative' difficulties concern an unresolved *aporia* left over from the sixteenth and seventeenth centuries. Does the Crown exercise civil sovereignty through Parliament, and ecclesiastical supremacy through the convocations in accordance with canon? Or does the Crown exercise legislative power in matters ecclesiastical through Parliament considered as a sort of synod of Christian laity? The latter theory has the enormous disadvantage that, since the opening of Parliament to those of all religions and none, it no longer corresponds to fact. There is a huge muddle in consequence, and among other disadvantages a danger that the morality of the State will be substituted for that of the Gospel, and 'good citizenship regarded as the ideal Christian life'.[7]

Yes, Anglicanism was feeling its way towards a new identity as a global communion. But meanwhile:

> Our individualistic outlook, a relic of Protestantism, the uncertain authority of the decisions of the Lambeth Conference, may account for Anglicanism as a whole displaying all the worst features of federalism, notably in its inability to function as anything more than a collection of dioceses; we cannot act as a whole.[8]

Here too, if there will never be an Anglican pope, only federalism can serve Anglicanism's turn. But 'we want the Eastern Church to teach us how to make it work, to show the various parts of the Anglican Church how to act together as a whole, as one body and one family'.[9] This was an extraordinarily frank essay by one who secured preferment in the Church of England, becoming vice-principal of St Chad's College, Durham, and, late in life, dean of Chester.

Anglican worship

Given that the Fellowship was predicated on encounter not only in didactic events but also, and above all, in worship, the question of how Anglicans understood—and practised—the eucharistic Liturgy would inevitably be raised. The third conference of the Fellowship, in April 1929, was to be devoted to the theme of the Holy Eucharist, the central liturgical action, and the *Journal*'s first issue of that year, appearing the month before, prepared the way. Gabriel Hebert of the Society of the Sacred Mission, writing under cover of his initials ('A. G. H.'), gave an excellent overview, considering the motifs of 'Thanksgiving', 'Corporateness', 'Commemoration', 'Sacrifice', and 'Mystery'. 'Thanksgiving' was for the redemptive acts, especially notable in the Scottish, South African, and 1928 English Prayer-Books. Corporateness or what he termed the 'Corporate-aspect' was dear to Anglicans not least through the congregational singing of hymns. 'Commemoration' was linked to the historicity of the Gospel events as well as to salvation-history more widely. 'Sacrifice' must be included since 'the risen Saviour Who ever lives as the eternal Sacrifice for man, sets forth in the liturgy His eternal Sacrifice under conditions of space and time', and here the writer deliberately avoided saying the Church offers Christ (she offers herself as we do ourselves)—a difference, there, from Tridentine Catholicism. 'Mystery' meant 'the Real Presence and the Heavenly Food': the author proposed that Christ the Priest is really present as the true Celebrant of the Eucharist throughout its course, whereas as Christ the Victim, he is present in the sacred Elements, after the Consecration, then—but 'not corporeally' so.[10] The account suggests the pre-Tractarian High Church doctrine of the Eucharist, rather than that of contemporary Anglo-Catholicism, though a more 'advanced' note is struck when 'A. G. H.' concluded:

> This aspect of Mystery finds its expression in the ceremonial of the Mass, and very specially in the silences of the Mass: also in all preparation for Communion, including the custom of Fasting Communion, and in the use of Penance before Communion, and in the confession of sin which occurs in the service.[11]

In 1936, the Reverend G. A. C. Whatton's 'Anglican Ritual Variations— An Explanation' seemed at first sight a fair-minded survey, granted an Anglo-Catholic standpoint. Whatton's was at one time a well-known name among 'spikes', being the author of a much-used 'Manual of Prayers and Instructions'.[12] The 'explanation' began from the observation that the 'ceremonial directions' of the 1662 Prayer Book were so meagre as inevitably to require supplementation. This might have been done through a general awareness of how to celebrate the eucharistic Liturgy—but the advent of Protestantism, both within and without the Church of England, had ruptured any such historical awareness. Two solutions appeared once the revival of eucharistic doctrine in the early nineteenth century made some resolution imperative. The first was to look to contemporary Roman models—the ceremonial of the 'Western Use'. The second was to make appeal to the ornaments rubric, placed before Morning Prayer in the 1662 Book, which itself drew attention to what was done in the 'second year of King Edward VI', which might be interpreted as either of the last year of the Latin liturgy or of the first year of the new English service. This strategy generates the 'English Use' with its debt to Sarum. Whatton gave a much fuller justification of the first programme for action: 'The English Use was only a local variant of the Western Rite as it then was, and ... the English Ceremonial Tradition was never in its fullness written down and consequently cannot be fully recovered', whereas the Western Rite has been carefully revised by experts 'familiar with a continuous tradition'.[13]

That is a matter of gestures, but what of words? Some set aside the Prayer Book text in favour of the Roman Missal in English (while retaining some elements of the Book such as its collects), arguing that the various Prayer Books were imposed by the State. Even if Convocation composed the 1662 Book, it never promulgated it by canon—and had it done so the then Church of England was so much a creature of the State as to make such an act non-authoritative. Other clergy add to the prayers of the 1662 Book *sotto voce*, appealing to the devout additions made in the period when the Roman sacramentaries were being enriched by extra devotional texts. Others again rearrange its prayers to conform better to the 1549 Prayer Book, which 'best represents the Anglican tradition unalloyed by foreign Protestantism'.[14] The Deposited Book of 1927-8 Whatton saw as vitiated by compromise with Protestantism and Modernism.

The Orthodox would probably not have gained a very edifying picture of Anglican liturgical diversity from this source. Indeed, a letter to the editor from Edward Every was scathing about Whatton's article, notably about his strictures on the Church of England's liturgical inheritance and his clear preference for the Western Use, namely the Roman Missal. Every defended the Deposited Book against charges of Modernism (making an exception, however, for its Marriage Service), and took the view that opting for Roman liturgical forms was just as much a matter of private judgment as any other course.

> Submission to the Curia and its organs is not necessarily submission to Catholic tradition in liturgical matters, any more than in exegetical and doctrinal matters. It is our business to deepen our study of the whole of the historical materials of Eucharistic Action, Eastern and Western, preparing in a 'soborny' spirit for the next authoritative revision of our Prayer-Book.[15]

Another correspondent enquired, Could the Fellowship be serious about attracting Anglicans of other viewpoints than the Anglo-Catholic if Whatton's was the attitude which would meet them?

On the credit side, the Orthodox were told of the social activism which had come to complement an emphasis on regular eucharistic worship of a doctrinally and ceremonially rich kind, notably in Anglo-Catholicism of Whatton's sort. Thus for instance, Father Basil Jellicoe in 'Knights of the Holy Table', likewise an early offering in the *Journal*, gave an ambitious description of a programme of social action (including not only an already realized model housing scheme, but also model farm, model factory, model public house and even model night club) that would befit an Incarnation that had chosen as the vehicle of continuing divine presence the daily bread of the common people. How to create a society and culture worthy of eucharistic participants was, in continuity with the social radicalism of the slum clergy of early Ritualism, Father Jellicoe's theme.[16] It probably struck a chord at Saint-Serge.

But the Orthodox continued to express dismay at the variety of Anglican views of the Holy Eucharist, and not simply the variability of ritual practice. A substantial article on 'The Eucharist in Anglican Controversy: Catholic and Evangelical', originally a lecture at the Abingdon conference of 1955, sought to enlighten them. Unlike the historic liturgies, the Prayer Book rite was composed *ad hoc* by the academically inclined and then imposed by the State. These were not ideal circumstances.

> It would not be unfair to claim that Cranmer and his colleagues intended the new *lex orandi* to express a new *lex credenda* of their own—while the Elizabethan government treated the *lex orandi* as a substitute for any *lex credenda* whatever. It is no cause for wonder if Anglicans of later generations, however much moulded by the forms of prayer to which they have become accustomed, have continued, consciously or unconsciously, to read their doctrinal beliefs, not out of their liturgy, but into it.[17]

Humphry Green thought the Anglo-Catholic liturgiologist Dom Gregory Dix probably right to say Cranmer's eucharistic theology was Zwinglian by 1552 if not by 1549, while the revisers of 1662, though helpfully amending the rubrics of the Book, did not feel politically safe in altering the prayers. The mixed result is that there can be no reconciliation of divergent theologies of the Eucharist in the Church of England 'merely by appeal to the true principles of the Book of Common Prayer'.[18]

Looking then to the two chief schools, Catholic and Evangelical, Green found neither especially easy to follow historically. The historical theologian C. W. Dugmore's *Eucharistic Doctrine in England from Hooker to Waterland* had demonstrated for the seventeenth century the existence of three streams: moderate Calvinism among the centrists, Zwinglianism among the rising Latitudinarians, and with the High Churchmen a trembling on the brink of the Catholic doctrines of eucharistic sacrifice and eucharistic presence.[19] That tendency could not go further owing to the 1689 oath on transubstantiation which 'not only made their doctrine of the presence elusive and difficult to pin down, but, by ruling out the notion of a true offering of the Body and Blood of Christ in the Eucharist, restricted the ritual sacrifice to the two points of a representation of the death of Christ by means of the bread broken and the wine poured out, and the association of the Church with his heavenly intercession.'[20] The Tractarians took a rosy view of the High Church writers responsible for the 1662 revisions, but even if they had been disabused they would not have worried. 'If a doctrine stood proved by the testimony of Scripture and the Fathers, it would not perturb them, as it had their predecessors, to find the same doctrine taught by the Church of Rome.'[21] Anglican Catholics today (that is, in 1955) are more agreed on the deficiencies of the Prayer Book than on the best way to remedy the situation.

What then of Evangelicals? Anglican Evangelicalism, explained Green, is home grown. It does not derive, as does Evangelicalism generally, from the 1859 American revival, and is best considered a continuation, in eucharistic matters, of the 'centrists', i.e. the moderate Calvinists, as described by Dugmore. It is historically crucial that the High Church wing of the Evangelical revival, led by the Wesleys, was lost to the Church of England in the break-away that was Methodism. The Evangelicals who stayed in the Church of England might still refer occasionally to High Churchmen for devotional resources. But their guru in matters eucharistic became the eighteenth-century Daniel Waterland ('the most erudite of English archdeacons'[22]), whose writings on this subject were comprehensively reprinted in 1868 as a counter-blast to Anglo-Catholicism. For Waterland, heaven is local, and Christ is now located there, not here. Waterland's preferred analogy for the Gifts was taken—via St Bernard on sacraments in general—from mediaeval property law. In the standard example, a ring or a crozier confers a privilege but only by symbolizing what it conveys. In any case owing to Christ's post-Ascension absence there cannot be real presence in our churches. Indeed, Waterland assumes that a sign always denotes an absence, which in the Eucharist means the absent crucified body of the Lord. The Lord's Supper is a participation in the Atonement once performed in history, not a sign of the glorified body as it now exists (to whose inheritance, though, devout sharing enables communicants to become fellow-heirs). As to eucharistic sacrifice, Waterland held that we do not offer Christ to God, rather God offers him to us, a maxim often cited by later Evangelicals although, as Green comments, there is an obvious equivocation here in the use of the word 'offers'. Waterland did, however, accept a certain number of sacrificial motifs. In the 'ante-oblation' (that is, the offertory), there is presented to God, he thought, three things: alms, an acknowledgement of God's creatorhood, and the elements for consecration. In the 'post-oblation' (that is, the post-consecratory commemoration), another trio appears. Offered to the 'view' of God, angels and men is the death of Christ. Offered to divine 'consideration', with our praise and thanksgiving, are Christ and his sacrifice, whose merits we plead. Offered too is Christ's mystical body the Church as a living sacrifice to God. Green comments, 'There is nothing in this, so far as it goes, with which a catholic would wish to quarrel, though he might be tempted to see it as a setting without its jewel'.[23]

What was decisive for Evangelicals was the way Waterland's primary stress lay on the memorial on its 'manward' side, though he did not deny a 'Godward' dimension. But, remarks Green, the movement of the Eucharist, as can be learnt simply enough from its name, is chiefly Godward. In their report *The Fulness of Christ* (an answer to the 1947 *Catholicity*), Anglican Evangelicals had maintained that apart from the alms the only sacrifice actually offered in the Eucharist is the offering of praise and self-oblation—thus, despite themselves, they place the emphasis more on the Bride than on the Bridegroom! In *The Shape of the Liturgy* Dix had compared Reformation liturgies with mediaeval eucharistic devotions: they have it in common that they are a devotional commentary on the actions of Christ, not their reproduction.[24] And Green predicted:

> Eventually [Evangelicals] will either be compelled to retreat into the position of Cranmer and present-day Barthians, who will have no offertory whatsoever, only a bare provision of bread and wine for the divine ordinance; or to accept not only an offertory but an oblation of Christ's sacrifice in which ours is taken up and its imperfections transcended. Without the latter the offertory is ultimately only one more instance of that Pelagianism against which evangelicals are so rightly on their guard.[25]

In terms of any overall trajectory of eucharistic doctrine in the Church of England, Orthodox readers—assuming they were able to follow the rather sinuous course of history as Green traced it—might be expected to find this a disappointingly agnostic conclusion.

Anglican approach to Scripture

Anglicans prided themselves, legitimately, on the carefulness and sobriety of their scholarly exegesis, which at its frequent best avoided both the scepticism of much Continental Protestant scholarship, notably in Germany, and the defensive conservatism of the officially permitted Roman Catholic scholarship, confined as this was by the stern dictates of the Pontifical Biblical Commission. Thus for example, the Anglican contribution to the topic of Easter at the Eastertide conference of 1929, by Herbert Kelly, the founder of the Society of the Sacred Mission, embodied this temperamental sobriety. Its title, 'The Resurrection', was only partially justified by its content, much of which concerned theodicy rather than the events of Easter Day. It spoke of those events with some perplexity as well as awe. The narratives, said Kelly, were not easy to harmonize, but neither are those of the Passion, or, for that matter, the reports that had emerged during the Great War about the Battle of the Marne. But the perplexity is also about the outcome, the response to the Resurrection appearances. 'There is no hint that these appearances were ever seen by unchristian eyes. It is never definitely said that they could not be so seen, but the narratives seem to imply it.'[26] And as to reaction to the Resurrection proclamation, if the story told 'does pass into faith, it also develops into a dogged anger and rejection.'[27]

Kelly's exegetical offering was itself reflecting the intellectual culture passed on by the Society's study-house at Kelham in Nottinghamshire. Its home-made theology course, issued on duplicated foolscap sheets and lauded as vastly preferable to anything offered in the university theology faculties or the other Anglican theological colleges, stressed the place of Church history, dogmatics, and ethics, even when studying Scripture. The theological (and philosophical) meaning of Scripture is what counted for them, inevitably so since Kelly defined theology as 'the science of life as a whole.'[28] Kelly himself has sometimes been regarded as a precursor of Barthianism in England, though he (and other Kelham teachers) also made much use of the work of St Thomas Aquinas. The historian of the Society of the Sacred Mission, Alistair Mason, would speak of a 'useful tension' between quite a fully developed philosophical natural theology (in the manner of Thomism) and a '"Barthian" rejection of all man's search'.[29] But Kelly was neither a Thomist nor a Barthian. His most revered master was the mid-nineteenth-century eclectic Anglican Frederick Denison Maurice, who (however he saw himself) was regarded by the early twentieth century as purveying an Anglican Catholicism of a moderate kind.[30] In Part Two of this book it will be explained how Maurice emerged, at the hands of a general secretary of the Fellowship, as an Anglican equivalent of St Gregory Palamas, the late Byzantine doctor most influential on modern Orthodoxy. Both divines were apostles of direct human-divine communion in knowledge as well as love.

Erastianism or disestablishment?

The weighty issue of the relation between the Church of England and the modern British State was taken up by the Fellowship in 1931—not long after a damaging debate in the country at large over revision of the State-authorized liturgical book. Herbert Hensley Henson, bishop of Durham and no stranger to controversy, gave the keynote address at the Fellowship conference in that year. It was, as it happened, at a crucial turning point in his career. Owen Chadwick explains.

> The conversion of Henson to disestablishment was the second turnabout of his career. In 1900–1 he publicly threw Anglo-Catholicism overboard to be a liberal Modernist and the leading defender of establishment in England. In 1927–8 he publicly threw overboard the theory of establishment and for the rest of his years advocated the separation of Church and State.[31]

The principal cause was indeed the rejection of the Revised Prayer Book by the House of Commons (twice; it was modified in the interim) during the weeks from December to June of those consecutive years. Henson believed what he called the 'Protestant underworld' was to blame.

> Before 1927 his attitude was, these godly and sensible Christians of the Reformation ought to have their say in our national church. After 1928 his attitude was, these bigots must have no part in our Church and the only way to get them out is disestablishment.[32]

Henson had in any case been moving closer to the 'Catholic' attitudes of his young manhood, notably in advocating auricular confession as a better way than the emotive public confessions of Dr Buchman's 'Oxford Group', and opposing in Convocation the bishop of Liverpool's permission to a Unitarian to preach in his cathedral. He had made very plain his detestation of Bolshevism during the Durham miners' strike and the General Strike, which was its most serious outcome. 'Driven into the wilderness by the events of 1927–8, he realized how he stood in kinship with those high churchmen who asserted the rights of the Church as a divine society.'[33] So his willingness to address the Fellowship was not so surprising, despite his early notoriety as a bishop who did not require of ordinands a personal assent to the two 'great miracles' of the Creed (the virginal conception and the bodily resurrection).

In that address to the Fellowship, a lengthy historical preamble ends with a percipient conclusion—and prophecy.

> The only functions left to the Church in the modern State are those which are technically religious, and as such lie outside the normal concern of citizens. Even those functions—the organization of public worship, the teaching of doctrine and morals, the enforcement of ecclesiastical discipline—are only tolerable in the modern State in so far as they have no bearing on the interests, policies and prestige of the State itself. So long, therefore, as the prevailing sentiment of the community is friendly to Christianity, the action of the modern State is likely to be considerate, and even sympathetic ... But if it should fall out, that Christianity were generally abandoned by the population, and that its distinctive procedures conflicted with prevailing currents of opinion, the relations of Church and State could not but become dangerously strained, and might very easily become actually hostile.[34]

The 'day of which the Hebrew prophet wrote, when "kings should be nursing fathers" of the Church, and "their queens nursing-mothers" has passed for ever.'[35]

In this setting, Parliament's rejection of the Revised Prayer Book naturally rankled. 'Parliament still retains the supreme authority over the Church of England which was only intelligible, though even then barely legitimate, when its Members and their constituents were legally required to be communicant members of the Established Church. We have recently witnessed the portentous spectacle of a Parsee communist voting in the House of Commons against the adoption of a Prayer Book which had been carefully revised by the authorities of the Church of England. The scandal is gross, extreme and dishonouring.'[36] And again:

> Few English Churchmen have been accustomed to think of the Church as a religious society, bound by principles which are independent of national preferences, interests, and sanctions, and committed to obligations which must finally override the requirements of secular citizenship.[37]

It was a damaging admission. It was also, fuelled by still un-pacified anger, an over-stated one.

Anglican sociology

In the first decades of the Fellowship, a strong point of English Anglicanism, especially in its High Church manifestation, was the emergence of a 'Christian sociology'. By this was meant a body of reflection about the civil order in the spirit of a renewed Christendom—not without its parallels in the Roman Catholicism of the time. Such figures as Christopher Dawson in England and Jacques Maritain in France, had the same idea, along with other authors, many of whom were represented in the series 'Essays in Order' published by the English Catholic publishing house Sheed and Ward. Anglican sociology of a comparable kind was of considerable interest to the Russian Diaspora intelligentsia. The question of how to reconstruct the cultural, social and political order on a spiritual basis in Russia after the much-desired fall of Communism was never far from their minds.

Maurice Reckitt, a weighty name in the 'Christian Sociology' movement—from 1931 to 1950 he was editor of its mouthpiece, *Christendom. A Journal of Christian Sociology*—wrote for the Fellowship's journal in the year he took on the editing of his own.[38] He stressed the 'dual allegiance' of the Christian, since thanks to a wise Hellenism, the State exists for the good life—just as does, albeit in a far higher sense, the Church.

Not that Reckitt thought the task of realizing this dual allegiance in a publicly effective manner an easy one, either practically or conceptually. As to the practical aspect: despite the Church establishment, Anglicans are possibly a minority of professing Christians in England, and in any case of the whole national community 'only a minority (albeit a large one) are systematic attendants at any organized Christian worship'. Moreover, of the latter it is likely that 'only a minority consciously attempt to relate their political ideas and practice to some clear conception of Christian values and ecclesiastical organization.'[39]

And as to the conceptual aspect: there is, to begin with, the difficult of deciding what is meant by 'the State'. Disagreement reigns as to whether the term should be taken

> (in defiance of the political 'pluralists') to cover every aspect of the secular community; whether to signify the organization of those aspects of affairs which (to adopt Mazzini's definition) 'affect men equally and in the same way'); whether as virtually synonymous with the policy-directing authority—i.e. the cabinet of the day (without prejudice to the question as to whether policy is in the last resort thus directed); or whether as identified with Administration, and the permanent machinery of bureaucracy, central and local.[40]

But for the Christian there is a more fundamental problem than one of mere definition, and it

> arises from the fact that while he acknowledges loyalty to a body which exists explicitly to concern itself with the supernatural end of man, he finds not only that some further organization is necessary to promote the justice and command the happiness of society, but that the proper functioning of that organization is highly important precisely from the supernatural standpoint.[41]

To Reckitt's mind, defining the legitimate scope of each of the Church society and the civil society ought to reduce the danger of tension or conflict between them. But to the extent that acceptance of ecclesial obligation diminishes in the population, the State can be expected to 'develop an ethos, and a legislative code founded upon it, which are at variance with the social outlook and precepts of the Church.'[42] In such a hypothetical but entirely possible and even probable case, it will not be right to say that the Church should simply reject the State, for the New Testament is clear that the powers that be are ordained of God (compare Romans 13:1). Reckitt accepted the lucid explanation of that Pauline text given by William Temple, later a regrettably short-lived archbishop of Canterbury, in his 1928 study *Christianity and the State*:

> Society is essentially a Fellowship of Persons..., and this is the arena wherein the moral and spiritual destiny of mankind is wrought out ... If, then, we believe in any divine Sovereignty of the Universe, we shall find here a sphere of divine activity; and to whatever has over this society an authority indicated by society's own need of such authority, we shall not hesitate to attribute a Divine origin and a Divine right.[43]

For his own part, Reckitt confessed he could find no better statement of the State's proper purposes than that provided by the Spanish Jesuit Francisco Suárez in his treatise 'On the Laws'. Such citation of a Counter-Reformation Latin divine should not astonish. The 'League of the Kingdom of God' to which Reckitt belonged was a decidedly Anglo-Catholic venture. Though a post-mediaeval Scholastic, Suárez, so Reckitt explained, had retained here the best of the Western medieval tradition. Those proper purposes of the State—the *regnum*—encompass

> the natural happiness of the perfect human community whereof the civil legislature has the care, and the happiness of individuals as they are members of such a community, that they may live therein peaceably and justly and with a sufficient of goods for the preservation of their bodily life, and with so much moral rectitude as is necessary for the external peace and happiness of the commonwealth and the continued preservation of human nature.[44]

It was not a dramatic statement, and would hardly have appealed to the more 'catastrophist' thinking of many of the exiled Russian thinkers. It also lacked any explicit presentation of the relation between the natural social order and the supernatural ecclesial order. William Temple, contrastingly, had been arguing ever since the 'Conference on Christian Politics, Economics and Citizenship' held at Birmingham in 1924, that 'the religious and political life of the community should not be separated, that the nation should once again move towards the goal of becoming a Christian commonwealth'.[45]

Reckitt devoted the remainder of 'A Dual Allegiance' to attacking 'State Absolutism', whether in Communist or Fascist form, for its denial of the rights of persons and associations. He had in mind more especially associations concerned with higher goods than those of which the State takes cognizance, established on its legal foundations though they be. The 'disarray of modern civilization' is no accident, but 'the logical result of turning away from the idea of Christendom in which an explicitly Christian culture is seeking to express itself in the whole of life'.[46] Here Reckitt captured, no doubt unwittingly, the idea of *otserkovlenie*, the harmonious 'ecclesialization of life' in its totality, which was so major a theme in the 'Russian Religious Renaissance' of the early twentieth century.

This 'turning away' should not, however, so Reckitt insisted, prevent the Church from seeking to frame a policy of its own towards this distinctively modern and regrettably de-ecclesialized civilization. Reckitt was glad to report a notable feature of the time in England. While the number of Christians is shrinking, the 'scope and intensity of Christian thought and conviction are expanding'.[47] One might think here of the contribution that T. S. Eliot, after his conversion to Anglican Catholicism, was shortly to make.[48]

Anglicans on Church authority

The comprehensiveness of Anglicanism meant not only some bewilderment for the Orthodox at the variety of approaches to the liturgy, and an anxiety as to its enthralment to a no-longer Christian legislature. Whether the Church of England could give a plain account of its own credentials to teach the apostolic faith was also a matter of concern.

In 1931, in the period when the Fellowship was still finding its feet, Canon Henry Leighton Goudge, an Anglo-Catholic who held the Regius Chair of Theology at Oxford, considered the issue of 'Authority and Freedom in the Church'. Goudge argued that Christ's Church is meant to possess an 'inherent self-evidencing authority both to teach and to command'.[49] 'As the Lord was felt to stand for God, so the Church ought to be felt to stand for the Lord, whose Body it is.'[50] Protestants excel on the call to individual witness, but have less sense of the corporate witness of the Church, whereas Romanism is certainly corporate in its self-understanding but the latter is vitiated by the over-sharp distinction between *ecclesia docens* (the Church that teaches) and *ecclesia discens* (the Church that learns). In this context, thought Goudge, Orthodoxy has things about right. He cautioned, however, that the authority in question is limited to the message with which God has entrusted the Church, i.e. to faith and morals. It does not extend to history and science. Moreover, if it is really *inherent* authority, then it 'depends for its continuance upon the preservation by love and obedience of the Spirit's presence', from which assertion he drew the conclusion that if contemporaries cannot recognize that authority this may be the fault of Churchpeople themselves.[51] Goudge considered that the Russian Church then under persecution enjoyed more genuine authority than at any time in its history.

Goudge, it could be noted, was a member of the carefully calibrated Joint Doctrinal Commission of Anglicans and Orthodox set up with a view to the forthcoming 'pro-synod' of the Orthodox Churches, an assembly (later to be called, more ambitiously, a 'Great and Holy Council') that was first postponed to 1932 and then indefinitely. The commission at any rate had actually met even if the synod or council had failed to do so. This was in October 1931 and its deliberations had been difficult. Though Arthur Headlam's 'Suggested Terms of Intercommunion' were endorsed in certain respects, on other matters and notably the question of Scripture and tradition, and of the sacraments in general, the Anglican and Orthodox positions were left side by side, while in the end nothing was affirmed about Orders or the Holy Eucharist.[52]

The authenticity of Anglican Orders

The claim of Anglicans that the consecration of their bishops, and the ordination by bishops of priests took place in the authentic 'apostolic succession' was a recurring topic in the early years of the Fellowship's existence if not only then not least because the claim elicited a variety of responses on the part of the Orthodox themselves. Some of these have already been registered in the opening chapter of this book. One Orthodox Church which had not yet spoken was the Church of Rumania. In 1935, so the journal of the Fellowship explained, an official commission from the two Churches had met in Bucharest and pronounced an agreed doctrinal statement on the strength of which the Rumanian delegation recommended the acceptance of the validity of Anglican ordinations. In March 1936 the Rumanian Holy Synod concurred on condition that the report was ratified by the Anglican Church and in June the Rumanian Patriarch Miron Cristea paid an official visit to the archbishop of Canterbury with this end in view. By January 1937, as Eric Mascall, then the editor of the Fellowship's journal, recalled in his autobiography, the 'Convocations had given the required ratification (though in the case of Canterbury in a subtly ambiguous form)'.[53] The subtly ambiguous form was provided by Headlam, who moved that the report of the Bucharest conference should be accepted inasmuch as it answered the question, Could certain statements of the Rumanian Orthodox be accepted by members of the Church of England—without necessarily implying that the answer was the only possible interpretation of the Anglican formularies.[54]

By contrast, the Church of Russia—without which, in the last analysis, nothing can be definitively done in world Orthodoxy—had not made an official response, nor was it ever to do so. In 1944 John Findlow, stressing the high quality of Paul Anderson's book *People, Church and State in*

Modern Russia,⁵⁵ drew attention to a striking citation it included on this topic from the newly enthroned Patriarch Sergius:

> The Anglican hierarchy has not received recognition by the whole of the Orthodox Church. However, if the renowned 'rapprochement of the Anglican Church with the Orthodox' were to go its normal ecclesiastical path, if the Anglicans, as a body, actually organized in seeking the True Church and grace-given priesthood; if the thought of achieving first of all recognition of their hierarchy, which the Roman Pope at one time so brutally condemned, did not confuse their search from time to time, in order, if achieved, to remain quietly just as they were—then the reunion of the Anglican with the Orthodox Church might very well take place, and the question of hierarchy, in all likelihood, would be answered in a positive sense.⁵⁶

Delvings in Anglican theology

In the pages of *Sobornost* there would be notable attempts to expound the work of Anglican theologians deemed likely to elicit Orthodox sympathy—and this extended in time to the founders of Methodism, which originally, after all, had been an Anglican movement in the persons of the Wesleys, John and Charles. The Cambridge professor Brooke Foss Westcott, later bishop of Durham, was one of the first of those chosen. Ivan Young wrote:

> It is scarcely necessary to point out that Westcott stands directly in the line which runs back to the Cambridge Platonists and therefore we should not be surprised to find in him distinct affinities with the strongly marked Neo-Platonic tradition which is to be associated with Orthodox Theology.⁵⁷

Like Maurice, Westcott had encouraged his readers to set a higher value on the Greek Fathers than on their Latin counterparts. It is not altogether clear how Young understood Westcott's aim in this regard. He implies it sought a Christology less concerned with what Christ taught about the Father, even in works as well as words, than with Christ as showing the Father: that is, as actually *manifesting* him.

Westcott's theology revolves around the themes of creation and Incarnation, on which he is a 'Scotist', holding that creation was *for* the Incarnation from the beginning, even absent the Fall—while also holding it an even greater mystery of divine Love that the Fall failed to frustrate the eternally willed End of uniting human beings with the eternal Son. Philosophically, he was an intuitivist on the issue of the existence of God, and presumably this non-rationalist approach was also regarded as appealing to the Orthodox. To Westcott's mind, a deep consciousness of God, underlying all thought, belongs to the very nature of man.

With more than a ritual genuflection to British empiricism, Westcott also allowed a certain role for experiential verification. The kind of purposiveness and meaning theism postulates may be confirmed in personal living and in history—and ultimately in the Gospel, 'Christ in the fullness of His Person and Life'.[58] The Gospel, however, is not merely a declaration of God's nature and will, or even a manifestation of it. It is the power of God unto salvation, and here Westcott's full-blooded doctrine of the sacramental mysteries would have struck a chord with Orthodox readers. The salvation in question is indissolubly linked to Baptism as a participation in Christ's death and Resurrection, and to the Eucharist as a partaking of the human nature of Christ united as this is to the divine nature in his single Person. The fruit is the union of Christians as bound together by 'mutual offices' of love.[59] Westcott saw the Holy Spirit as given precisely in order to animate this life of union. In that perspective, he felt sure the divisions of the Churches were only temporary. '[The streams] start from one source, and they will end in one ocean.'[60]

This essay started quite a search for other Anglican divines with whom Easterners might feel some affinity. It was an especial strength of Donald Allchin, who was unwearying in identifying such figures, sometimes largely forgotten by Anglicans themselves.

'Learning from the English'

The Anglican thirst for enlightenment from the Orthodox could be paralleled by an Orthodox desire to learn from Anglicans—and often from their national character as the English people (at any rate on an Anglican-centred reading of English history). This was so with George Fedotov in an article 'Meeting the English', which appeared in the final issue of 1937. It could just as well have been entitled 'Learning from the English'.

Fedotov was one of those who wanted the Russian Orthodox to take from the English example they encountered at Fellowship meetings a recognition that, here in Anglican Catholicism, was the 'Western

Orthodoxy' they should hope to experience if Orthodoxy truly is universal Christianity in embryo. 'The assimilation of everything which is true and good (Orthodox) in Western Christianity is certainly one of the tasks before us.'[61] Among the Western Churches, no doubt, Rome would have most in common with Orthodoxy, but her 'militant, proselytizing character' made relations impossible, while in the case of Protestantism, as distinct from Anglicanism, there was too much that divided minds.[62]

Most of Fedotov's essay was taken up by praising English attitudes at large: the sobriety and clarity of English thought, compared with Russian 'chaos' if also depth;[63] the moral seriousness and even purity which English church-people exhibit, compared with the oscillation between 'monastic holiness' and 'gypsy dissipation' among Russians;[64] the dedication to social service, notably among Anglo-Catholics, whereas in Russia, although a 'social pathos' inspired much theology from Khomiakov to Bulgakov, the 'monastic-pietistic tradition' was much more concerned with individual salvation only.[65] Fedotov even went so far as to call the politely endured comprehensiveness of the Church of England an English *sobornost*, in that people were unfailingly courteous to each other despite differences. 'The English social sense is that minimum of love (akin to courtesy), without which intercourse is impossible. This is the true gift, the *charisma* of the English people, which governs not only the ecclesiastical but the whole social and political life of England.'[66] It was a judgment which erred somewhat on the side of excessive kindness. Perhaps the fact that the original address was given abroad, at the Fellowship's Paris branch, encouraged the author to think he would not be factually contradicted in some of these claims. Be that as it may, Fedotov evidently agreed with words of William Temple, who, when the Russian historian was writing, held the position of archbishop of York: 'The Church of England, like other churches, has often failed to be completely Christian—always, indeed, if we take those words in all their proper depth of meaning; but it has never failed to be utterly, completely, provokingly, adorably English.'[67]

→ 5 ←

Forming a Spirituality

The Fellowship was keen to form the spirituality of its members, explaining the riches of the East to the West and vice versa, in terms of the inspiration of life. As usual, since most members of the Fellowship, for most of its life—until recently, in fact—were Anglican, the explanations to be given came chiefly—but by no means exclusively—from the Orthodox side. In the early years, at any rate, there was an evident concern for even-handedness where possible.

A Paschal spirituality

A homily on the Resurrection for 1929 by Metropolitan Evlogy, the Russian metropolitan of Western Europe in the exarchate of the Constantinople Patriarchate, struck a note that would become familiar to the *Journal*'s readers with its suggestion that the Western Church may have something of a Paschal deficit.[1]

> We Eastern Christians, and especially we Russian Orthodox, have always been surprised to find that the Feast Day of Easter, the Resurrection of Christ is not placed in the centre of the Church life of Western Christianity, that it is not its culminating point, that it is not its 'Feast of Feasts', its 'Triumph of Triumphs', as it is in the Eastern Church.[2]

And he went on to explain that

> Through a personal experience we live through this 'rebirth', this renewal, by our blessed participation in the immortal glorious life of the Risen Christ. And a realization of this consciousness is poured out in the inexpressible rapture and joy of our Easter services, and in the luminous, incessant and irrepressible rejoicing of the Christian soul.[3]

The invited preacher at the 1930 conference was Bulgakov, and he used the opportunity to call for the resurrection of the Russian nation and the manifestation of the glory of its Church.[4] For now the Church confesses only in silence, yet that silence is heard by living hearts—including in England. This was hardly what was normally meant by a Paschal spirituality. A more doctrinally appropriate address was given on the meaning of the Lord's Ascension by Georges Florovsky. Florovsky pointed out that Christ 'did not rise for the purpose of again returning to the usual earthly order of things, so as to again live and commune with the disciples and the people by means of preaching and miracles'.[5] With Christ human nature ascends to heaven and so, quoting St John Chrysostom, 'We, who are unworthy of earthly dominion, have been raised to the kingdom on high'.[6] Florovsky calls the Ascension the sign of the coming of Pentecost.

> For the gifts of the Spirit are 'gifts of reconciliation', a seal of accomplished salvation and of the reunion of the world with God. And this was finally accomplished only in the Ascension... Through glorification in the ascended Christ man's nature became receptive and worthy of the grace of the Spirit.[7]

Citing this time Bishop Theophan the Recluse, Florovsky continued, 'and unto the world He gives quickening forces through His human body'.[8] So the 'being ... of the Church is the fruit of the Ascension' and 'within the Church, through acquirement of the Spirit in the fellowship of Sacraments, the Ascension continues and will continue until the measure is full'.[9] This in turn means that the Ascension is not a sign of Pentecost only but also of the Parousia, the second Coming, when the 'mystery of God's providence and goodwill shall be fulfilled'.[10]

Two commentaries on Pentecost concluded the June 1930 issue—from Bulgakov again, meaty if short, and from the *Journal*'s editor, Ambrose Reeves. For Bulgakov, the first thing to say about Pentecost is that it is the 'birth of the New Testament Church', the whole life of which is 'an extended Pentecost', the new life of grace, the supernatural, inhabiting the natural, with each fresh member enjoying a personal Pentecost through the sacrament of Chrismation.[11] That a sacrament should be the means of such enjoyment is not unfitting, for 'The Holy Spirit is the inexhaustible fountain of spiritual gifts, which the Church conveys in its sacraments'.[12] More widely:

> The work of Christ has become effective for the Church by the power of the Holy Spirit, that is why salvation receives its fulfilment only in the descent of the Holy Spirit.[13]

Just as at the Annunciation, the Father sends, the Spirit descends, the Son is conceived, and so the entire Trinity epiphanizes (and this is reflected also at the Baptism of the Lord when the Father speaks, the Spirit descends, and the Son is baptized), so likewise at Pentecost through the Spirit the Father is revealed in the Son.

> A universal manifestation of God took place at Pentecost and not only for human nature, but for the whole of creation which has its head and centre in man; to betoken this we bring flowers and decorate the church with branches of trees—thus turning the whole of nature into a temple.[14]

The following day is devoted to the Holy Spirit, yet without a special service since 'this feast-day is like a sealed icon or a sealed book', the full meaning of which only to be revealed at the end of the ages when the 'actual face of the third Hypostasis shall be disclosed'. At present the person of the Spirit is known only in the gifts of grace, though that face is pre-contemplated in the Virgin Mary.[15] And Bulgakov added, rather more baldly, 'For the reason stated above the number of direct prayers addressed to the Holy Ghost are comparatively few.'[16]

Ambrose Reeves was less speculative, re-imagining Jerusalem on the Jewish feast-day in the year of the original Outpouring. The coming of the Spirit is expressed in the New Testament in the language of *dynamis*, the dynamic, but the power involved is 'only' the power of love. Love's powerful working by the Holy Spirit will mean 'pure thirst for God and complete self-giving to God', and 'love of the whole [human] creation for His sake'.[17]

In the life of Christians as in the life of Christ, exaltation follows humiliation. It was not possible to have a genuinely evangelical 'Paschal spirituality' without a prior spirituality of repentance.

A spirituality of repentance

The March 1930 issue was devoted precisely to the place of repentance in redemption. The spiritual teaching given was by a combination of Anglicans and Orthodox—for it should not be thought that early

Orthodox members of the Fellowship imagined that Church of England people were entirely deprived of spirituality. Frank Cross, later Lady Margaret Professor at Christ Church, Oxford, and editor of the well-known *Oxford Dictionary of the Christian Church*, spoke for Anglicans on repentance in terms of the 'change of mind', which is *metanoia*, while for the Orthodox Bishop Benjamin Fedchenkov, before the Revolution a lecturer at the Petrograd Theological Academy and now 'Inspector' of the Institut Saint-Serge, gave a thoroughly informative account of different aspects of the practice of repentance, or penance, in the Russian Church.

The essay by Cross was nothing if not straightforward. Repentance is an essentially human act. Something comparable to human repentance is at most rudimentary in the animal world, while by God 'repenting' of evil Old Testament writers are speaking merely of a 'differing manifestation of the Divine Purpose.'[18] Repentance entails relationship of some kind with the divine Personality. Its most powerful evocation is the Crucifixion of Christ, if what we are speaking of is repentance of the 'higher kind', which has 'passed beyond the mere feeling of sorrow that we have done something of which we are ashamed, to sorrow for sin against love.'[19] Lastly, the basis of repentance is the work of the Holy Spirit since it cannot operate without the gift of faith (which, in somewhat Lutheran fashion, Cross takes to mean trust), the gift of hope, and the gift of love. Penitence consists of cognition, affection, and conation: namely, knowledge of what sin costs the divine love, godly sorrow for it, and a forward looking determination to sin no more.

Metropolitan Benjamin based himself on the prayers recited by the Orthodox liturgically as well as the daily prayers for personal recitation commonly found in devotional books. Despite claims that the Orthodox Church is above all a Church of Resurrection joy, the bishop pointed out how its worship has a strongly penitent character, the invocation 'Lord have mercy' figuring countless times both liturgically and in the private prayers. The Jesus Prayer itself seeks mercy on the one praying precisely as sinner. The great penitential psalm of David, Psalm 51 (50) is read at almost every Hour of the liturgical day, because, he remarked, 'it is so loved by the soul of the Orthodox.'[20] Statements of helplessness and contrition follow on at morning prayer—and the evening prayers are even fuller in their sounding of these themes.

For an account of the importance for repentance of sacramental confession, the Fellowship looked for an Anglican standpoint to Father

L. Gage-Brown, vicar of St Cuthbert's, Philbeach Gardens, a well-known Anglo-Catholic parish in Kensington. The effective disuse of the sacrament of Penance in the eighteenth century, this writer explained, had obliged the Tractarians to look to Roman practice, 'though Anglicans are far from following much of the Jesuit and Liguorian moral theology'.[21] 'The expression of our sins to another in words brings them home to us in a way that neither a general confession of our sinfulness nor the secret confession of faults and transgressions can do. It stirs us up to a more genuine sorrow and a more thorough metanoia.'[22] He noted the tendency of Anglican penitents to include accounts of imperfections and not simply sins, so that their confessions are lengthier than is usual with Roman Catholics. He also emphasized the objective grace of the sacrament. Contrition and self-examination are essential but they are ways of corresponding with the grace of God; as to spiritual counsel given in the course of the sacrament, it is entirely secondary. In a clear statement, 'The sacrament of penance is the ordinary appointed means whereby sin is forgiven and life restored to the soul.'[23] One notices the absence of any reference to satisfaction by a canonical penance; the sacrifice of reparation is, it seems, the making of a humble confession itself.

Militza Zernov wrote on 'The Sacrament of Confession' in such a way as to 'describe the spirit of this tradition as it was expressed in Russian practice'.[24] She admitted that what she would expound is the ideal version, not 'deviations'. Preparation for Confession and Communion, called *govenie*, lasts roughly a week. Those who can may seek to spend it in a monastic setting, preferably in the countryside. Militza described pre-revolutionary Russia in Lent as like a huge monastery; theatres and other places of entertainment were closed, at any rate until about 1900. *Govenie* would include asking forgiveness from others for any offences, using a stereotypical formula ('Forgive me'; reply: 'God will forgive you'). Church attendance (if in Lent, the black vestments and especially austere chants were a feature) would be recommended along with fasting, almsdeeds, reading devotional literature such as the Sayings of the Desert Fathers, saints' lives, sermons of John Chrysostom, writings of St Ephrem and Isaac the Syrian, or works of modern authors like John of Kronstadt or Theophan the Recluse. Militza gave the impression that the only period when many confessions were heard was in fact Lent, and she went into some detail about the fasting arrangements in that period, as well as referring to its liturgical ethos.

Confession itself would usually occur on a Saturday evening or on Sunday morning. Beforehand the priest reads certain prayers, then the penitent approaches the table (*analoy*) with the Gospel book, a cross, and generally an icon of Christ, the priest standing by his side: a custom Militza linked to her case that the priest represents the *sobornost* of the community, for 'the sense of guilt before the whole church is very real to the Russian Christian'.[25] The manner of confessing is spontaneous rather than 'scheduled', though some priests would want to distinguish any general discussion from the confession proper. On its conclusion, the penitent kneels, the confessor places his stole on his head, and the prayer of absolution is pronounced. If the confession is made in the evening penitential prayers are recited at night. 'Measures of penance' (*epitimia*) are mentioned by her but not explained. Usually the confessor is the parish priest though some are keen to find spiritual directors especially helpful to individuals. She painted an attractive portrait of the spirit of such direction:

> Although the practice of Orthodox direction displays much tolerance and understanding of human weaknesses, the atmosphere of Orthodox spirituality is infused with a quality called *tresvennost*. This can be translated as 'sobriety', 'austerity', 'realism'. It is a vigilance against self-indulgence. It calls the Orthodox Christian to the highest commandment of perfection of the Heavenly Father, and preserves them from substituting for this ideal the superficial optimism of humanism.[26]

Tolerance is also needed vis-à-vis the priest though faith and the gift of prayer make up for many defects in the eyes of the faithful. But in any case the Russian Christian is certain that it is Christ who, present in the sacrament, receives the penitent and forgives his sins: 'This certainty is the fruit of the all-prevailing sense of Christ's Presence so characteristic of his worship'.[27]

Forgiveness of sins implies the reality of redemption. Lev Gillet wrote on the Orthodox understanding of redemption by Christ. Gillet, a Latin Catholic by origin, had been a priest of the Ruthenian Church united to Rome until his reception into Orthodoxy. He pointed out that the Orthodox Church has never committed itself to one particular theory of the redemption; it has repeated, rather, the words of the Creed, he was 'crucified for us'. The question is how to approach those words. In a somewhat startling but probably correct statement, it follows, he thought, from the notion of *sobornost* that 'Every intuition or experience, every insight common to all the faithful is true'.[28] So, then, what 'immediate data' present to common consciousness among the Orthodox 'answers this label: "Redemption by Christ"'?'[29]

For Gillet, the experience of redemption, as lived out by the Orthodox, comes across in four distinct modes. First, redemption is felt as part of a whole which reaches from Incarnation to Resurrection in a single process of salvation, with the transformation of human nature constantly in view. Secondly, redemption is regarded as something gratuitous. It is a gift which cannot be expressed in juridical fashion, not even in 'moderate' theories of 'satisfaction' on the Cross, since, if etymology be any guide, all such theories would mean is that the Saviour, when he hung on the saving Tree, was 'doing enough' (*satis-facere*). To the Orthodox, the language of debt-payment, or even exchange, feels altogether 'repugnant to the magnificent gratuity of Christ's act'.[30] Thirdly, redemption is registered as a positive endowment where 'something new is produced outside of ourselves and is communicated to us . . . by a kind of transfusion'.[31] Fourthly and finally, it is perceived as

> being in some way analogous to—though infinitely higher than—some very simple human experiences. Experiences of pity, of suffering love, of voluntary loss and pain, of wish to give one's life for others.[32]

Behind all this lies a 'common intuitive presupposition', namely that from what is sacrificed there springs a 'new stream of life'.[33]

Mme Zernov had already drawn readers' attention to Lent as the time of repentance *par excellence*. Archpriest Sergius Tchetverikoff took the reader on a tour of the Orthodox Great Lent, passing in review the key Gospels and prayers of the succeeding weeks of this season, in which, he remarks, the Church has 'enshrined . . . all the depths and riches of Her feelings of repentance and faith.'[34] This essay formed a complement, based on the annual cycle of the liturgy, to Metropolitan Benjamin's remarks on how the daily cycle included so many prayers of penitence. In Fore-Lent, the parable of the publican and the pharisee is read on the first of the Sundays and that week at Great Compline the penitential canon of St Andrew of Crete is recited; the parable of the prodigal son is used on the Sunday following, along with the 'Order of the Triumph of Orthodoxy' (in cathedrals), when heretics are anathematized and the confessors of the Orthodox faith praised; on 'Forgiveness Sunday', when the faithful ask forgiveness from each other, the Church reads Matthew 6:14–21, with its instruction on penitential practices and exhortation to lay up treasure in heaven. Once Lent begins numerous prostrations accompany the reading of psalms and prayers, the clergy use black vestments and the principal furniture of the church building is swathed with black too. During the Second Sunday St Gregory Palamas is recalled as the doctor of transfiguration, on the third the Cross is shown to the people for veneration, an anticipation of the climax of the Great Week; on the fourth St John of the Ladder is recalled, since the reading of his ascetic treatise is especially recommended in Lent. On the fifth Sunday he gives way to St Mary of Egypt, who stands for all notorious converted sinners. On the sixth Sunday the Lord's solemn entrance into Jerusalem is commemorated, and on the Saturday evening the raising of Lazarus. On Great Thursday during the combined celebration of Compline with the Liturgy the Last Supper is commemorated when in cathedrals the bishop washes the feet of twelve priests, and the same evening the 'twelve Gospels' are read to rehearse the narrative of the Passion. The following day the image of the body of the Lord as taken down from the cross is placed in the middle of the Church for veneration. Great Saturday is a day where the liturgy is suffused with feelings of rest and expectation. Compline, joined with the eucharistic Liturgy, is celebrated some time after midday, the dark vestments change half way through to light ones, and a deacon already reads the Gospel of the Resurrection. Then before midnight all hear the Acts of the Apostles read as the feast of the Resurrection dawns. The author understands the Great Fast as intended to enable the faithful to 'accumulate a small store of spiritual forces and spiritual experience which will serve us for the rest of the year'.[35]

The place of asceticism

Asceticism was a well-known concept to Anglo-Catholics influenced by early modern Latin Catholic spirituality—a topic which had become conventionally distinguished into two sub-departments of theology, 'ascetical' and 'mystical' theology.

In 'On the Prize of the High Calling', Florovsky put forward a characteristic position on the role of *podvig*—a word that has been variously translated 'exploit', 'heroic deed' or (surely too banally) 'effort'—

as vital to the Christian life. He distinguished here the 'charismatic' and the 'ascetic' moments in the movement of Christian holiness. Let the reader understand—he was not using the terms in their commonplace sense. For Florovsky, the 'charismatic' factor is the free gift of the grace of God and this is primary, yet the 'ascetic' factor, meaning our human works freely enacted on the basis of grace, is, though subordinate, also essential. Salvation in Christ is spiritual vivification through the Holy Spirit whose very name indicates he is the 'source of sanctification', taking place as sanctification does in the Church which is the 'mysterious Body of the Incarnate Word', its life manifested most especially in the sacraments. Florovsky spoke of 'sacramental acts in which the Holy Ghost is breathing', adding that 'through them is manifested the union with Christ and the contact with God'.[36] But the Spirit who is given must be appropriated, and in this sense acquired. This is the task of the Christian life in its exercise of freedom, and demanding freedom at that—hence the need for 'heroic deeds'. Interpreting Pauline teaching in Romans and Galatians, Florovsky remarked that sanctification is the gift of the God who calls and not the result of works, and yet it is 'not without works'.[37] Divine grace attracts but does not 'drag', and in that distinction lies the place of creative freedom in ascetic deed.

'The ascetic mystics were especially mystics of love—to a far larger extent than mystics of penitence.'[38] Love of Christ inspired the martyrs and the great monks to their difficult deeds. In venerating the saints we revere God's gift of grace to them, and also his grace in them which inspired their acts of love.

In June 1931 the *Journal*, following the line of that year's conference, returned to the theme of asceticism, this time in connexion with that of culture. On the matter to hand, Oscar Hardman, rector of Chislehurst, attempted to answer from the Anglican side the question 'What is Asceticism?' Hardman had authored two relevant works, *The Ideals of Asceticism* and *Psychology and the Church*.[39] His investigations into asceticism worldwide, not least the India of his own childhood, had convinced him that

> in spite of erroneous foundations, revolting forms and injurious excess, here is the hall-mark of religious earnestness and the truest evidence of a temper which specially fits men to be caught up by the Eternal Spirit into association with His ceaseless activity of redemption.[40]

For the 'Incarnate Son of God... being met with the same problem of evil solved it by the practice of an asceticism which is not entirely unrelated to the asceticism of these others, greatly as it corrects them in respect of false premises, misdirection of effort, and fanatic extravagance'.[41] Christians do not hold with the notion of an internally conflicted God, yet the Cross and Passion can speak of 'incomprehensible effort, patience, self-humbling and sacrifice' in the divine Being.[42]

Hardman frankly admitted that the description of the Anglican Communion as 'bourgeois and unheroic' was not altogether incorrect. While disciplinary asceticism as in seasons of fasting and almsgiving is certainly not unknown, 'so far as the asceticism of penitence and reparation and of mystical fellowship are concerned we are only just beginning again to go to school', and in this he hoped for good fruits from the revival of the religious life in Anglicanism.[43] Since Anglican religious already teach others how to pray, now they should inculcate in them ascetic zeal.

On the theme of asceticism and culture, Florovsky and Fedotov faced Harry Carpenter, later bishop of Oxford, and Dom Bede Frost, a prolific spiritual writer, at that time a monk of Nashdom, the Anglican successor to Abbot Aelred Carlyle's Benedictine foundation on Caldey Island. For Florovsky the 'history of Christian culture is by no means an idyll. It is enacted in struggle and dialectic conflict.'[44] By the time of Justinian a new Hellenism is created, 'churchifying' or transfiguring the Hellenism of the pagan world. Not for nothing does it coincide with the development of the 'Monastic Movement', which is a 'transition to another social plane and order', thus setting up a polarity between Desert and Empire.[45] But note well:

> The fact that monasticism denies and limits the design of the Empire does not imply that it opposes culture. In this case there exists a complicated antinomy. In an extraordinary way monasticism succeeded, much more than the Empire did, in preserving the true ideal of culture in all its purity and freedom ... [as] cliffs, deserts and caves become centres of the new theurgic aspects of wisdom.[46]

It was an ascetic milieu that brought forth the best of Alexandrian theology (presumably a reference to Origen and Athanasius the Great), while ascetic and 'creative' elements intermingled in the Cappadocians, real intellectual magnificence appears with St Maximus the Confessor (who was also an ascetic), and under the iconoclast emperors monks defend sacred art. Florovsky's explanation linked asceticism and creativity together. Asceticism 'contains the urge of infinity, an eternal unsatiableness and thirst, an eternally unquenchable aspiration',[47] an opening of the spirit, which in the humble exercise of freedom makes possible glorious exploits. In this way, asceticism expels the indifference, disappointment, disenchantment that disable creativity.

> [T]rue asceticism is inspired by the task of transfiguration and a reinstatement of the world in its originally created beauty, from which it fell into sin. It is because of this that asceticism leads to creativity and action.[48]

Florovsky realized this would sound counter-intuitive, and admitted that the task, historically speaking, has not been fully carried through. But he insisted that 'new and different problems of culture are disclosed through the ascetic trial, a new hierarchy of values and aims is revealed'.[49] Ascetic maximalism is 'transfigured apocalyptics' inspired by a presentiment of the End of history,[50] showing itself in an attitude to charity, to knowledge, to art—all of them things that are capable of undergoing eschatological transformation, which not everything can. For not everything has 'eternal dimensions'.[51]

> The idea of a churchified Empire did not succeed, for it fell to pieces in bloody conflict, degenerating in fraud, ambiguity and violence. But the Desert was successful. And will remain for ever to witness to the creative effort of the ancient Church—with its Byzantine theology, prayer and icon.[52]

Fedotov looked at the same question from the viewpoint of the Russian experience. The antinomy of culture and asceticism was unknown to mediaeval Russia, since both featured as elements in the treasury of the Church brought to them from Byzantium. It was books, precisely, those monuments of culture, that taught of 'ways to repentance' and 'how to acquire wisdom and temperance.'[53]

> The life of almost every Russian saint speaks of his achievements in literary learning: where natural aptitude is lacking, God miraculously bestows an understanding of science.[54]

The exception is the category of 'fools for Christ's sake' though even they did not actually stress the element of denial of culture as such.

Fedotov rather disapproved of the early modern philokalic revival in Russian monasticism insofar as it confirmed a lack of interest in learning and education. 'Mount Athos and early Eastern asceticism became its tutors, instead of the early Russian holiness.'[55] In consequence, by the end of the nineteenth century the liberal Orthodox tradition of philosophical and religious thought in Russia was distinctly hostile to asceticism; its mind-set can be seen in the 'Living' or 'Renovationist' Church in Russia today, i.e. in the early 1930s. In the wake of the Revolution, however, the Orthodox intelligentsia, now transported to the West, has altogether changed its attitude, and adopted a profoundly ascetic temper. Russian intellectuals, commented Fedotov sadly, tend to take an idea to an extreme. Yet the

> idea of an Orthodox culture has not died. It has found a mighty support in the dogma of the Church—which stands at the present time at the very heart of all theological and religious life. The Church must not be torn away from the world, it must transform it, and Christian culture is the form of this transfiguration. Culture is born of the Cultus—like the painting of the icon, the music of hymns, the exposition of the Word. Beyond the doors of the Church it unfolds itself in a whole system of values which serve to build life, in ideas of God which become rooted in the world, the world of the Logos. Such is the new Orthodox justification of culture, such is its creative task.[56]

The Anglican response from H. J. Carpenter, looking at asceticism in the context of Reformation communities, had necessarily to explain why the Reformers' theology discountenanced it.

> Any theological system in which the Lutheran doctrine of justification by faith alone is central can have no place for asceticism. For asceticism grows out of a view of salvation entirely foreign to such a system. For, first, asceticism implies that the soul can make progress in the knowledge of God and in conformity with the Divine Will. And, secondly, it implies that the human soul can by effort and self-discipline co-operate with divine grace to attain a fuller vision of God with its correspondent moral transformation.[57]

These ideas are hardly compatible with Lutheran (or Calvinist) doctrine.

> To them the idea of the possible benefits of ascetic practices appears to thrown doubt on the sole efficacy of divine grace, and to reintroduce, in however subtle a form, the idea of the meritorious contribution of the individual to his own salvation. Further, if progress in holiness is possible, then justification *sola fide* is only one

stage in redemption. It means that God is not ultimately satisfied with anything less than actual personal holiness on our part: His forensic acquittal and forgiveness in justification is indeed the preliminary and substratum of the Christian life, but not its full attainment. It is here that the typically Protestant and typically Catholic views of grace and salvation fall apart.[58]

Consonantly, the Reformers abolished all institutions and practices concerned with the ascetic life—a task facilitated by the mediocrity of the monasteries though, tellingly, their reform was not considered. Things were made worse by the notion that the monastic way was a more perfect one (a doctrine defined at Trent), and here Carpenter agrees with the magisterial Reformers: it should be considered 'rather, a vocation to be obeyed when it comes'.[59]

But the Reformation denial of a graduated approach to the vision of God also affected culture, for 'corporate human activities lost their sacramental significance as partial revelations of and partial steps towards the knowledge of God'.[60] The vision of a supernatural goal ceased to hold together in harmony the various dimensions of human living. The aimlessness of modern civilization points to the need to recover both the asceticism without which the soul 'cannot see beyond the things of this world' and a 'corporate religion which brings the individual into the life of a redeemed society, and consecrates all his activities to a common supernatural purpose'. Carpenter found in the nineteenth-century Catholic Revival solutions for both, and, to his mind, Bishop Gore had embodied both. There was less evidence that 'popular Protestantism' was accepting them.[61]

Bede Frost was expected to survey in this perspective the contemporary scene. He made his own task easier by defining asceticism—with support from the Buckfast monk Anscar Vonier—as the deliberate development of the potential of human nature, of which culture is the highest product. '[U]nregulated, undisciplined desire, the abandoning of the self to a vagabond life, makes culture impossible.'[62] The cultured man may have more possessions and opportunities, but he is also more detached from them. Rather patronizingly, Frost thought that public school boys in demanding situations, like wealthy candidates for the monastic life, adapted better to fewer amenities than did their less socially favoured contemporaries. Within the Church, both asceticism and culture are means to an end. Frost recommended the imitation of St

Francis de Sales, in whom 'culture and asceticism meet and intermingle' producing a model of both Christian humanism and holiness, an antidote to an age when 'a spurious culture, lacking the restraints and supports of asceticism, proclaims a freedom and a progress which are least the possession of its votaries'.[63]

Contemplation

Anglo-Catholics were schooled in early and mid-twentieth-century Roman Catholic literature. They knew that the other wing in the diptych of spirituality, after ascetical theology, was mystical theology, just as the complement to asceticism was contemplation.

Lev Gillet, whose addresses and celebrations were now appearing frequently in the Fellowship Notes, wrote on contemplation. It was from start to finish a Latin account, stressing the prayer of simple regard as the doorway to contemplative prayer, distinguishing between acquired and infused contemplation, defining mysticism in a Thomistic manner (it consists in the predominance of the Gifts of the Holy Spirit vis-à-vis human effort), speaking of the 'prayer of quiet', the 'prayer of union', and the 'spiritual marriage' in the standard vocabulary of Catholic authors. His stress on the possibility of living a contemplative life in the world belonged in the tradition of Francis de Sales—who, however, would no doubt have spoken more readily of a 'devout' life (more so than a 'contemplative' one), so perhaps there was an advance here. The citations were all from Latin authors: Bernard Ullathorne, Loyola, Bernard of Clairvaux, John of the Cross, Augustine.[64]

For once, then, there was no sea-change in moving from an Orthodox to an Anglican author, than which no better could be found on the subject than Father Gilbert Shaw.[65]

Gilbert Shaw was an increasingly respected spiritual director in the Church of England, and his essay of 1951 on 'Simplicity in Prayer', which among other things made reference to a book by Gillet on the Jesus Prayer reviewed in the previous issue, helps to show why. Shaw explained his title. He was not intending to speak about the 'prayer of simplicity' or 'prayer of simple regard' familiar from the early modern Latin treatises, but about simplicity in any sort of prayer, whether on the purgative way or the illuminative way or the unitive way: in other words, simplicity in prayerful expression generally. After all:

> The fundamental concept and activity of prayer is simple, for it is
> the soul's communication with the Divine Personality for which
> it exists.[66]

What complexity there is in describing the life of prayer does not derive from prayer itself but is due to 'the disordered mind, the self-centred heart, the pressures of worldly idealisms, the solicitations of doubts and fears, the temptations of the adversary who is for ever sowing tares and seeking to destroy the growth of righteousness and true holiness'.[67] The 'dissipation' of our nature after the Fall must be brought to a 'unity of attention,'[68] and Shaw would expect this to happen as a mind well stocked by meditation—especially through liturgical participation and the use of Scripture—seeks that 'simplicity of obedience and contemplation for which [man] was intended'.[69] Shaw was a psychological realist. Reverie or brooding are natural to us, and can be the way we meditate, and for those with pictorial imaginations something like the Ignatian method may also be natural too. But he was also in possession of a clear objective in guiding souls. He recommended the development of two spiritual attitudes, dependence and penitence, which can inform any and every prayer that is said on a day-to-day or even moment-to-moment basis. Referring to the example of St Seraphim (always a winner with the Orthodox), a few prayers of simple dependence and penitence are enough if 'well and regularly used'.[70] A childlike prayer of the heart is the best road to simplicity, for simplicity is only a means to an end and the end is God.

Challenges to such prayer will come, whether from within the self, from the environment, or from the Evil One. That will make it 'for the most part a prayer of overpassing or going through distraction or of enduring dryness and darkness of mind and spirit'.[71] Here Shaw appealed to the scheme of expected development in prayer worked out by the sixteenth-century Spanish Carmelite St John of the Cross. In the 'night of sense', where those who generally live by 'active' prayer are likely to find themselves, 'active purgation' will be when mind and heart choose and maintain right direction. In the 'night of spirit', which those drawn into 'contemplative' prayer are likely to experience, 'passive purgation' will be a call for the soul to 'hold to its spiritual nature as "oned" with God'.[72] Here the only thing to do is to depend: any other activity would lose simplicity.

> The greater the simplicity the more able is the individual to bear
> the knowledge and impact of the discordances, and so be enabled

in union with the Divine victory cheerfully and willingly to offer the fruit of the experience.[73]

Shaw said he was not proposing to discuss contemplative prayer except to say it is 'simple dependence'.[74] But he did not keep to this self-denying ordinance. Thus he told his readers how simplicity of this sort results in a 'flowering and fruition of an ever-widening complexity of knowledge of that which is contemplated'—quite unlike the sterility of Quietism.[75] He was evidently describing the illuminative way, since he spoke not only of 'heat', 'light' and 'song'—which could in principle be signs of the unitive way, but also of 'figurative and rationalized constructions which are showings of Divine truth' as with the late mediaeval anchoress Julian of Norwich, in whose *Revelations of Divine Love* suchlike analogies, assisted by the Holy Spirit, express a variety of truths about God.[76] Shaw remarked how this is a 'less perfect knowledge than the Divine dark'.[77] And since he then moved on immediately to speak of 'the "Cloud" method', a 'beating upon the cloud of forgetting' (a reference to that anonymous classic of the English Middle Ages, the *Cloud of Unknowing*) and also to the Jesus Prayer as another 'concentration method' (and one with the advantage of being 'an evangelical contemplation of Scripture rather than a philosophical direction', a prayer that is 'always instinct with devotion to the Person of the living and present incarnate Son of God'),[78] it seems reasonable to suppose that he was at least considering the prospect of a soul that is moving beyond illumination towards prayer-union with God in the fullest sense of the words. That said, he agreed with Lev Gillet that the Jesus Prayer should not be considered something reserved for the mystical way, as though its use with that intention could enable one to bypass any preliminary 'ascetical purifications'.[79]

This was both a sophisticated and a helpful spiritual theology in miniature, from which Orthodox readers, as well as Anglicans, could have learned much.

A monastic spirituality

Monastic spirituality, represented not least by the anthology known as the *Philokalia* with its commendation of the Prayer of the Name of Jesus, was increasingly formative in modern Orthodoxy, not just for monastics but for all the members of the Church. In the pages of the Fellowship's journal, it would become especially important in the latter decades of the twentieth century, championed above all by one of the translators into English of the *Philokalia*, Kallistos Ware. But it had made itself known from a very early date. Sergius Tchetverikoff, the chaplain to the Russian Student Christian Federation, was, though a married priest, the first to fill this gap. Writing in 1929, he concentrated on what was undoubtedly for Russian spirituality in the early modern period the most influential of the monasteries, Optino, whose spiritual fathers had made so great an impact on Russian pilgrims of all educational levels in the course of the nineteenth century.[80] Russian monasticism, as Tchetverikoff described it, was and is an ascetic institution, and in one tradition eminently so. Yet it is not for all that dualistic. To the contrary, Russian monasticism 'always had a joyful and serene outlook on the world'—the world, that is, in the sense of the cosmic creation, rather than human society, as the author's reference to the opening chapter of Genesis makes plain.[81] Tchetverikoff made no secret of his preference for the kind of monastic ethos which emphasizes the inner struggle with 'thoughts', the manifestation of conscience to an 'elder', and the contemplative recitation of the Jesus Prayer rather than stressing sheer physical austerities, heroic in character. The latter carry the danger of becoming ends in themselves rather than helps to spiritual growth. He recounted the story of Optino and its inspirer Paissy Velitchkovsky, a student at the Academy of Kiev in the eighteenth century who sought in vain from his teachers the spiritual wisdom—the inner transfiguration—for which he thirsted but was introduced to it, via the writings of the ascetic fathers of the Church, in the *Philokalia* as he encountered it on Athos. The monastery Paissy founded in Moldavia was a centre of spiritual practice, and also of editorial work on producing a sound Slavonic version of the philokalic texts. The monks trained there gravitated to a number of the great Russian monasteries which they penetrated with their influence, but nowhere was that influence more effective than in the hermitage of Optino, situated in the heart of European Russia, and closely linked at its foundation in the early years of the nineteenth century to the then metropolitan of Moscow, Platon. It was not the successive superiors of Optino who were important so much as the succession of *starets* figures, the elders or spiritual fathers. Tchetverikoff had the great good fortune of knowing the third and last of the great elders, Ambrose, who died in 1891, and an invaluable section of his article is the account of Ambrose's way of life, in all the detail of daily routine. No doubt hearers were impressed to learn that the countless visitors who came to his cell included Dostoevsky and Tolstoy. But for Anglo-Catholicism, where the revival of the religious life had principally taken 'apostolic' form (albeit with a strongly 'conventual' dimension in commitment to the choral celebration of the divine Office), it would have been cheering to hear of the *starets* Ambrose's foundations, which included a home and school for girls, a home for the aged and cripples, and a hospital. Tolstoy's sister was a nun in the convent he started, the 'last great achievement of his life'.[82] He was not to see the Revolution which destroyed his work, though his immediate disciples did.

In succeeding years, the topic of monasticism surfaced fairly regularly in *Sobornost*, even though the handful of monasteries as still existed in Soviet Russia were inaccessible, and the Holy Mountain of Athos at a very low point of its existence. So at this epoch, most references were historical. In the winter of 1956 a presentation of the outstanding monastic figure of mediaeval Serbia, St Sava, monk, bishop, writer, formed a suitable prelude to an attempt at an overview of Orthodox spirituality by Austin Oakley, which went out of its way to emphasize the monastic dimension. Oakley was knowledgeable on his subject, as was only right: he was editor of *The Christian East*, the journal of the Anglican and Eastern Churches Association. He paid tribute to the foundation of Orthodox mysticism in the sacraments (the 'mysteria'), in doctrinal theology, and indeed in the Scriptures. But the historic moment of the Desert Fathers, the 'flight to the deserts and the tombs of the Thebaid', which initiated the monastic life in the Church, was something both different and, for later ages, essential. To Oakley's mind:

> the whole course of Orthodox spirituality stems from this spirit-impelled movement of the ancient world, and may truly have still a cleansing and sanctifying work to do in the new world that is opening around us in this cataclysmic 20th century, when once again the Church finds the powers of the world massed against her, and with a similar sense of being the few against the many.[83]

The collecting and codification of the sayings and lives of the Desert Fathers began the process that underlies the development of the *Philokalia*. The keys are: purification from the passions and the cultivation of holiness, entailing a disciplining of senses, memory, imagination, intellect. For the Christ-centred man, a path opens to 'great simplicity and concentrated power in the spiritual life, thus gathered up, unified and used to God's glory' (one wonders whether there is some influence of the supernaturalist novels of the Anglican imaginative writer Charles Williams in the reference to 'concentrated power').[84] But even this is only preparation for that imageless contemplation, for which the Jesus Prayer is a most helpful 'method'. Oakley cautioned against neglecting the 'magistral importance' of Denys, not least as interpreted by St Maximus the Confessor and the fourteenth-century Byzantine polymath Pachymeres.[85]

A 'social-mystical way'

Perhaps in an effort to bring together the monastic/philokalic strand in Orthodox contributions to the Fellowship with the creativity theme dear to the Paris School, Fedotov identified a 'social-mystical way of salvation', by contra-distinction to a life of mystical prayer in solitude, lauding it as the way for those in the world to combine love of neighbour with love of God, for without the latter love of neighbour will not bring about salvation.[86]

> Herein the mystical life of the Church is given in its objectivity, as Grace which embraces us, which ceaselessly uses us for weaving the divine-human texture of the Body of Christ.[87]

In this context, the sacraments have three advantages: they are 'objective' in the sense of independent of my level of mystical experience, though not of my faith. They have an embodied nature suited to the human condition and indeed are 'an outward sign of the transfiguration of the whole of life in an eschatological plane'.[88] They are given in a social context and in this way their nature, at any rate in principle, 'sanctifies Christian society as a whole and in particular forms of fellowship', the corporate life, the *sobornost*.[89] These strengths also mask dangers: immoralism (moral indifference in their use), religious materialism; a weakening of the personal basis of religion, the 'flourishing of liturgics to the detriment of mysticism and ethics' (Fedotov thought some Orthodox and Anglicans subject to this).[90] This should serve as a reminder that sacraments nourish personal spiritual life, they do not replace it. 'Only an inter-penetration of the social-liturgical and personal-mystical (or ethical) way of Christianity can lead to a balance in the spiritual life.'[91] Fedotov's comments lead naturally into an account of a sacramental vision, which must mean the spiritual mediated by the sensuous in a union of body and soul.

Transfiguring the body

Writing in 1963, Timothy Ware, still a layman, produced one of his classic essays—on the transfiguration of the body. St Seraphim of Sarov was celebrated as an exemplar of humility, of poverty of spirit. But humiliation leads to exaltation. Seraphim was the recipient of the grace of transfiguration—here Ware could cite the 'conversation with Motovilov', which is so often reproduced *in extenso* in Orthodox spirituality, not least by Vladimir Lossky in *The Mystical Theology of the Eastern Church*.[92] By bringing forward other examples from East and West, Ware stressed how Seraphim's case was not isolated, even if it cannot be called statistically normal. (The most surprising case, since closest to home, is the Anglican spiritual writer Evelyn Underhill.) Such transfiguration, an extension of the Christological mystery to a member of the Mystical Body, shows how the physical body is not excluded from sanctification or divinization (*theosis*). It is also a pointer to the end of the age in the Parousia: while the glory of most saints is now concealed, the same was also true of the Saviour (except on Tabor), but transfiguration will be Christ's public condition at the Second Coming, as it will also be theirs. Those already transfigured now show that Christian eschatology is not entirely 'futurist'; rather is it 'inaugurated'.[93] The Lord's transfiguration included his clothes, i.e. utterly material things, and so likewise in the inaugurated eschatology of Orthodoxy the icons are also 'first-fruits of [the] all-embracing redemption of matter'[94]—though Ware admitted the notion of 'cosmic redemption' needs careful handling.

Boris Bobrinsky of Saint-Serge provided a mystical and sacramental complement to this physicalist and cosmic celebration of Seraphim in a study of the Byzantine lay theologian Nicholas Cabasilas (also canonized in modern times). Longer than most *Sobornost* articles and heavily laden with endnotes, Bobrinskoy gathered together what is known about Cabasilas's life but was chiefly concerned to argue that, despite the paucity of references to Palamism (or indeed to the wider Hesychasm) in his writings, this liturgically and sacramentally oriented, Christocentric, humanistically inclined layman belonged firmly with these dogmatic and mystical movements of his own day. Yet for Cabasilas, it is the sacraments of initiation—Baptism, Chrismation, Eucharist—that launch the believer on the way of illumination and union.

Forming a Spirituality

The fundamental belief of Palamas and the hesychasts that the Saints might after the manner of the Apostles contemplate the light of Christ on Mount Tabor with the eyes of their transfigured bodies, permits them to safeguard the reality of the divine life which is given us by the Church through its mysteries.[95]

The place of the eucharistic Liturgy

Those mysteries come to their climax in the Holy Eucharist. Forming a spirituality suited to both Anglican Catholics and the Orthodox could hardly dispense with an account of the Divine Liturgy.

Nikolai Arseniev, after his departure from Russia, taught Russian literature and history at Königsberg while holding a chair in New Testament and the History of Religion at the Orthodox theological faculty at the University of Warsaw. He was that comparatively rare bird, a Fellowship figure from the Diaspora Orthodoxy beyond the Paris hub. Now he furnished a spiritual commentary on the entire *déroulement* of the Divine Liturgy in the Byzantine ritual tradition.

Arseniev explained that the eucharistic Liturgy is not only the supreme manifestation of the Church's life or what he termed a revelation of the 'boundless condescension of God's love'. The Liturgy is also the source of the 'organic unity of the body of the Church'.[96] It is so not just outwardly but also 'in the deepest, real and mystical sense'.[97] The words 'real and mystical' take their bearing from a subsequent claim, namely that in this renewal of the Sacrifice of the Lord there is a breaking through the limits of our world so as to reach a 'higher and supernatural Reality'.[98] Arseniev's commentary on the Divine Liturgy is chiefly a description of its principal moments, gestures and texts—leaving, however, the nineteenth-century Russian author Nikolai Gogol (in his little treatise on the Liturgy[99]) to comment on the moment of personal communion. Arseniev included a large element of the allegorical interpretation customary since the later patristic period which—despite the sometimes negative reactions of liturgical historians—can play an important role in the spiritual inspiration the Liturgy provides. Thus the initial rite of preparation is a 'remembrance of our Saviour's early life which was also a preparation for his great work', and, like that early life, it takes place 'unseen and unknown to the people'.[100] The cutting out of the portion of bread that is to be consecrated corresponds to the birth of the Lamb, the table of the Oblation stands for the cave of Bethlehem. The Little Entrance, during the Liturgy of the Word, represents 'Christ Himself going out for the first time to His divine preaching'.[101] The Great Entrance with the pre-prepared Gifts 'typifies our Lord's path to His suffering and death',[102] their placing on the altar Christ's lying in the tomb. But at the start of the Anaphora or Eucharistic Prayer, when the celebrant unveils the offering, the altar represents rather the Upper Room, the 'chamber where the Lord's Supper was held'.[103] Between the words of institution and the epiclesis the altar becomes 'the mount of Golgotha where the great divine sacrifice has been made',[104] while after the epiclesis 'we have now on the altar-table Christ's true body, which had suffered on the earth and was buried, and had risen from the dead, ascended to heaven and is sitting on the right hand of the Father'.[105]

This was a useful guide to the spiritual significance of the Byzantine Liturgy by one who was a founder-member of the Fellowship, a participant in the original 1928 conference at St Alban's, and would be best known in England for his *Mysticism and the Eastern Church*,[106] though there were also later books along the same lines: *Holy Moscow*, and *Russian Piety*.[107] Zernov wrote of him, 'Both Muscovite and European, he harmoniously combined within himself the Slavophile and Westernizer traditions. He was equally familiar with German, French and English culture as with Russian.'[108]

The role of the saints

The veneration of saints was one obvious dimension of liturgical life on which Orthodoxy and historic Anglicanism (as distinct from the Anglo-Catholicism that succeeded the Tractarians) were at odds. Georges Florovsky made a good stab at explaining it in the second issue of the Fellowship's *Journal*.[109] Making play with the idea of the Church as the Body of Christ (central to Florovsky's ecclesiology as this was) he underlined the significance of the maxim *unus christianus, nullus christianus*. One can only be a Christian, united with Christ, if one is a 'co-citizen of saints', in the 'great throng' of those accepted into the Church, which is the 'Mansion of the Spirit'.[110] Catholicity, which Florovsky also calls the 'oecumenical' nature of the Church, is best thought of as 'all-timeness', i.e. as the Church 'running through all times'.[111] This emphasis on the diachronic is clearly pertinent to the topic of venerating saints, since the overcoming of time in the Church implies that 'men of different epochs and generations become our living contemporaries'. The Church should be regarded as a 'kind of mysterious image of eternity and a foretaste of the Resurrection of all'.[112] Understandably, then, biological death does not sunder the members of Christ. In support of these statements, Florovsky cited the prayers for the departed and the Order of Burial in the Orthodox liturgy with their clamant pleas for the intercession of 'our heavenly co-citizens in the Church'.[113] But who can, with certainty, be counted as among those co-citizens?

Here Florovsky had to confront the issue of what the East calls 'glorification' and the West 'canonization'. Florovsky did not stress, as might well be the case in a Roman Catholic writer, the juridical or forensic nature of the process involved.

> Reverently the Church watches for any signs of grace which witness and confirm the earthly struggle of the departed. By an inner sight the Church recognizes both the righteous living and departed, and the feeling of the Church people is sealed by the witness of the priesthood of the Church.[114]

Here of course the 'feeling' concerned corresponds to what in the West is called *fama sanctitatis* together with some evidence of 'cultus', while the hierarchical 'witness' amounts to the juridical process, with its weighing and sifting of testimonies, in the Latin canonical tradition. The Orthodox term 'glorification' carries a suggestion of doxology, and Florovsky cites St John of Damascus, who, faced with a critique of saint-worship by iconoclasts, considered that in every case it is 'the Lord' who is 'wonderful in his saints', for the glory ascribed to the saint is given ultimately to God. The sanctity of human beings attests the success of the Son's work of deification in his Incarnation, and the fulfilment of the economy of the Spirit in spreading grace abroad.

But—back to the topic of catholicity—the act of venerating the saints also affects others not just in the obvious sense of getting help from their intercession but in the more subtle respect Florovsky had already highlighted. All 'calling on them through communion in prayer, deepens the consciousness of the catholic unity of the Church'.[115] Florovsky's interpretation of the *Pokrov*, a vision of Mary, the Mother of the Lord, with the faithful sheltering beneath her 'Protecting Veil,' nicely supported this claim. Though the legend is Byzantine, its exploitation is Russian—and it corresponds closely to the Latin image of the 'Mantle of Mary', said to be used first in Cistercian circles in the West. The Protecting Veil is a 'vision of the unbreakable and ever-existent unity of the heavenly and the earthly Church'.[116] Florovsky stressed that the life of the saints is one of ceaseless intercession or mediation, and he links that intercession to the early Syriac writer Isaac of Nineveh's celebration of the 'pure heart' praised by the Saviour in the Beatitudes. It is 'a burning of the heart for all creation—for men, birds, beasts, demons and all creatures'.[117] In the eucharistic Liturgy, the whole Church, earthly and heavenly comes together, not excluding in the latter the angels, whom, Florovsky reports, 'great saints' (Seraphim of Sarov is mentioned) have sometimes seen con-celebrating with the earthly worshippers.[118] The iconographic decoration of the church building in any case speaks of this mysteric unity, of the presence of the saints with the faithful on earth.

The question of veneration of the saints continued to fascinate members, and, up to a point, to divide them. Some Orthodox could extract a great deal from the annals of the saints, to a point that more earthly minded Englishmen might find hard to grasp. Another Russian contributor, Vladimir Illiin, writing an introduction to the life of St Seraphim of Sarov, found in that life, and indeed in the saint's 'face' and 'ikon', an answer to the questions, What is Orthodoxy? What is Russia? What is the Russian idea?

> The saint flowered forth amongst us as an embodiment, an ikon of the complete transfiguration, which will come into the world outside time ... These anticipations, rooted outside time, are of the very nature of New Testament Catholicity, which presents life with history, and not *in* history (that is— not in servitude to history, not as prisoners of the world). This last again is especially characteristic of Russian Orthodoxy, which, though it was a living factor historically, transcends history and soars above it. This transcendence, this soaring, is the Passover, the fullness of which is known by Russia alone.[119]

As to that, an Anglican writer, William Martin Whitley (he had been curate at the amazingly High Church parish of St Silas, Kentish Town, and would later be warden of Liddon House, and curate at the Grosvenor Chapel, an austere early-eighteenth-century building in the West End of London's South Audley Street, skilfully Catholicized by the church-designer John Ninian Comper) took a very different—indeed a deliberately cosmopolitan—view. Whitley argued that the value of seeking the intercession of the saints lies, partly at least, in its supra-local (including supra-national) significance It emphasizes the unity of the Church, a 'common life drawn through the Incarnate Son, and a common bond of prayer for mankind'.[120]

> As we approach the Saints in prayer, we learn to sink lesser loyalties in greater demands and duties. The interests of a local or national church must be subordinated to the whole Church catholic of Christ.[121]

The other value of their cultus, for this contributor, lay in reminding Christians of the Church's true work on earth. This is to worship God, which leads to an understanding of his greatness; to make prayer and intercession, joining with the prayer of Christ who lives for ever to make intercession for us; to serve by knowing the will of God and doing it, and to know that behind and before all of these the call to personal holiness is heard. 'To expect the prayers of the saints is to accept the conditions of holiness which have brought the saints to perfection.'[122]

An anonymous contribution on the same subject taken from the *Feuillets de Saint-Serge* for 1931 defended direct petition for the intercession of the saints rather than simply what many High Churchmen who were not Anglo-Catholics were willing to concede, which was 'comprecation': asking God that the saints may help us rather than addressing directly the saints themselves. This writer based himself on an 'understanding of the Church of Christ as a union of the faithful, as a great and living Bond, bound by faith and love in Him' that is 'incomprehensible without the recognition of this mysterious act of the influence of souls on another soul'.[123]

Preparing for death

The redoubtable Militza Zernov may have the last word, in an essay on 'The Mystery of Death'. The theological preamble to her essay was perhaps predictable, speaking of death as it did as the supreme trial yet also the gateway to eternity, to a world beyond description (certainly not via the 'doctrine of purgatory... of the Romanists').[124] But despite the silence of doctrine there is quite a lot that can be said, so it turns out, on the basis of the liturgy. The Orthodox funeral services speak of death as a 'tragedy and an affliction', with a person falling into the hands of the living God in a way that makes those he or she leaves behind tremble, because (or despite the fact that) his or her destiny is undetermined so far as we are aware. When and how it is finally determined we do not know.

> We go on praying. And with us the whole heavenly Church is praying. The energies of the whole Church in heaven and earth are engaged in this crisis of a single soul.[125]

The prayer asks for pardon and rest in the land of the living.

Mme Zernov described the sacramental rites that precede the moment of death: the Holy Unction, Confession and Communion, as well as the canon to be recited at the parting of the soul from the body, which itself remains in the house for three days during which the *panikhida* service is repeated at intervals and 'the house assumes the atmosphere of a church'.[126] A special ceremony attends the deposition of the body in the coffin, with 'several reminiscences of the Holy Week service of the burial of our Lord'.[127] The body is treated as sacred as 'an image of the departed', which does not exclude a 'realization of the living presence of the soul of the departed'.[128]

> In this conception matter is not opposed to spirit but is penetrated by it. Accordingly, the cemetery or the grave is for an Orthodox Christian a place of rest and prayer, a place of closer communion with the departed. He is profoundly shocked at seeing a Christian grave deserted and untended.[129]

And she mentioned how St Seraphim invited his disciples to seek his help at his tomb.

As to the survivors of death, the Church opens for them a 'salutary expression of grief' as in the laments of the funeral rite and the mourning black, which is an 'emblem ... of the depth of mystery for which the departed soul has left the shifting lights and colours of this world'—but also in the way she encourages the mourners to shift their attention from themselves to the needs of the departed.[130] There is an earthly realism in her closing remarks. Prayer for the dead needs to become a life of reparation for them. Their example challenges us to extirpate in ourselves the faults they undoubtedly had themselves.

→ 6 ←

An Interest in Art

The growth of interest, academic and popular, in icons in the West more or less coincides with the life-time of the Fellowship's journal. So it is not surprising that an attempt was made to explain the icon and its veneration to Anglicans, both by illustrated lectures at the conferences—which depended on the acquisition of images not always readily available—and by articles in print. There was also a willingness to consider other art traditions that bore an analogy with the art of the icon—or coincided with its patristic beginnings, and some awareness of the wider issue of 'theological aesthetics' as such.

Evgeny Trubetskoy

The October Revolution placed under threat the rise of a theologically conscious approach to the traditional art of the Russian icon. Under Bolshevism, icons of outstanding artistic value were generally preserved, but this was on the ground of their historic importance for Russia's cultural patrimony. Any hint of their importance for a Christian world-view, unless delivered in dismissive or at best patronizing tone, was sedulously avoided. This cut off a promising development of the late tsarist period. Orthodox theologians, or at any rate religious thinkers, had begun to consider traditional icons precisely as objects of theological interest—indeed as theological objects, embodiments of theological meaning. The trio of lectures delivered by Prince Evgeny Trubetskoy in Moscow during the First World War encapsulated this trend.

In 1937 *Sobornost* published a translation of one such lecture. Here, Trubetskoy's topic was the cosmology implied by the Holy Liturgy and its setting—a setting which, most importantly, included iconography. Extracts from a text later published in its entirety in English under the title *Icons: Theology in Color* set out Trubetskoy's eschatological view of the sacred art of Russia's mediaeval age.[1] For Trubetskoy, the 'whole of ancient Russian religious art was conceived and nurtured in the struggle with [the] temptation' to fall down and worship Satan conceived as ruler of the 'Kingdom of the Beast', that is, a world where biological necessity—might is right—takes the place of the ethical principle. Both the exterior and the frescoed interior of ancient Russian churches proclaim 'that inner "soborny" unity which must overcome the chaotic divisions and enmities of the world and of mankind'.[2] Speaking of how the traditional icons combine sorrow and joy, Trubetskoy remarked

> The attenuation of the figures is a sharply expressed rejection of that very animalism which raises the satisfaction of the flesh to the level of the highest categorical imperative. For it is precisely this attitude which justifies not only the coarsely materialistic and cruel attitude of man to the lower animals, but also the right of every nation to engage in bloody combat with other nations, which obstruct its insatiable greed.[3]

Readers in England might well have been disturbed by Trubetskoy's perspective. The shadow of Hitlerism had already fallen over central Europe, and only two years would elapse before the outbreak of the Second World War.

As that War gained momentum, the journal published an essay in the more neutral vocabulary of conventional history-of-art writing: Eric Prehn's 'The Development of Icon-painting in Russia'.[4] Its manner differed *toto caelo* from that of Trubetskoy, yet, oddly enough, its conclusions were perfectly compatible with those of Orthodox enthusiasts for Primitivism in Russia's 'Silver Age'. Prehn found the fifteenth-century masters the apogee of this art, and the invasion by Western art-styles in the seventeenth and eighteenth centuries to be its downfall. Despite its sober tone, his essay would herald the kind of apologia for the icon, over against the religious art of the early modern West, produced in post-War Paris by Léonide Ouspensky and Paul Evdokimov.[5]

> The influence of Western Art, by nature so naturalistic, preoccupied with anatomy, perspective and the treatment of light and shadow, was in its essence so completely different from the art of Russian religious painting that its principles could not be incorporated in the latter. It dealt a final and fatal blow to the old style, from which there was no recovery.[6]

What Prehn did not foresee was the renaissance of the icon in the Diaspora and eventually, in the post-Soviet period, in Russia itself.

Joanna Reitlinger

An excellent example of Diaspora revival of the icon was soon forthcoming. Shortly after the Second World War ended, and normal communications could resume between London and Paris, Sister Joanna (Julia Nikolaevna Reitlinger), an artist who had been Bulgakov's spiritual daughter and lived at this time in a tiny attic in the Institut Saint-Serge, received an invitation. She was asked to provide the images for the Chapel of St Basil's House at 52 Ladbroke Grove, the Fellowship's newly acquired headquarters. This was not simply a commission for an iconostasis. The plan was to decorate the entire wall space of the room. Frescoes would be painted on plywood panels and mounted on wooden frames. Militza Zernov, herself an iconographer and a favourite lecturer on the topic of the icon at later conferences, described the work in a memorandum.[7] Post-War shortages added greatly to its difficulty. Artists' paints and paint-brushes were hard to find, eggs for the tempera still rationed, and plywood was unobtainable in England so it had to be brought from France. Sister Joanna started her task in the summer of 1947, returning to complete it in winter 1948. The carpentry was the work of a second generation émigré, Oleg Andronov, an engineer who had never before done woodwork. Collaboration cannot have been easy since Reitlinger was very deaf and most communication had to be in writing. She also had the disconcerting habit of locking herself in to the chapel so as to work undisturbed, her singing of Church chants while painting the only sign of her presence.

The iconographic scheme was well worked out. The lower walls portrayed the Church in its earthly history via groups of saints of various traditions and nationalities, mostly—but not entirely—prior to the Schism between East and West. The Conversion of St Paul, apostle of the Gentiles, began the series, which continued on the left hand wall with the Greek and Latin Fathers, and on the right hand wall with saints of the Balkans, the Caucasus, Britain, and Russia. St Birgitta of Sweden was interposed between the latter two—perfectly correctly from a geographical standpoint. On the upper walls a more theological scheme began with the creation of the world and man, to be followed by scenes from the Johannine Apocalypse and completed with a painting of the heavenly

Jerusalem. This was a daringly original scheme, suggesting a remarkably relaxed attitude to Orthodox convention in church decoration.[8]

Nicolas Lossky

The year after Reitlinger finished her work Nicolas Vladimirovich Lossky—I am presuming this was the son of the Paris theologian Vladimir Lossky, later the interpreter to the Orthodox of the 'Mystical Theology of the Church of England', and not an accidental editorial inversion of name and patronym—wrote in *Sobornost* on the topic of the icon. Nicolas Lossky would have been 19 or 20 at the time of publication: a not impossible chronology. The essay was a taster for the more extended account his father would provide, with Ouspensky as co-author, in the classic *The Meaning of Icons*, which appeared in German and English three years later in 1952.[9] In 'The Place of Icons in the Church', Lossky *fils* stressed that iconic art is specifically liturgical.

> Art in the Church is liturgical, not merely a frame for the Liturgy, but similar to it both in its content, and in its ways of expression. Liturgical art and the Liturgy complete one another and cannot be separated.[10]

Art must abandon any pretensions to independent value when it enters the liturgical arena. It should no longer be seeking to 'awaken aesthetic feelings' but remain content to be an 'objective expression of the Truth of the church'.[11] The icon closely identifies with the liturgical text, and it carries out a theological task which Lossky described in three ways.

In the first place, the icon may exhibit the dogmatic meaning of an event in revelation history. Secondly, it can tell of the particular way of serving God carried out by this or that saint: testifying, by images of the saints, that all the redeemed share in a single holy liturgy, in heaven and on earth. Thirdly—and this picked up Trubetskoy's emphasis—the icon images the transfigured world, for its artists understood what was meant by deification of the body in the Age to Come.

Lossky was clearly a traditionalist in his approach to iconography, and might not have approved of all of Reitlinger's work. Strict adherence to tradition was recommended, though not on grounds of conservatism for its own sake. It was for a more specific reason: 'the notion of the transfiguration, alive in the ancient iconographers, is not alive in us'.[12]

This was an excessively pessimistic conclusion if Tradition, in the theological sense of that word, remains animated by the Holy Spirit. His later career, including as it did major ecumenical roles on the Faith and Order Commission of the World Council of Churches and in Catholic–Orthodox dialogue, as well as bridge-building between the Patriarchates of Constantinople and Moscow (on ordination to the priesthood in 2006 he chose to serve in the Moscow jurisdiction while teaching at Saint-Serge under the exarchate) implies he was not as congenitally downbeat as this striking—not to say shattering—comment might suggest.

Vladimir Weidlé

In 1950 George Every of the Society of the Sacred Mission reviewed for the journal a major text on the genesis of Christian art by the Paris Diaspora literary critic Vladimir Vasil'evich Weidlé. Weidlé was that *rara avis*, a genuinely theological critic of the arts. His *The Dilemma of the Arts*, published two years previously, had described modern European culture in unflattering terms.[13] That culture showed every sign of what Weidlé termed 'the Great Refusal'. What he meant by the phrase was the refusal to be fellow-workers with God, accepting what is given in nature and human (and Christian) tradition, and thus co-creating rather than constructing solely from personal resources. Such an approach, he believed, was already prefigured as early as Leonardo. Subsequent to the Renaissance it was universalized in European Romanticism. Inexorably, judgment has fallen upon it. The judgment is 'Loss of Style', which entails cutting off from around the artist those who ought to be his audience. Schism from the hearer or beholder is exemplified in both 'Pure Poetry' and 'Abstract Art'. In traditional art, by contrast, there is always empathetic understanding between the work and the viewer.

Weidlé's *The Baptism of Art*, now under discussion in the journal, focused not so much on the art of the icon, a post-Nicene development, but on the Christian art of the third century. Essentially, this meant the excavated Christian church at Dura-Europos on the eastern edge of the Graeco-Roman world, along with the Roman catacombs. These primitive beginnings were, in Weidlé's perception, a new or at least newly employed visual language. What might seem a crude didacticism, or, in the case of catacomb art, a kind of visual telegraphese, should not be misconstrued. A certain mismatch between content and form was highly instructive. These painterly forms were brought into being in order to express thought within a religion. They should not be regarded as art proper, for it is constitutive of the latter that form and content are always totally fused.

Every suggested what he considered a better formulation for these first efforts at sacred art in the Church. In the sacramental approach which was characteristic of his own theological thinking he called them 'signposts to the mystery of grace in the baptismal liturgy',[14] thus turning the metaphorical 'baptism' of Weidlé's title into literal fact. But Every accepted Weidlé's view that something was lost when the simple 'signitive' art of the pre-Nicene age gave way to the more complex 'symbolic' art of the fourth and fifth centuries and beyond. There was a diminishment of the sense of the 'immediate presence of the Mystery Itself, of something that can never be embodied in any art form or thought form, at which we can only point'.[15]

Lev Gillet

George Every was of course a Western writer and was here correcting an Orthodox colleague. The Orthodox did not, at this stage of *Sobornost*'s life, have all their own way, either on this topic or on others. In the first place, even when an Orthodox was writing, he might have considerable criticisms of his co-religionists to offer, whether on or emanating from this topic. Thus Gillet, writing a review article on a book about the emergence of the image of the lifeless Christ on the Cross, sought to deconstruct a number of phil-Orthodox enthusiasms.[16] The Dutch Byzantinist L. H. Grondijs (whose narrative, it should be said, is not accepted in all respects by later art-historians) had insisted that the departure from the *Christus triumphans* on the Cross was essentially a Byzantine initiative. He noted, for instance, Cardinal Humbert's dismay at seeing images of the dead Christ in Constantinople on the ill-fated visit of 1054, and pointed out how, leaving aside Western copies of the new Byzantine manner, it was only much later that Franciscan devotion to the crucified Lord in his anguish took possession in the West. Originally Byzantine too was the depiction of the flowing of a fountain of blood from the wounded side of Christ—from which observation some large conclusions might conceivably be drawn. Gillet proceeded to draw them now.

> [I]n the 11th and 12th centuries the Latins move gradually from the contemplation of the side pierced by a spear to that of the Heart

wounded with love; and hence it may be said that the cult of the Sacred Heart, in which so many Orthodox see a Latin aberration, is partly based on Byzantine iconography and the dominant interests of the devotion which it expressed.[17]

Gillet agreed with Grondijs that modern Orthodox are too prone to downplay, by way of contrast with the Latin Church, the central sacrificial, Passion-oriented, themes of the liturgy and the liturgical year—though in a footnote he exempted from these strictures Sergei Bulgakov, whom Grondijs had invoked as among the culprits.[18]

Gillet then proceeded to criticize what he termed 'Orthodoxy-up-to-date'. He complained that many Orthodox, especially among the young, have lost the sense of original sin (however this be named in the Greek tradition) and the consequences thereof in concupiscence, i.e. 'the disordered, immoderate attraction of the human will to transient good'.[19] Modern Orthodox readers are treated to exquisitely beautiful accounts of man made in the divine image without being told that these apply properly to Adam before the Fall (Gillet had Berdyaev in view here). Their mind-set does not allot sufficient space to Redemption, as distinct from Incarnation, transfiguration, and deification. '[R]are are the Orthodox for whom Jesus Christ crucified occupies the central place given to him by St Paul.'[20] Gillet regretted that Metropolitan Antony Khrapovitsky, whom many in the Diaspora regarded as a touchstone of rigorous Orthodoxy, had adopted a moral theory of the Atonement more characteristic of Liberal Protestantism. Or, to put it somewhat differently, as Gillet went on to do, Khrapovitsky saw through the eyes more of Dostoevsky than of the Fathers. Nor did Gillet want to exclude from Orthodox preaching (and hence iconography) the ideas of expiation, reparation, satisfaction, which, in ascending order, explain the substitution of the Lamb of God for sinners.

> Those who speak of the 'juridical' Latin concept of the Atonement should realize that long before St Anselm, a genuine Oriental, Theodore Abu Qurrah, bishop of Haran in Mesopotamia at the beginning of the ninth century, upheld the most juridical theory of the redemption that it is possible to imagine.[21]

And Abu Qurrah—Gillet might have noted but did not—was the premier Arab Christian apologist for the holy icons over against Islamic criticism. The upshot for the spiritual life of this animus against the more searing kinds of Passion iconography, and of the theological motive for that animus, may well be grave.

> We forget that for man on this earth, the glory of the Transfiguration is an exceptional grace and a momentary consolation, and that our normal state as Christians is to be following after Jesus, carrying our cross, which is a sharing in His Cross.[22]

Byzantines and Pre-Raphaelites

A less controversial reminder of the visual aspect of the liturgical setting of Orthodox teaching followed a couple of years later. In 1956 an assistant was consecrated for the Greek archbishop in London. *Sobornost* took the opportunity to offer an architectural and iconographic study of John Oldrid Scott's Neo-Byzantine cathedral of St Sophia in Moscow Road. Confusingly, London's Greek cathedral has a Russian address. The street names in this part of Notting Hill commemorate the visit of Tsar Alexander I to London in 1814. The building, dating from 1879 (when it replaced a succession of smaller churches, the first, from 1837, at Finsbury Circus, the second, from 1850, in Winchester Street, London Wall) was praised by that ubiquitous describer of British architecture Nikolaus Pevsner, in his *The Buildings of England: London*, published in 1952.[23]

The *Sobornost* writer described the mosaics of the interior. 'Echoes of Byzantium and the Pre-Raphaelites intermingle. Prophets of angular austerity give place to angels represented in the Victorian manner. Thus the cathedral happily embodies the theological and liturgical vigour of the traditional iconography, but without the puristic uniformity that can be so edifying on paper and often so lifeless in execution.'[24] This was a warning against too ruthless an emphasis on that conformity to the canons of iconic art Lossky had counselled some few years previously.

Philip Sherrard

In 1962 an issue of the journal was largely dominated by theological aesthetics of one kind or another. This was explicitly so in an essay by the Orthodox lay philosopher Philip Sherrard on the art of the icon, and implicitly so in an essay by Donald Allchin on 'Creation, Incarnation, Interpretation', a paper at the Swedish conference of the Fellowship the previous year.

Sherrard's essay was an appeal to save the icon from aestheticization, for an 'icon divorced from a place and act of worship is a contradiction in terms'.[25] Echoing Nicolas Lossky, the art of the icon is essentially liturgical. It belongs to a 'visual system conveying and giving support to the spiritual facts which underlie the whole liturgical drama'.[26] This was a statement which might have been less unqualified, for domestic icons appear exceptionally early, and they continue to play their part in the devotional life of Orthodox households. The oversight was, however, forgivable. The domestic icon belongs tacitly to the wider scheme of right worship laid out in the liturgy. The same toleration cannot be extended, however, to Sherrard's claim that the two principal events of which the Eucharist, central to the liturgy, is the consummation are the Incarnation and the Transfiguration. The eliding of the Paschal Mystery of the Lord's Cross and Resurrection here was quite astonishing—a perfect exemplification of Gillet's comments on the *Christus passus* a decade before. The selective foreshortening of the mysteries of the life of Christ, omitting the Passion, may have been unconsciously motivated by the preference for mysticism over asceticism to which Gillet ascribed the iconographic pathology he had analysed. But consciously speaking, Sherrard's decision was dictated by the desire to speak in symmetrical fashion of the Incarnation as the entry of the Spirit into matter (identified with *natural* existence), and, balancing the Incarnation, of the Transfiguration as the consequence of this entry as such matter is spiritualized (thus producing an existence that is *more than natural* in kind).

Sherrard went on to explain the developed iconographic scheme of an Orthodox church. That scheme lays out an entire cosmology (shades of Trubetskoy and Lossky), which he also interprets, in a rather original fashion, as a reminder of what man is capable of becoming. The 'diagram in miniature of the universe ... is also a diagram of man's inner world'.[27] He takes the icons 'made without hands'—icons believed to have come into existence miraculously—to indicate symbolically the way that, in iconic art, the 'sacred subject' should be thought of as 'itself projecting or reflecting itself on to the material of the icon', rather than 'expressing the artist's own response to or observation of his subject'.[28] This does not, he insisted, depersonalize the act of artistic making, since there has to be an 'endless recreation within the life of the artist of the spiritual realities which are the subject of his work'.[29] Sherrard's way of expressing the sacramentality—in an extended sense—of the icon is to say it 'becomes in its turn a centre of power, an incarnation in its own right of the spiritual energy of its divine or deified prototypes'.[30] If this is certainly strong language, we may not be expected to take it entirely *au pied de la lettre*, since he has just said that 'as all images it is penetrated with something of the vitality of what it images'.[31]

Donald Allchin

Allchin's contribution to the third Scandinavian conference of the Fellowship on 'Revelation and Art'—he gave the same paper at the English conference at Broadstairs later in the year—was a little classic. The title he chose was deliberately Trinitarian: the Father is related to creation as the Son to Incarnation and the Holy Spirit to interpretation. In this overall perspective, he spoke first about divine creation and human sub-creation, and thus of man's artistic activities in their broadest form.

> Man sings, he composes verse, he paints, he carves... And he seems in some strange way to be participating, at his own level, in the divine activity itself. For God who is himself creator, has planted in man this desire and capacity to create. And if all human activity has a symbolic character, that is to say, points beyond itself to some further reality, then artistic activity of whatever sort, is particularly charged with this mysterious, symbolic quality. It is very evidently not self-explanatory. It contains and reveals meanings and purposes which are not apparent at the surface.[32]

He spoke in the second place about the redemptive Incarnation, and the human response thereto, and thus about liturgical art in the Body of Christ.

> The symbolic character of all artistic work receives its full expression, its true foundation, in the fact that God reveals Himself in particular events, in taking flesh, and in the sacraments of the Word made flesh.[33]

Finally he spoke about the Spirit as interpretative translator, as establishing a two-way communication between God and man.

> [W]hen we consider how much artistic activity is rendered fruitless and sterile by a failure to communicate and how often the shock of recognition which the Spirit brings about fails to take place, we see again in this particular sphere how necessary this work of the Spirit is.[34]

Those members of the Fellowship who were left cold by the art of the icon—presuming there to be such—were meant to take note of this.

Ancient Irish art

Allchin's self-selected remit had been extraordinarily wide. This breadth was not uncommon in the journal of the period. It should not be thought that *Sobornost* was entirely uninterested in Western sacred art. In the period when it was genuinely bi-focal, with Anglicanism and Orthodoxy at par, its editors might have been forgiven a degree of inattention to English Christian art, since so much of it had been destroyed at the Reformation and an aniconic attitude to visual art in church largely prevailed in the immediately post-Reformation centuries. Of course, thanks not least to the Gothic Revival, visual art in various media under Anglican auspices made a massive come-back in the course of the nineteenth and twentieth centuries. But on the whole, the Fellowship liked its Christianity presented through the mirror of *ressourcement*. So there was the earlier art of the Latin West to consider, not all of which fell victim to the strictures of Prehn, Lossky or Ouspensky.

In 1966, Daphne Pochin Mould, an Irish convert to Orthodoxy, contributed a rich article on the early Irish high cross. These stone crosses, often elaborately carved, correspond more to the 'ancient and once universal' spirituality of the Cross, now replaced in modern Ireland by the 'late western tradition' representing Christ not reigning from the Cross but dead there.[35] Unlike Gillet, she had evidently not read Grondijs, and was unaware that iconography of the dead Christ in Constantinople churches had disturbed the Latin visitors of the mid-eleventh century. Early Irish martyrologies, Pochin Mould explained, are pan-European in their comprehensiveness. But not too much should be made of direct Oriental influence on the ancient Irish Church. She drew attention to the challenge mounted to the thesis of such influence by recent scholars. They had pointed out that the principal overseas contacts of the Irish were with the Church in Gaul, Italy, Germany and Switzerland.[36] The 'Celtic Church' was, to a large extent, the creation of Victorian myth-making. In the islands of the North Atlantic archipelago the Church was a part of Latin Christendom that, through distance and the difficulties of communication, had developed distinct customs of its own.

Pochin Mould herself linked the blossoming of the Irish high cross to the Culdee monasteries (many of which later adopted the Augustinian Rule). Simple crosses, engraved on pillars, became stones shaped into a figured cross in a development dateable to the eighth century. Though other symbols were cut into rocks or pillar stones (the fish, the *chi-rho*, the letters alpha and omega, the *orans* figure, the ship of the Church with the Cross as mast), these carved crosses, some of which emulated jewelled crosses by the delicacy of their workmanship, were surely pre-eminent. The most common biblical scenes portrayed are Fall, Crucifixion, and Last Judgment. That hardly suggests the *Christus Victor* ethos she claims is supreme in this art. She herself admitted that the episodes of the Transfiguration, Ascension and Pentecost appear to be absent. But there were other panels that supported her claim, notably Old Testament scenes such the Ark, the Binding of Isaac, the Exodus at the Red Sea, Moses with arms outstretched while Israel was fighting Amalek, Jonah and the whale. These were redolent of the texts for the Byzantine feasts of the exaltation of the Cross.

The Syrian church model

Although there had been occasional Roman Catholic contributors to *Sobornost* before 1968, 1968 was the year when Allchin wondered aloud whether Catholics should be permitted to become full members of the Fellowship—and not merely guests at conferences or branch meetings. Appropriately, then, an issue of that year saw a Western Catholic writing on liturgical architecture, albeit with a distinctly Oriental slant.

Dennis Hickley was a practising architect studying for the priesthood as a late vocation at the Beda College in Rome. He had taken from the Orthodox theologian Alexander Schmemann an idea newly hatched in the latter's *Introduction to Liturgical Theology*, to the effect that, in the Christian religion, the liturgy of the Word reflects temporality, the liturgy of the Eucharist the Eschaton or Age to Come. Hickley argued that early Syrian churches embodied Schmemann's distinction. These churches typically placed the synagogue-derived 'bema'—a slightly elevated platform, horseshoe in shape, where the Word is proclaimed—in a central position in the nave. In various Syrian texts the bema appears as Christ preaching on the Mount of the Beatitudes, or from Jerusalem, the centre of the earth, while in the Byzantine sphere the ambo, despite its smaller size, had originally the same symbolism attached, for it occupied the same place as the bema in terms of the building as a whole.

The artists who decorated the nave made reference, accordingly, to the cosmic creation in the here and now. This they did by mosaic work on the floor depicting animals, birds and fish (sometimes in the vegetable shape of an 'inhabited vine') as well as symbols representing the heavens. In Hickley's Schmemann-influenced view, when the liturgical celebrants left the bema (and thus the nave) to move into the sanctuary, they were leaving the cycle of cosmic time to enter the time of the Eschaton. As Hickley put it, making use here of a ninth-century Syrian Nestorian text, the *Exposition of Church Offices*:

> This sense of the two times finds a spatial expression in the church building where the nave represents the time of Creation, of the seven-day week and the historical cycle of Fall–redemption–Return, and the sanctuary the breaking out of this cyclic pattern into the great Eighth Day of Salvation.[37]

In Syria the temporal dimension could be accentuated by mosaics showing the wheel of months and seasons either on the floor of the nave proper or in the aisles. Vault mosaics do not survive at these sites, but Hickley made the logical deduction (from the premises already laid out) that, where they existed, they must have been 'eschatological in character and expressed such themes as the Lord's coming in the Eighth Day beyond the time of this world, yet already present in it, in the Eucharist, by the power of the Holy Spirit'.[38] These were the (hypothetical!) images which stimulated the decoration of the domes of apses in the Byzantine world, where, however, the nave lost its autonomy and became something of a mere forecourt to the sanctuary. That was the result, Hickley thought, of the disappearance of the great ambo once central to the nave.

The implication of Hickley's essay was that new churches, even in the West, should seek to recover this arrangement, owing to its theological excellence. Alas, the burden of international Modernism, the functionalist style common in newly built churches for the Roman rite, continued to prevail. It gave the Orthodox good grounds for thinking that the Christian West was falling victim to aesthetic as well as theological apostasy.

→ 7 ←

The Sophia Affair

The concluding issue of the Fellowship's journal for 1935 opened with a worrying editorial. The much venerated Sergei Bulgakov, the Fellowship's greatest Orthodox priest-friend, was in difficulties. News had arrived of the censure pronounced by the *locum tenens* of the Moscow Patriarchate on Bulgakov's sophiological theology. Bulgakov's response, which rejected the accusations of heresy, was also to hand. The editor asked for prayers for him and for all dealing with the matter.

Reception of the ukaz

The publication of the *ukaz* was known to few people in the West. When news of it broke—surprisingly, this was in an English Roman Catholic weekly, the *Catholic Herald*—it was obviously necessary for the Fellowship's journal to make some appropriate comment. Zernov, with his profound commitment to Bulgakov, was dismissive of the intervention by Metropolitan Sergius. Sergius, after all, was only a caretaker for the vacant patriarchal throne and he was, moreover, obliged to do the bidding of the Soviet government, whatever that might be. But this reaction would not do. Paul Anderson wrote sternly to Zernov from the Russian Student Christian Movement Federation headquarters in Paris.

> I think you have not taken into account the fact that the Ukaz of the Metropolitan Sergius is only the most recent of the most concrete and authoritative of the various attacks on the teaching of Father Sergius. Several leading theologians in Yougoslavia, Roumania and Bulgaria have been raising the question. [W]e are facing a period in which the conservative and the more progressive forces in the Orthodox Church will come increasingly into conflict . . . It is clear to persons like Heriod, Hodgson and Tatlow as well as to Douglas, that we must take this into account, and that since not only the Life

and Work and the Faith and Order organizations, but also, in the Orthodox sphere, the YMCA and the Federation, are dealing with the Orthodox *Church* and not merely with individual Orthodox people we must be aware of and react to the mind and desires of the authorities as well as of individual thinkers.[1]

Zernov was not likely to be moved, holding as he did that 'Sophianic theology' expressed the most foundational 'conviction of the Russian religious mind', namely, the 'recognition of the potential holiness of matter, the unity and sacredness of the entire creation, and man's call to participate in the divine plan for its ultimate transfiguration'.[2]

A proxy battle

As to Bulgakov personally, no one wanted to kick a man when he was down—quite aside from the fact that the Anglican office-holders in the Fellowship largely lacked the linguistic ability to do justice to books written in the Russian language. But, though seeking to protect, or at any rate not undermine, Bulgakov's good name, there was plainly a degree of doctrinal discomfort nonetheless.

The more audacious side of Russian Diaspora speculation did not emerge unscathed in Eric Mascall's review of Alexis van der Mensbrugghe's *From Dyad to Triad. A Plea for Duality against Dualism and an Essay towards the Synthesis of Orthodoxy*, a work introduced by that indefatigable ecumenical diplomat, Canon J. A. Douglas.[3] If there is a true sense in which all created things are in God, Mascall preferred a more sober and doctrinally careful Western 'panentheism' to Van der Mensbrugghe's version. The latter, so Mascall asserted, placed the world inside God with a Logos who was always not simply 'incarnable' (a useful if ugly neologism) but also incarnate. The Logos was the 'Cosmic Christ' existing before all worlds. This review was a proxy critique of Bulgakov's Sophiology, though without mentioning the Russian theologian's name.

A spirited rejoinder from the Flemish priest was printed as a letter to the editor in the next issue. It touched on—again without explicit mention—various issues pertinent to the criticisms of Bulgakov's visionary system levelled by the Moscow Patriarchate and indeed, as Anderson had rightly said, by the Synodal Church with its central authority in Yugoslavia. There is in God as Creator no initial conceptual realization followed subsequently by realization in reality. God's thinking creates. Van Mensbrugghe was not seeking to deny the existence of evil, nor was he ascribing evil to God, for 'physical and moral evil arise in and through the relation of the created forms between themselves', a statement linked by somewhat impenetrable steps to his doctrine of the Wisdom of God as oscillating between 'Better' and 'More'.[4] Taking the war into the enemy's camp, van der Mensbruggle claimed that Mascall's own sort of panentheism is really polytheism in heavy disguise. It finds alongside God other, now autonomous, beings—and what is the right word for these if not 'gods'? Mascall had said that in creating the world God created what was 'outside' him. For Van Mensbrugghe this is to make God and the world 'numerically on the same footing, alongside each other'.[5] There was in his mind, he protested, no confusion of the sort Mascall had deplored between God's inner relations with himself as Trinity and God's relations with what is not himself, i.e. the world. He had not confused those two sets of relations because he had conjoined them—just as reality did. And lastly he made a spirited defence of the concept of the Cosmic Christ:

> If Sonship and Creatureness are only dual aspects of the same Cosmic Christ, of the Eternal Son born 'before the Ages' and yet 'the first-born of creatures', then generation of the Son and Creation of the World are only the reflection and the counterpart of these same dual aspects in the Father's Simple and Eternal Act.[6]

Sympathy for Bulgakov

Editorial sympathy for, as well as a certain distance from, Bulgakov's travails were signalled in the opening of *Sobornost*'s second issue for 1936.

> Sophiology may be a path which few Englishmen may be able to tread, but no Englishman of discernment can fail to note that behind its obscurities there is the passion to see the world in God, a passion which must in some form be the prelude to any constructive social revolution.[7]

Early in 1936 Bulgakov had spoken in France on the question of intellectual freedom in Orthodoxy, and this became the premier essay of the number. He made it plain he did wish to comment on his own case, offering instead some general reflections. The 'real content' of the dogmatic formulations, he proposed, is 'supplied by the true depth of the mystical life of the Church', such that one can speak of a 'dogmatic life of the Church [that] goes on constantly'.[8] The 'eternal divine content' of doctrine is given in a 'divine-human process of development', a process in which new questions are raised and fresh tasks faced. So 'dogmatic development itself requires freedom of thought'.[9]

The ecclesiastical hierarchy must guard the deposit of faith and act as its mouthpiece when truth needs to be affirmed. But strictly speaking there is no 'external organ' which can take it upon itself to proclaim such truth in all its binding force.[10]

> Many among us, and particularly many representatives of the hierarchy in our Church, have been sadly influenced by Romanizing tendencies, so that they actually regard themselves as so many Popes, or as a sort of collective Pope. This is a sin in Orthodoxy, and constitutes a real temptation to many. The Orthodox Church has no external dogmatic authorities.[11]

When doctrinal truth has to be determined, 'where, and in what way, the decision will become obvious no one can tell'.[12]

Turning to the case of the Church of England, or Anglicanism more widely, Bulgakov considered 'comprehensiveness' the 'corresponding principle' in the Anglican Church—but an 'ambiguous', 'dangerous' and difficult' one. In his estimation, the principle of comprehensiveness called into question the givenness of dogma rather than, as was the case with patristic pluralism (which might otherwise be compared with it), emphasizing various aspects thereof.[13] In Orthodoxy, concluded Bulgakov, the struggle for ecclesiastical freedom is not a struggle for liberalism. It is a struggle for truth in the Church.

Probably not by accident, the same issue contained a review by Mascall of the English translation of Bulgakov's *L'Orthodoxie*.[14] This work—where Bulgakov's distinctive theology is barely apparent, and Sophiology named only to be marginalized, begins, as Mascall pointed out, with the Church as life in Christ, and as living Tradition, whereof Scripture forms part. Bulgakov had described the Church's infallibility in this text as 'no mechanical thing but a manifestation of the Church's life'.[15] That might have referred, obliquely, to the circumstances of his own condemnation at Karlovci and Moscow.

Surprisingly, granted the tip-toeing around the Bulgakov case in which *Sobornost* writers were involved, there suddenly appeared an unmistakeable apologia. At the height of the crisis over Sophiology in the Russian jurisdictions, the printing of an article putting the case for the pro-Bulgakov side of the argument was likely to be deemed controversial and partisan. The editor, in announcing the decision to go ahead, admitted as much. 'It may seem strange that after preserving complete silence on the subject for so many years, the Journal should print an admittedly *ex parte* statement on a matter not only hotly controverted, but, at the moment, *sub judice*. It is this very fact which makes us consider the occasion apposite.'[16] The editor directed readers' attention to advice from Ignatius Loyola. 'It should be presupposed that every good Christian ought to be more ready to give a good sense to the doubtful proposition of another than to condemn it.'[17]

There could have been no better choice for author of the Bulgakov apologia than Leo Zander, who would later produce a two-volume study of his Sophiology which still remains the fullest exposition of Bulgakov's mature thought.[18] Zander's article, despite cutting by the editors, was an impressive rallying-cry. The central principle of Bulgakov's thought is sophianity: 'in God there exist the forms of the world, while in the world itself the likeness of God is imprinted. The sophianic attitude consists precisely in the establishment of this deep connection between God and the world. The world is not alien to God, but represents an expression of his glory, a ray of the divine energy, the image of his Wisdom.'[19]

> The beauty of creation, the harmony of nature, the rationality of man witness ... to the sophianic character of their very being, to their participation in their divine principle 'in their very essence'. The purpose of philosophy (*philo-sophia*, love of wisdom) therefore consists in discovering in every realm of thought and life its sophianic elements, in learning to understand all in the light of divine wisdom.[20]

The original element in Zander's essay lies in his argument that such a philosophy of wisdom enjoys a special affinity with the 'spirit of Orthodoxy'.

> The cosmic character of Orthodoxy, its positive orientation to the world, its anticipation of the transfiguration of that creation which it envisages as all going to make up the Church of God—this needs no proof. Its ritual, ceremonial and church art, all witness to this at every step. But if the outlook of the church is thus patent in its practice, it had never been propounded in theoretical form.[21]

The sophianic attitude—and by extension then the sophiological system—applies this 'experience of life in the Church to the interpretation of life as a whole'.[22]

> Accordingly it must be the sophianic attitude which is to provide the true basis for an Orthodox philosophy, for it is one with the primary intuition from which springs the whole Orthodox attitude to life, to nature, and to man.[23]

Turning his fire on Sophiology's critics, Zander complained they are guilty of an Orthodox version of Schleiermacherianism, the feeling-based theological system of the early nineteenth-century Lutheran theologian Friedrich Schleiermacher. The critics take offence at what they consider the dogmatic rationalism at work in Sophiology. For them, 'Orthodoxy should be no more than the rule of devotion'—and this is precisely what, by counter-distinction to their positive appraisal, Zander equated with Schleiermacher's 'pietistic sentiment'. While affirming the dogmas, the critics deny that the teachings of revelation have the capacity to illuminate the world of thought as a whole.[24] In so doing, they betray the entire Byzantine inheritance.

> Orthodoxy, in its dogmatic theology as in its worship, embodies all the best of the dialectic of Byzantium, which developed from the data of revelation both genuine philosophy and an incomparable literary and plastic expression in art. Every Orthodox, even the most unlearned, is a potential philosopher and theologian.[25]

Even worse is the state of mind of those who reject not only Sophiology but the wider sophianic attitude which underlies it. It is significant that this second type of criticism frequently has recourse to the language of either Thomism or Barthianism so as to formulate its objection to the account of the God-world relation found in sophianity. Zander regarded such critics, Orthodox though they may be in Church allegiance, as representatives of an 'acosmic Orthodoxy' which fails to correspond to Orthodoxy's spirit, and especially to the spirit of its liturgy.[26] The real criticism that should be made is constructive criticism. By this Zander meant the constructive effort to make of Bulgakov's presentations of doctrine the beginnings of an 'Orthodox "Summa".'[27]

Zander at least was in no doubt that systematic theology and the Orthodox liturgy are not alternative *foci* of Christian inspiration.

A wider discussion

The editor was bold in publishing Zander's *plaidoyer*—but many of his fellow Anglicans were still afraid to burn their fingers in the fire. The 1936 theological conversations between Saint-Serge theologians and Anglicans at Mirfield, held under Walter Frere's presidency, and the most important of the developments *Sobornost* had to record for the year, conspicuously abstained from drawing near to the furnace.

They were asking instead, was the Western patristic tradition alien to the Christian East? Florovsky said No, the East–West difference is post-patristic. There are no exclusively Western Fathers. Dix, Van der Mensbrugghe and Fedotov disagreed. Van der Mensbrugghe thought the patristic West had a psychological, the patristic East an ontological, concept of personality, and the difference lay there. Fedotov believed that the West had an anthropocentric bias, formed by questions of grace and freedom, faith and works, whereas the East, contrastingly, had a cosmological focus. Dix maintained that the West had a pure Hebrew monotheism, but the East worked with a dual concept of God and Godhead.

Did attitudes to theological freedom vary, then, as between East and West? Here it was hardly possible for Bulgakov's name not to be forming on all lips. For Lionel Thornton, at the time the leading dogmatic theologian of the Community of the Resurrection, the basic freedom was liberty to believe revelation in its entirety. Criticism was not of revelation but of the human attempts to grasp it. Bulgakov had in fact said something similar. Freedom must include recognition of the entire content of Tradition. Michael Ramsey claimed that, precisely owing to freedom in theological studies, the past's preoccupation with individual items of belief has given way to a healthier concern with membership in an organism which entertains orthodoxy as a whole. Van der Mensbrugghe was not so willing to give Anglican theology the benefit of the doubt. For him the essence of *sobornost* lay in a relation between theology and devotion, reflecting the way the faith was accepted from the Church as Mother. 'The average Anglican, he thought, has more opinion than knowledge, and even if he held right beliefs, held them as "theologoumena".'[28]

Arrière-pensées

In 1937 the journal tried again. It asked a writer with just the right background, combining theological *nous* with a knowledge of Russian, to review what was at the time Bulgakov's sole English-language book, *The Wisdom of God*.[29] A. F. Dobbie-Bateman advised readers to try substituting throughout for the name 'Sophia' the noun 'Nature'—even though the inclusion of the attributes of glory and love in the divine Sophia goes beyond what the phrase 'the divine Nature' would immediately connote in English.

Dobbie-Bateman did not necessarily think he would have many takers, even among members of the Fellowship. English readers might fear to approach the book at all. Instinctively, on opening it at random, they would consider it a work 'too profound to be understood and too original to be safe'.[30] He confessed that, for some of its elevated difficulty, Protestant mysticism and German philosophy must take both praise and blame. Yet regarded as a Christian text *The Wisdom of God* was far less deviant than Soloviev's musings on Sophia as described in Konstantin Mochulsky's great study of that flawed genius—also reviewed in this number of *Sobornost*.

Alongside, in a piquant juxtaposition, was reviewed one of the sharpest criticisms ever penned of both Bulgakov and Soloviev, Georges Florovsky's *The Ways of Russian Theology* (which existed, at this time, only in Russian[31]). As readers were informed, Florovsky had seen the All Russian *sobor* of 1917–18 as the Church's chance to escape from the theological 'kaleidoscope of Latin and German refractions'.[32] The reviewer made the interesting comment that the Russian and the Anglican Churches have it in common that 'they are so much the meeting place of influences which they do not originate that their children must ask anxiously at times whether they speak with their own true voice'.[33] Florovsky's prescription was return to the Fathers but in a free meeting with the West. Dobbie-Bateman had noted in the Paris School journal *Put'* Berdyaev's severe criticism of Florovsky's encyclopaedic history as sheer conservative reaction, and disagreed with Berdyaev on the point. 'Florovsky is not a primitive; he is post-exilic.'[34]

The continuing concern with Bulgakov and Sophiology may explain at least in part the writing of Thomas Parker's 'God and the World in the Light of the Doctrine of Creation', a paper read to the Fellowship's 'Theological Group' in April 1937. Parker, later dean of University College, Oxford, did not mention Bulgakov, and insofar as he has any named figure in his sights it was W. R. Matthews of St Paul's Cathedral who, in his 1930 study *God in Christian Thought and Experience*, held creation to be a divine necessity if God is to be fully personal.[35] Parker was in step with Bulgakov when he insists that the transcendence of God who creates absolutely *ex nihilo* is in no way compromised by the Christian Platonist notion of the 'divine ideas'. As Parker put it, expressing an Anglican 'sophianic attitude' of his own, 'the universe must be, to a greater or less extent, a reflection of God. It is an externalization of divine ideas and must therefore mirror the divine goodness'.³⁶ But Parker was also emphatically supportive of the divine autarchy—*pace* Matthews, though Bulgakov might also be in view. God is self-sufficient. Though the word 'self-sufficient' has a bad savour in English when used of human beings, it is entirely in place in relation to God. Were it not *le mot juste*, 'the attitude of worship' would be impossible, or 'at least becomes something less valuable than it might be, when adopted towards a creator who could not help creating'.³⁷

Dobbie-Bateman himself had had second thoughts. He returned to the topic of *The Wisdom of God*, already reviewed in the previous number, this time more harshly. 'It seems as if the more Fr Sergii explains himself, the darker is the case against him.'³⁸ His worst fear was that Sophiology may involve, at any rate psychologically, an 'involuntary substitution' of the name of Sophia for the name of Christ.³⁹ Had he waited, and read Bulgakov's dogmatic writings as a whole—the Great Trilogy and the Lesser Trilogy—he would have realized such an involuntary error was utterly inconceivable.⁴⁰

Meanwhile Vigo Demant, later Professor of Moral and Pastoral Theology at Oxford, ventured a sharp critique of Berdyaev's newly published *Spirit and Reality*.⁴¹ Berdyaev and Bulgakov should not, of course, be lumped together, yet the support the former gave the latter at the time of the *ukaz* and, more generally, their moving in the same Parisian circles, could give rise to condemnation by association. Berdyaev's book, thought Demant, would confirm the doubts of many about the wisdom of his philosophical positions while confirming their belief in the zeal of his desire for a spiritual reawakening.

> In spite of his repeated assertion that objectification is the work of the spirit he inclines to the conclusion that the objective world is the fallen world. And he is so jealous to preserve the Deity from being apprehended as an object that he is involved in the beginning of an infinite regress wherein behind God is primordial freedom and behind both is the unfathomable *Urgrund* of Jacob Boehme. This, it seems to me, is to court the very danger he wishes to avoid, that of making God an objective element of the natural world. The danger can only be avoided by the dogma of God as the Being of beings out of which come both freedom and nature, in the sense of the world of objects. The calamity from which Berdyaev wishes to preserve us, namely that of losing freedom to objects, can then be avoided by resolutely refusing to merge freedom and being into one another anywhere outside God.⁴²

In 1939 Bulgakov himself reviewed Zernov's life of St Sergius, the Fellowship's co-patron.[43] Sergius's vision of the Trinity underlies Rublev's famous icon of the 'Old Testament Trinity', the mysterious visitors to Abraham at the Oak of Mamre as described in the Book of Genesis. He took the opportunity to comment that Zernov's claim for the doctrine of the Trinity—it brought together 'religious transcendentalism and immanentism' and surpassed both by the 'principle of divine tri-personal love'—had omitted something. The something in question was, so Bulgakov believed, the key notion for such a surpassing: that of the divine *ousia* as self-manifested in 'Wisdom and Glory', at once 'the content of the divine life' and 'the ground of the creation of the world'.[44] It was for the journal a gracious farewell to Sophiology, at least for Bulgakov's lifetime.

Bulgakov's death

The second and last issue of 1944 brought sad news: Bulgakov's death after a long struggle with cancer of the throat. Dobbie-Bateman wrote an obituary for *Sobornost*, less formal than the editor's briefer one. He said one very memorable thing.

> When [Bulgakov] named the existential problem Sophia, we behaved like Greeks who thought that Anastasis was a goddess. Unfortunately, on our side liberalism had not died on us, nor had our biblical theology matured dialectically. It was not yet, and now never will be, possible for him to touch us just at the point where theologically we could have responded.[45]

Most of the rest of his comments were taken up by the intercommunion controversy. But he summoned up the figure of Florovsky, languishing in Belgrade. Dobbie-Bateman cast Florovsky in the role of the Anti-Bulgakov, for 'so active a personality produced its reaction'.[46] The two between them 'covered the whole life of the Fellowship'.[47] Bulgakov had died without any proper resolution of the Sophia dispute, and remained, outside the Russian exarchate of the Patriarchate of Constantinople, a suspect figure (even though many Orthodox in Russia itself, and thus in canonical obedience to the Moscow Patriarchate, stand by him today).

A panegyric essay followed in 1945, written by Zander, and translated by the lay philosopher Evgeny Lampert's wife Elizabeth.[48] A deep understanding of Bulgakov's project allowed Zander to write of the 'bond' between philosophy and theology in the mind of the deceased thinker, such that for Bulgakov philosophy that does not lead to dogma is false, and dogma which does not resolve the problems of philosophy is dead. Thus he aspired to formulate an Orthodox philosophy, or to put Orthodoxy at the basis of all knowledge of reality, of the world, of man and human civilization.[49]

Zander compared his thought for its 'range of content and the integral character of his theological system' to that of Aquinas.[50] Bulgakov reminded him, among Orientals, of Origen of Alexandria. There was a striking conclusion.

> [U]p to the present time, only individual people understand and value Fr Sergius. Nevertheless his thought is beginning to penetrate into the world of western theology, where it occasionally finds, especially in Roman Catholic circles, a great response and appreciation. It has always been a source of distress to me that the representatives of English theological thought who respect Fr Sergius as a priest and a brother in Christ, have not felt the need of acquiring greater insight into his theology. As a member of the Anglo-Orthodox Fellowship, who has been used to breathe the air of both traditions, I cannot help a feeling of regret that the first important translations of Fr Sergius's work are being produced not by the English but by the French; not by Anglicans but by Roman Catholics ... [T]he language of sophiology has not been up to the present made sufficiently intelligible to the English mind.[51]

# 8 /

Writing Theology

From early days, the Fellowship's journal was very serious about good theology. I consider below in the first place how a variety of contributors treated particular themes—specifically, theological epistemology, original sin and personal sin, asceticism and morals, the theology of the Holy Trinity, ecclesiology, and Mariology, before turning to the concept of theology as a whole and some of the main masters who predominated in the pages of *Sobornost*.

Theological epistemology: worship and reason

Eric Mascall, still a layman, contributed to its second issue an essay on 'worship and reason', which sought to reinforce what some Orthodox (though hardly Bulgakov, or Florovsky for that matter) might have seen as a distinctively Western concern for rationality. His essay begins

> The affective and the rational aspects of his religious experience are for the Christian the two most sharply contrasted of all. The one calling with irresistible force on all the powers of devotion of his soul, the other perhaps as strongly urging him never to accept what he does not see rigidly demonstrated; these have produced in many Christian souls an intolerable conflict.[1]

But 'great saints' never ran to these extremes, which are, in fact, so Mascall claimed, perfectly avoidable. It is not the case that reason 'necessitates one philosophy of the Universe while worship requires another'.[2] Reason is an instrument for moving to conclusions, it does not form the body of assumptions on which it works. Those assumptions are not, however, to be chosen arbitrarily. These 'must be such that their recognition carries with it immediate conviction of their truth'.[3] What, then, are they? The young Mascall was evidently not the Anglican Thomist he later became in metaphysics, for he finds the preliminary assumption of the reasonable life to be the 'fundamental facts' that are the 'sense-data of our acts of perception'—a theory borrowed, with due acknowledgement, from Bertrand Russell's book *The Analysis of Matter*.[4] It also happens to be a theory rejected in the course of the twentieth century by philosophers of nearly all persuasions, from Idealists to the disciples of Ludwig Wittgenstein. But Mascall at this point in time found here:

> a great opportunity for Christian theology. The experience of communion with Our Lord in prayer and the sacraments, our common unity in the life of the Church, are quite as immediate as, and indeed far more immediate than the mere experience of our senses.[5]

So the liturgical experiences of, say, the Orthodox are just as primordial as the sensuous experience of seeing a round red object as an apple. No doubt an atheistic scientist lacks that experience, but that is immaterial. No one supposes that not having visited Australia is a ground for denying Australia's existence. And here, in the primordial data, Orthodoxy is experientially richer than the Western Church. Whereas the 'great work of the Western Church has been in the sphere of reason, there can be little doubt that the Eastern Church has developed its capacity of corporate worship far beyond the Western.'[6]

What then of the faith of the Church (Western or Eastern) as expressed in her Creed? For the Mascall of this period, ecclesial faith is the unification of the experiences of individuals and therefore the equivalent of a satisfactory theory in natural science. 'We have listened to our Mother and found her counsel true.'[7] What has borne fruit in the Church's tradition cannot be spiritually illusory.

The predominance in the early meetings of the Fellowship of reform-minded Orthodox is reflected in Mascall's comments on the role of tradition in theological epistemology. It is the Orthodox, not the Anglo-Catholics, at those meetings, who have been saying that tradition is, not 'something rigid and unrelenting' (Mascall finds this 'what it has often seemed to be in the West'), but 'living and pulsating with the devotion and enthusiasm of the faithful', for the test of any present-day 'contribution to tradition' lies in its 'acceptability to the body of the Church.'[8] Here Mascall considers the 'Anglo-Catholic critical school' (he probably had Bishop Gore in mind) at one with Orthodox advocates of 'living Tradition'. But, as he recognizes, 'criticism' is not the word the Orthodox would be likely to use. Mascall defended the vocabulary nonetheless, realizing that in the context of modern study of the Bible a scholarly examination of the historicity and theological reliability of the texts is unavoidable.

> We [Anglo-Catholics of the critical school] do not attempt to build up our theology on a critical basis because we doubt the truth of our religion, but because we have been forced by our opponents to meet them on this ground and because we wish to show them that their destructive conclusions are invalid.[9]

'Tradition' in and of itself, though, was a topic on which the Orthodox and Anglican Catholics could do business.

Orthodox and Anglicans on Tradition

In a lucid exposition Henry Balmforth, principal of Ely Theological College, defined Tradition as the transmission of the original Gospel. For the Fathers, Scripture is the single most important means of such continuing communication, the 'decisive and regulative part' of Tradition.[10] Yet Scripture 'incorporates a faith and a practice which it did not create and it rests upon a worship which it everywhere presupposes.'[11] The New Testament, taken as fulfilling the Old, has to be seen in that light. If we ask what this means in concrete terms, Balmforth replies:

> [T]he organs through which that tradition expresses itself, the Liturgy, the baptismal Creed, the Rule of Faith, the Hierarchy, give us apostolic witness which was not derived from an existing Bible but was contained in the worshipping community and expressed itself not in a sacred book but in institutions, organic structures of the Body of Christ.[12]

Without denying that Tradition has a role in dogmatic formulation, he took its more salient feature to be its pertinence to Christian practice: specifically, in liturgical worship and in the life of charity. In regard to dogma 'its function is rather one of interpretation than origination.'[13]

How then does Tradition find authoritative utterance in controversies of faith? For Balmforth, it has no single centre but finds its outlet in a 'complex of media':[14] the apostolic ministry exercised from the bishop's chair of teaching, or by the bishops together in council; the mind of the Church/consent of the faithful, for 'the business of the ecclesiastic and the theologian is not to impose unfamiliar or novel truths upon the Church but to interpret and make explicit what lies deep in its heart and mind';[15]

and lastly, the 'consecrated reason'[16]—as exemplified in the great Fathers and the high-mediaeval Scholastics. Balmforth warned, however, that the channels of Tradition may become clogged, citing a dictum of the French Jesuit Henri de Lubac's that it may be 'necessary to remove the sand from its [river] bed'.[17]

Father Jean Meyendorff (still a professor in Paris; only later when moving to America did he anglicize his first name as 'John') was offered more space for a substantial two-part theological essay on what he termed 'The Sacrament of the Word'.[18] This was in effect an enquiry into the transmission of revelation through the tradition of the Church. The Roman Catholic Church, said Meyendorff, has a very clear concept of what is included in revelation. The contents of revelation are indicated by the 'magisterium': they are those doctrines which are accepted by the Roman see. Other communions seek to find some analogy for this in order to forward their own claims. In the case of Orthodoxy, this is done by reference to the ecumenical councils. Meyendorff wished to nuance this assertion. Of course, no one could be Orthodox who did not accept the teaching of the first seven ecumenical councils—but that is because Orthodoxy has recognized the truth of Christ in them. In themselves, the councils were essentially organs of the Christianized Roman empire, later the theocratic Byzantine State, which owing precisely to its own 'ecumenical' pretensions, would not hold them without some Western participation or at least connivance. The Church, via its episcopate, did not, however, begin to entertain revealed truth only when the era of the councils commenced, nor did she cease to hold the revealed truth when that era ended. Not every formally ecumenical council was Orthodox, nor is it the case that only such councils can promulgate true doctrine.

> It is remarkable that the Orthodox Church of the East, after the separation with Rome, although according to Byzantine theocratic conception no oecumenical council could be held without the Westerners, never ceased to consider herself as a witness to the true doctrine of Christ in its fullness.[19]

The winter issue of 1952 brought the second part of Meyendorff's essay, which considered—still under the overall title 'The Sacrament of the Word'—the 'Bishop in his See'. Meyendorff's account aimed to 'underline one particular aspect of [the episcopate] which has often been obscured by an excessive anti-Romanism among Orthodox and Anglicans'.[20] And this is the charism of infallibility enjoyed by the bishop when teaching authentically from his liturgically presidential chair. The bishop must not only liturgize and administer, he must also teach the Word.

> The way in which divine Truth is manifested in the Church is a sacramental way, which is not separated from the whole sacramental life of a local Christian community, of which the bishop is the head. Along with the other sacraments, there is a sacrament of the Word; one cannot recover its true significance, unless the true conditions of exercising his function are recovered by the head of every local Catholic Church.[21]

Meyendorff rejected the idea that presbyters had ever been equal to bishops. Referring to two of the principal ante-Nicene sources, the monarchical episcopate is not only attested by Ignatius of Antioch, it is clearly implied by the more geographically uncertain figure of Hippolytus as well. The conjunction of the two 'renders very improbable any collegiate episcopate in primitive times'.[22] In the ordination prayers preserved by Hippolytus the bishop alone has the dignity of high priest. For Meyendorff, episcopally transmitted tradition knows 'two different Apostolic Successions: succession through predecessors, and that through consecrators'.[23] The first is too often forgotten though for the ancients it was the more important as a criterion of orthodoxy—crucial as this is to the bishop's magisterial office.

A theological debate about sin

The Fellowship's *Journal* for December 1929 was devoted to thinking through the topic of sin, and its contributions were weighty from both the Anglican and the Orthodox side. It gives a good idea of the equilibrium between Anglican and Orthodox contributions in the *Journal*'s early years. Both the Orthodox articles, by Bulgakov and Evgrafy Kovalevsky, later known for his efforts to create a Western-rite Orthodoxy in France, are unusual presentations in different respects, though both of them (but chiefly Bulgakov's) are indebted to Augustine.

Kovalevsky's text is unusual in the first place in its categorization of sins: those which can be forgiven, through faith in the Christ's first Coming, and those, the 'blasphemies against the Holy Spirit' and, adds Kovalevsky—thinking here of words of Jesus about offences against 'little ones' (compare Matthew 18:6)—blasphemies against the Church, which cannot be so forgiven and are forgiven, if at all, only via hope in his second Coming.

Into the former category, forgivable sins, come all sins of pride (all striving to be apart from God in and by oneself) and self-indulgence (all striving for what is not oneself, which, granted the loss of God, can only be for what is below the self). By re-establishing the unity of the human creation and God, Christ makes it possible not only to be forgiven but to sin no more, in these respects. Into the latter category, unforgivable sins, comes the willful destruction of self, either of the body by physical suicide or of the possibility of repentance by spiritual suicide. The tendency of despair towards non-being indicates the depth of the power that is freedom of the will. The sin against the Church or the 'little ones' consists in the attempt to draw others into one's own despair. 'Those who tempt thus are bishops of the Church of Satan whose god is non-being.'[24]

Kovalevsky also considered the question of freedom and predestination, and here too what he had to say was surprising. Seeing this 'eternally Western' question as a matter of 'practical asceticism', the East responds to it on two planes. In Christology the Eastern Church emphasizes its rejection of Monothelitism (presumably because that heresy would only allow one will, a divine one, in the Word incarnate and thus deprive the human freedom of the New Adam of any consistency properly its own). In pneumatology the East, after the time of the Seven Councils and up to the fifteenth century, develops a theology of the Spirit's gifts (relevant, one assumes, since it is those gifts that enable freedom and grace to enter into synergy: presumably he had the doctrine of Symeon the New Theologian and the Palamite synods in mind). Yet since the fifteenth century, in Kovalevsky's view, Orthodox writers have in fact tended to either a Protestant or a Catholic view of the matter—to the degree that one might even speak of 'Orthodox–Protestantism' and 'Orthodox–Catholicism', with Russian writers seeking at times to synthesize the emphases of both. These statements were too cryptic to be fully satisfactory.

Bulgakov's contribution ('On Original Sin'), as its title suggests, considers chiefly the proto-parental sin, though it extends to a view of personal sin as well. Bulgakov's theology of original sin, and of the Fall, is determined by his theology of Adam, the proto-parent *par excellence*. Adam is created with the 'possibility of a life not only in God and for God, but also in the world and for the world'.[25] So much is common teaching. But in Bulgakov's own formulation, the choice lies between either being the friend of God or a 'natural being, immersed in the world (in "cosmism")'. And Bulgakov terms the latter 'practical atheism'.[26]

> In turning away from God man lost his strength and the fountain of life within him and, becoming impotent, he could no longer bind and control his body. Death entered into the world. Simultaneously to this, being the ontological centre of the world, its soul, he likewise lost his faculty of 'dominion' over the world. The world became an orphan.[27]

Subjectively, this meant guilt. Objectively, it meant 'diseases, labours, sorrows and death'.[28] The repercussions were universal, for Adam was not so much an individual as 'the all-man who by his own decision *determines the condition of his nature*'.[29] He was the 'hypostatical bearer of humanity', the 'decider of the destiny of human nature'.[30] This follows from his being the 'first' in a truly primordial sense. 'It is precisely this one that opens the count for all further hypostases, while itself not included in this order—it founds it and commences it out of itself.'[31] This claim gives Bulgakov's doctrine a character (and an interest) all its own.

> And so we come to the conclusion that Adam's own individuality did not exist before the Fall, although the hypostasis was there, as a personal centre, a possibility of love. Adam's individuality as such, as that of one among many, possessing its own particular destiny and place, arises only with the Fall and as a result of it ('ye shall be as gods, knowing good and evil'). And it is then also that Adam and Eve likewise come to recognize themselves as separate, severed, unrepeatable, and already impermeable centres. But instead of remaining as one, though multi-hypostatic body— one nature with many hypostases—mankind broke up into numerous individualities, separate representatives of mankind, who are even apt to ask themselves—whether mankind does exist as one body?[32]

Objectively speaking, this process produces a 'deep abnormality' in Adam's descendants,[33] who are, in this regard, sin's 'involuntary prey'.[34] Subjectively speaking—the more tricky question, since the modern Orthodox have generally rejected the Latin notion of an inherited guilt—each new-born child carries within it a 'deep awareness of some immemorial self-determination, as of something undue given', which serves as 'a witness of our personal participation in Adam's original sin'.[35] It was Bulgakov's belief that each human soul underwrites a 'freedom of man against his own nature',[36] not so much in a pre-existence, as with Origen of Alexandria, but nevertheless on the threshold of time. This ineffable decision transpires for Bulgakov 'on the edge of time ... not in eternity but not as yet within time' in the moment when the soul 'acquiesces in its own existence'.[37] Audacious as this speculation may seem, Bulgakov thought it necessary in order to explain the practice of infant baptism, acceding to the teaching of the Council of Carthage on this matter during the Pelagian crisis in the West. After the Fall,

> [a man's] spirit does not sufficiently take possession of his body at birth, so that already since the time of his birth simultaneously with the energies of life the energy of destructiveness is developed and stored.[38]

This 'weakness', which is the consequence of original sin, is, however, 'not yet in itself personal sin'—as can be seen from the fact that the Sinless One took it upon himself, took on the likeness of sin, the debility of our nature after the Fall. Thus too the Virgin shares the same weakness, and in this sense she bears the burden of original sin. Yet she is free from 'any participation in the creation of evil', thanks to the working of divine grace.[39] Bulgakov was early concerned with the Catholic doctrine of the Immaculate Conception, its rights and wrongs. (It formed the topic of the first volume in his two trilogies, which is rather less than the complete Mariology its subtitle might insinuate.[40])

The Anglican writers were less daring than Bulgakov but they were forceful all the same. Defining will as 'the whole personality organized for action' (is there here, one wonders, a covert allusion to Maurice Blondel's classic *L'Action*?), Father R. C. Langdon-Davies, a member of the Community of the Resurrection, proceeded to argue in a very Augustinian-Thomist fashion that 'perfect freedom is the final state of the soul set upon God ... [T]he will is ever less free in proportion as it is set on ends the further removed from that end for which man was created'.[41] Langdon-Davies thus understood original sin as 'an inherited infirmity which prevents us from setting our wills upon God'.[42] That formulation avoids what he described as the 'extreme' Augustinian thesis about 'original guilt'—a concession aimed at the Orthodox, yet the thesis in question was one which Bulgakov, admittedly in his own way, had just accepted. Using a very British metaphor Langdon-Davies concluded that human faculties are no longer team-players. Those faculties may be temporarily harmonized by combined concentration on some object less than God. But experience indicates how 'in the majority of cases no lasting harmonization of the soul can be effected if it be set upon any object this side of the Eternal Object, and that unless it advance from the fairly satisfying to the wholly satisfying it must in the end recoil upon itself'.[43] The use of the notion of 'natural grace' in Langdon-Davies's account of 'temporary harmonization' may be a sign of Neo-Calvinist influence on this writer—or perhaps he had been reading Bulgakov, who uses the phrase to denote the 'sophianity' of creation, its reflection of the Uncreated Wisdom of God. At any rate, for this author it is Christ who, by revealing the Will of God, set human feet fully on the path to authentic freedom.

Ralph Foster, apparently a lay contributor, provided a second Anglican response, writing on 'The Conflict between Good and Evil in the Personal Life'. That the Word assumed the entirety of human nature is enough to show that no essential appurtenance of that nature can be intrinsically evil. The struggle against evil is not against some aspect of our nature but 'a fight to make the whole of our human nature serve the end for which God created it'.[44] Accepting the (Dionysian) notion of, if not exactly three 'ages' of the spiritual life, then at any rate three 'aspects'—'purifying', 'illuminating', 'uniting', Foster found the purifying mode to consist in enduring and overcoming the 'great attack of evil through penitence, mortification, and detachment'.[45] What or who is the subject of such attack has not yet been explained, but in the next sentence we hear of the 'limitations, discords and evil with which we are surrounded'.[46]

Asceticism and morals

Kovalevsky had thought it necessary to invoke the concept of asceticism in order to throw light on the relation of human freedom to sin and grace, though his account was too assertoric to be much help. In the closing months of 1930 the *Journal* turned to consider the question of asceticism and the foundations of morals in its own right. Tchetverikoff, writing on 'Asceticism in the Lives of the Saints', placed Christian ascetic practice in the right context, that of growth in holiness—for it is in holiness that the virtues ultimately have their *raison d'être*. During the 'active' phase in the process of sanctification the saints are 'on their guard so as not to become prisoners and slaves of this temporal life, and so as not to forget for its sake the eternal life which is to come, about the "heavenly Jerusalem"'.[47] Such active life—and therefore asceticism—is necessarily lived, he explained, in a social context, since contact with others provides the opportunities for acquiring meekness, forbearance, and other virtues. But if virtuous socialization is not to descend to the level of mere sociability, it will involve vigilance in regard to the thoughts of the heart, accompanied by an interior life of prayer in which the Jesus Prayer will surely find a special place. He could cite Paissy Velichkovsky, the compiler of the Slavonic *Philokalia*, on the priority to be accorded this sort of attention, aspiration, and spiritual effort, rather than heroic feats of physical endurance.

For the Anglicans, Edmund Morgan, warden of the College of the Ascension at Selly Oak, Birmingham, and later Frere's successor at one remove as bishop of Truro, attempted to place Christian asceticism in a much broader historical context, starting with the Hellenes. Disciplined training of *body and mind* is generally accepted as a desideratum in a host of cultures. What is disputed is, rather, the disciplining of the *soul*. He admitted there could be a pathological version of such asceticism, exhibiting its symptoms in a 'morbid desire either to suffer or to inflict pain'. But there is also, he claimed, a healthy version—indeed a sacramental version, based on the belief that the flesh should be the 'instrument of the spirit'.[48] Morgan found voluntary poverty, chastity of heart and 'holy obedience'—the latter understood as a 'check to and protest against willfulness, violence and self-assertion'—to be authentic features of Jesus's preaching and practice, and either examples of the ascetic way or, at the least, closely related thereto.[49] Although by the conduit of Gnosticism a purely 'Oriental' (and thus non-biblical) form of such asceticism made its way into Christian culture, the Church sought to purify and control it.

There were, Morgan suggested, four lessons the Church both learned and inculcated. First, genuine asceticism is not self-regarding but Godward in its reference. Secondly, it is freely accepted. Thirdly, it can be lived in some form in the world. Fourthly, it is essentially positive while making use of the negative—notably by the eschewing of excessive comfort. Morgan's account was not merely sensible. It also accepted certain mystical implications of the ascetic way. The 'outward act of self-denial may become a means of joyful communion with the Passion of our Lord', and, furthermore, there 'is a mysterious sense in which people are called to take their share in filling up what is lacking in the sufferings of Christ'.[50] The members of the Mystical Body are invited to share the sorrow of God

at the continuing estrangement of the world. '[I]n some mysterious way
... [this] helps to lift the burden of sin and fulfil the victory of Christ'.[51]
Morgan's essay showed how an Anglican view of asceticism could come
within hailing distance of an Orthodox perspective.

Anglicans could do still more than this, serving as guides to the practice
of the Orthodox themselves. A persuasive picture of Orthodox asceticism
on the specifically monastic journey to God was painted by Edward Every
in an account of the Holy Places, visited for the feast of the Invention
of the Cross and ending at the monastery of Mar Saba in the Judaean
wilderness. 'To the true monk... "reality", wherever he sought it before
he came to the desert, is the prayers that never stop running on in his
heart and his sub-conscious mind, because with so many hours in church
he has become so deeply marked with them.'[52]

The asceticism described in these articles could be said to transcend
moralism: it seeks to show a way out from the semi-continuous repetition
of the vices, rather than restrict itself to tut-tutting. On this subject
the journal had reprinted an article from *Put'*, the Russian-language
publication of the Paris Orthodox—to which, reflecting the importance
of that constituency for the Fellowship's knowledge of Orthodoxy, it
was more than once indebted for its materials.[53] Before the Revolution,
Boris Visheslavzev had been professor in the faculty of law at Moscow
University, where he specialized in the history of political theory. Now
he taught moral theology at Saint-Serge. Reflecting St Paul's argument
in the Letter to the Romans, he pointed out that

> Law combats sin by means of judgment and condemnation, but it
> cannot make that which was as if it had not existed, it cannot bestow
> compassion, forgiveness, or grant 'justification freely'.[54]

'The law cannot love sinners.'[55] Concepts like repentance and redemption
are meta-judicial (Visheslavzev's word), and that which gives life is
greater than that which—even justly—destroys. This author was not an
antinomian, but he was conscious of the limits of the rational appeal to
the good which the law makes.

> It may be that the law is useful in practical life for the purpose of
> distinguishing that which is recognized as a transgression ('by the
> law is sin recognized', the *ratio cognoscendi* of crime), but it never
> descends to the depths, where the *ratio essendi* of the crime is buried.
> These depths are irrational, unfathomable and impenetrable so far as

the law is concerned. The law is a rational rule, directed to the mind, to the conscious will, but not towards the irrational, unconscious and subconscious instincts and desires.[56]

In a distinctly contemporary touch, Visheslavzev regarded St Paul's concept of *sarx*, 'the flesh', as virtually equivalent to the 'sub-conscious, with its sensually coveting, erotically vibrating nature, as described by Freud'.[57] Hence the use of the characteristically Freudian term 'sublimation' in his title, though he was also willing to call the subconscious, with Paul, 'the inner man' or, with the Hebrew Bible, 'the heart' or 'the bowels', and preferably the latter for 'the heart' also denotes what is above ordinary consciousness in the spirit as well as what lies below it. '[I]ts irrational depths constitute the sphere of the higher mystical experiences, no less than the lower, subterranean, sensual desires and longings.'[58] There is here, he wrote, a 'chaos' which can be shaped into either the ugly or the beautiful. Though Freud is not denied his say, Visheslavzev held that Plato surpasses him, for the Platonic teaching on eros should be accounted an essential corrective to Freudian theory. Eros is far more than sexual libido as was already noted by Jung, for whom it is the fundamental psychic energy, just as for a third ground-breaking psychologist, Charles Baudouin, it means 'affective potential', and for a fourth, Alfred Adler, a thirst for power and lordship. Visheslavzev was willing to concede the utility of all three definitions since, on his Plato-derived view, he took eros to be a 'function of striving, which moves into eternity and is multiform as to content, but always directed to an augmentation of existence and to the enhancing of its value'.[59] Yet none of them suffice.

> [U]ltimately Eros is a thirst for the Incarnation, the Transfiguration and the Resurrection, a thirst for the God-man, a thirst for the true 'nativity' in 'beauty', a thirst for deification and a faith that 'beauty shall save the world' (Dostoevsky). And Christianity has said this for it is the religion of the absolutely desirable.[60]

Freud was looking for sublimation but it was Plato who actually found it in its vast dimensions. Where one's highest value lies, there is one's eros focused, so sublimation can include all culture and religion. And through Denys the Areopagite, followed by St Maximus, Christianity at last gave Plato's teaching its highest fulfilment.

> Out of love, the Creator of nature united this force with His own Hypostasis in the incarnation, so as to 'bring to an end its restlessness'

and draw it to Himself. In this way Maximus the Confessor expresses the sublimation of the restless chaos of natural forces, and this sublimation is both an incarnation of the divine and a deification of the natural.[61]

From here Visheslavzev moved on in a fashion all his own. The restoration of the original Godward-directed form in man is the restoration of the image—but the power which grasps this is the *imagination*, itself inspired by the 'image of Christ standing before us'.[62] Imagination

> possesses a special gift of penetrating into the subconscious, and of a special organic similarity with Eros. And this is due to the fact that the subconscious is simultaneously the subterranean spring, from which the stream of fantasy bursts forth, and the dark cistern into which the glittering images fall again so that they may go on living there and moving in the impenetrable depth.[63]

In Christ our imagination has the pre-existing divine Wisdom in human form before it, drawing to itself all the powers of the soul in the ultimate sublimation.[64] Thus morals are at once secured and transcended.

Trinitarian theology

Granted that the Filioque had been one of the chief causes of the schism (if not, indeed, the principal cause), in matters of Trinitarian doctrine could East and West be one again? The Mirfield theologian Lionel Thornton discussed 'The Revelation of the Trinity with Special Reference to the Procession of the Holy Spirit'. Though Thornton thought he had made it clear in his analysis how 'the threefold revelation through creation, redemption and sanctification is a revelation which unveils to us the interior life of the Blessed Trinity in so far as it is possible for that ultimate mystery to be disclosed to our finite minds',[65] he did not actually claim to resolve the issue of the Filioque. His principal concern was with how the Spirit is manifested in the three economies of creation, redemption and sanctification, and this led him to defend the notion of the Spirit as bond of union between Father and Son (sometimes regarded by Orthodox writers, despite its use by St Gregory Palamas, as depersonalizing the Spirit, just as the Filioque is said to diminish the Spirit's divinity). Economically, 'the Spirit 'reproduces in us the likeness of the Son by conforming us to his filial nature, so that we cry "Abba, Father"'.[66] But this must be 'referred back' to the eternal Trinity: as God acts, so is he. From this the conclusion is drawn:

> If the Spirit proceeds from the Father to the Son, he also proceeds back once more from the Son to the Father. The Spirit opens our hearts to the Father after the pattern of the Son. There is an eternal response of the Son to the Father, and the Spirit is the bearer of that response in the Son to the Father.[67]

And with that mediating statement, members of the Fellowship would have to be content.

The Fellowship conference in 1956, the year Thornton's paper had been read, had taken as its overall topic God the Holy Trinity. Thornton's discretion had, it seems, marked it throughout. Timothy Ware, the future Bishop Kallistos, at this time an Anglican layman, had written the report.

> The 'filioque' controversy remained for the most part in the background; and though it was often mentioned, no main speaker dealt specifically with the differences between Eastern and Western theology over this use. Perhaps this was as it should be, and made it possible to see the whole subject in proportion; but it was felt by some that difficulties and differences were being covered up when it would have been better to bring them into the open.[68]

Maybe this was what Ware was referring to when he wrote in his conclusion that despite friendship there was 'also a feeling of loneliness and separation. Many members were acutely conscious of a sense of strain.'[69]

A further offering from that conference was delayed in its published form until 1957. Father Basil Krivocheine's 'The Holy Trinity in Greek Patristic Theology' was published in two parts in the two issues of that year. Despite its length it was a selective account, eschewing, for instance, the major figures for the subject of St Gregory of Nyssa and St Cyril of Alexandria. But justice was done to others among the Greek divines.

Krivocheine had benefited from the Origen revival in Western scholarship. In his judgment, the 'core and central idea of the whole spiritual system' in Origen is

> transition from the contemplation of the crucified Jesus and of the humanity of Christ to the theology and mysticism of the Eternal divine Logos, the Image of the Father, and from here even farther to a direct vision of the Father.[70]

Krivocheine could say, accordingly, that despite the problems with Origen's orthodoxy as speculative metaphysician and theologian, he 'exercised a decisive and lasting influence on the formation and development of the mystical theology of the Eastern Christians'.[71] Krivocheine explained how Origen's doctrine of the divine image can assist progress on this path, while noting a degree of pneumatological deficit in his writing and the replacement of longing for vision of the tri-personal divine Being of the Gospel revelation with an aspiration to the Father as the ultimate Monad.

Evagrius was the next figure to whom Krivocheine directed his readers' attention. A monastic teacher—unlike Origen, whose intellectual background he otherwise shared, Evagrius naturally gave more thought to experiential description of such spiritual progress.

> [T]he contemplation of the Trinity is practically identical for Evagrius with pure mental prayer, when the mind is immediately united with God without any imagination. Such a rejection of imagination in mental prayer and in the vision of the Holy Trinity is very characteristic of Evagrius and the Eastern Christian spirituality in general... [I]n the mystical theology of Evagrius it is in Its unity, as a Monad, that the Holy Trinity is mainly contemplated by the mind in its highest elevation—a mind which after an ascetic 'exodus' from all that is visible and invisible, ascends by the grace of the Holy Spirit through the scale of contemplation to an immediate vision of the Trinity, a mind which is restored in its 'natural' purity and simplicity and united in pure, not imaginative, prayer with the simple Triune-Divinity, who overshines the mind and appears to it in 'the place of God'.[72]

Krivocheine's survey of 'The Holy Trinity in Greek Mystical Theology' concluded with two further giants: Maximus Confessor and Symeon the New Theologian. Maximus both synthesized and 'doctored' Origen, Evagrius and Denys the Areopagite in the interests of a truly Orthodox account of how, through the action of uncreated grace, the mind goes out of itself in a mystical loving union with the Holy Trinity in the experience of pure prayer in the 'Sabbath of Sabbaths', an expression used by Maximus in his *Capita theologica et economica*.[73] Krivocheine was fuller on Symeon, whose writings, at that time rather neglected by the Orthodox, he knew especially well. Symeon's not just vivid but wonderfully lyrical accounts stress not only the distinct personalities of Father, Son and Holy Spirit but also the circumincession of the Three. He can speak too both of the light of the Trinity as produced through the Spirit, who reveals in us the Son and the Father, and of union with Christ as bringing us to union with the Father and the Spirit. Symeon often addresses prayers to the Spirit, which is not so usual in the ancient writers. But he also stresses the place of the Incarnation in Trinitarian contemplation: Jesus Christ, and not simply the eternal Word.

Krivocheine thought the Swiss Catholic patrologist and dogmatician Hans Urs von Balthasar, writing on St Maximus, had underestimated the Trinity-centredness of these mystics, perhaps because of expectations derived from the mediaeval West.[74] He considered a comparative study of West and East highly desirable in regard to the theology of the Trinity well beyond the limited issue of the Filioque. He could already identify some relevant points. There is more apophasis in the East. There is in the East a Monad, who is, however, always a Monad-Triad. The East stresses the Father as Trinitarian Source. The West is concerned for the never merely provisional humanity of Christ. The West accepts imaginative prayer and places greater emphasis on the value of sensuous visions.

Ecclesiology

Ecclesiology was prominent as early as the twelfth issue of the *Journal*, in 1931. Bulgakov addressed that classic topic the 'four notes of the Church'—classic since already contained in the clause on the Church of the Creed of Nicaea-Constantinople, the 'Nicene Creed'. For the first such note, the Church is 'one', and Bulgakov was strong on unity. '[The] oneness of the life [of Christ and the Spirit] in the Church does not allow of the different local or particular churches remaining separated or independent.'[75] In consequence, there is a natural tendency to develop this oneness into a 'kind of uniformity and exterior reunion', a 'concentration of churches' which attains its apogee in the West through the Roman doctrine of the *monarchia* of the pope.[76] But the Eastern tradition does not connect oneness with concentration in this way. Rather, it connects oneness with mutual recognition, via dogmatic unanimity, identity of sacraments, and a hierarchy based on apostolic succession. With regard to the latter: a bishop must be consecrated by other bishops—that signals how, since a bishop is 'the representative of his church, in his person the whole of his church participates in mutual relations'.[77] In the situation of divided Christendom, the only feasible approach is to acknowledge both the existence of one true Church (somewhere on earth) and some sort of authentic Church-existence for the other denominations. Bulgakov does not admit even as a possibility the 'branch theory' whereby Catholicism, Anglicanism and Orthodoxy are all

> in some sense equivalent as an expression of the Church's life, while at the same time each one of them is one-sided and in a sense not true. Such sceptical relativism means nothing else but the absence of the true Church and the impossibility of the appearance of the Church's pure truth in the world. Such a view means that the true Church has become lost in the course of history and instead of the pure truth we have only fragments of it.[78]

That would contradict the promises of the Saviour.

Bulgakov is not, then, in any doubt. 'The Orthodox Church is the true Church for the whole of the Christian world.'[79] Yet since the Church's identity is not restricted to her visible organization, it is possible to think of 'the Orthodox Church as existing beyond the limits of the Orthodox Church', through a common treasury of life: of faith, hope and love.[80] That overspill is the ground of ecumenism, but it is also what hinders true fullness, even for Orthodoxy itself.

> Our soul has a mystical organ of the feeling of one Church—not only as a mystical body but as a social and historical one, and both feelings are identical in us. In this sense one can say that the feeling of the one Church, which existed before the division of the Eastern and Western Church, was a fuller, richer, and more real one than we have now. This period in the history of the undivided Church remains for us a lost paradise, which must be regained again.[81]

Bulgakov then unfolded his programme. True ecclesial unity can only be found in Orthodoxy but this does not mean incorporation into any local Orthodox Church. Intercommunion, or external union, with the Orthodox Churches would be an important stage, but not a decisive one (as it would for Roman Catholicism).

> The restoration of Orthodoxy, or the return to the life of the undivided Church, must be first achieved in the life of different Churches. In that sense it can be said that Anglicanism in its tendency towards the restoration of the ancient Church, as a reaction to Protestantism, is already becoming more and more Orthodox, and this process is naturally a way to its reunion with historic Orthodoxy. And, generally speaking, there exists no other way to reunion than

a restoration of Orthodoxy in the inner life, because 'being one' for the Church really means 'being Orthodox'.[82]

In Orthodoxy 'unity' does not signify (as with Rome) obedience to the power of one Church, but 'one life in love, and freedom and holiness'.[83]

Bulgakov was equally forthright on the topic of the Church as 'holy', the second of the Creed's four notes. 'There exists no natural holiness without [i.e. outside] the Church, because holiness is a supernatural gift of God, though in actual life the word is often applied to express natural righteousness or the moral health of man.'[84] Everything that belongs to the Church is holy because holiness is an attribute of the Church's substance. The Church is the Body of Christ, who lives in it in his holy humanity, and the dwelling of the Spirit, who likewise abides there. The presence of sin and sinners is no argument against but follows inevitably from the fact that sanctification is only in process now, not complete. The rest of Bulgakov's presentation of the second note concerns devotion to the saints. 'It is included in our faith in the Holy Church that the saints do exist in it, as a kind of golden girdle, during the whole time of its existence without any interruption.'[85]

What of the Church as 'catholic', the third note? He privileges qualitative catholicity over quantitative. All local Orthodox Churches are catholic in the same degree. In fact the word 'branch', whose theological force he denied when it was used in the 'Branch Theory' now comes into its own. '[T]he degree of the catholicity of a Church does not depend on the dimensions of the Church, but merely on its fidelity to the truth.'[86] By a providential mistranslation, in Church Slavonic 'catholic' was rendered *sobornoia*, implying a 'oneness of many in love and freedom', for 'the truth is only revealed to such a unity'—a claim for which some evidence is forthcoming in the invitation to mutual charity which precedes the recital of the Creed in the Liturgy of St John Chrysostom.[87] Authority lies more with the whole Body than with the hierarchy, and as in the Sophiological controversy Bulgakov deplores the fact that so many Orthodox ascribe infallibility to the corporate episcopate, as a kind of collective pope. That is hardly compatible with the 1849 Letter of the Eastern Patriarchs to Pope Pius IX, which stated that the preservation of the Church in truth is entrusted to the entire *laos*, not to hierarchs alone. Bulgakov goes so far as to express the 'deepest conviction that the idea of any external dogmatic authority in the Church is a superstition which must be set aside for all time'.[88] The bishops in council are representatives and witnesses of their

Churches and their definitions are to be received by the whole Body (or not, as the case may be). In any case doctrine is handed down in the Church by more means than councils.

There remains the fourth note, 'apostolic'. Bulgakov defends the notion of apostolicity of ministers via episcopal succession even though he is (unnecessarily) sceptical about the claims of an apostolic institution of the threefold ministry as known in later times.

> The first consecrator was Jesus Christ Himself, Who ordained the Apostles as the first hierarchs of the whole Church, when on His appearance He 'breathed on them and said to them: receive ye the Holy Ghost' (John 20:22). This general ordination received its full strength and confirmation at Pentecost and was realized for the whole of the Church in the apostolic succession in a general sense. This is the Divine fact which the Church has in [the] historic episcopate.[89]

There is also the question of apostolicity of doctrine and practice if not in a 'full and set form' dating from the Twelve.

> Such an unhistorical interpretation stands in complete contradiction to the very idea of holy tradition, because tradition is not a passive and obedient conservation of external law, but always a living inspired extension of the past in the present.[90]

Bulgakov accepted doctrinal development so long as it is not understood as novel teaching. He adds, moreover, a third dimension of apostolicity (after apostolic doctrine, and apostolic practice) which enables one to understand that 'livingness' of Tradition, and this is what he terms the 'fulness of apostolic gifts'.[91] Pentecost should be considered 'a continued act in all times of the Church's existence', and it means for her 'apostolic power and inspiration', one element of which, he thinks, is now the movement for reunion, for Christian unity.[92]

That might almost have been a cue for Florovsky's 1932 essay 'The Work of the Holy Spirit in Revelation', which culminated in an ecclesiology of the Spirit as well as of the Son. It was a wide-ranging essay that both contributed to Florovsky's dogmatics, his 'neo-patristic synthesis' and also disclosed something of the underpinnings of his wider conceptual scheme.[93]

Florovsky began by distinguishing the manifestation of God in nature and the human soul from revelation in the 'direct' meaning of the word.[94] The traces of God in the world at large are a testimony that prompts a search for God, not a theophany which gives knowledge of him. Only in 'the super-natural', in 'what is above nature', does God 'appear' in his 'transcendence', revealing himself by his word, whether to those who heard it directly, 'the great initiated [sic] and prophets', or those who heard it through their mediation.[95]

> The Scriptures transmit and preserve for us the Divine Word such as it had been heard, such as it sounded in the receptive soul of man. The mystery of Divine inspiration is not only that God spoke to man, but also that man was listening to God and heard Him.[96]

If there is a certain anthropomorphism in the outcome, it is not only through adaption to human weakness, it is also by way of anticipation of the Incarnation. Natural theology is really philosophy; it is through revelation that proper theology at last becomes possible and in Scripture we find human beings not only listening to the words of God but responding to them. This is a prerequisite of the Covenant, the path of God with man in history, whose highpoint is the Flesh-taking by the Word. There '[t]he Old Testament is finishing—the history of flesh and blood. The history of the Spirit is beginning—the Kingdom of Truth and Grace opened' (compare John 1:17).[97] Yet because the Law is not destroyed but fulfilled the books of the Hebrews remain sacred. Florovsky said he could not pause to consider higher criticism in its relation to the Old Testament. But he also said the issue is ultimately non-essential.

> Scientific criticism cannot prove the sacred value of the Bible; cannot refute it. Divine inspiration presupposes a certain rupture in the natural order. It is not a category of autonomous science.[98]

To become aware of the Breath of the Spirit in Scripture we must have spiritual insight through a 'transfiguration of consciousness', which is only possible in the Church, thanks to the latter's 'spiritual charismatic completeness', on the basis of Pentecost.[99] The Gospel in its fourfoldness is a verbal icon painted by the Spirit. And the Spirit is sent to us to enable us to read it. 'No man can say that Jesus is the Lord, but by the Holy Ghost' (I Corinthians 12:3).

Florovsky has laid great stress on the Scriptures as the inspired record of Revelation. But now he needs to speak about a further dimension.

> The words of Scripture do not exhaust the whole fullness of Revelation; do not exhaust the whole fullness of Christian experience

and of the charismatic reminiscence of the Church ... For those
who abide within the Church, the testimony of the Spirit makes
Scripture clearer; this testimony once more lives in their personal
experience. And this is why we must not speak of the 'self-sufficing
quality' of Scripture.[100]

In strong language, Florovsky terms the Church the vehicle of this further dimension.

> In the Church, Revelation becomes an inner spiritual experience. The
> Church in itself is already a Revelation. From the Day of Pentecost,
> when the Holy Ghost entered the world to abide in it, Revelation
> has become an uninterrupted continuity.[101]

The reality of revelation is expressed in two ways—in images and symbols (he calls this 'charismatic theology'), or in the conceptions of the mind (here he is content with the standard expression, 'dogmatic theology'). Preaching (which he apparently assumes to be imagistic or symbolic in form) and dogma (its conceptual complement) are 'the two ways in which the Church bears witness to Truth, to that inner Revelation which is still continuing in the Church by the power of the Spirit abiding in it'.[102] Dogma itself Florovsky terms the 'logical icon of Divine reality'. As such, both the 'inner word' of revelation, its true contemplation, and the outward choice of literal words, items from the dictionary, are important to it.[103] In an alternative formulation to Bulgakov's, but one that maintains the same principle of continuity-in-discontinuity, dogmas can arise but they cannot be developed.

> There is a predogmatic period of Church consciousness; then the
> language chosen is one of images and symbols. But after this comes
> the time for bearing dogmatic witness. For truth of faith is truth
> of reason as well, and thought must enter 'into the knowledge of
> truth'. In doing this it becomes creatively transfigured—the very
> realm of thought becomes transfigured, sanctified and renewed.[104]

Words which may have been borrowed from a habitual philosophical vocabulary become 'eternalized and stabilized' by the power of the Spirit either at ecumenical councils or 'through the silent reception of *ecclesiae sparsae* [Churches dispersed across the world]'.[105] The Truth of the Church's experience is not exhausted in definitions of this sort but it is nonetheless 'determined and protected'.[106] The experience of the Church is wider than the dogmatic word, for there is 'much to which the Church witnesses even to the present day in images, symbols, and similes, in symbolic theology'.[107] Whereas the Church was given the fullness of truth from the beginning, its gradual expression is itself, in St Paul's words about the vision made possible by faith, only 'in part' (I Corinthians 13:9). As in St Paul's looking ahead to the End, the 'exhaustive fullness' will not be disclosed until the Parousia.[108] That still leaves many mysteries for which there is as yet no dogmatic formulation: hence the role of theological research and speculation. Though there is room even for fresh understanding of the dogmata themselves Florovsky warns against 'subjective arbitrary mental choice'.

> Once more we want to remind you that the dogmas of faith are the truths of experience and life—therefore they can be unfolded through no logical synthesis and analysis, but only through *spiritual life*, through actual participation in the fullness of Church experience.[109]

Teachers of the Church must embody catholicity, or (in a favoured phrase) 'Catholic transfiguration' whereby 'personality ... receives the faculty and strength of feeling and expressing the consciousness and life of the whole'.[110]

Mariology

In 1937 Bulgakov gave *Sobornost* a paper (enhanced by new prefatory comments) he had read as a lecture at the Edinburgh Faith and Order Conference of that year. Against the grain of that overwhelmingly Protestant assembly, he insisted, to their irritation, on the importance of the veneration of the Mother of God. His preamble for the Fellowship journal was instructive. 'The way in which the whole Protestant world suddenly ceased to venerate the Virgin Mary was the most mysterious and real spiritual event of the age of the Reformation.'[111] Evidently the speeches made by Bulgakov and Metropolitan Evlogy on the Orthodox side, supported by two representatives of the American Episcopalians, did not have the desired effect, for the resolution they proposed was whittled down. It started out promisingly enough. 'The place of the Mother of God was considered ... and all agreed that she should have a high place in Christian esteem. We commend further study of this question to the Churches'. But in the event it was, in effect, kicked into the long grass. 'The way in which we should understand the words, "All generations shall call me blessed" (Luke 1:48) was considered. No agreement was reached, and the subject requires further study.'[112] But at least this was a more positive response than when he had raised the same issue at the Lausanne Conference in Faith and Order ten years earlier. At his first experience of the ecumenical movement, his attempt to bring it to delegates' attention had simply been declared out of order.[113]

At Edinburgh Bulgakov explained that the veneration of Mary in Orthodoxy 'rests not on any dogmatic definitions besides the definition of the Third Oecumenical Council, as the Mother of God (*theotokos*) but rather on the tradition of piety, explained dogmatically in theological doctrine.'[114] But he also showed how this single dogma is virtually sufficient to explain the veneration that followed.

> The Incarnation is achieved through the action of two persons of the Holy Trinity: of the Holy Spirit who is incarnating the Logos, and the Logos Himself who is incarnated; and through the action of the blessed woman who was able and holy enough to receive the conception of the Logos. Through this action of God Himself, the Mother of God in the Incarnation came into perpetual, eternal and indissoluble connection and nearness with the Lord Incarnate.[115]

The icon showing her with her Son in her arms is the icon of the Incarnation—and in this aspect she is the personal heart of humanity, its 'Holy of Holies'—a statement which was in some danger of challenging the place as New Adam of the humanity of the Son. She needs salvation, and in the Magnificat recognizes God as her saviour (Luke 1:47), but she does not turn original sin into personal sins since she is holy from her birth (not from her Conception, note) and especially from the Annunciation, her 'personal Pentecost'—a notably Bulgakovian claim.[116] As the one who gave Christ human flesh she is glorified and resurrected, indeed she is 'in the state of the last glorification which is predestined for the creature.'[117] Bulgakov calls her queen of heaven and earth: 'in a certain sense the centre of the whole created universe.'[118] She belongs to the communion of saints as the 'head of this holy company',[119] yet she cannot simply be included in it owing not just to the completeness of her glorification but to her nearness to Christ. Bulgakov admitted that this 'whole practice of piety and the corresponding teaching' is given in Scripture 'only in a limited degree'. But nevertheless it 'has an axiomatic character, as a necessary conclusion of the experience of the church which was and is enriched from age to age'. It is a 'development' due to 'Holy Tradition.'[120]

Theology in a broad perspective

These were particular themes, and important ones. But the Fellowship was intellectually adventurous, and it did not hesitate to attempt overviews of divergent or convergent perspectives on theology as a whole. A report on the theological conference of the Fellowship at Oxford in December 1943 corresponds well enough to that description. The conference subjects had been three, and they divided proceedings accordingly. The first section was entitled, 'Historic Facts of God's Revelation and their Apprehension'. Here the speakers were Vigo Demant, then Chancellor of St Paul's Cathedral; Austin Farrer, at that time a Fellow of Trinity College, Oxford; and the metaphysician and writer on modern Russian culture Evgeny Lampert. The second section was labelled 'Convergence and Divergence of Local Traditions of Theological Thought'. The speakers allotted to this subject were Alexis van der Mensbrugghe, then lecturer at the Institut Saint-Irénée of the Western-rite Orthodox in Paris, and the poet, novelist and critic Charles Williams. The conference's third and closing section considered 'Integration of Heathenism and Unbelief into the Life of the Christian Church', to be addressed by H. A. Hodges, Professor of Philosophy at Reading, and an Armenian cleric who had already contributed to *Sobornost* a summary description of Armenian Church history and life, Tiran Nersoyan.

On the first theme, 'Historic Facts of God's Revelation and their Apprehension': Demant saw the major forms of unbelief as deflections from the fundamentals of Nicene faith such that the Christian task today is to show the inter-relation of the eternal and the temporal. In Lampert's way of doing precisely that, divine revelation is an encounter of two worlds, the meaning of this world lying in the other. Christology and history thus belong to each other as answer does to question. '[T]o think Christologically is to describe that concrete point at which the eternal enters history and so transcends its apparent meaninglessness.'[121] From this Lampert drew the conclusion that 'Historical revelation is itself apocalypse: Christ is Conqueror, and history is seen as the triumph of the Kingdom of God.'[122] Lampert's doctrine of reciprocity entailed that in some sense God becomes in time, just as time is to be eternalized in God. Farrer was quick to mount a challenge. If there were a real reciprocity of this order, then creation and redemption would not be pure agape—gratuitous love—but necessary to God's fulfilment. 'So pure agape belongs to God alone and constitutes His absolute transcendence. Thus it is the denial of reciprocity in creation which establishes God as personal Love.'[123] But he agreed with Lampert's biblical realism, and his stress on God's self-revelation through historic acts.

On the second theme, 'Convergence and Divergence of Local Traditions of Theological Thought', Van der Mensbrugghe asserted that Orthodoxy is the wholeness of truth, and 'raced' through the topics of the metaphysics of creation, the Trinity, Incarnation, Atonement, ethics, spirituality, politics, Church order, and sacramentalism, to show how this might be.[124] Charles Williams, never a conventional thinker,[125] proposed that the unity of theology could not be realized unless the discipline comes to include the 'theological experience of the body'. We are generally unaware how body and soul form a single composite on which physical death is an unintended assault. The contrast with the perfect unity of the God-man in all his powers is something the Christian imagination has failed to grasp in its full actuality. 'We were bidden to consider "that divine and unwounded identity" which was the Incarnate, "with horror regarding the temporary splitting of His identity".'[126]

On the third motif, 'Integration of Heathenism and Unbelief into the Life of the Christian Church', Nersoyan, the Armenian contributor, took Western secularism to be a consequence of the Renaissance in a highly specific, and rather unusual, sense. The rediscovery of 'Hellenistic' culture, i.e. the culture of Late Antiquity, had not been accompanied by any intellectual re-appraisal of social and economic developments. This disabled an integrated natural-supernatural ordering of the world.[127] For H. A. Hodges too there had been a *débâcle* but in his view its location was the realm of pure thinking. He provided a summary of his own lecture, reported as 'a daring attack upon traditional Christian metaphysics as a pagan invention.'[128] Certainly the statement that the hammer of Hegel breaks the idols of Aquinas sounds somewhat less than encouraging for any supporters of the *philosophia perennis* who might have been present. Hodges' starting-point was intriguing.

> A pure Christianity would have everything to teach to the rest and nothing to learn from them; but a damaged Christianity has to submit to learn from its rivals and even from its persecutors, as an erring Israel had to accept judgment from Nebuchadnezzar and deliverance from Cyrus.[129]

What Hodges attacked was 'metaphysical theology' understood as 'the theory that the existence and chief attributes of God constitute a body of truths which can be established by quasi-scientific reasoning as a pendant to physics, astronomy and ontology'.[130] Hodges accepted the Italian Idealist Giovanni Gentile's belief that the law of thought is immanent self-criticism, and for Hodges this is also the law of the Cross in the life of thought. We must de-construct in the light of the revelation of God in the Cross of Christ, but we must also construct in the power of the Resurrection. When we do so an interesting thing happens: the metaphysic which is wrongly sought as a preliminary to revealed theology can be found—in a different shape—as a consequence of it'.[131]

Nothing could be less sympathetic to this standpoint than the editor's own *He Who Is*, subtitled 'A Study in Traditional Theism',[132] which was published that same year, 1943, and reviewed in this number of *Sobornost* by Lampert. Admiring the coherence of Eric Mascall's work, Lampert found himself (as 'an Orthodox belonging to the Russian theological tradition') bound to disagree with its 'presuppositions'. The epistemology is that of Thomist realism, as though the 'Critical Philosophy' (the work of Kant) had never existed. Missing too was any acknowledgement of the 'Existentialism' which should also be taken into account by a modern theologian (a movement, Lampert calls it, 'largely anticipated by Russian philosophy of the nineteenth and twentieth centuries').[133] But he approved of Mascall's criticisms of Logical Positivism. Lampert also left more or less unscathed Mascall's presentation of the proofs of divine existence even though these were seen in the perspective of the Thomism for which the author had made such high-falutin' claims as 'altogether the final synthesis of the Judaeo-Christian tradition with Greek philosophical thought; or, more precisely with Aristotelian rather than Platonic thought'.[134] Yet in the book's discussion of creation, the God-world relation, and the issue of immanence vis-à-vis transcendence, 'a conflict with Orthodox thought' struck Lampert as 'quite inevitable'.[135] For Lampert, Mascall's assertion that the essential activity of the Christian God is not to create but to be (creation as such, then, is quite gratuitous) fails to do justice to the doctrine of the divine ideas, ruling out of court as this doctrine does any opposition between God as transcending the creation and God strictly as Creator. 'To be God is also to be Creator. Creation is surely first and foremost an act of love, of supreme transcendent love; and God *is* love, not only "has" love, or loves'.[136] Thomism's denial of 'real relations', i.e. reciprocally causative relations, between God and the world condemned it, in Lampert's view, to the status of a Monism. Thus Lampert as an anti-Thomist took the diametrically opposite tack to the anti-Thomism of that other Orthodox commentator on Mascall, Van der Mensbrugghe, for whom Mascallian Thomism had constituted not Monism but polytheism! (Their 'spat' was described in Chapter 7 above.) Where Lampert most sympathized with Mascall was when he saw the Anglican Thomist 'struggling in [the] teeth' of this metaphysical inheritance by insisting on the divine intimacy, notably in contexts where mysticism is in question.[137]

From Mascall to Lossky

The change of editor, from Eric Mascall to the dyarchy of Patrick Thompson and Helle Giorgiadis, had coincided with the start of a new 'series' of *Sobornost*, and the contents of the second issue suggested a new orientation. The journal was looking to the figure of Vladimir Lossky as to one who might take the place of the deceased Bulgakov as the Orthodox theologian of predilection for the Fellowship. Certainly Lossky was as interested in ecumenism as Bulgakov had been—but he was also less eirenic or at any rate less of a seeker for common ground. In his memoirs, Mascall described Lossky as 'a quietly vivacious, stocky little man, always ready for a theological discussion'.[138] In Mascall's 'Ecumenism Exemplified', an item in his book of comic verse *Pi in the High*, the original Palamite and Thomist who inspired the inconclusive theological debate whimsically presented by way of a parody of Edward Lear's dotty *The Walrus and the Carpenter*, 'were not the Orthodox monk and Dominican friar of Barbara Jones's admirable illustration but Vladimir Lossky and myself; indeed the original version of the poem was recited by us together at an informal concert at Abingdon'.[139] (By 'Abingdon' was meant the Fellowship summer-school at St Helen's, the Wantage Sisters' school in that Berkshire town south of Oxford.)

But if Mascall and Lossky were the 'Thomist and the Palamite' of the Fellowship, the future of *Sobornost* would lie more with the Palamite Lossky than with the Thomist Mascall. This was not only because the Anglican Thomism Mascall sought to communicate—involving as it did the integration with the metaphysics of Aquinas of the 'theologians of ressourcement', practitioners of return to the Fathers in the Western tradition—failed to create a school of thought in the Church of England.

Contrastingly, Lossky's neo-Palamism and advocacy of apophatic theology had no shortage of followers in the world of Eastern Orthodoxy. It also reflected, on a long view, the waning interest of newly self-confident Orthodox, and Orthodox converts, in the Western Christian heritage, and the transformation of the journal into an organ of Orthodox self-expression. But before that happened, some instructive exchanges worthy of record took place.

In 1947 Gillet offered the readers of *Sobornost* a masterly summary of Mascall's complex yet lucid book, *Christ, the Christian and the Church. A Study of the Incarnation and its Consequences*, which had appeared the previous year.[140] He stressed Mascall's distinctive standpoint in relation to the currents of his time.

> As to Revelation, the theologian does not examine it from outside; he is actually in the Revelation, i.e. in Christ and in the Church, or at least he should be so. His theological adequacy will depend ultimately upon the maintenance and nourishment of his union with Christ. The really great theologian must be a saint. The breaking down of theological liberalism and the impasse reached in the critical study of the Bible show the necessity of another approach. Theology must be free from the subjectivity and ephemerality to which liberalism is exposed, and also free from the violent repudiation of reason which has appeared in some other quarters. Only in the Spirit-bearing Body of Christ the human mind, rescued from error, reaches its highest activity and becomes able to contemplate the Ever-blessed Trinity.[141]

Gillet also drew attention to Mascall's fellow-travellers, cited in its pages. These were chiefly Roman Catholics (Anscar Vonier, Maurice de la Taille, Jacques Maritain, Emile Mersch, Henri de Lubac, Eugène Masure, Yves Marie-Jean Congar, Étienne Gilson), but there were also some Anglicans (Sir Sir Edwyn Hoskyns, Gregory Dix, Lionel Thornton, and more remotely Richard Hooker and Robert Wilberforce). As to Orthodox influences, certain voices, Bulgakov, Florovsky, Arseniev could be heard if in muted fashion. Among the Greek patristic writers, Leontius of Byzantium and John of Damascus were important for Mascall. 'But the dominant influence is incontestably Thomas Aquinas.'[142] Gillet would have liked to see more Hebrew influence deployed (following his own preferred approach[143]). He also found Mascall's use of 'Mystical Body' language (like Mersch's) too vague. The phrase itself was foreign to the patristic tradition (which, if true, did not stop Florovsky using it, one might add in parenthesis). Gillet ventured one especially important criticism, namely that Mascall saw incorporation into Christ only on the level of grace and not on that of nature. The Greek Fathers, by contrast, saw that incorporation operating in both. The New Adam was renewing human nature already at Christmas, he did not in every sense await the total regeneration of Easter and Pentecost.

> This physical incorporation into Christ, distinct from the incorporation which grace procures, is a consequence of the Incarnation; it is linked, in the thought of the Greek fathers, in the first place with the ideal immanence of the whole creation in the Logos and the universality which, in consequence, the Logos confers on the flesh that he assumes, secondly with the dogma that the Logos united himself not to a human person or to a particular human nature but to human nature itself, thirdly with the ontological relation between an archetype and the beings of which it is the model.[144]

The final gripe was that, despite the commitment to Thomas, no explanation is given as to why the author of 'one of the great works of Anglican thought'—namely Mascall himself—is not a papalist.[145]

Also in 1947, publication of an English version of Lossky's essay 'Redemption and Deification' was accompanied by a lengthy review by Derwas Chitty of Lossky's most celebrated work, the *Essai sur la théologie mystique de l'Église d'Orient*.[146] Chitty evidently knew at once he was in the presence of a classic. The *Essai* has retained its status more obviously than the Mascall book reviewed by Gillet, who, however, used of the Anglican study that very word. Chitty characterized it as unapologetically Eastern, albeit written 'by a scholar who has had sufficient Western training to enable him to make his points clear to Western readers'—and, moreover, very much wants to make them clear since he thinks the 'schism did involve a conscious taking of sides in matters of faith, and therefore in ways of the spiritual life'.[147] As has already been noted in Chapter 2 above, Chitty himself wanted to see what one might call the 'Orthodoxification' of the Church of England. Yet even he recognized that, here and there, Lossky had gone too far in stressing difference from the West—notably in his denial of devotional Christocentrism (but what else is the Jesus Prayer or the Akathist called 'O Jesus sweetest Christ'?) and the existence of any Eastern practice of the 'imitation of Christ'. Both points were connected with a more serious weakness, in the reviewer's eyes, and this was a certain (no doubt unintended) downplaying of the incarnate Life of the

Saviour. Otherwise, Chitty goes all the way with the apophaticism and the Palamism, as well as the distinctively but not exclusively Losskeian notion of the Spirit as non-manifest until the Parousia, and the—surely over-facile—way Lossky links the Church as one Body to the Son, as many persons to the Spirit.[148]

Not that Lossky was so foolish as to dismiss everything that emanated from the Latin West. Had he been so, he would hardly have devoted his doctoral research to the figure of Meister Eckhart, nor would there have been a foreword by the historian of mediaeval thought Étienne Gilson for the posthumous publication of his Sorbonne thesis.[149] In fact, Lossky was among those Orthodox who had considerable time for St Thomas Aquinas. Reviewing for *Sobornost* Mascall's *Existence and Analogy*, Lossky praised Mascall's decision to begin, in the footsteps of Gilson, from the notion of *esse*, the 'act of existence'. Authentic original Thomism was 'rich with new perspectives which the philosophical herd, giving into the natural tendency of the human understanding, was not slow in conceptualizing, and changing into School Thomism, a severe and abstract doctrine, because it has been detached from its vital source of power'.[150] Enquiry into the *esse* which causes 'that which is' to come into 'existence' (i.e. enquiry into the contingency of everything created) requires going beyond the realm of substantial being.

> In order to express, in terms of metaphysics, this distinguishing mark of created being, it was necessary to discover—without destroying the Aristotelean world—in the forms themselves (which remain fully acts in the substantial order) some potentiality in relation to the first act which makes them existent beings.[151]

Transcending the plane of essences, acts of existing 'cannot be expressed in concepts, but they are stated in judgments of existence'.[152] Lossky warned, however, against neglecting essences altogether, and he disagreed with Mascall's presentation of analogy. For Thomas (whom he always refers to as 'Saint' Thomas), analogy was not a doctrine but a 'tool for the theologian' to use.[153] He noted Mascall's own criticism of the lack of clarity in the natural/supernatural distinction in Orthodoxy. Lossky wrote a rejoinder to that.

> There is no continuity between nature and grace, if one is created and the other uncreated; that is a clear enough distinction. On the other hand, created nature is ordered towards grace, and it is not

truly as it was meant to be by the Creator, except when it is in the order of grace; this kind of inherence excludes opposition.[154]

He ended by raising the issue of Palamism, in which Mascall had anticipated him in his book:

> With Fr Mascall, I ask himself to what extent the God of S. Thomas Aquinas, knowable in His cosmological relation, i.e. on the plane of His creative energy, can be made to resemble the God of S. Gregory Palamas, unknowable in His essence, as distinct from His energy. If the question is to be answered we must resolutely make our way outside the boundaries of Natural Theology, and that would oblige us to leave the subject of Fr Mascall's book, We shall hope to take up this further question, *Deo volente*, another time.[155]

Lossky died prematurely in 1958. Mascall wrote a memorial tribute to him for *Sobornost*.[156] In his autobiography he remembered Lossky warmly, and thought that behind even the most fundamental of their disagreements a real union of minds lay hidden. 'Vladimir remained as convinced of the incoherence and inadequacy of the Western concept of the created supernatural as I was of the unintelligibility of the Eastern distinction between the divine essence and energies ... And yet he was ready and anxious to assert that he and I were both trying to express in the limited and halting terms of human speech the same mysterious and inexhaustible reality, namely the participation by a creature in the life of the Holy Trinity without destruction of its creaturely status.'[157] But it would be Mascall's Thomistic view, not Lossky's Palamite one, that would disappear from the journal's pages.

Augustinians and Palamites

Gerald Bonner, later lecturer in Church History at the University of Durham would become a major contributor to *Sobornost*. In 1960 he appeared in its pages for the first time, writing on Augustine's doctrine of the Spirit—certainly a vital topic for any investigation of the Filioque dispute.

Bonner made some excellent points. The challenge of Western Arianism must always be borne in mind in assessing Augustine's doctrine of God. As the French scholar Irénée Chevalier's work had made plain,[158] Augustine was by no means ignorant of Greek Trinitarian theology, nor was he 'divorced from the teaching of the Greek Fathers.'[159]

Indeed he was indebted (in translation) to all five of Athanasius, Basil, Nazianzen, Epiphanius, and Didymus the Blind. Augustine inherited a Latin theological patrimony which was, on the procession of the Holy Spirit, 'undecided, but tending towards some statement of a double procession'.[160] He rejected any notion of the Filioque for which the Godhead has two principles from the beginning, and/or for which the Holy Spirit might be called 'Grandson' of the Father.[161] The heart of the matter is this: Augustine distinguishes between, on the one hand, an eternal *procedere principaliter* from the Father, a phrase Bonner translates as a proceeding 'from the Principle [of the Father]', and, on the other hand, an equally eternal *procedere per donum Patris*, a proceeding 'through the Father's gift'. And in the latter case, had there been another Latin verb available, Augustine might well have employed a different term for such proceeding 'through the Son'. Here is Bonner's key statement. Augustine, Bonner writes,

> distinguishes as firmly as Gregory of Nyssa between the Father, who is the Cause, and the other two persons who are Caused. Moreover, he rejects any interpretation of the procession which would imply a Neo-Platonist system of emanations, and make the Holy Spirit, as it were, the grandson of the Father. We must not be misled on this point by the text-book assertion that it is a cardinal premiss of Augustine's theology that whatever can be predicated of one of the Persons can be predicated of the others. This is undoubtedly a truth; but it refers to their qualities 'according to substance', not 'according to relationship'. We must remember Augustine's warning that, while nothing which is said of God may be said accidentally (*secundum accidens*), since God can have no accidental attributes; yet not everything that is said is said substantially (*secundum substantiam*), for the relationships of the Persons within the Trinity are *secundum relativum*, relative to one another. Such relationships are not accidental, for they are eternal. Now, it is in this relative sense, that Augustine holds that the Father is the Source of whole Godhead, and warns his readers that, when we say that the Holy Spirit is not begotten, we must avoid saying that he is unbegotten, lest we should introduce two Fathers into the Trinity, or two Persons who are not from Another; hence it seems to me that Augustine's doctrine of the Holy Spirit is a great deal less revolutionary, and a great deal closer to the thought of the Greeks, than he has usually been given credit for, whether for praise or blame.[162]

This was something for the Orthodox to ponder, since their attitude to 'blessed' Augustine (the more generous honorific 'saint' was commonly withheld) left something to be desired.

Heralded already in Lossky's *Essai* from a decade or so earlier, another master was now emerging from the shadows: the fourteenth-century Byzantine theologian St Gregory Palamas. His rediscovery would strengthen the theological convictions of the Orthodox that the Latin tradition had not done justice to the Christian doctrine of God. In the year of Bonner's lecture, Donald Allchin hailed Jean Meyendorff's *Introduction à l'étude de Grégoire Palamas* as a 'milestone' in the recovery of mediaeval Greek thought comparable to the rediscovery of the genuine Aquinas in contemporary Thomism.[163] With so many historic variations (Florovsky would say deformations) of Orthodox thought behind us, now at last, said Allchin, it is possible to take up again 'a living Orthodox tradition of theological thinking at the point at which it was so abruptly cut off'.[164] This assumes Allchin was correct to say that Palamas has 'gathered together into one whole the many strands of Eastern theology and mysticism', in a manner comparable to the synthetic power of Thomas—which might, perhaps, be questioned, given the occasional nature of Palamas's œuvre.[165] Despite comparative studies in certain limited aspects, notably the doctrine of grace, it is still John of Damascus who is customarily compared with Aquinas in this respect.

Florovsky himself had just been at Thessalonica receiving an honorary doctorate and celebrating the sixth centenary of the death of Palamas, who was archbishop of that see. After Allchin's glowing review of Meyendorff's book on the saint it was unsurprising that, as editor, he had asked for this lecture to appear in *Sobornost*. Florovsky, doyen of neo-patristic theologians, did not disappoint.

Florovsky began from an encomium of the Fathers at large before moving onto a statement of Palamas's place in their company. 'The *didaskalia* of the Fathers is the formal and normative term of reference ... Only by being "Patristic" is the Church truly "Apostolic".'[166] In explanation of this identity (apostolic/patristic) Florovsky quoted some lines from a hymn for the office of the three Hierarchs (Basil, Nazianzen, Chrystostom): 'By the word of knowledge you have composed the dogmas which the fishermen have established first in simple words, in knowledge by the power of the Spirit, for thus our simple piety had to acquire composition.'[167] He cited the French Oratorian Louis Bouyer: the Church is 'not just the daughter of the Church of the Fathers; she is and remains the Church of the Fathers'.[168] He also emphasized the existentiality of patristic theology: it was oriented to spiritual knowledge and experience—even if it was also furnished with intellectual arguments and logically set forth. It is not enough, Florovsky stressed, to quote patristic texts. One must acquire the mind of the Fathers. He complained that the Orthodox outlook had been affected by the idea of a 'pattern of decay' in Church history such as Protestants had applied to the pre-Reformation tradition.[169] The phrase 'The Church of the Seven Councils' as used by many Orthodox is almost as restrictive as the *consensus quinquesaecularis* (the 'five-century consensus', meaning up to the Council of Chalcedon in 451) of many moderate Protestants (including Anglicans). Seriously adopted, these notions would disqualify any Byzantine (i.e. mediaeval Greek-speaking) Christian from being a Church Father. The devout, using as they do the texts in the *Philokalia*, cannot make sense of such an idea. Florovsky believed they should be heeded. We ought not to regard the epoch of the Fathers as ended so long as there live those who are witnesses and teachers sharing the mind of the Fathers.

Gregory Palamas is a perfect example of Florovsky's point: not a speculative theologian but a creative extender of ancient tradition who proposed as the key to the spiritual experience of the Church an 'intimate intercourse of man with God, in which the whole of human existence is, as it were, permeated by the Divine Presence'.[170] How so? 'In His "energies" the Unapproachable God mysteriously approaches man. And this Divine move effects encounter'.[171] With a tacit reference to Meyendorff, Florovsky concluded that while calling Palamism an 'Existentialism' might mislead insofar as it could associate him with the twentieth-century movements that come under that label, St Gregory was certainly opposed to all theologies that 'fail to account for God's freedom, for the dynamism of God's will, for the reality of Divine action'.[172] One would expect as much, for he was a successor of the Fathers in such a way as to be a Father himself.

Enter Dumitru Staniloae

After Gregory Palamas, Allchin made another discovery. And this was the revival of Orthodox dogmatics in Romania (by the 1960s the current orthography was in place) thanks above all to the work of the indigenous theologian Dumitru Staniloae, no less than three of whose essays were included in an issue of *Sobornost* in that year. From 1936 to 1947 Staniloae had served as rector of the Theological Academy of Sibiu, while from 1947 to 1968 he had held a chair of 'Ascetica and Mystica' in the Theology Faculty of Bucharest University. He had been in England in the winter of 1968–9, visiting Oxford and the Jesuit athenaeum of Heythrop College. As editor of the journal Allchin made the most of the opportunity, believing as he did that Romania as a Latin nation had a special role to play between East and West. Allchin also liked to note how the Orthodox Liturgy was more accessible to native speakers in Romania than elsewhere, having been translated into the vernacular as late as the seventeenth century. For most Anglicans this was a selling-point.

What was Staniloae's contribution to *Sobornost*?[173] A short statement of salient characteristics of Orthodoxy; an elegant lecture on Tradition and the development of doctrine; and a rather daring presentation of theological cosmology, close in spirit to (and indeed citing) Alexander Schmemann's *The World as Sacrament*.[174] Orthodoxy is ancient, said Staniloae, yet it meets the religious needs of its adherents, which mystifies propagandists for *aggiornamento*—the sort of rather compromised 'bringing up to date' the Second Vatican Council had attempted in the Church of Rome. Staniloae's explanation ran, 'Orthodoxy has preserved the mystery of salvation in its living richness',[175] such that not having entered on the way of 'intellectual explanations which on the one side complicate things and on the other empty them of their mystery,' it does not need to 'disentangle itself from those explanations which have been left aside by the progress of the human mind'.[176] Orthodoxy is richer symbolically than is Western Christianity, but it is also more conscious of life in the Holy Spirit, and hence of foretaste of the Resurrection which makes it, therefore, more cosmic in character.

> Jesus Christ renewed in himself the sacramental and eucharistic character of the whole world. All things are gifts and words of God towards us, and gifts and words of ours towards God and amongst ourselves.[177]

Staniloae calls the Orthodox faith 'doxological not theoretical', eschewing speculation about God, and in relations between man and God, and man and man, stressing love not justice, which is why it is 'par excellence, ecumenical'.[178] This was a rather hopeful assessment of Orthodoxy's ecumenical readiness.

'The Orthodox Conception of Tradition and the Development of Doctrine' was in the lecture genre and so more nuanced than the above. In courteous opening remarks, Staniloae noted how Anglicanism was committed to the early patristic centuries, but also wanted to speak to later generations. Orthodoxy 'also wishes to make the treasure of early Christianity accessible to the man of today without sacrificing anything of its essence'.[179] He then explained his concept of Tradition. Tradition comprises the whole of revelation as climaxing in Christ and does so not simply as texts and monuments (Scripture and the rest) but as a content really given to the Church's faithful to experience, above all in the sacraments. Though subjectively God can come nearer to this man or that, objectively God cannot come nearer to mankind than he has done by becoming the subject of human nature in Christ.

> This is why we do not move into a new revelation, but remain under the brightness of the same sun, of the accomplished revelation, the sun which began to shine in the Incarnation, Resurrection and Ascension of Christ, who has given us the power of knowing him through the sending of his Holy Spirit.[180]

Christ is drawing history towards the end he has promised, and here Staniloae paused to enter a somewhat naïve account of historical progress and the wisdom of future-orientedness in present-day culture. In Tradition there is not only a '"living memory" constantly relived by the Church' but also 'a tension and a constant self-transcendence towards the eschatological goal' and consequently a 'progress in the knowledge of the divine activity'.[181] That is a presupposition of an Orthodox account of the 'development of doctrine' which, though, also has other explanatory or at least characteristic features. One obvious one is that the fullness of the saving mystery cannot be adequately expressed so 'new expressions are justified'.[182] Staniloae assumes these new expressions will be more delicate and subtle, more articulate and adequate both to the richness of the mystery itself and also 'to the more profound problematic of a humanity which is spiritually more advanced'[183]—though he at once added this must be, in the words of Vincent of Lerins, *progressus in idem*, i.e. advance in the same, self-identical meaning. The new expressions must be incorporated with the ancient, both to refresh the latter and to attest to their own veracity. No inner contradiction is permissible here. This is exactly what a Roman Catholic theologian of the 'homogeneous' development of doctrine would say.

Staniloae now qualifies his progressivism. The overall eschatological orientation of history should not mean there cannot be temporary reversals. Accordingly, the organic metaphor—seed into plant—is misleading, for the development is on a spiritual level where 'liberty and choice' play their part.[184] The examples of such reversals in Church history that occurred to him were mediaeval Scholastic theology, whose idiom he deemed 'below the level of the spiritual relations existing amongst the faithful' and the sixteenth-century Reformation for its 'individualistic mentality'.[185]

What, then, of his third piece, on 'The World as Gift and Sacrament of God's Love'? A philosophical meditation on the discovery of the world as a common possession, but a highly ambiguous common possession, in terms of being and non-being, sense and non-sense, concludes with these words:

> The meaning of the world lies precisely in its inherent necessity of finding its fulfilment from a source which possesses the power to grant fullness of meaning, since it gives completion of being.[186]

This is the basis of Staniloae's (theological) affirmation that the world is 'gift', the gift of God. Precisely as God's gift the world discloses the value of the human person who perceives it as a gift from God. And this raises the issue of death, for how can someone 'involved in absolute value' die?[187] Here Staniloae borrows, with acknowledgement, from the German Jesuit Karl Rahner. By death we make way for those who will follow us, with new talents for penetrating the world. Hence death is a sign of trust in God and love for man.

This problem overcome, Staniloae feels able to assert that, as the gift of God, the world becomes a bridge for meeting God. Indeed, he goes on:

> The whole world ought to be regarded as the visible part of a universal and continuing sacrament, and all man's activities as a sacramental, divine communion.[188]

Only if a gift is received as such, is it the means of communion—but this is the case we are considering now. And this leads Staniloae, albeit briefly, into the topic of the Holy Eucharist. Because man can only give back to God, in gratitude, what he has received, every gift to God is a sacrifice of something of this world, But God will answer this with 'still greater love and blessing, because man is in the position to receive it'—having made his own gift, Staniloae means.[189] And this in turn means, then: 'When man offers a sacrifice to God he receives a sacrament at the same time.'[190] And is not the Eucharist a sacrifice-sacrament?

Where Staniloae approaches (one would have thought) the frontiers of heterodoxy is in his further speculation that the world may be called the Body of God.

> If the world is sustained in being through the power of God; if in its rational, complex and adaptable organism the ever-living speech of divine love is reflected, then the world is a kind of body of the Word of God, of the divine Logos and of the powers of God, of which some are actualized in the world, while others stand ready to be actualized according to the choice of each individual person, and of all together, from ever fresh possibilities.[191]

Each individual can 'actualize this body in a personal manner, but only in working together with all'.[192] That description leads to a prescription. 'Every single person must use the whole world and contribute to its common development—but for all and together with all.'[193] Here one sees what Staniloae is attempting. He is seeking to find a better account of human solidarity than that offered by Marxism-Leninism, which at this time was of course the official ideology of the Romanian State. He believed his version to be deeper, more humane, and more likely to be efficacious, as well as, compatible (if at one major point only arguably so) with Orthodoxy itself.

The discovery of modern Greek theology

Sobornost's discovery of modern Greek theology was made first by Allchin, though it would be seconded by Kallistos (especially on its monastic side), and confirmed by Rowan Williams, future Oxford professor, Welsh bishop and Anglican primate. The stage was set for the advent of the new Greek writers in person, and among them, most notably, Christos Yannaras and John Zizioulas.

Allchin, looking into modern Greek theology, found a distinct advance compared with the dry but competent Orthodox writing typical of the late nineteenth and early twentieth centuries. Orthodox theology had been academic, lay, often German-trained. It was cut off from monasticism, from the Liturgy, and from consulting in depth its own liturgical and philokalic sources. This was now changing, as appeared from a book edited by Elias Mastroyiannopoulos, which, while not entirely Greek in production (there were essays by the Russians Florovsky, Lossky, Schmemann and Meyendorff, as well as the Serb Justin Popović), showed a new spirit. That was plain from the editor's own essay, which called for a theology that was lived, prayed, and ecclesial. It was seconded in a contribution from the professional ecumenist Nikos Nissiotis—for whom theology, whatever the scientific character of its preliminary disciplines, concerns (in Allchin's summary) the 'death and resurrection of human categories and ways of thought, as the mind opens itself in praise and adoration of the revealed glory of God',[194] and another from Demetrios Trakatellis, later a bishop in the Greek metropolia in North America, speaking of the need for a theology of the living God who incarnated himself for the whole world, and gave his word as 'Yea and Amen'.[195] These essays specified existential demands on the theologian as much as, or more than, they indicated any particular content for the theologian's work. Allchin regretted no university teachers had been included, some might have proved sympathetic. He thought the essay-collection could help toward monastic renewal, and, potentially, re-make bonds with the hierarchy that were relevant to the education of the clergy. Moreover, a revived theology in Greece would give new conversation partners to the Fellowship, for—though this was not stated in so many words—it could be that the day of Saint-Serge was passing.

A paper on 'What is Theology?' by the holder of the chair of New Testament studies at Thessalonica, originally written in Greek for the journal *Ekklesia*, and now offered in English to *Sobornost* subscribers, gave the best idea of what this new spirit might mean. Savvas Agourides thought that

> the break in the stream of patristic theological thought caused by the Turkish domination and the lack of an indigenous theology in the Greek State has been the primary cause of our more general spiritual alignment with the West and of the alienation of our spiritual and intellectual leaders from our people's medieval and neo-Greek roots.[196]

The situation was changing, not least owing to contacts with 'Western thought', by which Agourides meant Russian Diaspora theology and the ecumenical movement.[197] Agourides began from the axiom that 'theology has divine revelation as its starting-point and guide, not only formally but essentially'.[198] Theology has two aims: to interpret and elucidate the content of the faith, and to project it in language the age understands—

which includes, moreover, the defence of the faith against 'the world's attacks'.[199] Over against pietist influence (a coded reference to the Zoe Brotherhood), Agourides stressed that the person has to appropriate the content of faith—namely, salvation—through 'the total experience of his life' and therefore of the 'logical processes' which form part of that life. Agourides expected that would include tolerating antitheses in experience—but also explaining its unity. He called theological interpretation a 'spiritual liturgy',[200] explaining in the light of Johannine teaching on the Paraclete that

> historical study and knowledge of the content of the faith cannot lead to understanding of it from the standpoint of faith without the Spirit of Pentecost.[201]

Like, he asserted, is only grasped by like, and the Gospel 'has nothing like itself by relating it to which it may be understood'.[202] Here, thought Agourides, is where much modern Protestant theology goes wrong, relating Jesus and the message of the Kingdom to either Jewish or Hellenistic backgrounds, without taking into account the Tradition of the Church—so necessary for an interpretation, an understanding, that operates by the Holy Spirit, active as the latter is in the sacramental and agapeistic life. The misdirection in question, Agourides added, is likely to become even more misleading owing to the human condition after the Fall.

The greatness of the theological enterprise so conceived threw a poor light on ecclesiastical officialdom in Greece. The latter, remarked Agourides, seeks theological counsel only when it is a question of inter-confessional relations or canon law. The 'Christian Movement' or 'movements' in modern Greece have shied away from theology as a dangerous realm, and ended up, despite their undoubted if circumscribed regenerative force, with moral or religious generalizations that are needed yet insufficient. The word 'platitudinous' seemed to be hovering over the page. '[S]ince it was bereft of theology [the Church of Greece] left the world of letters, art, social legislation and ecclesiastical organization completely unmoved.'[203]

So far Agourides has had little to say about the 'projective' (or, for that matter, the 'defensive') role of theology, and what he now says is perhaps too brief really to be helpful. He considers Existentialism and socialism the predominant trends of the age, and expects that theology can usefully be beamed at unbelievers or semi-believers using 'the presuppositions and in the terms' of either.²⁰⁴ Here the sympathetic observer might wish to know how, in this strategy, the integrity of theological content is to be preserved, especially when the writer adds that 'the most precise test of the orthodoxy of a theology is ... how much it helps men and society to be transformed by the Gospel'.²⁰⁵ This looks like pastoral pragmatism, though Agourides tries to defuse criticism by citing the dominical logion, 'By their fruits ye shall know them' (Matthew 7:20).

When in 1965 *Sobornost* began its fifth series Allchin again noted positive developments in Greek theology. A new journal, *Sunoro* ('Frontier'), had for its moving spirit Christos Yannaras, who was soon to become well known for his mixture of Greek patristic apophaticism and Heideggerianism, while *Orthodoxos Parousia* was more consciously ecumenical—but by implication just a trifle dull.

The new Greek masters: Yannaras, Zizioulas

Yannaras was definitely the first of the coming men. What was his distinctive style?²⁰⁶ In the first place, he was in debt to the German philosopher of being (not, however, in the Thomasian sense) Martin Heidegger. Yannaras, a lay philosopher who never held a theological post as such, took his cue from Heidegger's *Holzwege*.²⁰⁷ That essay collection was Heidegger's first post-War publication, after emerging from a period of enforced silence, a penalty for his collaboration, when rector of the University of Freiburg, in the anti-Semitic policies of the Third Reich. The fourth item in that collection was entitled 'Nietzsche's word: God is dead'. Pondering this essay, Yannaras came to the conclusion that the 'socio-political appearance of the Church' (he may have had in mind the rather staid ethical renewalism of the Zoe Brotherhood in the Greece of his day) no more expresses the 'faith of the New Testament' than the 'God of European metaphysics' expresses the 'God of Christian revelation'.²⁰⁸ The ostensibly Christian West had rejected the way of unknowing, the apophatic way of the Greek patristic tradition. It had not sought for God in a darkness beyond thought. Consequently, it had taken the only possible alternative way, a way which leads to the 'death of God'. In the West, the God of standard theism has been gradually replaced by metaphysics, a metaphysics which itself has led by the equally gradual reduction of being, once considered so substantial, to the status of an ontologically ungrounded 'value', or 'set of values', and thereby, through an inevitable logical progression best associated with the name of Nietzsche, to a nihilist conclusion. For Yannaras, official Byzantium had been pre-eminent—which means in context even worse than the West—in looking on God as the extension of civic religion. But by a fortunate chance there was something else in the East Roman civilization which was able to preserve apophasis nonetheless. This was monasticism, considered by Yannaras a breakwater against the rolling theocratic waves. Here the name of Denys surfaces—though no case is made for treating Denys as a monk and the scene soon shifts to Palamas (unnamed), whose teaching Yannaras sums up in a lapidary statement. 'Though God is completely unknown and inaccessible in his Essence, yet we can approach him and participate in him through his Energies.'[209]

The most disputable aspect of Yannaras's thought is surely his underwriting Nietzsche's programme of going beyond the 'objective values of good and evil'.[210] That is possible, he wrote,

> because Orthodox Spirituality looks towards repentance, which is a reality of a different order from ethics—that which emphasizes the person as against the law, and which goes beyond a juridical relationship to one which involves a 'knowledge' of persons, that is to say, a personal relationship with Jesus Christ.[211]

The phrase 'as against the law' in this citation indicates an antinomianism from which (to hark back to an early *Journal* essay) Boris Visheslavzev's 'The Ethics of Sublimation as a Means for Overcoming Moralism' (discussed above) had been conspicuously free. Since, for Yannaras, the Church is 'not an ethical socio-political institution, but a liturgical, eucharistic and doxological community', its holiness, he claimed, is 'not a matter of virtue but an ontological reality'.[212] Virtues, meant only for keeping legal precepts, are sub-evangelical. One wonders what, say, St Maximus would have made of the notion that virtues developing under grace are not an ontological matter, and in no sense a participation in the virtue of Christ.

Yannaras represented an apophatic approach to the real, equally applicable to God and to the communion of human persons. He sedulously avoided both traditional Christian metaphysics in the Catholic sense—which had also been that of Byzantine Thomism, and an ethics of the virtues—though the latter were equally prominent in the ascetical vocabulary of East and West. There would be more to come—much more—in the 1970s and later, as Yannaras pursued his theological project and his books became available in English, and were regularly reviewed in *Sobornost*'s pages.

John Zizioulas, who began his theological teaching as a layman (in the United Kingdom as well as in Greece) would become a commanding figure in the world of bilateral dialogue between Orthodoxy and the Western confessions, and, as a consequence, was ordained a bishop in the Holy Synod of the Ecumenical Patriarchate under the title Metropolitan John of Pergamum. Zizioulas would also become known for his revisionist theological and anthropological metaphysics.[213] But in the 1960s he was familiar to readers of *Sobornost* for his thinking about the sacraments of initiation—Baptism, Chrismation or Confirmation, Eucharist—some agreement on which was high on the list of priorities of the World Council of Churches at this time.

Zizioulas explained that the East has typically seen the three within the single mystery of Christ, whereas the West has looked at each for its own sake. What, then, is the unity of these mysteries? It is not an easy question to answer, but a start would be to say that for the ancient Church the sacraments of initiation are contextualized in a 'Christology which summed up in itself the entire history of salvation as it was not only seen but also eschatologically realized through the Pentecostal outpouring of the Holy Spirit'.[214] Zizioulas criticized the Western tradition for regarding Chrismation as the perfecting ('confirming') of Baptism, as though Baptism were not yet pneumatological. Rather, Chrismation makes a person a layman in the true sense, i.e. one anointed to be a member of the holy *laos*. But he also criticized modern Orthodox practice for communicating the baptized and confirmed outside the *Synaxis*, the eucharistic assembly.

> By entering into Eucharistic communion the baptized and confirmed person enters into the realization of the capacity of the 'layman' which he acquired in the first two stages of Christian initiation ... The Eucharist, therefore, following immediately Baptism and Confirmation is the expression of the summoned People of God in a certain established and charismatic order in the unity of the Body of Christ.[215]

The Body of Christ, in which the Son of Man is at once personal yet corporate, reflects the way the divine Persons, by their relationships, found an ineffable communion as the one God, and how that communion enters human history through Incarnation and Pentecost.[216]

As with Yannaras, much more would be heard of Zizioulas's thinking in the later decades of the Fellowship's journal, though, unlike Yannaras, he was a man of the essay, not of the book. Like Yannaras, Zizioulas was an opponent of *ousia*, of substance, and a believer that relationship is all.

As the luminaries of the Russian Diaspora were gradually extinguished, and the great masters of the Anglo-Catholic (or Anglican Catholic) theology of the inter-War years, and the 1950s, died off without replacement, a vacuum was created in the Fellowship dialogue of East and West. Through their admirers, and (dare one say it?) *faute de mieux*, these Neo-Greek theologians, despite their metaphysical strangeness, entered in and took possession. It was one of the ways in which *Sobornost*, in future decades, would distance itself from its own past.

→ 9 ←

Ecumenical Prospects

From the start, the Fellowship had been concerned not only to inform Anglicans and Orthodox about each other but also to bring them into closer *rapprochement*, if not indeed to outright union. The hope of 'Reunion', at any rate on the horizon though not yet in reach, shaped its ethos, gave warmth to its meetings, and generated the zeal of a number of its more active members. This was true above all of the years before the Second World War.

The 1920s

Eric Mascall had ended his first contribution to the *Journal of the Fellowship of St Alban and St Sergius*, in the opening year of its existence, by an expression of hope in the future reunion of the Churches. But he also knew that 'misunderstandings' required removal, and 'apathy' had to be turned into 'brotherly love'.[1] It was not simply that 'differences require explanation'. His essay served as an overture to Nicolas Zernov on 'Psychological Barriers to Reunion'—union, that is, between Orthodox and Anglicans—in an article which followed Mascall's plea.

For Zernov, while the dogmatic barriers are the more important, they are also the easier to overcome. They will 'not be the stone against which we will be dashed'.[2] He listed the more serious obstacles. First came 'national pride', or 'failure to grasp the Oecumenical nature of the Church'. '[O]nly a nation which deeply feels the oecumenicity of Christianity can wish for and can bring about the reunion of the Churches.'[3] Neither England nor Russia quite met this description. Next came what he termed 'Church "restfulness"': resting, he meant, in ignorance of each other. Historically, not a great deal would have brought English Anglicans and Russian Orthodox into contact—but now this had changed thanks to the Diaspora, so there was some chance of interrupting the 'rest' in question. The struggle with State atheism had made the Orthodox in Russia more concerned with links with Christianity internationally. And in England, the advances of Roman Catholicism and what Zernov called diplomatically 'some of the complications arising within the Anglican Church itself' had prompted more interest in schemes of reunion with separated episcopally ordered Churches abroad.[4]

Then there was the obstacle of cultural differences. The English, Zernov observed, feel superior to the Christian East, while the Orthodox East has had too many painful experiences of both Roman Catholic and Protestant proselytism to feel inclined to open itself to Westerners of any description. Zernov drew from this a wise inference. 'Only examples of disinterested help rendered to one another, of Church fellowship in love and respect of the stranger's tradition and culture can overcome this obstacle.'[5]

Finally, there was the barrier constituted by divergent conceptions of what Church reunion might mean. Anglicans tend to think of mutual recognition of sacraments, with everything continuing as before, not grasping that the Orthodox will reject a union where dogmas and practices incompatible with their own persist. Orthodox, at least in Russia, tend to think of a total makeover of Anglicanism so that it will resemble Orthodoxy in every least particular, not appreciating the difference between 'that which is eternal and unchangeable in the Church' and 'that which can be freely changed in different epochs and by different nations'.[6]

Writing from France, Zernov counselled against wrongly motivated attempts to circumvent these 'barriers' by hasty action, which might be driven on the Orthodox side (especially at Constantinople, Antioch, Alexandria, Jerusalem) by a hope of extracting material assistance, and on the Anglican side, by a desire to strengthen the political position of the British Empire and to find allies in a common front against the Roman Catholic Church.

A rather different note was struck by Verrier Elwin, chairman of the third conference, in April 1929. In his closing address, while he emphasized the Anglo-Russian and Anglo-Catholic/Eastern Orthodox character of the Fellowship, he refused to be bound by these limits. Citing the prophet Ezekiel's vision of the river of life flowing from Temple to wilderness, he said:

> So must the spirit of our Fellowship flow out into that dry and arid world that is about us: it must go out to Roman Catholics and Protestants as well as to Anglo-Catholics and Orthodox; among all kinds of people we must be centres of love and peace.[7]

The son of a colonial bishop, Elwin had originally been an Evangelical Anglican. From the post of vice-principal at Wycliffe Hall in Oxford he had progressed to become a Fellow of Merton College. A self-taught ethnologist, he had gone to India in 1927 as a member of the 'Christian Service Society' (hence the letters 'C. S. S.' that followed his name). Via the Mahatma Gandhi, India had cast its spell, and in 1935 Elwin embraced a wider ecumenism than any the Fellowship could recognize, abandoning Christianity for Hinduism.

The 1930s

In 1930 the Fellowship's conference, its fourth, marked a significant advance, since it was honoured by the presence both of Metropolitan Evlogy, the bishop with the care of Russian parishes in Western Europe, and of the archbishop of Canterbury, Cosmo Gordon Lang. This was a double sign of the Fellowship's 'arrival'.

Lang's address was far from being a formality. In two major paragraphs it outlined the commonalities between the Orthodox and the Anglican Churches. In the first place, the common points were doctrinal.

> We have the same creed, which lies at the basis both of our faith and of our ritual. We have the same Scripture to which we look with reverence as the Guide of our thought. We have the same sacraments which we reverence, I trust, with the same constancy of devotion. We have the same orders preserved by us and you throughout the centuries. We have the same conviction that we stand together for a conception of the unity of the Body of Christ illimitably deeper and more beautiful than that which is associated with the great Roman Catholic Church.[8]

From this the primate drew the conclusion that Anglicans and Orthodox have 'very much the same duty to fulfil in Christendom'.

Moreover, the structure of the two communions was similar. Without using the full technical vocabulary customary among the Orthodox, he spoke of the twenty (or so) 'autonomous branches' which made up the Orthodox Church world-wide, held together by 'nothing more rigorous than by common traditions, and, what is even more powerful, though it cannot be as easily defined, a common spirit, and also by a reverence for the ancient tradition and primacy of the oecumenical Patriarch'.[9] Similarly, the Anglican Church represents globally a multiplicity of autonomous

Churches, and these too are united by common traditions, spirit, and reverence for an ancient see—not Constantinople but Canterbury. And the archbishop did not fail to mention that, as a sign of this convergence of destiny, the ecumenical patriarch was arranging for a delegation from the autocephalous Churches to attend the next Lambeth Conference which at the time of speaking was imminent.

The Fellowship, said Lang, embodied this 'brotherhood'.[10] Its Eastern members would be likely to teach their Western counterparts the lesson that the Church is a 'communion of the Seen with the Unseen', the Western to teach the Eastern how 'in the midst of this very modern world, with all its complexities' to 'adjust themselves to life about them'.[11]

This speech fitted well with other addresses about ecumenism Lang made in the first years of his primacy. In 1934, for instance, addressing the Canterbury diocesan conference in a speech which, according to his biographer Robert Beaken, 'he knew would be reported outside his diocese, and which was entirely his own composition',[12] Lang explained how the Church of England could be considered a bridge Church: 'At one end it has an affinity with the great Latin Church of the West and the Orthodox Churches of the East; and at the other end it has an affinity with the Protestant Churches'.[13] The latter affinity was, however, circumscribed, since the absence of episcopacy, to be counted quite as essential for Church-life as are the canon of the Bible and the Creeds, could never be acceptable in 'any united Church of which the Church of England can form a part'.[14] Beaken considered that his happiest relations, ecumenically speaking, were in fact with the Orthodox, though Lang (a convert from the Church of Scotland to a Catholic-minded Anglicanism) 'always spoke respectfully of the Roman Catholic Church'.[15] In 1931 Lang hosted a discussion about reunion with Anglican and Orthodox participants at Lambeth Place, but

> [T]he hopes of some on the Church of England side that a meeting of the Pro-Synod of the Orthodox Churches 'will lead to the various Orthodox Churches following the example of the Ecumenical Patriarch in pronouncing Anglican Orders to be valid (*bebaios*) and that inter-communion *kat' oikonomian* will be permitted' were never fulfilled.[16]

As to the fourth conference itself, Zernov was frank about problems of communication.

Ecumenical Prospects

> The majority of English students find the Russian way of approach unusually complicated and they are rather lost in the number of ideas presented and in the too scientific and abstract terminology of the Russians. From the other side the English addresses were unsatisfactory in a different way—they did not penetrate sufficiently into the nature of the problems.[17]

In fact he described the addresses in question as 'more suitable for an ordinary parish meeting'.[18] Yet overall Zernov felt positive.

> The most important result of this last conference was undoubtedly a clear vision that behind our work stands already a small but energetic group of people who not only are conscious of the necessity of reunion between the Anglican and Orthodox Churches, but also have the firm desire to become personally active workers in this field.[19]

And he added, plausibly enough:

> I think that in the history of the Christian Church it is perhaps the only instance where the members of two very different Christian communities which never before had any common religious life came to the conclusion that the reunion of their bodies in not only important but urgently needed and quite possible. I believe that many of us realized during this conference for the first time in our lives that between some of the Anglican and Orthodox Christians not a single fundamental difference exists.[20]

The obstacles he had listed earlier had not prevented 'a group of younger theologians' from taking on 'the task of striving for corporate union within their lifetime'.[21]

In Zernov's view only three possible schemes for a reunited Christendom were on offer: the Roman scheme, characterized by 'the spirit of authority and obedience'; the 'extreme Protestant' scheme, with its attempt to 'modernize Christianity, deprive it of all Creeds and make it more like a moral teaching than a dogmatical and sacramental religion', and the 'free Catholic' scheme, which will 'preserve the traditional creeds, sacraments and Church ministry, but at the same time will consist of self-governing national Churches with inner freedom and the possibility of independent spiritual development'.[22] Only the third had the sanction of ancient Christianity—with which one might agree were it not for the use of the word 'national'.

In the last issue of 1930 in an account of 'The Orthodox Delegation to the Lambeth Conference' J. A. Douglas applauded the advances in Anglican/Orthodox relations. Douglas was associated chiefly with the diplomatic effort to secure recognition of Anglican ministerial Orders by various Orthodox entities. So it may have surprised some to find that his piece was critical of reunion 'simply by ecclesiastical negotiation' or through forming 'as it were a bloc of churches arrayed against another bloc'. For reunion there has to be a desire for 'essential unity with all true believers in Christ' and the wish to 'join with them in driving back evil and in bringing in [Christ's] reign upon earth'.[23] Yes, there must be dogmatic agreement, which will signify 'the formal recognition that their conceptions of the mystic life of the Church are the same and that the essential external features imparted by Christ to His Church are present in them both'. But this must be 'preceded by the will to Reunion in the great body of the people', and this was evidently the context in which he saw the Fellowship's value.[24]

> The work of the theologian is to test whether the Faith of two churches permits their Reunion. The work of the ordinary Christian is to create the love, which will enable them to unite.[25]

In the summer 1933 issue of the *Journal*, Zernov noted how in a collection of essays published by the Russian YMCA Press, attitudes to reunion were spread along a spectrum: rigorist, moderate, audacious, of which the latter was represented only by the Paris Diaspora. Even this statement was rather optimistic, as he was about to discover. The 1933 conference would be notable for Father Sergei Bulgakov's first airing of his ideas on intercommunion, ideas that were to prove so controversial for a number of years ahead.

To grasp Bulgakov's approach to intercommunion some doctrinal background is necessary. Unity had a very special place in Bulgakov's mind, for his Christology entailed a 'multi-unity' of all human beings. More than a hint of this has been given in the account of his theology of the Fall in the previous chapter. For Bulgakov, Jesus Christ in his humanity is not only an individual but in some sense contains all men—all the fullness of Adam's nature and all its hypostatic images, just as the first Adam potentially contained in himself all the individualities of future mankind'.[26] In the Redemption the humanity of Adam becomes that of Christ, and insofar as human beings are united by life in Christ they constitute a 'living "sobornost"', a 'harmonious existence'.[27] The *sobornost* of the Church, union in love, *is* this existence as in process of being accomplished. It is therefore 'the guiding principle and ideal for the fellowship of mankind'.[28] In the (Jerusalem) Church of the beginnings, 'church love' spread out into the whole of life, knowing no limit, leaving nothing to lower principles to govern. This epoch when the fire of ecclesial love melted all in itself remains unforgettable since 'All the members of the Church ... have this power of the Incarnation, for they are bound to Christ in His Body', and this is the reality which acquires its 'direct and immediate fulfilment in the Sacrament of the Body and Blood, in the Divine Eucharist'.[29] In the High Priestly Prayer recorded in St John's Gospel, Christ, so Bulgakov wrote, 'seems to throw open before His disciples the gates of the temple—of the Upper Room—calling on them to share with the world the treasures which they have received—the divine Eucharist'.[30]

In 'By Jacob's Well' Bulgakov set out, on these presuppositions, his proposal for limited intercommunion. In a text which was slightly abridged from its Russian original, Bulgakov argued that 'The Church is one, as life in Christ by the Holy Spirit is one. Only participation in this unity can be of varying degrees and depths'.[31] Prayer, the Word of God, especially the Gospels, the spiritual life, the sacrament of Baptism: these constitute between Orthodoxy and Protestantism the content of an invisible communion. 'A more direct and true communion in sacraments with the Protestant world is hindered by the absence of a rightly ordained priesthood: this is the threshold over which Protestantism must pass, the re-establishment of an Apostolically ordained hierarchy'.[32] But where there is such a hierarchy, as seemingly in Anglicanism, as well as in Roman Catholicism and the separated Eastern Churches, more can be said. In their cases: 'The Churches which have preserved such a unity in sacraments are now divided canonically in the sense of jurisdiction, and, dogmatically, through a whole range of differences; but these are powerless to destroy the efficacy of the sacraments'.[33]

Bulgakov found it congruent with this observation that the general rule whereby dogmatic agreement precedes unity of sacramental life be not treated as the law of the Medes and the Persians. 'Why should we not seek to surmount a heresy in teaching through superseding such a heresy of life as division?'[34] That is a statement which concerned in explicit terms Orthodoxy and Rome (between whose clergy Bulgakov sought, at this date, concelebration of the Liturgy). Yet in the context of the 1930s the only possible contender for a Western correspondent was Canterbury.

Behind the scenes, A. F. Dobbie-Bateman, Anglican layman and senior member of the British civil service, had been taking soundings in early October among the Orthodox in Paris—the centre, after all, of Bulgakov's jurisdiction, its Fellowship 'branch' the *alter ego* of the London organization. He now sent the Fellowship executive a lengthy confidential note based on these personal conversations.

> The general question may be put more specifically in the form whether it is possible to proceed to partial inter-communion by 'capillary' or 'molecular' action. Here a beginning or process ('partial') is contrasted with the endeavour to obtain full inter-communion in one act by the 'diplomatic' method. I found complete disbelief in the diplomatic method, based on two considerations. The first is that reunion must be a spiritual act, unobtainable by negotiation. The second is that in any case the diplomatic method is in point of fact powerless within its own sphere. If the diplomatic method is to prevail then the situation is hopeless, since the Orthodox Church has not succeeded in achieving diplomatic coordination within her own body.[35]

Georges Florovsky commented sharply, almost by return of post. The proposal amounted to Orthodoxy being in communion with some Anglicans and not others. It was 'uncatholic, particularist and even sectarian' to attempt to 'achieve intercommunion within the limits of an individual and arbitrary group, such as the Fellowship, regardless of its size and the conditions of intercommunion'. Yes, indeed, *sobornost* is a 'spiritual attitude', not a 'magnitude in space and time'. But just for this reason it was uncatholic to 'let the image of the fellowship overshadow the reality of our Churches, Orthodox and Anglican.'[36]

The June issue of 1934 saw its editorial dominated by the Bulgakov proposal: the executive wanted the next conference to give serious thought to the idea of a mutual sacramental blessing of ministers leading to Intercommunion within the Fellowship. There had been enough sheer talk. Dom Bede Frost on 'Prayer and Reunion' echoed this conviction, basing himself on the analogy of the fruitless machinery of peace conferences in Europe at this time.[37] By the issue of December 1934 it was plain to the editor that the study groups set up at the conference were generally favourable to at any rate some act of partial intercommunion.

But the editorial also recognized the need to have regard to the views of those who were opposed. Henry Leighton Goudge, Regius Professor of Divinity at Oxford, wrote for those who were unconvinced by Bulgakov's proposal. The idea of a sacramental blessing was unclear. It might mean nothing more than prayer for one another. And in any case to attempt some form of intercommunion is to act without authorization from the entire Churches involved.

> Let us not forget that both the English Church and the Orthodox Eastern Church are far less united in their own ecclesiastical life than they ought to be. Our own party-divisions are a serious hindrance to Christian unity, and the national divisions of the Orthodox Easterns are perhaps even more serious. It would be a great mistake for our Fellowship to take any action which might give wide offence to either of the Churches to which our members belong.[38]

By way of consolation, he observed that there was in the Fellowship a unity of spirit which transcends the divisions, while in 'irregular communions our minds might easily be fixed more upon ourselves, and what we are doing, than upon the Lord whom we came to receive.'[39]

Anton Vladimirovich Kartashev, professor of Church history at Saint-Serge, in 'The Path towards the Reunion of the Churches', argued against Goudge. Kartashev's was a weighty voice. He had been the last Procurator of the Holy Synod, appointed by the Provisional Government in February 1917, whereupon he immediately abolished the post and became instead the first Minister of Cults in Kerensky's administration. Modern history, said Kartashev, offers no examples of unions achieved by Churches at parity. Mutual recognition, simply as such, is too difficult psychologically for most Church members. The Uniate Churches have been absorbed, rather than united in the best sense of the word. Admittedly, the administrative union of Reformed Christians and Lutherans in Germany seems to have worked, and the recent (1931) agreement between Anglicans and Old Catholics is another apparent exception to the rule. But the German Protestants were similar to each other anyway, while the Old Catholics had not been in existence long enough to feel themselves self-sufficient. Perhaps the continuing union of long-standing parties in the Church of England is a genuine exception— but it hardly comes without a degree of 'inner tragedy' and anyway would be unthinkable outside the common life of a single nation.[40] Churches that are great quantitatively and qualititatively can hardly be expected to sacrifice their principles to each other—though this is what the 'diplomatic' method of interchurch negotiation silently presumes.

So what can be done? Kartashev's answer ran, prayer, working towards rapprochement, and above all imbuing the great masses of Church people with a consciousness of their mystical unity in the 'one, invisible and only Universal Church'.[41] But he believed there was also need for a creative act (shades of Berdyaev's philosophy!), since only the latter, not evolutionary development, truly overcomes tragedy. It can happen that a 'word or an act which is born in one part of the Church is later complied with by the whole Church' (the glorification of a saint was Kartashev's chosen example: canonized at one location, the cult may spread to many).[42] Yes, the danger of anarchy in spontaneous partial processes is real. Yet 'when this way emerges through an actual, burning need in the life of the Church, and when it is accompanied invisibly by the power of the Grace of God's Spirit, then we can surely describe it as a path that is, in truth, both Catholic and "soborny" the inevitable consummation of which will take place at an official council'.[43] If someone is not convinced of the weakness of the present-day divided Church in a secularized culture and has no sense of eschatology then of course he or she will be happy with the slow diplomatic route. Otherwise, some examples of 'eschatological daring' are needed, like Soloviev's (a rather controversial illustration).[44] Direct action between the Orthodox and either Anglicans or Old Catholics is the way forward.

That Establishment figure Tissington Tatlow, who had been of invaluable assistance to Zernov in getting the Fellowship going, gave a context for the discussion so far as Anglicans were concerned. It was a report on official developments 'on all fronts' since the end of the Great War—an upbeat report, as well it might be at that time.[45] Tatlow took the 1920 Lambeth 'Appeal to all Christian People' to be the turning of not only a page but the tide. The 1920 conference had already acknowledged the apostolic succession in the Church of Sweden, encouraging mutual reception of Communion and co-consecration of bishops. Still on the Scandinavian (and Baltic) Lutherans, the 1930 conference had received a request to extend the same recognition to the Churches of Norway, Denmark, Finland, Estonia and Lithuania—but this was more difficult (owing no doubt to the rupture of the succession) and work was ongoing. Tatlow ascribed the Malines Conversations of 1920 to 1925 to the influence of Lambeth 1920, while admitting they were only unofficial meetings. The death of the Malines archbishop, Mercier, in 1926 was unfortunate; even more so the 1931 encyclical *Mortalium animos*, which Tatlow claimed was triggered by the 1930 Lambeth assembly. Tatlow cited Randall Davidson as remarking that he had never read a document less attuned to the spiritual needs of its times. The situation with the Orthodox was far rosier. Following the 1920 conference, Constantinople, followed by Jerusalem and the Church of Cyprus had accepted the validity of Anglican ordination (this was probably to misunderstand the appeal to 'economy' by the hierarchs, but the degree of recognition it entailed was certainly confirmed by the presence of the patriarch of Alexandria at the 1930 conference). The 1932 report of the Anglican–Orthodox doctrinal commission set up by that conference was provisional, but it reported 'much underlying agreement' while referring to the governing authorities of the respective Churches any agreement on intercommunion which should be based, it said, on 'unity of faith'.[46]

The upshot of Lambeth 1930 for relations with the Old Catholics was, said Tatlow, more encouraging still. The Bonn 1931 meeting had resulted in mutual ecclesial recognition, warranting full participation in the sacraments of each by the other, while also declaring that intercommunion 'does not require from either communion the acceptance of all doctrinal opinion, sacramental devotion or liturgical practice characteristic of the other, but implies that each believes the other to hold all the essentials of the Christian faith'.[47] The signatures on the agreement were of the members of the conference—but Tatlow felt sure it would be a model for other Churches to follow in due course.

The 1920 Lambeth Appeal had resounded among the Free Churches in England also, especially with the provisions for occasional episcopal authorization of preaching by the non-episcopally ordained, and the admission of unconfirmed communicants from 'non-episcopal congregations working for unity'.[48] This had raised high hopes. Cryptically, Tatlow describes their disappointing at the 1930 conference as 'through circumstances largely accidental, partly the result of misunderstanding'.[49] Talks were resumed in 1931 and in a document of 1933 the archbishop of Canterbury and the moderator of the Federal Council of the Evangelical Free Churches spoke of common witness to the central truths of Christianity as a basis for joint mission. The Scottish Presbyterians, on the other hand, had suspended dialogue. Tatlow's greatest enthusiasm was reserved for the South India scheme, though it was too complex a subject to enter into except to say that if successful it could be adapted and adopted in England. What this made clear to those who could read was a salutary warning. Not all movement towards one separated body is necessarily movement towards the others. One wonders what Zernov made of it. Probably he saw it, despite the difficulties discreetly noted, as a sign of imminent reunion all round.

So far as Zernov personally was concerned, at this date a certain nervousness attended his position. He was an office-holder not only of the Fellowship, a private organization, but also of the Russian Clergy and Russian Church Aid Fund, an official agency of the Church of England.[50] Douglas, in his capacity as general secretary of the Council for Foreign Relations on the Church of England and secretary of the Russian Church Aid Fund, was displeased with Zernov's tendency to depart from his brief. It was no part of his job as appeals officer for the Fund to introduce the Reunionist aspirations of the Fellowship into his public propaganda. Douglas had made his criticisms rather intemperately, supporting them with the further consideration that, owing no doubt to his association with Bulgakov as well as his advanced ecumenical proclivities, Zernov was persona non grata at Karlovci. But his *démarche* was unsuccessful. The president of the Fund, Lord Charnwood, took the opportunity of the dispute to replace not Zernov but Douglas, alleging a conflict of interest between his two secretaryships. Yet this was not the end of the affair. In June 1934 the acting honorary secretary of the Russian Church Aid Fund, W. Tudor Pole, wrote to the Fellowship's secretary, Eric Fenn:

> Until Douglas spoke, I did not know that Zernov was regarded with such suspicion by the Metropolitan Anthony and his wing of the émigré Russian Church, and under those circumstances it might be difficult for him to become *officially* associated with our Fund and the Fellowship.[51]

And indeed the change of secretary at the Fund did not solve the problem of Zernov going off-script. So much was apparent a year latter when Anderson wrote to Fenn on the subject from Paris.

> One of the most difficult things for Zernov will be for him to recognize the limits, and perhaps the restrictions, imposed upon him in speaking for the Fund in matters which concern the policy of the Church of England and other Churches with reference to the Russian and other Orthodox Churches.[52]

A couple of months later. Anderson was writing again, this time to Tudor Pole:

> It would appear that last year the purposes and programme of propaganda of the Fellowship led Zernov, as its secretary, to include in his lectures ideas which extended beyond the range of the official approach of the Church to these questions ... There is evidently the tendency in his lecturing to develop interest along the lines of the problems of Church relationships, without fully effecting a transfer of interest to the practical task of supporting the Russian Clergy and Church Aid Fund.[53]

In fact Zernov's mind was not fully focused on either job, since at this time he was negotiating with Spalding about the possibility of the latter endowing a lectureship in Eastern Christian Studies (originally, 'Slavonic Church History') of which Zernov would be the first holder. Not that Zernov was proposing to lay down his baton at the Fellowship; indeed, both he and Spalding envisaged the Oxford Lectureship combined with the creation of an Oxford headquarters (to be dedicated to St Basil) for the Fellowship's work. Dobbie-Bateman was much exercised at the prospect of Zernov over-extending himself, and went to see Spalding on the topic. Spalding was unimpressed by his protest, writing to Zernov:

> My view still is that we should if possible have a lectureship for you here starting in October 1935 and leading to St Basil's House, and that the Fellowship ought to work in with this scheme.[54]

This must have been a relief, since in March of that year Zernov had come away from a visit to Spalding at his North Oxford address anxious that the bigger fish Spalding now had in mind of bankrolling a university chair for the world religions would lead him to 'forget relations between Eastern and Western Christians' as altogether too parochial in comparison.[55]

The dream of a 'house' at Oxford had been in Zernov's head for at least three years—not, however, quite consistently, for his fertile brain was ever considering new schemes. In 1933 he produced a memorandum for a different 'St Basil's House' to be located in Canterbury and to be run as an inter-Orthodox foundation, with the resultant need to contact the heads of each of the autocephalous Orthodox Churches and their theologians. In practice, this would have meant the leaders of the Orthodox countries in the Balkans. Even Zernov quailed somewhat at the notion of asking each such Church to propose a candidate as principal, with the dangerous possibility of stirring up nationalist feelings of an unmanageable kind.[56] The Second Balkan War, where Serbia and Greece had fought Bulgaria, was only a quarter of a century past, and the Great War which set Bulgaria against Romania and Serbia, even less, while the Second World War would prove their animosities still active. Perhaps fortunately, at least at this period in history, no more was heard of the idea.

In 1934 the long-awaited 'Fellowship Book'— *The Church of God. An Anglo-Russian Symposium*, edited by Mascall, with a preface by Frere, finally appeared from the Society for the Promotion of Christian Knowledge,[57] and was reviewed in *Sobornost* by an Anglican, S. C. Carpenter, later dean of St Paul's. Carpenter praised the brilliance of style and glowing piety of the Russian writers but was in two minds about their intellectual coherence. On the one hand, they 'move among great ideas with sure step', on the other they seem to 'hold irreconcilable or anyhow antipathetic ideas together'.[58] He was sure the Orthodox had influenced their Anglican co-writers, and thought it at least possible that the reverse was also true. Florovsky's qualitative view of catholicity came as a revelation to him. Had Newman held it, thought Carpenter, he would not have been so undermined in his Anglican allegiance by the Roman Catholic Nicholas Wiseman's citing of the maxim *securus iudicat orbis terrarum*, 'the whole world is a safe judge'. It was the Donatist crisis in the North Africa of the fourth and fifth centuries which make quantitative catholicity paramount in the West.

The second issue of the newly renamed journal was dominated by the Bulgakov proposal, as would be the conference of June that same year. But the editor noted how sacramentalism is possible without much in the way of personal experience of the power of the Holy Spirit. Perhaps that is why the more 'churchy' articles were preceded by a presentation, translated from a 1917 article by Bulgakov, of Symeon the New Theologian's *Hymns of Divine Love*. Symeon, as Bulgakov described him, was 'as a writer ... not anything exceptional'. He was not learned. The hymns are devoid of both metaphysical speculation and 'religious moralism'. Nonetheless, they 'give us a testimony of religious experience, shattering in its grandeur, vividness, and power. This experience may even terrify some of us, and serve as a stumbling-block because of its daring.'[59] They are certainly at some remove from the discussion of innovative ways to ecclesiastical reunion which followed.

Bulgakov's own 'Ways to Church Reunion' re-stated the case already made in 'By Jacob's Well' but with renewed, and rather original, argumentation. The eucharistic sacrament could be efficacious in acts of intercommunion if only there was no demand for maximal dogmatic agreement first. A minimal dogmatic agreement should suffice, and this Bulgakov defined not in the rather airy terms which Headlam had conjured up in the interests of Anglican comprehensiveness (compare Chapter 1 above) but in terms, rather, of what he called the 'dogmatic-canonical postulate[s] of the truth of the Eucharist'. He meant by that: any dogmatic truth demanded by the reality of the Eucharist must be accepted by all concerned. Bulgakov argued that the teaching of the Seven Councils comes into this category, since the dogmatic definitions of those councils state the Christology without which the eucharistic presence does not make sense. So does the doctrine of Holy Order as a sacrament, since what is at stake there is the 'efficacy of the celebrators as of the hierarchy of the "apostolic succession".'[60]

What, then, should be said of the status of other doctrines? Bulgakov replied:

> In the general context of dogmatic differences which separate the Churches, we must learn to discern the essentially important dogmatic teaching which finds its expression in Eucharistic dogma, and contrast it with other dogmatic assumptions which should be set aside as calling for further consideration and elaboration as theologumena. And we must also have faith that a union in Eucharistic love before the Holy Chalice will give us greater power to overcome them than tournaments between theologians which will *never* result in complete union, for the 'human', the all too human, always dominates them.[61]

There is in any case a 'certain hierarchy of order' in doctrine: not everything is equally important. This, the 'hierarchy of truths', would be a motif contributed by Yves Congar to debates on ecumenism at the Second Vatican Council,[62] after which gathering it soon became clear it was easily redefined by liberals to mean that not all truths are worth defending. Bulgakov anticipates the objection that these distinctions between doctrines as eucharistic or non-eucharistic, and more important or less important, would have the effect of undermining all claim of the Church to infallibility in teaching. He replied that such infallibility is misunderstood, in this objection, as a 'formal abstraction'.[63] Rather, it should be considered as the ability of the Church to meet the needs of dogmatic consciousness in each and every age.

His proposal might seem an assault on canonicity. Yet the alternative official route of 'diplomatic Reunion' would also require, to be successful, the consent of Church members. What he envisaged was movement into intercommunion not for any idiosyncratic *ecclesiola* on either side but for one, or more, entire dioceses, with their bishops, respectively Orthodox and Anglican. He put forward in embryo what would later be termed an ecclesiology of communion, proposing that the Church is to be conceived as a 'union of bishoprics'.[64]

How would Michael Ramsey, later archbishop of Canterbury at a high point of Anglicanism's opening to both Orthodoxy and Rome, seek to respond in 'Reunion and Intercommunion', his own contribution to this debate? He did not address Bulgakov's thinking directly though it is impossible to suppose he was unaware of the Russian theologian's mind on the matter. Ramsey's starting-point was the doctrine of the Church as the Body of Christ. In its light, much contemporary concern with Reunion was, he thought, 'full of sentimental and un-Catholic ideas', especially the notions that 'unity is a matter of human feelings and that the Eucharist is the focus of the Christians' feeling of fellowship rather than the act of Christ in His one Body'.[65] The Eucharist *is* the act of the one Body. Accordingly, Ramsey was not in any doubt. The proposal before the Fellowship could only augment sentimentalism. It would undermine the gain in eucharistic consciousness so far achieved in England. 'Looking for results' is not the way ahead, but if results are in view let there be a continuation of the conferences and an expansion of the educational work that surrounds them. He felt that 'the Orthodox consciousness is growing in the English Church' if 'not always in terms of Eastern Orthodox language and thought'.[66]

Bishop Frere, still the Fellowship's president, though he had little time to live, pointed out how the field of Reunion went beyond Anglicans and Orthodox, and there was need for patience. Could such a new shoot as the Fellowship expect to heal ancient divisions? God intends unity, yet he has also brought good out of the evil of division, in permitting a diversity which prevents a hard narrowness of thought. On a Parliamentary analogy, he suggested the Bulgakov proposal should go into a committee stage where it would be considered line by line. The Reverend C. S. Gillett, principal of Chichester Theological College, asked to respond in print as an attendee, supporting Ramsey's negative opinion, cautioning against the divisions that acts of intercommunion would create in the Anglo-Catholic movement. It would subvert the latter's opposition to the adoption of 'Open Communion' policies towards Free Churchmen on the part of Low Church Anglicans.

But the Bulgakov question had to be resolved in one way or another. In 'Intercommunion and Doctrinal Agreement' Gabriel Hebert maintained that these two factors are obviously linked.

> The liturgy as a whole may be called a great and complex confession of faith essential to our claim to be called Christian. Clearly then the doctrinal affirmation required of those who receive Communion can be none other than the common faith of the Church of God, into which we were baptized.[67]

Hebert did not care for any distinction even approximating to that between essential and non-essential articles of faith. Right belief is one and simple because it is response to the Gospel of God, even though all human understanding is only partial. A service of intercommunion attended by the specially qualified would be an outrage or at any rate a retrograde step—'less "catholic" than the liturgy as now celebrated by the members of those churches in the present state of schism'.[68]

Ramsey's address at the Fellowship conference at High Leigh in July 1938 on 'The Significance of Anglo-Orthodox Relations' sought to move away from this irresoluble dispute. Starting from a reading of the public ministry of Christ, Ramsey argued that a schism between doctrine, worship and life lies deeper than the inter-confessional schisms of Christendom. The Latin Church, which did not emerge well from this presentation, proposed to solve the problem of de-Christianization by the Thomist revival. 'Thomism claims to lead us to the wholeness that we need and to deliver us from the schisms of the intellectual life—but in fact it is, in relation to inward Orthodoxy, schismatic through and through.'[69] Revelation and faith become propositional, grace quantitative, the Church a corpus or institution. '[T]he Thomist revival can lead us far away from those Biblical and Greek conceptions which we so greatly need to recover.'[70] And criticizing Rome more generally, 'Authority and Infallibility lie not in a dogmatic scheme but in our Lord who dwells in us and is Himself the Truth'.[71] The Eastern Church *does* convey a sense of the unity of truth and worship and life: this is what Anglicans through the Fellowship have discovered. Perhaps the Orthodox can learn from Anglicans... Ramsey hesitated to say the importance of morality but 'that the Anglican tradition of moralism does contain an important orthodox truth'.[72] Did he know, one wonders, of an alleged remark by Charles Gore on returning from a visit to the East: 'Well, perhaps the Eastern Church beats us by being certainly in the Apostolic Succession, but we beat them by having the more Apostolic morals'?[73]

Dobbie-Bateman reported that a spat had broken out on the last evening of the conference about 'Latinism'. No doubt it was provoked by Ramsey's words.[74] Writing from South Africa, the Mirfield-trained G. W. H. Hewitt undertook to describe the forms sympathy for the Latin Church took among Anglo-Catholics. 'Many who profess a strong opposition to what is distinctively Roman Catholic are far more Roman than they realize; and often the most "moderate" church will show clear traces of Roman influence in decoration and ceremonial.'[75] More widely, the influence can be of seven kinds: private-devotional, beginning with Pusey who realized the need for models of popular prayers; ceremonial, among those who thought the Sarum revival antiquarian, and such a practice as genuflection before the Blessed Sacrament has entered even 'Prayer Book Catholic' churches; aesthetic, in the shape of vestments, altar arrangements, statuary—though a reaction against much of the common form of these in the Roman Church itself has disconcerted some; ascetic, in relation especially to the revival of the religious life and the practice of retreats; liturgical, in the use of parts at least of the Roman Missal, the acceptance of public devotions such as Benediction and Stations of the Cross; 'ecclesiastical' where loss of confidence in the English Reformers, awareness of the importance of reunion, and admiration for the doctrinal firmness of Rome have produced an Anglo-Papalism; 'dogmatic' in the form of openness to Scholasticism, systematic moral theology, and the writings of such distinguished authors as Maurice de la Taille and Friedrich von Hugel.

> Orthodox members of the Fellowship may find these considerations of use to them in their efforts to understand the Church of England. Anglican members, who have the advantage of acquaintance with another venerable Christian tradition, may well ponder which, if any, of the foregoing modes of Romanism they may with wisdom make their own.[76]

In the last issue of 1938, Thomas Parker's 'The Vision of Unity', subtitled 'The Future: Hopes and Fears', argued that the Russian Diaspora had already influenced Christian thought in the West in the direction of a 'rediscovery of the *differentiae* of Christianity and (in New Testament phraseology) "the world"', over against a 'tendency to equate or harmonize Christianity with the natural spirit, the very essence of Liberalism',[77] something not unknown in England since Newman had attacked it throughout the Tractarian revival—as his *Apologia pro vita sua* makes plain. The Diaspora influence could hardly have been fertile in the West had the ground not already been prepared, through the patristic and liturgical revivals in Tractarianism (the *Library of the Fathers* series, the liturgical work of John Mason Neale), and in Roman Catholicism through the Thomist revival and the movements of patristic and liturgical *ressourcement*. The Christian reaction has been 'by a return to the fountain heads of authentic Christianity, the Bible, regarded as the Word of God and not a vaguely inspired literature, the teaching of the Fathers and the sacred Liturgy, the living expression of Christian tradition.'[78] The Russian Diaspora helped, since a 'profound belief in the supernatural character of Christianity is the foundation of Russian religion, and is most perfectly expressed in the Byzantine liturgy, in which we find our deepest inspiration.'[79] What is needed now is time for the Church of England to expel the last remnants of Liberalism from her system. Parker admitted that intra-Anglican unity in the Church of England was not an immediate prospect, clearly disapproved of its official liturgical revision attempts ('illogical liturgical uniformity'[80]), and agreed that 'the fogbank of vagueness which recently engulfed Anglican theology is only beginning to lift.'[81] He took the opportunity to commend to the Orthodox the 'profundities of the Scholastic synthesis',[82] something Ramsey had just pooh-poohed. He also thought the connexions with Rumanian Orthodoxy—a Latin culture like our own ('the Church of England is Latin to the core')—providential,[83] not least because it would form a bridge to Greek and Slavonic Orthodoxy as well. In this regard, Parker had already divined what Allchin would discover—in the context of Staniloae's rise to fame and fortune—thirty years later.

The first number of the fateful year 1939 included Zernov on 'Obstacles and Opportunities'. Part of what he wrote he had been saying for some time, especially about ignorance (sometimes hiding behind a superiority complex) and prejudice or group fantasy. He noted that the pre-Great War political obstacles whereby the policies of Lambeth, the Phanar, and the Petersburg Holy Synod were determined by the politics of England, the Porte, and Russia were no more. But ecclesially speaking that by itself guarantees nothing. Not only is there an anti-Western Eastern prejudice, which assumes the West cannot but be heretical. There is also a Roman 'phantasy' which may be either excessive hatred, spilling over into dislike of the East for its sharing of much in Roman Christianity, or excessive liking which fears union with the East will introduce new problems into the search for union with Rome. Others again are pro-East because anti-Rome, seeing in the Orthodox world an ally against the Roman Church. Yet Zernov still thought an alliance of Anglicans with the Orthodox the only forward for Church reunion, since Rome will only have union by submission, while most Protestants will only have it in a diluted form of practical cooperation. The *soborny* or Orthodox–Catholic view of the Church is the only one able to 'provide the vague but widespread desire for unity with a sound theological foundation', for it stresses 'not so much the geographical universality of the Church as the all-embracing quality of its life in which each individual and every nation can find its proper place'.[84] It helps that (assuming the adequacy of the Bonn Conference of 1874–5 in resolving the Filioque dispute) Anglicans and the Orthodox have the same basic understanding of Bible, Creed, sacraments. Only the clause of the Creed on the Church really separates them and Anglican theologians should do more work on it. Thus the ever-optimistic Zernov.

Throughout these discussions the editor of *Sobornost* had been someone more theologically oriented to the Roman Church than he was (even) to the Orthodox. In the third issue of 1939, Eric Mascall's editorial advised looking at Clément Lialine's pamphlet *De la méthode irénique* (reprinted from *Irénikon*, and appearing in English dress in the *Eastern Churches Quarterly*) for 'any of our readers who may still be under the impression that Roman Catholics can do nothing as regards reunion beyond maintaining an attitude of incomprehending intransigence'.[85]

The 1940s

In the opening issue of the 1940s, the philosopher Evgeny Lampert offered a retrospect on the history of the Bulgakov proposal on intercommunion, giving the pros and cons as these had emerged over years of discussion.[86] As things turned out in the 1930s, the time had not been ripe. Opposition was too strong. Lampert gave his own comments in a sequel. Canonical invalidity does not equate with 'mystical and sacramental invalidity', and in terms of practice,

> The Church in various times and places has been far from uniform and has often gone beyond canonical qualifications in its relation to the sacraments performed in other confessions.[87]

As to dogmatic unanimity as a precondition of intercommunion:

> Dogmatic unity is primarily unity of experience, in love and unity of thought, it is *sobornost' realized in soborovanie* [the actualization of harmony], which may happen at many times and in many ways and as we have seen is often achieved partially.[88]

So, then, why should there not be such a thing as 'partial intercommunion'? But even Lampert thought the actualization of harmony needed to make some progress in relation to the understanding of the Church and the ordained priesthood, the sacraments (and notably the Eucharist itself), as well as in questions of Christology and Pneumatology, and the cult of the Mother of God. And this might be easier said than done.

As if in aid of this admonition, an anonymous missive specified ways in which Rome and Anglicanism were closer to each other than to Orthodoxy, and ways in which Rome and Orthodoxy were closer to each other than many Anglicans might like to suppose. Two robust letters, from Moss and Edward Every respectively, were received in reply. Moss repeated his warning not to let Roman Catholics into the Fellowship: they could not be trusted to refrain from proselytism.

In 1943 Brandreth returned to a topic he had considered before which sounded alarm-bells for pro-Orthodox Anglicans. This was the issue of Presbyterian-Anglican union, under active consideration in the United States. He investigated for readers the deficiencies in a 1942 document, 'Basic Principles proposed for the Union of the Presbyterian Church in the USA and the Protestant Episcopal Church in the USA', which treated the bishop/presbyter distinction as one of administrative functioning not ministerial order, and gave hostages to fortune in the brevity of its reference to Bible and Creeds as the rule of faith. Brandreth commented on the implications for Orthodoxy.

> The relations between Anglicanism and the historic Orthodox Churches have been steadily improving during the past hundred years and this movement for Anglican–Orthodox rapprochement is not just the work of a small and extreme section of the Anglican Church, it is the work of the whole body led by its responsible leaders. These good relations, moreover, have been achieved because of definite assurances given by the Anglican Church at various times as to the way in which Anglicanism generally interprets the doctrines of the Church, the Ministry, the Sacraments, and so forth, as set out in the Book of Common Prayer. Is Anglicanism now to turn round

and deny the validity of all those assurances made on her behalf in good faith, ratified in her synods, and accepted at face value by those to whom they were made? Such a step would be inconceivable if it were not now, apparently, contemplated.[89]

In 1948 there was poor news, ecumenically speaking, on a variety of fronts: Amsterdam, Moscow, and Lambeth. That year Florovsky had addressed the first Assembly of the World Council of Churches in Amsterdam, but the Ecumenical Patriarchate which he helped to represent was somewhat minoritarian among the Orthodox Churches in sending participants. Moscow, and the Churches in the Soviet satellites stayed away. Florovsky found in ecumenism as currently organized a lack of Christian initiative: 'we face the challenge of the world instead of challenging the world ourselves'.[90] And in any case agreement on secular issues, could it be reached by Christians, would only suggest that doctrinal disagreements were of no vital importance. A 'common Christian front is not yet ... the *Una Sancta*'.[91] Only a deep theological consensus would do. Florovsky warned against thinking this could be pan-Protestant or indeed non-Roman, for, like Moscow, Rome was self-excluded. Rome, thought Florovsky, must be included—not 'the present Rome, but the truth and heritage for which Rome stood and is still standing, in spite of all that should be said against "Romanism"'.[92] But 'one step' might do for now, citing Newman's 'glorious verses'.[93] The speech was not the sour grapes of an outsider to official ecumenism. Florovsky, who had made his name as an ecumenist at the 1937 Edinburgh Conference on Faith and Order, had been elected, while in Scotland, a member of the 'Provisional Committee to Prepare for the World Council of Churches', and had regularly commuted to Geneva for the two previous years on this account. His criticisms did not prevent his election while in the Netherlands to the Central and Executive Committees of the new World Council, and reappointment to its Continuation Committee on Faith and Order. And he could console himself that he was one of those responsible for getting through the Assembly a formula important to the Orthodox (and also to Roman Catholics, for that matter): 'God has given to His people in Jesus Christ a unity which is His creation and not our achievement'.[94] Michael Ramsey, already important to the Fellowship and later, as bishop and archbishop to be more so, was there as well. His biographer Owen Chadwick commented, 'The cold war condemnations of Moscow and the obsessive rigidity of Rome elevated Florovsky, on that stage, into a

Ecumenical Prospects

mouthpiece of the eastern Catholic tradition, and elevated Ramsey into a mouthpiece of the western Catholic tradition' in his turn.[95]

Zernov had also been present at Amsterdam. While paying tribute to its spiritual atmosphere and the intellectual quality of the addresses he described it as 'essentially the meeting ground between the broken fragments of those Churches which passed through the Reformation'.[96] It was dominated by Americans and the British. Lutherans failed to find a voice of their own, some tending towards 'Catholic', some towards 'Reformed'. The absence of the Orthodox except for the Church of Greece and for Constantinople was striking. Neither the World Council of Churches as currently existing nor 'the Eastern Churches as they stand at present' are ready for 'full cooperation'.[97] As to the Anglicans, their divisions on the subject of Church and ministry were painfully apparent. Several of their bishops communicated at the Calvinist service where the celebrating minister had warned that those who invoke dead saints, angels or other creatures have no place at the Lord's Table. In Zernov's view this did not help. The poor attendance at any eucharistic services held on weekdays showed the delegates had not learned the lesson of the Fellowship.

That was Amsterdam, what of Moscow? By 'Moscow' was meant in this context the five-hundredth anniversary celebrations of Muscovite autocephaly—though the meeting was avoided by the representatives of Constantinople and Greece, whereas the Churches of Georgia, Serbia, Rumania, Bulgaria, Albania, Alexandria and Antioch took part. Edward Every's report in *Sobornost* was downbeat, understandably so given the negative comments about Anglicanism in the patriarch's address. The patriarch had been asked by Canterbury to recognize Anglican Orders; he declined to do so, citing the lack of compelling arguments. The sacramentology of the 39 Articles does not correspond with that of Orthodoxy. The recognition of Anglican Orders by other Orthodox Churches was conditional. The question of validity cannot be answered without an authoritative confessional act of Anglicans affirming unity of faith with Orthodoxy. On the World Council the patriarch was stronger still: 'Efforts by means of social and political activity and the creation of an Oecumenical Church as an international influence are like falling into the temptation which Christ refused in the desert'.[98] The reduction of the requirements of World Council membership to confession of Christ as Son of God do not go beyond what is possible for the demons (compare

James 2:19, 'Even the demons believe—and shudder'). Every made the best of it. Anglicans should have noted the conditionality the Orthodox always attached to their recognition of Anglican Orders. At any rate nothing was said negatively about the tactual succession or the ordinal. And it is as well that Anglicans should realize how

> doubts are arising as to whether our church believes in the sacramental character of ordination and in the apostolic succession as a matter of doctrine, and that these doubts, for some people at least, affect the question as to whether we actually have the succession in any significant sense.[99]

That left Lambeth, on which a member of the Fellowship wrote anonymously. Much of the comment was critical of the lack of clarity about faith and order in the new 'Church of South India' which had absorbed large numbers of Anglican clergy and laity from the four dioceses of Madras, Travancore and Cochin, Tinnevelly and Dornakal. Little had been said at Lambeth about the Eastern Churches, though there had been a request for a new commission to work with Constantinople. The unnamed reporter was inclined to think that, in the context of the revival of Moscow, the singling out of that see might be unwise.

Around this time *Sobornost* showed several signs of fissure in the traditional High Anglican/Orthodox hegemony in the Fellowship. Two articles in 1949 indicated a continuing openness to a wider Protestantism. Jack Newport discussed his time as a Congregationalist observing Parisian Orthodoxy: '[O]ur Fellowship has a part to play in building up a new confidence between the Orthodox–Catholic position and the Reformed, as well as in exploring the somewhat different problem of the relationship between Anglicanism and Orthodoxy'.[100] And Eric Segelberg reported on the Whitby conference of that year between Anglicans and Swedish Lutherans.[101] Meanwhile, Allchin, attending his first Fellowship conference, noted the presence at the 1949 Abingdon gathering of Bouyer, Lialine, and Winslow—all Roman Catholics. This was the conference where, among very varied activities, Mascall launched his comic poem 'The Thomist and the Palamite', no doubt part of what Allchin was lauding when he wrote:

> One could not be struck by the wisdom which had shaped the Fellowship, and realized that only in common life do the diverse parts of a single Christian tradition, let alone of many, fall into a proper perspective.[102]

Ecumenical Prospects

Finally, the twenty-first year of the Fellowship's life and the end of the 1940s found Helle Giorgiadis in reflective mood.

> If there had been hopes of 'reunion in our time' for Orthodox and Anglican, these have receded in the last fifteen years. It has been the proof of the Fellowship's vocation that its vigour has not depended on the nearness of its objective. Looking back on past disappointments one might even say that the very failure of the responsible authorities of the two traditions to effect a more positive understanding has preserved the Fellowship from the temptation of exclusive provincialism.[103]

Evidently, she had participant Congregationalists and Lutherans, as well as visiting Catholics, in her mind. Was, then, the Fellowship to enter an ecumenical melting-pot? In the wake of shifting tectonic plates in the wider ecumenical movement, soon to include Roman Catholics as it was, the question might have been considered open.

The 1950s

The Zernovs began the decade in Greece, on their first visit, undertaken in part so as to make contacts for the Fellowship. They reported that the 'apostasy of the westernized classes and the ignorance of the common people' had been 'convincingly met' by the twentieth-century movements for re-evangelization and visited the printing house of the Zoe Brotherhood, where the noted Greek dogmatician Panayiotis Trembelas showed them round.[104] They claimed a 'distinct return to the Church among intellectuals in Greece, both professors and students'; these included Fellowship members.[105] They approved of a newly built neo-Byzantine Athenian church, Hagios Dionysios, richly provided with mosaic and fresco, as a sign of the revival of the style after the decadence of the nineteenth century, and were moved by popular piety on the islands, notably Tinos, the 'Lourdes' of Greece. The world is conflictual, yet permits human lives to cross in a remarkable way. 'It is not by chance that we found our way to Athens through London and Oxford, and that the Fellowship starting in snow-bound England when Russian and English students met in 1928 has found its footing in remote and sunny Greece.'[106]

Meanwhile Zernov had been perusing the papers and resolutions contained in 'The Acts of Consultation of the Heads and Representatives of the Autocephalous Orthodox Churches', the official title of the gathering held under Stalinist auspices in 1948 in connection with the fifth centenary of the autocephalous existence of the Russian Church. Zernov skipped the section on Roman Catholicism which had given offence to ecumenically minded Catholics, notably in France. More forgivably, he also avoided the discussion of the Church calendar. He concentrated on the sections devoted to 'The Anglican Hierarchy' and 'The Oecumenical Movement and the Orthodox Church'. The discussion of the former had been heated. The conference resolution 'expressed the readiness of the Orthodox Church to recognize Anglican orders if and when the Anglican Church formulates more precisely its teaching on the sacraments in general and on Holy Orders in particular'.[107] On ecumenism more widely, a Romanian professor urged full participation commending the work of the Russian exiles in Paris; Metropolitan Stefan of Sofia explained it was owing to the political activities of Reunionists that the Bulgarian Church had not gone to Amsterdam, and a Russian archpriest appealed to other Orthodox Churches to follow the example of Moscow and refrain from all official involvement, since for the Church the 'establishment of social justice by means of international agreements and political actions is outside its proper sphere'.[108] Zernov put a brave face on it. The meeting 'showed the underlying unity of Orthodox thought and the keen interest of the Orthodox world in Christendom at large'.[109]

The first issue of 1951 was prefaced by a letter from the president, Bishop Rawlinson seeking to allay an anxiety. In his book *The Problems of Reunion* he had given priority to organic union with non-episcopal Protestant Churches: 'Evangelical Christianity'.[110] He explained this was only because it was the most feasible of the Reunion propositions—but, he said, it made all the more necessary growth in knowledge of, and contacts with, the Orthodox and Roman Catholics as a 'corrective against any mere sliding into "Pan-Protestantism"'.[111] The opposition he aroused has been charted in Chapter 2 above. Some Fellowship members looked back longingly to the days of Bishop Frere and the great Anglo-Catholic congresses.

A start to the journal's interest in Methodism, or at any rate the hymnology of the Wesleys, was made by Hodges who found in the Wesley brothers a 'lost Anglican doctrine of the spiritual life'. What he had in mind was the concern of the Wesleys with both evangelical conversion (here they were influenced by their encounter with the pietism of the Moravian brethren) and with Christian perfection or 'scriptural holiness' (an inheritance from the Catholic tradition in the Church of England).[112] Hodges pointed out that the former is generally dependent on a strict doctrine of justification by faith alone, while the latter is often regarded as incompatible with such a doctrine since it will always tend to bring in 'works righteousness', the implacable foe of *fide sola*, by the back door. It was the genius of John Wesley's sermons and Charles Wesley's hymns to synthesize these two seeming incompatibles—and the fact that the Wesleys were lost to the Established Church was, in this perspective, a spiritual tragedy. Hodges mused on what the Church of England might have been had it married to the nineteenth-century Catholic Revival a 'Methodist Order' of evangelical enthusiasts. Hodges argued that Anglicanism cannot become more than a set of parties until it recovers a synthesis between the Evangelical Protestantism of the 39 Articles and some of the Tudor *Homilies* and the writing of its divines, on the one hand, and the Catholic spirit of the *Book of Common Prayer* on the other. This essay was deep but easy to read.

In 1952 Zernov reported on the Third Faith and Order Conference in Lund. Some five years previously the Faith and Order Movement had been transformed into a commission of the World Council of Churches. Zernov considered that, paradoxically, the growth of the ecumenical spirit was accompanied by an 'accentuation of the impediments to reconciliation'.[113] He listed them for readers. The number of ecumenists had increased so that they were now at very different stages of development in their understanding and expertise. Delegates were now Church officials, with the theologians present only as consultants. Discussion of intercommunion— owing presumably to the two factors just mentioned—was lacking in nuance; the mental comparison was surely with the Bulgakov proposals. Yet Zernov thought the tiny Orthodox contingent had an influence altogether beyond its numbers.

There was clearly some irritation in the Fellowship at what was seen as Zernov's apparently limitless ecumenical optimism. In 1953 Derwas Chitty produced a lengthy and rather ruthless review (effectively a review article) of Nicolas Zernov's latest manifesto, *The Reintegration of the Church*.[114] Chitty recognized Zernov's contribution to ecumenism as unique, yet warned that 'the Fellowship should not be too closely identified with his statements and policies'.[115] Identifying weaknesses as logician, historian and dogmatician, Chitty felt that Zernov 'has become too much acclimatized to the twilight of a student liberalism—a world which is really not his own ... the world which is shy of the compelling objectivity of the Truth, the world of puzzled Christians'.[116] The chief point of Zernov's study had been to re-make the case for some version of Bulgakov's proposals on intercommunion. This testified to the purity of Zernov's ecumenical zeal but not necessarily to wisdom or indeed to an orthodox mind-set. Yet in the chapter of the book on 'the Healing Power of the Eucharist', so Chitty wrote,

> we feel that we are here very near the heart of the personal religion of one who, however much he may outwardly take on the colour of his non-Orthodox surroundings, remains at heart a simple and humble Russian Orthodox believer. We might criticize in detail. We might perhaps ask whether he has fallen in some measure under Western influence in concentrating his attention *in* the Eucharist rather than looking *through* it, with a certain resultant loss of proportion in regard to the totality of the Life of the Church of which it stands at the heart. But we prefer not to criticize here. We know that our friend writes of that which is of all things the most precious to him; wherein he rightly feels the key of unity to life; and which he yearns, generously and passionately, to share with others.[117]

Writing in 1954, Zernov defended his re-launch of Bulgakov's proposal, now under the name 'controlled intercommunion', emphasizing not only the healing power of the Eucharist but also the fact that within any Church there will always be those with sinful habits and heterodox views who nevertheless communicate at its altars. He suspected Chitty of thinking that the health of a Church depends on its correction or expulsion of such members. He had come across another review, also in an Anglican source, which advised those wanting the genuine Orthodox standpoint to avoid lay theologians (such as Zernov of course was), and deplored the lack of concrete detail in what he envisaged as 'control'. Zernov accepted this latter criticism. He now put forward the idea of a 'Sacrament of Reconciliation' to be constituted from elements of the sacraments of Penance, Chrismation, and Ordination, as a means of entry to communicant status in another Church-body. It might work even between episcopal and non-episcopal bodies, but would require discernment of those 'duly prepared for the work of reconciliation'.[118] The Fellowship did not rally to these proposals, finding the said 'sacrament' to be disturbingly vague.

Realism in ecumenism was the hallmark of Helle Giorgiadis's report as Orthodox secretary of the Fellowship that year. Speaking of an additional conference that July in Stamford, she wrote, 'At the end of four full days everyone knew exactly where each stood, and though this in practical ecumenics usually means deadlock, spiritually it bears fruit in deeper integrity of friendship'.[119] She recommended emphasis on home ecumenism rather than globetrotting: 'those at home are quick to detect imperfections in our good intentions'. She added, 'Because the Fellowship is concerned with persons and not with institutions, we have, as an unofficial organization, great opportunities for seeking unity in truth and love'.[120] Her Anglican opposite number evidently agreed with her. '[I]t may confidently be assumed that the day of large-scale theological interchange has passed', as a result of succumbing to the 'new totalitarianism' which 'does not permit or require the atmosphere or the method in which serious understanding must be sought'.[121] The temper of Eric Hayman's words was clearly reaction to a perceived shift at Lund towards a federalist concept of Reunion, which, frankly, fitted best the concept of the World Council with its own quasi-federal structure. Hayman called the theological atmosphere of Lund 'eschatological despair'.[122] It ignored the worship of God to concentrate instead upon a pilgrim people—defined by the writer as a refugee people whose only living tradition is grief. There was 'no apparent knowledge of [Christ's] continuing presence in the Church by His sacramental grace'.[123]

The new president, Michael Ramsey, then bishop of Durham, would not have agreed. In a brief but telling message, summarizing the story of Orthodox–Anglican relations since 1920, he gave it as his belief that 1955 marked the start of a new and hopeful phase. The Church of England was about to starts talks with Moscow, while the Church of South India question, over which many Anglo-Catholics had agonized (and some had 'gone over' to Rome[124]) now lay behind them. 'The need is for the continuance in the Church of that interior quest for Orthodoxy within her own life, which must go hand in hand with friendship with the Holy Orthodox Church.'[125] If changes come to the Church of England, it should be a matter of giving fuller expression to the 'orthodox life' she has always possessed.[126]

As already noted, *Sobornost* and the wider Fellowship had previously shown some interest in the Non-Chalcedonian Eastern Churches, though the latter were not, at this stage of its history, fully part of its remit. On the other hand, some of the Chalcedonian Orthodox (who *were* its remit) had recently demonstrated enthusiasm for rapprochement with their Non-Chalcedonian separated brethren, and thus the 'Oriental Orthodox' swam by an indirect route into the Fellowship's ken. In 1954 a special Committee of the Fellowship had been formed to look into this; it included a Jacobite and a Copt. The Assyrians were not in question, so a general adhesion to Cyrillianism could safely be maintained. The question could be raised, however, how Cyrilline was Chalcedon? This is not an issue where professional patrologists speak with one voice. Not surprisingly, then, the account of the Committee's deliberations in this number reported a degree of deadlock.

> Most of the Orthodox members of the Committee felt that even if the Credal orthodoxy of the Oriental Churches was to be conceded, the value of the Chalcedonian definition remained... The Orthodox Church regards the Seven Councils as inviolably sacred and they cannot at the moment come into communion with any church which does not have the same attitude to the Councils.[127]

C. A. Abraham, evidently expressing the Syrian Jacobite view, raised a question more associated with Roman Catholics:

> How would the Orthodox explain the discontinuance of the Councils after 1054? What valid distinction can be made between the rejection of Chalcedon and subsequent Councils by the Oriental Churches and the rejection of the Councils held by the Roman Church after 1054 by the Orthodox Church?[128]

Abraham hoped that use could be made of the modern ecumenical movement to go beyond the historic stalemates. The despatch of an elaborate questionnaire under the joint names of Zernov and himself (replies to Zernov, care of Keble College, Oxford) suggested that one means to 'better understanding and closer co-operation between our two groups' might be 'joint support of the societies working for Christian unity, e. g. The Fellowship of St Alban and St Sergius'.[129]

There was not long to wait for a follow-up to Zernov's new enthusiasm for relations with the Oriental Orthodox. It transpired that 'informal discussions' between the Orthodox and the Oriental Orthodox had been held in Kottayam (in Kerala) in 1953 to 1954. The Syrian Orthodox of Malabar—until 1910 under the jurisdiction of the Syrian metropolitan of Homs, but since that date with an autonomous Catholicos—were calculated to be some 350 thousand in number with ten bishops and 250 priests and deacons. They had already shown active interest in ecumenism, and more especially in contact with the Russian, Serbian, and Greek Orthodox Churches. Zernov had himself been a member—but presumably was asked to treat the dialogue as a confidential matter. In 1956, however, extracts from the discussion had appeared in the *Journal of the Moscow Patriarchate*, and Zernov reproduced these for *Sobornost* readers in the summer of 1957. A writer in the Patriarchal jurisdiction, professor at the Leningrad Theological Academy, admitted that 'the Malabar Christians have retained some formulas akin to the Monophysite doctrines', but concluded that 'nevertheless they hold the true teaching about the unity of two natures, Divine and human, in the single hypostasis of our Lord Jesus Christ'.[130] The 'Group' (as already mentioned, discussion was informal) recommended the adoption of the terminology 'Byzantine' and 'Oriental' Orthodox, proposed a reconciliation with unity of doctrine but diversity of liturgy and identified three key problems: the language of Christology, the number of the ecumenical councils, and disparity in recognizing or failing to recognize certain fathers of the Church 'and some other liturgical and canonical distinctions'.[131]

The conclusions were, on Christology, that the 'nature of the incarnate Lord is mono-dual, one and two at the same time ... without forming a third nature' (and the same was asserted of the question of the will or wills of the Saviour);[132] on the councils, that the Oriental Orthodox agree that the 'positive decisions' of the Fourth, Fifth, Sixth and Seventh Councils contain nothing *contra fidem*, and will after reconciliation with the Byzantine Orthodox consider what elements from the decrees of those councils they can incorporate by synodical decision; on the saints (where Dioscorus was for them a Father, and Leo a heretic) that each side will remove from its service books any condemnation of figures respected by the other. These results were not significantly advanced by further, more official, dialogue, in later decades, including up to the present (2018).

Of more immediate consequence for the Fellowship was Michael Ramsey's report on the Anglo-Russian theological conversations of 1956 in Moscow. He recognized the conversations had not been easy. The Russians remained dissatisfied with the 39 Articles. They insisted on the wholeness of Tradition. They saw Creeds and Councils as more than safeguarding or expressing orthodox faith, for Creeds and Councils were essential to its content. Ramsey felt they had not really grasped the role of historical context, or the limitations of theological language. But he was, he said, 'not made anxious'.[133]

Patrick Rodger, at one time Scottish Episcopal Chaplain to students at Edinburgh University (and later bishop of Manchester), a Scot by birth, and indeed from a Presbyterian family, reported in his turn on the 1957 joint report of conversations between Anglicans and Presbyterians (following on those of 1932 and 1934, between English Anglicans and Scots Presbyterians only, which were abruptly broken off owing to disagreement about ministry, and exchanges in 1950–1 which had included voices from the Scottish Episcopal Church and the Presbyterian Church of England). Rodger supported the Church of South India, so he was looking for a diplomatic success of which the 'South India Scheme' would be the model. The aim was full communion and mutual recognition of ministries. The proposals were: moderators to be superseded by 'bishops in presbytery'; episcopal Confirmation to be optional, and perhaps shared by the bishop and the parish minister acting together. Anglicans were not happy about the latter, and, though Presbyterians recommended greater freedom of self-governance for the Church of England, more stress on the preaching office, and smaller dioceses, it turned out that the Scottish Press was up in arms about the whole thing. That was owing to 'the immense force of a so-called non-theological factor, that of Scottish nationalism—*not* political separatism [this was yet to come], but the insistence on a way of life, including religious practice, which must at all costs be distinctive and different from that of England'.[134] Whether influenced by the journalists or not, most Presbyteries rejected the plan, though it had been given another year for consideration by the General Assembly. At the time of writing (1959), the Church of England had yet to speak, since Anglican leaders wanted the Lambeth Conference to comment—though some said the delay was in the hope that Presbyterian intransigence would kill off the scheme first.

The Fellowship's 1959 conference had also taken the ordained ministry as its topic. Various clouds no larger than a man's hand were spotted. A Swedish Lutheran spoke about the determination of the Swedish State to impose the ordination of women. Derwas Chitty said, rather surprisingly, that no complete reunion scheme was possible without attending to the primacy of Rome, and raised a cheer. There were alleged to be 'an increasing number of Anglicans who look more and more to the Orthodox for guidance and help in the very difficult times through which the Anglican Communion is passing'.[135] That raised the possibility of some Western members of the Fellowship jumping ship. The advent of the 1960s increased the chances of that happening exponentially, for in the course of the decade, which was marked by profound cultural corrosion and the construction of that vast ecclesial building-yard the Second Vatican Council, the Western Churches sometimes gave the impression they were on the verge of melt-down.

The 1960s

The opening number of the 1960s offered an overview of the current state of ecumenical affairs. Much was made of the meeting on Rhodes of representatives of the Central Committee of the World Council of Churches together with representatives of the Orthodox autocephalies, including Moscow. The activities on the island of two Roman ecumenists—Mgr Jan Willebrands, later archbishop of Utrecht, and Père Pierre Dumont of the 'White Fathers', in due course a fixture at the Secretariat for the Unity of Christians where Willebrands would be for a while the head—had been construed as a Vatican plot to 'separate' the Orthodox from the World Council.[136] Some conservative Roman Catholics might have commented, 'If only'.

Sobornost's summer 1961 editorial could boast that the Fellowship's president had been translated to Canterbury—and he was no ordinary president at that. 'No Archbishop of Canterbury in recent times has been as devoted to overcoming the schism between East and West as the 100th Archbishop, Arthur Michael Ramsey,' wrote a member of the International Commission of the Anglican–Orthodox Dialogue (that sobriquet would replace in 1989 a previous title, 'The Anglican–Orthodox Joint Doctrinal Discussions'); here William Green was looking back from the vantage point of the early twenty-first century.[137] Looking ahead, *Sobornost*'s editor, Donald Allchin, rightly saw 1962 as likely to be significant for ecumenism. It proved to be more so for relations with Rome than with the Orthodox. Allchin wrote an enthusiastic article-length review of the two-volume *Mission et unité* by the (now sadly underrated) French Dominican ecumenist Marie-Jean Le Guillou.[138] After hailing the work's 'amazing spirit of charity and balance, its continuous effort for universality, comprehensiveness and fullness of understanding', Allchin went on to remark:

> by standing apart from the main activity of the movement for Christian Unity, the Roman Catholic Church has given to some

of its members a possibility of seeing that movement as a whole, and discerning the true proportions and significance of its work.[139]

Le Guillou's work represented 'an ecclesiology which while faithful to the Roman position will do justice to all that is positive in other concepts of the church'.[140]

The Pan-Orthodox Conference on Rhodes in the autumn of 1961 had been the other reason why Allchin thought East-West relations were entering a momentous phase. Now it had happened and was anonymously reported in the first *Sobornost* of 1962. All autocephalous Churches were represented except Albania, though Georgia was there via Russian proxy. The meeting was concerned, however, only with drawing up an agenda for a future pro-synod (faith and dogma; worship; ecclesiastical order and administration; inter-Orthodox relations; relations between Orthodoxy and the rest of the Christian world; social problems)—so this was hardly a general council in a teaching sense, though that did not prevent it from promulgating a 'Message'. The Message was given in the name of 'our One and Undivided Church' but it described the communion thus designated as 'our local and national Orthodox Churches' and 'our local national Orthodox sister Churches'—even though there has been, historically, some very reasonable Orthodox resistance to using the word 'national' as an epithet of 'Church'.[141] The identification of de facto Orthodoxy with the de jure undivided Church was dispiriting for Anglicans, but it did not necessarily impair ecumenism on the affective (as distinct from effective) level. Ramsey had sent the participants a message of his own in which he said, 'From the day of my Enthronement as Archbishop of Canterbury there has been no desire in my heart greater than to see deeper friendship with the Holy Orthodox Church'.[142]

That confession fitted well with Ramsey's lecture 'The Ancient Fathers and Modern Anglican Theology', given to a gathering of Anglicans and Old Catholics on the same day as he wrote to Rhodes (19 September 1961), and now made available in *Sobornost*. Whatever the speaker's friendliness to the Orthodox, the lecture could certainly not be described as eirenical vis-à-vis Rome. It started uncompromisingly: 'It was the desire of the English Reformers of the sixteenth century to recover the doctrines of Holy Scripture, and to show that these had been the doctrines of the primitive Church in contrast with Roman innovations and errors'.[143] Ramsey then rehearsed the familiar story (already set out in the early pages of the present study) of Anglican attraction to patristic inspiration. Ramsey gave a distinctive Anglican–Catholic spin to the formal position in fundamental theology when he declared that 'while Scripture was the supreme standard of faith, the Fathers represented the tradition of the Church by which Scripture was rightly interpreted' (and did not merely, then, confirm the authentic voice of Scripture arrived at by intra-biblical means).[144] He stressed the way that seventeenth-century Anglican divines, not sharing the obsession of Continental Protestants with the issues of justification and predestination, were able to recover the Incarnation-centredness of the 'Fathers of the Nicene age', and, moreover, to be saved from 'western narrowness' by emphasizing the Greek patristic contribution, which in turn created the desire to reach out to Eastern Christendom.[145] Inevitably Ramsey had to praise the Tractarians for their 'massive' deployment of the texts of the Fathers but he also suggested they sometimes 'lacked historical discrimination' in regard to both 'facts and concepts'—citing the example of Newman (was this accidental?) on apostolic succession, in the first of the *Tracts for the Times*. Ramsey admitted that the authority Anglicans accord the Fathers is less defined than with the Old Catholics who in that respect are closer to Orthodoxy than is Anglicanism, but he also pleaded for Old Catholics and Anglicans together to reach out to the Christian East.

In winter 1962 *Sobornost* notched up a new writer for its pages, one who was distinguishing himself as that lonely petrel a Greek ecumenist. This was Nikos Nissiotis, already mentioned in the last chapter as one of the bright young things among the new generation of theologians in the Church of Greece. Speaking at the 1961 New Delhi Assembly of the World Council of Churches Nissiotis addressed the issue of 'The Witness and the Service of Eastern Orthodoxy to the One Undivided Church'.

> The unique contribution of Orthodoxy to the discussion on Church unity lies in its simple reminder that the unbroken continuity of the life of the historical Church has a far greater authority than any confessional statement of a local church which attempts to explain and justify its separateness. The life of the Church in itself and by itself is the most solid authority because it perpetuates the event of Pentecost[146]

when the Holy Spirit 'accomplished the communion of mankind in Christ'.[147] He described the service of unity as an 'obligation arising from the very essence of Orthodoxy itself',[148] giving as his first concrete example the unlikely one for a Greek Orthodox of the Roman primacy:

> The Orthodox *martyria* for unity must include psychological and theological preparation for the restoration of this function of the undivided Church as one of the most fundamental means of preserving unity.[149]

Boris Bobrinskoy, professor of dogmatics at Saint-Serge, had spoken at New Delhi on much the same theme, and turned his presentation into a sermon preached in a Calvinist church in Paris for the 1962 Unity Octave, with Catholics officially present some months before the Second Vatican Council opened. Bobrinskoy was generous in his remarks to both Protestants and Catholics but they would have been disappointed if they were expecting a less than complete statement of the unique claims of Orthodoxy. It was, however, a dogmatic claim rendered in a remarkably humble and even penitent tone of voice. Through their separated brethren the Orthodox were discovering their own tradition in its fulness. They owed Protestants and Catholics gratitude and admiration, just as they should also show penitence for their inattention to the best that 'Rome and the Reformation have produced in spirituality, in doctrine, in Biblical exegesis'.[150] Such penitence should also extend to the way the Orthodox have failed to give value to the spiritual experience of the saints of their own Church—all of which constitutes a common patrimony for Christianity as a whole, as can already be seen in the way, for instance, Taizé uses the Rublev icon, or a Catholic ashram in India discovers the Jesus Prayer. But, he went on, 'these borrowings seem only partial and peripheral, and to lack the cement which might join the fragments of a homogenous tradition into a harmonious and organic Christian life'.[151] By contrast, in Orthodoxy everything is connected up—'asceticism, spirituality, the doctrine of the Trinity, the mystery of man, ecclesiology, liturgical forms and artistic expression',[152] though the Orthodox must show humility, indeed self-effacement, vis-à-vis the 'reality of God and ... the beauty of his house' if they are to be effective witnesses to this truth.[153] Bobrinskoy recommended his fellow-Orthodox to make an end of 'sterile polemics' and to abstain from calling the separated brethren to return to the first eight centuries, for 'the time of history is irreversible'.[154] Still, there was here a call to the non-Orthodox to discover a communion with an Orthodoxy itself renewed.

Ecumenical Prospects

The Second Vatican Council was soon in full session and Canon Roger Greenacre applauded the Melkite patriarch Maximos IV's edition of speeches made in its aula during its opening phase.[155] The need, highlighted by Maximos, to have a double but equal loyalty (to Rome and to Byzantine Orthodoxy) had a parallel in the situation of the Anglo-Papalists in the Church of England—who, so Greenacre believed, ought to show more *pietas anglicana*.

The council ended its sessions in 1965 but *Sobornost*'s first editorial for that year was dominated rather by reportage of the visit of Patriarch Alexei of Moscow to Britain in the autumn of 1964, a return compliment for Ramsey's visit to Russia in 1962. It was the first time a Russian patriarch had visited Britain (just as Ramsey was the first archbishop of Canterbury to go to Russia) so the space spent on formal speeches, and descriptions of ceremonies was justified. At Lambeth on 28 September 1964 Alexei declared:

> both on the part of the Church of England and on the part of the Russian Orthodox Church the will to holy brotherly union does not weaken... The Russian Orthodox Church attaches the greatest importance to efforts to elucidate the real prospects of Orthodoxy and Anglicanism coming together on the path to unity of faith.[156]

A joint theological commission was, accordingly, essential both between the two communions as a whole and in the form of conversations between the two national Churches in particular, and here the patriarch did not hesitate to stress that progress in friendly contacts would have wider social and political implications for the United Kingdom and the Soviet Union.

Not that, by making so much editorial space for the Muscovite visit, Allchin intended to draw a veil over the contemporary happenings in St Peter's. The Conciliar decisions were clearly set to be transformative for the Roman Catholic Church and would have implications, not all of them by any means happy, for Anglo-Catholicism in the Church of England and elsewhere. For the spring 1965 issue Allchin wrote a major essay on 'Ecumenical Perspectives'. By this time Paul VI had met Athenagoras I in Jerusalem (neutral territory), and the Conciliar documents *Lumen gentium* (on the nature of the Church) and *Unitatis redintegratio* (on Christian unity) had been promulgated. They could only herald a new era, the latter in ecumenism, the former by softening the authoritarian and juridical image of the Roman Catholic Church at large. The November 1964 meeting of the Orthodox on Rhodes seemed disappointing by comparison, but it did at least decide to reopen conversations with Anglicans (no doubt Alexei's words in London were effective) and with the Old Catholics. And by simply deferring a like decision in regard to Rome until after the council had ended it had not flung shut the door. But it did not act on the 1964 Aarhus consultation between the Chalcedonian and Non-Chalcedonian Orthodox, hopeful as this had seemed for overcoming the schisms dating ultimately from 451.

And now Allchin grasped a thistle. The World Council was worried about the possibility that Rome would seize the initiative in ecumenical matters, and notably that it would seek an Orthodox–Catholic dialogue separate from the rest, even to the point of detaching the Orthodox from the World Council altogether. This was not a total fantasy. Some bishops at the Vatican Council *did* think in terms of a new ecumenism concentrating on Churches of a Catholic type. The general secretary of the World Council and its representative at the council were tempted to propose instead a Protestant-Orthodox coalition of all who rejected the Roman primacy. This would-be counter-measure did not please the editor of *Sobornost*. The Orthodox, and many Anglicans for that matter, did not reject the primacy for the reasons classical Protestants did. Their reasons were less radical. The Orthodox and the Roman Catholics recognize each other in a way that neither of them recognizes Protestants or even Anglicans. To say they should not be permitted a bilateral dialogue of their own was odd. The World Council had no official blueprint for unity, but its trend in such matters was undoubtedly chiefly Protestant in character. It must become in the future, Allchin urged, 'more genuinely ecclesiologically neutral'.[157] This was also a plea for the Orthodox, and not just for Rome. Orthodoxy, he went on, is not an undeveloped form of Romanism, but nor is it an inarticulate Evangelicalism or the archetype of via media Anglicanism. It must be heard on its own terms, and Western Christians must allow it do so.

In September a conference at Nottingham recommended the members of the British Council of Churches to join together by covenant—some saw this as an option against *both* Orthodoxy *and* Rome. Allchin felt it need not be read in that light. There were Anglicans who thought the imperatives to join up with the Reformation Churches and with Rome were not contradictory in character. Still, there must be realism. If there were to be union with British Protestant bodies it must be made clear that the Church of England hopes ultimately for reconciliation with the Roman centre of unity and has been engaged for a century on pro-Orthodox ecumenism. This was an attempt to overcome the old division in the pre-Ramsey Fellowship between Rawlinsonians and their opponents. Perhaps, mused Allchin, Protestant theologians and leaders will come forward to say they welcome just such a Church of England, one that looks to the rock—or rocks—from which it was hewn.

> Our old and too limited conceptions of how unity may be brought about have to be broken and reshaped under the guidance of the Holy Spirit.[158]

Meanwhile, behind the scenes, there were rumblings about plans—if they existed—for a British Orthodox Church more user-friendly to indigenous converts in these islands. In October 1965 the general secretary of the Church of England Council on Foreign Relations wrote to his opposite number at the Fellowship, Basil Minchin, conveying the news that Metropolitan Athenagoras of Thyateira had expressed to the Archbishop of Canterbury his concerns about English-language celebrations of the Liturgy at St Basil's House. Here the chaplain, Father Vladimir Rodzianko, was said to be the culprit. Metropolitan Athenagoras feared that Rodzianko had introduced this practice so as to 'win converts from the Church of England' and was anxious lest 'other Orthodox priests are accused of this sort of proselytism which is strictly against the policy of the Ecumenical Patriarchate.'[159] Minchin replied in an undated note, blaming Gillet and calling the suggestion 'a figment of Father Lev's malicious imagination.'[160]

That the unity of the Orthodox among themselves could not be taken for granted was admitted on a larger stage than this. Elias Mastroiannopoulos, writing originally in the periodical *Aktines*, made an urgent plea for greater knowledge of each other; for more fellowship through, for instance, common pilgrimages to Jerusalem and Constantinople, as well as to (why not?) Alexandria, Damascus, Mount Sinai and even the Lavra of St Saba; co-operation in, for instance, catechetical schools, youth movements and camps, Christian journalism, liturgical matters, charitable activity; unity of prayer by, for example, calendrical reform so that the saints of other Orthodox Churches would be more fully celebrated. He wanted as soon as possible closer contact between Athens and Constantinople, and then with the rest of the autocephalous bodies, together with annual (not just periodic) inter-Orthodox meetings and the holding of a pro-synod. Also, the theologians must come together more (a conference of Orthodox theologians was to be held in Bucharest, but its only predecessor, the Athens congress where Florovsky launched the neo-patristic movement, pre-dated the Second World War). The one bright feature Mastroiannopoulos found in the present scene was Syndesmos, the Pan-Orthodox Youth Movement which lived up to its name. All of this should be given priority over relations with the heterodox, he concluded.

In summer 1966 *Sobornost* was able to register the Joint Declaration of Paul VI and Athenagoras I of 7 December 1965 whereby the mutual anathemas of the fateful year 1054 were cancelled. Those excommunications had been of persons not of sees. The consequences, however unexpectedly, had been far-reaching and dire. They were now, pope and patriarch declared, 'committed to oblivion'.[161] Of course the same could not be said for the major Church-dividing issues. The two hierarchs hoped that with the help of the Spirit 'those differences will be overcome through cleansing of hearts, through regret for historic wrongs, and through an efficacious determination to arrive at a common understanding and expression of the faith of the Apostles and its demands'.[162]

A second declaration, from 23 March 1966, was by Pope Paul and Archbishop Ramsey, announcing their intention to 'inaugurate between the Roman Catholic Church and the whole Anglican Communion a serious dialogue which, founded on the gospels and on the ancient common traditions, may lead to the unity in truth for which Christ prayed'.[163] On the agenda, the two men said, should be not only theological matters but practical issues that had been found to raise difficulties (probably 'mixed marriages' were in view). Yet a third declaration emanated from the ecumenical patriarch on the 9 June 1965, and it concerned the Chalcedonian and Non-Chalcedonian Orthodox Churches. In the wake of the third Pan-Orthodox Conference of the Eastern Orthodox and the Addis Conference of the Oriental Orthodox, Athenagoras pronounced himself in favour of a theological commission parallel to those between the Orthodox and Anglicans (and Old Catholics), to look at the historic causes of the schism, the contemporary Christological teaching of the two bodies, and 'other general points of dogmatic, historical, or canonical character (regarding Church Order, administration, jurisdiction, etc.). Once detailed findings had been finalized they would, so the patriarch envisaged, be submitted to the hierarchs of the two communions and, if found acceptable, undergo discussion at a Pan-Orthodox and Pan-Oriental Conference (meeting separately). This would then be the preamble to an ecumenical council which would produce a Decree of Union, followed by universal rejoicing at a concelebrated Eucharist. This programme was the most optimistic of those found in the three Declarations—and it would be the least observed.

After the Second Vatican Council, partly in view of its provisions but mainly owing to the crisis it unleashed in the Roman Catholic Church, some Orthodox found themselves considerably nonplussed by Rome. Kallistos Ware, in an account of 'Intercommunion. The Decisions of Vatican II and the Orthodox Standpoint', revisited the Bulgakov question of what the conditions may be under which we can be visibly united as one Body at the Holy Eucharist. The topic had returned to the agenda owing to two Decrees of the Second Vatican Council, *Unitatis redintegratio* on ecumenism and *Orientalium ecclesiarum* on the Eastern Catholic Churches, where a limited intercommunion between Orthodox and Catholics was envisaged. Ware posed two well formulated questions.

> First, do the Vatican decrees envisage only economic intercommunion—that is, in cases of necessity—or is their scope wider? Secondly, is it assumed in the decrees that Orthodox and Catholics are already at one in all the essentials of the faith, and therefore intercommunion is possible in virtue of a *realized* unity? Or is intercommunion viewed as a means of *rapprochement*, a stepping stone to a unity not yet fully attained?[164]

As he points out, on the first question *Orientalium ecclesiarum* seems somewhat contradictory. It allows for Catholics to request Orthodox sacraments if in the absence of Catholic sacraments some 'necessity or a genuine spiritual benefit' recommends it. But it allows the Orthodox to receive Catholic sacraments in any situation whatsoever (so long as the initiative is from the Orthodox side).[165] On his second question, *Unitatis redintegratio* gives as ground of intercommunion the degree of unity with the Orthodox Church that already exists, while *Orientalium ecclesiarum*, recognizing that this unity is seriously deficient, understands intercommunion as a way of promoting union.[166] This looks like, then, economic intercommunion—but in view of the preparation of unity, and hence an unsatisfactory mixture of two quite different rationales. Here, so Ware observes, the council was in advance of the most advanced theologians of the previous decade, citing the ground-breaking Dominican ecumenist Yves Congar writing in 1952 and his confrère Christophe Dumont, founder of the Parisian institute *Istina*, writing in 1959. Both men had explained why there were profound reasons why the introduction of intercommunion would be an inappropriate step.

What do the Orthodox think? Economic communion can be either a matter of non-Orthodox, in certain circumstances, receiving Orthodox sacraments, or of Orthodox, in certain circumstances, receiving non-Orthodox sacraments. Confining himself for the moment to the case of Anglicans, Ware thought it is feasible for the Orthodox to give permission, in cases of necessity, for Anglicans to receive, so long as they confess the truth of the eucharistic conversion (bread and wine into the Lord's Body and Blood), but not for Orthodox to receive from Anglicans—for this would raise the question of 'ecclesia extra ecclesiam', and there is no known instance (excepting a Syrian Jacobite in America who had to eat his words) of any Orthodox hierarchy granted formal permission for this. The nearest to such an act would be the expression of opinion (only) by the 1931 Joint Anglican–Orthodox Theological Discussions at Lambeth (where, importantly, the Moscow patriarchate was not represented).

Is the Roman Catholic case any different from that of Anglicans? When the question is one of Catholics receiving Orthodox sacraments in certain well defined situations, they could hardly be treated more rigorously than Anglicans. But what about the other way round? Might the Orthodox, who may not receive Anglicans sacraments, receive Catholic ones? Not necessarily, for many Orthodox hold the Cyprianic view that there are no authentic sacraments outside the visible unity of the Church. And even where that ecclesiology is not in vigour, there is a widespread phobia about 'Rome' which would see the invitation to receive Catholic sacraments as yet another form of proselytism. Moreover, no Orthodox authority has yet given formal permission for members of the Orthodox faithful to receive Catholic sacraments or indeed, for that matter, for members of the Catholic faithful to receive Orthodox sacraments. Consequently, there is a unilateralism about the Conciliar decrees which is, surely, undiplomatic to say the least. Indeed, thought Kallistos, it is likely to be counter-productive and lead to a resentment which will 'prejudice the wider cause of unity'.[167]

Theologically, on the wider question of intercommunion as goal and means, Orthodox writers have taken the 'conservative' view espoused before the council by Congar and Dumont, and have given exactly the same reasons as they. It is a view which has been consistently maintained by the Orthodox at the World Council and was reaffirmed with Rome in

1965 at the time of the lifting of the anathemas of 1054. The more liberal view, as would be well known to readers of the Fellowship's journal in the 1930s, was represented by Bulgakov, and continued to be held by Zernov; up to a point, as Kallistos was aware, Bishop Cassian Bezobrazov and Paul Evdokimov of the Institut Saint-Serge agreed with them where intercommunion with Catholics was concerned—that is, Cassian thought it a disciplinary issue only, while Evdokimov considered the questions of the Filioque and the Immaculate Conception should be resolved first (not the Roman primacy, surprisingly, for he believed it to be only a matter of canonical ordering). Ware indicated his disagreement with these figures. It is not enough to invoke the healing power of the Eucharist in a context of 'eucharistic ecclesiology'. The Eucharist is itself 'indissolubly bound to the whole content of the faith'.[168] In the setting of continuing dogmatic disagreement it would be 'somehow unrealistic—a kind of self-deception and a refusal to face the bitter facts'.[169]

Meanwhile in September 1966 an Inter-Orthodox Theological Commission, meeting at Belgrade, produced some useful stock-taking pertinent to *Sobornost*: a list of topics on which agreement had been reached between some Orthodox Churches and the Anglicans; a list of topics which had been examined but without full agreement; a list of topics which had not yet been examined; finally, a list of topics which must be given priority at the opening of any dialogue with Anglicanism in the future. So far as the latter were concerned the Commission had identified four: the implications of Anglican intercommunion with Old Catholics, Swedish Lutherans, and possibly Methodists; an account of how union in faith with Orthodoxy is to be understood; an explanation of how decisions reached will bind the entire Anglican Communion; a decision about the status of the 39 Articles.

In 1967, Athenagoras of Constantinople, whom Michael Ramsey had befriended five years earlier in Istanbul, came to London. 'Never since Theodore of Tarsus in the seventh century was there an Archbishop of Canterbury so capable of penetrating and valuing what the Ecumenical Patriarch stood for, and never before was there an Ecumenical Patriarch so capable of penetrating and valuing what the Archbishop of Canterbury stood for.'[170] The Fellowship's general secretary, Basil Minchin, accompanied by Bishop Oliver Tomkins of Bristol, went to greet him at Lambeth. They told him they welcomed him 'with special honour and affection, not only because of his position in the church, but because he has always stood for just those principles that the Fellowship has tried to work out in its life'.[171]

To Archbishop Ramsey's disappointment, the plenary Anglican–Orthodox Joint Commission—representing all the Orthodox Churches and all the provinces of the Anglican Communion, though much desired by the Patriarch, would not meet until 1973. By then Athenagoras was dead, and Ramsey himself on the edge of retirement, while the issue of the ordination of women had become a drag.

As the Fellowship moved into the 1970s, the waters ahead were going to be choppy, and, despite the work of the bilateral ecumenical dialogues, they would become more so in the years to come.

PART II

A VOICE FOR ORTHODOXY:

THE LAST FIFTY YEARS OF THE JOURNAL *SOBORNOST*

→ 1 ←

The Continuing Story

I resume here the 'story' which ended with the close of the 1960s in Part One of this book, 'The Encounter of East and West'. It will exhibit continuities—but also show significant discontinuities with the first forty years. More and more, the theme of 'A Voice for Orthodoxy' wins the day.

The 1970s

The 1970s began with a retrospect. To mark the twentieth-fifth anniversary of Sergei Bulgakov's death, the Fellowship had published a collection of his pieces in early numbers of the journal. Donald Allchin, as editor of *Sobornost*, found the words 'prophetic gift' highly applicable to his work.[1] He also thought—and this was hardly irrelevant to Bulgakov's legacy—that more attention should be paid to the question, what grounds the sense of affinity between Anglicans and Orthodox? 'When we go beyond diplomatic and surface reasons', asked Allchin, 'can we discern a genuine similarity or relationship at the theological and spiritual level between the two traditions?'[2] He believed we can, belonging as he did to the school of Michael Ramsey on that subject. It was important to try to achieve clarity in this regard since, in the combined atmosphere of accelerating cultural change and ecclesial disorientation in the West the ecumenical movement was showing signs of taking unexpected directions and generating unforeseen difficulties.

Like Eric Mascall, Allchin believed that office-holding in the Fellowship mandated travel. In the winter–spring issue of 1970, the last of *Sobornost*'s fifth series, he produced a felicitous travelogue describing his recent experiences of the Orthodox world. He had been in Istanbul where, with excellent taste, he found the church of the Saviour *in Chora*, with its mosaics from the age of the Palaiologan dynasty to be the highlight.

'In its last century the Eastern Christian Empire seems to have gained in inward vision as it lost in outward power.'[3] He had visited the theological seminary at Halki on the Îles des Princes where the Patriarch Athenagoras I, though he had not long to live, was the undoubted star. 'He has given back to the Patriarchate of Constantinople an honour and a renown which it has scarcely known since the fall of the city in 1453.'[4] At Thessalonica, he inspected Moni Vlatadon, the newly created Patriarchal Centre for Patristic Studies with its library of manuscript images and microfilm from Athos, and its biennial publication *Kleronomia* ('devoted to the renewal of Greek theology on the basis of a living rediscovery of the patristic tradition'),[5] under an abbot, Stylianos Harkianakis, who was the author of a study of *Lumen gentium* as well as of World Council of Churches papers. On Athos itself he was saddened by signs of decay yet the Holy Mountain had the 'look of a place that has been loved, been prayed in.'[6] He ended up at Athens, and more particularly in the church of Kaisariani at the foot of Mount Hymettos with rich frescoes from this 'vital Orthodox seventeenth century of which we know so little'.[7] The Greek leg of his trip completed, he mused on how different the standard Greek academic theology would have been if the first modern students to go West had gone to the England of *Lux Mundi*, the ambitious manifesto of Liberal Catholicism in the ancient Universities, and not to the Imperial Germany of Adolf von Harnack, the founder of a minimalizing and anti-metaphysical liberal Protestantism.

In Romania, where the Communist regime was, on patriotic grounds, relatively generous to the Church, Allchin visited monasteries. At Neamtz, in Moldavia, he paid his respects to the grave of Velichkovsky, translator into Church Slavonic of the *Philokalia*, and thus the foster-father of the nineteenth-century Russian spiritual revival. In Transylvania, he called at the former Habsburg city of Sibiu (Allchin thought it looked a mediaeval German town), where after reintegration in Greater Romania and the re-absorption of the Uniates into Orthodoxy, the Romanian translation of the *Philokalia* emerged at the start of the 1950s at Staniloae's hands. At Bucharest itself, Allchin visited the patriarch at his palace, and mulled over Romanian history. He explained that while the patriarchate was an invention of the 1920s, the Phanariot princes who ruled Wallachia (Valachia) and Moldavia under Turkish overlordship in the seventeenth and eighteenth centuries allowed the Church a latitude which made it useful to a wider Orthodoxy. Thus, for instance, the erudite Patriarch

Dositheus of Jerusalem had his theological works published here. Allchin also mentioned the inter-Orthodox Synod of Jassy in 1642, but not its Latin Catholic tendencies in theological style.

The 1969 Broadstairs conference had discussed the future of the Fellowship, looking at such possibilities as extending the use of St Basil's House, conscious recruitment, especially of young people, and the offering of full membership to Roman Catholics and Free Churchmen.[8] It was surprising to hear (assuming the conference reporter was well informed) that the latter at least had not been 'full' members previously. Protestant Nonconformists of various stripes had been involved from the Fellowship's beginnings, and in Eric Fenn they included a general secretary. The next issue would describe Fellowship participation in a course of lectures organized by the Roman Catholic equivalent body in England, the Society of St John Chrysostom. Both Derwas Chitty and Michael Paternoster, the latter now general secretary, were among the lecturers, along with another Anglican, Henry Brandreth of the Anglican and Eastern Churches Association. Three Catholic speakers made for a half-and-half affair, a sign of the breaking of the ice in relations between the Church of Rome and both Anglicans and Orthodox after the Second Vatican Council.

The summer 1970 issue, the first of the sixth series of the journal, came out with a completely redesigned cover. Like the newly introduced Western liturgies of the period, the design was radically simplified. A decade for which the word 'neophilia' might have been invented was a time for new beginnings. Taking stock was part of this. Appropriately, then, *Sobornost* borrowed from *St Vladimir's Theological Quarterly* (formerly *St Vladimir's Seminary Quarterly*, but Crestwood's 'theological' credentials were by now well established) a recent analysis of the developing theological scene in the Orthodox world by the dean of St Vladimir's, now John (rather than 'Jean') Meyendorff.

Orthodox theology, so Meyendorff reported, had left its linguistic ghettos. Currently, it existed in French and English quite as much as it did in Greek or Russian. Its principal imperatives were to remain faithful to Tradition and to be open to the contemporary theological world. In the latter he saw two prevailing tendencies. The first was that of 'late' Barth, the Karl Barth of the last volume of the *Church Dogmatics*, and his more existentially oriented Lutheran contemporary Paul Tillich. In revolt against an Augustinianism dominated by the contrast of nature and grace, they were keen to emphasize a presence of God in creation independent of—though doubtless also related to—the Incarnation. This, thought Meyendorff, was not unlike the Russian Sophiologists, but Sophiology had few attractions for younger Orthodox theologians. The latter preferred to 'overcome the nature–grace dichotomy along christocentric, biblical, and patristic lines', after the manner of Florovsky, no doubt.[9] The other principal *Tendenz* was biblical hermeneutics as shaped by the great demythologizer, Rudolf Bultmann. Bultmann's exegesis had tried to combine the *kerygma*, the basic proclamation of the 'Good News', with, in the matter of Christian origins, a meagre set of historical facts. Meyendorff thought this an unfortunate mix. It had led to a subjectivization of the Gospel. The Church's message was caught between a 'gnosis without objective criteria' and a 'determinism' whereby God 'can only follow the laws and the principles he himself has established' as to what can or cannot happen in everyday empirical history. Meyendorff did not want Orthodox theology to follow either of these leads. He wished it to concentrate instead on a theology of the Holy Spirit capable of uniting nature and grace, Tradition and liberty. It should synthesize five great themes which are both essential to the Orthodox witness and also what 'people' are seeking, consciously or otherwise. And these are: a non-divine cosmos that needs salvation; a theocentric anthropology; a Christocentric theology; a personalistic ecclesiology; a Trinitarian concept of God. The Church that carries such a theology will avoid superficial ecumenism, but it will also eschew behaving as a denomination or a sect.

Meanwhile, in Moscow, Patriarch Alexei (Simansky) had died, and Zernov wrote his obituary, describing him as the last living link between the pre-revolutionary Church where he had been a bishop in the diocese of St Petersburg and Novgorod and its Soviet successor body. In the absence of any 'behind the scenes' accounts, it was impossible to adjudicate between the very varied interpretations of his collaboration with the State authority under Stalin, and the meaning of his withdrawal from the public eye when renewed persecution set in under Nikita Krushchev. While conceding that Alexei's actions often appeared opportunistic, Zernov drew attention to his great public popularity in the years 1945 to 1953, and a 1960 speech at a Kremlin peace conference where he sought to resist the new anti-Church pressures. Zernov could testify personally to the strong sense of presence he conveyed on the two occasions he met him, at Moscow in 1960 and London, as Ramsey's guest, in 1964.[10]

The Continuing Story

Sobornost sought to gain insight into the workings of the Soviet Russian system, especially as it affected ordinary Church-people. In this connexion Sophie Koulomzin's 'Encounter with Russia', describing a return trip after fifty years to Leningrad, her place of birth, and to Moscow, her last Russian home, was memorable. She noted the riddling mode of speech people adopted to avoid direct statements; described a woman who, asked what the greatest difficulty was in Soviet life, wrote the word 'lie' in French on a piece of paper and immediately tore it up; and reported how a friend had volunteered the opinion that, harder to bear than the arrests and exiles, were the unworthy vocations to the priesthood in the relatively brief period at the end of the War when Stalin's favour smiled on the Church, and a clerical career was lucrative.[11] Sharper in tone was Philippe Sabant's 'The Weakness and Strength of the Russian Church'. After 1966, with the ending of the Krushchev era, church closures and the harassment of priests had ceased and in 1970 a small number of Bibles and prayer books were printed. Yet very few of the churches closed by Krushchev had reopened, the five suppressed seminaries had not been recovered, and it was still the case that no religious instruction could be given by the clergy. Moreover, in recent months, measures of 'atheist education' had been stepped up, especially among young adults. But perhaps this was positive for the Church, since it could be interpreted as a sign of official anxiety. Religious belief, stimulated by the Liturgy, could be returning in a new generation.

> It is indisputable that, through their beauty and spiritual intensity, the religious services in the Russian churches act as the best means of official evangelization left today at the disposal of the Church. This has been repeatedly stressed both by the anti-religious propagandists and by Russian clergy.[12]

Sampling methods used by Soviet sociologists produced statistics distinctly encouraging to the Church not only in the countryside but also in the urban centres. Sabant disagreed strongly therefore with the novelist Alexander Solzhenitsyn who, in his 'Lenten Letter', warned the new Patriarch, Pimen, that the Church's faith was draining away from Russia. The only question was whether its mass base allowed for a successful challenge to the State or whether such a venture would put in deadly peril the ecclesial institutions still remaining.

The annual general meeting of 1970 recommended seeking Roman Catholic, Free Church and Non-Chalcedonian Orthodox representation on the Fellowship's council. It was reported that the number of branches was growing steadily, though in fact while some fruited others withered on the vine. So, for instance, Southampton came into existence as Canterbury threatened to pass out from it. But this was generally the case with local branches or groups throughout the Fellowship's history, Oxford being the great exception.[13]

In 1971 Allchin reflected on the sudden rise to popularity in theological circles of the word 'celebrate'. The Fellowship, gathered in conference at Broadstairs, heard Allchin speak of the contemporary discontent of Western youth: 'this movement of protest, instinctive, unorganized, sometimes muddled and naive' which, he thought, was nonetheless leading young people to look elsewhere than to the 'cult of efficiency and acquisitiveness' for 'quality of life'.[14] Shockingly (but it was the early 1970s after all), Allchin brought together the revival of the gift of tongues with the use of hallucinogenic drugs as a possible way to the 'apprehension of spiritual realities'.[15] The American Catholic layman Michael Novak's name was invoked in support of the notion that drug use may bring people closer to the world as perceived by artists, mystics and primitive peoples: less in terms of function, more in terms of being. Novak was correct to say we need to 'find ourselves in a more intimate, co-inherent relationship with others and the world around us'.[16] Moving into his more accustomed mode, Allchin brought together texts from Sophronios of Jerusalem, St John of Damascus, the Byzantine Liturgy, the eighteenth-century Welsh Methodist Ann Griffiths and the Anglican divines Jeremy Taylor and Mark Frank, to show how such 'coinherence' is achieved in the divine Economy the Church carries through history, such that, as the 'language of function and utility recedes', the 'language of being and rejoicing comes to the fore'.[17]

The last editorial of 1972 noted the death of Patriarch Athenagoras and the accession of Dimitrios I, and the three-day meeting of the Orthodox and Anglican Commissions for Joint Doctrinal Discussion at Chambésy, Geneva—though a communiqué indicated the participants were still only moving towards the formation of an agenda.

The closing issue of that year opened with a sermon by John Saward on 'The Folly of Peter and Paul'. Preached to the Anglican Sisterhood of the Love of God at the Convent of the Incarnation ('Fairacres') in Oxford, its papalism pointed ahead to his move to the Church of Rome, its argument to his forthcoming study of the 'fools for Christ's sake' in

East and West, based on the book that came out of his Oxford doctorate, *Perfect Fools*.[18]

> Peter and Paul are a scandal. So are all who share their ministry and vocation. The primacy of the Pope in the college of bishops is scandalous folly; so is the bishop in the diocese, the priest, deacon or religious in the whole body of Christ; the Christian in the world.[19]

The fools for Christ occupied a category of saints especially important for the Russian East, though Saward would be ingenious in finding Latin parallels.

Saward was followed in this issue by Professor Donald Nicholl, a Catholic lay philosopher, who was fast becoming a Fellowship favourite. Nicholl had spoken to the Oxford branch on the significance of St Seraphim of Sarov for the 'science of the heart', a concept he was developing as a tool for describing the search for holiness, or at any rate for spiritual truth, in the world religions. The range of reference was wide, including especially Jewish and Buddhist traditions, a token of the eclecticism of the period. Nicholl's conviction that the sacred 'largely falls outside the normal categories of historical method' was indebted to the anti-Positivism of the same years.[20]

There were more travelogues: Garth Fowden, secretary of the Fellowship's Oxford branch, had been in Jerusalem, and Stephen Parsons, an Anglican curate who had written on Zizioulas's theology, in the Lebanon and Syria. Both sets of impressions were illuminating, but a striking point they had in common was their anti-Roman tone. Ten years after the inception of the Second Vatican Council that might seem rather out of step with the editorial policy of *Sobornost* at large—though probably not with majority thinking in the Fellowship itself. Fowden was not uncritical of either the Greeks or the Armenians in Jerusalem, but he considered the Latin patriarchate had no real rationale.[21] Parsons was admiring of the Orthodox patriarchate of Antioch, and notably its youth movement, had almost nothing to say about the Maronites, and reported major divisions among the Melchites—the Chalcedonian Orthodox in union with Rome, where for one strand of opinion the establishment of the Uniate patriarchate had been a travesty which needed unmaking as soon as possible. Parsons rather took it for granted this party would enjoy *Sobornost* readers' support.[22]

But if anti-Romanism was still predictable, other things were not. For Brian Frost, a London-based lay ecumenist, writing on 'Living in Tension between East and West' in 1973, emerging trends in theology might render irrelevant the ancient divides between Latin Christian and Oriental Christian thinking. He had in mind such new phenomena as 'social theology' (compare 'political' and 'liberation' theology) and 'ecological theology' (a term Frost claimed as his own invention). Only certain themes, he implied, were likely to survive at all helpfully into the Christian future: among them unknowing, struggle, hope, transfiguration.[23]

The journal's final number for that year coincided with some notable events: most obviously, the long prepared initial plenary meeting of the Anglican–Orthodox Dialogue at Hertford College Oxford; a 'Cistercian-Orthodox Symposium', also taking place in Oxford—this was a Roman Catholic/Orthodox event with some Anglican participation but subsidized by the Fellowship in a clear expression of its new openness to the Latin tradition; and, last but not least, Nicolas Zernov's seventy-fifth birthday, marked in *Sobornost* by the inclusion of a characteristic essay by the man himself. Meanwhile Patriarch Demetrios had issued a statement for the twenty-fifth anniversary of the founding of the World Council of Churches. He ascribed to Orthodox influence the fuller doctrinal outlook of the World Council in recent years and sought to overcome the polarization between, on the one hand, those who were more interested in turning the organization into an instrument of social politics and, on the other, those with traditional ecclesiastical concerns.

Nicolas's seventy-fifth birthday item took as its subject 'The One Holy Catholic and Apostolic Church and the Anglicans'. What else would one expect? Most Orthodox theologians, declared Zernov, would have difficulty in saying whether Anglicans were in that Church or out of it. The Orthodox sense of unity is not based on authority, as with Rome, but on a 'particular corporate experience' where 'worship and teaching, liturgy and customs' form an unbroken web—on which each Eastern Christian tradition is a recognizable variant.[24] The *Catholica*, accordingly, is identical with what Zernov called the 'Orthodox Ethos'.[25] Where the signs of that ethos are apparent, even a schismatic rupture, as with the Bulgarians before 1948, does not un-Church. Where the signs of that 'ethos' are not apparent, the Orthodox observer has difficulty in recognizing the Church at all. Of course there can be such a thing as a manifest falling away from the Church, as with heresiarchs. But in Zernov's view, Western Christianity, with a different tradition in worship and teaching, liturgy and customs, can lack the Orthodox ethos without for all that being outside the

Catholica. Western Christians have not been synodically condemned as heretics. 'Neither Roman Catholics nor Protestants have been condemned or excommunicated as such.'[26] The lack of synodical condemnation is from one viewpoint positive, but it also means the absence of a common policy—and hence the tergiversations of the Orthodox Church as to whether to baptize Westerners on their reception into Orthodoxy or not. Zernov believed that the policy of rebaptism, when in use, was essentially a defence against Western aggression—significantly, it was not customarily applied to Uniates even though these belonged to the same communion as Latins. The conventional teaching of Orthodox writers had no answer to the 'fact' of schisms within the Church (compare the pre-War Bulgarians)—and hence should be less willing to affirm the existence of schisms from the Church in other cases.[27] That is what leading hierarchs such as Patriarchs Athenagoras and Demetrios of Constantinople and Patriarch Alexei of Moscow have tacitly conceded, whenever they use elevated ecclesiological language about other Christians, notably in regard to the Church of Rome. Eastern Christians should 'recognize that Western Christians who do not share the Orthodox Ethos with them, possess a much greater treasure—the Sacramental life of the Catholic Church.'[28]

The Fellowship was not to forget its own history, in which the Institut Saint-Serge, through its professoriate, formed an essential part. In this opening issue of 1975 not only was there Zernov's obituary of Arthur Fitzroy Dobbie-Bateman, the Russian-reading layman who, as Chapter 7 of Part One described, had been a first-hand witness of the Sophiological controversy (on retirement from the Whitehall Civil Service he became, so it transpired, an Anglican cleric). Altogether in the Zernov mode was the obituarist's summing up of Dobbie-Bateman:

> He felt equally at home in the balanced scholarly atmosphere exemplified by Bishop Frere and in the mystical and speculative world of Saint Seraphim and Father Bulgakov. His own life contains proof that the Anglican and Orthodox can in the future form one community without losing their distinctive characteristics, both being inspired by the same Holy Spirit and united round the sacred meal of the holy Eucharist.[29]

It was true that Dobbie-Bateman wrote admiringly about Seraphim of Sarov, but his enthusiasm for Bulgakov's thought was far less obvious.

There was also Paul Anderson's obituary of the American Presbyterian Donald Lowrie, a key player in enabling the foundation of the Russian

YMCA and the first historian of the Institute, while in the same number Zernov reviewed a new history of the said Institute by its then rector, Father Alexis Kniazeff, noting, significantly, that

> the Professors and students have never been a uniform community. There have always existed diverse tendencies among them, but they all remain within the framework of the same tradition. This has been particularly clear in regard to ecumenical contacts. Some of the Professors and students have been enthusiastic supporters of the work of unity, others have kept aloof from it.[30]

At a time of growing theological radicalism in the West the Institute laboured under a difficulty in the wider Orthodox Church. Some sought to blacken all its staff, past and present, with the same tar-brush, splashing around accusations of 'Modernism' or declaring it the home of 'Protestantism of the Eastern Rite'.

The lay convert from Protestantism to Orthodoxy Elizabeth Behr-Sigel, no avoider of controversy, wrote on how Western European Orthodox, mainly young adults, had been taking refuge from jurisdictional divisions at a gathering near Dijon (the Russian Synodal Church did not attend).[31] Behr-Sigel was the spiritual daughter of Lev Gillet whose biography she would write. In 1975, while she was reporting on the Dijon assembly, Gillet (under his nom de plume, 'A Monk of the Eastern Church') was publishing in *Sobornost* the text of an appendix he had written to his bestselling *Orthodox Spirituality*. Gillet was never afraid to show his colours, not least in his endnotes. He called his own book, by then thirty years old, a 'clear and objective presentation of what one might call traditional Orthodoxy'—not referring, therefore, to its considerable borrowings from Western Catholicism, which one could also note, without too much difficulty, in other of his writings.[32] This perhaps understandable reticence did not detract from the pertinence and, often, acuteness of his comments in a new supplement to his minor classic.

Gillet found the Russian emigration the principal, if not the exclusive, bearer of Orthodox spirituality to the West. He was thinking of the influence of St Seraphim and John of Kronstadt, Russian iconography, Sophiology, the Symbolist poets, and even certain strands of a 'questionable mysticism, eroticism, and occultism'. Dostoevsky, Berdyaev and Bulgakov had been treated, wrongly, as typical Orthodox thinkers. Vladimir Lossky was a different kettle of fish, but he 'identifies too one-sidedly the spirituality of the Orthodox Church with Palamism' and his 'rejection [of] a human imitation of Christ goes against the whole spiritual teaching of the Fathers'.[33] Gillet was kinder to Paul Evdokimov and his French disciple Olivier Clément. He seemed to approve of American Orthodoxy in its younger 'more rigorous' theological generation.[34] And he wondered whether the cultus of the Name of Jesus (which his own writings had assisted!) might carry 'some danger of the symbol ultimately replacing the reality, or at least veiling it'.[35] He liked best the simple evangelical Orthodoxy of St Tikhon as described by Nadejda Gorodetzky in her biography of that holy bishop,[36] and saw Mother Maria Skobtsova (St Maria of Paris) as its most recent embodiment. He noted the renaissance of Hesychasm in Romania, the emergence of new monastic leaders in Greece, and the demise of the Zoe movement, condemned for its pietism, while harbouring doubt as to whether those who had brought it to its knees would do any better. Rather damningly, he saw among some Orthodox a divorce between a sense of moral duty and high spiritual/intellectual aspirations, as though personal conversion on the ethical plane was somehow dispensable. He felt the non-Orthodox did much better than the Orthodox in articulating a Christian position on justice (including human rights, freedom, dignity) and on sexual questions. The most practically minded Orthodoxy was that of the Arab patriarchate of Antioch. Few Orthodox, he complained, had learned anything at all from Western sanctity or theology, whereas, especially in England, many non-Orthodox have opened themselves to Orthodox inspiration in these regards. On liturgical reform, he was inclined to think that the Liturgy of St John Chrysostom met admirably all the desiderata of liturgical scholars or pastoral experts, even if it might need slight tweaking here and there. The thirst for authentic icons he found real, and offered the opinion that modern non-representational art might lure viewers into the world of the icon. The charismatic movement, at any rate in North America, had had some mild effect in Orthodoxy, not especially pernicious since confined to groups for prayer and silent meditation, whereas recent radical theology in the West had been, for the most part, rightly ignored. Finally, there was Orthodoxy behind the Iron Curtain, about which we can only say we would like to know. Along with Albania, the Soviet Union had much the most secrecy-inducing regime, as shown in Trevor Beeson's study of the Churches in Eastern Europe, *Discretion and Valour*, commissioned by the British Council of Churches, on the basis of a mass of carefully assembled specialist reportage and reviewed in this same 1975 number of *Sobornost*.[37]

The Fellowship conference in the summer of 1975 had taken as its theme 'Prayer and Mysticism: Christian and Non-Christian'—very appropriate for the return of prayer after the horizontalist later 1960s/early 1970s in what survived of the Christian West. David Balfour, convert from Catholicism and former Orthodox priest, commended the Charismatic Renewal to his fellow-Orthodox in rather undiplomatic terms and touched on its affinity with the writings of Symeon the New Theologian. The Cistercian Hilary Costello, a monk of Mount St Bernard's, put the Fellowship's way by that Cistercian/Orthodox conference of 1973, spoke on spiritual darkness and its fruits. Father Kallistos dealt with 'Athonite Spirituality Today'. The Reverend A. O. L. Hodgson spoke about the refounding of Little Gidding and its closeness in spirit to Nicholas Ferrar (though by 1981, only six years later, a 'community of "Christ the Sower" was formally established there, with ecumenical worship, for members from the Roman Catholic, Anglican and Free Churches and the utterly non-sacramental Quaker tradition',[38] which is not what is usually associated with the Caroline Revival). Donald Nicholl's presentation of *scientia cordis* persuaded the conference chronicler of the value of including the non-Christian religions in the conference's purview but the same chronicler expressed dismay on hearing another speaker opine that a member of the Church of England could still retain his churchmanship were he to become a Buddhist. Geographical scope was well served by Edward Every on the Middle East, Roger Cowley on Ethiopia and the Russian Orthodox layman, released from the Gulag in 1973, Anatol Levitin-Krasnov. Not for the first time, criticism was made of the unrepresentative character of the Fellowship's Anglican worship, with its borrowings from Rome. Presumably now it was the *Novus Ordo* of Paul VI rather than the earlier quasi-Tridentine 'English Missal' that was the target.

In 1976 a second Pan-Orthodox theological congress had been held in Athens (not in Romania as originally planned), and in 1978 the papers appeared—also at Athens. Nicholas Behr, a parish priest in the Orthodox Church of America, would review it, a trifle belatedly, for *Sobornost*; he saw it as a plea for the disagreements among the Orthodox to be openly aired.[39]

Allchin stood down as editor in 1977, to be succeeded by Father Sergei Hackel, assisted by two Anglican priests, John Saward and Hugh Wybrew. Allchin's farewell after sixteen years (but as chairman of the Fellowship council he was not disappearing) spoke of a 'great and sometimes frightening movement of convergence, untidy and unpredictable in its dynamism.'[40] A key to his editorial mind is found in his claim that 'We have always tried to combine spiritual with theological ecumenism, practical collaboration with a concern for popularizing', since Christian unity is 'not for experts alone.'[41] Very suitably, Allchin had been invited to receive an honorary degree from the Bucharest Theological Institute (he was, after all, responsible for introducing Staniloae to the readership of *Sobornost*). He gave them in return an ambitiously conceived paper on 'Trinity and Incarnation in Anglican Theology from the Sixteenth Century till Today', in which he put forward David Jenkins as a theologian whose lively Trinitarianism showed a historic feature of Anglican theology was still alive and well. This was before Jenkins became the *bête-noire* of classical Anglo-Catholics (and conservative Evangelicals) by casting doubt on the virginal conception and bodily resurrection of Jesus on the eve of his consecration to the see of Durham. Charles Gore would not have been amused.

Edward Roche Hardy, an American Episcopalian but Fellow of Jesus College, Cambridge, wrote on the background to the founding of American branches of the Fellowship. Good relations between Orthodox and Episcopalians were nothing new in the United States by the time Nicolas Zernov first set eyes on St Albans in 1926, though organizationally speaking those relations were haphazard. A 'Russo-Greek Committee' established in 1862 by the General Convention of the Protestant Episcopal Church of the United States of America lasted only until 1874; an American branch of the Anglican and Eastern Churches Association struggled on for some years until 1916. More important were the numerous Orthodox priests who had studied in the seminaries of the Episcopal Church. Successful lecture tours by both Bulgakov and, later, Zernov also figured in Hardy's account, as did the name of Frank Gavin, professor of Church history at General Theological Seminary, New York, whose *Some Aspects of Contemporary Greek Orthodox Thought* Hardy describes as dating 'from the end of the period of scholastic Orthodoxy', though Gavin, who died young, was not to know this.[42]

Also in 1977, Ramsey's successor as Archbishop of Canterbury, Donald Coggan, had visited Patriarch Demetrios at the Phanar, and their respective speeches of greeting were included. Demetrios spoke of Paschal joy, but also warned against the innovation of ordaining women to the presbyterate and episcopate. 'We would have wished that devotion to the Theotokos might have increased on the part of all Christian peoples, rather than the movement towards the ordination of women,'[43] he said with dignity. Coggan told him Anglicans had no wish to impose it, but those who saw such a move as right should be free to carry it out.

Demetrios had other matters to worry about, as Philippe Sabant's 'On the Way to the Pan-Orthodox Council' indicated. Sporadic interest in such a council, bringing together, at least ideally, the heads of all the autocephalous and autonomous Churches, had emerged before the Great War. In 1930 an Inter-Orthodox Committee, assembled at the Athonite monastery of Vatopedi under the stimulus of Constantinople, took some cautious steps in this direction. In 1961 at a meeting in Rhodes the desirability of such a council was finally agreed on in principle. Now, at the end of November 1976, the First Pan-Orthodox Pre-Conciliar Conference had been held at Chambésy, with all Churches represented except the Church of Georgia, which was impeded by the lack of visas, and two bodies whose canonical status were disputed: the Autocephalous Orthodox Church in America and the Autonomous Church of Japan, both initiatives of the Moscow Patriarchate without a stamp of approval from the Ecumenical Throne. Sabant reported:

> Some theologians thought the decision was premature, either because of the conditions in which the Council would have to meet owing to the position of the Churches in the Communist countries, or because Orthodoxy as a whole was not yet sufficiently prepared internally for such an event, and the real problems confronting the Church in the present age were not yet sufficiently clear to all parts of the Orthodox world.[44]

He stressed that 'most' reactions to the Conciliar project had been supportive—but rather undermined the claim by adding 'leaving apart, of course, the ultra-conservative elements, afraid of anything that might upset the routine of centuries'.[45]

The agenda was more controversial. The 1961 list was long, from fundamental dogmatics to student exchanges, but in the meanwhile (at a gathering, also in Chambésy in 1971) a shorter list was devised, based on the notion that such a council should be brief, concerned 'only with a few questions of immediate practical importance, leaving aside theological issues except insofar as they had a bearing on the former'.[46] But the Moscow patriarchate was keen to keep some of the wider questions on the table. So a return was made to the Rhodes agenda, eliminating topics which fewer than seven Churches wanted to include. The final list ran as follows: the Diaspora; how autocephaly is proclaimed; the diptychs; the calendar; obstacles to marriage; fasting rules; relations with the rest of Christianity; the ecumenical movement; contributions to peace, freedom, international and racial brotherhood. Four topics were recommended for another day: the sources of revelation, the idea of the Church, codification of the canons and canonical rulings; *oikonomia* and *akribeia*, the latter corresponding more or less to what in the Latin West would be canons governing dispensation (and its withholding). The Chambésy gathering of 1976 anticipated in part the ecumenical issues on the proposed agenda. As reported in *Sobornost*, it approved continuance of the official dialogues with Anglicans, Old Catholics, and the Oriental Orthodox Churches. It agreed to the initiation of dialogue with Lutherans and Roman Catholics. It was critical of the policy of the World Council of Churches.

The Fellowship could have told them something about Lutherans based on its by now historic experience of branches in Sweden and Denmark, and, by coincidence, there appeared for the first time in the pages of *Sobornost* some account of a small Norwegian branch, including a reference to Kirkelig fornyelse, a movement devoted to making Norwegian Lutheranism more classically Christian, and its journal *Lære og liv* which in due course had High Church Lutheran, Orthodox and Roman Catholic contributors. (Forty years later, in 2017, owing to departures from the Church of Norway for destinations in Catholicism, Old Catholicism and Orthodoxy, Kirkelig fornyelse, which had stressed the eucharistic basis of its unity, felt obliged to close its doors.)

The Fellowship's secretary, Gareth Evans, hailed 1977 as a bumper year. There were members if not branches in fifty-six countries, and a six thousand strong circulation list for *Sobornost*. After the annual general meeting three 'traditional fixtures' would follow: a celebration of the Orthodox Liturgy in St Albans Cathedral, the Fellowship retreat at Pleshey in Essex, and the conference, to be, as so often, but by no means uniformly, at High Leigh in Hertfordshire. These were the high points of the Fellowship year, in a pattern by this date long established.

Despite all this activity, the first issue of 1978 opened with distinctly anxious 'Editorial Notes' from Hugh Wybrew. The ordination of women, or agitation for it, continued to snowball in various Anglican provinces. He feared it was about to become the mortal threat some had warned of. At the time of writing it was not yet clear whether the Anglican–Orthodox Dialogue would resume or be broken off *sine die*. There was little he—or anyone—could say that would bridge the gap between possibilists and impossibilists, including among Anglicans themselves, for they were at loggerheads. Hackel took this opportunity to correct misleading reporting of the 'Agapia Consultation' which had brought women from the Orthodox and Oriental Orthodox Churches to discuss the wider topic of women in the Church at a Romanian monastery in 1976. In the course of 1977, the *Church Times* had claimed that the consultation showed tell-tale signs of division on the matter among the Orthodox too. So Hackel published Elisabeth Behr-Sigel's paper (on which the *Church Times* had based its reporting) for its true proportions to be discerned. They were less than overwhelming. Though her name continued to crop up in this context, her own position on the priesting of women was agnostic.[47]

For 1978, the fiftieth anniversary of the Fellowship's founding, George Florovsky had been invited to send a paper, and his role in its early years was graciously acknowledged. In the spirit of return to the origins, Nicolas Zernov sought to revive interest in Bulgakov's proposal for limited intercommunion. Less controversially, Gareth Evans, as general secretary, noted that St Basil's House in London was open daily, and an Orthodox Liturgy held each Saturday. Within a short time, that would change, since by the early 1980s Archimandrite Kallistos was drawing attention to the infrequency of celebration.

Sobornost's next number (still in 1978) reported the imminent incorporation of the *Eastern Churches Review*, itself founded by Barbara Fry in 1966 so as to continue in a new format Dom Bede Winslow's *Eastern Churches Quarterly*. Robert Murray and Father Kallistos, who had been editors of the *Review*, would now join the board of *Sobornost*. John Saward resigned from that board, and was replaced by Norman Russell, then a priest of the Brompton Oratory. The Fellowship's most viscerally anti-Roman counsellor, Claude Beaufort Moss, was doubtless spinning in his grave.[48] Nicolas Zernov, as always, was graciously accommodating:

> The presence of two Roman Catholics among the editors was a new departure for the Fellowship. It reflected the special emphasis of *The Eastern Churches Review* which was always strongly supported by Roman Catholics, but it also reflected the widening scope of the Fellowship itself.[49]

And he reflected further:

> As the Fellowship embarks on its sixth decade it embraces Anglicans, Orthodox, Roman Catholics, and many other traditions, all of

them trying together to understand more deeply the problems preoccupying them, and meeting in a wider field with renewed confidence in the healing power of the Holy Spirit.

As if to comment on Zernov's revival of the Bulgakov proposal at the fiftieth-anniversary celebrations, Kallistos Ware published a revised version of a talk he had given the previous year, at the Fellowship conference of 1977. This was 'Church and Eucharist, Communion and Intercommunion', in which he reiterated the negative conclusions on the topic he had already aired a decade previously. Since then the Orthodox had become more isolated on the topic and the spokesman in question more severe.

> Vatican II has greatly mitigated the previous rules, while the actual practice of Catholics in many places goes far beyond anything that the Council envisaged. Theologically and canonically, there has been nothing short of a revolution in the Roman Catholic view of intercommunion. This in its turn has had a profound influence on the theory and practice of High Church Anglicans and Old Catholics.[50]

'The grave theological arguments in support of the "traditional" view are now very largely forgotten or misunderstood, even by some of the very people who not long ago found such arguments convincing.'[51] Going back to first principles, Kallistos points out that 'As a Eucharistic organism, the Church realizes and maintains its unity through the act of Holy Communion.'[52] In ecclesiology, no text is more decisive than First Corinthians 10:16–17, the celebrated 'one bread, one body' passage, which unites Paul's thinking about the Eucharist to his view of the Church. Citing both early Christian witnesses and contemporary Greek and Russian theologians, Kallistos affirmed that eucharistic unity presupposes unity in the faith and unity in the bishop. Though expressing 'anguish' at eucharistic disunity, he went on to speak trenchantly of the modern concept of intercommunion understood as 'sharing in the sacraments, on an occasional or even a regular basis, by Christians belonging to ecclesial communities that are still officially separated.'[53] 'The Bible, the Fathers and the Canons know of only two possibilities: communion and non-communion. It is all or nothing.'[54] Admission to Holy Communion and admission to Church membership are one and the same thing. Communion in the Eucharist cannot compensate for non-communion in faith nor, for that matter, for lack of communion with a bishop who possesses the Orthodox faith. Nor can there be a simple appeal to a mutually recognized Baptism, for 'One cannot be baptized into the Catholic Church without belonging at the same time to a local Church, and here at once the problem of disunity confronts us: for it is precisely as members of local church communities that we are separated'.[55] He went so far as to call those who advance the cause of intercommunion ecclesiological Nestorians, separating the invisible and visible aspects of the Church. 'A sound Eucharistic ecclesiology ... so far from involving the acceptance of intercommunion, implies rather its repudiation.'[56] This otherwise clear-cut position was somewhat muddied when readers were told that Dumitru Staniloae was willing to relax the principles involved in the case of the Oriental Orthodox. Here the claim ran: there is already unity of faith, issues like the number of ecumenical councils being 'problems of church order'.

The 1980s

The 1980s opened with some notable losses in the Orthodox world. Well-focused obituaries enabled readers of the journal to take the temperature of Orthodoxy at this time. Three high-profile figures had died: a hierarch, Athenagoras (Kokkinakis) of Thyateira and Great Britain, Orthodox co-president of the Fellowship, and two dogmatic theologians, one of whom was closely associated with the Fellowship, George Florovsky, while the other, Justin Popović, was not.

Athenagoras, a Patmian and monk of the Monastery of St John on his home island, so Kallistos Ware explained, was eminently qualified academically, with American university degrees in philosophy, philology and theology. He had previously been dean of Holy Cross College, in Brookline, Massachusetts, the teaching institution of the Greek Archdiocese of North America. In London he totally transformed the administration of the diocese (from 1968, it was an archdiocese), founding many new parishes, a youth organization, auxiliary sisterhoods for pastoral work, and a priests' association with insurance and pension schemes, though the energy with which these schemes were decided on and implemented had unfortunately alienated 'many leading members of the Greek community, both clergy and laity'.[57] His obedience to the ecumenical patriarch in refraining from public criticism of the military Junta in Greece brought him massive adverse reaction from Cypriots in Britain at the time of the Junta-backed coup against President Makarios which triggered the Turkish invasion of 1974. Though he wanted children to learn as much Greek as possible in the parish schools, he did not stand in the way of priests who wished to introduce some English into the liturgy, and was the first Greek bishop in Britain to ordain Western converts. He was much involved in ecumenical efforts, even though his own ecclesiology was strict, especially in the early years—but also in the last years—of his episcopate. At his death no member of the Holy Synod was permitted by the Turks to attend his funeral, which was conducted by Metropolitan Meletios of France. 'Fellowship Notes' announced the advent of Methodios Fouyas, the new Archbishop of Thyateira and Great Britain, as Orthodox co-president.

George Florovsky was given two obits, one by Mascall and the other, on his theological work, by Rowan Williams. Mascall remembered him from the Fellowship's earliest days, and drew an entertaining as well as moving picture ('it was plain that the source of his theology was his Orthodox faith and not just his academic competence, great as the latter was'[58]). He also recorded his comment that Augustine was 'really an Eastern Father',[59] which later on was much quoted. Rowan Williams rightly remarked that he should not be regarded simply as a walking patristic encyclopaedia for he had a 'complex and sophisticated theology and philosophy of history', a judgment thoroughly borne out by later Florovsky scholarship.[60]

Elizabeth Hill, emerita Professor of Slavonic Studies at Cambridge, wrote knowledgeably about Popović, an intransigent Orthodox dogmatician and controversialist, but also a devoted monk who helped inspire a revival of women's monastic life in Serbia after the Second World War. Descended from seven generations of priests, he had studied at St Sava Seminary in Belgrade under Nikolai Velimirović, the founder of the religiously coloured nationalist ideology termed *Svetosavlie*, was professed as a monk in 1916 and sent to Petrograd Theological Academy for further training. In Russia he fell under the influence of the Slavophiles, Leontiev, Soloviev and especially Dostoevsky on whom, after a premature transfer from Petrograd owing to the Revolution, he wrote a thesis at Oxford—not accepted for a higher degree since he refused to tone down his criticisms of Catholicism, Protestantism and the West in general.

> It is not surprising that his Oxford years had not turned him into a foreigner aping the English for whom he had little sympathetic understanding and of whose traditions and culture he had little knowledge. He was convinced that Western Europe was no model

for Eastern Europe: the West was fast becoming spiritually barren; the decline of European civilization was already obvious.[61]

Instead, he returned to teach theology at Sremski Karlovci, the seat of the Russian Church in Exile, where he came into contact with its presiding bishop, Antony Khrapovitsky, whom he revered as a man who did not know the meaning of the word 'compromise'. His own immovability was legendary. The last number of the Serbian Orthodox journal *Christian Life* which he edited was devoted to criticizing as non-Orthodox innovations changes mooted at the 1927 Pan-Orthodox Congress in Constantinople. The abortive Oxford study of Dostoevsky was published (there would be another Dostoevsky book in 1940), the harbinger of his three-volume dogmatics (*Orthodox Philosophy of Truth: The Dogmatics of the Orthodox Church*) and the twelve-volume hagiology of all Orthodox saints which lay ahead. Meanwhile he was involved in the movement to recover Uniates for Orthodoxy in Subcarpathian Rus, then part of Czechoslovakia. In 1934 he became lecturer in comparative theology at Belgrade, but in 1948 when, owing to the advent of the Communist regime in Yugoslavia his academic career was finished, he retired to Čelije near Valjevo, a mediaeval monastery with a handful of nuns to whom he became the priest-confessor. He continued to write, not least his 'The Orthodox Church and Ecumenism', published in 1974 at Thessalonica in Serbian and Greek, a work in which he delivered his highly negative judgment on Orthodox participation in the ecumenical movement. In 1976 he completed the third and final volume of his dogmatics. He died on his birthday, 25 March 1979. It was salutary for the Fellowship to know that Orthodox theologians of this stripe existed.

Meanwhile, Sister Benedicta Ward considered Kallistos Ware's popular handbook *The Orthodox Way*, commenting that given the number of (post-Schism) Western sources cited it might as well have been called 'The Christian Way'.[62] Possibly this was the beginning of the suspicion with which some Orthodox were starting to view his alleged 'liberalism'. Zernov reviewed Lossky's posthumous essay collection *Orthodox Theology: An Introduction*.[63] He did so generously enough but did not fail to remark, as befitted an admirer of Bulgakov, that 'there exist other schools of thought within Orthodoxy which disagree with [Lossky's] outlook'. Zernov summed up the latter rather witheringly as 'an entire commitment to patristic thought together with an unwillingness to consider a number of new theological problems'.[64] A life of Mother Maria Gysi, originally a Swiss

Methodist, by the two remaining nuns of her small monastic foundation at Whitby was based on her letters.[65] The sisters noted her love for the Cambridge (and other) Platonists. Archimandrite Barnabas Burton, a Welsh convert from Anglicanism via Roman Catholicism, praised her Ware-like desire to integrate, not spurn, the Western inheritance.

In the subsequent issue of the combined journal—the last of 1980—two women writers at Durham sought to make honourable amends for the lack of material in the public domain on H. A. Hodges who had made such a massive contribution to the Fellowship in its first forty years (see especially the closing chapter, 'Ecumenical Prospects', in Part One of this study). Anne Beacock Borrowdale, who had written a Durham thesis on Hodges' thought, and Ann Loades, a lecturer at the University of Durham, collaborated in writing on Hodges, who had died some four years previously. A Yorkshireman with a nominally Methodist background, reading Greats at Balliol, he became a Catholic-minded Anglican, finding in the Church of England milieux he frequented a satisfyingly full sacramental life and a rich tradition of spiritual teaching. Hodges would later find these qualities even better represented by Orthodoxy, which, moreover, had not, in his judgment, separated theology from spiritual life. After a year spent in an Oxford lectureship he moved to the University of Reading where he stayed until his retirement from the chair of philosophy in 1969. An autobiographical fragment in manuscript form spoke of a discovery of 'the Great Invisible', then of the Incarnation, and finally of a conversion from sin to newness of life, reversing the normal Evangelical sequence, which was also that of Wesleyanism. His view of philosophical enquiry was distinctly *sui generis*.

> For him the true form of philosophical argument was 'this must be true if the questions in which I am interested are to be capable of the kind of answer I hope for'. In other words, he drew attention to the connections between arguments, feelings and desires, and the way in which deep self-analysis uncovers fundamental attitudes to life and the world.[66]

For Hodges a philosopher is someone who chooses to be himself in a consistent manner: not perhaps the best way to create a sapiential consensus. But this otherwise quintessentially Alban and Sergius figure—committedly Anglican yet passionately phil-Orthodox—offered philosophy to others as a therapeutic exercise. At his hands, it aimed to track beliefs and principles to their roots, clear up muddle, and get a handle on how others see matters so differently.

Death reared its many-headed form in this same second issue of the combined *Sobornost/Eastern Churches Review*, since Lev Gillet, Alexis van der Mensbrugghe and Nicolas Zernov had all passed away that year, 1980. Helle Giorgiadis's obituary of Gillet would prove controversial. A convert to Rome herself, she claimed Father Lev had never been asked to renounce specifically Roman Catholic doctrine on being received into the Orthodox Church. The offending passage was the following:

> His transfer in 1928 to the Russian Orthodox Metropolitan Evlogii in Paris 'by concelebration' is one of the mysteries of Fr Lev's life, and his friends have placed various interpretations on his adherence to the Orthodox Church. His personal affirmation was that he identified himself with Solov'ev's position: that there is no intrinsic incompatibility in being Catholic and in communion with the Russian Orthodox Church because the two Churches were separated only by historical vicissitudes and not by any canonical impediment. Metropolitan Szeptytski and the then Archbishop Evlogii had known one another in Lvov, and Fr Lev maintained that his move had the full knowledge and approval of Szeptytski. It would seem from Fr Lev's address at metropolitan Evlogii's memorial service in 1945 that this understanding was also shared by Evlogii. I have attempted elsewhere to elucidate the logic of Fr Lev's ecumenical attitude, which he maintained throughout his life. His vocation was visionary and prophetic rather than an invitation to others to copy his example. It was not for display but an interior, personal offering for the Lord to use and make fruitful as he chose.[67]

Whatever his inner attitude St Basil's House would soon feel his outer loss. In the course of 1982 Bishop Kallistos wrote a memorandum deploring how little use was now made of the chapel at St Basil's House for celebrations of the Orthodox Liturgy. The council of the Fellowship was then invited to submit a name or names for an Orthodox chaplain, the appointment of whom lay in the hands of Metropolitan Methodius of Thyateira and Great Britain (this was required by the 'deed of hallowing' by Archbishop Germanos in 1949). It was thought advisable that Metropolitan Anthony Bloom should also be consulted, as a courtesy to the Moscow Patriarchate.[68]

Elisabeth Behr-Sigel, who was to be Gillet's biographer, sought to explain the 'Clamart concelebration' which Giorgiadis had spoken of in her obituary of Father Lev as a kind of Solov'ev moment in reverse. For Giorgiadis, Gillet became Orthodox without, in his own mind, ceasing to be Catholic whereas Solov'ev had become Catholic while, so far as he was concerned, not ceasing to be Orthodox. What Giorgiadis had left out, in Behr-Sigel's view, was the shock administered to Gillet by the encyclical *Mortalium animos* (on the ecumenical movement) of January 1928, so different in its negative tone from the 1924 letter *Equidem verba* by the same pope, Pius XI, which encouraged Benedictine abbots to work for unity between East and West, and, in so doing, gave his specific vocation to the young hieromonk Lev, sometime secretary to the great Uniate archbishop Andrei Szeptytsky. The harshness of the encyclical alienated him from the Roman system. What seemed to support Giorgiadis's version is that, firstly, Gillet went forward to the concelebration with a tacit blessing from his former bishop, and, secondly, did not make any explicit renunciation of Catholic doctrine, a point he had stressed in a letter to his mother. However, he also told Mme Gillet, and Behr-Sigel quotes these words, 'It would be deeply disloyal on my part to remain in the Roman Church now that I am convinced that the fullness of Christ's light is to be found in Orthodox Catholicism'.[69] But puzzlingly, until he became a parish priest he continued to name Metropolitan Szeptytsky in the Liturgy, perhaps an expression of affection for a spiritual father and thus an act which did not commit him ecclesiologically. Behr-Sigel had to admit in her conclusion, a 'certain amount of darkness and mystery continues to envelop this period of the life of Fr Lev'.[70]

In 1982 David Balfour offered his own 'Memories of Lev Gillet', dating from their time together at Farnborough when that Hampshire monastery was an abbey of the French Solesmes Congregation. Abbot Cabrol's successor, Bernard du Boisrouvray, had, according to Balfour, little time for the patristico-mediaeval studies of his predecessor, much less for Orientalizing aspirations vis-à-vis Russia, and not all the professed monks were convinced of Gillet's stability—in the secular sense of that term. This explains his enforced departure when the issue of solemn vows arose, and his subsequent transfer to the 'neo-Studite' monastery of Univ in Galicia. Balfour in effect followed him there, and found him in crisis. 'If he stayed in Galicia but refused to conform to the hybrid Ukrainian framework, he would find himself obliged to undertake on his own a process of external and internal self-russification which was beyond him. Small wonder that he felt frustrated and later escaped to mix with the Russian emigrants of Western Europe.'[71] Balfour was unable to confirm or deny Giorgiadis's dual claim that Szeptytsky had approved the 'concelebration of Clamart' and that Evlogy shared this understanding. Yet her version, thought Balfour, had some merit. It could account for the lack of insistence on the normal canonical form for reception: a general confession, public and specific renunciation of doctrines rejected by Orthodoxy, together with chrismation. He was inclined to think she was right about the continuing ambiguity of Gillet's attitude. He had been seen in Paris emerging from a Catholic confessional. He continued to publish, albeit anonymously, through the good offices of the bi-ritual Catholic monastery at Chevetogne. He did not openly take sides in Catholic/Orthodox doctrinal disagreements. His book on the Jesus Prayer avoided espousing Palamism. He would not let Bulgakov express his thanks in print for his help with the beautiful French of *L'Orthodoxie*. In later years he enquired at Rome how his ecclesiastical position was understood and was shown his dossier. Balfour thinks he might have returned to the Roman fold towards the end of his life but for a supernatural voice heard on the shores of the Sea of Galilee. He was 'a stormy petrel of the ecumenical ocean'.[72]

> His was, it must be recognized, a somewhat subversive influence: he disliked the pride of Rome and its inquisitorial traditions and he encouraged people to think for themselves and to think boldly. When I finally became Orthodox myself in 1932, it was under quite other immediate influences, which I recognized as providential and submitted to during a visit to Mount Athos; but I have always looked on Fr Lev as the person who had given the original impulse to my gradual conversion. However, as I joined the jurisdiction of the Patriarchal Church of Moscow through the strict synodal procedure and not the liberal/ecumenical world of the 'Evlogians' into which Fr Lev had managed to insert himself but with which my Church was not in communion, I did not see much of him at first, though resident in France, as he also was, in 1933 and again in 1935.[73]

The promised obituary of Alexis van der Mensbrugghe also appeared. The scion of a deeply Catholic and highly clerical family in eastern Flanders, he became a Benedictine monk of St André at Bruges, and was taught at Mont César by two leading liturgical historians Dom Capelle and Dom Botte before transferring his stability to Amay (the later Chevetogne) thanks to attraction to the Byzantine rite. Sent to be chaplain to Benedictine nuns at Kylemore in County Galway so as to cure him of Orthodox fever, his exile had just the opposite effect. 'Dom Maurus' was received at Saint-Serge by Metropolitan Evlogy in April 1929, taking the new monastic name of 'Alexis'. During the 1930s he made his home in England, as a chaplain to two Scots convert ladies living in Gloucestershire and commuted to the Bodleian Library and the British Museum to do research. Thence arose his book *From Dyad to Triad* whose status in a proxy war over Sophiology was described in Chapter 4 of 'The Encounter of East and West', and also his discovery of the Fellowship.

Father Alexis became a British subject. Links to Evlogy necessarily interrupted by the Second World War, he served instead under the Greek bishop in England, Germanos of Thyateira. After the War he removed to Paris, to become professor of patristics and liturgy at the Institut Saint-Denis, and involved himself in attempts to create Western-rite parishes. In 1960 he was made an auxiliary bishop of the Moscow Patriarchate with the title bishop of Meudon, in 1968 became bishop of Philadelphia, and, on the abolition of the patriarchal exarchate in the USA in 1970, looked after patriarchal parishes elsewhere in the world, initially in Mexico and then in Germany. From 1971 he acted as archbishop of Düsseldorff until his retirement in 1979, when he was terminally ill.

The most loved of this trio of figures was Zernov, memories of whom dominated the first issue of 1981. There was a very full obituary by Bishop Kallistos, already drawn on in Part One of this book. That obituary was written *con amore* and indeed with gratitude, because Zernov was the first contact of the gifted English schoolboy, from an army and Anglican background, with the Orthodox Church. Kallistos declared *The Russian Religious Renaissance of the Early Twentieth Century* to be Zernov's best book, given life by the conviction that 'this movement had a universal message, a significance for humankind as a whole'.[74] That message coalesced with Zernov's Oxford studies of Church unity (and disunity) in the early Christian centuries, as found in his doctoral thesis 'The Unity of the Church and the Reunion of the Churches: A study of the problem of church unity from the end of the first until the close of the fourth century'. On Ware's reading of that thesis, Zernov had stressed the twin elements of 'freedom and interdependence', seeing the ante-Nicene Church as fundamentally a family of self-governing communities whose unity was the gift of God—a state of affairs menaced both by Cyprian's over-rigorous theory of the collective authority of the episcopate and by the alliance of Church and State to come.[75] Ware noted how this account was implicitly sympathetic to Khomiakov's ecclesiology, on which Zernov would also write, but surprisingly silent on the role of the Holy Eucharist, which later would become for him utterly central. It would be impossible to describe Nicolas Zernov, wrote Ware, without stressing his cordiality and genius for friendship, both tested in the crucible of dreadful experiences of penury, even near-starvation, in the chaos of Russia in the Civil War.

Important postscripts carried some useful judgments. The first concerned his attitude to the divisions in the Russian Church abroad. In 1926 when Metropolitan Evlogy was expelled from the Karlovci Synod Nicolas remained in his diocese, and did so again when in 1931 it was brought under the *omophorion* of the Ecumenical Throne. In 1945 Evlogy accepted the authority of the Patriarch of Moscow—but on his death the following year the French parishes reverted to Constantinople. The exception was London and therefore Nicolas.

> [W]hile loyal to the authorities of the Patriarchal Church in Russia, at the same time Nicolas was never a partisan. He always spoke of the non-Patriarchal Russian groups in an objective and generous way and strove for co-operation across jurisdictional barriers.[76]

His patriarchal allegiance did not prevent him from plain speaking about the incompatibility of Marxism-Leninism with Christianity.

The second postscript concerned his writings (listed in a bibliography that followed). These were, Kallistos explained, sometimes hurried because Zernov was a man with a mission who started late (he was forty-nine when given an academic post). Moreover, he did not regard academic writing as its own justification, but sought to 'kindle a spark' in others which might go further.[77] He was accused of unrealistic optimism in matters of Church unity, yet he always upheld Church canons in practice.

> Nicolas was totally convinced that non-Orthodox share in divine grace, and therefore he rejected as absurdly inadequate any approach which simply dismissed them as being 'outside the Church'. But he also believed, more especially towards the end of his life, that there are personal situations where it is right for other Christians to become Orthodox. However great his affection for the non-Orthodox Churches, especially the Anglican, he did not hold a facile branch theory. For him Orthodoxy was unique: it was 'the Mother Church of Christendom'.[78]

In 1983 an editorial took the opportunity of a change of general secretary (from Gareth Evans to Hugh Wybrew) to ask what the Fellowship's role should be given the 'current proliferation of ecumenical bodies, conferences and publications'.[79] Members could hardly doubt it had one, but could it be properly defined? At the 1983 conference Militza Zernov had warned of a crossroads, expressing a feeling in the air of 'expectancy touched with foreboding'.[80] Why? Part of the answer was that 'serious discussion ... sometimes revealed deep-seated differences in participants' understanding of the Christian faith'.[81] But Wybrew also alluded to financial difficulties and the deterioration of St Basil's House. In the opening issue of 1984 Kallistos wrote about the first quarter-century of the House of St Gregory and St Macrina at Oxford: ecumenical centre, parochial centre, residential student hostel. Perhaps he had a premonition that St Basil's House would soon be no more. The secretary's Notes explained that henceforth the finances of the Fellowship would receive expert management from a professional accountant, and he himself would draw his salary only in part since he would be working for the Anglican Consultative Council in his capacity as secretary of the Anglican–Orthodox Dialogue, in addition to which he was associate secretary for Ecumenical Affairs at Lambeth Palace. The creation of branches in Orthodox countries (a chapter had opened in Athens, with explanatory literature in modern Greek) was the most obvious way of making good the dearth of exiled Russians crossing the Channel. The numbers of those who could even remember the Revolution of October 1917 was growing small.

It was Colin Davey whom Wybrew succeeded as secretary to the Anglican–Orthodox Dialogue. So Davey suitably provided an article now on 'Anglicans and Eastern Christendom', originally a lecture at Milan to mark the 450th anniversary of the Act of Supremacy, and thus the split of Canterbury from Rome. Much of the factual material has been outlined in the opening chapter of 'The Encounter of East and West'. But Davey's account of motives was the most original aspect of his presentation. In brief, and in chronological order, the motives for Anglican–Orthodox rapprochement were: desire for alliance against Rome; hope by High Churchmen for recognition of Anglican Orders and intercommunion; the desire to learn from the Orthodox tradition of prayer and spirituality. Davey did not fail to mention in the third case the role of the Fellowship, making use of the Zernovs' *Memoir* in so doing. Two of these historic motives were clearly *passé*. The Orthodox were as much in dialogue with Roman Catholics as they were with Anglicans, and Anglicans with Roman Catholics as much as with the Orthodox. And the need to make sure the full spectrum of Anglicanism (and not just the Catholic-minded) was properly represented in such dialogues was universally acknowledged. Of course the prayer and spirituality were still needed, and Davey thought they had kept the Anglican–Orthodox Dialogue on the road when the issue of women's ordination could well have derailed it. But what was it possible to hope for? He thought it might be possible to recognize each other's Churches as enough of a *"provisional* embodiment of God's purpose" with sufficient faith in common to open the way to a closer sharing of life in Christ.'[82]

Another trio of deaths led to instructive revelations about those closely involved in the Fellowship's course. Basil Krivocheine—encountered in Chapter 8 of Part One—had died, aged 85, as the Moscow Patriarchate archbishop of Brussels. The son of the tsarist minister of agriculture in the years 1908–15—for a period Alexander Krivocheine was head of civil administration in the Crimea when the latter was held by the White Army, Vsevolod Krivocheine had been a student of philology at St Petersburg at the time the tsardom was overthrown. By 1920, a former soldier in the White Army, he was evacuated to Egypt and thence made his way to France to join what remained of his family. In 1925 he began theological studies at Saint-Serge but later that year decided to go instead to Athos where the Russian monastery of Saint Panteleimon still boasted over five hundred monks. He remained there until 1947 using his linguistic gifts as their 'Greek' secretary, a member of the monastic council and eventually the representative of his monastery at sessions of the 'Holy Community', the central administration of the Mountain. On Athos, in Kallistos's words, he 'laid the foundations of his exceptional knowledge of the Fathers',[83] which bore fruit in his ground-breaking study of Gregory Palamas and later of Symeon the New Theologian. Misunderstandings of his role during the War (he was accused of collaboration with Germans and Bulgarians) and after the War (when he was termed a 'friend of Moscow') led to his expulsion from the Mountain, condemnation by a Greek court and imprisonment. On release he was invited to Oxford to work on the Patristic Greek Lexicon in progress at the University Press, and there was ordained deacon and priest by a Serbian bishop acting for the Patriarch of Moscow. He became assistant to Father Nicholas Gibbes at the Russian parish of the Annunciation and took up residence in the church house, 4 Marston Street. In 1959 he was consecrated auxiliary in the Russian patriarchal exarchate of Western Europe, and a year later archbishop of Brussels and all Belgium. Between 1966 and 1984 he represented the Russian Church in the Anglican–Orthodox Dialogue. He died on a visit to Leningrad in September 1985 and was buried in the St Seraphim cemetery there. It had been a quite extraordinary life.

Paul Anderson had also died, he who brought the Zernovs from Belgrade to Paris, and had so much to do with the help given by the YMCA to Russian émigrés after World War One (his name appears in Chapter 1 of 'The Encounter of East and West'). An obituary covered his own writing, including a 1985 memoir which recorded his first hand experiences of the Revolution of October 1917 and its aftermath.[84]

Elizabeth Hill, emerita Professor of Slavonic Studies at Cambridge, wrote a touching piece on the life and work of Gorodetzky, emphasizing that this latecomer to academe's book on *The Humiliated Christ in Modern Russian Thought* also expressed her own spirituality and way of life—itself much indebted to her encounter with Gillet which turned a rather conventional allegiance to Orthodoxy to something more profound.[85] Fleeing from Russia as a sixteen/seventeen-year-old, and mislaying her parents at Kiev on the way, she ended up in Yugoslavia. Exactly where and how she lived is unknown, as is whom she married (and divorced). Moving to Paris, she wrote novels and short stories, a study of Charles Péguy, and also translated Gillet's book on the historical Jesus. The Zernovs knew her there and in 1934 Nicolas Zernov, now ensconced in England, promised to see whether he could find some way of extending her theological education. He found her in fact a scholarship at the College of the Ascension, Selly Oak, the erstwhile institution of Edmund Morgan, one of the Anglican theologians who contributed to the journal's earliest numbers, as indicated in Chapter 8 of Part One. Serge Konvalov, who combined the chair of Russian at Birmingham with teaching at Oxford enabled Gorodetzky to enter the B.Litt. programme at the latter. Thus there appeared her book on the *kenosis*—and the corollary of Christ's self-emptying, the acceptance of suffering—in relation to Russian writing of the nineteenth and early twentieth centuries. In 1944, a member of St Hugh's College, she completed research for a doctorate on St Tikhon Zadonsky, eventually published in 1951. She had already given some lectures at Oxford on Russian religious thought (and written an article on the Jesus Prayer for the Oxford-based Dominican journal *Blackfriars* in 1942—before, then, Gillet's book which introduced the Prayer more widely to a non-Orthodox readership). In 1945 she became university lecturer in Russian, and in 1956 professor at Liverpool. She returned to Oxford for her retirement, part-owner of a large house on Banbury Road, living in a flat which on her death passed at her wish to the use of the priest of the Russian parish at 1 Canterbury Road. One wonders what became of her manuscript on Zinaida Volkonskaia, the aristocratic Russian convert to Rome whose Roman palazzo was a haven for Russian historians of art abroad.

Such brief lives naturally made readers ponder the rationale of Orthodoxy in the West. George Theokritoff made two interesting comments in a review of a World Council of Churches publication on 'Orthodox Perspectives on Mission'. The first concerned Orthodox Westerners.

> Orthodox Church in the West are categorized as *diaspora*. But one wonders how many indigenous western Orthodox see themselves as *diaspora*. There certainly is no need to do so in western Europe, in lands adorned with numerous ancient saints of the undivided Church.[86]

The second concerns the question, Why be Orthodox? His answer ran:

> Apart from those sections of the Church of Rome touched by the Jesuit Pierre Teilhard de Chardin, it is only the Orthodox Church that has a complete view of the wholeness of creation and a sense of the sanctity of matter.[87]

That might have been disputed by E. C. Miller, author of *Towards a Fuller Vision: Orthodoxy and the Anglican Experience*, which, very much in the manner of Allchin (who wrote its Foreword), found affinities between various Anglican writers and the Orthodox,[88] though the *Sobornost* reviewer, Gerald Bray of Oak Hill Theological College, was critical of the methods involved.

> First, one takes a well-known Anglican author of classical vintage (Andrewes) and demonstrates how aspects of his thought converge with another tradition (Orthodoxy), even though everybody knows that such connections are either coincidental or the result of a common dependence on a much earlier patristic tradition. Then one finds a number of obscure characters who in their own day were either unknown or regarded as eccentrics, and uses them as representatives of Anglicanism.[89]

This obtained a robust rejoinder from the said Allchin.

In 1987 Wybrew of the many hats announced he was leaving to become dean of the Anglican Cathedral in Jerusalem. His Orthodox counterpart Elizabeth Briere was given not a co-secretary but an administrative assistant in the shape of Mary Cunningham, described as theologian and Byzantinist, which indeed her numerous writings on Byzantine saints' lives and homiletics, and her co-editing of the *Cambridge Companion to Christian Orthodox Theology* showed her to be.[90] It was announced that the Fellowship had inspired a 'Fellowship of St Hendrik and St Arseni' for Lutherans and Orthodox in Finland. Allchin described the St Theosevia Centre for Christian Spirituality in Canterbury Road of which he had become the first director. Purchase of an additional house was made possible by Gorodetzky's legacy, a fund in Nicolas's honour, and a gift from Militza. Nicolas's books were to be housed there. Basil Minchin had died and received a gracious obituary from the bishop of Bristol, Oliver Tomkins, who had recommended him for the post of secretary of the Fellowship, knowing of his longstanding interest in Orthodoxy. At Mirfield, Lionel Thornton had marked Minchin's essays with the comment, 'You have again taken the Eastern Orthodox standpoint'.[91] Minchin's liturgical and musical interests were praised. It had all helped at 52 Ladbroke Grove: 'The little chapel with its contemporary yet traditional icon screen, Fr Lev Gillet as celebrant and Basil as cantor: here was an island of Orthodox spirituality in the unlikely setting of Bayswater.'[92]

Michael Ramsey died in 1988, and two tributes followed. From Owen Chadwick came the memorial address at Westminster Abbey, which took as its theme Ramsey and the beatific vision, for his authorized biographer described the late prelate as endowed with a strong sense of the closeness of another world. His favourite feast, we hear, was the Transfiguration, on which he wrote a largely exegetical short book.[93] It was when his discourses touched on heaven that they took off in beauty of words. Allchin, addressing the Fellowship, concentrated on Ramsey's Orthodox connexions. He had wanted a Christianity that breathes with both lungs and was afraid of any merely English Church-unity based on the lowest common denominator of English religious feeling.

The 1990s

As the new decade began, the Fellowship's general secretary was Elizabeth Theokritoff, who over the next quarter-century would make her name as an Orthodox theologian in her own right. (She was Mary Cunningham's co-editor in the *Cambridge Companion*.) But it was also announced that she would be, professionally speaking, short-lived, and relinquish her post after that year's conference had ended. She used her secretaryship to draw attention to the transient character of most of the Fellowship's branches. If the list published in the opening issue of 1990 seemed considerably shorter than usual that was owing to her determination not to include purely notional groups with no actual activities. She recommended that each group should have at least one Orthodox and one Anglican among the 'active' members—then at any rate they would be less likely to collapse on the withdrawal of a sole dynamo.[94]

That first issue of 1990 included a report from a Sourozh diocese study group on whether the Orthodox should take a public stand on contemporary issues. The view of participants was that 'The Church is too sacred and too central to human life to be assimilated to secular institutions. Individual Orthodox, however, should be encouraged to discuss political and social issues within the Church, and to take an active part in such issues whenever possible, outside her.'[95] The Orthodox Diaspora, it was pointed out,

> is spread through liberal, democratic countries, where anyone may say almost what he pleases and where religious bodies make use of that freedom to the full. Most Orthodox have an instinctive negative reaction to this, a reaction which we have come to believe is largely justified. The danger of institutionalization of the Church as one more secular player, only under clerical leadership, exists even when we are speaking of intercession against oppression. How much more does it exist when we are speaking of democratically elected governments, already subject to public criticism and accountability?[96]

This helps to account for the dearth in the journal of articles on issues of the day. But the conference of that year on the Christian in the world suggested to Theokritoff a twofold lesson.[97] The world must not be allowed to set the agenda, true. But neither should we ignore its needs and demands in the name of spirituality.

The second issue of 1991 furnished an important contribution for any history of the Fellowship. This was Robert Murray's 'Symbiosis and *Sobornost*: The Eastern Churches Review Trust and the Fellowship of St Alban and St Sergius'. In 1990 the Fellowship, after just over a decade of the joint journal, had agreed to meet the wishes of the trustees of the *Eastern Churches Review* to amalgamate the two organizations, at any rate to the degree that the law of trusts allowed. Murray had been the last chairman of the Eastern Churches Review Trust and was an editor of *Sobornost*—and so a living and personal link. It was his memory of events he sought to set down.

Murray's narrative now unfolded. Dom Bede Winslow, monk of Ramsgate, who had died in 1959, had founded the predecessor of the *Eastern Churches Review*, the *Eastern Churches Quarterly*—initially as a supplement to the review of the Prinknash Benedictines review *Pax*.[98] He had done so against the backdrop of the 'irenic Catholic ecumenisn' of the 1920s and 1930s, fostered as this was by, in particular, the bi-ritual Benedictines of Amay (later Chevetogne) in Belgium and the French Dominicans.[99] After Winslow's death his Benedictine legatees turned the *Eastern Churches Quarterly* into the pan-ecumenical journal *One in Christ*. But his 'disciple' (as Murray terms her) Barbara Fry, who died almost ten years later in 1968, wanted to keep the specifically pro-Eastern element in Winslow's inheritance alive. She established the *Eastern Churches Review* with this in mind, giving the editorship into the hands of Kallistos, George Every and Murray himself, while after her death Mary Claudine Scott, a London headmistress, brought into existence the Eastern Churches Review Trust to manage its affairs. Winslow's roots had been Anglican and according to Murray he 'never ceased to appreciate... the importance of the Anglican feeling for the Orthodox East which his own movement parallelled'.[100] Before the Second Vatican Council this was not a popular attitude among English Roman Catholics, where there was 'suspicion of any policy other than individual proselytizing'.[101] Winslow himself wrote little for except two manifestos which, however, were crucial: the 1945 'Integral Catholicism and the *Eastern Churches Quarterly*' and the posthumously published 'The General Principles of the *Eastern Churches Quarterly*'. His notion of 'integral Catholicism' implied that the existing Roman Catholic Church was not the fullest possible actualization of catholicity, which requires the integration of all 'catholic' traditions, including (above all) those of the Eastern Orthodox, for the realization of its complete potential.

The *Eastern Churches Quarterly*, so Murray reported, included of set purpose both academic articles and more popularly written accounts of visits to churches and monasteries in the East. This declined in the *Eastern Churches Review* as it had likewise done in *Sobornost*—and this he ascribed not to policy but to the fact that 'Those who edit scholarly journals side by side with other occupations inevitably accept material of good quality as it comes in'.[102] He regretted it nonetheless. Yet he evidently regarded the ground-breaking articles the *Quarterly* had contained (such as those by the Czech Church historian Francis Dvornik, redeemer of the reputation, in the Latin West, of Photius of Constantinople) as more potent in clearing road-blocks and rectifying conveniently forgetful historical memory than any other. Murray was inclined to regard Winslow as the only real predecessor of Vatican II's ecumenical spirit in Britain. Abbot (later Bishop) Basil Christopher Butler of Downside, who was also from an Anglican background, had come on board only as the council unfolded. Much in the council's documents proved that 'emphases characteristic of Orthodoxy have been absorbed',[103] even if popular reception was patchy and had given rise to turbulence. Murray deplored the increase in Roman interventions under Pope John Paul II, over against the 'highly collegial vision of the Church of *koinonia* rather than subordination which was worked out in the ARCIC talks'.[104] Seemingly, he did not notice that most of those Roman interventions were undertaken to protect the classically Christian norms of doctrine and practice shared overwhelmingly with the Orthodox (as well as with Anglicans of a Catholic stamp). There was an important coda, triggered by recalling Winslow's love of the Eastern Catholic Churches. Murray did not wish to open up controversy unnecessarily. Yet he felt he must ask about Uniatism:

> If something had much that was wrong about its origins, yet subsequently has borne fruits of holiness, how long does it have to go on being condemned, and what spirit is at work in such condemnation?[105]

But as I suggested in the Preface to *Alban and Sergius*, the absorption of the *Eastern Churches Review* did not halt the movement of *Sobornost* in the direction of an Orthodox 'monophony'—and neither did Murray's plea.

Meanwhile, on home ground, as the 1980s drew to their end, it was announced that St Basil's House would have to be evacuated, and the chapel and library temporarily closed, owing to the discovery of rot.

Not all had been well at Fellowship headquarters in other senses either. Dietrich Schuld had only lasted a year as secretary in succession to Elizabeth Theokritoff before leaving to be Anglican chaplain in Bucharest. The new secretary was a priest-convert to Orthodoxy from the Church of England. This was Graham Kendall, then a teacher at Manchester Grammar School, but he could not take up the duties immediately. The acting general secretary, Donald Savage, noted a chronic decline in attendance at the annual general meeting: hence the decision to combine it with the annual conference. Donald Allchin stood down as chairman after twenty years. Hugh Wybrew replaced him but also resigned, pleading pressure of work at Oxford. John Binns, later Vicar of Great St Mary's Cambridge, who became a noted writer on the Eastern Churches, especially that of Ethiopia, succeeded Wybrew. Allchin had not attended the annual conference, for the first time in two decades. Nor had Militza Zernov, who was hospitalized. The speakers had included Jews and Muslims, a choice which not everyone appreciated. There was also some murmuring at the number of Roman Catholic speakers (three out of twelve), perhaps because the rise of ill-feeling over Uniatism in Eastern Europe had poisoned the atmosphere. Sebastian Brock's wife Helen felt that 'Our Fellowship has perhaps not made the most of the change in Roman Catholic attitudes'.[106] Few Orthodox were actually present anyway.

In 1993 it was explained in the secretary's report that St Basil's House, for so long the Fellowship's physical and indeed spiritual centre, was definitively to close—and be either leased or sold. The secretary's Notes, dealing with that traumatic question, noted how special thought would have to be given to the library, where there had been no consistent policy of buying, and the chapel, itself little used in recent years by the Fellowship as distinct from London's Bulgarian parish. Later that year 52 Ladbroke Grove was put on the market, and it was announced that the Fellowship's headquarters would move to Oxford in the January following. The Fellowship would not be commandeering the entirety of the House of St Gregory and St Macrina but it would rent a large office on the ground floor and sufficient basement space for archives and periodicals. The library, thinned out by removing books outside the Fellowship's proper domain, would be housed where the Zernov collection had formerly been located, for, with the opening up of the former Soviet Union and the liberation of the Church, Zernov's books had been shipped to Moscow. Where to 'reconstruct' the chapel had not been decided.[107] Here the fate of

Sister Joanna Reitlinger's decorative scheme was crucial. The Fellowship's archives contain a document of 1994 on the topic which shows with how much care those responsible proceeded. The crux of the matter was stated at the outset. 'It is very unlikely that a building will be found with dimensions close enough to those of the original St Basil's Chapel to accommodate the wall paintings and iconostasis without considerable adaptation.'[108] The Fellowship was advised:

> Where the panels are of partly awkward shapes, such as those around the windows, it may prove best to make new panels which do fit the building synthetically, and on these to paint copies of Sister Joanna's apocalyptic symbols. However, it should not be unduly difficult to inlay the paintings themselves merely extending the background colour around them. It is not possible to discuss such adaptation in any detail until the new site is chosen, but no such site can be regarded as suitable for the paintings if it would necessitate a rearrangement that would obscure their significance.[109]

The general secretary reported Militza's death on 3 February 1994. It must have seemed the end of an era. Perhaps, for those who entertained a generous vision of Orthodoxy, and its possible relations with the Western Christian world, there was some consolation in the fact that, on a visit to London, the new ecumenical patriarch, Bartholomew I, had denounced nationalism as the 'bane of our ecumenical Church'.[110]

Life, as always, had to go on. By the second issue of 1994 the general secretary was writing that the Orthodox must adjust their witness, pastoral structures and cultural understanding to a West which, in the shape of disaffected Western Christians, was knocking at their doors, while at the same time huge political changes were a massive challenge for them in Eastern and Southern Europe. 'The Fellowship's role amidst all this is to provide opportunities, not to take sides or make partial judgments. We are not the official handmaiden of any one group: that is one of our greatest strengths. We are neutral, and were created to promote understanding in every direction.'[111] The sale of 52 Ladbroke Grove had made more money available for bursaries. The candidates sought were men and women overseas with a history of active Church involvement, to come for relatively short periods so as to experience a British equivalent. It was noted that that year's conference, on 'Giving a moral lead? The Church in the modern world' attracted an exceptional number of speakers from the Russian Federation. This was a harbinger of a possible new future ahead.

The Continuing Story

Not that the ecumenical scene beyond the Fellowship's bounds was exactly encouraging in the mid-1990s. Wybrew, thinking in the first instance of the Anglican–Orthodox Dialogue, was downright pessimistic. It was unrealistic to expect any major advance in relations between the two Churches:

> While among many Western Churches the concept of growing together by stages has been accepted, for the Orthodox it is difficult to envisage any intermediate stage in ecclesial relations, there will be unity and sacramental communion when there is doctrinal agreement, and without such agreement there can be no kind of interim mutual recognition leading to some degree of communion.[112]

And he went on:

> It is probably not untrue to say that some of the enthusiasm for dialogue on the Orthodox side has evaporated. The earlier stages of the dialogue have revealed that Anglicans are not quite what the Orthodox supposed them to be when the dialogue began. They are capable of ordaining women, and of a degree of theological liberalism or radicalism unacceptable to the Orthodox. It is the case that various developments have taken place within Anglicanism since the dialogue began, and the Anglican Church is not quite what it was, or what it seemed to be. To some extent it is true of all Western church life, which has changed, and is changing, at a rate which many Western Christians find bewildering and upsetting.[113]

He was right about the latter. The General Synod of the Church of England had agreed to the ordination of women to the priesthood. After the vote, a number of Anglicans were seeking to become Orthodox. The Orthodox bishops met and published a communiqué. They would not automatically re-ordain all Anglican clergy; the needs of the Orthodox community would be paramount. They rejected the idea of a Western-rite Orthodoxy while noting there were various views on the matter. They expressed sadness at Anglican difficulties and a disinclination to profit by them.

Wybrew went on to say that Orthodox problems in relations with Rome had also been exacerbated, specifically by the Uniate issue, which Robert Murray had raised in his history of the *Eastern Churches Review*. In any case, the new amity of the Byzantine Orthodox with the Oriental Orthodox meant that, in future, this would be the ecumenical priority of Orthodoxy—if it had one. But perhaps it would *not* have one, since the new freedom the Orthodox were enjoying in the Communist world had also brought extraordinary challenges, pushing ecumenism way down the list of things to do.

It was probably a relief to look back to what seemed a happier time. An occasion was provided in the shape of the centenary of Lev Gillet's birth. Bishop Kallistos offered both a personal memoir, and, in a separate article, an evaluation of the most frequently reprinted of Gillet's works, the anonymously produced Fellowship booklet *On the Invocation of the Name of Jesus* which he commended for its sobriety while deploring its lack of interest in Palamism.[114] But he had already said of Gillet that it was characteristic of him always to avoid polemical issues that had bred *odium theologicum* in the Church.

> In both his writings and his talks, he carefully avoided the polemical issues that have divided Christians over the centuries, and stressed only what could heal, reconcile and unify.[115]

Gillet, in writing of the Jesus Prayer, was not afraid to depart from what might be considered Orthodox norms. He recommended the use of the Holy Name Jesus by itself, as was done by such Western mystics as Richard Rolle. He also counselled connecting the prayer with particular episodes in the life of Christ, though Kallistos was quick to add that 'he does not intend to turn the Jesus Prayer into a form of "discursive meditation" on the Ignatian or Salesian model, but merely to give content and richness to the personal feeling with which the Prayer is to be suffused'.[116] And Gillet linked the Prayer with intercession, another novelty, proposing the invoking of the Name on any human beings with whom we come into contact, whether in a sustained way or even casually, as with passers-by on the street. He told his readers too that they are not to try to pray this prayer come what may, but to pray as they personally find best—an expression of his spiritual freedom which Kallistos dwelt on in the memoir.

> Fr Lev's position within the Fellowship of St Alban and St Sergius afforded him in particular one very precious gift: it enabled him to keep his freedom. He was free from administrative responsibilities; free to keep in touch with people entirely outside Fellowship circles; free to make long journeys abroad, particularly to the Lebanon; free in his talks and writings to explore unusual and even controversial ideas, which might have got him into trouble had he held a more official position within institutional Orthodoxy. He was free to remain always a pilgrim.[117]

Understandably, Elisabeth Behr-Sigel's very full biography of Gillet was given a substantial review (by Sergei Hackel). The review underlined Father Lev's radicalism, which went beyond even David Balfour's frank account: attending Sunday service with Quakers or the French Reformed, seeking to locate latent Christianity in the non-Christian religions, and in a letter to Behr-Sigel writing, 'Orthodoxy, its structures, its rites, have little significance. Only the Gospel matters.'[118] As to Kallistos, he would speak what was probably his last word on the enigmatic Gillet in 2005 at the Institut Saint-Serge. Scanning the occasional references to ecclesiology in Gillet's writings, Kallistos finds they can be summed up in three words: love ('Those who refuse to love others cannot worthily confess the love of the three divine Persons'[119]), tradition (here, using words of Gillet applied to French Orthodoxy, Bishop Kallistos made a plea for a specifically English Orthodoxy, incorporating not only pre-schism saints but later figures that are good and noble), and freedom ('He detested all forms of ecclesiastical bullying'[120]). Kallistos adopted Behr-Sigel's description: universality without relativism. As Gillet wrote to his brother about his entry into the Orthodox Church, 'I have gone where I have found—I would not say *another* light—but the same light of Christ *to a purer degree*.'[121] The general secretary's report included the news that the Fellowship was subsidizing an English translation of Behr-Sigel's life of Gillet, and that the paintings in St Basil's Chapel, where he had celebrated so often, would be removed to the monastery of Christ the Saviour in Hove. It was described as 'an Anglican foundation, associated with the Community of the Holy Trinity, Crawley Down, and with a distinctive spirituality rooted in the Eastern tradition',[122] where they would remain accessible to Fellowship members in a chapel of roughly the same dimensions as at the house in Ladbroke Grove. (The Crawley Down brethren could not, in the end, sustain this daughter-house and the paintings would be moved yet again, to an Orthodox church in Northampton.)

In the last issue of 1995 the editor, Sergei Hackel, asked whether people would like to meet C. S. Lewis. This was not a proposal of necromancy, but a question put to him by Nicolas Zernov. It had been mentioned in the obituarizing of Militza that the couple were close friends of the literary historian and Christian apologist. But though Hackel himself never in fact met Lewis, Lewis had been a Fellowship member in the period 1949 to 1953. Now Kallistos was asking whether he was a hidden Orthodox.[123] His contacts with Orthodoxy were few and far between.

He cites Orthodox writers not at all, unless one is to go as far back as either Denys the Areopagite (and then it is a matter of Denys's influence on the medieval West) or Athanasius (but he only wrote a preface for the translation of the *De Incarnatione* by Sister Penelope of Wantage because she was a friend).[124] Yet despite Lewis's comparative indifference to both Churchmanship and formal worship and his avoidance of Mariology, Kallistos believed there were distinct convergences—which explains why he is almost the only non-Orthodox writer stocked in many Orthodox bookshops. It came down to four matters: apophaticism, despite the stress on reason and universal moral law; the Incarnation and Trinity, though the latter is only weakly present in Lewis's fiction; the sacramentality of creation; and the vocation of the human person to *theosis*.

Philip Sherrard had died at the age of 72 and Kallistos wrote his obituary, rightly recording that he should be remembered 'as a translator and exponent of modern Greek poetry, and as a creative interpreter of the spiritual tradition of the Orthodox Church'.[125] Sherrard's family was linked through his mother to the Bloomsbury Group, but he was diametrically opposed to Bloomsbury in his rejection of agnosticism and desire to recreate a sacral consciousness in the West. In his approach to the poets it was their world-view, their attitude to truth, which concerned him. This was an unusual viewpoint in modern literary studies, and perhaps a signal that he would not remain forever in academe. After seven years at King's College London and the School of Slavonic and Eastern European Studies, he decided he preferred the 'greater liberty—and the greater insecurity' of living and working in rural Greece as a freelance writer and translator.[126]

Meanwhile, John Binns as chairman of the Fellowship had been in Moscow, in which city Friday 17 March 1995 was

> a working day at the Library of Foreign Languages, where Nicolas Zernov's books are now kept, well arranged in a room of their own. There is a complete run of *Sobornost*, and we spent much of the day at a table piled high with volumes of back numbers, discussing the contents of a projected volume of translations into Russian. My host Alexander Kyrlezhev's plan is that this *Sobornost* anthology will include articles by Orthodox theologians not yet available in Russia, material about the Church of England, and some on the ecumenical movement. Also Nicolas and Militza Zernov's brief history of the Fellowship. The work of translation should begin immediately.[127]

This was more encouraging than his visit to the Department for External Relations of the Moscow Patriarchate at the Danilov monastery where he learned that 'the Russian Orthodox Church is generally anti-ecumenical, with little sympathy for other Churches, due to the aggressive proselytizing by sects and new religious movements. Relations with the Church of England are poor, worse than with ECUSA [the Episcopal Church of the United States of America]. This is due partly to the decision to ordain women to the priesthood, partly to a lack of sympathetic involvement at the senior reaches of the Church of England.'[128] He had a warmer reception at the 'Alexander Men Open Orthodox University' where a course on the English religious novel had reached as far as Chesterton. But then it occurred to him that developing relations with that particular institution might queer the pitch with other Orthodox in Russia.

Graham Kendall, still general secretary, reported that financial help had been given the newly founded *Eastern Churches Journal*. It incorporated *Chrysostom*, the modest bulletin of the Society of St John Chrysostom, which had as its patron the Melkite patriarch, Maximos V, and was published at London and Fairfax, Virginia, under the editorship of a Uniate priest, Serge Keleher, who was definitely its *spiritus movens*. Its editorial board included members with strong Fellowship connexions, not least Bishop Kallistos. But it had a primarily Catholic (and above all Eastern Catholic) orientation. Meanwhile *Sobornost*'s first issue for 1996 issue would announce Kendall's resignation, and return to the Church of England as a parish priest. 'Being an Orthodox layman is a fine thing, but some of us even after seven years have to accept that perhaps we do not have what it takes to be one in the problematic circumstances that make Orthodoxy what it currently is in the West.'[129] On 27 April 1996 the Fellowship council made Deacon Stephen Platt of the Sourozh diocese the general secretary. This ended the succession of short-lived General Secretaries which cannot have been good for policy, or Fellowship morale. He would still be in place a quarter of a century later.

Platt was soon reporting on that year's conference 'Aspects of Prophecy' and his visit to Moscow on *Sobornost*'s (and the Fellowship's) behalf. He had more hope of branches in Moscow (soon achieved) and Belgrade (in process) than in London (though the latter was a real possibility). America had become a *terra incognita*, though this did not necessarily mean that nothing was happening Fellowship-wise. Branches were not good at sending information. Perhaps, in the future, e-mail, so economical and easy, would help. Moreover a website was under construction. The increasing emphasis on '*Sobornost* overseas' had led to the appearance in Greek of an anthology of its articles under the title, *Enotes en te poikilia*, 'United in Diversity'. In 1997, the possible London branch became actual, meeting in the Jerusalem Chamber at the Abbey, just in time for the centenary of Zernov's birth. Appropriately enough, the 1997 conference had as topic the tradition of faith with especial reference to the contemporary Russian Church, and a second conference on much the same theme took place in Oxford shortly after. In his annual report the new general secretary put the word 'Orthodox' in the phrase 'Orthodox countries' into inverted commas. Soon he would be relaying that John Binns had come to the end of his term as chairman and Father Gregory (Graham) Woolfenden had been appointed in his stead. Woolfenden was a tutor at Ripon College Cuddesdon, an amalgamation of High Church and Liberal theological colleges. Originally a Latin Catholic, he had moved across to the Byzantine-rite before subsequently becoming Orthodox, indeed a priest of the diocese of Sourozh with responsibility for the Russian Orthodox communities in Bristol and Portsmouth.

The 2000s

In 2000 Stephen Platt was busy re-founding the Athens branch of the Fellowship, which had evidently fallen by the wayside. When his term of office was renewed for a further five years, routine administration was hived off so that, now a priest, he might have more time for the needs of the Russian parish in Oxford.

2001 began with a spirited editorial on beavers who nibble away at the wooden supports of ecumenical bridges. This was Hackel's way of referring to two documents. The Roman Congregation for the Doctrine of the Faith's letter *Dominus Jesus* had affirmed not just the divinely sanctioned uniqueness of Christianity in general but that of Catholic Christianity in particular. The Moscow Patriarchate had issued a similarly restrictive text, 'The attitude of the Russian Orthodox Church toward the other Christian confessions', though, as Hackel admitted, the latter was trying to defend at least a 'degree of ecumenism' from the attacks of 'Russian diehards'.[130]

Stephen Platt had been in Copenhagen and reported that the fifty-year-old Danish branch remained strong. Then he was to be found in Bulgaria, opening a branch of the Fellowship in Sofia. He could now confirm that the Fellowship's Moscow base was up and running in the crypt of St Andrew's Anglican church. Its office was manned by a reader in the patriarchate who had translated most of Cranmer's liturgical texts into Russian and written a thesis on the Anglican daily Offices. In 2002, he was able to report on a Fellowship retreat in Greece, for the Athens chapter, reviving an idea from the 1980s which it was hoped might now be realized as an annual fixture.

In 2003 Andrew Walker, a convert to Orthodoxy, flew a kite for another sort of revival: a revisiting of something akin to the Bulgakov/Zernov proposal on intercommunion. Appealing to apophasis and the principle of economy, he argued for the possibility of true ecclesiality beyond the Orthodox fold. In his editorial Hackel noted that in 1969 a synod of the Moscow Patriarchate (but under State pressure?) had declared it was not prohibited to give the sacraments to Catholics and Old Believers, though nothing was said about Anglicans. But subsequently this concession was rescinded. Hackel also mentioned that, in the wake of the 1847 Concordat between Nicholas I and Pope Gregory XVI, exiled Catholics in the tsarist domains could, according to a statement of the Holy Synod, have recourse to Orthodox sacraments when cut off from their own. Philaret of Moscow had been a party to it, and Walker had named him, over against Khomiakov, as an Orthodox who thought there were 'etiolations of the one true Church' in the non-Orthodox Christian confessions.[131] Walker's proposal went far beyond those of the 1930s. He wanted an Orthodox 'open table' for all Trinitarian Christians with a personal faith in Christ as Lord. That would presuppose, he explained, a minimal dogmatic statement as a precondition for communion, yet 'fellowship', not doctrinal unity, should be the keyword.

Metropolitan Anthony Bloom of Sourozh was dead and there had to be adequate mention. He was born in Lausanne, the son of a tsarist diplomat; his mother was half-sister to the composer Alexander Scriabin. In 1923 the family fled from Tehran, his father's last posting, to France, enduring dreadful conditions on the way. When he came to England as a lay participant in the 1947 Abingdon conference of the Fellowship he had no intention of becoming a priest, rather than a medical doctor, the training for which he had received in Paris. The idea was given him by Gillet. A Russian-speaking priest was certainly needed with the death in 1950 of Father Vladimir Theokritoff who had celebrated at the former exarchal church, a building loaned by the Church of England, in Buckingham Palace

Road. Since 1931 Bloom had belonged to the patriarchate—in Paris at the church of the Rue Petel, its only parish—and never to the exarchate. In 1991 he would be nominated as a candidate for election as Patriarch but since he was not a Soviet citizen it was impossible. He was a wonderful speaker but a poor administrator. His chosen means of 'writing' was to record broadcasts, and the considerable Russian-language works now available in print indicate their extent. On ecumenism the anonymous biographer wrote, 'Though the young Fr Anthony came to Britain in the van of the ecumenical movement, he gradually ceased to be an enthusiast or even a supporter of the cause. Least of all was he comfortable about any ecumenism which involved the Catholic Church. He had apprehensions of putative Catholic endeavours to dominate the Christian world.'[132] In 1997 he sent to Moscow a negative letter on Catholic–Orthodox relations which had its hoped-for effect on the bishops. His last year as metropolitan was disturbed by the quarrel over the succession at London's Russian cathedral (also acquired from Anglicans) at Ennismore Gardens in Knightbridge. In 2006 Gillian Crow's memoir of Anthony Bloom would be reviewed in *Sobornost* by Rowan Williams, who brought out the forbidding as well as attractive elements in Bloom's personality. Writing at the height of a crisis in the affairs of Sourozh (Bishop Basil, the *locum tenens*, had sought to bring it under the *omophorion* of Constantinople, rather than Moscow), Williams hoped the acute, and litigious, resistance to Osborne's plan would not end in making of the Russian diocese an 'exotic import'.[133] That would have reversed Bloom's policy of Anglicization. Williams mentioned Bloom's Cold War politics (he favoured the retention of the nuclear deterrent) yet nuanced attitude to persecution in the USSR (he disliked Keston College which monitored Church affairs in the Soviet bloc in a manner useful to Western powers but admired Solzhenitsyn, one of the Soviet system's most implacable critics). For Metropolitan Anthony, 'the Church's business was not transitory politics'.[134]

By 2004 the general secretary had a much-increased parochial workload with the withdrawal of Basil Osborne from the Oxford community—first to London and then, after the partial failure of his canonical strategy, into retirement as a married layman. That year the annual conference took place at Ushaw College, Durham, formerly the great nursery of the Northern Catholic clergy, and the participants were able to see for themselves the decline in English Catholicism. The formation of a Romanian branch of the Fellowship had been approved by Patriarch Teoctist at a meeting with

Stephen Platt. The Romanian branch duly opened in Bucharest, at an event covered by Romanian television. A Russian conference of the Fellowship was held in the Patriarchal Library in Moscow, and Kallistos began it by entering the controversial waters of how the Orthodox generally should relate to other Christians. On the island of Mykonos (in Greece) the Fellowship sponsored a conference on the contemporary practice of Confession in the Orthodox Church. The incoming archbishop of Canterbury, Rowan Williams, was made 'patron' of the Fellowship—a new office created in recognition of the services to mutual Anglican–Orthodox understanding he had rendered through his writings.

Sergei Hackel died unexpectedly and Matthew Steenberg, then a Fellow of Greyfriars Oxford but later the London-based bishop of the Russian Orthodox Church outside Russia in its British incarnation, was obliged as assistant editor to steer the ship. The first issue of 2005 had more of Roman Catholic interest than was usual, perhaps by chance.

There was discussion of where the theological inspiration for the Fellowship had been coming from. Marcus Plested, director of the Cambridge Institute of Orthodox Christian Studies, founded in 1999, disagreed with any setting at odds of the newer, Florovskian, Neo-Patristic school and the older, more adventurous, Russian school, mainly Sophiological, of the 'fathers' of the Russian Religious Renaissance. Paul Valliere's newly published *Modern Russian Theology* sought to make that contrast programmatic, and to promote the notion of going beyond patristic Orthodoxy so as to forge a 'philosophic Orthodoxy for new times'.[135] Plested commented judiciously. 'I am not convinced that Valliere has fully allowed for the potentialities of the understanding of tradition as the opportunity for a creative re-affirmation and re-appropriation of our scriptural, liturgical and patristic inheritance—an understanding we can find delineated in both neopatristic and Russian schools.'[136] A similar message emerged from a contribution by Anastassy Brandon Galaher on a seemingly unlikely topic: an exchange of letters about Seraphim of Sarov between Florovsky and A. F. Dobbie-Bateman, that important behind-the-scenes figure from the Fellowship's early years. Florovsky had insisted on the need to interpret Seraphim's words Christologically, for all we are given by the Spirit is 'christoform', a statement which influenced Dobbie-Bateman's own account of the saint in his 1970 *The Return of St Seraphim*.[137] Dobbie-Bateman wrote to Florovsky, accepting his Christological interpretation of the saint's life, by which 'the Pentecostal interpretation seems to lose its disturbing, almost sectarian, vagueness'.[138] The letter touched on other themes from which Galaher singled out that of patristic authority, and this was relevant to Plested's disagreement with Valliere.

> The catholic consciousness or 'patristic mind'... is the living, eternal and faithful experience of Christ being wholly in the midst of his church in both head and members. In figures like St Seraphim, we see saints (called 'doctors and fathers') who are unique in that they have attained a level of catholicity, a completeness of the patristic mind, which allows them personally to witness for the whole Church 'from the completeness of a life full of grace'.[139]

Galaher pointed out that neo-patristicism of this kind, where the 'global gospel vision of the fathers' is not simply verbal but pneumatic could be described as common teaching for all the 'Parisian' theologians, despite the great differences between Bulgakov and Florovsky in some other respects.[140] In the letter, reproduced in its entirety in the article and copiously annotated, Florovsky went so far as to say of the *consensus patrum*, 'I do not like this phrase. The "authority" of the Fathers is not a *dictatus papae*. They are guides and witnesses, no more. Their *vision* is of authority, not necessarily their words'.[141]

Hackel was now obituarized. He had been born in Berlin, the son of a German-Russian convert to Orthodoxy who was a post-Revolutionary emigré. In 1940 his mother brought him to England, where he found his way to Lincoln College Oxford to read Modern Languages. After a decade of school teaching, he became lecturer in Russian at the University of Sussex in 1964 and continued in post until 1988. Ordained by Bloom in 1965, he edited the weekly religious broadcasts of the BBC Russian service. An early visit to Russia during Krushchev's anti-religious campaign sowed the seeds of his distrust of the Moscow Patriarchate. He became an outspoken advocate of the patriarchate's liberal wing, defending not only Father Alexander Men but also the unconventional nun Mother Maria Skobstsova, later St Maria of Paris, whose life he wrote.[142] He was fully committed to the ecumenical movement and saw his editorship of *Sobornost* in that light.[143]

The general secretary could report on the successful establishment of a branch of the Fellowship in St Petersburg and ambitious plans to open no longer just a 'chapter' but a 'bureau' in Athens (with office for enquiries, programme of lectures and events, sponsorship of new publications). The new editor of the journal was to be the distinguished patristic scholar Andrew Louth, then at Goldsmith's College, London, but later holder of a chair in patrology at the University of Durham. Andrew Louth's first editorial gave the journal—and by implication the Fellowship—a new orientation.

> For in the new millennium, the encounter between east and west is less between those from the east and those from the west (though this encounter has, indeed, been renewed in a different way), but rather for most Orthodox in the west an encounter within ourselves between what we owe to the east and what we owe to the west, Indeed, what is meant by 'east' is broader than simply the Orthodox of the Byzantine tradition; it needs to embrace, too, those of the Oriental Orthodox Churches, many of which are equally finding themselves at home in the West... Perhaps this is the way that our journal, *Sobornost*, should go: to be not so much a place of encounter between those of the east and those of the west, clearly distinguished, but rather a place where two kinds of belonging may be explored and developed—first, probably, among the 'western' Orthodox, whether western by destiny or by origin, but also among those who find in the traditions of eastern Christendom keys to the riches of their own western Christian tradition.[144]

Andrew Louth's second editorial confirmed what he had hinted at in the first. '*Sobornost*, as a primarily English journal, will increasingly be a voice for Orthodoxy in the West.'[145] Not that this remark was made in an anti-ecumenical spirit, for apart from gracious reference to all that the Orthodox had learned from Western scholarship there was also to be discussion in the issue of relations between Jews and Orthodox and between Evangelicals and Orthodox too. But there was little now, other than a historical retrospect, to suggest a continuing privilege for the relation that started the whole thing off—the relation between the Orthodox and the Anglicans. Symbolically, this seemed confirmed by a visit of Stephen Platt to Moscow where, speaking on the theme of the history of Christianity in the British Isles, he had met with the secretary of the patriarchate's commission for canonizations to discuss how early British saints might be included in the calendar of the patriarchate. It was a declaration of an alternative Christian history of England.

In 2007, the general secretary's report could not avoid mentioning the crisis in the Sourozh diocese, but he felt it premature to comment further other than to say it highlighted not only matters of Church governance but 'a whole host of questions that relate to the nature and place of Orthodox Christianity in Western Europe',[146] especially about what sort of Orthodoxy would best promote the message of the Gospel in this particular setting. But he pointed out that before the Second World War Russians of different jurisdictions had met in friendly ways in the Fellowship.

Gregory Woolfenden, now rector of St Mary's Ukrainian Orthodox church at New Britain, Connecticut, and teaching at Yale and St Sophia Orthodox University, New Jersey, drew attention to the recent reunion (not administratively) of the Russian Orthodox Church Outside Russia and the Moscow Patriarchate and explained how this might add to the already considerable complexity of Orthodox Church life in the United States, where differences in, for example, the calendar and liturgical practice can already lead to a degree of estrangement. Appropriately enough, an obituary was printed of Metropolitan Vitaly Ustinov, a leading (and perhaps the last) exemplar of the 'White' tradition in the Synodal Church of which he was the 'First Hierarch'. Not too much was known about this strand of Russian Orthodoxy in England—as distinct from in the United States—but it was obviously an important topic for *Sobornost* to treat. 'With Vladyka Vitaly's repose, so vanished ROCOR's last living link with pre-revolutionary imperial Russia and the tradition of resisting a Moscow which still supported the decisions of Metropolitan Sergii. Metropolitan Laurus signed the Act of Canonical Communion with Patriarch Alexey II on the feast of the Ascension in 2007, prompting the further splintering of the ROCOR. In death as in life, then, Vladyka Vitaly bore both the ideals and the contradictions of the White Russian movement itself. Nevertheless, his most important contributions—the preservation of liturgy, of monastic life, of Church Slavonic, of religious publication, of strict private asceticism and active community work—fulfilled crucial roles in the survival of the Russian Orthodox tradition.'[147]

Stephen Platt and Tim Grass of Spurgeon's College, London, had prepared an exploratory meeting for an Orthodox–Evangelical dialogue which met at Oxford in April 2008. A second meeting also in Oxford, specifically on ecclesiology, was scheduled for September of that year. This was an important development: if the Orthodox in the West wanted interlocutors who could be trusted not to stray from credal fundamentals, conservative Evangelicals were a safe bet.[148] It was also a return to an element in the Fellowship's earlier life, where some had sought a Protestant counter-balance to an unrelieved diet of High Anglicanism.

The Continuing Story

The editor's *Greek East and Latin West. The Church AD 681–1071* was a major work, not marred by the polemics of the almost identically entitled book by Philip Sherrard from 1959 which had caused such a stir in the Fellowship when reviewed so acerbically by Gerald Bonner in *Sobornost*'s pages.[149] Now, in 2008, Bonner was still on the job. He found notable Louth's comment on the events of 1054, the year so often quoted as marking the Schism's beginning. Except for a few isolated figures in the West it was quickly forgotten—and yet the controversy over the 'azymes' (unleavened altar-breads), in itself hardly worth mentioning, indicated an 'apostasy' inasmuch as neither side was willing to enter the symbolic universe of the other.[150]

The year 2009 began on a truly delicate topic, the primacy. The editorial noted what had become gradually obvious from the general secretary's reports, namely that his policy was to promote the 'worldwide' interests of the Fellowship—rather than, though Louth does not say so explicitly, its English branches. The 2008 conference had been held in America, at St Vladimir's, and took primacy as its subject though only two of the papers were available for publication. The editorial also noted that with the elevation to the patriarchate of Metropolitan Kirill of Smolensk, Bishop Hilarion Alfeyev had become head of External Affairs of the Russian Orthodox Church and Archbishop of Volokamsk. It was he who grasped the nettle of 'The Orthodox Understanding of Primacy and Catholicity' in this issue.

In Alfeyev's view, the primacy of Rome, and later of Constantinople, was entirely based on the political (imperial) significance of these cities and argues nothing for any jurisdiction beyond their own localities (later, patriarchates). Alfeyev admitted that the current situation in global Orthodoxy is problematic inasmuch as there is no 'supreme arbiter in cases when differences or conflict arise over ecclesiastical questions between two or more Local [i.e. autocephalous] Churches',[151] nor is there (at any rate as yet) any authoritative way of resolving the distinctively modern issue of multiple jurisdictions in the Diaspora. The only possible way is a pan-Orthodox council but none is likely since the Churches do not agree about its 'status and agenda'.[152] Yet catholicity is maintained through eucharistic communion, unity in doctrine, and meetings or the exchange of letters between regional (Alfeyev says 'local') primates. In Orthodoxy, Alfeyev explained, the notion of catholicity is linked more to the church of the bishop who is in his own place successor of Peter than to the geographically universal Church. The connexion with the universal Church is that the local bishop cannot embody its catholicity aright unless he is in concord with all other local bishops—to the extent that Alfeyev can accept Cyprian's view that there is only one episcopate in which each shares. As to primates, they have no direct jurisdiction over dioceses not their own but only a coordinating function exercised in union with their synods.

Alfeyev did not think that in the East, ecumenical councils were regarded as requiring the confirmation of the Roman bishop. Nevertheless, he was willing to put forward a 'general outline of the framework in which the primacy of the Bishop of Rome might be acknowledged by the Orthodox Churches, should the Christians of the East and West unite in one Church'—rather startling, after what had preceded.[153] First, the dogmatic unity of the ancient Church must be restored—citing the recently canonized fourteenth-century St Symeon of Thessalonica. '[T]he Catholics must prove that their faith is identical to that of the ancient undivided Church.'[154] What then? Only an Orthodox–Catholic dialogue could say, and before it happens the Orthodox must find a single voice on the issue of what primacy means on the level of universality since at the present time Constantinople and Moscow certainly do not agree on that. One might hazard that it will be a primacy of honour, not of jurisdiction, with, however, the possibility of 'fulfilling certain coordinating functions', which would not amount to acting as the single head of a worldwide Christianity.[155] Nor can there be any question of accepting the infallibility of the Roman bishop 'independent of acceptance by the Church' since for Orthodoxy it is precisely acceptance by the Church which guarantees the truth. Just as Catholics are surprised by the fact that Orthodoxy has not broken up in fragments, the Orthodox are surprised that Catholics continue to bother to have councils of bishops at all.

A review essay by Louth looked at three books on historic contacts between Orthodoxy and Anglicanism (all three were used by the present writer in 'The Encounter of East and West'). Reading these works by Pinnington, Doll (as editor) and Wheeler touched a chord. 'Relationships between Anglicanism and Orthodoxy have always been at the heart of the Fellowship of St Alban and St Sergius.'[156] Louth outlined the history of the relation of the English or British to Orthodoxy, rather relentlessly stamping on historical fantasies, and culminating in a statement of the status quo. 'We are probably now in a further period, marked by a growing confidence in the Orthodox voice, freed from the shackles of communist oppression, and a growing liberalization of world Anglicanism—a striking, though probably chance, synchronism—that is seeing a further period of estrangement between Anglicanism and Orthodoxy, occurring—strangely—at a time when the leader of world Anglicanism, the Archbishop of Canterbury, has probably a deeper understanding of and sympathy with Orthodoxy than any of his predecessors.'[157] And later: 'At least in the English-speaking world, it seemed for a time that there was an especial affinity between Anglicans and Orthodox, an affinity that seems to have been dissipated in recent years'.[158]

Reviews that year included *The Cambridge Companion to Orthodox Christian Theology* whose list of contributors reads like a catalogue of *Sobornost* editors and writers.[159] Its modest length made impossible chapters on a variety of important topics, from ethics to Mariology, and it was noted that though nearly all the contributors were Anglophone Orthodox, Anglophone Orthodoxy itself was largely ignored.

The 2010s

Arthur Macdonald Allchin had died and was obituarized by his friend Bishop Kallistos who recalled the sixty-three years of their friendship. Allchin's postgraduate research at Christ Church took for its subject the revival of religious life in the Church of England and it was the beginning of his great admiration for Father Benson, the founder of the Cowley Fathers. Kallistos thought the resultant *The Silent Rebellion*,[160] and indeed Donald's other works, a little lacking in theological thrust. He was at his best when 'exploring in a free-ranging manner the interaction between spirituality and poetry'.[161] He had joined the Fellowship as a schoolboy, and strengthened his links with Orthodoxy by getting to know the Lossky family, notably Nicolas, initially through the 1949 Fellowship conference—which in 'those more spacious days' lasted for three weeks.[162] The translation of *The Mystical Theology* was done by Nicolas, Allchin and Peter Hammond; Madeleine Lossky, Vladimir's wife, thought it read better than the French original, it was less heavy. In the mid-1950s Allchin got to know Hellenic Orthodoxy, and later Yannaras, and then in the late 1960s Staniloae. He was High Church but not an Anglo-Catholic. His only pastoral charge had been as curate at St Mary Abbots in Kensington, from 1956 to 1960. From 1960 to 1969 he was a

Librarian at Pusey House, and it was then that he developed his link with the Sisters of the Love of God at Fairacres. That looked ahead to the years 1986 to 2008 when he was warden of the Society of the Sacred Cross at Tymawr; the Welsh location fitted with his love of David Jones, Ann Griffiths, Gwenallt, and R. S. Thomas. By the end of his life he was fluent in Welsh. In between, from 1973 to 1987 he was a residentiary canon at Canterbury, and in this period he became a member of the International Anglican–Orthodox Doctrinal Commission (until 1984), and from 1987 to 1994 the first director of the St Theosevia Centre for Christian Spirituality. Kallistos describes him as 'Anglo-Orthodox', a perfect Alban and Sergius man. Allchin had said he would become Orthodox when the Anglican Communion did so.[163] His study of the Danish hymnwriter Nikolai Grundtvig, published in 1997, has been called the best book on that figure in any language. He was much influenced by two Cistercian monks, Dom André Louf of Mont des Cats and Thomas Merton: he was the first president of the Thomas Merton Society of Great Britain and Ireland. He also had a great sympathy for Methodism.

Two years later, in 2013, the editor took stock. It was natural to have in *Sobornost* articles on Orthodoxy and on East–West dialogue (like one on William Blake and Orthodoxy in the issue before him) but odd to have an article simply on Western Christianity as such yet there was one (on the Church–State relation in Protestant and especially Evangelical theology). This would *not* have been thought odd in the journal's earlier life, a sign of the move from Part One to Part Two of its story. There were several articles of specifically Russian interest and this too was only right given the Fellowship's origins. Liturgy in principle and in practice had always been one of its concerns, though an article on liturgical dance was a novelty, as indeed was an anonymous funeral rite produced in Greece.

Gerald Bonner, who kept the flame burning for the Latin tradition over many years in *Sobornost*, had died at last. It was while working as a Keeper of Manuscripts at the British Museum that he discovered Augustine of Hippo who would be the great scholarly love of his life. His *St Augustine of Hippo. Life and Controversies* in two volumes had led in 1964 to an invitation to join the Durham Theology Department.[164] From that there flowed his writing on the Northumbrian saints, in whom there was otherwise little academic interest. He was deeply attached to the traditional Anglican liturgy and a friend, albeit critically so, of the Orthodox. Louth reports

The Continuing Story

he had no time for attempts by the Orthodox to claim for themselves the Anglo-Saxon saints.[165]

2014 had been the centenary of the birth of Metropolitan Antony Bloom. The first issue of *Sobornost* for 2015 carried two of his addresses, one not previously published. The editor rightly recorded in his opening remarks that Bloom's 'faith, steadfast but intellectually searching' became something of a beacon in the disoriented 1960s and 1970s, and remarked on how his contribution to a university mission at Oxford at the end of the 1960s had outshone the principal missioner and left on many a lasting impression of a man of truly living prayer.[166] The present writer can bear this out for he was one of the hearers.

As this story comes, for now, to its conclusion, five members of the Fellowship council attended a conference in Moscow on the influence of St Sergius outside Russia. Nicolas Zernov, who wrote lovingly on the saint and helped choose him as patron at St Albans, will have been there in spirit.[167]

→ 2 ←

The Wider East

In the half century which stretched ahead from 1968, *Sobornost* did not forget its Russian roots. It consolidated the interest it had shown before or by that year in Greek and Romanian Orthodoxy. It continued to be concerned for the Non-Chalcedonian Churches, including not least Ethiopia, a topic not easily pursued owing to the exoticness of culture and language. And it showed a special predilection for the Syrian Orthodox, which meant both their present-day plight and their historic literature. This was in the first place, the contribution of two specialist Syriac scholars: Sebastian Brock, an Oxford Anglican, and Father Robert Murray, a London Catholic. The two men were admirable translators of, and commentators on, the wonderful verse of the ancient Syriac theologian-poets.

Old Russians

Much as Georges Florovsky may have regretted it, the zest of English Anglicans for the Russian Orthodox in exile was owed in part to a fascination with the 'fathers' of the Russian religious renaissance—in which connexion one could also speak of 'grandfathers': such figures as Khomiakov, Soloviev and Dostoevsky.

Writing in *Sobornost* for 1972, Zernov compared Dostoevsky with the contemporary figure of Alexander Solzhenitsyn. Both were novelists of freedom before God, but writing in such different situations that their *métiers* seem far apart. 'Solzhenitsyn is the master of preaching without a sermon; he challenges his readers in such a way that they are obliged to rethink their position', whereas Dostoevsky 'wrote for people brought up in the Christian tradition and familiar with the Biblical language and thought'.[1] Zernov sought to demonstrate the importance of the latter for two novels, *The Brothers Karamazov* and *The Possessed*, not only by concise analysis of five strata in the writing, the deepest of which, he believed, was the theological, but also by investigation of the possible significance attaching to the names Dostoevsky gives his chief characters. Both authors, Dostoevsky and Solzhenitsyn, describe the most brutal degradation, but they are not pessimists, knowing that the 'spark of Divine Light cannot be finally extinguished'.[2]

In 2009, Avril Pyman, biographer of both Pavel Florensky and Anthony Bloom,[3] wrote on Dostoevsky's novels. In a complex paper, offering a conversation about joy and tragedy that drew in a variety of figures from the critic Mikhail Bakhtin to the Staretz Silouan, her view of Dostoevsky ended with Rowan Williams and Bloom. For Bloom, in broadcast talks now translated into Russian, Dostoevsky was unable to describe an evangelical perfection that went beyond his own experience. In *The Brothers Karamazov* his Starets Zosima is saccharine compared with its model, St Tikhon Zadonsky. 'Yet far from condemning the great novels as profane, [Bloom] valued their insight, took psychological examples from them as he did from his own experience to illustrate his teaching, to awake at least the longing for redemption in his listeners, to demonstrate the horror and emptiness of perdition and to suggest albeit fleeting insights into the beauty of holiness which can shine forth in the most unlikely places.'[4] For Williams, 'Dostoyevsky is concerned as a writer to show what belief and unbelief are like rather than to conclude either argument'.[5] As for herself, she believed that 'Dostoyevsky, an artist, not a saint, used his great gift not to reveal the Light which he himself sought, but rather to reawaken the desire for it in the hearts of indifferent or forgetful readers, not least by showing a whole world of sinners beloved and potentially saved—for whom sin is a dead end, holiness a life-giving perspective'.[6]

The ordained Oxford Russianist Mark Everitt wrote on 'Vladimir Solov'ev: A Russian Newman?' He thus picked up the title of an impressionistic study of Soloviev by the *éminence grise* of the secret papal mission to immediately post-Bolshevik Russia, the Jesuit Michel d'Herbigny—but added an admonitory question-mark.[7] The ecumenical importance of Soloviev's vision made this article an important one for the journal. Everitt gave an excellent overview of Soloviev's career against its rather unpropitious background in the reign of Tsar Alexander III. His main focus was Soloviev's essay 'Dogmatic Development of the Church and the Union of the Churches', originally intended as an introduction to his major unfinished theological work, which itself was meant to cover the entirety of biblical and Church history and to be entitled 'The History and

Future of Theocracy'. In the articles that made up the essay, Soloviev had two problems especially in view: the schism of the Old Believers, and the hostility of Slavophiles to the Roman Church. Discussion of the latter, 'The Great Quarrel', aroused in Russia, so Everitt claimed, the same sensation that Tract 90 caused in England in the early Victorian era. According to Soloviev, the early Slavophiles laudably expressed 'the idea of the Church as a living, substantial unity', rather like in the West the early Catholic Tübingen school theologian, Johann Adam Moehler, whom Khomiakov had read. But these lay theologians, or religious philosophers, committed the fallacy of misplaced abstraction. In Everitt's words, paraphrasing but also translating from Soloviev's essay:

> [The Slavophile writers] defined the essence of the Church magnificently, but not how to realize it amidst the 'paucity of love, the decay of faith, and the fierce religious divisions which are what we actually see'. Faced with this dilemma, Khomiakov retreated into Orthodox exclusivism, accused the whole of the West of being perverted by rationalism, and came to the 'monstrous conclusion that we alone are in possession of absolute truth, and all the rest are in absolute falsehood'.[8]

Soloviev considered in sober fashion the two main Latin heresies, the Filioque and papal infallibility. Khomiakov had seen the Filioque as the primordial 'fratricidal act' of the schism, an all-determining Cain and Abel moment. Soloviev disagreed.

> There was no standard Latin translation of the creed and in the Spanish texts it is an early, and a constant feature. There is a clear implication that it is intended to express the faith of the fathers of Chalcedon. In any case, Chalcedon recommended *four* documents as enshrining 'the faith of Nicaea', not especially stressing the present creed (whose Greek text is not constant either), or insisting on its verbal integrity. At the Seventh Ecumenical Council, a creed was read by Tarasius [the Constantinopolitan patriarch], and approved, in which the Holy Spirit is said to proceed 'from the Father through the Son'.[9]

As to the pope, Soloviev maintained that no general council had ever condemned the Latin view of monarchical Church governance and the teaching authority of the Roman bishop. After his 1885 visit to the pro-Orthodox Bishop Strossmayer of Diakovar, in Bosnia, Soloviev composed an open letter in French, nominally addressed to that worthy. In it he gave his view on the reunion of the Orthodox Church with Rome. In terms of doctrinal theory, he wrote:

> We are united with Catholicism by all that we ourselves recognize as absolute and unalterable truth, whereas the errors which separate us from Catholic unity are only opinions which have no higher authority even in the eyes of those writers who put them forward. As for the mass of the faithful of the Eastern Church, they cannot be accused of any definite error, since their faith is the same as the Catholic faith, apart from their ignorance of certain doctrinal definitions made in the West since the separation.[10]

In terms of the practicalities:

> It must be considered a very favourable circumstance that the Eastern Church, and in particular the Russian Church, has never been part of the Western patriarchate so that the uniform centralization of jurisdiction which has developed within the Latin Church cannot rightly be imposed on us in all its rigour.[11]

And Soloviev added that the position accorded in Russia to the Orthodox emperor must stay intact.

This insistence did not mollify the tsar's censors. An extended ban on Soloviev's journalism (though not his lecturing) had as compensation increasing interest in his ideas abroad. It was now that he received the invitation to write, for a French publisher, *La Russie et l'Église universelle*.[12] In that work he maintained that Byzantium had remained Orthodox in doctrine but had failed to establish a State on consistently Christian principles. The Roman pope combined with the Russian tsar could surely do better. A compressed version, *L'Idée russe*, reached pope and emperor.[13] Leo XIII described it as beautiful but, short of a miracle, impossible. Alexander III was less entranced, calling it sad that a son of his own tutor should come to think thus. In any case Soloviev himself became disillusioned with the monarchy after the feeble reaction to the famine of 1891 and the renewed pogroms against the Jews. In *Three Conversations* he turned to apocalyptic, seeing the reunion of Christendom as reserved for the final persecution, and the last days of the world. Yet his own act of requesting sacramental Absolution and Communion from a Catholic priest, Father Nicholas Tolstoi, at Moscow in 1896 was in his own mind a prophetic gesture towards this end—and *the* End likewise.

Comparing, then, the approach to Church history of Soloviev and Newman (the latter in the *Essay on the Development of Christian Doctrine*),

Everitt would say that Soloviev starts further back—from the apostolic preaching as found in the sermon material in the Acts of the Apostles. He also continues further than Newman in the celebrated Essay, right down to the last commonly recognized ecumenical council, in 787. Everitt found Soloviev the fairer critic of the two. He has nothing comparable to Newman's 'wresting' his description of the state of the early Church to fit the state of the Roman Church in his day. What Soloviev *does* have is a master-idea for his whole narrative, 'which he sees all along as a progressive unfolding of the necessary implications of the fundamental doctrine of the divine-manhood'.[14]

In 'The Spirit of the Age to Come', Rowan Williams looked at the great Russian theologians on the Holy Spirit but in an unexpected light. He began with some striking phrases from St Gregory of Nyssa. On Williams's interpretation of that fourth-century Church Father, 'the Holy Spirit [is] that mode of the divine presence and activity which is associated with the coming Kingdom'. Accordingly, Williams went on, the Holy Spirit is 'primarily to be apprehended and experienced in the dimension of *hope*, the sense of a promise of the future which is in no sense conditioned or determined by the limits of the present and the past'.[15] He entered a plea—mentioning now one of his Russians, Sergei Bulgakov, writing in *Sobornost* for 1939 on the 'Spirit of prophecy'[16]– that we not confuse the truly eschatological with the parody of it that is the chiliastic, an 'essentially finite historical utopia'.[17] The Son descended into this 'age' or 'world' (*saeculum*) so as to redeem it, and the transforming work of the Spirit can no more be sundered from the Son's redemptive work than the redemptive work of the Son can be sundered from the creative work of the Father. Beware the pseudo-eschatology which sacrifices present generations, or claims to supersede normative morality.

Yet hope is needed when the resources of the present cannot suffice. Williams wanted to locate true hope more specifically in the context of tragedy, for that was where his reading in literary criticism and recent moral philosophy had led him. What is tragedy if not a conflict between two goods which cannot now be pursued together? So it is in Sophocles' *Antigone*, where the good of the polis and the good of the family are at odds. Or again, the self-fulfilment of two persons may appear exclusive, the one of the other. The Welsh Wittgensteinian D. Z. Phillips took moral dilemmas to be essentially tragedies where, it seems, evil will come, whichever choice is made. Others, such as the German Protestant

Existentialist thinker Karl Jaspers, believed that Christianity has no place for tragedy. Williams summoned his old supervisor, the Scottish Episcopalian Donald Mackinnon, to argue the opposite case. Insofar as God enters a 'humanity whose mode of being is God-less-ness', the very Incarnation itself is tragic, something expressed in the cry of dereliction (if that is what it was!) from the Cross. Here Williams's supporting reference was again from Bulgakov, in a sermon on the Resurrection in *Ultimate Questions: an Anthology of Modern Russian Religious Thought*, a collection edited by Alexander Schmemann.[18]

Tragedy generates a cry of longing for the Spirit—the cry that, at the Pentecost of the Risen One was heard. But the cry continues to go up, and for the Church that is supremely so in her Liturgy. Interpreting the Byzantine Liturgy more than its Western counterpart, and indebted especially to Paul Evdokimov's writings, Williams declares that, as the ritual comes to its close, 'We have claimed the fullness of our incorporation in the Word by opening ourselves to the transforming power of the Spirit, and so are placed in full communion with the Father'.[19] The significance for the issue of tragedy can now be spelt out. '[T]he action of the Spirit ... here bestows the possibility of transcending that collision of individual absolutes, individual imperatives, which we have remarked to be the dominant characteristic of modern expressions of tragic experience.'[20]

And this is where Vladimir Lossky's theology of the Spirit comes into its own. Lossky's understanding of the work of the Holy Spirit turns not only on a contrast of human *persons* with human *nature*—for in Lossky's view the redemption of human nature at large is the task of the Son. His pneumatology also turns on a contrast between human *persons* and human *individuals*. To Lossky's mind, individuality is at best a poor sketch of true personhood, and at worst an obstacle to its emergence in all its rich relationality. The Paschal Mystery, climaxing in Pentecost, makes possible an inter-personal communion transcending the clash of individual identities. That does not make the Christian life, sentimentally, all peace and joy. It may be, rather, a 'communion in horror and glory'.[21] In 2008 the editor of *Sobornost*, Andrew Louth, would find Rowan Williams's suggestive *pensées* on the Holy Spirit in Russian theology—a tiny bilingual English/French book published in Quebec under the title *A Margin of Silence*—perhaps the only way to speak properly of the Holy Spirit. The sources were mainly Bulgakov, though Florensky and Lossky played their part, and the latter had given Williams its title. It was surely indebted to this *Sobornost* essay of forty years before.[22]

New Russians

The 1988 conference theme was the 'Russian Spirit and the Universal Church'. It was the millennium of Rus, and readers could look forward in the next couple of issues to some Russian topics for a change from the Greek subjects that had become more frequent of late. The concluding issue of 1988 opened with a stirring address by Archbishop Robert Runcie of Canterbury where he read from a letter of Metropolitan Platon of Kiev to a previous Primate of All England, Edward Benson, exactly a century before. From this it transpired that the Church of England was the only Western Church which had sent congratulations on the ninth centenary of the baptism of St Vladimir. These were the 'deep roots' that Runcie had in mind when speaking of Anglican/Russian relations.[23]

'Same homeland, different future' was the laconic title of a crucial article written under a pseudonym by a Muscovite member of the Russian Church and sent for translation to the United Kingdom. Not only was its writing in the year 1988 significant, its date in July was too, so rapidly was the scene changing. The situation in Russia was volatile, with *perestroika* succeeding to *glasnost*. But how long will this last, asked the author, before some reversal intervenes caused by shifts in the balance of power in the ruling party? Every day counts for the present and the future of the Church. The article stressed the reality (but not necessarily the enduring reality) of the change and its top-down character.

> Those very Soviet bosses who had hitherto feared so much as to set eyes on a priest suddenly began, as if on command (come to think of it, it was on command) to praise all that related to the Church, from icons to saints. It was a tribute to the obedience of the minions of the Party apparatus: no sooner said than done. The persecutors switched role to become custodians.[24]

As during the Second World War, the Communist Party, faced with national disaster, turned to the Church for help, 'Feeling the chill dread of imminent chaos and disorder throughout the land'.[25] Gorbachev's hugely positive speech of 29 April 1988 at his official meeting with the patriarch and the members of the governing synod suggested to the writer the possibility of a 'new Edict of Milan', 'according to which the

State, admitting its errors and impotence, would free Christians from all prohibitions and limitations, allowing the emergence of a new symphony, laying the foundations for the peaceful coexistence and cooperation between former persecutors and their erstwhile victims.'[26] There were already strong hints of new legislation to permit the revival of religious education, and charitable work by the Church, as well as the building of new churches indicated by the registering of parish communities with officialdom. Some surviving churches and at least two monasteries had already been returned. But after the drastic closures of the Krushchev years the numbers needed would, at the present rate of building, take several decades to provide, above all outside the western Ukraine, which had largely escaped the pre-War assault on churches.

The writer's prophecy for the future was not well founded. He thought the most likely scenario to be a '"Bulgarian version" [of Communism], combining firm State controls with a degree of Church autonomy.'[27] This of course assumed the continuance of Soviet power. The true outcome (as could be seen by the second decade of the succeeding century) was noted only as a marginal possibility: an alliance of the Church with Great Russian nationalism. That became a recipe for governance once it became clear there would be a large-scale revival of Orthodoxy in the Russian lands. That in turn implied re-conversion. The writer recognized that conditions might be favourable for re-evangelization. 'The godless masses seek a way out of the moral dead-end... spiritual desolation, cynicism and bitterness.'[28] Not that he thought the institutional Church well placed to take advantage. Zeal had been emasculated, priests were self-censoring, the Orthodox intelligentsia had little confidence in the hierarchs, there was a division among the former between liberals and nationals comparable to that between Westernizers and Slavophiles under the tsardom.

> The liberals in that community advocate a careful recreation of the Renovationist experiment; whereas the nationalist wing stands for a strict preservation of Orthodox traditions and popular historical customs, allowing any innovations only after much careful thought. A great part of the clergy and laity support this latter tendency.[29]

In September 1988 a Fellowship pilgrimage to Russia was made up of both Anglicans and Orthodox, who could thus see for themselves. The Anglican reporter noted the lections in both Slavonic and the vernacular at the cathedral of Kiev; more young women and men at the Liturgy; much renovation work in progress; optimism about forthcoming legislation on the part of patriarchal officials; a tendency among Intourist guides to touch on the spiritual (and not just cultural) significance of icons.[30]

Runcie gave a circumstantial account of his participation in the Russian millennium celebrations, and reported on a *sobor* at Zagorsk, which he cannot, however, have attended personally except for the ceremonial functions. Despite passing useful statutes including the restoration of the chairmanship of parish councils to parish priests, it had refused for the time being to canonize the martyrs of the Bolshevik period. The archbishop felt that 'the Church has not yet quite abandoned the caution it has learned in a very hard school'.[31] His 'one major misgiving' ran: 'Was the identification of the Orthodox church and the Russian culture too close? What of other Christian groups? ... What of Jews and Muslims? A bishop from West Germany said, "I understand the Byzantine tradition of the Russian Church. But for us since the Nazi era this degree of patriotism is unthinkable".'[32] He made a visit to the so-called Christian dissidents, who also had interesting comments to make. The Church must now get modern teaching materials for enquirers after adult baptism. And it must encourage centres of spirituality and holiness as beacons of light in a materialist society.

Sergei Hackel shared Runcie's anxieties about the future direction of Moscow. In 1997 Hackel recorded his dislike of Yeltsin's restriction of the religious freedoms offered by the 1993 Russian Constitution, a restriction carried out at the behest of the Moscow Patriarchate which on this was allied with both Nationalists and Communists. In 1998 he took the opportunity to criticize the Russian record on anti-Semitism when speaking in St Petersburg at a conference on 'Theology after Auschwitz and the Gulag'. During and after the Second World War the Soviets had suppressed mention of the special victimizing of Russian and Baltic Jews by the Nazis, not least because Slavs and others had given a helping hand. The Orthodox needed to hear more of the Shoah east of Poland. Hackel wanted oral historians in Russia to seek out candidates for the status of 'righteous Gentiles', an official Israeli categorization. One Hackel could think of immediately was Metropolitan Andrei Szeptycky, but of course he was a Uniate. Hackel held up the example of the Roman Catholic Church as a model in its response to the Shoah in the Second Vatican Council's declaration *Nostra aetate*. The 'Catholic world' had accepted 'responsibility for teachings and attitudes which helped to provide the context, even the "justification" ... for the horror'.[33] He stressed that in the preamble to Vatican II there had been dialogue with at least one

Jewish scholar, Jules Isaac, as well as the president of the World Jewish Congress. In the council's eventual programme, anti-Judaism was to be removed from the pulpit and supersessionism reconsidered since the latter was not the plain message of the Letter to the Romans where the issue of non-Christian Jewry was raised. Had this been heeded among the Russian Orthodox? Hackel was depressed. Relations with Rome were bad, anti-Semitism endemic, all ideas of reform tainted by association with Renovationism—they were said to amount to 'Neo-Renovationism', *neo-obnovlenchestvo*, though the original Renovationists had no interest whatsoever in the question of the Jews. Of course Scripture and Tradition must be carefully weighed. But that would include looking again at the pejorative use of 'the Jews' in the Gospels and Acts; rhetoric from, for instance, Gregory of Nyssa and John Chrysostom; the canons, such as one from the Council in Trullo requiring segregation; the services for Holy Week—which use the term 'deicide' avoided by the historic liturgies in the West; the willingness of the official canonizations committee of the patriarchate to consider 'Jewish ritual murders'.

Hackel's laudatory obituary of Father Alexander Men, appearing a few years previously, had to be relevant to his words. Hackel had touched on Men's Jewish ancestry, his baptism in the underground Church by those refusing any dealings with the Soviet State, how when approaching ordination he was helped by a metropolitan dismissed during the Krushchev persecution, the publication under a pseudonym of his voluminous writings by the Brussels publishing house Vie avec Dieu, and his sudden propulsion to television fame under Gorbachev and Yeltsin. He ended his account with Men's murder on 9 September 1990 en route to celebrating the Liturgy in his parish of the Presentation of our Lord at Novaia Derevnia, between Moscow and Zagorsk, and the failure of the police to make any progress in tracing the culprit. Men had more of a link to the Fellowship's history than might meet the eye. A correspondence with Sister Ioanna Reitlinger, the iconographer of St Basil's Chapel, was published after both their deaths. '[F]ollowing his advice, she lived to create the main icon of her life—the icon of her soul.'[34] He valued her link with Bulgakov, who, like Men himself, was inspired by Soloviev. And she gave him the vestments she had made for Bulgakov and his letters to her, telling him they would be a spiritual heritage for him. Men counselled her in her increasing blindness and in her difficulties with the Church in Tashkent, telling her in return of the connexion between accepted suffering and those one loves. Her true blessing was to be surrounded by those who needed her. Urging people to be free and fearless had been at the heart of his ministry of spiritual direction. This blithe spirit was obviously Hackel's *beau idéal* of an Orthodox priest.

In the remaining issue of 2001, Hackel gave an account of what he termed, not very flatteringly, 'Managerial Patterns in a Patriarchal Church'. Not only under the Soviets but in the post-Soviet period, there was no realization of the 1917/1918 *sobor*'s vision of a patriarch assisted by an elected synod of bishops and a 'supreme Church council' consisting of three bishops chosen by the synod plus six clerical and six lay representatives elected by the 'most recent local [i.e. national] council of the Russian Church'—the councils in question to be summoned at intervals of no more than three years. The thesis of Byzantine law that decisions of the court of the patriarch are subject to no appeal or review since that court is the 'foundation and source' of all ecclesiastical courts whatever, had been too influential.[35] The new statutes of the Moscow patriarchate operate with a notion of 'sacred headship', *svishchennonachalie*, which the then patriarch, if correctly reported, applied in 1997 in no uncertain terms to his own claim to authority over the thinking of the clergy. Not that episcopal collegiality was the only issue at stake here. Such authority would be no more 'conciliar' in the sense of the 1917/1918 *sobor* even were it oligarchic in form, i.e. enacted by a group of bishops acting alone.

The Soviet period statutes of 1945 and 1988 and the post-Soviet statutes of 2000 give the patriarch with his synod an 'exercise of power ... hardly subject to scrutiny, discussion or control'.[36] In the latest statutes, the bishops are empowered to call a national council—but only if they consider it necessary (though at least there had been no truth in the rumour, circulating in 2000, that the national council would be dropped altogether, on the grounds that simple priests and laity had never attended an ecumenical council). To make matters worse—from Hackel's perspective—the selection of new bishops is in the hands of the synod, not the diocesan assemblies envisaged in the *sobor*. *Sobornost* (the quality, not the publication!) is 'too often banished to the fringes of church life'.[37] This, so Hackel believed, was paralysing the ability of the Church to draw new members. It cannot be said that the demographics of the Russian Church in the years after 2000 have verified this claim, since its growth has been staggering by the terms of almost any other Christian body in the world.

Philip Walters of Keston College returned readers to the nitty-gritty of what was happening in Bulgakov's beloved Russia today. After the collapse of Communism there had been a fairly widespread religious revival of a somewhat eclectic kind in which missionaries from abroad had space to make headway. Those who congregated around them did not, however, constitute stable denominational groups. Nevertheless, the diffusion of Protestantism had been considerable, affecting especially 'actors, artists, musicians, journalists and teachers of humanities',[38] while newly opened or reopened Catholic parishes, intended for ethnic Germans and Poles transported onto the soil of the former Soviet Union, may have as many as sixty per cent ethnic Russian membership—not the result of missionary effort, for this was minimal, but by way of spontaneous adherence. There had been a struggle between 'restoration' and 'innovation' among those representing religions long established on Russian soil. The Soviet-era restrictions meant that the Orthodox have missed out on mainstream Western Christian trends which now shock them, not excluding the ecumenical movement itself. Ecumenism had been exploited by Soviet authorities to further their global agenda. As a consequence it is profoundly tainted as 'e-communism' or 'economism'. Sects with a North American origin are seen as 'elements in a US-backed market-orientated neocolonialism'.[39] However, the Orthodox themselves still have problems with regional or local officials stuck in a Soviet mindset, and sometimes ally with Muslims to gain concessions.

In 1990, Walters reminded readers, a year before the collapse of the Soviet Union, a generous law of religious freedom was passed, and in 1993 this was reflected in the new constitution of the Russian Federation. But encouraged by the patriarchate, various regions passed more restrictive legislation against proselytism, which led eventually to the 1997 law reining in religions other than Orthodoxy, Islam, Buddhism and Judaism. 'Religious groups' can practise private worship, but 'religious organizations' must succeed in registering if they are to own property, run schools or bring religious literature into the country. Concern for 'totalitarian sects' was used to pass the 1997 law, but these are so little apparent that one expert has called this battle a battle with shadows. Indigenous Protestant sects who do not want to be under the umbrella of a centralized organization are the main victims in practice, though Catholics have also suffered through the denial of residence permits to priests and bishops born abroad. The patriarchate's claim that all the Russian lands are its canonical territory gives credence to these moves. Groups with a nationalist agenda can take shelter under this concept, since the Orthodox Church stands for Russia, tradition, and 'non-Westernism' as well as Christianity. It is unclear whether over time a process of familiarization will set in whereby confrontation between 'traditional' and 'new' religions will diminish, or whether world trends will militate against this. The post-Twin Towers re-activation of the United States on the world stage had generated in the patriarchate a new fear of 'globalization' understood as 'a secularizing neocolonial agenda which will impose an unacceptable uniformity, based on materialist consumerism'.[40] This is why the spokesmen for the patriarchate are now stressing the need for a world pluralism of national cultures each with its own value-system (compare 'communitarians' in the West).

Walters ended with a notable discussion of the rights of conscience. '[W]hile for liberals the concept of "difference" stands for individual freedom, for communitarians the concept of "difference" involves the role of the group in limiting the individual freedom of its members.'[41] So the 2000 document 'Foundations for a Social Concept for the Russian Orthodox Church' could state that the principle of freedom of conscience means the privatization of religion and testifies to society's loss of religious aims: indeed, to the civil order's de facto indifference to the Church's activity. The introduction of that principle was little short of a cue for mass apostasy.

New Greeks

The condition of new theology in Greece became a regular preoccupation of the Allchin years, and it never again went away. Anthony Koumantos, graduate of the University of Athens studying at King's London, and writing in 1974, furnished an attempt at overview. His analysis of the background was instructive. In the newly independent Greek State people sought roots in the Western Enlightenment. Ecclesiastically speaking, they created a Greek Church that was defined as companion of the State, with, in its wake, pietistic movements seeking to save both nation and Church by promoting a morality suited to a Greek-Christian civilization on a scheme that left little to the revelation of the Word through salvation via his Body in the Holy Spirit.

Of course academic theology can help students get a first grip. But its merely human wisdom must give way to existential illumination through the eucharistic *synaxis* for the sake of a new world. Koumantos touched on the recent Athonite renewal, which had chiefly come about through trained theological students in three of the monasteries: Stavronikita, Philotheou, Simonopetra. In time, he thought, one can expect there to be a parting of the ways between the renewed monastic theology and the desideratum that a renovated Greek theology must address 'all the aspects of life'.[42]

John Zizioulas has already been mentioned as an increasingly important ecumenical figure and among the reviews from 1974 was his 'The Unity of the Church in the Holy Eucharist and the Bishop, in the First Three Centuries' in its Greek original, which took the form of an Athens University doctoral thesis from 1965. Stephen Parsons gave a very competent run-through of its contents, noting how at times the argument was pressing New Testament evidence to the limit, and occasionally lacked satisfactory logical form. Nonetheless the book, as he rightly divined, was of huge ecumenical significance. It overcame the dichotomy the eucharistic ecclesiology of the Saint-Serge teacher Nikolai Afanasiev had introduced between an 'Ignatian' and a 'Cyprianic' view of the Church—the first, biblically entirely correct, based on the Church as local, the second, biblically rather less correct (despite, say, Acts 9:31 with its reference to 'the Church throughout all Judaea and Galilee and Samaria'), based on *Ecclesia* as universal. As Parsons explained, for Zizioulas, 'The unity of the Church would be a unity of full Catholic Churches fulfilling one another, each having the genuine Apostolic tradition and the Eucharist'.[43] Not least 'the office of the bishop is what links one church with another, since they all possess it in common.'[44]

The Catholic theologian Paul McPartlan had written, under Kallistos's supervision, a study of Zizioulas and the French Jesuit giant of *ressourcement* Henri de Lubac, for they shared the view that the Church, to be understood as communion, must be exhibited primarily in the Eucharist.[45] But Hugh Wybrew pointed out some notable divergences between de Lubac and Zizioulas, even if he began by affirming a point in common.

> Both reacted against individualism. But de Lubac was concerned to de-individualize Christians, by emphasizing that Christians are always related with God as members of the Church. Zizioulas, by contrast, is concerned to de-individualize Christ, who is not to be understood apart from Christians.[46]

Moreover, while 'de Lubac understands human destiny to be fulfilled in a relationship with God above time and space, Zizioulas sees our transcendent destiny as ahead rather than above'.[47] Whereas for de Lubac there is a substantial presence of Christ in the consecrated elements, for Zizioulas the eucharistic presence is through mystical identification with 'the Christ who comes'.[48] There were other contrasts too. A reader of the review might wonder whether the two writers could usefully be paired at all.

Towards the end of Part One of the present work, 'The Encounter of East and West', I pointed to another Greek writer who would tower over the pages of *Sobornost* in the future. John Saward now reviewed Christos Yannaras's 'The Metaphysic of the Body in John Climacus'. Yannaras's study was a *tour de force*. It turned on its head a natural reading of St John's *Ladder of Divine Ascent*, that early Byzantine classic of the ascetic life. Yannaras argued that, despite the depreciatory language, this typically monastic theologian was hugely positive about the body and 'eros', working not with a dualism of matter and spirit but with a contrast of life and death, incorruptibility and corruption. Saward was disappointed that Yannaras's interest in Heidegger had not moved on from *Sein und Zeit* to the later writings where the Freiburg thinker made appeal to the *Gelassenheit* of the German mediaeval mystics (notably Meister Eckhart, so fruitfully studied by Lossky). Saward thought bringing the Eastern ascetic tradition together with this partially contemporaneous Western spiritual tradition might be of value. His own—even more audacious—contribution was to suggest a parallel with D. H. Lawrence's anthropology. The work reviewed was a thesis in French of which a Greek translation had been published at Athens.[49]

More influential was Yannaras's *De l'absence et de l'inconnaissance de Dieu*, published by the Paris Dominican house du Cerf,[50] and discussed in the same number by George Every who, once again, demonstrated his many-sided intellectual competence. Yannaras was seeking to enlist Heidegger and Denys against the historic thinking of the Christian West, and Every noted a Catholic commentator (it was in the second number of *Istina*, the French Dominicans' 'Russian' journal, for 1972) who had found here a 'Greek Slavophilism', not a true opening to Tradition. Yannaras had brought together the divine darkness of Denys and Heidegger's *das Nichtige*, 'Nothing'. In the existential nihilism of modern man (*Sobornost* had presented a Yannaras essay on the 'Death of God' in 1966), he thought he saw the logical outgrowth of the element of theological rationalism in the Western way of doing theology. Every's own conclusion, while expressed in measured terms, was rather damning.

> My doubt is partly about the clear lines that are drawn between Eastern and Western apophatic theology, and partly about the existential interpretation of the divine darkness in terms of 'the absence of God' in the Western post-Christian sense. I am quite sure that for some the nihilism that denies the metaphysical foundations of belief is a necessary stage in the destruction of idols, and so in the return to faith, and I am grateful to Yannaras for calling attention to Heidegger's own awareness of the distinction between Christianity (*Christianisme*) and the New Testament faith. But I am not sure that it is legitimate to give to his analysis this theological slant. This is an intensely stimulating book, but this use of Western ways of thought for defensive ends is perhaps more reminiscent of the modern Greek theology that he rejects than Yannaras would like to think.[51]

Rowan Williams's article 'The Theology of Personhood, A Study of the Thought of Christos Yannaras', was esoteric in its philosophical vocabulary, but far less so in its doctrinal content. Williams opened by detecting links in Yannaras to the personalism of Vladimir Lossky, on whom Williams was still writing his great thesis (never published, except in Russian translation, but much consulted, both in the Bodleian Library and 'online'). He would close by calling Yannaras's thought a 'development and maturation of Lossky's ideas', albeit one in not altogether happy subservience to a particular secular metaphysic.[52] The rest of his account would be taxing. He summed up his overall conclusion in advance. Yannaras synthesizes the Greek patristic tradition, up to Palamas and other mediaeval writers, with modern phenomenological thought. Williams called it a genuine alternative to the language 'customary in the Latin tradition and its offshoots', adding that 'alternative' does not necessarily mean 'superior'.[53]

There followed a careful exposition of Yannaras's ideas. On the theme of the book, they start out from etymology. Thus *prosopon* ('person') comes from *pros hopôs* ('in relation to [something]'), which gives Yannaras his cue for coining for the use of modern Greek a Heidegger-influenced term, 'ek-static', meaning 'inherently open to what is other than oneself'. Applied to a personal God this has definite implications. 'If [God] is personal, we must see Him as creative energy relating to creation in the present', and not as 'a "First Cause" external to his effects'.[54]

Likewise, for creatures, the 'emergence of beings into personal relation' is crucial to their reality-quotient,[55] such that the being of humans is diminished when, owing to their fallenness, they come to exist only in a 'state of "atomistic" self-consciousness'. In that situation, there are 'only individual entities existing in "distance" (*apostasis*) from the whole'.[56] When 'mutual absence is the basic ontological category', then the 'idea of Being is ... reduced to that which exists, opposed to that which does *not* exist' and to that extent 'nothingness is, as it were, introduced into the definition of Being, as a possibility'.[57] The call to fallen man is to enter into relation and so become truly personal, by way of invitation from the God who is always personal communion: the divine Trinity. Here there is offered to man a 'change in nature ... conveyed to us through the Sacraments', and leading by *metanoia* (conversion) to the attaining of true freedom.[58] There is a message here for ethics of a somewhat antinomian kind.

> [T]he experience of sin is not primarily an experience of the violation of law, but an experience of Nothing, as existence-in-isolation, the outside (*ektos*) of communion... [A]n individually orientated ethic inevitably involves an ontology based on encapsulated individual entities.[59]

Williams found Yannaras's presentation of certain elements in Trinitarian theology good, but was less sure how helpful his scheme could be in Christology where he only had brief and somewhat riddling remarks to make. Drawing on his own research (where Lossky's unsympathetic treatment of John of the Cross figured), he applauded Yannaras for showing how the 'experience of the absence of God' is by no means the same as the 'absence of the experience of God'.[60] If one were to accept Palamas's distinction between the divine essence and the divine energies (for Williams a rather large 'if') then one could find in this book a satisfactory way of expressing the mutually (and not merely logically) real relations between divine and human persons without any danger of involving the divine *ousia* in the finite world in a way that threatens the latter's createdness. Williams was favourable to Mascall's Thomistic notion of replacing the 'energetic' in God according to Palamas by the 'esse' that is God of the Thomist school—and notably one of its twentieth-century masters, Lossky's supervisor Étienne Gilson. He thought that Yannaras was dependent on analogy-thinking for his talk of communion as both human and divine, despite the Greek theologian's rejection of the 'Western' principle of the analogy of being. Williams was surprised by the absence of a pneumatology.[61] He found Yannaras's dependence on Heidegger not unlike that of nineteenth-century Russian theologians on Hegel, and, as with Every, endorsed the *Istina* writer who had spoken critically of 'Hellenic Slavophilism'.

Williams provided the Christological spadework Yannaras's scheme needed so as to show the place of Incarnation and Atonement. Drawing on Maximus the Confessor's distinction between natural willing and gnomic willing (the latter a consequence of the post-Fall situation when alternatives can seem equally attractive), Williams suggested the following:

> 'Since the Fall' man has been capable of ek-stasis, of genuine personal communion, only by conscious exercise of his will to escape 'atomicity'. In Christ, the possibility of existence-in-communion which is *not* merely dependent on our continuing struggle against atomicity is established. There is still an ongoing *metanoia*; but what we are given is authentic personal freedom, freedom to *be* persons, freedom from the threat of existence-in-isolation. This seems to be what Yannaras means: but I, for one, should be grateful for exposition, at some future date, of how this is to be related in detail to the Chalcedonian definition, and, indeed, to the general Byzantine tradition in Christology.[62]

In 1973 Stephen Parsons looked at Yannaras's quasi-book-length essay from the previous year, 'Theology in Greece Today'.[63] While for some Westerners Yannaras represents the best of Greek theology today, there are also, Parsons pointed out, Greek Orthodox commentators for whom he approximates to a quasi-heretic. Yannaras's abrasive dismissal of Scholasticism and academicism is central to his attempt to revive what he sees as a more participatory style of theology—which he ascribes in its origins to Plato for whom truth itself is participated in, rather than objectively regarded by, the subject. This struck Parsons as a rather Existentialist reading of an ancient thinker. Trembelas's 'Patristic Scholasticism' had come in for much criticism at Yannaras's hands, notably for its lack of specifically Orthodox spiritual themes, ignoring of the Russian émigré theologians of the Paris school, and indifference to modern trends in Western philosophy. Parsons noted Yannaras's dislike of the Zoe movement for what he considered its individualistic notion of salvation and borrowings from Protestant Evangelicalism. Positively, Yannaras wanted an apophatic and mystical theology, a philokalic treatment of ethics and devotion, an emphasis on the eucharistic and liturgical (not institutional) side of the Church, and a theology of icons. It is not a list of desiderata which would sustain the 'quasi-heretical' case against him.

Old Greeks

In more recent decades, *Sobornost* has become a major source of articles and (especially) reviews on what I will term, perhaps discourteously, the 'Old Greeks', since this title suits the structure of my chapter. By 'Old Greeks' I mean in the first instance the Greek Fathers, including the ascetic theologians of the patristic period, and the later Byzantine doctors, homilists and saints. As to the Fathers, it is not that there was ever a conscious policy to exclude the Latin patristic authors. It was simply that the interest of editors and review editors—above all, in this second period of *Sobornost*'s existence, did not lie with the Latin Fathers (except Cassian, who could be regarded as an Oriental with Roman speech). And similarly with the mediaevals: it is not impossible to find notice taken of monographs on Western authors, but their Byzantine equivalents dominate the field.

One vitally important legacy of the Byzantine period was Athonite monasticism. Though the revival of Athos from the 1970s onwards was new, the Holy Mountain itself was patently not. It had celebrated its millennium in 1963, and the spirituality of its monks reached back deep into the patristic age. Father Kallistos had lectured to the Fellowship's 1975 conference on 'Athonite Spirituality Today', but what appeared in the second issue of that year was, rather, an article by Garth Fowden on 'The Revival of Monasticism on Athos': an update on his survey of two years earlier, 'Is there a Future for Mount Athos?', which had noted strengths in some of the coenobitic monasteries, and weaknesses in their idiorhythmic competitors.[64] Fowden's earlier article, while noting the new difficulties—the religious apathy in Greek society, the inescapable economic exploitation of the peninsula which followed on the loss of monastic estates in the rest of Greece—was by no means a lament for the coming inevitable extinction. But this time he was able to speak about actual resurgence, as his choice of title indicated.[65] Stavronikita, distinctly intellectual in outlook, and Philotheou, larger and very strict, continued to consolidate their strengths. Esphigmenou remained a bastion of Old

Calendarism and hostility to ecumenism. Various largely idiorhythmic communities had ardent pro-coenobitic minorities. The absence of abbots, and especially of spiritual men as abbots, in idiorhythmic monasteries, was a drawback. Yet 'sketes', or hermitages located at a distance from the historic houses, were sometimes the most impressive sites of all. The new Greek government had been somewhat more receptive to the idea of foreigners coming than had the now dissolved Junta of 1967 to 1973, but the obvious way to make up numbers—from the Soviet Union—was equally obviously impossible. Casual tourism remained a threat to the life. Fowden thought the idea of a great exhibition of a permanent kind on the border of the monastic republic might be a solution, as well as responding to a possible wish by the Greek State to see some tourist return on its financial aid in restoration work.

Bishop Kallistos went to Athos in 1992, his eleventh visit but his first for ten years. His report was overwhelmingly positive. Whereas before, in some monasteries, you could hardly see any monks with black beards, now you had to look for a monk with grey hair. The buildings are being repaired (though not always judiciously); the food and sanitation are better; the theological life has been transformed: a few tracts on Freemasonry or the calendar question have been replaced by patristically inspired texts on liturgical and mystical theology. The only problem is extra noise, roads, tourists or at least visitors in large numbers, and monks using portable telephones, though Kallistos saw no (or at any rate less) objection to the use of electricity, central heating and hot water. There is also the issue of the large minority who are Zealots at Esphigmenou and many of the sketes and hermitages: Kallistos was not asked to take part in their services. He also deplored the way the Ecumenical Patriarchate had persuaded the police to help expel monks in the Russian skete of the Prophet Elias who had ceased to commemorate the patriarch: they were not even allowed to collect their personal possessions on expulsion. The Greek State was deliberately blocking the arrival of non-Greek candidates for the Russian, Serbian, Bulgarian and Romanian monasteries.

But Athos had its spiritual theologians again. The higumen of Stavronikita, Father Basil, was a new star in an old universe. In his 'Dying and Behold We Live' he attempted to sum up the essence of the monastic life. In a personally thought-through account, he describes a monk as one who has some experience of the Resurrection.

[I]n the end, in the midst of much labour, of ascesis and vigil which often does go beyond human endurance, a shoot comes to birth, a shoot of new and unfading life which gives fruit a hundred-fold. And then you bless all pains and sufferings. You sacrifice all things, because the joy which has appeared is a gleam of the age to come, which gives light and life both to the present and the future. Thus spontaneously you come to search what is harder, more sombre, more lonely in order to go forward towards this true consolation which does not deceive, towards this light which does not set, but which makes men able to communicate with all men and with all things.[66]

The mysteries of repentance and charity generate in the monk true humility which measures by the measure of the salvation of all.

The Syriac poets

The East is not only the Greek East. 1974 saw the first of a number of notable contributions to *Sobornost* by the Syriac scholar Sebastian Brock.

In 'World and Sacrament in the Writings of the Syrian Fathers', St Ephrem dominated the writings chosen. In Ephrem's vision, the world and Scripture are, in symbols and types, the great co-witnesses to creation—and thus to the Creator. The disclosure they offer comes to a twofold climax, in Incarnation and Parousia, an oscillation between the temporal and the eschatological recurrent in early Christian thought. Brock felt the impoverished symbolic content of modern Western baptismal ceremonies might prejudice the reader against his claim that, for the Syriac Fathers, Baptism is re-entry into Paradise, not simply by a spiritual rebirth for the individual person but by an entering into relation with the original Paradisal world. In self-defence, he cited the prayer of consecration for baptismal water in the Maronite rite, which has just this sense. The crossing of the Red Sea and the passage over the Jordan, in this liturgical poetry, are both baptismal types. But whereas one leads to the wilderness wanderings, the other gives access to the promised fruition. Here again is a tension of temporal and eschatological, for the Paradise-garden is pledged to the baptized but not fully given over to them. Ephrem sees the reborn life as, above all, a life of praise; the newly reacquired freedom to praise he calls the 'robe of glory' or 'robe of praise' of baptismal existence. 'Everything in creation is clothed by the Holy Spirit with new meaning',[67] a flower-bud, for instance, taking on resurrection significance, as in certain of Ephrem's

Hymns. Thus the cosmic meanings are deepened through baptismal faith, both as they appear in creation and as they look in Scripture. In the fourth of the *Hymns on Virginity* Ephrem speaks of Christ as 'Lord of the symbols', the 'harbour' where they come to rest.

In 'The Poet as Theologian', a Fellowship conference lecture, Brock was, despite his title, not generalizing. He had Ephrem the Syrian constantly in mind. Ephrem is 'probably more like what we expect of a conventional theologian than many other great poet-theologians', he wrote,[68] for his poetry is specifically religious and while not systematic takes as the frame for its symbolic language the Christian mystery centred in the paradox of the Incarnation, the 'Great One who became small'. Brock stressed Ephrem's approach to sacred time, seen as the point of convergence of the moments of ordinary linear time, as well as an anticipation of the 'time' of the Age to Come. A comparison might be attempted with the view of time and its relation to eternity in T. S. Eliot's *Four Quartets*.

In 'The Mysteries Hidden in the Side of Christ' Brock focused on St Ephrem's *Commentary on the Diatessaron*. At John 19:34, which, in the course of the Johannine Passion narrative, describes the piercing of Christ's side with a lance, Ephrem's commentary reads:

> Through the side I pierced with the sword I entered the garden fenced in with the sword. Let us enter in through that side which was pierced, since we were stripped naked by the counsel of the rib that was extracted. The fire that burnt in Adam, burnt him in that rib of his. For this reason the side of the second Adam has been pierced, and from it comes a flow of water to quench the fire of the first Adam.[69]

Brock describes Ephrem's exegesis of the Piercing as 'looking back ... to the Paradise narrative of Genesis, and forward to the new Paradise, the sacramental life of the Church'.[70]

Similarly, Jacob of Serugh, a second Syriac theologian-poet whose life context Brock would summarize in a later piece, stressed the relation between Eve and the Church-Bride in the miraculous birth-giving in Eden and on Calvary.

> Christ slept on the cross, and Baptism came forth from him; the Bridegroom slept, and his side was pierced in his sleep, he gave birth to the Bride, as happened with Eve, in Adam his type. The stillness of the sleep of death fell upon him on the cross, and from him came forth the other who gives birth to all spiritual beings.[71]

While Jacob also associates the birth and betrothal of the Church with the Baptism of Christ (and not only with the Crucifixion), this is because the Lord's Baptism and the flow of water on the Cross are conceived by him as one single unit in 'sacred time', whatever the chronological distance between them.[72] The baptism of each Christian enables the same ecclesial marriage imagery to be applied likewise to the individual soul. As sacramental Baptism climaxes in the Holy Eucharist, the 'blood' of the Passion must also figure in this account. Pentecost too comes into the picture, for those who mocked that the apostles were filled with new wine were by no means wholly wrong: the Chaldean Breviary says: 'the sheep, saved by the pure Blood, became drunk with the wine that was pressed out by the sword'.[73] Here another imagery enters in, the grape cluster that Caleb brought back from the Promised Land in Numbers 13:23, and the grape in which blessing was hidden according to Isaiah 65:8.

Brock concluded this essay with the Marian dimension often alluded to in the Syriac tradition. (He would return to it more fully the following year.) Mary's role is complementary to that of the Church and her sacraments, and necessarily so.

> The descent and miraculous birth of God into the world requires the co-operation of an individual human being with the Holy Spirit; only then can the miraculous birth of the sacraments from Christ's side effect the ascent of man to God.[74]

Father Robert Murray, in his first contribution to the combined journal—*Sobornost* with *Eastern Churches Review*—gave a splendid translation, with commentary, of a hymn by St Ephrem to Christ. The hymn is litany-like, its imagery always striking but often densely complex. An example may be offered.

> O Master Mariner
> who has conquered the raging sea!
> Your glorious Tree is a sign;
> it has become the oar of salvation.
> The wind of your mercy blew,
> the ship set out on its course,
> away from the raging sea
> to the haven of peace.
> Blessed is he who becomes
> the mariner of his own soul
> and preserves and unloads his treasure!

Murray concluded his commentary, 'Systematic theology has to come, and is necessary, but imagination lives closer to the sources of faith, both in the beginning and whenever a believer is reborn'.[75]

In 'Mary and the Eucharist: An Oriental Perspective', Brock shared more of his lovely translations from the Syriac, though his lens was wide-angle, considering the East as a whole, if hardly, in a short article, comprehensively. Prima facie, the New Testament does not connect these two themes, but the Syrian Liturgy of St James, like certain other anaphoras, draws a parallel between the overshadowing of the Spirit at the Annunciation and the Spirit's working in the eucharistic epiclesis. At the former, so the ninth-century commentator Moshe bar Kopha says, the Spirit 'descended on the womb of Mary... and made the body of God the Word from the flesh of the Virgin, so too the Spirit descends on the bread and wine on the altar and makes them into the Body and Blood of God the Word which originated from the Virgin'.[76] Brock invoked typology to help sustain this comparison, citing for example, one of St Ephrem's *Hymns on Unleavened Bread*: 'Mary has given us the Bread of rest/ in place of that bread of toil which Eve provided'.[77] With the consent of the individual believer to the Spirit's work in the sacraments, Christ can be conceived in the heart—for which Brock quotes at length Symeon the New Theologian's commentary on St Matthew's parable of the marriage feast in his *Ethika*. Symeon was not, of course, a Syriac writer, he was a Byzantine one. Brock nevertheless used Symeon's work to sum up his own overall message.

> On the one hand, Mary corresponds to the Church as the source of the sacraments, in that she herself gave birth to Christ, the fountainhead of these sacraments. On the other hand, she corresponds to, and provides the model for, the individual Christian who receives the vivifying sacraments. Whether they will allow the Holy Spirit to transform their lives through the sacraments, depends on whether they make the same reply as Mary at her Annunciation. If they do, they will become, as Symeon hints, 'mothers' of Christ.[78]

In 1980, Murray offered another reading of a hymn by Ephrem, this time Hymn 9 in the collection 'On the Church'. It concerns the relation of reason and—not faith but—love, and Murray's explication was of theological interest. A teaching song (*madrasha*), the hymn dealt with the contrast yet unity of the apophatic and the cataphatic ways. On the one hand, there is 'the realization that our finite minds cannot grasp God or encapsulate him in human terms'; on the other, 'the experience that Christ, the Scriptures and the created world in their respective ways do speak to us truly about God and therefore allow us to respond in a way which cannot be entirely invalid'.[79] A follower of Lossky would no doubt cry 'Thomism!' when Murray goes on to say that the 'traditional balance' the believer finds between the apophatic and the cataphatic turns on the judgment that human language can be applied to God 'analogically'.[80] But what is surprising in Ephrem's poem is that love speaks cataphatically and reason apophatically, and not, as we would expect, the other way round. In this 'dramatic contest' (the genre of which was ancient in Mesopotamia and continues in modern Syriac),

> Reason insists—almost brutally—that the attempt to penetrate the nature of God is both folly and blasphemy, while Love simply has to praise and respond to the revelation and experience of himself which God himself has given.[81]

The contrast of the hidden and the revealed is typical of Ephrem, who also anticipates St Maximus in his sacramental notion of created nature. But more to Murray's point is the way the Syriac word *raz*, while it means first of all 'secret knowledge' or 'mystery', then proceeds to indicate symbolic concepts or language before going on finally to denote the sacraments of the Church. Ephrem has no theory of symbolism. Yet Murray ventures the suggestion he would have rallied to Paul Ricoeur's maxim 'The symbol gives to think'—not by rationalizing, or demythologizing, or even by elaborate allegorizing, but 'in its own way, feeding the mind by warming the heart'.[82]

In 1981 Sebastian Brock introduced a long poem by Jacob of Serugh on the 'Veil of Moses'. Jacob, we now learn, was an older contemporary of the much better-known Greek liturgical poet Romanos the Melodist. Born in the Euphrates Valley in the year of the Council of Chalcedon, he was apparently among the 'hesitators' who preferred to the Chalcedonian formula the version 'one nature out of two', though some scholars infer from the date of his consecration to the episcopal see whence he takes the name by which Church historians know him ('of Serugh'—he occupied it only briefly before his death in 521) that he was a Chalcedonian, appointed by the robustly pro-Chalcedonian emperor Justin I. Still, not only the Syrian Orthodox but also the Maronite Church regard him as saint and doctor. (We are not told how he is regarded by the 'Jacobites' in union with Rome.) The poem that follows is an example of his verse homilies or *memre* of which some three hundred are extant, and it exemplifies perfectly the typological approach typical of Syriac Christianity. In Jacob's theology, 'This is what the veil on Moses' face symbolizes:/ that the words of prophecy are veiled;/ the Lord covered Moses' face for this reason,/ that it might be a type for prophecy, which is also covered ... The whole Old Testament is veiled after the fashion of Moses;/ in him all the prophetic books are depicted.' With the Incarnation the veil is lifted. 'Our Lord shone out as sun in the world, and all received light;/ symbols and figures and parables, all were explained./ The veil that was placed on the face of the scriptures was removed/ and the world now sees openly the Son of God.'[83]

Murray had spoken of the 'dialectical' hymns of Ephrem, but there were also, in a variety of writers, hymns 'dialogical' in genre. These are popular hymns, sometimes, it is thought of great antiquity, which share a structure:

> [A]fter a few introductory verses the main body of the hymn consists of a dialogue, normally argumentative in character between two biblical characters (or at least personifications); at the end the argument is resolved and the last verse is normally some form of doxology. The verses are short and very often they incorporate an alphabetic acrostic.[84]

The earliest examples are from Ephrem but he was modelling himself on Mesopotamian literature where 'precedence disputes' can be found in Middle Iranian, Akkadian and Sumerian. The genre continues in modern Syriac. Brock had found forty examples in liturgical manuscripts, judging those occurring in both the West Syrian and East Syrian tradition to be the oldest. A prominent group is assigned to the Night Office of Holy Week: for example, Palm Sunday has Church and Sion, and Church and Synagogue; Thursday the Sinful Woman and Satan; Friday the Two Thieves; Saturday the Cherub and the Penitent Thief, and Death and Satan. The other major cluster is in the Advent season called in Syriac tradition 'The Annunciation'. They were successful because, as Brock explained, 'While appealing to popular taste in their outward form, the Syriac dialogue hymns often succeed in conveying something of the dilemmas posed by the paradox of the Christian message.'[85] For instance, the Unrepentant Thief says to the Repentant Thief, 'It is astounding on your part that you do not see the flail marks all over his back, yet here you are proclaiming the man's glory. Who will believe what you are saying?'[86]

Brock thought the change from contest poem to argumentative dialogue might be a 'conscious Christianization of the genre',[87] for 'the dialogue poem is ideally suited for depicting, in popular form and by means of a series of different episodes, the state of disjunction between God and the created world effected by the Fall. It is equally well suited to depict the resolution of that state of conflict brought about by the descent of the Divinity into this creation, a descent that was initiated by a love that is utterly unexpected.'[88] He added:

> In late antiquity Syria was a centre of creativity in a whole number of different fields: in art, architecture and liturgy, as well as in hymnography. It is a striking fact that most of the early Byzantine hymn writers, among whom Romanos of Homs is but the greatest, came from Syria or Palestine; many of these will have been bilingual in Syriac and Greek, and so been fully aware, without the need for translation, of the riches of Syriac hymnography. The full extent of the debt of Greek writers such as Romanos to the hymns of St Ephrem, and to Syriac hymnography in general, still remains to be properly explained. But enough is already known of Romanos's sources of inspiration that we can be certain that these included several works in Syriac.[89]

Sobornost was not so absorbed in these poetic beauties to be unconscious of the difficulties besetting the successors of these figures in their homelands. In the year 2000, Stephen Griffith, *apokrisarios* of the archbishop of Canterbury to the Syrian Orthodox, visited Tur Abdin, bandit country much of it in the control of Kurdish oil smugglers, but the erstwhile patriarchal seat. The restrictions placed by the Turks on the monastery of Deir Zafaran, the spiritual and educational centre of the life of the 'Suriani', contradicted the provisions of the post-Great War Treaty of Lausanne about religious liberty in the remaining Turkish portions of the Ottoman Empire, though Griffith admitted that the Syrian Orthodox are not mentioned by name in the treaty, nor in the 1932 Act which defined the position of non-Muslim minorities in Turkey. He also reported that, owing to the tourist value of the sites, government officials are becoming milder, but not necessarily in a consistent way across the various relevant departments. The Syrian Orthodox in Istanbul are supportive of villages and monasteries, but much of the Diaspora is too far away—in the West, and in Australia.[90]

Romania

The year 1970, when Donald Allchin wrote up his grand tour of Orthodox Romania (see Chapter 1 above), was also the year when Archimandrite (later Bishop) Antonie Plamadeala wrote on monastic renewal in that country for *Sobornost*. The revival, described as a 'renewed monasticism [which] has found the means of adaptation as well as of faithfulness to the tradition', was counter-posed, somewhat gloatingly, to the confusion Plamadeala had identified in attempts at *aggiornamento* (bringing up to date) and *ressourcement* (going back to the sources) in the religious life of the West. He had been a doctrinal student at Heythrop College, in the rural Oxfordshire incarnation of that Jesuit institution. Though the situation of Romanian monasticism at the end of World War Two was anything but rosy—in many monasteries, idiorhythmism was not only an individualistic way of life but a rather self-indulgent one, Plamadeala was inclined to ascribe the success of the monastic renaissance under Patriarch Justinian to the 'simple fact that we have kept the tradition',[91] whereas Western Orders, committed to 'some medieval or post-French Revolution renewals' have 'lost the meaning of their pristine tradition as well as the meaning of the present renewed world'– where the term 'renewed' refers, one supposes, to Socialism, as exemplified in the then Romanian 'People's Republic',[92] though conceivably it might mean the world after Pentecost.

Though, as Plamadeala agreed, a monastic renaissance cannot be produced to order, Justinian's programme for monastic revival was so well thought out it contributed mightily to this end. By a combination of synodical legislation and moral persuasion, coenobitism was reintroduced, in a spirit of poverty and fraternity. With care taken not to damage the life of prayer, in the Liturgy and in the cell, monasteries were assisted to become self-supporting either by working the land or by developing arts and crafts in workrooms or small factories. The educational level of both monks and nuns was dramatically raised by creating schools of monastic theology which could give their students diplomas in spirituality and the theology of the monastic life. Where suitable candidates emerged from this process, they might be sent on to a faculty of theology for a full degree. The buildings of the monasteries, nearly all of them historic, were restored with State as well as Church aid. The Church aid was not only financial but entailed the creation in the monasteries themselves of schools of painting, woodwork, and metalwork, not to mention schools for vestment-making or the design of 'other objects for the decoration of the Church'.[93]

At the same time, the valuable elements of the older generation were preserved, by which Plamadeala means chiefly the election of abbots who, though not able to profit personally from the patriarchal programme for monastic entrants, were wise guides for the young, such that a new generation of spiritual fathers began to emerge. The author was clear that an abbot should principally be a spiritual guide; other gifts, such as administration or cultural preparedness are secondary. The monasteries became newly attractive to the laity seeking for confession and counsel as well as a livelier spirit of prayer.

Plamadeala's account would have been sobering reading for those responsible for the post-Conciliar reordering of religious life in the West. He was not impressed by what he saw among many Catholics; he thought the attitudes among Anglican and Protestant religious (presumably the last is a reference to the Taizé Community) were healthier. The latter showed a movement towards Tradition, the former seem often 'to be more interested in the world than in the Tradition'.[94] Some, he agreed, would say that in modernity the Romanian monastics will eventually fall victim to similar disintegrating factors as had afflicted their Catholic counterparts. He rather doubted it; their convictions were too deeply implanted. He hoped the West would find what he termed a 'principle of permanence' as well.

Romania's premier theologian, Dumitru Staniloae, had been in England again, at Fairacres Convent, and he spoke to the community about the meaning of the Cross. His words to them were recorded and he supplemented them to make an article. The Sisters, whose spirituality, though they are Anglican, is chiefly Carmelite, told him they had found St John of the Cross and St Teresa in his address. Staniloae had said, for instance, 'it can ... happen that God does really withdraw himself from our vision in order to prove and strengthen the tenacity of our love for him',[95] and this was certainly a Carmelite-sounding remark. Staniloae's dependence on St Maximus explained, said Allchin, how a Franciscan present could also find in the lecture an illumination of the life of Francis, for it combined love of creation, devotion to the Cross, and joy in the resurrection. The friar in question probably had in mind a passage near its end:

> The cross completes the fragmentary meaning of this world, which has meaning when it is seen as a gift which has worth, but only a relative and not an absolute worth. The cross reveals the destiny of the world as it is drawn towards its transfiguration in God by Christ.[96]

Ion Bria's 'A Look at Contemporary Romanian Dogmatic Theology' made it possible to contextualize Staniloae's work. Bria underlined his importance, treating him first. He called Staniloae 'the most representative dogmatic theologian in this [post-War] period', bringing a 'new spirit into present day Romanian theology, a spirit characterized by the organic inter-penetration of doctrine, spirituality, and the social life of the Church'.[97]

Staniloae's hallmark is a combination of depth and analytic power. The insistence that dogma is the foundation of spirituality, the prominence given the doctrine of the divine energies, the ontological dimension of redemption (not least in its cosmic character), and an ecclesiology of *sobornost* are among the salient features of his theology. Of Staniloae's generation, Nicolae Chitescu seemed closest, notably in his rejection of a Scholastic approach to the topic of grace and his interest in Khomiakov's ecclesiology. Isidor Todoran's theology was characterized by a dialogue with Protestantism, many of whose personalities and theological currents he introduced to a Romanian readership. Among the younger writers, Bria named first himself and at most length—perhaps defensibly in the context of the journal (though one can hardly imagine an English chronicler doing this!), since his chief interest was ecumenism, and he had written a good deal on Anglican–Orthodox relations. Bria's 'The Ecclesiology of Communion' clearly anticipated much Roman Catholic writing on the same topic, emphasizing as it did the Church's Trinitarian basis and 'organic and spiritual character'.[98] Bria's own pro-ecumenical bias appeared in his summary statement that 'In opposition to the past, present day Romanian symbolic theology has abandoned the stage of purely comparative or even polemic exposition and has reached the point where it now lays stress on the positive contribution of the other confessions in their relationship with the Orthodox tradition'.[99]

In 1977, Staniloae had a chance to provide a more fully worked out staurology than he could give at Fairacres, and this he did in 'The Cross in Orthodox Theology and Worship'. It confirmed Bria's characterization of his theology. He began from the statement that the Cross is already victory, is virtual resurrection. But how so?

> The cross reverses the end of death, in making that which puts an end to life into a death which annuls and transcends itself, in delivering life from the reign of death ... The resurrection of Christ constitutes the full manifestation of the power which he has exercised in his voluntary passion on the cross.[100]

The radiance of the Cross's power is always present in the risen Christ and this is why it will be the sign of the Son of Man's final victory at the End. The Cross teaches us to live as 'those who, in communion with God, strengthen their spirit, go beyond themselves and by a death-resurrection transform nature into an offering'.[101]

This is not merely a moral lesson. So much became apparent when Staniloae spoke not only of the significance of the Sign of the Cross but of the 'power' of a blessed cross—pointing out how in Orthodox practice the water with which a cross is blessed has itself been consecrated by the immersion in it of a previous cross. This is a staurological, rather than apostolic, succession, setting up a quasi-identity between the cross of Golgotha and the cross used here and now in this or that church or household. The energy of Christ's Cross is not however magically contained in the cross as devotional object. It is present there through the gift of the Holy Spirit, invoked in the blessing of the water.

He turned to the Holy Spirit in his own right in 'The Holy Spirit in the Theology and Life of the Orthodox Church', translated from the French Orthodox journal *Contacts*. Staniloae took his theology of the Spirit's origination in the Trinity from the thirteenth-century Constantinopolitan patriarch Gregory of Cyprus. It mediates between Monopatrism and Filioquism, declaring that the Spirit 'proceeds from the Father and shines forth from the Son'.[102] Economically, the Spirit illumines the Son by enabling human consciousness to know the Son. Staniloae combines this notion with a companion idea drawn from Palamas: the Spirit 'represents the joy of the Father for the Son and the joy of the Son for the Father'.[103] This joy, adds Staniloae, constitutes the splendour of the Holy Spirit. Economically, the Spirit, illuminating the Son for human beings, also, then, inflames human beings with joy.

These mediaeval doctors have, no doubt, their own standing. But Staniloae provided no indication of the scriptural basis of their concepts, attractive as they are. Possibly, by linking these ideas to the doctrine of the divine Energies—affirming, in fact, that it is the Spirit who makes the divine Energies effective for creatures, we are meant to infer from the gifts of, specifically, *light* (compare Gregory of Cyprus) and *joy* (compare Gregory Palamas) which the Spirit brings to the souls of the redeemed that these are the crucial cues to the essential nature of the Spirit's role in the Economy and even to the manner of his origin in the Trinity itself.

In the Christian life, declared Staniloae, the Spirit ensures 'sensitiveness' to both God and one's fellows. Here there has been a twofold translation, from Romanian to French, and from French to English. The word used is plainly key to Staniloae's thought in this essay—as can be seen from the fact that he defines faith itself as the 'first stage in sensitiveness'.[104] It is the fundamental building block of his epistemology of grace. Staniloae went on to identify his chosen term with *aisthesis* as found in the ascetic theologian Diadochus of Photike—and this in turn led him to see the development of 'sensitiveness' in terms of both 'love' and a 'keen sense of responsibility towards God', where the latter embraces a 'whole range of feelings ... produced by the Holy Spirit' for both ascetic and mystical progress and mission.[105] It is because the Spirit represents the perfection of relationship in God that he can thus fortify human relations—both between human beings and with God himself.

Staniloae explained the descent of the Spirit at Pentecost in its relation to Christ's Ascension. Only when the Son has achieved in its entirety his capacity, as man, for communion with the Father and with other human beings can he confer the Holy Spirit in power. Through the Spirit God will realize his plan for the world's salvation as the Church guides the world to its *telos*, its true end. Salvation works itself out in synergy—hence the crucial role of prayer in the Church's life, above all liturgical prayer. Every prayer of the Church is in some way an epiclesis, but the full revelation of the Spirit as 'divine and divinizing energy and glory' comes only at the End.[106] Still, worship itself is 'an opening into eschatology'.[107] Staniloae concluded by pen-pictures of three 'spiritual men', i.e. spiritual fathers, of the Romanian Church in the modern period, ascribing their perfection of life to the inspiration of the *Philokalia*.

> These 'spiritual men' feed not only on the Church's liturgical and private prayer, but also on the ascetical and patristic writings which they know sometimes through reading, but more often through the lives of their spiritual fathers, who are actual embodiments of these writings. In this way they learn the doctrine of the purification of the passions and the way of uninterrupted prayer. By these means they make their natures spiritual, so that they become permeable

to the Holy Spirit and to the divine light, as Christ was on Mount Thabor.[108]

He added rather tartly that they do not 'band together in charismatic groups, apart from other members of the church, because one of the passions from which they are purifying themselves is pride'.[109]

In 2016 Andrew Louth produced an overview of Staniloae's *Orthodox Dogmatic Theology* (called by its American publishers *The Experience of God*), the sixth and last volume of which had been Englished in 2013. It was, surprisingly, 'the only comprehensive account of Orthodox theology written in the latter half of the twentieth century'.[110] He passed on a suggestion from a Romanian source that the standard text-book format may have been adopted so as to reassure the Communist censors that it was nothing new. But as to content it was not a standard manual for there were some splendid insights of Staniloae's own. Thus in volume I, '"Scripture and Tradition" is a traditional enough theme, but Staniloae treats it in the context of what he called "the dialogue of the Church with Christ", not as sources of knowledge of God, but aspects of the continuing and deepening relationship between Christ and the Church and those who seek to be his disciples'.[111] Still in volume I, the advantage of the apophatic is that it 'forbids us to follow natural ways of thought and the formal concepts that would usurp the place of spiritual realities'.[112] From volume II, readers of *Sobornost* with a good memory would be reminded of Staniloae's Fairacres lecture when they find Louth reporting, 'The gift of the world is marked by the cross: in blessing and also a sign of contradiction, a sign that receiving the gift involves an ascetic movement on the part of the receiver, lest the gift degenerate into a mere possession.'[113] In volume III, the person of Christ is revealed in his work, these are not two quite separate Christological treatises, as so often. In volume IV, the Church as communion in the Holy Spirit is Christ's Body—a neat way to express at once pneumatological and Christological approaches to ecclesiology. In volume V Louth notes that the famous 'toll booths' of (some) Orthodox eschatology, the somewhat folkloristic Orthodox version of the Intermediate State, do not get a mention. But the overall verdict was that Staniloae's was a real achievement, and the judgment was offered by one who was himself no slouch.

… 3 …

Anglicans and Latins, and their Critics

In this chapter I consider how the journal looked at the Anglican patrimony, and its principal historic source—traditions deriving from Latin Christendom, and did so by relating that patrimony and those traditions, wherever possible, to Orthodoxy. Some contributors wrote on behalf of the Western Churches. Others looked at the West more critically, even adversarially. There were sticking points. There were also examples of convergence and even mutual enhancement.

Anglican ressourcement

In the early period of *Sobornost*'s life, as was mentioned in my thematic survey in 'The Encounter of East and West', Anglicans had sought to locate figures from their own tradition whom they guessed the Orthodox would find congenial: so, for instance, Brooke Foss Westcott of Cambridge and Durham was put forward as an obvious example. During his editorship, Donald Allchin was especially interested in developing the 'latent Orthodoxy' in Anglican writers. He thought he had made a good start in a small book of his own, *The Spirit and the Word*, where he looked in this perspective at two comparatively minor figures, Thomas Hancock and R. M. Benson.[1] The second of these—the founder of the Cowley Fathers (properly, Society of St John the Evangelist)—he had long known from the research that went into his master's thesis on 'The Silent Rebellion. Anglican Religious Communities, 1845–1900'.[2] Allchin hoped for the day when the Orthodox would have made such figures so much their own that it would be they, and not Anglicans, who would write in *Sobornost* of the 'classical Anglican writers' of, say, the seventeenth and nineteenth centuries. Allchin went on to offer a wider judgment—which also posed a question.

> [F]or the development of a Western, English-language Orthodox tradition it will be, in the end, essential to assess and recover all that is Orthodox in the long centuries of English Christianity from the schism to the present day. Will it be possible in the future perhaps to see Lancelot Andrewes as an Orthodox father, just as it has been possible to see an Isaac of Syria, who in his lifetime was a Nestorian bishop, as an outstanding influence in the development of Orthodox spirituality? It was at least interesting in a recent Greek theological book-catalogue to see *The Cloud of Unknowing*, which has recently been published in a Greek translation, described as the work of 'an unknown, fourteenth-century, English Orthodox writer'.[3]

This was the more desirable since the official Anglican–Orthodox Dialogue, as reported in the same 1970 issue, was slow to make progress.

Michael Paternoster, at that time the Fellowship's general secretary, wrote an essay which Allchin signalled in advance as the sort of Anglican writing he wanted to see. Paternoster's piece could be thought of—evidently, Allchin *did* think of it—as an Orthodox reading of Frederick Denison Maurice, the influential mid-nineteenth-century Churchman difficult to locate on the Anglican spectrum and best remembered for his role in the beginnings of a theologically grounded Christian Socialism. Paternoster proposed an analogy between the Palamas/Barlaam quarrel in the Byzantine Middle Ages and the dispute between Maurice and Henry Longueville Mansel, Waynflete Professor of Metaphysical Philosophy at Oxford and, later, dean of St Paul's Cathedral in London. Mansel's 1858 Bampton Lectures to the University of Oxford had been published under the title *The Limits of Religious Thought*.[4] They caused a certain stir. Mansel was a philosopher engaged in arguing that God was largely inaccessible, for epistemic reasons, to the human mind. Barlaam had been a Scholastic philosopher who objected, also on grounds of epistemology, to experiential claims made by some Athonite monks, namely, that they had glimpsed the Uncreated Light. Both Maurice and Palamas were opponents of epistemic miserliness. This was the ground of the comparison.

On the other hand, there was a problem. Dom Gregory Dix, a supporter of the Fellowship, who, though dead, was still much revered in Anglo-Catholic circles, had bracketed Palamas with such heresiarchs as Marcion and Arius for making a common 'Hellenic' mistake never made by the 'Syriac' mind.[5] Palamas himself, Dix pointed out, had denied that man can ever see God in the sense of coming to know the divine Essence. For Dix, the typical 'Hellenic' error in divinity was to hold that 'in so far as

[God] is approachable he is less than ultimate', while 'beyond him is the impersonal unknowable absolute'.[6] Paternoster's reply was twofold. On the one hand, the word 'impersonal' is out of place in Palamas's account of the divine Essence, for the Essence is the Essence of, precisely, the Holy Trinity. And on the other hand the term 'absolute'—taken as signifying the non-dependence of the divine on anything other than itself—is for Palamas quite appropriate for the divine Energies themselves, and not for the Essence only. So Mansel's notion that the revealed idea of God tells us not what God is in himself but only how he wills us to think of him, could hardly be equated with Palamas's view that in revealing himself God enables us to know his Energies but not the *ousia* from which these Energies spring.

For his part, Maurice, though in all likelihood totally unaware of Palamas's existence, had seen immediately that Mansel's view (compare Barlaam's) destroys any authentic or 'direct' cognitive communion between God and man in Christian revelation. Dix, a century later, had failed to grasp how this experiential communion with the essentially mysterious triune God, was the real issue at stake in the Palamite controversy. In Paternoster's words:

> It seems to me that Palamas takes whatever is true in the Hellenic outlook, and absorbs it into a coherent and illuminating defence of the essential truth of the Syriac insight. You may or may not regard this terminology as helpful—I do not myself regard it as sacrosanct—but it is surely clear that he is using it to assert the same thing as F. D. Maurice.[7]

From here it was easy for Paternoster to move to a wider statement about the nature of theology.

> False theology is just an academic exercise, which could quite well be carried on by an unbeliever, if he happened to be interested: an exercise which does not nourish the spiritual life and is not expected to. True theology springs from a love of God and a desire for God and a conviction that God is real and living and knowable: it is drawn out of the deep wells of experience.[8]

Also in 1970, Vladimir Lossky's son Nicolas attempted an 'Orthodox Approach to Anglicanism'. Lossky *fils* had a key idea. Where agreement on doctrinal formulae is faltering, try excavating the spiritual experience underlying the formulae, for this may be more profitable as an avenue of *rapprochement*. The writings of the Anglican divines, the texts of the Book of Common Prayer, and the *English Hymnal* (did Lossky realize the latter's controversial nature on its first appearance, one wonders?) are the right way to approach the bare and theologically unpromising language of the 39 Articles, object of unflattering assessment by the Orthodox as these had sometimes been, notably in Russia. Thus for example, chapter 56 of the Book Five of Hooker's *The Laws of Ecclesiastical Polity* testifies to a deep consciousness of the mystery of the Church as Body and Spouse of Christ—especially if we bear in mind what Nicolas Lossky called 'Hooker's natural reserve in verbal expression and great care in choice of words'.[9] Lancelot Andrewes's First Sermon on Pentecost had spoken equally eloquently of the Church as the Church of the Last Times instituted at the first Whitsun. Lossky thought a passage in his father's essay 'Rédemption et déification', reprinted in *À l'image et à la ressemblance de Dieu*, was little other than a 'continuation' of the passage of Andrewes he had just cited.[10] Donald Allchin was enthusiastic for this approach. Probably he suggested it to Lossky whose subsequent book on Andrewes, entitled, with obvious reference to his father's masterpiece, *La Théologie mystique de l'Église d'Angleterre*, Allchin oversaw in its English translation.[11]

In the second issue of 1970 Allchin returned to the study of Benson, an Anglican figure with a hidden Orthodox mind-set. Benson was born in 1824, and had no contacts with Eastern Orthodoxy. But Allchin took his cue from Charles Gore, who had praised Benson for the patristic caste of his mind in spiritual letters, retreat addresses, and the like. Unlike many Anglo-Catholics, Benson was thoroughly 'patristic'—that is, on Allchin's interpretation of the term, decidedly pre-mediaeval and pre-Reformation—in outlook. The contrast cannot have been quite as sharp as Allchin insinuates. To take only one example: the custom of making 'preached retreats', where Benson made his mark, itself derives from the Catholic Reformation. Yet Allchin was able to make Benson's outlook sound not only Orthodox but sympathetic to Rome in her more recent mood.

> [I]t is precisely those elements of Counter-Reformation devotion, liturgical practice and theological opinion which sixty or more years ago were being eagerly and uncritically introduced into the Church of England in the name of Catholic 'advance', which are now coming under serious scrutiny within the Roman Catholic Church, and if not being rejected as 'deterioration and corruption' [words of Gore

at Benson's centenary celebration], at least being left aside as less helpful secondary developments which need to be corrected in the light of the witness of the Bible and the wholeness of tradition.[12]

Benson thought that, beginning with St Anselm, Scholasticism had started to cut the roots of 'theological science' in 'prayer and liturgy', making itself an 'increasingly arid speculation on metaphysical truths'.[13] This was an odd, though not an unexpected, comment on St Thomas and St Bonaventure, however much the hat might fit, for example, William of Ockham. Over-confident theological reason had then bred the agnosticism and apostasy of modern times. As Benson memorably put it in his devotional conferences to religious, *Followers of the Lamb*:

> The use of intellect is, that by knowing the things of God we may attain to the experimental knowledge of God's love. Otherwise our learning is only like a staircase leading to the top of a ruined tower.[14]

Benson was a dogmatic Christian, but he thought dogma worthless apart from the spiritual life it represents. Dogma can only be understood by participation. In Allchin's view, this was why Benson kept away from the ecclesiastical controversies of his day, for whose movers and shakers one could be perfected by pamphlets. Argumentation always risked bringing divine revelation within all too human bounds. The Church was the pillar and ground of the truth for one very simple reason—she is the pillar of *life*. Allchin found this a very Orthodox thing to say—though one has to admit the library of the Fathers would be much reduced if anything amounting to argument about Christian doctrine were excised from its volumes' pages.

In Allchin's contribution to the 1973 Oxford Orthodox–Cistercian symposium, 'Monastic Life and Unity in Christ', he would celebrate the figures of Gore and Benson (and to a lesser extent Frere and Hebert), thus appealing to all three of the Mirfield, Cowley, and Kelham traditions of religious life for men in the Church of England. In a briefer exercise in finding 'latent Orthodoxy', he claimed his heroes had recognized 'a certain wholeness and balance in the period of the first twelve centuries, which provides a criterion by which later developments may be measured and in some sense judged'.[15] The cut-off point of the twelfth—rather than the eleventh—century was chosen to safeguard the place of St Bernard as the 'last of the Fathers'. (In any case, it could be argued that the real century of the start of schism between East and West was the thirteenth, beginning with the Fourth Crusade.)

In 1977, as noticed in the previous chapter, Allchin had received an honorary degree from the Bucharest Theological Institute and in return given them a paper. The Bucharest event was an obvious opportunity for rehearsing 'Anglican *ressourcement*' to an Orthodox audience. Allchin pointed out there were no magisterial reformers in the English Reformation. Cranmer was a liturgist, not a dogmatician. Not until the mid-seventeenth century did a 'distinctive theological viewpoint' emerge in the Church of England,[16] though this chronology was not easily compatible with his statement that the 'most influential writers of the classical period of our theological literature' were Hooker (who died in 1600) and Andrewes (who died in 1626).[17] At all events, the classical Anglican way is Scripture interpreted with the aid of the undivided Church. Hooker had focused on the Incarnation, and at his hands the concepts of mutual participation and conjunction imply coinherence and *perichoresis* between the human and the divine. Hooker's 'balance and proportion' are echoed in Andrewes,[18] whose liturgical sermons speak of *theosis* as the Incarnation's rightful consequence. Nicolas Lossky had understood him well. Andrewes's 'remarkably dynamic definition of the state of grace' as a constant going forward (a sermon for Pentecost was under scrutiny) influenced T. S. Eliot, as is 'revealed above all in his *Four Quartets*'.[19] The axis of Trinity, Incarnation, Church, Sacraments then reappeared in Samuel Johnson of Connecticut, the 'outstanding representative of our tradition in the eighteenth century', albeit in the American colonies.[20] Above all, that catena of themes typifies the Oxford Movement, which 'gave rise to new understandings of the implications of this doctrine, both for the inner life of man, and for life in its social and national dimensions'.[21] Here Allchin referred to Maurice and his disciple Hancock—who were not, strictly speaking, in the Tractarian succession, but mattered to Allchin for their looking 'beyond the Church, to the whole of humanity and the whole creation'.[22] And here too he brought in R. M. Benson, 'the outstanding monastic theologian of our Church since the Reformation'.[23] He then made allusion to his near-contemporary David Jenkins, seeing his work as a pure continuation of the best of the previous four centuries. He was not to guess that a few years later, at the meeting of the Anglican–Orthodox Doctrinal Commission in Dublin in 1984, Jenkins's thought on the Conception and Resurrection of the Saviour, officially unchallenged by the Church of England, would become a thorn in the Commission's side.

Allchin ended by wondering—on the basis of the cluster of themes he had identified—whether there might be a special link not just between Anglicanism and Orthodoxy in general, but, quite especially, between English Anglicanism and Romanian Orthodoxy: 'due in part to the mediating positions held by our two nations'.[24] But he went on to qualify this remark. In a 'world which has suddenly become one, not only at an economic but also at a spiritual level, the old distinctions of East and West have very largely ceased to be meaningful'.[25] This was rather a strange comment unless he imagined the *pot-pourri* of articles in *Sobornost* during his editorship represented an emerging universal consciousness.

At the end of the 1970s, Andrew Louth was still an Anglican—and very much of the Allchin mould. So much emerged from 'The Hermeneutical Question Approached through the Fathers'. This article had begun life as a lecture where, in effect, he was explaining Anglican theology to German Lutherans. Modern biblical exegesis in England, he said, was not approached theologically, but theology itself was still approached patristically, an inheritance from the English Reformation with its lack of major confessional documents. Yet no fundamental divide was discerned between the Church 'in and for which the Scriptures were written and the Church of the Fathers'.[26] Of course as everywhere in Europe the Reformation stressed the sufficiency of Scripture. But as Louth saw it, the way in which, for Anglicanism, the Scriptures instruct the Church 'rests on *no principle*'.[27] And here is where the Fathers can enter. They can provide a sort of hermeneutical lens, or at the least an ethos, for the approach he wanted to commend. It was 'an approach in which one can discern a certain directness in expounding Scripture, a certain boldness—*parrhesia*—in [the Fathers'] expounding of the mystery of the faith', which enabled the doctrines of Trinity and Incarnation to emerge and endure.[28]

Classical Anglican theology follows that 'way', which means, in the first place, interpreting Scripture by the rule of faith with, at its centre, the mystery of Christ drawing our hearts and minds. Louth understood this in a manner that heralded his later conversion to Eastern Orthodoxy—and not, say, to the Latin Church.

> Before any articulation of our confession of Christ, there is an inarticulate closeness to Christ, to that creative silence out of which the Word comes, to that stillness (*hesychia*) in which are wrought the mysteries that cry out. This is the ultimate meaning of interpreting Scripture in accordance with the rule of faith: not

> simply subordinating Scripture to the articulated faith of the Church, but listening to the Scriptures from a contemplative stillness that is being with Christ. And this is something given and known in the life of the Church, in the tradition that is the movement of the Spirit in the Church.[29]

That fitted quite neatly with the other feature of the way of the Fathers he highlighted. This was the allegorical method of interpreting Scripture, understood broadly as including typology, and where the 'sole truth' is Christ and all else shadow, having value only inasmuch as it points toward him.[30]

> The use of allegory is a recognition of the fact that here is not the whole truth, but a partial reflection of it through which we might be enabled to discern the truth itself. Allegory ... helps us to discern through Scripture a truth not contained in Scripture, but simply witnessed to it by it.... Such an approach to Scripture is not 'scientific' and *is not meant to be*: it is contemplative, it is a way of prayer.[31]

What some would call 'allegory' is really, then, 'openness to God's manifestation of himself in Scripture so that we are responding through it to the mystery to which it is a witness.'[32]

In 1984, Louth, still, seemingly, an Anglican, wrote on a related topic, 'The Oxford Movement, the Fathers and the Bible'. Here was an example of Anglican *ressourcement* in very pure form. The connexion between the Oxford divines and the Fathers is obvious—their Library of the Fathers was the basis for the two later series of patristic texts in English translation, the Ante-Nicene Christian Library and the Library of Nicene and Post-Nicene Fathers. But where does the Bible fit in? As Louth confesses, 'The Oxford Movement was not noted for biblical scholarship.'[33] Pusey published on the Minor Prophets. Isaac Williams produced a devotional commentary on the Gospels. There were Littledale and Neale (the latter unconnected with Oxford) on the Psalms. The biblical scholar William Sanday felt Newman would have made an excellent exegete, given his 'innate kinship of spirit' with the Gospels, but unfortunately he lacked the scientific preparation.[34] Louth thought otherwise. Newman was unlikely to have found the preparation worthwhile. The Oxford fathers were on the defensive vis-à-vis modern exegesis. They were seeking to salvage an older and, in their opinion, a better way.

Louth based himself especially on Keble's Tract 89, and Pusey's unpublished lectures 'Types and Prophecies of the Old Testament' (a manuscript in the keeping of Pusey House in Oxford), though he also made references to various writings by Newman. Partly, the Oxford divines wished to remain true to the approach to the Bible of the Fathers. Partly, they had inherited a mind-set from English Romanticism. Here Louth was rather tentative, though the final sentence of this citation is important.

> The Tractarians... share something of the Romantics' approach to understanding, but will, it would seem, develop these insights in rather a different way, in a way that lays more emphasis on tradition than the individual talent. What this involves could be developed in a variety of ways, and it would be interesting at some stage to embark on a thorough comparison of Wordsworth and Keble: to show how much they have in common in their grasp of the tentativeness of any human knowing, even though their initial emphases are rather different (with Keble anxious not to lose a sense of objectivity mediated by tradition, Wordsworth more willing to trust to the genius of imagination). Certainly, one point of fundamental similarity between the Tractarians and the Romantics might be mentioned: their common stress on the moral conditions of real human knowledge, something derived from their common indebtedness to Greek wisdom.[35]

Louth was right to stress the hermeneutical importance of moral and spiritual qualities, qualities that render a reader responsive to Scripture, especially, perhaps, simplicity and purity of heart.

Then he made an extraordinary claim. Seeking to grasp Scripture via sensitivity to type and symbol is less a method of acquiring information and more a 'realization of the Communion of Saints', since by it 'we are united to all those who have similarly heard God's voice and responded— both with those of the Old Covenant and those of the New, and especially with those who formed part of our Lord's immediate company during his earthly life'.[36] This assertion could appeal to Pusey for support. In the unpublished lectures, Pusey had argued that we understand the Old Testament better if we see it as prefiguring the New Testament, for then we 'grasp the living continuity that holds together all who have sought to respond to Christ's coming, whether as prefigured or as already taken place'.[37] Louth challenged the critics on their own ground. Sensitivity to type and allegory when 'combined with a humility which does not exalt the modern over the ancient' entails treating the past with more, not less, respect than modern historical critics do.[38] It put him in the company of the Syrian poet-exegetes commended by Murray and Brock.

Critiques of the Latins

Derwas Chitty, that stalwart of the Fellowship's first forty years of existence (it was he who introduced Ramsey to its gatherings), died in 1971. *Sobornost* that year included not only an obituary by Edward Every and a tribute by Donald Allchin but a reprint of a Chitty manifesto from *The Christian East*, the journal of the Fellowship's predecessor and occasional partner, the Anglican and Eastern Churches Association. In later life, Allchin opined, Chitty would have been somewhat less anti-Latin than in this 1929 essay. That would not have been difficult for in 'The Spirit of Orthodox Christianity' the monstrosities committed or permitted by the Latin Church are remorselessly piled high. They include the use of a non-vernacular language in the Liturgy; a doctrine that is no more than philosophy; worship that is emotional expression; the individualism of hierarchs; the legalistic concept of works of supererogation; tolerance of the notion that those called to the mystical way are only some Christians, not all; doubt whether the Incarnation would have happened without the Fall; the clergy as an elite caste; making the Church a ruler of States rather than the animator of patriotism; calling the Anastasis, the Jerusalem church of the Resurrection, the 'Holy Sepulchre'; the deficiencies of the Oberammergau Passion Play; caution about 'deification' talk; moralistic sacred art; lack of interest in the feast of the Lord's Baptism; eucharistic consecration by the words of Institution rather than the prayer for Descent of the Spirit. Even the word 'sacraments' is wrong, or at least not half as good as 'mysteries'.

For Chitty, these shadows must be cleared away if we are ever to see the sun of Orthodoxy shining. He had some fine things to say on that 'sun' (the article comes from the period when he was considering becoming Orthodox himself.) Thus on the fear that theology will disrupt the 'simplicity of Christ's intimacy with us' he comments:

> The Orthodox also understand this fear. But their answer as a Church is to throw all the fullness of their theological thought into their worship. Its very bulk suggests the awful fullness of God and makes us afraid to dwell on any single point too long, lest it should upset the balance and simplicity of our approach to and worship of God.[39]

That throws light on his otherwise rather baffling claim that 'the Liturgy itself is the final authority',[40] though he could also write a little later, 'to the Orthodox only the Spirit is the criterion of doctrine.'[41] In the words of Edward Every, Chitty

> saw the Anglican Churches in terms of their special relationship with the Orthodox whom they, in their independent life [i.e. after the break with Rome], have not condemned as heretical or schismatic or 'Unreformed'. His view of Anglicanism recognized her vocation to provide a bridge to authentic Catholicity which all Protestants can use. Thus his attitude to the Anglican–Methodist negotiations and to approaches towards the inclusion of Non-Episcopalians in the Episcopal Church was, on the whole, positive.[42]

And if Every was *amical* but understated, Allchin's tribute was lyrical.

> Wholly given as he was, in heart and mind, to the service of Orthodoxy, he yet continued to live in and through the faith and worship of the Church in which he had first known Christ, and in which he had received the gift of priesthood.[43]

Every and Allchin were courteous debaters. They also saw the problematic nature of adopting a systematically anti-Western attitude, for they were themselves ordained ministers of a Western Church. That cautionary consideration did not apply to lay converts to Eastern Orthodoxy. Thus when in 1976 Philip Sherrard wrote on 'Christian Theology and the Eclipse of Man', he laid the blame squarely at the door of the Western Church for the disappearance in modern culture of a theocentric doctrine of man. That such a doctrine has evaporated into thin air can hardly be gainsaid. 'Modern man's chief heresy about himself consists in the fact that he is or can be man without any inner dynamic relationship with God, without that reciprocity and interpenetration of the divine and the human of which the model is the incarnate Logos.'[44] Sherrard's question was. Could this deplorable state of affairs have an inner-Christian source? He found one—in the 'Aristotelian revolution' of the high mediaeval West. The introduction of the philosophy of Aristotle had expunged—historically it would be more accurate to say had reduced the role of—participation-thinking. When Aristotle criticized Plato for minimizing the independence of substances, he was a menace to metaphysical coinherence, and introduced to European civilization that sense of the 'separateness and self-contained, or self-enclosed nature of concrete things' which disables the human awareness of the communion of all things in God.[45] Thomas Aquinas was the villain of Sherrard's piece. Though Thomas meant to continue a classical Christian understanding, simply replacing Platonic language with Aristotelian (here Sherrard has the history significantly wrong), the traditional view buckled under the strain.

Sherrard sought to recover that traditional view, but in so seeking, he invoked a different theme. Four years earlier, in 1972, he had reviewed Eric Mascall's Gifford lectures, *The Openness of Being*.[46] Though Sherrard was not as dismissive of Mascall's version of a Thomist approach to God as he might have been of other 'Thomisms'—Mascall had spoken of a 'contuition', made possible by wonder, of God-and-the-world in the 'cosmological relationship', and this entailed a distinctly contemplative approach to metaphysics—he was not convinced. In his view, there was a more important distinction than the distinction between natural and revealed knowledge with which Mascall, and most other Anglican and Latin authors, were accustomed to work. This other, more significant, distinction, lay between

> the exercise of the reason, divorced from its roots in the higher faculty of man's spiritual heart or intellect (*nous*), on material delivered to it through the senses and regarded as purely natural (i.e. independent of grace or revelation), and the exercise of the reason on material delivered to it through this higher faculty from the latter's direct and supra-rational apprehension of divine realities both in creation and in the Word of God.[47]

Man, for Sherrard, is 'a being endowed with precisely this [latter] noetic faculty, actualized by the Spirit through prayer and invocation, which is superior to the reason' such that 'independent of this noetic faculty the conclusions of the reason have no necessary connection at all with the knowledge of God'.[48] That 'diremption' within reason would certainly make dispute with unbelieving philosophers easier—by ruling it out of court! When volume four of the English translation of the *Philokalia* appeared (it was the longest, owing to enormous chunks of Palamas), Andrew Louth, while recognizing the difficulty in matching English to Greek, thought that a certain unnamed person among the editors—surely this was Sherrard—was responsible for the decision never to translate *logos* as either 'word' or 'reason', owing to the 'idea that English, as a corrupt Western language, naturally cannot represent the wisdom of the East'.[49] Coleridge and Newman, said Louth, would have disagreed. To insist that 'reason' in English can only be the discursive power (*dianoia*) impoverishes the language yet further. It also makes it impossible to grasp

Palamas's insight that there is a trinity in the human mind of intellect, reason and spirit (ultimately this goes back to Nazianzen, Louth pointed out) with its affinity to Augustine's triad of *mens, intellectus, amor*.

In an essay of 1976 Sherrard asserted the existence of a supra-rational organ capable of directly experiencing 'spiritual or metaphysical realities' by knowing the 'uncreated idea or type or energy' of which realities here below are the expression.[50] It is through this faculty that man becomes a 'deified being', and without it, he claimed, the whole notion of deification 'falls to the ground'.[51] Unfortunately, so expressed, this was a sub-Christian theology with no place for faith—or indeed for grace. The connexion with the discussion of Aristotle's criticism of Plato, though, was now made plain.

> For St Thomas, God cannot be directly present in man, in such a way that he is the active subject of man's being, because he—God—being a substance in his own right, cannot be present in another substance, man, without displacing or destroying it.[52]

One recalls Mascall's retrospect on his dialogue with Vladimir Lossky: '[H]e and I were both trying to express in the limited and halting terms of human speech the same mysterious and inexhaustible reality, namely the participation by a creature in the life of the Holy Trinity without destruction of its creaturely status'.[53] The article was an object lesson in how differently (to put it charitably) the historic sources could be understood.

But Sherrard, at this time a lecturer at London University, was not going to let go his mission to rewrite Christian anthropology in what he deemed its most authentic, but now concealed, form. In 'The Christian Understanding of Man', published in 1977, he proposed to take Christology as the starting-point for anthropology—and to do so by re-launching the notion of Christ's 'divine humanity', a phrase which, as the Sophiological controversy would have reminded older readers of *Sobornost*, requires very careful handling. Sherrard chose to speak of the 'eternal humanity' because, in his view, '[e]ternal truths, not historical events, are the proper subject of theology'.[54] This was not too well formulated given the salvation-historical element in Scripture. Yet something like it was needed if Sherrard was to make good his claim that human beings are essentially sons of God by virtue of their created imagehood of the eternal God-man—and not, as might otherwise be supposed, by 'adoption', via the redemptive effects of the life and death of the Word specifically as human: as an agent, indeed, in human history.

Just as Aquinas was the villain of the piece in Sherrard's earlier essay, so now that honour fell to Thomas's single most important predecessor in the Latin tradition, St Augustine.

> It is one of the paradoxes and also one of the tragedies of the western Christian tradition that the man who affirmed so strongly the presence of God in the depths of his own self and so the ultimate independence of the human personality from all worldly categories should as a dogmatic theologian have been responsible more perhaps than any other Christian writer for 'consecrating' within the Christian world the idea of man's slavery and impotence due to the radical perversion of human nature through original sin. It has been St Augustine's theology which in the West has veiled down to the present day the full radiance of the Christian revelation of divine sonship—the full revelation of who man essentially is.[55]

Augustine risked returning Christian sensibility to an Old Testament condition at its worst, with man regarded as 'derivative and dependent ..., impotent to save himself from his own nothingness and from the tragic dereliction of his life upon earth.'[56] Platonic participation thinking about the image's share in the archetype could have saved Augustine from this reversion. Sherrard did not pause to consider how Augustine might have combined his commitment to Christian Platonism with his doctrine of grace.

By insisting he will start out from Christology, but a Christology of the 'eternal God-man', rather than the Word incarnate, Sherrard ran a risk all his own in directing to this end his use of the Chalcedonian Definition. For Sherrard understood the union of the divine and human natures in the person of the incarnate Word as the *perichoresis*, or interchange, of those natures, speaking of their mutual penetration as if it were the very actuality of the person concerned. This was just the sort of misunderstanding of Chalcedon which the Fifth Ecumenical Council, Constantinople II, sought to exclude by insisting that the unique 'person' whose existence the Chalcedonian Definition had affirmed is none other than the eternal (exclusively) divine hypostasis of the Trinitarian Son. From his own, idiosyncratic, rendering of the Definition, Sherrard drew conclusions which were hardly compatible with Christian orthodoxy, whether of the East or of the West.

> This means that in becoming human God is fulfilling a potentiality in His own nature as such, while in becoming divine the human is

fulfilling a potentiality which is fully in accord with human nature as such.

Moreover, the divine can only fulfil this potentiality in union with the human, just as the human can only fulfil it in union with the divine.[57] Or again, 'God and man are in some sense exemplars or paradigms one of another, to such an extent that the qualities possessed by the one may be also be possessed by the other'.[58] If man is not divinized his human nature is 'truncated'—just as the divine nature is 'truncated' and 'less than divine' if it is not humanized. The aim is an enhypostatization of each and every human being on the model of Christ's own. 'God is always seeking to work the miracle of His incarnation in all men.'[59]

Turning to the question of a theory of consciousness that would fit this scheme, Sherrard returned to that unique noetic faculty he had described earlier. Now it was re-conceived as 'capable of apprehending the divine and penetrating into it'.[60]

> Such an organ may be 'created' in the sense that it depends on God and is not God: but it may also be termed 'uncreated' in the sense that it is not entirely other than God or entirely separate from him: there must be some kinship or affinity between the two, for otherwise any real communion and union between them would be impossible.[61]

This organ beyond rational thought is the spiritual intellect, the 'divine image and what in the deepest part of himself [man] is'.[62] Appealing to Augustine, but in an unreferenced text, it is 'the mysterious eye of the soul'. Though Sherrard wants to identify with this power the image of God in man, he also wishes to maintain that soul and body too are apt for inclusion in 'man's eternal nature'.[63] As he recognized, the language of 'the soul' is too much for most modern philosophers. But his own account, though he claims it draws on ancient springs, renders the soul remarkably insubstantial. He calls it 'that highly charged complex of thought, feeling and sensitivity with which God endows us at birth'.[64] Yet the soul so understood can, through union with the image or spiritual intellect, be carried 'into the Godhead'.[65] It will not, it cannot, leave behind the body in so doing, for the union of soul and body is indissoluble. The body as we normally understand that word decomposes at biological death. Yet the 'body formed of gross material elements is really a kind of condensation or husk or outer wrapping of a body of a far more subtle texture'.[66] It is this more sophisticated physique, reminiscent of the astral body of Theosophy, which endures.

Sherrard's conclusion that man is a microcosm owing to the uniting of spirit, soul and body has, at any rate, authentic patristic warrant, and on this basis he can legitimately say that the Incarnation has taken the whole created world into God, seizing it at the point of *enanthropesis*, the 'enmanment' of the Word. But Anglican readers of the journal who were well instructed on the Creeds could be forgiven for wondering where an 'Orthodoxy' of this sort might be leading.

Contributions of the Latin Church

Positive statements about the Latin Christian tradition in *Sobornost* might be expected to come from Anglican Catholic or Roman Catholic contributors. But this was not invariably so. In some ways Father Lev Gillet might be called a 'Latin Orthodox'. His little book of retreat addresses, *The Burning Bush*, given to Fellowship members at Pleshey, showed him once again as a living synthesis of West and East, with much of his early Latin formation still intact. This was so not least in the Thomist account of God as Pure Act, and the Augustinian emphasis on prevenient grace (albeit not by that name). *The Burning Bush* was given for review to Helle Giorgiadis, now a Roman Catholic and secretary of the Society of St John Chrysostom, the modest Catholic equivalent to the Anglican and Eastern Churches Association. The 'Latinisms' did not strike her, perhaps through a difference in background.[67]

Ernest Michael Beaumont was also something of a synthesis of East and West: an Orthodox priest who took for his academic specialty—he was Professor of French at University College, Dublin—the Catholic literature of France in the modern period. In 'Man's Creative Spirit and the Holy Spirit', a 1973 contribution to *Sobornost*. Beaumont dealt with the relation between literary art and the *Creator Spiritus*, the ultimately creativity of God. As Beaumont noted, anyone who holds a broadly 'Romantic' view of art, if he or she is a Christian, needs to explain how the artist can be a sort of *magus*, mediating intuitions about a world beyond the everyday. But a Christian with a robustly non-Romantic, or even anti-Romantic, view of art also needs to ask about art's relation to 'the manifestation of the divine energies', its connexion with 'God's redemptive plan for the world.'[68] Beaumont wrote now about Léon Bloy and Paul Claudel,

Catholic writers who held, respectively, negative and positive views of the relation between art and the Holy Spirit.

In *La Femme pauvre* Bloy outlined his negative view that 'if Christian art existed, then a door would be open on the lost garden of Eden', a theological impossibility.[69] Artists, thought Bloy, seek to 'efface the memory of the Fall', so as to create a 'factitious earthly paradise'; they therefore make false idols.[70] Art can never be fully Christian but it can to some extent be redeemed by making of itself an instrument of the Church, obedient to her teaching. Claudel's positive view stands in a degree of contrast to Bloy's. For Claudel, the poetic word can spread the redemptive Word. Drawing on the last of *Les Cinq Grandes Odes*, Beaumont wrote:

> The poet's function by his creative word is to present the world again to man, the world that God has created and redeemed. In this re-presentation of the world, the poet is according to Claudel's view to act consciously as an emissary, as it were, of the Holy Spirit. He is to show the world according to God's plan as he understands it.[71]

Claudel seems rather to take it for granted that his understanding as a poet will coincide in all essentials with the divine scheme. But he does not suppose that his poetic mission exempts him from the obligation of trying to be holy. In the Fourth Ode, his 'muse' underlines the inadequacy of merely celebrating the world poetically. The poet must 'give himself entirely, wholeheartedly, to God, in utter self-giving'.[72] Beaumont was persuasive on the value of both these artists.

Gerald Bonner was a lifelong Anglican. As long as he was alive and able to contribute to *Sobornost*, the claims of the catholicity of the West would not go wholly unnoticed. That was well illustrated by the lecture on 'Anglo-Saxon Culture and Spirituality' Bonner gave at the Fellowship conference at Winchester in 1973. Among English converts to Orthodoxy there can sometimes be noticed a tendency to idealize the Anglo-Saxon period in an insular fashion—not recognizing, for instance, the role of French monasteries in St Dunstan's tenth-century monastic revival. The Norman Conquest, which, by accident, more or less coincided with a spat at the other end of the Mediterranean involving the patriarch of Constantinople and papal envoys, appears accordingly as a complete *débâcle*. On balance, said Bonner, the English gained more than they lost through the Norman Conquest—but they *did* lose something.

The Old English state which came to an end at Hastings was far from being the uncultured polity of Norman imagination. In many fields—for instance in book-painting and embroidery, and in the development of a vernacular literature, the English were superior to their conquerors, while the English church was by no means the decadent and simoniacal institution depicted by the propaganda employed by William of Normandy to justify his aggression.[73]

The Anglo-Saxons had experienced the coming of Christianity as access to a higher culture—that of the Christian Roman empire—whether the missionaries were from Rome, Gaul or Ireland. Unlike Cyril and Methodius, the Roman and Irish missionaries 'did not attempt to give their converts a vernacular bible or liturgy'.[74] But the Latin culture the Old English accepted had a stamp which was decisive for Anglo-Saxon spirituality. It was monastic, and it was biblical. It regarded learning as ordered to the praise of God in the public worship of the Church and the expository study of the Scriptures.

Bonner stressed that the 'programme of study required for the acquisition of such a culture did not provide for any acquaintance with the Latin classics'.[75] One went from the Latin grammarians to Bible and the Fathers without a spell of study of secular Latin authors in between. That did not make its culture inferior, it made it specific—as can be seen from such breathtaking works of art as the Lindisfarne Gospels, the Codex Amiatinus (probably the finest Latin uncial manuscript extant), and the Benedictional of St Aethelwold. All of these were made for specifically religious ends in the monastic spirit. Bonner extols the creativity borne of the contact between the Roman and Irish missions in the Lindisfarne Gospels, the Ruthwell and Bewcastle Crosses, and the works of St Bede. The Irish asceticism remained notable in Chad, Cuthbert, Guthlac, the last dying only in 715, and it continued the spirit of St Martin of Tours and the monks of Egypt. The art of the northern crosses too was 'at once expressive of the native genius of Christian Northumbria and also of the common Christian culture of Europe',[76] the latter apparent in the vine-scroll ornamentation, so patently Mediterranean in origin. The strength of devotion to the Cross was exemplified in *The Dream of the Rood*, extracts from which appear on the Ruthwell Cross. Rosemary Woolf had argued in the late 1950s that

> the Dream of the Rood is a carefully argued orthodox formulation of Christ's dual nature and the contrasting aspects of the Crucifixion,

divinity and triumph on [the] one hand and humanity and suffering on the other, which takes account of the Monophysite and Monothelite controversies which were still raging in the Greek East in the seventh century.[77]

It was a nice idea, but Bonner was inclined to think the Old English, though orthodox Chalcedonians, not up to these subtleties.

The coenobitic monasticism Bede represented was, in Bonner's view, an 'active' one, concerned with the pastoral and missionary life. Bede himself, after all, is described as teaching and translating up to his dying day. The Anglo-Saxon mission to Continental Europe belongs with this. Bonner draws attention to the continuing influence of the Irish monastic notion of *peregrinatio pro Christo*. The Northumbrian Egbert, who pioneered the notion of the mission to Germany, did so after first embarking on such a 'peregrination' to Ireland. Bonner emphasized how the English missionaries communicated abroad the 'same concern for monastic culture which marks the home-church' (the Echternach Gospels, the production of English uncial and miniscule manuscripts in German scriptoria, Charlemagne's summoning of Alcuin to be his learned counsellor).[78]

Bonner underlined 'various pointers to the future', and this would have been, perhaps, less pleasing to those who were not 'Anglo-Latin' in outlook. He had in mind pre-Conquest anticipation of such features of high mediaeval Church life as the cult of the real presence and eucharistic oblation, the public veneration of the Virgin, and—not least—Filioquism.

> [I]t was the English Council of Hatfield of 680, meeting under a Greek Archbishop of Canterbury, Theodore of Tarsus, which in its denunciation of Monothelitism, solemnly declared its belief in the double procession of the Holy Spirit from the Father and the Son—a belief which could be found in Latin theologians from St Augustine of Hippo onwards, but which was not at the time professed by the Roman see.[79]

A pleasing footnote to this encomium on the Anglo-Saxon Church was Bonner's address, thirteen years later, to the Fellowship on 'The Saints of Durham' as listed in an Anglo-Saxon poem, the 'latest datable poem in Old English', written before 1109.[80] They are saints from the church of Lindisfarne whose relics lay in Durham cathedral: Cuthbert, Oswald, Aidan; bishops Eadberct, Eadfrith, Aethelwold (the latter two were respectively scribe-illuminator and binder of the Lindisfarne Gospels),

Boisil of Melrose (who trained Cuthbert) and Bede—whose relics were brought to Durham in the eleventh century and who had no connexion to Lindisfarne. Yet, says Bonner, Bede's devotion to Cuthbert, whose life he wrote for Eadfrith, and his *Ecclesiastical History* 'entitle him to be regarded as a representative of the Hibernian strain in Northumbrian Chrstianity no less than the Roman.'[81]

In 1977 Bonner was addressing the conference again, this time on 'The Church and the Eucharist in the Theology of St Augustine'. Augustine's attitude to the Real Presence can be confusing because he took from the Western tradition both realist and figurative language and combined them without any sense of incongruity—as had Tertullian, Cyprian, Optatus in North Africa and, at Milan, Ambrose. The seeming lack of devotional warmth towards the Presence (adoration was expressed in reverent reception and consumption) is to some extent offset by his doctrine of eucharistic sacrifice, notably in *The City of God*, where we also see in clear perspective his view of the Church. In the Eucharist, Christ is Priest and Oblation, but the 'Church also offers herself as the oblation through Christ, because he is the head and she the body.'[82] In this text,[83] Augustine speaks of a daily offering—so he knew of daily Mass, though elsewhere he shows he knew the custom not to be ubiquitous. The idea of the Holy Sacrifice offered specifically for the dead, already a practice in possession (compare his mother's dying wish in the *Confessions*) is 'wholly in keeping with Augustine's theology, for it is "the whole of the redeemed city"—*tota ipsa redempta civitas*—which is offered by Christ the High Priest to God, both living and departed, for it is only sin, and not physical death, which can separate us from God.'[84]

Bonner concluded with an appeal to the Orthodox to accept Augustine wholeheartedly as a Father of the Church just as he, Bonner, did the Greeks—any of whom could have written the words Bonner has been citing (though to say this rather reduced the impact of *The City of God*'s more original formulations).

In 1982 Bonner made a second attempt to commend Augustine to the Fellowship in this later period of its existence. 'The spirituality of St Augustine and its influence on Western mysticism' was a paper given first to the Fellowship and then to the Durham Lightfoot Society, where it was pointed out to him that little if anything he had said departed from the mind of the Greek Fathers. In a note which Bonner prefaced to the essay he wrote:

I am only too happy to agree with this observation, which confirms my own view that theological differences between the Greek and Latin Fathers are commonly exaggerated and that there is a patristic tradition common to East and West alike. I would, however, defend the propriety of the term 'Augustinian spirituality' in the present context, since in the first place it is not clear that Augustine owed any *direct* debt to Eastern theology in developing his own; and, secondly, it is certain that Western spirituality in the early Middle Ages was dominated by Augustine, and by his popularizer, Gregory the Great, and owed relatively little to the Greeks until the work of Dionysius the Areopagite was made available by John Scotus Eriugena in the ninth century.[85]

Within, as it were, a definition of spirituality as 'an orientation of the mind and will to God expressed in a man's life and teaching', Bonner offered a sub-definition of mysticism—rather a wordy one—he had borrowed from a French philosophical dictionary. Mysticism is 'belief in the possibility of an intimate and direct union of the human spirit with the fundamental principle of being, a union which constitutes at once a mode of existence and a mode of knowledge different from and superior to normal existence and knowledge.'[86] Scholars were divided on the question, Was Augustine personally a mystic? Bonner did not seek to settle the question. Moments of illumination at Milan and Ostia were not necessarily repeated later when 'Augustine's heavy commitments as a presbyter and a bishop, together with his enormous literary output, might well have prevented any development of his contemplative capacity'.[87]

That did not prevent Augustine owning a spirituality. Bonner considered its primary quality to be 'a sense of frankness and intimacy with God devoid of any element of sentimental and vulgar familiarity'.[88] Augustine's spirituality was Christocentric and its goal was deification. This followed from his doctrine of creation in the image of God, and the restoration of that image through participation in the grace of Christ. Important for him were the interior illumination of mind by divine truth, a sense of apophasis (already noted by Vladimir Lossky), an emphasis on ejaculatory prayer (see the lengthy 'Letter to Proba'), and humility and fraternity, well expressed in his monastic Rule.

Augustine Casiday in an article dedicated to Bonner, presented his namesake, Augustine of Hippo, as a theologian of deification. He placed him in the group of Western theologians of deification including Bernard, William of Saint-Thierry, Thomas Aquinas—and Martin Luther, on whom more anon from other writers. Casiday recognized he was not the first to ascribe such a doctrine to Augustine, believing indeed that the repackaging of Augustinian teaching in such terms is a fruit of the dialogue between Western and Eastern Christians. But he also thought that the 'broader historical perspective' created by the proliferation of patristic study 'seriously complicated the attempt to assign responsibility for developments (or deviations) to any one person'.[89] The twenty-six newly discovered homilies, found at Mainz by François Dolbeau, include one, on Psalm 81, which is a classic statement of preaching deification by grace over against the false divinities of pagans. Casiday translated it to illustrate his claim. Both by its content, and its dedication to Bonner, his article raised the question of 'mutual enhancement'. The Orthodox could profit from meditating on Augustine's sermon—and Latin Christians could usefully apply to it the developed thinking of the modern Orthodox on *theosis*.

Marcus Plested's *Orthodox Readings of Aquinas* sought to dissuade the Orthodox from defining themselves by caricaturing Aquinas's methods and content. For *Sobornost*'s reviewer, Christopher Villiers, Plested 'disproves the notion that Aquinas was an Aristotelian rationalist alien to patristic theology'.[90] St Thomas had made a rich use of Eastern Christian sources. And in any case, 'From Cyril of Alexandria onwards, syllogistic reasoning and Patristic citation loomed large'; here Villiers does not hesitate to call St John of Damascus 'the epitome of Patristic scholasticism that infused Byzantine thought'.[91] Plested went on to consider the reception of Aquinas in Byzantium, which was in fact a significantly smoother ride than in the high mediaeval West. 'Where Aquinas is not forgivably affected by the errors in which he was raised as a Latin, he is regarded as a divinely inspired theologian of surpassing excellence.'[92] It is in the wake of the Slavophiles, with their programmatic definition of Orthodoxy over against the West, that Aquinas begins to be excoriated, a process which continues, more or less, among such otherwise divergent figures of the Russian Diaspora as Lossky and (especially) Bulgakov. A sharp contrast between mystical Greek wisdom and the rationalist hubris of the West also typified the writing of John Romanides and Philip Sherrard, and somewhat less dramatically that of Christos Yannaras. By contrast, Georges Florovsky sought to right the record and commendably so. (Readers of the present book may think here of Mascall's memory of Florovsky's dictum on Augustine as an Eastern father, recorded in Chapter 1 above.)

Positive benefit

Occidentals could benefit positively from the East, Orientals from the West. That there was a *lumen orientale* had been acknowledged in Western Christendom since the early Middle Ages. *Sobornost*, especially in its latter decades, certainly did it justice. But it did not, for all that, deny the occasional shining of a *lumen occidentale* as well.

John Eudes Bamberger, abbot of Genesee abbey in New York State, had been a contributor to the 1973 'Cistercian-Orthodox' symposium, and his essay 'Thomas Merton and the Christian East' was perfectly modulated for *Sobornost* readers. Merton always carried on his person a Greek icon with on its reverse a *Philokalia* text about the spirit 'naked to God' (might it be a text from Evagrius?). This fitted well Merton's longstanding devotion to St John of the Cross. The 'naked knowledge' spoken of in both East and West was increasingly important to him.[93] He had always thought of the city of Rome as Byzantine as well as Latin, thanks to its art monuments. The art of the icon stirred him more than others (though in the source quoted, *Conjectures of a Guilty Bystander*, a note of hesitation is also sounded about this asseveration.[94]) At an early period in Merton's monastic life, the *Sayings of the Desert Fathers* became influential, and, probably through Gilson's *The Mystical Theology of St Bernard*, he grasped the role of the Greek Fathers in the tradition which formed Bernard's mind.[95] He reflected on Hesychast spirituality, notably Palamas, and saw the 'light of Tabor' as ultimately the light of Easter. In his classic study, *The Climate of Monastic Prayer*, he seems to have alternated Western and Eastern authors quite deliberately.[96] He contributed an essay on John Climacus to a new translation of the Sinai master, claiming that his spirituality had influenced the Russian literary tradition, notably in Dostoevsky.[97] The words 'ferocity and paradox' were used. He felt a huge admiration for St Seraphim of Sarov. His desire, granted in his last years, for a hermit life-style could also be regarded as testifying to this multiply attested Oriental bent, though of course there is a noble story of Western hermit-monks to be told. Very Seraphim-like is the statement that the 'purpose' of the spiritual life is to 'attain to possession of the Holy Spirit, by the free gift of God in Christ'.[98]

> He was convinced that when we attain to this greatest of all gifts through ascetic preparation and through prayer of the heart we would discover that in the Holy Spirit we are already united, already

one, and in this realization we would receive the light and strength to give corporate expression to this unity so that, in the end, we would be fully united in the Whole Christ.[99]

This was expanded two decades later. Donald Allchin, now described as chaplain to Anglican nuns at a location in Wales, was at his best in 'The Worship of the Whole Creation: Merton and the Eastern Fathers'. Merton's death in 1968, Allchin explained, did not obliterate his memory, not least owing to the subsequent publication of five volumes of letters, and, more recently, after a twenty-five year Cistercian moratorium, the first three volumes of his diaries. But his appeal to the Eastern tradition had not yet been fully studied: notably his use of Maximus and Palamas, and some nineteenth- and twentieth-century Russian writers, including Theophan the Recluse and Alexander Schmemann. And finally there was his evident determination to appropriate the monastic tradition in its entirety which could not conceivably leave out the Christian East where the roots of monasticism lay. What made it easier to fill this lacuna was the access Allchin had received to his unpublished 'Lectures on Ascetical and Mystical Theology (given at Gethsemani Abbey in 1961) and the 'Working Notebooks' archived at Bellarmine College, Louisville (both in Kentucky). In the lectures, the chapter 'Contemplation and the Cosmos' is devoted to Maximus of whom Merton wrote, 'He has the broadest and most balanced view of the Christian cosmos of all the Greek Fathers, and therefore of all the Fathers'.[100] 'The vision of *theoria physikē* is essentially sophianic. 'Man by *theoria* is able to unite the hidden wisdom of God in the things with the hidden light of wisdom in himself'.[101] Allchin commented:

> It would be tempting to expound at length Merton's understanding of *theoria physikē* as he develops it under the guidance of Maximus. He sees it as an expression of Christian faith in the inherent goodness of things which remains despite all the ravages of sin—and in the power of divine grace which is always at work to make up what is lacking and to heal what is wounded in the creation of God. He sees the relevance of all this, not only to our contemplation of things, but to our use and transformation of them. And he comments on the dangers of our advanced technology when it is ruled by the desire to exploit and manipulate. He speaks about the role of the artist, and of the way in which he, of all people, must be in touch with the *logoi*.[102]

As to Palamas, Merton knew him via Meyendorff, and found St Gregory's account of the role of the spiritual senses more plausible than any he had previously encountered. '[T]he spiritual senses are ... the senses themselves, but spiritualized and under the sway of the Spirit rather than new spiritual faculties.'[103]

The Notebooks give the lie to those who feel Merton's late interest in inter-religious dialogue attenuated his Christian faith. Allchin tied Merton's continuing Christ-centredness to his references in these diaries to Theophan the Recluse, texts from whom are, moreover, underlined in Merton's copy of that Orthodox anthology *The Art of Prayer*. As to Schmemann, he also appears, in the guise of the author of *The World as Sacrament* which fitted well Merton's own developed view of monasticism as neither flight from the world nor capitulation to the world. In the Notebooks Merton returned to the early monastic sources, finding special inspiration in the account of the meeting of Anthony and Paul in Jerome's life of Paul of Thebes.

In his conclusion Allchin was in danger of exhausting laudatory epithets. Merton was a profound theologian in the Evagrian sense and in the sense of a servant of the Word. He was a mystical and experiential theologian, a 'great historical theologian, with a firm grasp of the main outlines of the development of Christian doctrine and a remarkably detailed knowledge of the development of monastic life and thought'.[104]

In 1976 there was another exercise in convergence between East and West when Neville Clark, an Anglican priest in the diocese of Guildford, Surrey, wrote on the Prayer of the Name. Clark placed its Oriental origins within the wider experience of prayer in desert monasticism, noting the role of the heart in the anthropology of the Pseudo-Macarian Homilies, and the early (mid-fifth-century) mention of invoking or remembering the name of Jesus recommended by Diadochus of Photike.

> The type of prayer which best spans the levels of extension and intension is monology; this repetition allowed the monk to dwell, as it were, in two realms at once: the outward and the inward. He could carry on some simple work while praying unceasingly at the deepest level, in a way which was not possible with the more varied programme of vocal prayer.[105]

In calling on the name of Jesus, invocation became evocation, and the *nomen*, the verbal name, actualized the *numen*, the Lord's own presence.

Of this highly specific prayer Clark said:

> It had the conciseness of the best monologic prayer; it contained the name of Jesus; it was a cry for help and a means of effecting that help; it achieved constant memory of God and was full of adoration and affection; it looked to the divine glory and at the same time was aware of human sinfulness, yet in this recognition it contained also the hope of remedy.[106]

Unsurprisingly, it became a focus for Orthodox spirituality in the centuries ahead. But so it did in the twelfth- and thirteenth-century West, notably in the 'Jesus Psalter' of Richard Whytford, even though there is 'no developed theory of the workings of the prayer in the West, and no record of the use of the standard Eastern form of the prayer'.[107] Since the fifteenth century, Clark went on, 'Western spirituality had concentrated more on structured meditation than this simple affective prayer, and this tradition is very distant from the Eastern technique'.[108] He suggested that in the Rosary the *Ave Maria* acts more like a mantra while the mind discourses on the mysteries, whereas in the Jesus Prayer the name engages the whole mind and imagination is discouraged. So despite the use of prayer-ropes in both, the similarity is less than it might look.

Kallistos Ware returned to this topic in 1982 under the title 'The Holy Name of Jesus in East and West: The Hesychasts and Richard Rolle'. For Ware, as for Clark earlier, Diadochus of Photike is the crucial figure in the East:

> Diadochus preserves the Evagrian insistence upon imageless prayer; but by proposing the use of a monologic invocation containing the name of Jesus, he offers a practical method for attaining imageless prayer in a way that Evagrius himself fails to do. Thus in the *Gnostic Chapters* of Diadochus, there can be found for the first time the essential elements of the Orthodox tradition of the Jesus Prayer.[109]

Ware found Hesychius of Sinai to be the closest Easterner to Rolle. Hesychius had seen the invocation of the Name of Jesus not as penitential (an expression of *penthos*, compunction) but 'more as an expression of gladness and gratitude for sin forgiven'.[110] In Rolle's case, the Holy Name is pronounced by itself or with an adjective, as was also recommended by Hilton and the Cloud author. This, said Kallistos, is unknown in the Greek East. 'The Holy Name, so most Orthodox feel, is almost too powerful, too concentrated, for it to be used "undiluted" over a prolonged period'.[111] The most marked difference from the Hesychasts is that while Rolle 'believed that the imagination should be controlled... he nowhere suggests that it should be transcended. On the contrary, his use of the terms *calor*, *canor* and *dulcor* [heat, song, sweetness], whether or not these be regarded as purely physical experiences, clearly implies the continuing use of the imagination.'[112] To find something comparable to the Byzantine Hesychasts in fourteenth-century England one must combine Rolle with the Cloud author, for whom the 'aim of this monologic prayer is precisely to attain non-discursive contemplation, to "smite down all manner of thoughts" and "beat upon" the cloud of divine darkness'.[113]

Positive benefit could come about through scholarship too. In 1980 Kallistos reviewed the English translation of Irénée Hausherr's classic book on the Jesus Prayer (and related prayer modes), *Noms du Christ et voies d'oraison*, originally published at Rome in 1960.[114] Ware had no hesitation is describing this Alsatian Jesuit, who had died in 1978, learned in Greek, Syriac, Armenian, Slavonic, as 'for more than a quarter of a century... the greatest living authority on the history of spirituality in the Christian East'.[115] It appealed to Ware that Hausherr was a man of the heart and not just the head, conscious of the practical and pastoral and not simply the historical and doctrinal dimensions of his subject. At one time, we are told, Hausherr had been less than enthusiastic about some aspects of hesychastic prayer, but in the 1960s when the Uniate monastery at Grottaferrata was bringing out a new edition of the Byzantine Office, his voice was raised to include the feast of St Gregory Palamas, the Hesychast doctor and a major figure in the Orthodox Lenten season, who had been omitted from previous Catholic versions on doctrinal grounds. The saint's proper texts were duly added, albeit in an appendix. Ware compared Hausherr's study of the Jesus Prayer with Gillet's, tending to agree with the former rather than the latter on some disputed points of its history. The Prayer started out not from devotion to the Holy Name but as an expression of *penthos*, compunction, in the desert manner. The American editors of Hausherr's book had not updated its bibliography; Ware went to the unsolicited trouble of doing this for them.

A further example of a sought-for Eastern benefiting from Western sources came in 1978, in the shape of a study of Julian of Norwich in the light of Orthodoxy. The author, an American Lutheran, who noted at the outset Julian's recent popularity in the Anglophone sphere but also the seemingly heterodox character of some of her statements, looked especially at her doctrine of the Trinity seen as generating an 'ontological understanding of divine love, and therefore of sin and salvation'.[116] He found not only doctrinal orthodoxy with a lower case initial letter, but a teaching attuned to Orthodoxy with an upper case initial too.

On Julian's account of the Trinity-in-itself, Brant Pelphrey had this to say:

> Although Julian could not have known it, her picture of the constant motion within the Trinity, which is at the same time the stillness of indwelling, reproduces the concept historically known in Orthodoxy as *perichoresis*. It is even more remarkable that Julian recapitulates the historical applications of the term first to the indwelling relationship of divinity and humanity in the person of Jesus, and then (as revealed in the Son) to the Being of the Trinity. Thus the nature of God the Trinity—which cannot be seen by any human being—is made manifest in the Person of the Incarnate Son; and the Being or 'substance' of God is identical with his love: 'Charity unmade is God'. We note, incidentally, that if the substance of God is love, then it is impossible for God not to love. Hence Julian's conclusion, also echoing the Orthodox saints, that there can be no wrath in God.[117]

That is said of God in himself. But what about the triune God's relation to space and time, and thus his relations with what is not himself? In Julian's visions, God speaks of the same events as past, present and future, owing to his non-temporality of view. Pelphrey argues that Julian teaches not an eternal creation (perhaps of some element in the human composite—shades of Sherrard!) but an eternally situated purpose of God in creating man. So likewise, taking a God's eye view, always purposive in scope as this is, she identifies the fall of Adam with the Incarnation and Atonement, when God's Son fell into the Hell of sin to overcome it.

That is helpful, but what about her view of salvation history where, by hinting there is a final stage not as yet disclosed in Scripture or Tradition, she sometimes seems to undercut the revelation that *has* been given in those media? Audaciously, Pelphrey linked her to Palamism—not of course as an influence, but as an affinity—her seeing two 'secrets' in God. One remains hidden to us as creatures, while the other is revealed in Christ for our salvation. This was somewhat problematic. It did not really take into account those texts where Julian says the 'great' secret will be revealed eventually. Pelphrey compares Julian's account of the revealed 'workings' of God with St Gregory's divine 'Energies', but for the contrast with the ever unmanifested divine Essence of Palamism to work, one would need Julian to speak of a secret that is never to be shared with humans. But that is not what she says. Much later, Bishop Kallistos would introduce a Russian translation of the *Revelations of Divine Love* and argue in his own way for the 'latent Orthodoxy' of Julian's text.[118] He stressed the Trinitarian and Marian dimensions of her theology of the Cross, comparing her on these points to Philaret of Moscow and the Staretz Silouan, respectively.

In 1979 Bonner, who more customarily presented himself as a man for the Latins, wrote on 'St Cuthbert as a Western Orthodox Saint', instituting a comparison between the Northumbrian monk-bishop and St Seraphim of Sarov. So here was another example of positive benefit, operating this time through mutual enhancement—for the insight offered could be enjoyed by each saint's devotees. Both Cuthbert and Seraphim were highly ascetic. Both were thaumaturges. Both were consolers of the sorrowful. Both were lovers of animals. Each emerged from reclusiveness for ministry, though Cuthbert's only lasted two years, Seraphim's (as a spiritual father) for eighteen. Bonner is, accordingly, reduced to suggesting that 'Cuthbert's solitary life on Farne may have been of greater value to the people of Northumbria than his more active ministry as bishop of Lindisfarne. God alone knows.'[119] But perhaps this is an unnecessary agnosticism, since Bonner reports on the basis of Bede's *Life of Cuthbert* that many people came to him on Farne for counsel. 'He is the English saint of the earliest period of Northumbrian Christianity who preeminently calls us to the life of prayer as the foundation of Christian living.'[120]

An essay by Andrew Louth, 'The Influence of Denys the Areopagite on Eastern and Western Spirituality in the Fourteenth Century', sounded promising for convergence, but turned out to be less hopeful after all. He summed up at the outset Denys's theological vision.

> It is presented to us in the *Corpus Areopagiticum* which consists of the two works on the *Celestial* and the *Ecclesiastical Hierarchies* respectively, the *Divine Names*, the *Mystical Theology* and ten letters. They all have a single aim: the union of the whole creation with God by whom it was created, a union in which the created order attains perfection, or becomes divinized, as Denys is fond of saying. The different works (which are presented to us as the surviving works of a more extensive corpus) seek to achieve this goal in different ways, though all ways follow a threefold pattern: of purification, illumination and perfection or union.[121]

The difference of 'ways' would be crucial for Louth's essay, since he regards the Byzantine use of Denys as integrating more of his teaching on the Christian life than do mediaeval Latin authors, notably by adding the liturgical way to the way of personal prayer. But even on the way of personal prayer there is a change of climate when we reach the Cloud author, for whom *nous* is not so much purified and simplified as displaced by love. In the Victorine school (Thomas Gallus, abbot of Vercelli, is important here) and, above all, among those influenced by St Bernard, the 'Dionysian notion of knowing through unknowing came to take on a fresh twist: to know through unknowing is not to know with the intellect at all, but to attain to a felt union through love'.[122] In the West, paradoxically, Denys's influence made possible the pursuit of non-Dionysian ideas. Louth presented a second striking instance. In the writings of Thomas Gallus, in Richard of St Victor's *Benjamin Maior*, and St Bonaventure's *Journey of the Mind to God*, Denys's *Celestial Hierarchy* is linked to the *Mystical Theology* in what can only be called a distinctively Western fashion. The ranks of the angels are allegorized, so as to become an image for the interior hierarchical structure of the soul. Thus in Gallus's scheme, nine degrees of activity, natural or supernatural—this is activity ultimately based on receptivity—are related to Denys's ninefold angelic orders. That explains the keen sense among the English mystics of the fourteenth century of how the angels assist contemplation. But it is not quite the historical Denys's teaching.

The main contrast between East and West in the utilization of Denus concerns his liturgical influence. In the East, via Maximus, Germanus, Cabasilas, this was potent in a manner hardly possible in the West since the pattern of the Western rite did not really fit Denys's liturgical scheme. That Cabasilas only deals with three sacraments, Baptism, Chrismation, Eucharist—though in *The Life in Christ* he spends time on the rite of consecration of a church—can be explained readily enough. Denys has three 'initiations': Baptism, Eucharist and the oil—and on the latter Denys too refers to the consecration of a church. More importantly, the Areopagite strengthened in the East a sense of the Liturgy as essentially a corporate enterprise. 'Denys's understanding of the hierarchies is the vision of a *society*, mutually supporting and supported, and the Liturgy is a dramatic enactment of the events of our redemption, events which established the ecclesiastical hierarchy, and in this enactment all participate.'[123] Louth doubted whether in the West this was ever understood.

Louth also reviewed an important work for East–West relations: Jean-Claude Larchet's *Maxime le Confesseur, médiateur entre l'Orient et l'Occident*.[124] This too might have been an exercise in mutual enhancement but, as things turned out, it was not. Maximus was a Byzantine theologian who, unusually, spent a lengthy period in the West, in North Africa and Rome, in the character of an exile. The book concerns his view on the Filioque, the papacy and original sin. With regard to at any rate the first two topics, his position has been claimed by Roman Catholic scholars as endorsing the stance of their Church. The third motif has not been much discussed in this context but, as Louth points out, the Augustinian doctrine (or what is taken for it) had been under attack both from the Orthodox and from Western liberals. Louth thought Larchet had disposed of the Roman arguments on the first two issues, though he was sceptical of the French writer's grasp of Augustine's Triadology.[125] Larchet's rejection of a notable attempt by the Dominican Jean-Miguel Garrigues to solve the Filioque dispute (it was more or less officially taken up by the Holy See and endorsed by, among others Olivier Clément and Boris Bobrinskoy on the Orthodox side), was something of an ecumenical setback. As to original sin, Larchet had already discussed the ancestral sin, as seen by Maximus, in the pages of *Sobornost*.[126] Here he added a complaint against modern Orthodox who have taken a sunny view of the Fall based on the Antiochene divines Theodore of Mopsuestia and Theodoret of Cyr. Meyendorff was especially criticized for reliance on Christologically suspect figures. Louth noted in passing that Larchet was impatient of Russian Emigré theology in general.

By the 2000s, Latin themes were not often heard in *Sobornost* (and Anglican themes even less), so it was good to have Marcus Plested on the theology of grace in Augustine and the Pseudo-Macarius. Plested, who had just published his *The Macarian Legacy. The Place of Macarius-Symeon in the Eastern Christian Tradition*,[127] argued that in richness of doctrine on this topic Macarius can well be compared with Augustine. More especially, he had in his sights possible affinities between their teachings. The difference between East and West on the theology of grace may have been exaggerated. Plested hoped to 'make a small contribution to the better appreciation and understanding of Augustine among the Orthodox and, concomitantly, to meet in some modest way what Oliver Clément characterizes as the West's need to "reinsert Augustine's voice into the patristic symphony"'.[128] Usefully, he listed points the two writers have in common. They were: a high doctrine of Adam's pre-eminent condition; a 'certain transmission of guilt to humanity through the fall'—plain in Augustine, insinuated in Macarius;[129] an 'inner presence of evil ... not immediately removed by baptism'—for both 'reject the Pelagian thesis that baptism restores us to the state of sovereign liberty of Adam',[130] although it is 'through baptism that evil is extirpated bit by bit' in the holy warfare in the soul;[131] a rejection of ontological dualism and fatalism. On the issue of grace and freedom—especially neuralgic between East and West—while Macarius says God does nothing without the free will of man, Augustine could well say the same, since even for the later Augustine of the the Pelagian controversy, grace liberates freedom and does not suppress it. The African doctor does not teach the 'irresistible' grace of Jansenism or Calvinism, and Macarius himself, in a passage preserved only in Arabic, maintains that '[t]hose who have been found worthy of the true good must not attribute to themselves the power of grace'.[132] Does that mean, then, that nothing at all distinguishes the African doctor from the Byzantine Father? No, for Macarius does not have a doctrine of predestination except insofar as he says God fore-chooses those who will love him.

And the Filioque

When the talk of the day is 'Anglicans and Latins, and their critics', the topic of the Filioque will inevitably raise its head. Here was a sticking-point indeed. For the first joint issue of *Sobornost* and the *Eastern Churches Review* Edward Every had been thinking about the Filioque in the context of Anglican concessions to the Orthodox. He hit on the idea that the Latin verb *procedere* has to do service for more than one Greek verb—this was actually the basis of the 'solution' to the Filioque problem laid out a generation later by the French Dominican Jean-Miguel Garrigues and semi-officially adopted by the Roman see.[133]

Every was knowledgeable about the Anglican phase of this disputed history. In the mid-seventeenth century, John Pearson, whose *Exposition of the Creed* was long influential, 'condemned the addition to the Creed made by the Latins "without the consent and against the protestation of the oriental church"'.[134] Yet Pearson defended the Filioque doctrine as true while admitting its lack of explicit New Testament sanction. He strongly opposed those who condemned its absence in the Greek form of the Creed and in a footnote opined that the schism between East and West would never be healed until the clause was omitted. In the proposals for Prayer Book revision in 1688/9 there was reason to believe, so Every told his readers, that some members of the Royal Commission wanted the insertion of a note meant at the least to indicate the objections of the Greeks, if not the desirability of suppressing the clause altogether. It *was* suppressed in a liturgical book published by the Non-Juror bishop Thomas Deacon in 1734. In 1968 the Lambeth Conference had recommended for study a report which suggested consideration of the restoration of the original form. The American Episcopalians had already emended their Creed in this sense the previous year though they changed their minds again in 1976. In 1976 the Moscow Agreed Statement of the Anglican–Orthodox Doctrinal Commission asked for the excision in all the provinces of the communion. Hard on its heels, the 1978 Lambeth Conference invited thought on the matter from Anglicans at large. As to Every himself, he was inclined at this date to think both forms of the Creed should be preserved—and this despite putting forward an argument (in the last published number of the *Eastern Churches Review*) that on the basis of the Annunciation and Baptism of Christ (as distinct from Pentecost) one should assert the issuing of the Spirit from the Father alone.

Such havering will not have pleased the Orthodox. In *Church, Papacy and Schism*, Philip Sherrard had found in Christological and Triadological errors, among which the Filioque was preeminent, the cause of the Latin Church's wrong turnings in ecclesiology, among which the claims made for the papacy figured prominently.[135] Norman Russell was not convinced.

> The error in Christology is held to arise from a distorted view of the Fall which places too great a gulf between God and man so that the divinity and the humanity in Christ cannot really form a single person. Rome, however, would agree with Sherrard that the humanity is enhypostatized in the Logos without change, or confusion, or mixture.[136]

And as to Triadology, Sherrard's 'account of the Latin doctrine is … somewhat one-sided. He says that in Roman Trinitarian theology "the primacy of the essence is asserted over the concrete reality of the persons". This was certainly a tendency in Latin thought, but it is not found in its best exponents.'[137] Russell was inclined to think Sherrard less indebted to the Fathers than he believed, and more influenced than he realized by such modern Orthodox writers as Khomiakov, Lossky and Romanides.

Russell was establishing himself not only as the best translator into English of contemporary theological Greek (he had a Greek mother) but as a fine scholar of Greek patristics, so his opinion was worth having.

For his own part, Russell also wrote on the Filioque and the union of the Churches—but in the twelfth century dialogue between Anselm of Haverberg, a Premonstratensian bishop from northern Germany (though he died as archbishop of Ravenna), and Nicetas archbishop of Nicomedia. The two had met in Constantinople where Anselm was engaged on a diplomatic mission to explore means whereby Lothair III and John II might cooperate against Roger II of Sicily. The religious atmosphere was clouded. The issues disputed between Latins and Greeks had aroused bitterness on both sides. Anselm was unusual for his spirit of 'humility and conciliation'.[138] The debate was detailed and thorough, and Russell explained it comprehensively with copious citations. The original point in Anselm's case was the attempt to explain Gregory Nazianzen's Trinitarian theology by reference to Augustine's. Against the odds, the discussion ended in agreement.

> Anselm was content if Nicetas would admit that the Son is not excluded from the eternal procession of the Holy Spirit which is properly from the Father. Nicetas, for his part, wanted to hear a formulation of doctrine which upheld the primacy of the Father as the source of divine being. Anselm was finally able to satisfy him by saying that the Holy Spirit proceeds from the Father and the Son but properly and principally (*proprie et principaliter*) only from the Father.[139]

Anselm had found the phrase in Peter Abelard's *Introductio ad theologiam*, and Russell considered it bold of him to 'utilize the work of such an advanced thinker'.[140]

By 2004 the North American Orthodox–Catholic Theological Consultation, so *Sobornost* noted, had issued an agreed statement, 'The Filioque: A Church-dividing Issue?' After a careful survey of the biblical and historical background to the Filioque notion, the 'consultors' distinguished between the theological (Triadological) and ecclesiological aspects of the problem. As to the first, they declared in an excellent statement:

> The Greek and Latin theological traditions clearly remain in some tension with each other on the fundamental issue of the Spirit's eternal origin as a distinct divine person. By the middle ages, as a result of the influence of Anselm and Thomas Aquinas, Western

theology almost universally conceives of the identity of each divine person as defined by 'relations of opposition'—in other words, its mutually defining relations of origin—to the other two, and concludes that the Holy Spirit would not be hypostatically distinguishable from the Son if the Spirit 'proceeded' from the Father alone. In the Latin understanding of *procedere*, after all, it can also be said that the Son 'proceeds' from the Father by being generated from him. Eastern theology, drawing on the language of John 15:26 and the creed of 381, continues to understand the language of 'procession' (*ekporeusis*) as denoting a unique, exclusive, and distinctive causal relationship between the Spirit and the Father, and generally confines the Son's role to the 'manifestation' and 'mission' of the Spirit in the divine activities of creation and redemption.[141]

The ecclesiological issue was more briefly dealt with. It concerned, of course, the pope. '[T]he Catholic tradition accepts the authority of the pope to confirm the process of conciliar reception, and to define what does and does not conflict with the "faith of Nicaea" and the apostolic tradition.'[142] The manner of the Spirit's origin should be regarded as still awaiting 'full and final ecumenical resolution'; meanwhile, the Catholic Church should use the Greek text in catechetical and liturgical translations.[143]

A coda on Lutherans

The Finnish theologian Jouko Martikainen, in his essay 'Man's Salvation: Deification or Justification? Observations on Key-Words in the Orthodox and the Lutheran Tradition', raised for *Sobornost* readers the question of theological method which at one point had looked like derailing the debate described by Russell. In 1976 the 'Finnish interpretation' of Luther was hardly known outside Finland itself. Indeed it can be said to have arisen out of the Russian Orthodox–Finnish Lutheran Dialogue of 1970 to 1974, and more specifically during the last of that dialogue's sessions, which concerned soteriology.

For Martikainen, Lutherans have favoured personalist categories and neglected ontological, while the Orthodox have favoured ontological categories and neglected personalist. So the strengths of each could in theory be combined in the future. While not excluding other descriptions of salvation, the East makes *theosis* central, at the same time placing great weight on the freedom of man who was made in the divine image and with a dynamism that points toward such deification in the 'likeness'.

Both emphases are prima facie alien to Lutheranism. For Luther, as is well known, the central soteriological concept is justification. Justification 'follows man's experience of standing before God who is speaking to him. God's direct call leads to a radicalization of sin and grace.'[144] Yet Luther's personalism did not prevent him emphasizing the 'est' ('This *is* my Body') of the eucharistic conversion, so evidently he was not opposed to ontology on principle. In eucharistic theology 'consubstantiation' is quite as ontological as is 'transubstantiation'. How, beyond this, to show the complementarity of justification and deification in soteriology was the challenge for the future.

Some Finnish Lutherans went further. They held the view that Luther himself might be brought to the witness-stand to give evidence for the doctrine of deification. It was not simply, so *Sobornost* readers were informed, that justification and *theosis* could be considered, in an ecumenical spirit, two complementary views of salvation. 'Recent Lutheran ecumenical theology has discovered an unexpected motif of deification and a pneumatological concept of grace within Luther's own writings. The so-called Mannermaa school at the University of Helsinki has provided a promised (and also to some extent controversial) claim about *theosis* being one of the images Luther used to describe salvation.'[145] That Christ is really present in the faith of the believer—this can also be expressed by saying that the *Spirit* of Christ is really present there—opens up the perspective of deification even though the word itself may be rare in Luther's usage. Veli-Matti Kärkkäinnen, who provided this information, also looked farther afield, finding links between the Anabaptists and the East, for the former understand grace as 'a transforming divine energy'.[146] John Wesley had been described as 'open to the idea of deification and to a pneumatological understanding of the concept of grace', since he was 'less interested than Reformation theology in the permanent justification of the sinner, and more interested in the process of a moral renewal',[147] and this emphasis was passed on to the 'Holiness' and 'Pentecostal' movements in modern Protestantism. Kärkkäinnen noted that Pentecostal theology and spirituality are not, as is often mistakenly thought, Spirit-centred. They are Christ-centred, yet the Spirit draws people to Christ and assimilates them to him. But 'Free Churches have been so eager to identify themselves with the Reformation doctrine of justification that they have not seen how much at variance their anthropology and view of human responsibility is with the view of the Reformation' itself.[148]

Anglicans and Latins, and their Critics

In 2012 Norman Russell, author of a substantial volume on *The Doctrine of Deification in the Greek Patristic Tradition*,[149] asked a Greek audience, at the 'progressive' Volos Academy for Theological Studies in Athens, why it was that *theosis* fascinated Western Christians. In the lecture he offered his own answer. After describing the historical emergence, development, and later vicissitudes of the *theosis* concept, culminating in its recovery by Catholics in the 1940s (if not slightly earlier) and beyond, Russell wrote: 'The recovery of a version of *theosis* by the Roman Catholic Church is perhaps not surprising given its respect for Tradition and the Fathers, Greek as well as Latin. What is more remarkable is in the strong interest that Protestants have shown in *theosis* in recent years'.[150] In the German-speaking world, this might be ascribed to the vacuum caused by the Nazi-period collaboration of the Lutheran and Reformed Churches with a paganizing State, and the consequent founding in 1948 of the Evangelische Kirche im Deutschland as a federation of Churches wishing to make a theologically new start. 'Both Jurgen Moltmann and Wolfhart Pannenberg have looked eastwards in their attempts to redefine what it is to be human in the light of the Holocaust and Germany's traumatic wartime experience',[151] turning notably to Yannaras and Zizioulas. Of course the ecumenical movement encouraged such looking outward, and nowhere with more impact than in Finland. Here Russell describes the advent of the Finnish school of Luther interpretation forged as this was (at any rate in part) in the context of dialogue with the Russian Church. American Protestants have now, he reported, picked up the torch. Yet it remains a moot point whether the *theosis* teaching can be detached from its 'broader dogmatic matrix',[152] and used as a 'helpful analogy that can throw light on any given Protestant's soteriology'.[153] It was all very well to say that man must be defined in terms of the call to deification. But there must also be Trinitarian and Christological orthodoxy, and a true understanding of the doctrine of grace, of the sacraments, and the moral and ascetical life if this definition is to be of any earthly use.

↛ 4 ↚

The Dialogues

The period covered by 'A Voice for Orthodoxy' was an age of dialogue in the Churches. 'Bilateral' dialogues, in particular, sprouted on every side. Addressing as they did both 'left' and 'right' on the ecclesiastical spectrum (these labels are theologically thin yet can serve as convenient ciphers), the ecumenical representatives of the Churches had to keep a large number of balls simultaneously in the air. Remembering to tell differing conversation partners fully compatible things was not always easy. And behind and beyond it all lay the more amorphous 'multilateral' dialogue—perhaps it should be called a 'polylogue'—presided over by the World Council of Churches, through its Commission on Faith and Order. *Sobornost* was not 'The Journal of Ecumenical Studies'. It had no brief to keep up with attempts at reunion all round. But it naturally had a special concern for what the Anglicans and the Orthodox had to say to each other, and to the Oriental Orthodox (though the latter were, for obvious historical reasons, less important for Anglicans than they were for the Byzantine Orthodox themselves). And after the absorption of the *Eastern Churches Review*, a horse from a Roman Catholic stable, it could hardly avoid considering the dialogue of the East with Rome.

The 1970s

Not all dialogues are official. In *Sobornost*'s first issue for 1970 Donald Allchin reviewed with substantial excerpts a set of 'dialogues' between the lay theologian Olivier Clément and the Patriarch Athenagoras published by the Paris house Fayard the previous year.[1] The theme of the reunion of Christians was especially prominent, and Athenagoras gave eloquent expression to his desire that, notwithstanding doctrinal difficulties, the whole spiritual atmosphere ought to be changed. Restoring mutual love would enable disputed questions to be seen in a different light. Allchin's extracts were not restricted to the ecumenical arena. They included internal criticism of the Orthodox Churches for their lack of fraternity, either as strangers or, worse, as rivals. Bulgakov would have been pleased by the Patriarch's espousal of economic intercommunion, though the adjective was not used. The simple and emotionally charged language may have been Clément's anyway. This was not a transcript of interviews, but Clément's summary of both sides of a lengthy set of exchanges.

In 1972 one voice sought to speak for both parties, Anglican and Orthodox. This was Richard Hanson, who had professed theology at the University of Nottingham and was now bishop of Clogher in the Church of Ireland. Hanson contrasted 'Orthodox Dogma and Anglican Vagueness' and found them, despite everything, not so far apart. Both are unwilling to 'separate doctrine and life, theology and piety'.[2] That was a fair enough statement. Both regard 'concord, Christian peace and harmony, as a greater thing than mere theological correctness'.[3] That was rather more dubious as regards the Orthodox, both historically and today. Both revere Tradition. Certainly. The Church of England was not created *ex nihilo* in a break with the mediaeval past. Instead, an attempt was made to 'accept the late mediaeval Church and to try to modify it according to the Scriptures'—for which the best evidence is the continuance of the threefold office of bishops, priests and deacons.[4] Both venerate the Fathers, and though Newman could ask his former co-religionists (ironically) whether the Spirit had left the Church in the fifth century, 'so far as dogma goes we have all the dogma which we need in the doctrinal development of the first five centuries'.[5] Hanson admitted the Orthodox had developed dogma beyond this, but expected them to agree there was particular importance in that early period. No doubt they would.

Michael Ramsey, still archbishop of Canterbury, gave a presidential address on 18 March 1972, with Zernov chairing. It fell to him to give dialogue a context. He spoke of three phases, so far, both of his own thought about the ecumenical movement and of the ecumenical movement itself. For him personally, the first phase was one of romantic attraction to Orthodoxy.[6] On that honeymoon he had been excited by, especially, Orthodox attitudes to worship, to the Communion of Saints, and to the nature of theological thinking. In a second phase, under the impact of the first, his own theological thought became 'more Eastern than Western'.[7] The key texts were the New Testament, the Greek Fathers and those of the Anglican divines who had been influenced by Greek patristic teaching. The third and current phase involved a swing to the West, for which his explanation was more pragmatic than theoretical. He had become (as bishop of Durham, presumably) a 'professional ecclesiastic' in a Western Church.[8]

What of the three phases of the movement itself which are more significant (except for a Ramsey biographer of course)? The first phase, suggested Ramsey, was dominated by a rediscovery of the doctrine of Church-hood, and lasted until the first assembly of the World Council of Churches at Amsterdam in 1948 or perhaps its successor gathering at Evanston in 1964. The second phase focused more on mission, and for the West this entailed a shift from investigating the ontology of the Church to seeing the Church as 'event'. That must have been a short phase, or one that overlapped with another, since Ramsey regarded the third phases as initiated by the World Council of Church assembly at New Delhi, in 1961, and the Second Vatican Council, held by the Church of Rome in the years 1962–5. The emphasis now lay on 'renewal'. Renewed churches were expected to be 'more obedient to Christ in their form, their behaviour, their mission'.[9] Such renewal was also to look outward, beyond the Church, to the world the Church exists to 'serve and re-create'.[10] It was perhaps as well Ramsey added the words 'to re-create' since by itself the expression 'to serve' suggests an all too worldly Church that takes its point of reference from what is as yet unevangelized. Ramsey was aware of this danger, admitting that the social activism seen at the World Council gathering (one is tempted to write 'jamboree') at Uppsala in 1968 looked to many like 'left-wing political activism', though he did not accept this characterization himself.[11] To speak of the transfiguration of the created order, as do the Orthodox—here Ramsey cited Zernov and Bulgakov—avoids the danger of subservience to the world's standards found in the West in the concept of the Church as 'servant'. But simultaneously with this turn towards the world, there had been an outburst of charismatic Christianity which also ran a risk—that of finding its home outside institutional Christianity itself. Ramsey felt Orthodox modes of thought might help here. If we think in terms not of the Church and her boundaries but of the world that-is-being-re-created, it seems more reasonable to suppose the Spirit can operate outside the 'precise frontiers' of the Church's fellowship as well as within them.[12] And secondly, a view of the Church as 'once given' yet also growing towards 'further plenitude' can allow for charismatic or other movements assisting in that movement towards greater fullness.[13]

Clément, Hanson, Ramsey, were all offering personal comments to ease the way. But the way itself was one of official dialogues, which, so far as the Anglicans and the Orthodox were concerned, began in 1973. Allchin had been speaking to the Anglican and Eastern Churches Association about the separate meetings of the Anglican and Orthodox members of the Joint Doctrinal Commission, which took place at Chambésy, in the run-up to the Commission's first plenary meeting at Oxford in that year. There were, he admitted, some grounds for pessimism.

> The tensions between those who see the salvation of the Church as lying in change, and those who see it as lying in resistance to change, have certainly increased.[14]

This augmented the problematic factor in Anglican–Orthodox *rapprochement* but it also intensified the urgency of reconciliation. The Chambésy meeting was preparing for a dialogue that was at once Pan-Orthodox and Pan-Anglican. The future would not resemble the 1937 conversations with the Romanians or those of 1958 with Moscow, which were confined to just one autocephalous Church and the Church of England. Allchin explained that the slowness of the progress followed from the non-centralized nature of both Orthodoxy and Anglicanism, and the political obstacles to communication for some Orthodox bodies. The Anglicans had sought to make themselves representative of all schools of thought in the communion. The Orthodox had tabled four issues.

> How the Anglican Churches would understand their union with the Orthodox Churches. What was the possibility of union between Anglicans and Orthodox in view of the measure of intercommunion practised between Anglicans and some other bodies. In what way would any decisions reached by the Joint Doctrinal Commission become binding on the Anglican Churches, and What was the status and authority of the Thirty-Nine Articles within the Anglican tradition.[15]

The Anglican members had been working on how they themselves understood 'comprehensiveness'. The full commission, consisting of forty to fifty members, was to gather in July 1973. It was rather large and Allchin hoped sub-groups would be allowed on particular topics, which could meet at different venues world-wide. He saw reason to think they would begin not from special controverted issues but from the great common dogmata—the Trinity and the Incarnation. If so, given the very different character of their Church life, that would already be a powerful witness.

The first *Sobornost* issue of 1973 was able to print the two Orthodox contributions which had emerged from that first plenary meeting at Hertford College, Oxford, the Anglican papers having already appeared in the journal *Theology*, associated with King's College, London, the flagship Church of England foundation within London University.

Basil Krivocheine, by this date Archbishop Basil of 'Brussels and All Belgium', wrote on 'Christ's Redemptive Work on the Cross and in the Resurrection'. After outlining the unity of the saving work from Incarnation to Pentecost, and stressing its mysteric character, he launched into an attack on St Anselm's theory of redemption—which erred not least by seeking to rationalize the 'unfathomable mystery of the Cross'.[16] For Krivocheine the notion of outrage against the divine majesty, and the need to render satisfaction for dishonour, were concepts alien to the patristic understanding of redemption—and unacceptable to Orthodoxy, though he went on to add, '[More] acceptable to us is the idea of satisfying God's justice'.[17] The Cross, he insisted, is a manifestation of both God's anger and God's love, not that Anselm's treatise really denied that claim. More pertinent was the objection that, on Anselm's account, the Resurrection is lost to view. Yet despite his criticisms, Krivocheine could not bring himself to conclude that the Anselmian theory was altogether false. It is perfectly faithful to Scripture and Tradition to say that the divine Son chose to suffer for sin on the Cross and redeemed mankind by his Blood.

Krivocheine anticipated his own account of the triumphant aspect of the Cross and—and so of the Resurrection—when he cited a famous text from a Good Friday sermon of Philaret of Moscow. Philaret had spoken of 'the crucifying love of the Father, the crucified love of the Son, the love of the Holy Spirit triumphant in the power of the Cross'.[18] The Cross exhibits the 'Divine power of love and self-sacrifice on which the world rests',[19] for, as the Sacrifice of the Son to the Father through the Holy Spirit, it shows forth the entire divine Trinity, itself the world's beginning and its continuing foundation. To call the Cross a unique, a 'once for all', Sacrifice, is to draw attention to the way it 'marks the beginning of a completely new relationship between God and man'.[20] Krivocheine cited Hebrews 10:12 as to how the Cross-sacrifice marks the beginning of Christ's Glorification ('When Christ had offered for all time a single sacrifice for sins, he sat down at the right hand of God'). That was the cue for his statement of the inseparability of the mysteries of Cross and Resurrection. Krivocheine understood the Resurrection as both an historical and a meta-historical event, a 'divine–human act which creates and transforms not only history but also meta-history'.[21] It is certainly not a matter of 'subjective visions of the Risen Christ which reflected [the apostles'] inner state',[22] nor is it mere resuscitation, a replay, as it were, of the raising of Lazarus. Rather:

> Christ's Resurrection is a creative transformation of the natural body into a spiritual body possessing new qualities, belonging to the future age and therefore only visible for eyes illumined with the light of faith.[23]

Christ's Resurrection is the start and the principle of general resurrection, an 'all-embracing transformation of the cosmos and its transition from the plane of material being to that of spiritual, but by no means disembodied, being'.[24] Its saving power starts at once with the Ascension and Pentecost. It initiates the eternal life on earth, above all through Baptism. It prepares the way for the resurrection to come which the Holy Eucharist announces by its expectation of Christ's second coming, It is manifested in the souls and bodies of the saints. This paper was well received by the Anglican delegates.

In the remaining Orthodox contribution to the Oxford meeting, Metropolitan Stylianos Harkianakis, director of the Patriarchal Institute of Patristic Studies at Moni Vlatadon in Thessalonica, whom Allchin had encountered on his 1969 tour (see Chapter 1 of 'A Voice for Orthodoxy'), considered 'The Holy Spirit as Interpreter of the Gospel and Giver of Life in the Church Today'. From the beginning he struck an eirenic note. A Western commentator had called the lack of personal prayer to the Holy Spirit a demonstration of a pneumatological deficit in the West. The Greek archbishop thought it unlikely that many Orthodox frequently invoked the Holy Spirit either—despite the marvellous hymnography of the East about his Person. The basic problem is not a West/East divide, for understanding the place of the Spirit is 'the thorniest problem in the whole of Christian doctrine and the most incomprehensible to the human intellect'.[25] A complete pneumatology would need to discuss creation, redemption and justification—but it is, he says, in effect the last which 'the Anglicans' have asked to be addressed.

They wished him to consider that dimension of pneumatological understanding which 'speaks of the work of the Spirit in the Church after Pentecost'.[26] The terms 'Interpreter' and 'Giver of Life' apparently came from the Anglican side, but Stylianos found them the words an Orthodox might prefer anyway. The beauty of the combination lies in the suggestion that the life the Holy Spirit enables necessarily reproduces the Gospel the same Holy Spirit interprets. Or, to put this another way, the Spirit's giving of life to the Church makes possible right interpretation of the truth of the Gospel. Orthodox commentators in the modern period had been slow to recognize the difference in the Farewell Discourse in St John's Gospel between the Holy Spirit 'bringing to remembrance' and the Holy Spirit 'teaching'—for fear they would introduce into readers' heads the notion of a supplementary revelation by the Spirit to augment the revelation by the Son. But so long as, with the Cappadocian Fathers, we affirm the consubstantiality of the Spirit with the Son there should be no problem in recognizing that the 'work of the Holy Spirit, as teacher of the faithful, is to supplement and complete the teaching given by Christ'.[27] In St Basil the Great's words, the Son 'does not need the cooperation of the Spirit but chooses to bring things to completion through the Spirit',[28] just as the Father does not need the Son to create yet chooses to create through the Son. The Holy Spirit carries out this task in the way he builds up the life of the Body of Christ, the Church—and Metropolitan Stylianos gently corrects Vladimir Lossky's suggestion in *The Mystical Theology of the Eastern Church* that the Spirit works on persons, the Son on human nature as a whole. This is correct only if we add that the action on persons is so that they may contribute to the organic life of the Church-body as a whole. Indeed, for Stylianos, the Spirit's work as Interpreter finds its fruit more in the 'moral' than the 'intellectual' activity of Christians. What, then, of the Holy Spirit as 'Lifegiver' in the Church?

> If we begin from [the] identification of our Lord as Light and Life which is made by St John, the theologian par excellence, we can say already that to the extent that the Holy Spirit, as interpreter of the Gospel of Christ, enlightens the faithful and so contributes to His glory, in the same measure we should consider that he brings true life to the Church in every age. This life is manifested constantly in the variety of gifts he bestows on the Church, gifts and graces which make up the Church's total spiritual life.[29]

The presence of the Spirit preserves, and guarantees, the Word and the sacraments. The intimate connexion between the two explains the Orthodox 'conviction that wherever the totality of the Faith is lacking, it is impossible to have *communio in sacris*'.

The official communiqué from this meeting was frank. On 'comprehensiveness' the Orthodox were not fully convinced. But they were at least encouraged by what Anglicans had said. The Anglicans, for their part, wanted to know whether the Orthodox acknowledged the Spirit's activity beyond the canonical limits of Orthodoxy—and indeed in the world at large. More work had to be done on what could constitute an 'Agreement'. It was suggested that the decisions of the Dialogue might become incumbent on Anglican Churches in a gradual way. As to the Articles of Religion, in many Anglican provinces their place was being re-thought. In England the new Declaration of Assent for the ordained referred to the 'faith which is revealed in the Holy Scriptures and set forth in the catholic creeds and to which the historic formularies of the Church of England bear witness'. Everyone was happy with the account of the Paschal Mystery given by Archbishop Basil. For the future, it was announced, sub-commissions would be appointed on 'Inspiration and Revelation in the Holy Scriptures', 'The Authority of the Councils' and 'The Church as the Eucharistic Community'. Allchin thought Anglicans would have to look again at the place of the Filioque in the Creed—and at the claim that the Fifth, Sixth and Seventh Councils form a unified whole.[30]

Inevitably, there would be grumblings. Frank Weston, then principal of the College of the Ascension in Birmingham, and later of Coates Hall in Edinburgh, namesake and descendant of that celebrated High Church warrior the Bishop of Zanzibar of the Kikuyu Controversy and the great Anglo-Catholic congresses, wrote on 'Orthodox Critiques of Western Ecumenism', an important and little studied topic. Weston looked at the 1973 declaration of the Ecumenical Throne for the World Council of Churches' twenty-fifth anniversary, and the less congratulatory comment on the 1972 Bangkok meeting of the Division of World Mission and Evangelism of the Council, which Patriarch Pimen of Moscow addressed to the ecumenical body's central committee. Juxtaposing these two texts with the essay 'What is Salvation?' by a Russian theologian, Vitaly Borovoy, published in the *International Review of Mission* for January 1972, Weston concluded that the real dis-connect between Western ecumenism and the world of Orthodoxy was a view of salvation based on *theosis* and leading to the salvation of all creation.

> The question for Western ecumenists is ... how far their priorities for mission spring from a philanthropy insecurely based in traditional Trinitarian theology and the question for Orthodox ecumenism is ... how far does their monumental system go to meet the burning questions of our time, for which perhaps their notion of philanthropy is somewhat inadequate.[31]

In years to come, there would be a burst of *theosis* language in Protestant Church-bodies—but not all Orthodox were happy for them to have the concept without what they considered its proper context. There would also be, among Orthodox radicals, especially in Greece, an itch to answer those 'burning' philanthropic questions.

The Oxford meeting was meant to look ahead to a further gathering at Moscow which might hammer out an 'Agreed Statement'. *Sobornost* published two doctrinal papers produced in this hope. Mark Santer, then principal of Westcott House, Cambridge, and later bishop of Birmingham, wrote on 'Scripture and the Councils'. Scripture, always interpreted by the Apostolic Tradition, is the starting-point for the Councils. '[A]lthough scripture is the rule, it is understood by all that scripture must be read in an orthodox sense.'[32] But while the interchanges at the 268 Council of Antioch are largely unknown to us, a survey of the subsequent Councils suggests that Scripture's direct role, immense as it was at Nicaea I, receded progressively. Of more immediate importance to later Councils was the authority, and the right understanding, of those assemblies that had preceded them, as well as faithfulness to the fathers (the bishops) who had spoken at them or been appealed to by them. And this implies that the later Councils' reliance on Scripture was increasingly tacit in character. That is not so obviously the case for Nicaea II—but Santer wanted to diminish the significance of that particular council. He had a low opinion of the exegetical powers of its members (or those of the Iconophile doctors who influenced it), and wished to commend its conclusions to Anglicans only in a limited sense.

Comparing the patristic epoch with the English Reformation, he found that the 39 Articles teach the sufficiency of Scripture for all things needed for salvation, the limits of the Church's authority (which cannot contradict Scripture), and the dependence of general Councils (themselves errant) on Scripture for their own authority. Mediaeval Western theologians did not necessarily disagree with any of these statements—so, granted the assumption that there *was* novelty in the Reformers' position, everything turns on how those basic assertions are understood. Here Santer called to the witness stand Richard Hooker and, more emphatically, his namesake and contemporary Richard Field. Hooker was chiefly concerned with appeal to the 'light of nature'—the light of reason—in interpreting Scripture, an anti-Puritan preoccupation. It was Field who, in Anglican–Orthodox dialogue, is more to the point. Field accepts the infallibility of the Church but not that of councils. The latter are 'not possessed of that infallibility of judgment which the Church as a whole enjoys'.[33] Instead Field appeals to a set of 'rules' or norms or criteria for judging a council's value. These are: the infinite excellence of God; the articles of faith; the Scripture, and the 'uniform practice and consenting judgment of them that went before us, as a certain and undoubted explication of things contained in the scriptures'.[34] Field uses a standard distinction of mediaeval theology, especially stressed by Aquinas, when he speaks of the Spirit inspiring the authors of Scripture but assisting (merely) those attending councils. This does not, however, lead him to take councils lightly. When a council has been lawfully constituted, with the participation of all the patriarchs, and its proceedings conducted in a regular fashion, then 'we are so strongly to presume that it is true and right that which with unanimous consent is agreed on in such a council, that we must not so much as profess publicly that we think otherwise, unless we do most certainly know the contrary'.[35] Field acknowledged all Seven Councils of the patristic epoch though he was wary of the seventh, which 'was not called about any question of faith, but of manners' and which may inadvertently have opened the way for later, i.e. mediaeval, superstition.[36]

Santer commended Field's approach. But he departed from him in aggregating Scripture and Councils, arguing there is no difference in their 'mode or degree of inspiration',[37] though this was more by way of minimizing the Bible's than by maximalizing the Councils'. The real difference, suggested Santer, is that Scripture records the primary witness to Christ, whereas councils 'expound and interpret that witness.'[38] Santer could not have eliminated the reference to a difference in mode had he accepted, among the councils of all the ages, the First of the Vatican, whose constitution on faith, *Dei Filius*, addresses among other things this very question. It is not of course likely that an Anglican writer would cite the First Vatican Council when writing for the Orthodox. Yet Santer did in fact cite the *Second* Vatican Council, and notably the notion of a 'hierarchy of truths' as described in *Unitatis redintegratio*, its 'Decree on Ecumenism'.

He applied the notion of a hierarchy of truths to the evaluation of the Councils at large, downplaying on this ground the *horos* of the Seventh Council which, he said, does not require of Christians 'unaccustomed to the veneration of images . . . that they should necessarily adopt the cult, but that, if its rejection involves the implicit denial of the more fundamental doctrine of the incarnation which legitimizes the cult, they should not reject it'.[39] He also applied the same notion, and rather more ruthlessly, to the Scriptures themselves.

> Some elements in the prophetic and apostolic witness [i.e. the books of the Old and New Testaments respectively] are central, others are peripheral. The peripheral must be interpreted, sometimes to the point of practical exclusion, in the light of the central. Nothing is dispensable in its character as witness; much may be dispensable as normative formulation of doctrine or prescription of behaviour.[40]

For all practical purposes, handing a neophyte a Bible is insufficient. The 'definitions and doctrines of the Church . . . add . . . an order and an integration which is more than a mere addition or summary of what is to be found in Scripture', though they contribute 'no new elements'.[41] In other words, Scripture is materially sufficient but formally insufficient, to use the terms preferred by the modern Roman Catholic debate on this topic.

Constantine Scouteris addressed the same question for the Orthodox. Scripture is created for the Church, for the 'edification of the faithful and for the salvation of the world'.[42] By defining the biblical canon the Church accepts the 'Word of truth'. There is a mutual relation which Scouteris puts cogently in the language of first Trinitarian and then Christological discourse, speaking of the 'perichoresis' of Scripture and Church in the image of the Trinity,[43] and of the way Church and Scripture are 'neither separated nor confused, being united without confusion' as in the Chalcedonian Definition of the being of Christ.[44] It follows from the reciprocity between Bible and Church that the Church alone can identify the Bible's true meaning. This she does in basing herself on the original apostolic tradition—always possible to her since she is the bearer of Tradition with an upper case 't'.

> By saying that in Orthodoxy the Bible is interpreted and understood through Tradition, we mean that the Apostles through the Church interpret themselves. This is so, simply because the Apostles, along with and parallel to the Scriptures, left Tradition to the Church to safeguard their teaching. It is precisely this Tradition, preserved

living through the energy of the Holy Spirit, that interprets Holy Scripture and is interpreted by Holy Scripture.[45]

Scouteris spoke of the Church as a synod continuously in session, 'constantly vigilant, and always active, in order to express the truth being experienced within her own Tradition'.[46] This can be put in terms of 'eucharistic' ecclesiology. From the beginning

> [T]he whole Church, under the Apostles, clergy and laymen, participated in such sacramental assemblies of the people of God, in which the totality of the Church, animated by the spirit of unity and love and convoked by the Holy Spirit, constitutes a constant ecumenical and living synod.[47]

An abiding, eucharistic, synodality underpins the occasional happenings that are the actual episcopal synods. That sheds light on how it is the 'people of God' as a whole that constitutes the 'ultimate criterion' for the ecumenicity of a Council'.[48]

These substantial essays were not written in a vacuum. The difficulties Anglican–Orthodox dialogue was beginning to encounter were signalled in an open letter from the council of the Orthodox Church in America, the former Russian metropolia, dated 13 November 1975, which now appeared in *Sobornost*. The eminent Church historian John Meyendorff wrote a short explanatory piece to introduce the missive. The letter stressed the excellent relations which pertained between Orthodox and Anglicans hitherto. It feared these were now to be eroded by innovations in the Anglican Communion, especially the introduction of women presbyters. Anglicans, said Meyendorff, now 'face a dilemma, which involves their very belonging to this "Catholic" Tradition of the Church'.[49]

Nonetheless, the first Agreed Statement between Anglicans and Orthodox—the 'Moscow Statement'—was on the point of appearing.[50] Allchin agreed that the ordination of women, not a topic on the official agenda, had started to overshadow the discussion. More serious for the imminent future, to his mind, was a loss of confidence in the reliability of the Church of England's Commission on Doctrine. Its latest product *Christian Believing* caused misgivings.[51] In effect, the text absolutized the present period of historical culture. It also seemed to discount the corporate knowledge that arises from the interplay of reality and experience in a shared way of life and worship. On both these matters Orthodox sensitivities were thoroughly engaged. Allchin commended in this regard a new book, *The*

Contradiction of Christianity, by David Jenkins, then director of Manchester's William Temple Foundation.[52] A wider diffusion of Jenkins's kind of thought would greatly assist Anglican–Orthodox *rapprochement*. That did not seem likely after the *débâcle* of Jenkins's début as a bishop-elect of Durham attended by Christological denials, some years later.

As already mentioned in the opening chapter of 'A Voice for Orthodoxy', some Anglican organs were inclined to point a finger at the Orthodox for concealing their own dissenters on the issue of women's ordination. Elisabeth Behr-Sigel's paper on the subject had aroused controversy beyond the confines of the Orthodox Church. Hence the need, so *Sobornost*'s editorship felt, to hear her entire case, and not just snippets taken out of context. She certainly believed the 'women's movement' was challenging the Church of today.

> It may have profound significance to see the woman as the mother, the heart and soul of the family. But is it not also a smoke-screen of words to obscure the emptiness of the lives that many women lead, especially in modern social conditions with nuclear families reduced to the parents and one or two children who quickly become independent, an increasing number of single or divorced women who are unmarried but feel no call to follow a monastic vocation?[53]

Putting this question did not make her a feminist. In demanding equality so aggressively, many modern women are, she thought, copying the 'old man'; the militants of Women's Liberation are becoming 'petty chiefs'.[54] Behr-Sigel was asking, rather, for a 'new style of relationships and new structures in which free men and women can join together in their common task in a spirit of fraternal or conjugal love, respecting one another's dignity and distinctiveness'.[55] Her perspective was one of enabling Orthodox women to serve more efficaciously the growth of God's Kingdom. She thought this enquiry would proceed with more serenity than in other Christian bodies. Orthodox women 'do not experience the Church as a pyramid of power, we experience it at the deepest level, linking us in fellowship with Jesus Christ through the Spirit, as a community of prayer and love. The mysterious presence of a woman, the Mother of God, shines through the Church's whole life'.[56] The 'equality of women with men in the order of sanctity has never been denied—and it is this and not the hierarchy which forms the axis of the Church'.[57]

At this date, she found Evdokimov's reflections on woman (and women) the most promising among Orthodox writers. For the Russian lay-theologian, woman has 'preserved the mystery of her being and spiritual gifts, which St Paul symbolically describes as a "veil" (First Corinthians 11:6, 10). It is this mystery she must "unveil", decipher, so that she may understand her destiny "conjugally" with man.'[58] Moreover, in his study *La Femme et le salut du monde*, Evdokimov

> goes even further and suggests a certain relationship or analogy (constantly to be corrected, however, by apophaticism, for God is the Wholly Other), between the masculine principle and the Logos which structures on the one hand, and the feminine principles and the Holy Spirit which incarnates, inspires, consoles on the other.[59]

Had not that ancient document the *Didascalia Apostolorum* related the deacon to Christ, the deaconess to the Holy Spirit?

But then there came a change of mind. In 2001 Elisabeth Behr-Sigel would write on 'Mary and Women', criticizing Evdokimov for ignoring *anthropos* when he made an 'absolute' of biological differentiation and transposed it into the 'spiritual sphere'.[60] The sounder tradition of the Russian Diaspora theologians, echoing the Greek Fathers, is to say person transcends gender. Ranging Mary and the Spirit's charismata on the one hand against Christ and the sacraments on the other has the effect, Behr-Sigel now protested, of excluding women from authority and thus decision-making in the Church (does this follow?), and downgrading the role of the Mother of God in representing all humanity as the 'matrix of humanity renewed'.[61] She would also object to glorification of Mary's physical motherhood rather than her typical disciple's faith. Mary's Assumption/Dormition is not a glorification of womanhood but a sign of the 'telos for which humanity as a whole was created'.[62] She had always drawn the line at ideas of the 'Eternal Feminine' which, though well intentioned, seemed to 'cast women, in the Church and in society, as specialists in sacrifice and devotion, a kind of universal welfare worker with Mary as the universal prototype'.[63]

Even in 1978 Behr-Sigel had predicted an increasing role for women in the management of Orthodox parishes. Thanks to their 'particular charismata', this should have the desirable effect of turning parishes into 'welcoming fellowships'.[64] Owing to their catechetical duties women in parishes needed access to good theology. There would be little difficulty in restoring the order of deaconesses though in the Byzantine Church they neither baptized nor preached. The Greek bishops had a college for them but in no sense are they ordained. The Copts on the other hand *do* confer *cheirothesis*, a laying-on of hands 'signifying the consecration of their work by the Church'.[65] She did not admit an 'ontological' difference between ordained and non-ordained, as a Catholic writer would be expected to do. But she granted a certain weight to the idea of the iconic role of the priest as representative of Christ. Along with Bobrinskoy, Clément and Nicolas Lossky she signed a letter of protest to Patriarch Bartholomew I deploring the fact that recommendations of various inter-Orthodox gatherings about the restoration of the women's diaconate had been ignored.[66]

Kallistos Ware was never afraid of handling hot chestnuts and he supported Behr-Sigel in her pursuit of the question of women deacons (and, with more discretion, presbyters). He now addressed another troublesome point, stimulated by Constantin Patelos's book, *The Orthodox Church in the Ecumenical Movement, Documents and Statements 1902–1975*, published by the World Council at Geneva in 1979. Far from confining himself to a summary of its contents, Kallistos launched onto the open sea of the questions it raised. Had Orthodox participation in the World Council had any real effect? Had the Orthodox profited from it (other than financially, which most certainly they had)? Should they leave the World Council altogether, negotiate a separate relation, as the Roman Catholics had done, or leave things as they were?[67]

He was inclined to think the Orthodox *had* made some impact. More effectively than Old Catholics or High Anglicans, they had stopped the World Council from simply being a Pan-Protestant federation with a liberal Protestant view of reunion. He also thought the Orthodox themselves had benefited in a wider sense. Their isolation, not least from each other, had been diminished. Their regrettable tendency to assume that the non-Orthodox are simply un-Churched had been weakened. True, there were major problems with the current set-up. He listed some of them: financial support for revolutionary movements in the Third World and the 'theology of violence' used to justify this; a feeling among the Orthodox representatives of increasing marginalization, owing partly to the large number of new Protestant Churches that were granted membership; the discovery that some of their candidates for World Council commissions had been blacklisted as unsuitable. In the future, he thought, bilateral dialogues would probably be more important, above all (in terms of likely success) with the Non-Chalcedonian Orientals, and also (in terms of possibilities, however remote) with Rome. Kallistos thought the Orthodox would be wise to concentrate on such dialogues, without however abandoning the World Council completely. It was two cheers for the ecumenical movement.

The 1980s

The Catholic–Orthodox dialogue had officially opened at the end of May 1980, and Norman Russell, in covering the event for *Sobornost*, called the first meeting of the Mixed Commission in Greece from 28 May to 4 June 'probably the most important meeting of Catholics and Orthodox since the Council of Florence in 1439'.[68] A diplomatic hurdle had to be removed first. A declaration by the Orthodox made it plain that the presence of Eastern Catholics on the Catholic 'team' was not to be taken as tacit acceptance of 'Uniatism'. The Catholics responded that the question of Uniatism could not be decided without the participation of Eastern Catholics. The dialogue members then got down to business. Officially outlined though this was in a joint communiqué published in the Athenian publication *Ekklesia kai theologia* (with a French translation in Chevetogne's journal *Irénikon*), its substance was more frankly conveyed in Russell's interview with Père Louis Bouyer, theologian of the Oratoire de France and a member of the Catholic delegation.

Bouyer made several valuable, indeed historically noteworthy, points. First the insistence on representation by bishops—with theologians as mere advisers—and thus the impression given of a quasi-synodal event, came from the Orthodox side. Secondly, theirs too was the proposal to investigate first the common ground. The Catholics had assumed the Orthodox would only be willing to discuss points that were historically disputed. Thirdly, the original venue chosen had been Patmos, both because the monastery of St John came under the direct jurisdiction of the ecumenical patriarch, and also because the pope (by now John Paul II) liked the idea of renewal by reference to the eschatological future, symbolized in St John the Divine's apocalypse-vision on that island. This last perspective was unexpected. Fourthly, the exchange over Uniatism, already mentioned, was, so Bouyer stressed, distinctly courteous in tone. Fifthly, it was the Orthodox who had decided that representatives would only come from traditionally Orthodox countries:

> on the grounds that the people in the diaspora either were represented by the delegates chosen in their mother country, or could not be

considered fully representative of Orthodoxy by the very fact that they were living apart from the sources of the Orthodox Church.[69]

This had the unfortunate effect of excluding some well-known theological names, not least names familiar to readers of the Fellowship journal. Bouyer set out the dialogue's programme.

> We came to the decision... to start our study with the local Church, and especially with the way in which the local Church finds both its expression and its realization in the Eucharistic celebration. We thought that by a common study of the two traditions of East and West of the way in which the local Churches live in and by the Eucharist we could be brought to the question of the unity of the local Church with the universal Church, then to the problem of communion between the bishops, and subsequently to the role of pope and patriarchs. We thought that by a discussion of the Eucharistic liturgy itself we would be brought to the problem of the procession of the Holy Spirit in relation to the Son, and that this problem would be illuminated by a study of the Christological aspect of the institution, and of the memorial of the institution, together with the pneumatological aspect of the epiclesis.[70]

Looking ahead, Bouyer hoped that some way would eventually be found to let autocephalous Churches co-exist with a papacy—for even Photius had insisted on the special role of Rome. Owing to the Iron Curtain, Churches in Eastern Europe saw the 'importance there could be in a unity that is perfectly independent of the State'.[71] Another positive factor was the sympathetic way Paul VI and John Paul II had dealt with Oriental hierarchs. Over-optimistically, Bouyer believed that most Orthodox clergy and laity wanted to see unity restored—a view he had taken from an unnamed Russian bishop. He admitted the Greek Church was a hard nut to crack, but if one takes the phrase to mean not just the Church of Greece, then the patriarchal sees still in the hands of Greeks outside Greece were not so rigorist as Church opinion in Greece itself. That was probably true for Antioch and Alexandria.

What, then, of the Anglican–Orthodox Dialogue, which, historically speaking, was, for the Fellowship, of greater concern? In 1979 its steering committee reported that, despite the difficulties created by the accelerating ordination of women, the Dialogue was still continuing, but now without the aim of immediate full communion. In 1980 the work resumed at Llandaff in Wales. Three distinct sub-committees were considering the

Church and the Churches (unity and diversity, and intercommunion), the Communion of Saints and the departed, and the Filioque. *Sobornost* heard that, on the issue of intercommunion, there was, unsurprisingly, little agreement, while discussion of the Filioque concept did not get far, though the Orthodox were pleased to learn of the deletion of the Filioque clause in various Anglican provinces. By contrast, on the topic of the saints and prayer for the dead a high degree of consensus prevailed. The editor, now Sergei Hackel, believed what had made it possible was the taking into account of Anglican and Orthodox liturgy and spirituality—a 'mode which the Fellowship of St Alban and St Sergius adopted from its earliest days ..., a mode to which this journal gives expression and support'.[72] Kallistos ventured the expression a 'Second Spring' for the Dialogue—but, prudently, he also added a question-mark.[73]

The principal spokesman for the Anglicans at Llandaff, Edward Roche Hardy of Jesus College Cambridge, had died just prior to the printing of his contribution. As graciously expressed as it was learned, it made a good case for the view that Anglicanism, even without later nineteenth-century Anglo-Catholicism, has been open to a discreet acknowledgement of prayer for the departed and to the 'comprecation' of saints (i.e. asking God that the saints might pray for us, rather than asking the saints directly). His starting-point was late-mediaeval piety—not yet seen through the kinder prism which, for example, Eamon Duffy's *The Stripping of the Altars* would provide for it.[74] 'One can understand, if not approve in all detail, the reaction which led to a severe restriction of the formal commemoration of saints and the memorial of the departed in the Church of England.'[75] The Prayer Book of 1552 was more ruthless than that of 1549, but, contrary to an Evangelical reading, it did not rule out prayer for the dead altogether. The Burial Service ends with a prayer

> that we with this our brother and all other departed in the true faith of thy holy name may have our perfect consummation and bliss, both in body and soul, in thy eternal and everlasting glory.[76]

The prayer after the communion of the people, later called the Prayer of Oblation, ends by asking that 'all thy whole Church' may benefit from the Passion, and Hardy implies this is meant to include the dead.

Hardy drew on the writings of Lancelot Andrewes and John Cosin as background to the 1637 Scottish Prayer Book and the revised Book of Common Prayer of 1662. In the latter's order for the Visitation of the Sick there is a commendation at the point of death which asks that 'whatsoever defilements [the soul] may have contracted in the midst of this miserable and naughty world ... being purged and done away, it may be presented pure and without spot before thee'.[77] Cosin, so Hardy recalled, had commented on Monica's death-bed wish for remembrance at the altar in Augustine's *Confessions* that it was not done

> to fetch her soul so much the sooner out of purgatory (for the papal purgatory fire was not then kindled, nor known), but ... that by the prayers of the Church made at the celebration of the Holy Eucharist, and by virtue of Christ's death and sacrifice therein commemorated, she might obtain a joyful resurrection of her body out of the grave and have her perfect consummation of glory both in body and soul, in God's everlasting kingdom.[78]

That is all very fine, but as Hardy points out

> There do not in fact seem to be any reference to memorial or requiem Eucharists in Anglicanism from the early days of Elizabeth I until the revival of the practice in the mid-nineteenth century, except for an interesting survival in the Obit Sunday service of the Order of the Garter which is still held quarterly, I believe, at Windsor.[79]

Queen Victoria played a part in his narrative since the use of the Orthodox *kontakion* of the departed at her funeral spread—and the Great War produced an almost irresistible desire, despite Evangelical opposition, to pray for the fallen, thus influencing Prayer Book revision in the 1920s. As is well known, the 'Deposited Book' failed to gain Parliamentary approval, but the awaited day came with the Alternative Service Book in 1980. Hardy provided a comparative study for other provinces.

As to the saints, the Edwardine Prayer Book's 'red letter days' were the biblical items from the Sarum liturgy's 'doubles', mostly apostles, while in 1561, after the accession of Elizabeth, Matthew Parker added the 'black letter days' which more or less corresponded to the 'greater simples' of Sarum. These belonged to various categories: ancient Roman commemorations such as Augustine had brought to Kent; French saints reflecting contact with the Gallican Church; English saints from Augustine of Canterbury to Richard of Chichester. After the Restoration, the 1662 Prayer Book added the names of Alban and Bede, but did not venture to give any of these 'black letter' saints actual liturgical texts (this was done, unofficially or otherwise, from the later nineteenth century onwards).

Comprecation was the practice of the Scottish Prayer Book of 1919 and the American Prayer Book of 1979, while the 1958 Lambeth Conference says that among traditional elements in Anglican worship is 'the honouring of the saints without invocation'.[80] Indeed, citing Pearson, Ken, and Keble:

> It is of the nature of Anglicanism to allow a wide variety of understanding and expression of the faith. Doubtless many Anglicans are not greatly interested in the matters we have been discussing while others would at least in their private devotions go further than what appears in their official books.[81]

A section of Hardy's paper considered whether the Church of England can commemorate its own 'worthies', using the precedent of the celebration of Charles the Martyr, included with other 'State Services' in the Prayer Book from 1662 to 1859.

An essay by Kallistos Ware on the same topic had points of comparison with Hardy's offering in that it made use of some Anglican material (Pearson, Pusey, William Temple). But its title—'"One Body in Christ". Death and the Communion of Saints'—enabled it to include the topic of preparation for death which was barely touched on by Hardy.

The Orthodox 'Service for One at the Point of Death' makes grim reading—or, rather, hearing. That, said Ware, using a favourite term of Florovsky's, is because 'To die well is a *podvig*, an ascetic feat, a specific Christian act in the face of strong temptations and assaults'.[82] Describing the Orthodox funeral rite, he touched on the rationale for the prohibition on cremation: 'abruptly and violently to destroy the body in a furnace'.[83]

What Latins call the 'particular judgment' and 'Purgatory' correspond to some extent to the Orthodox notion of the journey of the soul, accompanied by its guardian angel, through twenty-two *telonia* or toll houses, each concerned with a different sort of sin. A journey and a judgment ushering in a state seem very different notions, but they have something in common. In both conceptual schemes death is 'the moment of truth.'[84]

> As the soul comes to the toll house in question, it is examined rigorously concerning that particular sin: demonic customs officers inspect its spiritual luggage; scrolls are produced on which all our thoughts, words and actions are recorded; we are confronted with things that we have long forgotten or that we never noticed at the time.[85]

He added in a footnote 'For an imaginative description of this theme of self-discovery after death, see Charles Williams, *All Hallows' Eve*'.[86] The notion of these 'toll gates on the air-way' (to use an expression of George Every's[87]) has patristic roots in Origen, Athanasius and other Alexandrians, reaching full expression in the little-known tenth-century writer Gregory of Thrace. Kallistos insisted that 'while it is not a dogma of the Church, it is far more than mere legend or pious opinion'.[88] As to Purgatory proper: for the most part, Orthodox since the thirteenth century have rejected what 'they understand to be the Roman Catholic theology of purgatory' (note the careful wording). This is chiefly on account of three objectionable elements—Purgatory as place, suffering as by fire and especially material fire, and making 'satisfaction' for sins, notably doing so in an 'expiatory' way. Of these three disputed points the last is the most important. One might say the first is utterly unimportant: souls before the general resurrection cannot occupy space! The second can be polished off quickly. St Paul's reference in I Corinthians (3:13) to the 'fire' that shall 'try every man's work' can only mean, wrote Ware, the uncreated divine Energies, or, in less Palamite language, the divine fire of love. The real problem came with the third issue: *satispassio*, which is the better term in Latin dogmatics, since *satisfactio* denotes penitential satisfaction here and now. Orthodox writers do not accept the distinction between forgiveness of the eternal guilt of sin and the maintenance of a role for its temporal punishment on which the idea of expiation in Purgatory depends. Ware noted that not all Roman writers think of Purgatory in judicial or punitive terms (major exceptions included Newman and Catherine of Genoa), and here he could draw on the English Dominican Robert Ombres's *Theology of Purgatory*, which had just been published.[89]

Here Orthodox and Anglicans could agree. A distance opened up, however, when Kallistos began to describe the intensity and frequency of Orthodox prayer for the departed: during the *prosthesis* of the eucharistic Liturgy, after the Gospel, at the Great Entrance, and after the epiclesis; in the special memorial offices called by the Russians *panikhida*, especially on the anniversary of death; at the general commemorations on the penultimate Saturday before Lent and the Saturday before Pentecost. But—hence his title—Ware wants to understand all this 'not in juridical terms, but as the natural expression of that mutual love which binds together all the members of the one Body of Christ'.[90] Strictly speaking, the Orthodox only pray liturgically for other Orthodox but many clergy will exercise *oikonomia* about this. And as if to confirm the liberality of outreach, on the Sunday of Pentecost prayer is made at the 'Vespers of Kneeling' for those in hell—i.e. for a diminishment of suffering of the damned, though, he adds, many Orthodox consider the gates of hell are open, for release, until the final Judgment.

An Anglican report had recommended a prudent theological reserve on prayer for the dead, given the limits of our knowledge about the condition of the departed. Ware insisted this should not function as a reason for ceasing to pray for them.

> Equally we cannot tell how exactly how the saints become conscious of our prayers; but surely it is sufficient for us to reflect that they share 'the mind of Christ' (I Corinthians 2:16).[91]

Sobornost thought it helpful to append to these papers from the Anglican–Orthodox Dialogue the text of a lecture by Michael Ramsey on the Communion of Saints, which he opened by expressing gratitude to Derwas Chitty. From Chitty he had learned that the saints are not 'isolated meritorious mediators' but 'a family created by the birth of the God-Man through the Holy Spirit and the response of Blessed Mary'.[92] Ramsey went on to decode the Latin expression *communio sanctorum*.

> [T]wo uses, masculine and neuter, together tell of the Christians participating in sacramental gifts which are holy and in one another's lives which are holy. And when they so participate it is across the frontiers of earth and paradise and heaven.[93]

He explained the history of the appearance of this phrase in the Apostles Creed, seeing it as a late addition to the baptismal creed of the West. He had to admit it is unknown to the East. But no matter!

> For Orthodoxy the participation of the Christians in the holy gifts and their participation in fellowship with one another irrespective of death is just a ceaseless part of the Christian life and of the tradition which is the essence of Orthodoxy.[94]

Though, like Ware, Ramsey cites Andrewes and Pearson, his emphasis is placed not on the Anglican divines but on the Byzantine liturgy and the cult of the icons it presupposes.

> [T]he holiness of God is seen as invading the created world both in persons and in things. Both material things and persons may reflect the holiness of God in its graciousness and in its awe and

demand. The icons are venerated and they are both symbols of the saints and symbols of God's sacramental world. It is the deep intermingling of holy persons and holy things in God's creation which lies behind this.[95]

The passage was a testimony to how Orthodox the presiding primate of the Anglican Communion could be.

Of work on official dialogues there is no end. The Joint Commission had now to start thinking about what might go into an (at this stage entirely hypothetical) 'Dublin Agreed Statement' some years on. An interim communiqué, again from Chambésy, explained there were ongoing commissions on ecclesiology (emphasizing the role of the Eucharist and bishop); on sharing in the grace of the Trinity (where the Anglicans were proving eirenic on the Filioque while warning against dogmatic super-certitude), and on Tradition (on which both sides valued commitment yet also affirmed freedom). Meanwhile Edward Every gave a full account of the papers of the World Council of Churches' Faith and Order Commission on the Filioque, with a mixture of Orthodox, Roman Catholic, Old Catholic and Reformed theologians among its participants along with one Anglican—that was Allchin. The memorandum produced by the Commission agreed on the desirability of deleting the Filioque from the Creed, though the Catholic members were only willing to subscribe on condition that the Orthodox–Roman Catholic dialogue had resulted in agreement about Trinitarian doctrine first. Among the Reformed, the Scots Presbyterians shared their reluctance, agreeing with them that deletion implies prior doctrinal consensus—but then the Reformed make little liturgical use of ancient creeds. Casting aside caution, Every took the nineteenth-century German Liberal Protestant Albrecht Ritschl's view that the Creed 'is not a statement of metaphysical principles.'[96] He wanted the Anglicans to follow the Old Catholics without further ado, i.e. without getting agreement from other Westerners, particularly the Latins.

In 1982 Colin Davey reported on further preparatory Anglican–Orthodox interim discussion, this time at Canterbury. Now that the pressure for quick results was off, there could be, he thought, 'growth in depth'. But 'a reminder that we are still at the very first stage came when the Greek Orthodox Liturgy was celebrated at Margate in the presence of the archbishop of Canterbury and Anglican delegates, but without any *public prayer* for him or them, or for the Churches of the Anglican Communion.'[97] Kallistos's fuller account of the same proceedings mentioned that, surprisingly, John Romanides—rather an 'ultra' in Orthodox terms—insisted the Filioque could be understood in an Orthodox sense. Kallistos had participated as a newly consecrated bishop of the Constantinopolitan patriarchate, the first British-born person to have that honour.

In 1985 the long-awaited 'Dublin Agreed Statement' (itself dated 1984) made its appearance in published form.[98] Hugh Wybrew looked at its ecclesiology for *Sobornost*. While recognizing many excellent passages, he felt the statement reflected Orthodox convictions more fully than it did Anglican, notably in a tendency to compare Orthodoxy's strengths to Anglicanism's weaknesses, or ideal Orthodoxy to *de facto* Anglicanism. Furthermore, it was too easy for both parties to agree in criticizing the Roman primacy and its manner of exercise while at the same time not admitting any need for a universal ministry in the service of unity for their own divisions. He drew attention to Orthodox statements about the canonical limits of the Church. Did these coincide with *ecclesiological* limits in the full sense of that adjective? Dimitrios I did not seem to think so when addressing John Paul II.[99]

The widowed Militza Zernov, now 86 but indomitable, took up Wybrew's theme in 'Unity and Disunity today'.[100] New obstacles to Anglican–Orthodox unity were looming—here she was not original for she instanced women's ordination and the necessity of faith in the bodily Resurrection, a covert reference to the crisis over David Jenkins's appointment to Durham. The Orthodox were experiencing divisions of another kind. She dilated on the Slavonic adjective for 'one' Holy Catholic Church in the Creed. In confessing the mystery of the Church, the Orthodox should retain the sense of 'whole' contained in the word 'one' but abandon that of 'unique': they had now so much positive experience of non-Orthodox Christian bodies, not least through the Fellowship, of course. Sounding ever more like her husband, she wanted the insertion into the Liturgy of a prayer before Communion specifically for repentance for the sin of division. She offered a shortened form of one Bulgakov had composed for the Fellowship's use.

Militza Zernov was right to say that internal Orthodox divisions were themselves an obstacle to Christian unity. In the autumn of 1986 a third Pan-Orthodox 'pre-Conciliar' conference at Chambésy considered rules for fasting, relations with the non-Orthodox, ecumenism and social questions, leaving for a successor gathering four other topics: autocephaly and autonomy, the diptychs, and the Diaspora.[101] By the time the period covered by the present book ends, 2018, and despite the best efforts of the Ecumenical Patriarchate, a genuinely pan-Orthodox council had still not been held, for none could without Moscow.

In 1988 there was a Lambeth Conference and Bishop John Zizioulas of the Holy Synod had addressed it on the future of ecumenism, and *Sobornost* carried his speech. He outlined the difference between the mentalities of Christian West and Christian East in 'theology and church life'. They amounted, he said, to a 'different ethos'.[102] From the time of Tertullian on, the Latin West has been typified by 'a strong interest in history, a pre-occupation with ethics and a deep respect for the institution, sometimes to the point of being legalistic about it'. Augustinianism had added a 'dimension that was bound to create a dichotomy in Western Christianity ever since, namely the importance of introspectiveness, of consciousness and the inner man, from which sprang the important mystical, romantic and pietistic movements of the Christian West'. By contrast, the East had an 'eschatological meta-historical outlook that tends to relativize history and its problems'. This could have deleterious effects, not least in diminishing missionary effort. But it has also turned out positive. 'Authority in the Church was always placed in the context of worship, particularly the Eucharist, and was thus conditioned by the eschatological outlook in two main respects: through pneumatology, which makes of the institution an event, and through communion, which makes the authority of the institution constantly dependent on the community to which it belongs'.[103] There was a good deal of Zizioulas's personal theology in these last remarks, but he gave his hearers something to think about when he added that, as a consequence, clericalism, the Pentecostal movement, and argument about women's ordination have been absent from the Orthodox Church. It might look, then, as though West and East have little to say to each other but in an increasingly interdependent world we cannot be content with that. Though not all the Fellowship's Anglican (and Catholic) members would necessarily have recognized themselves in Zizioulas's characterization of the Christianity of the West, this at least was music to Fellowship ears.

Zizioulas went on to make two main recommendations to Anglicans based on recent Orthodox practice or thinking. The first concerned the need for synodality (or autocephaly) to be balanced by primacy, not only regional but even universal—though the word 'pope' was not breathed aloud. Evidently the modern Anglican notion of 'provincial autonomy' was at issue in this. The second point concerned women in the Church, and here he counselled delay, since at the ecumenical level the necessary theological reflection had hardly begun. He ended by commending an eschatological outlook of the sort that his own theology reflects, where the Alpha is not considered except through the lens of the Omega.

The 1990s

As the 1980s closed, the joint commission for dialogue between the Orthodox and the Oriental Orthodox had been meeting at Wadi-el Natrun in Egypt. It had come up, so *Sobornost* reported as a new decade opened, with an excellent Christological statement, which tweaked a famous formula from St Cyril of Alexandria. The Saviour is 'one incarnate *physis* (*hypostasis*) of the Logos'. The commission explained that the term *hypostasis* 'can be used to denote both the person as distinct from nature [*physis*], and also the person with the nature, for a *hypostasis* never in fact exists without a nature'.[104] Distancing themselves from both Nestorianism and Eutychianism, its members went on:

> Those among us who speak of two natures in Christ do not thereby deny their inseparable, indivisible union; those among us who speak of one united divine-human nature in Christ do not thereby deny the continuing dynamic presence in Christ of the divine and the human, without change, without confusion.[105]

This dialogue was contextualized in a wider setting of dialogue meetings by William Taylor, Anglican chaplain in Amman. That was in a subsequent comment which looked ahead to the Anglican–Oriental Orthodox Forum due to take place in the same Amba Bishoi monastery in March 1990. A quarter century later, for the wheels of ecumenical agreement may be slow to grind, the Anglican–Oriental Orthodox Theological Commission had produced an agreed statement on Christology, but it proved to be a remarkably Monothelite-sounding text. *Sobornost*'s editor would comment acerbically, 'the danger with ecumenical agreements between parts of divided Christendom ... [is] of reaching a statement of union that is ... union against some other part of divided Christendom'.[106] Father Gregor Sneddon, a Canadian Anglican, sought to clarify the issues involved against the background of the dyothelitism of St Maximus. 'The Anglican Church roots itself in the Chalcedonian tradition and the first four ecumenical Councils. Yet, for historical reasons, it is less clear on the authority of subsequent councils. This is a significant challenge for the Anglican Church's theological self-understanding and ecumenical efforts. The Sixth Ecumenical Council has not been a fundamental element of the Anglican Church's Christology and the resulting incomplete Christological expression has significant consequences. Clause 8 of the shared statement, "He who wills and acts is always the one hypostasis of the Logos incarnate with one personal will", falls outside dyothelite Christology as articulated by St Maximus and the Sixth Ecumenical Council. Is it time for the Anglican Church to affirm its Christological position and to establish further dialogue to explore how this shared statement with its Oriental Orthodox sisters and brothers can be realized, without compromise, in order to maintain a truly Chalcedonian Christology?'[107] Sneddon clearly thought it was.

Meanwhile, Hugh Wybrew felt that the Anglican dialogue with the Byzantine Orthodox—always the Fellowship's chief focus—had entered by the early 1990s a newly hopeful stage after the dip into the Slough of Despond in the mid-1980s.[108] The dialogue was fortified by Metropolitan John Zizioulas's robust sense of what made for a constructive programme. At New Valamo in Finland it was resolved to begin again, this time from the Holy Trinity as Source of the Church, and then to look at the Church in relation to Christ, all of this before considering such disputed topics as the ordination of women. The process was to be initiated in a further gathering at Toronto, and the delicate topics of feminine language for the Trinity as well as the inevitable Filioque were to be included in the first round. It was a variant on the procedure adopted from the start in the dialogue between Orthodox and Catholics, which also bore Zizioulas's hall-mark.[109] As little as two years later Wybrew was by no means so sanguine, as his synoptic essay on 'Anglican–Orthodox Dialogue: Its Past, its Present and its Future', already cited in my chapter 'The Continuing Story', made plain. In the face of the disaffection with various aspects of historic Christianity in the West it was dialogue with the Oriental Orthodox which enthused the Orthodox now, if any dialogue did.

In contrast, the Orthodox–Catholic dialogue was not going too well, and *Sobornost* knew why. The resurgence of a suppressed Uniatism in Ukraine and Transylvania and consequent quarrels over buildings had caused trouble. Via Wybrew, the journal covered a colloquium at Chevetogne which took a broad view of 'Uniatisms' of various kinds:

relations between the Russian Church and those Old Believers who had been brought into communion in the late tsarist period; the varieties of 'Thomas Christians' in India; Western-rite Orthodoxy, and the existence of some sort of Uniatism in the mediaeval Byzantine Church, though what was meant by the latter was not spelt out.[110] The papers must have confined themselves to factual reportage, since Wybrew noted the plan for a follow-up to explore the ecclesiology concerned. Meanwhile a draft document on Uniatism of a sub-committeee of the Orthodox–Roman Catholic International Commission was published (it would eventually become the 'Balamand Statement', named for the Lebanese monastery where its final form was settled) and commented on, largely favourably, by Archimandrite Serge Kelleher, an Irish-born priest of the Greek Catholic Church in Ukraine, who, however, considered both its account of history and its language open to improvement at points.[111]

The English Jesuit ecumenist Edward Yarnold, reviewing a collection of official texts and unofficial essays respectively from or on the Orthodox–Roman Catholic dialogue, found it a trickier enterprise than Anglican–Roman Catholic dialogue since disaffection, mutual or unilateral, had twice as many centuries to develop and the autocephalous Orthodox Churches, unlike Anglican provinces, had no equivalent to the Lambeth Conferences to bring them together on a public platform. He found considerable overlap between the two sets of negotiations even though the dialogue with the Orthodox had chosen to begin from shared fundamentals rather than—as had been the case with the Anglican–Orthodox Dialogue before Zizioulas—historic disagreements.[112]

Father Boris Bobrinskoy might be called the remaining major name left by the combined attrition of emigration and death at the Institut Saint-Serge. A heartfelt and much noticed address on Catholic–Orthodox relations delivered in Paris in 1991 was given to *Sobornost* readers in English translation in 1993. Looking back, the start of the decade had been difficult owing to developments in Eastern Europe, but he did not propose to embark on discussion of the Uniate issue, 'not least because one needs to have a great deal of information in order to get to the bottom of things in this painful situation.'[113] Much of what he said in his address was commonplace in the history of the subject, and his analysis of the dogmatic differences was not especially original, centering as it did on the pope and the Filioque. Although he spoke of the Filioque as 'insufficient' and a 'reduction' (not terming it, then, a heresy), he aligned himself with Vladimir Lossky's view that a defective Triadology had baleful consequences in the life of the Western Church. If the Spirit is simply the agent of the Son 'we are deprived of a direct relationship with the Spirit, which should be that of the Church'.[114] One consequence is that no individual hierarch can be the 'repository of the truth by himself'.[115] This was the ground of the Orthodox rejection of the 1870 'Vatican Decrees'. Yet 'should Rome return to conciliarity, Orthodoxy would rediscover the pope'.[116] Bobrinskoy mentioned the number of Catholics seeking to become Orthodox in France for 'many Catholics are disorientated by impoverished preaching and truncated worship'.[117] He recorded his reservations about the expansion of the Latin Church in Siberia, which, he believed, had triggered a counter-reaction of Orthodox intransigence or what he termed 'a tendency to fundamentalism' that would deny denied all sacramental grace outside Orthodoxy itself.[118] As if in deliberate contrast, an Orthodox priest in northern Russia figured next in this issue of the journal, commenting in sceptical terms about the revival of the concept of 'Holy Russia' in the Moscow Patriarchate. He thought it based on an over-narrow view of the sufficiency for the present day of mediaeval Russian spirituality and liable to link up with ultra-nationalism in the post-Soviet Russian Federation.

Like the Eastern Orthodox and the Anglicans, Roman Catholics were in dialogue with the Pre-Chalcedonian Churches. But in the mid-1990s something new emerged. Sebastian Brock had been attending a 1994 'Pro Oriente' consultation in Vienna on 'Orthodoxy and Catholicity in the Syriac Tradition'. Its novelty was the place given to the Antiochene Christological tradition in the shape of the Assyrian Church of the East. Hitherto dialogue with the Oriental Orthodox had meant Chalcedonians talking with those in the Alexandrian tradition, and the latter, at least in the case of the Copts, resisted any extension of reunion attempts to the Nestorians. In Vienna this changed. At last they had their say—represented by Mar Bawai Soro, their bishop in the Western United States. After the failure of Catholic–Nestorian or Chaldean–Assyrian negotiations he would later be received into the Roman Catholic Church as a bishop of the Chaldean rite. But that was years ahead. In his presentations in the Austrian capital, he made two important points. In the first place, the 'Vienna Christological formula' devised between the Oriental Orthodox and Roman Catholics (and it did not depart from the consensus of Oriental and Byzantine Orthodox) spoke of the 'faith' of Ephesus alongside that of

Nicaea and Constantinople. But Ephesus had been a 'council convened by the Roman emperor, and was not applicable to the Church of the East in the Sassanian empire', while in the absence of any Ephesian creed what might be meant by the phrase the 'faith' of Ephesus was ambiguous.[119] And in the second place, the theology of Mar Bawai's Church was not obviously Nestorian. Only one of Nestorius's writings, his *Second Apologia*, had ever been translated into Syriac, and that was around 540, almost a century after the split. Theodore of Mopsuestia had exercised far greater influence, while Nestorius was looked on more as a symbolic 'martyr' figure for the Antiochene Christological tradition than an actual authority on Christology.[120] In any case, the focus should be on how the Church of the East itself expresses the Incarnation, not the putative influence on it of ancient theologians from the Greek-speaking world. So could there be a new agreed formula, please? The consultation thought about it, and Brock believed they could have devised one, but they shelved the idea, worried it might be open to misunderstanding.

At the end of 1994 a common Christological declaration had been made by John Paul II and Mar Dinkha, catholicos-patriarch of the Assyrian Church of the East, expressive of a 'common faith in the mystery of the incarnation'.[121] In Christ, they said, 'has been preserved the differences of the natures of divinity and humanity, with all their properties, faculties and operations. But far from constituting "one and another", the divinity and humanity are united in the person of the same and unique Son of God and Lord Jesus Christ, who is the object of a single adoration'.[122] Yet since unanimity in all aspects of the faith has not yet been attained there cannot be a common eucharistic celebration. That there might be such consensus was the reason for instituting a mixed committee for theological dialogue on the same occasion.

Sebastian Brock reported on a second Viennese Pro Oriente consultation, which made progress on the Christological issue. In late 1994, the Assyrian Church had at last been accepted into the Middle East Council of Churches, and this, together with the joint Declaration with the Roman pope, had given it, Brock felt, a new assurance. It was located with the Catholic Churches rather than the Orthodox, Oriental Orthodox, or Protestant. This seems at first sight very odd, but as Brock notes, it 'makes good sense from the point of view of doctrinal history, Rome always having been the strongest defender of a more strictly dyophysite position in Christology'.[123] *Sobornost* printed the final communiqué, but Brock wanted to underline its three most salient aspects. First and foremost, the Vienna Christological formula (between Roman Catholics and the Oriental Orthodox) was acceptable to all participants as a starting point. Secondly, as proposed, amazingly, by an Assyrian, the 'theological contents [of the Council of Ephesus]' were deemed to be a possible basis for uniting the Churches of the Syriac tradition in 'the same faith in Jesus Christ'.[124] But as Brock pointed out, an element of ambiguity attached to this allusion, since there could be more than one interpretation of what the 'theological contents' of Ephesus (a council with no creed save Nicaea's) might be. Then thirdly, the communiqué wished to make 'an absolute distinction between the doctrinal position of the Assyrian Church of the East and the position, recognized by all to be heretical, which holds that there are two Sons, two *prosopa* in the one incarnate Christ, a position which is traditionally described by the Chalcedonians and the Oriental Orthodox as "Nestorian"'.[125] The Syriac *qnoma* should not be taken as equivalent to hypostasis (and thus to *prosopon*). *Qnoma* for the Assyrians (not necessarily for other Syrians!) means 'individuated but not personalized nature'.[126]

Sobornost readers could probably be expected to have more time for dialogues of these highly focused kinds than for the windier exchanges at World Council of Churches events or those of their imitators. The Anglican theologian Gerald Bray could always be relied on for a bracing douche of cold water on that topic. He was characteristically forthright in reviewing a study entitled *Together on the Way: A Theology of Ecumenism*,[127] just published by the British Council of Churches.

> For those not in the know, ecumenism is rapidly becoming a kind of super-theology, going beyond what any of the individual Churches teaches to embrace the whole diversity of the modern world. It is not syncretistic because it does not seek to combine different elements in an irrational hotch-potch. Rather is it transcendental. It rejects traditional theologies as 'divisive' and 'limiting', bound in many cases by historical prejudices which have no place in today's world. In place of these it posits the notion of 'unity' which has the status of a new gospel in itself.[128]

Bray suggested it might be salutary to take as goal not so much unity as truth. He admired, however, the persistence and ingenuity which had brought a very wide spectrum of Christian bodies, most of them spectacularly Protestant, to sign up to the Lima Declaration on 'Baptism,

Eucharist, Ministry', the sources of which were firmly located in the patristic world. The 'Faith and Order Commission must be congratulated in having got so far with an apparently hopeless task'.[129] But two other publications elicited a severer view of the World Council of Churches itself, as distinct from that more particular body of which Roman Catholics were also members.

> It has been clear to many for some time that the WCC is dominated by a radicalized elite, largely of Western European and American provenance, which promotes different leftist causes and is largely out of touch with grassroots feeling in its member Churches. The Orthodox in particular have been highly critical of this ... What is sad is that the orthodox elements within the Protestant Churches are seldom allowed to have their say in any WCC forum. This inevitably isolates the Orthodox in what appears to be an exotic conservatism, which the main body of the WCC can then proceed to ignore, at least in practice. This highly unsatisfactory situation needs to be addressed if the WCC is to retain any credibility as an ecumenical institution.[130]

A World Council publication on 'Justice, Peace and the Integrity of Creation',[131] which had become the World Council's mantra, and reviewed in the same issue, drew from Elizabeth Theokritoff the comment, 'It would not be fair to dismiss this book as a piece of political theology, but it would be an easy mistake to make'.[132]

A colloquium on problems of mission had taken place at Chevetogne (presumably this corresponded, more or less, to the pre-announced colloquium on issues of ecclesiology raised by Uniatism).[133] The abbot of Chevetogne, Michel van Parys, commended the 1993 Balamand Statement and noted favourable reactions to it in Ukraine, unfavourable in Romania and Slovakia. A priest representative of the Department of Foreign Relations of the Patriarchate of Moscow deplored the lack of information-sharing with the Orthodox by the Roman Catholic Church: new bishops for the Latin rite in Russia were announced, it was claimed, without the Vatican informing Metropolitan Kirill of Smolensk, whom the pope had met the day before. A priest of the Ukrainian Catholic Church reported on the 'informal Kievan church study group, which brings together bishops and theologians of the ecumenical patriarchate and of the Ukrainian Greek-Catholic Church of Kiev.'[134] Colin Davey had been there in person: 'In reply to a question of mine, Fr Andrei [Onuferko, the speaker in question] added that the Greek-Catholics in communion with Rome would prefer a greater autonomy than they now possess. Their present stance is closer to Orthodox ecclesiology than Orthodox or Roman Catholics seem to appreciate.'[135] The speakers had been from far more varied Church backgrounds than simply the Orthodox and Byzantine-rite Catholics.

Colin Davey looked at the Balamand statement of 1993, and John Paul II's *Orientale lumen* and *Ut unum sint*, the last two both in 1995, and the addresses given during the visit of Bartholomew I to Rome that same year. He found two major developments being encouraged: 'the deepening of mutual respect and recognition of one another as sister Churches,' and 'joint exploration of universal primacy for a re-united Church.'[136]

Meanwhile the unity of the Orthodox themselves was severely tried. Bishop Kallistos found the Estonian crisis in relations between Moscow and Constantinople in the spring of 1996 exceptionally worrying. There should never be suspension of communion over jurisdictional issues. If the clash had been over Ukraine, it would hardly have been resolved in a few months. The 'heart of the matter' as Kallistos described it concerned the need for a functional primacy.

> It is easy to say that the Eucharist creates the unity of the Church. But does not Eucharistic ecclesiology prove in practice unworkable unless it is accompanied by a firm and viable doctrine of primacy? Of course I am not suggesting that we Orthodox should accept the ultramontane understanding of papal primacy, as endorsed in 1870 by the first Vatican Council. But even if we dislike Vatican I, do not we Orthodox need to articulate more clearly some form of primatial authority? And if we fail to agree on this, shall we not find ourselves facing in the future a whole series of crises similar to the recent Estonian conflict?[137]

Meanwhile the ecumenical patriarch had been to the pope and read the riot act over Uniatism, saying his speech should not, however, be published—yet it was so published in Greek in *Episkepis* for 31 July 1995 before appearing in English in *Sobornost*. Putting together the rather underwhelming impact of Balamand and the impression given in *Orientale lumen* that the Uniate communities are at parity with the ancient Orthodox Churches, Bartholomew felt obliged to draw his own conclusions. '[T]he Church of Rome has considered the irregular ecclesiastical situation of the existence of uniatism today—which has only been accepted "by economy" as a *temporary measure* in accordance with a *special dispensation*—somehow to have been given a total amnesty by you, as if uniatism has at last been given canonical status and a lawful ecclesiastical form within the context of our mutual relations. Yet this is something to which we assuredly will never *consent or agree*, despite our immovable stance for peace and our readiness for reconciliation at all times in the spirit of the Gospel.'[138]

If Catholics were disappointing the Orthodox they were also failing to attract the Evangelicals. Reviewing Peter Hocken on revival or 'renewal' movements of the 'Holiness' variety, Gerald Bray was incisive. The book focused on Evangelicals and Catholics, at the expense of mainstream Protestants and the East. Bray commented:

> In many respects, evangelical movements in the Protestant world are a reaction to the liberalism of these bodies, and there are many evangelicals who are wary of Rome because they feel that a similar liberalism may be creeping in there as well. The opening of the Roman Church to biblical studies, for example, has not reassured them, because so much of what passes for Catholic scholarship is little more than a rehash of Protestant liberalism, and often an outdated variety of it at that. Post-Vatican II Rome appears to many of them like a Protestant Church, facing an internal battle between liberals and conservative in which the latter are on the defensive and are likely to lose in the long run. This analysis may be wrong, but it needs to be addressed, since Rome is not what it used to be.[139]

Wybrew reviewed John Turner on the present state of the Church of England: he was a traditional Anglican with the kind of anxieties for the future Bray had pointed to, but Wybrew noted that many of the most vigorously growing kinds of Christianity at present sit loose to much in tradition.

Wybrew also reported on the Anglican–Orthodox dialogue in Bucharest in 1998. The Romanians, he said, had always been the friendliest of the Orthodox to Anglicans, along with the Ecumenical Throne. It was a comment elicited by the sad absence of so many, Jerusalem and Georgia because they had withdrawn from ecumenical activity more widely, but no reason was given for the non-appearance of the Russians, Bulgarians and Serbs. For the first time the convention of alternating Anglican and Orthodox worship was dropped.[140]

The Dialogues

The new millennium

In 2008, Colin Davey, seasoned Anglican ecumenist, looked at the 'Ravenna Statement' of the Orthodox–Roman Catholic Dialogue.[141] He described the diplomatic build-up which overcame the jam caused by the re-emergence of the Uniate Churches in Eastern Europe, and the clash between Moscow and Constantinople over the status of Estonian Orthodoxy which led to the withdrawal of the Russian delegation at Ravenna and the premature publication, on the website of the patriarchate's representation to the European institutions in Brussels, of the still embargoed agreed text. This lengthy but necessary preamble in place, Davey came at last to an analysis of the (2007) Ravenna Statement itself. He described how it saw the basic ecclesiological principles of authority, conciliarity, primacy operating at local, regional and universal levels. At the last of these, the neuralgic area for the text, authority may be exercised by a synod (which raises the question of how ecumenical councils are recognized as such), or it may be wielded by a 'protos' of the patriarchs. East and West do not agree on how the authority of any given council can be affirmed, nor are they of one mind as to how the role of such a *protos* should be understood. An agreed way of understanding the latter would doubtless solve the problem of the former. But none exists.

Hence the way the Statement ends, with two questions for the future. 'What is the specific function of the bishop of the "first see" in an ecclesiology of *koinonia* and in view of what we have said on conciliarity and authority in the present text? How should the teaching of the first and second Vatican councils on the universal primacy be understood and lived in the light of the ecclesial practice of the first millennium?'[142] How indeed! Davey sought to compare the Ravenna Statement with helpful comparable portions of documents from the Anglican–Roman Catholic International Commission ('ARCIC') but no blinding light was shed.

Could there be an answer? In 2015, Andrew Louth reviewed Adam DeVille's *The Orthodox and the Papacy*, the subtitle of which ran '*Ut unum sint* and the Prospects of East–West Unity'.[143] A Uniate, DeVille had surveyed twenty-four Orthodox theologians who had touched on the issue of the Roman primacy in the years 1960 to 2006. In *Ut unum sint* Pope John Paul II had appealed to separated Christians to say what kind of universal primacy they might envisage. That appeal had been received in silence by the Orthodox, Olivier Clément being an honourable exception. So DeVille tried digging in their archives.

Rather surprisingly, he found six points held frequently if not absolutely universally. Once set in sequence, the six sounded substantial enough. In Andrew Louth's summary, they were: 'acceptance of the historical fact of the Roman primacy; an appreciation by some of a contemporary necessity for some kind of primacy, presumably to be exercised in a united Church by the Roman pope; an acceptance of the historic appellate jurisdiction, conceded to Rome in the first millennium; furthermore, there is a feeling among Orthodox that the notion of universal jurisdiction is quite foreign to an Orthodox mentality; that an ecclesiology of communion, which has become accepted by most Orthodox in the twentieth century, demands that primacy be exercised in communion with the whole episcopal order; and finally that it is as bishop of Rome that the pope exercises primacy'.[144]

Noting the sudden abandonment of the title 'patriarch of the West' in the Vatican Directory (*Annuario pontificio*), and the rather inadequate explanation of this action given later by the Pontifical Council for Promoting Christian Unity, DeVille, nothing daunted, pressed on with his scenario for the future. Perhaps predictably, it turns on recognizing a distinction between the Roman bishop as pope and as patriarch—but also on subdividing his patriarchate. The distinction between pope and patriarch would make it clear that the Petrine office is for the rarest of occasional use, unlike the patriarchal role which belongs to ordinary Church governance. The subdivision of the patriarchate would not only make it more manageable in the various continents whither the Latin Church has travelled. It would also trim the economic resources of the papal office to more modest proportions better suited to a servant of the servants of God—and less intimidating to the Orthodox for that reason.

With this work by a Catholic author Louth coupled an Orthodox study, *The Invention of Peter: Apostolic Discourse and Papal Authority in Late Antiquity*.[145] This was from the hand of George E. Demacopoulos, a scholar specializing in the study of Gregory the Great. Invoking St Peter, claimed this author, was 'a form of discourse that was fashioned for immediate purposes', starting in the late third century, when other means of commending the authority of the see of Rome were faltering.[146] Louth rather agreed with him, though he did not buy Demacopoulos's claim that no evidence exists for Peter's Roman sojourn, much less that he died a martyr there. It was a *canard*, if a long-standing one (the famously antipapistical Claude Beaufort Moss, major player in the Fellowship's early years, had been convinced of it by a Cowley Father as young man). In Louth's opinion, the kind of forensic rigour Demacopoulos brought to the issue could just as well be used to 'prove' the marginality of the Eucharist to the early Church. But it all went to show that the overcoming of schism, for which DeVille thought he had the recipe, would be no easy affair.

Meanwhile, it could be noted that the journal was in no great hurry to assess the two documents produced by the official Anglican–Orthodox dialogue in the new century: the Cyprus Agreed Statement, 'The Church of the Triune God' of 2008 and the 'Buffalo Agreed Statement', 'In the Image and Likeness of God. A Hope-filled Anthropology', of 2016. A detached observer might be forgiven for thinking its attention was elsewhere.

→ 5 ←

Commending the Liturgy

The Orthodox had always impressed Anglican members of the Fellowship by the numinous character of their worship. In modern liturgical revision in the Western Churches the emphasis was increasingly placed on the community-building power of a liturgical life of worship that—if the thinking were sociological in a conventional manner—was 'horizontally' conceived. But the Orthodox continued to insist on the primacy of the 'vertical'—not that this convenient spatial shorthand is especially illuminating for the saving mystery.

Eastern...

Kallistos Ware had little desire to modernize Orthodox practice when he wrote in *Sobornost* on 'The Theology of Worship'. Writing in 1970, a year after the introduction of a simplified *Missale Romanum* in the Latin Church, he was no doubt aware of challenging the emerging liturgical outlook of contemporary Western Christians on more than one score.

His starting-point, from Bishop Theophan the Recluse, sounded innocent enough. 'The principal thing is to stand before God with the mind in the heart, and to go on standing before him unceasingly day and night, until the end of life', a maxim cited from an anthology of Orthodox teaching on prayer, reviewed a few years earlier in the journal.[1] But the 'standing' in question is not just that of a man talking boldly with God as with a friend. It is also the stance of someone drawing near to the Dweller in light unapproachable. This duality, taken from Symeon the New Theologian, enabled Ware to make the point that, although God has opened himself to man in intimacy, nevertheless God remains the *mysterium tremendum et fascinosum*. He is near yet other. Putting that in terms of divine attitudes to man, God is good yet severe, merciful yet just. Not just hope and confidence but fear and awe as well are needed, then, in man's answering worshipful response. 'As we worship, we are both slaves before the throne of the King of heaven, and children who are happy to be in their Father's house.'[2] The latter part of this statement was verified in 'progressive' liturgical circles, but scarcely the first.

There was, though, more to come. Theophan had spoken of worship with the 'mind in the heart'. Ware comments on both 'mind' and 'heart' in this formulation. As to *mind*, worship 'involves our understanding and our intellectual powers',[3] and this is where words come into play.

> If our words possess no literal meaning—or if we recite them in such a way as to render the meaning unintelligible—then our worship will degenerate into magic and mumbo-jumbo, and will no longer be worthy of logical sheep [an expression Ware had found in Clement of Alexandria].[4]

But mind is to be in the *heart*. The intellectual is to be 'integrated with all the other layers of our personality', which Ware takes to include 'subconscious instincts', 'emotions', 'feelings', 'aesthetic sense', and 'that faculty of intuitive understanding and of direct spiritual awareness which far surpasses the discursive reason'.[5] Consequently, more than the literal meaning, or the immediate impact, of liturgical words will be involved. Associations and undertones will be important, as in poetry, and, beyond words, other media will necessarily be employed. The Liturgy also takes its effect

> through music, through the splendour of the priestly vestments, through the colour and lines of the holy icons, through the articulation of sacred space in the design of the church building, through symbolic gestures such as the sign of the cross, the offering of incense, or the lighting of a candle, and through the employment of all the great 'archetypes', of all the basic constituents of human life, such as water, wine and bread, fire and oil.[6]

Here modern liturgists, already suspected of verbal minimalism, received a second smack over the knuckles. These further dimensions constitute a

> point which many liturgical reformers at the present time need to keep in view. Worship is more than a form of proclamation through the spoken word, and the liturgical assembly is more than a public meeting with speeches and announcements.[7]

For his part, Ware felt that the Byzantine liturgy, despite influence by the 'social and artistic conventions of particular eras', nevertheless 'in its essence transcends these limitations and speaks to the fundamental condition of man, whether ancient or modern, eastern or western.[8] Joy and beauty are among its inalienable features. One thing Ware did approve of in the contemporary Western Church was its attraction to the art of the icon—in which such joy and beauty are often palpable. Citing Alexander Schmemann, Ware wrote, 'In the Eucharist we are standing in the presence of Christ, and like Moses before God, we are to be covered with his glory'.[9]

There remained to be discussed, albeit more briefly, Theophan's reference to prayer 'at all times': in other words, the spilling over of prayer into the rest of the twenty-four hours. Here Schmemann could be cited again, as could the English Metaphysical poets George Herbert and Thomas Traherne.

Thirty years later, a period of time in which the banality of much modern Western Catholic worship became only too well known, Bishop Kallistos remained firm. Two years on from the bi-millennium he was speaking to an Orthodox congress in Belgium on the Liturgy as 'heaven on earth'. He stressed the mysteric character of the Eucharist, which 'should be honoured with apophatic reticence',[10] though the liturgical character of its celebration entails not only mystery but participation. He emphasized its corporate nature, for the use of 'I' is generally reserved to the priest's 'private' prayers or, in the Slavonic use, texts that originally belonged to private preparation for Communion by the faithful, an exception being in the Creed where Kallistos suggested the Orthodox might follow some Western liturgical revision and replace 'I' with 'we', as in the original Creed of Nicaea. He also drew attention to the repeated bows at the commencement of the Liturgy which imply mutual forgiveness, a condition of unimpaired participation. He speculated about ways in which the sense of active participation by the worshippers could be enhanced. But the issue which gave rise to his title was the suggestion that the Liturgy is simultaneously being celebrated in heaven where Christ ontologically offers himself in silence eternally and everywhere, while clergy and people offer bread and wine verbally through words and gestures as an event in time at particular places on earth. In the anaphora—he would say specifically at the epiclesis—these two levels are united. Hence: 'heaven on earth'. The liturgical role of the icons is to draw attention to this union. The words 'It is time for the Lord to act' tell us that the true celebrant is Christ the invisible priest. The role of the Son reminds Kallistos to speak also about the role of the Spirit who does not only 'concelebrate', culminatingly at the epiclesis, but can be regarded (here the ceremony of pouring hot water into the chalice is crucial) as really present with the Son in the elements. In the 1440s Mark of Ephesus was asked to comment on priests who added the words 'receive the Holy Spirit' to the formula 'The servant of God receives the most precious and holy Body and Blood of the Lord', and replied it was liturgically unlawful but doctrinally correct. (But the reason given—that Son and Spirit are inseparable—could surely also be regarded as a reason for saying the Father is present also!) And indeed Kallistos maintains that the Father is co-involved in the Divine Liturgy, but does not say he is eucharistically present, rather that it is 'from him that all proceeds and to him that all returns'.[11] Finally, he comments on the social implications, the 'liturgy after the Liturgy' of service to the needy (compare John Chrysostom on the two altars: the altar of the sanctuary, the altar of the poor).

But Father Kallistos did not only theologize about worship—and, of course, celebrate it. He also translated its textual resources. George Every, no mean poet, as no less a critic than T. S. Eliot had recognized, was appreciative of the combined translating efforts of Ware and Mother Mary (of the Russian exarchate's French monastery at Bussy-en-Othe) in the *Festal Menaion*, a liturgical book which deals with nine of the twelve Great Feasts of the Byzantine rite.[12] Their translation style took its departure-point from the Authorized Version of the Bible, whilst not treating the latter as absolutely definitive. Speaking as a modern Anglican—but the Roman Catholic he later became could have said the same, Every commented, 'If our liturgy had the kind of combination of exuberance and precision characteristic of the Orthodox tradition our prayer would flow out of it and be consummated by it'.[13]

A few years later Hugh Wybrew commended the *Lenten Triodion*, companion to the earlier *Festal Menaion*, from the same translators.[14] His review made it plain that the book contained less than the entirety of the Byzantine rite services for Lent and Holy Week. Yet the translators were expecting a use for these books in English-speaking Orthodox parishes. So presumably they had truncated the texts at the points where they thought celebrants would do likewise. (Omitted passages were available on application to the Monastery of the Veil of the Mother of God.)

Not all commentators relished the Neo-Jacobean style. Nigel Gotteri, lecturer in linguistics at Sheffield, considered in the pages of *Sobornost* how the Orthodox ought to approach translation into the vernacular for the purposes of the liturgy. Though many English Orthodox like 'ecclesiastical English spiced with Hellenisms, slavonicisms and other barbarisms', they are neglecting the fact that as an exotic community, not tarred with any particular social image, they are freer to make an impact on the country generally—if they can find the evangelistic language in which to do it.

> Our advantage as Orthodox is that we are not so much revising our English as translating into modern English a variety of Christian expression which has evolved without reference to English conceptual frameworks. As a result we should be able to avoid outworn clichés more easily than most; we may use well-established words if we are sure that they have retained their full content, but we are not tied to them by our own traditions or by feelings of nostalgia.[15]

Gotteri argued that, in Orthodoxy, the combination of building, music, ceremonial, icons and incense creates sufficient atmosphere for language not to need adding to the mix. He opposed 'traditional church English and parsonic diction', and in particular any aping of the Book of Common Prayer.[16] Priority should be given to what the 25–30 age group found aurally clear; to the uninitiated not the initiated hearer; to non-ambiguity, in the sense of not relying on capitalization, punctuation or spelling, in establishing meaning; and to clarity when a text was read 'without an intonation pattern' if otherwise it was meant to be sung.[17] He did not entirely discount the aesthetic, but thought that, quite apart from clarity which is already a form of beauty, it could be adequately respected by the rhythmic character of the prose used.

In a second article Gotteri returned to the issue of translating of Orthodox liturgical texts, chiding critics and issuing a plea to the 'consumer' to be aware that 'the translator is carrying out difficult work on texts which he takes as seriously as you do: refrain from criticism until and unless you know the original at least as well as he', and that 'texts central to tradition serve and even demand a variety of translations'.[18] This at least was likely to please everyone.

Or so one might have thought. David Balfour produced an enormously detailed critique of a translation of the Liturgies of St John Chrysostom and St Basil and the Liturgy of the Presanctified, together with personal prayers for Communion, which had just been produced by Oxford University Press.[19] Dubbed modestly 'a few reservations',[20] this remorseless text was based on his own undoubted competence in Church Slavonic and Greek. He admitted the work under review was elegant, majestic even, often ingenious and original in word-choice, well edited and printed. But he regretted that the translator, a Russianist, lacked sufficient knowledge of the two most pertinent languages (apart, of course, from English). Balfour's denigration of Rosemary Edmonds's errors—these might more kindly be called choices—in her liturgical translations was then queried by a nun of Tolleshunt Knights. In 1985 Balfour wrote against the offending nun who had dared to challenge him on philological points.

Liturgical matters are notoriously likely to flame up from embers into fire. Hugh Wybrew reviewed a major piece of research into liturgical history. An Hispanic Jesuit, Juan Mateos, had written a comprehensive history, in French, of 'The Celebration of the Word in the Byzantine Liturgy'. Now his pupil and fellow Jesuit, the American Robert Taft, soon to overtake his master in fame, had written a history of the next part of the Orthodox rite.[21] *The Great Entrance* explained how the processional entry with the dedicated but not yet consecrated Gifts is likely to have emerged from the Oriental custom whereby the people handed their offerings of bread and wine to deacons on entering church, rather than, as in the West, bringing them to the chancel rail after the Liturgy of the Word. The humble practical need to transfer the gifts to the altar over some distance (before the tenth century the Constantinopolitan sacristy was a separate building) produced in time this solemn entry, compared by Byzantine and later commentators with Christ's own going to his Passion. Taft's study of the further ceremonial elements, between the procession and the anaphora, suggested some liturgical confusion had entered in, and he made proposals for a modest reform. Wybrew did not think the Orthodox would appreciate them. 'Fr Taft writes as a western Christian, influenced by the modern western view that the structure and content of the rite should express clearly the basic meaning of the Eucharist.'[22] That 'view' might seem to state a desideratum that was surely unchallengeable—but it was rudely challenged a generation later by a young co-religionist of Wybrew's when Catherine Pickstock of Emmanuel College, Cambridge, produced her defence of traditional unclarity—at least of a 'linear' kind—in *After Writing. On the Liturgical Consummation of Philosophy*.[23]

...and Western

An antidote to a unilateral Byzantinism in matters liturgical was furnished by Edward Roche Hardy who wrote on 'The Transfiguration in Western Liturgical Usage'. This American Episcopal priest, whose compendious essay on the commemoration of saints and the departed in Anglican liturgical books made an appearance in my last chapter, began encouragingly: 'The mystery of the Transfiguration has received more attention in Western liturgical usage than is often realized'.[24] The absence in the West, for many centuries, of a separate feast of the Transfiguration does not amount to the omission of its liturgical celebration. In the Old Roman liturgical cycle, 'the mysteries of redemption were celebrated at appropriate points in the calendar *de tempore* rather than by feasts attached to dates in the civil year, like those of the saints'.[25] Thus the Annunciation and Visitation were celebrated on the Wednesday and Friday of Advent Ember Week to prepare for the Nativity, the Transfiguration on the Saturday of Lent Ember Week to prepare for the Passion of the Lord. Hardy waxed lyrical over Leo the Great's sermon for this Lenten Vigil, which assembles as in a mosaic all the relevant themes, linking the patristic pope's Christmas preaching to his teaching on the Passion and Resurrection. In Hardy's summary of the Leonine masterpiece:

> The voice from the cloud asserts the unity of the Father and the Son, and calls on us all to follow him whom the Law and Prophets proclaimed, who saves us by his blood, and who opens the way to heaven *per crucis supplicium*, by the suffering of the Cross... Peter's desire to remain on the Mount was not improper but out of order; this is the time of endurance rather than of glory.[26]

The text was read in later Roman usage on the following Sunday as well. The modern Roman Lectionary retains this latter practice for the Second Lenten Sunday, the Ember Vigil having disappeared in the reform of 1969.

As a feast of summer time the Transfiguration is a Western import, but an early one, appearing in the eighth-century Calendar of St Willibrord, and a slightly later Irish martyrology, where it was celebrated on 26 or 27 July. In at least one diocese in ninth-century Spain it was ranked with Christmas and Easter, possibly under Mozarabic influence. Soon the date settled on was 6 August, possibly via the Greek monasteries in southern Italy. The Crusades gave it greater prominence, for the Latin kingdom of Jerusalem made Mount Tabor, the traditional site of the original event, more accessible to Western pilgrims. Abbot Peter the Venerable expanded its texts, sometimes by very economical means such as modifying the Christmas Preface to read 'the mystery of the transfigured [replacing 'incarnate'] Word'. In fact the Transfiguration was treated as a kind of

Christmas of summertime just as the Assumption was an Easter of summertime. It remained however largely a 'monastic specialty' until with renewed contact with the East and fresh emphasis on the humanity of Christ the papacy started to sponsor it in the mid-fifteenth century. Hardy goes so far as to call Calixtus III's promulgation of the feast for the entire Latin Church a consequence of 'ecumenical relations' in the age of Ferrara-Florence.[27] In the English Reformation the feast disappeared so far as a proper celebration was concerned though the date was recorded in Matthew Parker's calendar of 1561. It returned in the Catholic revival in the Church of England, when liturgical books drawing on Sarum or Roman usage replaced, or supplemented, the official texts.

This was a good choice for an article in *Sobornost* on the Western Liturgy. It could presume an attraction by Eastern-oriented readers to the Transfiguration mystery.

In the summer of 1978 two Anglican priests deeply engaged with the Fellowship, Michael Paternoster, former general secretary, and Hugh Wybrew, then editor of *Sobornost*, had an instructive exchange about the merits or otherwise of frequent eucharistic celebration (and encouragement to Communion) in a parish context.[28] Paternoster made the case for a pattern of worship where for most Sundays an 'Early' celebration of the Communion was followed up by Mattins as the principal morning service, with occasional Masses on weekdays. This corresponded better to the devotional instincts of most Anglicans—and also embodied the balance the makers of the Prayer Book had sought between the Divine Office and the Eucharist. Wybrew had some sympathy with Paternoster. He cited Michael Ramsey's misgivings when archbishop of York about the sudden wildfire spread of the parish Communion as the principal (or even exclusive) Sunday service: Ramsey had expressed anxieties that this kind of worship gave disproportionate expression to the human aspect of the celebration and lacked depth in terms of an reverent and even awe-filled approach to the sacrament. Wybrew countered that, while Paternoster's case might be persuasive in terms of the attitudes of individuals, from a corporate point of view the advent of the parish Communion as the Sunday staple was vastly preferable, especially if one bore in mind the entire story of Christian worship, West and East. Between the fourth and twentieth centuries people might have communicated rarely, but the texts of the liturgies made it apparent that the contrary was expected. If there is a worry that some attendees are pressured into making an act they are not yet ready for, it is Baptism (and Confirmation?) that should be celebrated more discerningly, not the Mass. Eucharistic celebration is not only privilege, it is also duty.

The article was instructive not least for students of the history of the Fellowship and its journal. It presumed a substantial Anglican readership, and an Orthodox readership that would think it worth their while to listen in on two Anglican priests discussing their parish timetable. It pointed back to the earlier epoch of the Fellowship's life, as chronicled in my Part One, 'The Encounter of East and West', rather than pointing on to a future period when *Sobornost* was more exclusively 'A Voice for Orthodoxy'. It was perhaps a sign of the times in the Fellowship that the distinguished Orthodox liturgist William Jardine Grisebrook, writing in 1990 on R. C. D. Jasper's *The Development of the Anglican Liturgy 1662–1980*,[29] felt he had to justify reviewing the book in the pages of *Sobornost* at all.[30]

Liturgical reform

Alexander Schmemann had died in 1983, but his *The Eucharist: Sacrament of the Kingdom* had been published posthumously in an English translation.[31] Jardine Grisebrook thought it too cautious on liturgical reform of the Byzantine rite. While acknowledging the 'disastrous' character of much liturgical reform in the West, he believed the renaissance of understanding of the liturgical heritage that Schmemann had called for was not only a precondition of good reform, but in any popular guise would have to entail some revision of the rites.[32] Schmemann had emphasized the integral character of the eucharistic Liturgy—it must be understood as a whole, and also the way it neither repeats nor represents but, rather, enables us to 'ascend' into the life and salvation won through the mysteries of Christ.[33]

Hugh Wybrew had written a guide to the Orthodox Liturgy which the Syriac scholar and former Catholic Ephrem Lash commended, feeling its author's discreetly positive attitude to liturgical reform and frequent Communion echoed Schmemann's. 'Fr Hugh is not uncritical of certain tendencies in Orthodox eucharistic practice, and much of what he says echoes the thoughts of the late Fr Alexander Schmemann, especially in his posthumous book on the Eucharist. Living things change and grow, sometimes they need pruning, sometimes they need training, and this is true of the Orthodox Liturgy also. More frequent Communion is now encouraged, and in at least one Athonite monastery the monks communicate four times a week, in others at least weekly, and in view of the well known Athonite distaste for ecumenism in all its manifestations, this is hardly to be attributed to Western influence. There is a greater emphasis on preaching, and increasingly in the traditional place after the gospel. In many churches there is more "active" participation by the people, the opposition to which often comes from the singers and the choirs with their vested interests in 'concerts' and other such manifestations. An eminent Russian theologian in Paris remarked to me many years ago that the ceremony surrounding the bishop at the Liturgy was in drastic need of simplification. But the well-known distaste of the Orthodox for over-systematization makes it unlikely that there will ever be the sort of formal liturgical reform that has characterized many of the Western Churches in recent years. This makes it all the more vital that the members of the Orthodox Church, clerical and lay alike, are well instructed and informed in both history and theology, and to this process Fr Hugh's book will make a notable contribution. It will also enable those Western Christians who attend Orthodox Liturgies to do so with greater understanding, and perhaps to attend their own churches' Eucharists with a better appreciation of what it is Christians do when they assemble to celebrate the Lord's Supper.'[34]

Gregory Woolfenden, by 2002 Orthodox and teaching at Cuddesdon, thought a study by a Chevetogne monk on non-spontaneous development of the Byzantine liturgy rather overstated its case.[35] It was, he felt, a typically Eastern Catholic as distinct from Eastern Orthodox 'take' on the possible wisdom of deliberate revision of rites from above. Historically, the Greek changes took place over a long period, while the Slavic were unhappy. The warning was given, with evident reference to the situation in the Roman rite, 'Returning to the norms of the holy Fathers often means turning to the firmly or sometimes less firmly based theories of particular scholars'.[36]

An essay by Father Dominic White of the English Province of the Order of Preachers on the history and anthropology of religious dance ended with a hint that people in the Church might consider taking up religious dance, and the implication is in the first place liturgical. 'Regarding the (re-) integration of dance into worship, the evidence of the tradition suggests that liturgy did not so much "include" dance, but *was* choreographic. Nevertheless, since all but the strictest liturgists would include the inclusion of appropriate, liturgically oriented hymns and organic music in the Western liturgy, even though they are technically extraneous to the liturgical texts, so appropriate choreographies might have a similar place.'[37] The Orthodox Church is hardly a Church given in modern time to liturgical reform—apart from the disastrous Renovationism in early Bolshevism, though one does hear of occasional radical steps in North America, such as celebrating the Liturgy of St John Chrysostom outside the iconostasis. Doubtless it was Roman Catholics and Anglicans Father Dominic had in mind.

That Orthodoxy is not entirely immune to liturgical 'itchy fingers' was demonstrated by Andrew Louth's presentation of a proposal for an alternative funeral rite in the Church of Greece, to pair the alternative marriage service he had described in an earlier issue.[38] (At this point the identity of the author of these would-be liturgies was still unknown.) The new liturgical rites offered anonymously to the Church of Greece in the years 2007–12 turned out to be by none other than the acclaimed theologian Christos Yannaras. Whereas officially discussed liturgical reform in Greece means modernizing the ancient or mediaeval language, here it meant accepting wholly original texts as an alternative to those found in the Byzantine Liturgy not only for the Eucharist but also for baptisms, weddings and funerals. And as Sotiris Mitralexis points out, as the production line went forward the audacity of the hidden author became more pronounced: above all, then, in the eucharistic Liturgy, the last to be written.[39]

It should be made clear that 'wholly original' does not mean without patristic allusions, for the texts are rich in them even though the Baptism rite also has clear traces of Yannaras's own 'prosopocentric theology' and the allied eucharistic ecclesiology of Zizioulas. But 'wholly original' *does* mean 'hitherto unknown in Orthodox worship'. The author found a semi-parallel in the late nineteenth-century adoption of the Liturgy of St James for an annual celebration in some parishes. Though the text was ancient its use was not, and it is carried out, apparently, outside the iconostasis facing the people. The texts suggested were beautiful—but they were also unprecedented. That a Church wedded to tradition could adopt them, even *ad experimentum*, or as alternative worship-forms to those in place, seemed most unlikely. The comparison that sprang to mind was 'pigs might fly'.

→ 6 ←

The Icon Again

In the first forty years of its existence, the Fellowship's journal had shown a sporadic but intense 'interest in art', to which I devoted a chapter of Part One, 'The Encounter of East and West'. This was one tradition which remained solid in the history of the journal, reaching something of a climax in its most recent issues.

Icons from Moscow to Canterbury

By the start of the 1970s the Rublev icon of the Holy Trinity had won for itself a sudden and extraordinary popularity in reproductions in the Christian West, to the point of becoming dangerously overexposed. This is where a good theologico-aesthetic exegesis of an image might help restore the eye. Rublev had been said to paint not with colours but with lights. The Trinity icon is not chromatically vivid, nor does it include striking contrasts. Why so? Militza Zernov, addressing herself to this question, cited an observer who saw it in 1930, when it was still in the Lavra of Sergei Posad. The unnamed viewer had remarked that the icon evokes the 'heat of the day of the Biblical narrative', when in air 'pulsating with heat the approaching angels were seen in silhouette on the midday sky'.[1]

Militza described the geometry of the composition. The most important element is the circle of angelic figures, a symbol of eternity. 'The three persons of the icon, holding equal sceptres of power, are in deep communion round the Eucharistic cup of Divine Love.'[2] She admitted that interpreters are divided as to how to assign which angel to what Trinitarian person, herself inclining to the view that the central figure is the Father—who will reveal himself in his 'two arms' (a variant on the Irenaean expression 'two hands'), the Son and the Spirit. She also presented the icon as the summit of Russian iconography:

> After the time of Rublev there was quite a flourishing of so-called 'theological speculative' icons in Russia, but they gradually lost the unity of artistic expression with the depth of theological intuition. They became rationalized and lost the beauty which permeates the icons of the fifteenth century.[3]

The best part of forty years later, *Sobornost* was still fascinated by this wonderful object and its history. Against the backdrop of the fate of the mediaeval icon in early modern and modern Russia, and the notable role of Old Believer connoisseurs of avant-garde French art in its rehabilitation, Charles Lock described the 1904 cleaning of an exceptional icon 'said to depict the Holy Trinity' and ascribed in an inventory of the Tretyakov collection to Rublev. Lock noted that no provenance was given, as would presumably be usual.[4] Given the Old Believer tendency to ascribe to Rublev any venerable icon he was surprised no one had taken up Gervase Mathew's challenge in *Byzantine Aesthetics*—Mathew thought it 'Constantinopolitan of about the year 1400'.[5] When he came to deal with the (putatively) Rublev icon in and for itself, Lock chose to depend quite substantially on a monograph by the Swiss Benedictine patristic scholar Gabriel Bunge, Englished by Andrew Louth as *The Rublev Trinity*.[6] But, as Lock points out, the value of Bunge's book is in one respect diminished by his apparent ignorance of the occlusion of the traditional icon in the period before the late nineteenth century (Bunge had not raised the question of attribution).

The 'Hospitality of Abraham' had been depicted in the fourth-century catacombs. But in an eleventh-century Greek psalter now in the Vatican (and Lock makes out a case for the influence on this of an Armenian gospel book, the 1088 Gospel of Vehap'ar, first exhibited at the 2001 British Library exhibition 'Treasures from the Ark'[7]), the figures of Sarah and Abraham are removed by a partition—thus leaving the divine Three in splendid isolation. Bunge stressed the transformation this sort of iconographical change entailed, for the imagery becomes exclusively theological and cosmological, not at all narrative or biographical. But in the Greek and Armenian examples important to Lock, a central, larger angel bears a cross in his nimbus, whereas Rublev reverted to the earlier scheme where the angels are of the same dimension and there is no cross to be seen. For Lock, this militates against the thesis, accepted by Militza, that the artist intended each angel for a specific divine person. For Bunge the perspective of the icon presumes that we the spectators are moving around the altar,

The Icon Again

and he combined this with the opinion that the central angel is the Son, the High Priest, the angel on the left is the Father, that on the right the Holy Spirit. To Lock's mind, identifying the figures in this way weakens *perichoresis*, the mutual identification going on in the dance. That insight gave Lock the title of his article, 'The space of hospitality: on an icon of the Trinity ascribed to Andrei Rublev', for 'only in such an exchanging of space, by such room being made, can strangers be entertained'.[8]

Readers wishing to know more of the 'logic' of such icons could turn to the article that had followed Militza's. This was by Joseph Frary, an American member of the Society of St John the Evangelist (the Cowley Fathers) on this very topic. After an excellent précis of the early Byzantine and modern Orthodox doctrine of the icon, Frary turned to his key term 'logic'. Three questions arise: 'How are human beings related to icons? How are icons related to the Kingdom? How are men related to the Kingdom through icons?'[9]

As to the first question, Frary replies: human beings are related to icons inasmuch as icons are cognitive, leading viewers to knowledge of the realities of the Kingdom, and this is possible because the 'conventional signs and techniques which go into the painting of icons . . . are the appropriate ways actually to link up this world and the Kingdom'.[10] As to the second question, he says: icons are related to the Kingdom by the way they are symbols; they are constituted both by the world and by the Kingdom, for these two constituent elements combine in the icons' case to make a symbol an entity in its own right. As to the third, he answers: men are related through icons to the Kingdom of God by way of the iconographer, who is the 'instrument for realizing icons by means of person, prayer, art, and obedience to the Holy Tradition'.[11] This was helpful.

Not all icons are necessarily Oriental. Christopher Pierce Kelley wrote on 'Canterbury's First Ikon', the image brought from Rome by Augustine in 597. In his *Ecclesiastical History of the English People* Bede describes it as a 'likeness painted on a board'.[12] Clearly, it was a panel icon, and Bede also makes it plain that its customary use was processional. The icon has long since vanished but Kelley thought the Christ-image in the *Sancta sanctorum*, well known to students of palaeo-Christian art, may be the closest thing we have to it now. Possibly Pope Gregory I acquired that image at Constantinople when he was *apokrisarios*, and gave it to the Lateran cathedral, where it was permanently housed. It may have been, Kelley suggested, a copy of the miraculous 'Kamouliana' image, one of the earliest of the images called *akheiropoieta* or 'not made by hands', for that image had been brought to the East Roman capital in 574 just before Gregory arrived. It was likely enough that on or after that occasion numerous copies were made. Since the original fell victim to early Iconoclasm, we cannot be sure of its appearance. Somewhat illogically, Kelley claimed that, since the Kamouliana belonged to the 'not made with hands' category', it must have resembled the Mandylion of Edessa, another *akheiropoieton*, though the causality of the image surely says nothing as such about its artistic form. Kelley also accepted Ian Wilson's controversial identification of the Mandylion with the Shroud of Turin.[13] In the sixth century, he speculated, unwillingness to show Christ naked brought it about that below the neck such a figure (a figure like the Man of Turin) would have been portrayed clothed and enthroned. That, he argued, fitted well Bede's description of the Canterbury icon. It was an image of 'our great King and Lord'.

The status of the 'Icon Council'

In Anglican theology, historically considered, the Fifth and Sixth Councils were largely ignored, while the Seventh Council was frequently rejected. This was an obvious disparity between the Church of England and the Orthodox East. Allchin had written a paper on the subject for the Anglican–Orthodox Joint Doctrinal Commission. He thought the Western tradition of iconography had been weakened by never fully assimilating John of Damascus on the images. Thomas Aquinas (who in fact had a good acquaintance with John of Damascus through the Latin *de Fide orthodoxa*) misconstrued the Byzantine teaching, holding there is a sense in which *latria*, the worship given exclusively to God, may rightly be ascribed to an image of Christ. Thomas's account of the veneration of images magnified the danger of idolatry and led to a negative reaction on the part of the Reformers. Subsequently, English Protestants did not distinguish between Roman Catholic and Eastern Orthodox malpractice. Up to and including the 1888 Lambeth Conference, defenders of Nicaea II found themselves rebuffed.

Allchin ascribed to the scholarship of H. R. Percival, who prepared the volume on the Seven Councils in the Library of the Nicene and Post-Nicene Fathers, much of the reason for a change of mind. Percival vigorously advocated acceptance of the ecumenicity of the 787 Council by Anglicans. Since Percival's time there had also been increased Anglican experience of how the Orthodox use icons in faith and worship. In the 1921 consultation of English Anglicans with Constantinople, the issue of the problematic status of the council was dropped. There remained from it only a modest request that the West should have liberty to continue its own custom of 'figures of Christ and the Saints... carved and sculptured'.[14] This was quite a *volte-face*.

The Orthodox might ask, why the change, and if so complete and swift (for some Orthodox saw three-dimensional images as a step too far) was it really serious? In a sense, the alteration in attitude was not so swift as all that. Anglican apologists had long abandoned the claim that Rome was idolatrous and therefore not a Church. In the Laudian revival they had come to revere church buildings and to replace lost stained glass. It was not in any case likely that corporate Anglicanism would start to venerate icons in the Orthodox manner. But, thought Allchin, Anglicans may well be brought to recognize the rightness of the 'Icon Council', to see the link between a genuine Christian art and the Gospel of the Word made flesh. And this could give the art of the West help it sorely needed if ever it was to be useful again to the Church.

> The present crisis of sacred art in the West, which is hardly less grave than that of the sixteenth century, may well arise from a failure to recognize the necessary character of an art which is meant directly and explicitly to serve the proclamation of the Gospel of the Word made flesh.[15]

The Greek theologian Constantine Scouteris largely agreed with Allchin. His paper 'Icons and their Veneration' was given to the Anglican/Orthodox Dialogue in session at Odessa in 1983. He chose to present the theology of icons via three liturgical texts from the Sunday of the Triumph of Orthodoxy. Scouteris stressed a select number of brief phrases. The first was patently Christological. 'The uncircumscribed Word of the Father, taking flesh, became circumscribed.' Over against iconoclast accusations that Iconodules were either crypto-Nestorians or crypto-Monophysites, the Orthodox confessed that it is the person of the God-man, the hypostasis of the incarnate Word, who is depicted in the icons. The next gobbet was anthropological. 'He [God in Christ] has restored the sullied image to its ancient glory, filling it with the divine beauty.' Scouteris noted that for Diadochus of Photike, ecclesial man is given the possibility, through inner action and the grace of the Holy Spirit, to 'to repaint his own likeness on the image of God'.[16] A third formula was soteriological. 'We confess the salvation in deed and word, and we depict it in the holy icons', which Scouteris took to be a statement that salvation is confessed through words in Scripture and through depiction in the icons. 'Both indicate the revelation, although revelation itself transcends words and images alike.'[17] A fourth sentence selected ran, 'We depict the likeness of thine outward form, venerating it with an honour that is relative'. This was the *timetikê proskynêsis* which Aquinas had spoken of as *adoratio relativa*, 'relative adoration', leading a synod of 1450 Hagia Sophia to accuse the Latins of idolatry, thus turning the tables on the accusations of idolatry laid against Byzantines by Charlemagne's theologians in the 'Caroline Books', and the source of Allchin's claim that Aquinas should be blamed for Reformation-period iconoclasm, not the Greeks. Then Scouteris cited the words, 'The honour shown to the icon passes to the prototype it represents'. Here he recalled how Stephen of Constantinople in his life of a martyr of the iconoclast crisis had called the icon 'a door opening our mind'.[18] Finally, he chose the formula, 'Following the holy traditions ... from thine icon we receive the grace of healing'. This he interpreted as a claim that 'the icon is a living *memorandum* of the divine energy and even more a *medium* for receiving healing and grace'.[19] It was an object lesson in how to use the Liturgy fruitfully in theological debate.

Christopher Walter (Father Julian Walter of the Augustinians of the Assumption) wrote on the icon before, at, and after Nicaea II, a revised form of a Heythrop lecture under the auspices of the Eastern Churches Review Trust. He wondered how important the Second Council of Nicaea had been, speculating that it might not have been much noticed had not St Photius numbered it as the seventh in his letter to the Bulgarians of around 866. '[T]he council legitimized the production of likenesses of Christ, although it did not inspire further speculation as to the relationship between the image and the prototype, nor any new departure in the iconography of Christ.'[20] Any 'new departure', in the course of the iconoclast crisis, was, arguably, Palestinian, not Constantinopolitan. That innovation took the form of a 'clipeate' image of Christ, connected with his virtual presence in the visions of prophets and Christian saints, as found in illuminated Byzantine 'marginal' Psalters. This stood over against more familiar rectangular form associated with the 'standard' icon of the Saviour. It could have been quite a cause of confusion in icon theory, for it implied a distinction between 'a picture used as a sign of Christ's presence and a picture of Christ actually invested with his *character*',[21] which term Walter explained as standing for the 'undivided totality of Christ's characteristics' an Orthodox Iconophile would hope to express in the painterly image.[22] But when the 'clipeate image was revived in the twelfth century in representations of the Holy Face on the Mandylion, the danger of confusion had lessened. It is unlikely that the artists who painted the Mandylion in so many Byzantine churches were aware that the iconographical type which they were using for Christ's features had once been used to symbolize his virtual presence.'[23]

Exhibitions and critics

Not all Eastern Christian art came from the Byzantine stable. In 1980 the Oxford Byzantinist Nicholas Gendle, fast becoming the art critic of the *Sobornost* of this period, looked at Armenian art through the eyes of its greatest living exponent—especially as that art was found in illuminated manuscripts—Sirapie der Nersessian.[24] He regretted her inability to get permission from the Turks to photograph at Ani and Kars, and the lack of comment on influence from (or on) Byzantium, Georgia and the Islamic world. Students of the iconoclast crisis would be interested to read that

> Wall-painting . . . is not so developed as in the Byzantine Empire (though here one must be cautious owing to comparatively slight survivals); and certainly icons do not have the same importance as in the Orthodox world. Instead, the cross seems to be the basic focus of devotion and artistic elaboration. In this connexion it is interesting to recall that there were iconoclastic sects in Armenia in the early seventh century, several generations before the iconoclast crisis in Byzantium.[25]

Two years later there was excellent writing by Gendle about an icon exhibition at London's Temple Gallery. He noted the esotericism which occasionally raises its head in Richard Temple's catalogues. 'Mr Temple does not always bear in mind sufficiently the objective (liturgical and dogmatic) nature of icons as expressions of theological Tradition.'[26]

Nicholas Gendle also reviewed Christopher Walter's collected essays, gathered together as *Art and Ritual of the Byzantine Church*.[27] Though sceptical of the attempt at semiological analysis which opened them (it was probably a concession to the spirit of the times), he praised their subordination of interest in style to concern with subject-matter. Walter recognized the primacy of the cult for Orthodox iconography. The book is a huge compilation on bishops and liturgical rites in Byzantine art, but it also has a thesis: namely, that in the Comnene period an increasing emphasis on the Liturgy and its ministers reflects a growing emphasis on Church not empire, with a 'move away from images of Christ as universal ruler, enthroned amidst his heavenly court, to a concept of heaven based in the sanctuary of the Church, where Christ presides as universal patriarch. This is epitomized in the Communion of the Apostles with celebrating bishops below them in mid-Byzantine and later apses'.[28]

Finally, Gendle wrote a masterly review of Otto Demus's four-volume work on the mosaics of San Marco.[29] Though only roughly a third of the mosaic surface is original, and much of that has been damaged by inept restoration, it is possible to trace the relations of the mosaics to Constantinople, which perhaps sent mosaicists for the early (eleventh-century) work, while there are also hints of contact with later (Palaeologan) Byzantine stylistic development. There is too, in Gendle's words, an 'older Venetian tradition ... often evolving with decidedly Western elements of an early Gothic character'.[30] And there is the extraordinary *tour de force* in the cathedral's Genesis cycle of translating into the mosaic genre the miniatures of that that ancient figured manuscript the Cotton Genesis. (Here Demus left the demonstration to the historian of the icon Kurt Weitzmann.) Gendle noted that what is described throws light forward, onto the 'background of the Venetian Renaissance painters'.[31]

As the decade of the 1980s drew to its close, another name took his place. Jill Storer reviewed a French translation of Trubetskoy's Great War essays on the Russian icon, which she found usually over-romantic but sometimes stimulating.[32] (One of the essays, it may be recalled, had initiated the journal's interest in art, as far back as 1937.) She clearly preferred Father John Baggley's *Doors of Perception*, a work by a former Anglican, now Catholic, which was sympathetic but sober.[33] Even then she pricked some bubbles: 'The majority of painters were probably motivated by fidelity to the tradition in which they had been formed and by the obligation to express sound Orthodox doctrine, rather than by spiritual experience', and it should suffice to say of many icons of poorer quality that they 'fulfilled the more modest functions of helping to realize the presence of Christ and his saints, and giving the worshipper the opportunity to venerate them.'[34] She was doubtful of the influence of Hesychasm—the *Philokalia* recommends imageless prayer—save on some changes in portrayal of the Transfiguration (and an increased number of representations of the episode). Theology and art history, she concluded, writing in 1989, are still too far apart.

The following year she gave a very thorough account of the World Council of Churches essay collection *Icons: Windows on Eternity*,[35] reporting 'much repetition of the clichés of iconology' yet 'too many contradictory view-points'.[36] Two further remarks were especially noteworthy: 'Much is now being asked of the icon—paradoxically, more, perhaps by the Western sympathizer or convert than by the majority of native Orthodox, who value the icon chiefly as a means of contact with the holy, and more rarely have the desire, presumption or opportunity to study it in detail'.[37] And then she cited a 'modest proposition' which should be 'commended to all concerned with icons'. 'There is need for a certain transparency, achieved by a clear composition, simple forms and harmonious colours as well as faithfulness to the traditional features of the saints.'[38]

In 1995 she considered the British Museum's winter exhibition of Byzantine art in British collections. Though the exhibition was much praised, only fifteen painted panels were included, of which half were Italo-Byzantine or even post-Byzantine, but the reason is simple. 'Not only have few wooden panels survived from the Byzantine era, but regrettably few of those are in British public collections.'[39] The Museum was congratulated on starting a national icon collection in this context. She was also good value on *Icons of Cyprus*, by Sophocles Sophocleos, published in Nicosia.[40] Notable is the book's account of the 'ornate carved iconostases that developed in the sixteenth century and include Gothic and Italian Renaissance motifs as well as Byzantine . . . They are simpler and lower than the Russian iconostasis, with only two or three tiers, are always crowned by an important crucifix flanked by the *lypira*—figures of the Mother of God and St John after the fashion of the western medieval rood.'[41] Evidently they could have been included in the 'Mutual Enhancement' section of my Chapter 4 above, 'Anglicans and Latins and their Critics'.

'Beauty will save the world'

These words of Dostoevsky's gave Metropolitan Kallistos his title in *Sobornost*'s opening issue of 2008. He recognized the ambivalence of beauty but thought it better to concentrate on its 'life-creating potentialities rather than its temptations'.⁴² Beauty expresses the attractiveness of God, relying here on the etymological link between *kalos*, 'beautiful', and *kaleo*, 'I call', and thus the connexion between beauty and love, as in Augustine's grieved expostulation that he had not loved the divine beauty. In the Psalter, the beauty of God (27:4) is reflected in his holy place (96:6) and thus in its worship (29:2), and also in his self-revelation (50:2), which leads into the beauty of the theophany of Christ. On Tabor, the mountain of the Transfiguration, in Matthew 17:4, Peter says 'it is *kalon* for us to be here', which Kallistos understands as 'This is a place of beauty'—just as Lev Gillet liked to translate John 10:11 not as 'I am the good shepherd' but 'I am the shepherd, the beautiful one'. For Denys, the divine beauty is the source and goal of all things, and Kallistos cited St Thomas Aquinas's commentary on Denys's *On the Divine Names* to this effect.

As to created beauty, it is found in nature, in the beauty of the angels and saints, and in the beauty of liturgical worship of which Kallistos remarked that the sequence of fasts and feasts is time made beautiful, the architectural ordering of the church building is space made beautiful, the icons are sight made beautiful, and the chant is sound made beautiful. All forms of created beauty are diaphanic: that is, beauty 'causes the distinctive truth of each things, its essential meaning to shine through it'.⁴³ Beauty also makes things theophanic, so that God shines through too, and this is its sacramental power and the right sense to give to the statement 'Beauty will save the world', whatever Dostoevsky's character may have meant by it.

But in order to avoid escapism, we must add in conclusion that the divine Beauty as manifested in the God-man is 'sacrificial and kenotic' though Kallistos did not quite take the final step with the Swiss Roman Catholic dogmatician Hans Urs von Balthasar and say that therefore glory—divine beauty—is ultimately love.⁴⁴

A great overview

In 2010 Louth reviewed Larchet's *L'Iconographe et l'artiste*,⁴⁵ finding it excellent on the spatial perspective issue (the Renaissance versus the icon), not so convincing on 'temporality' where Larchet saw the time of the icon in terms of the Romanian anthropologist Mircea Eliade's cyclical time rather than the Bible's eschatological time which is surely more pertinent to this topic. Larchet had defended Gregory Krug's icons as a development of tradition; Louth wondered what Larchet would have made of Sister Joanna Reitlinger's artworks—so well known as these had been to members of the Fellowship—where the relation to tradition is 'perhaps more troubling'.[46] This review was also a preview of Louth's truly magnificent piece on the icon which would follow a few years later. The first issue of 2017 was able to announce in its editorial that the Zernov Lectures, fitfully realized in the past, were to be resumed on an annual basis, and the editor himself was the first to speak, in 'The Recovery of the Icon'.[47]

Recovery implies a prior loss. Louth opened with some illustrations of the loss of the traditional Russian icon in Russia itself. Dostoevsky does not mention icons in his novels; Bulgakov's mystical-artistic experience as a young atheist was in front of the Sistine Madonna at Dresden, scarcely a Byzantine image; St Seraphim's icon of the Mother of God, kept in his monastic cell, was a Frankish work. The stimulus to change of the Nikonian reforms—Peter the Great's Westernization policy—occasioned a massive alteration in the appearance of the icon, and even the traditional icon villages, homes to large number of craftsmen, may have lost the ability to paint in the style Old Believers preferred—though this is perhaps a more moot point than Louth suggests. But towards the end of the nineteenth century and in the early years of the twentieth century art historians such as Nikodim Kondakov 'realized the importance of the Byzantine icon for Russian culture'.[48] It was pertinent to the Fellowship that Sister Joanna had been, as Julia Reitlinger, one of Kondakov's students in post-Revolutionary exile in Prague. New cleaning techniques, from the mid-nineteenth century onwards, enabled the sensitive restoration of mediaeval Russian works, and wealthy connoisseurs, sometimes of Old Believer background, began to add ancient Russian icons, to their collections, of modern, largely, avant-garde art. Louth noted the great 1913 exhibition which formed part of the tercentenary celebrations of the Romanov dynasty and the dual legacy of destruction and conservation left by the Bolsheviks. Evgeny Trubetskoy's trio of essays on the icon (rather pooh-poohed by Jill Storer) was the first major reflective, and even theological, reaction, placing 'contemplation in colours' at the centre of ancient Russian spirituality which set the radiance of the icon against the foil of the darkness of the Tatar period. A few years later Pavel Florensky was writing on the icon—though his materials were not published until many years after his death. Louth comments on his sometimes startling ideas about the uniqueness of the traditional Russian icon and the floor-to-ceiling iconostasis of which they so often formed part:

> Although the works in which these ideas were expressed remained unpublished until well after the period we are considering, memories of the impressions left by the talks on which they were based must have circulated, and notions of 'reverse perspective' and the central role of the face in the icon are encountered in those who furthered the recovery of the icon.[49]

As to new icons, the Russian tradition had to be recreated in the Diaspora. Here Léonide Ouspensky and Gregory Krug are the most prominent figures. Louth did not have the time to expound Ouspensky's *Essai sur la théologie de l'icône dans l'Église orthodoxe*,[50] whose title (he points out) must surely have been meant to mirror that of Vladimir Lossky's *Essai sur la théologie mystique de l'Église d'Orient*. But he pauses to consider the Ouspensky and Lossky joint work *The Meaning of Icons*,[51] an influential book, which assumes that the 'Russian icon has been recovered, so that modern Russian icons can be placed alongside the icons of the classical period.'[52]

The prominence of the Paris Diaspora does not mean, however, that the icon renaissance was purely Russian. For there was a one-man band in Greece, Photios (Fotis) Kontoglou, born in what is now Turkey in 1895—but not without a Parisian connexion since he studied fine art there during the Great War. Louth thinks it was the destruction of the Anatolian Greek communities (Kontoglou's own) in the ill-fated Greek 'Anatolian adventure' which made him look for Greek roots of a quite different kind by studying Byzantine (and post-Byzantine) art, initially in a spirit of Hellenism not Orthodoxy. (Kontoglou himself compared the Theotokos image to that of the ancient Greek goddesses.) After the Greek Orthodox Church banned the production of Italianate frescoes and icons in 1938, demands on Kontoglou soared, and like Ouspensky he sought to put the case in prose, 'summed up in his major work, *Ekphrasis*—Expression, or better, Image Interpretation—in two volumes, intended as a replacement for Dionysios of Fourna's *Ermeneia*, or *Painter's Guide*, for which Kontoglou had little time.'[53]

Like Ouspensky, Kontoglou was negative about Western art, while thinking Ouspensky's icons too Russian and Ouspensky himself wrong not to concede primacy to Byzantine painting. To Louth's mind, both men took fifteenth-century models, either Russian or Athonite and Cretan respectively, rather than what might have been a more obvious and universal choice, namely Palaeo-Christian art. Louth suggests this was because neither of them wanted to work in mosaic. Louth finished by considering two later offspins from Paris: the art of Mother Maria Skobstova (St Maria of Paris) and Julia (Sister Joanna) Reitlinger. Louth found in Mother Maria traces of the Douanier Rousseau, Marc Chagall and the English water-colourist (and writer of nonsense verse), Edward Lear. Though Sister Joanna was more traditional he thought there were touches of 'magic realism' in at least some of her icons.[54]

An ending: St Maria of Paris

Mother Maria Skobtsova has already been mentioned and she is a good place to end. Paul Ladouceur, teaching Orthodox theology in Quebec and Toronto, wrote in *Sobornost* on Maria of Paris's artwork which as with her literary production came in a great variety of genres: watercolour, pen and ink, pastels, icons, frescoes, embroidery, liturgical vestments.

His account is woven deftly into a narrative of her life. The work she did prior to her exile was unknown until 1977 when some sixteen items were donated to the Russian Museum in Petersburg. Their exhibition in 2000 (and a book by the organizer Xenia Krivochein) prompted a gift of many other items which went to the Anna Akhmativa Museum, also in Petersburg. They vary hugely in quality, and also in style, for some are realist, others symbolic. Subject matter is also highly variable. Some exemplify Hindu iconography, on which Ladouceur comments that, though her writings show no sign of Hindu influence, Hinduism 'featured in the religious scene of late imperial Russia and at least one well-known Orthodox religious personality, Symeon Sakharov (Archimandrite Sophrony, 1896–1933 [the founder of the Orthodox monastery at Tolleshunt Knights in Essex and biographer of St Silouan the Athonite]) went through a seven-year phase of Hindu spirituality, prior to returning to Christianity in Paris in 1924'.[55] Two works may be based on Graeco-Roman mythology, which is less surprising. Though in this period she was estranged from the Church, over half have biblical themes. One appears to be sophiological, representing Sophia as a crowned woman attended by two angels above the dome of a crowded church. Another is liturgical, with a two-tier celebration of the Divine Liturgy, by a priest on earth and by Christ in heaven.

From her exile, which coincides with her return to the Church, about ninety works survive, forty-nine of which as line drawings for a book of her poems. Much of her religious art, painted directly onto the walls of provisional chapels, has been lost, but her finest work appears to have been her embroidered icons, and scenes illustrating the major feasts of the Mother of God sewn into vestments.

Even in Ravensbrück she managed to make an embroidered scarf as a gift; it was secreted on the person of the recipient, another prisoner, and survived. She also drew the 'head of the Crucified Christ, with the crown of thorns, on a piece of an old shirt, using a charred stick'; this was discovered and led to punishment for the prisoners of her 'block' in the prison.[56] She is the Orthodox Edith Stein of the Nazi camps, a philosopher not, however, in the realm of the concept, as was her fellow-martyr, but in that of the image, both verbal and—above all—visual.

7

The Rise of Green Orthodoxy

Kallistos Ware took 'The Value of the Material Creation' as the topic of his contribution to the 1970 conference at Durham on Christian responsibility for the world. It was an early example of 'Green Orthodoxy', long before the Patriarch Bartholomew acceded to the Ecumenical Throne of Constantinople and earned the sobriquet 'the Green Patriarch'. It was a harbinger of things to come.

The Ware manifesto

Ware's introduction to the 1970 essay not only reflected the social preoccupations of the period, but was an early indicator of ecological concern as well. (The World Council of Churches would famously adopt the mantra, 'Justice, Peace and the Integrity of all Creation', often abbreviated to the mnemonic formula 'JPIC'.) Ware looked at the issue of the value of materiality from two standpoints: creation, and the New Creation.

Taken creationally, the world is, in an extended sense of the word, a 'sacrament', and man is its 'king and high priest'.[1] Man is 'king' because unlike the animals, he 'can reshape and alter the world, giving to it fresh significance and purpose'—though Ware considered such enhanced meaning already 'present potentially' in created things, things which in any case already have their own *logoi* or purposive idea which deserves to be respected.[2] That qualification was clearly meant to inhibit the technological exploitation that might be licensed by the original statement which it emended. Man is creation's 'high priest' because, unlike the animals again, he 'can bless and praise God for the world'.[3] The new liturgical day in the Byzantine rite begins at Vespers with Psalm 103/4, a paean of praise for the wonder of the world.

Then there is looking at that world in terms of the New Creation. With the Fall,

> The material creation ceased to be transparent, and it became dense and opaque; it ceased to be a sacrament and a means of communion with God and it became a barrier and an occasion of temptation and stumbling. Yet, just as the divine image in man was never destroyed by sin but only obscured, so the primal beauty of the creation was never utterly obliterated but only grievously impaired.[4]

Restoration in Christ will mean then the recovery for material things of the capacity to mediate sacramental communion with God, and man's return to his position as kingly high priest of the creation.

The Incarnation, the Baptism of Christ, the Transfiguration, the sensuous media Christ used in his public ministry, climaxing in the institution of the Holy Eucharist, all underline the critical importance of the material creation, while in his Ascension the God-man takes matter home to the Father, just as he will return with it in the glorious Parousia whose consequence is the general resurrection. That condition of risen materality is anticipated, so Kallistos noted, in the transfigured facial appearance of some of the great saints. The high-priestly role in redeemed humanity is apparent in the offering of the gifts at the Liturgy and in iconography. So as to avoid seeming 'unduly ecclesiastical or "aesthetic"', Ware identified a kind of analogue in scientific enquiry—without explaining, however, how the latter, as currently practised, can be said to follow from the restoration of the order of creation after the Fall.[5]

Modified rapture

Ware's overture to eco-theology found some resonance among *Sobornost* writers. Philip Sherrard had been writing about 'The Rape of Man and Nature', finding that a flawed Western theological and philosophical tradition (beginning, naturally, with Augustine) had led to the 'dehumanization of man and the desanctification of nature'.[6] Sherrard believed that, human invention as it is, the catastrophe can be undone by humans. But Andrew Sherwood, his reviewer and, so readers were told, a Green Party Parliamentary candidate, considered him short on prescription for the future. But of course Sherrard's foundational thesis, on the need to recover the sense of the divine significance of man, was scarcely amenable to legislative programming. In the early 1990s an Australian deacon, John Chryssagvis, noted that in a follow-up work, *Human Image: World Image,* Sherrard seemed to have recognized that not all the blame 'should be laid only on Western Christianity: no single cultural area or historical era can assume sole responsibility for the green-house effect or the depletion of the ozone layer. This is why it is gratifying to note how Sherrard has advanced in this work from the lamentation over the horrendous consequences of Western philosophy, theology and science, to a crucial synthesis between physics and metaphysics'.[7] Meanwhile Sebastian Brock was seeking to base a Syriac-inspired eco-theology on St Ephrem, Isaac of Nineveh and the modern day Indian Syrian-Orthodox Metropolitan Paulos Mar Gregorios Verghese, but especially the first of these. Ephrem, said Brock, teaches an 'inherent interconnectedess' within humanity, within creation as a whole—and thus between man and the environment, and between the material and spiritual worlds. In a rather unattractive image, all things conspire to form a 'vast multi-dimensional spider's web'.[8]

Not all Orthodox were convinced, especially if a World Council of Churches deemed short on doctrine was doing the attempted convincing. Even when it was the 'Council of Churches in Britain and Ireland' that was responsible, it might turn out that World Council thinking was *de rigueur*. In the mid-1990s, two books on 'JPIC'—one from each of these organizations' publishing houses—were reviewed by *Sobornost* in the doubtless well-founded opinion that some readers of the journal would be grinding their teeth.[9] Elizabeth Theokritoff gained the impression that 'the working out of a theological basis for Justice, Peace and the Integrity of Creation seems to be regarded as an optional extra'.[10] The upshot was (predictably, she thought) typical of the World Council: 'ill-thought-out generalizations, and the blurring of theological affirmations into social and political desiderata with only the most perfunctory attempt to show how the one necessitates the other'.[11]

Other Orthodox too were working on the matter. Zizioulas had been the leading light of a seminar on the environment at Halki, in 1994. It was convened by Bartholomew I, with support from H. R. H. Prince Philip, Duke of Edinburgh (himself a Greek by birth), on behalf of the World Wide Fund for Nature. Zizioulas regarded Western Christianity as a major contributor to an exploitative view of the natural world and thought the Greek tradition could combat this by its view of man as priest of creation, its treating salvation as cosmic, and the Eucharist likewise, and its affirmation of asceticism. These had also been Kallistos's themes. But Zizioulas recognized that, at the popular level, pertinent awareness among the general body of the Orthodox was very low. An 'environmental consciousness' must be formed, based on Orthodox teaching, and 'specific Church-sponsored environmental activities' initiated, though these appeared to replicate policies increasingly usual in advanced societies in the West.[12]

At the turn of the millennium John Chryssavgis, by then of Holy Cross Greek Orthodox School of Theology in Massachusetts, and religious adviser to the Ecumenical Patriarchate's Religion and Science Commission, reported on Patriarch Bartholomew's ecological overtures,[13] while Gerald Bray, now Anglican Professor of Divinity at the University of Stanford in Birmingham, Alabama, reviewed Chryssavgis himself on ecology. Bray praised his attempt to respond to the ecological crisis in the spirit of the Greek Fathers on the *Hexaemeron*, the six days of creation.[14] But he also commented sharply, 'As with most writers who exalt the goodness of creation, he has little to say about sin and evil'.[15]

Theokritoff was somewhat more positive about another World Council of Churches publication, *Living with the Animals: The Community of God's Creatures*.[16] The co-authors were Charles Birch, a biologist, and Lukas Vischer, a theologian, indeed a former director of the Faith and Order Secretariat. But she rebuffed Vischer's assertion that cosmic suffering in the animal creation should not be considered bound up with the Fall. That thesis was hard to square with the 'manifest ability of many saints to reduce the level of violence in the animal world around them'.[17] She also took issue with his statement that after the year 1500 little is heard about the spiritual community of the saints with animals. The remark could only be made by someone ignorant of the Christian East. By contrast, she approved of Birch's call for return to an economic system that looks to human and animal wellbeing and not simply to expansion. It must surely mean a return to asceticism.

Theokritoff, who was rapidly developing a specialized expertise in this literature, liked the discussion of sustainable development in another World Council product, *Earth Community, Earth Ethics* by Larry Rasmussen.[18] But his overall approach for which 'viable earth faith requires re-rooting virtually all religious and moral traditions' had led him to do with theology and ethics what he said should never be done with nature—namely, treat it as a 'mere bank of resources to quarry as required'.[19] Theokritoff was far kinder to Edward Echlin's *Earth Spirituality* than to most books on eco-theology sent her for *Sobornost* review.[20] Its subtitle, 'Jesus at the

Centre', sounded reassuring to adherents of classical Christianity. The author seemed to her unusual among eco-theologians in so obviously loving the countryside. 'Fr Alexander Schmemann remarks somewhere that theologians talk about matter in connection with sacramental life, but one rarely gets the sense that they actually *like* matter very much. Edward Echlin, however, is a theologian who ... likes matter as it is embodied in our real surroundings: in the countryside, the kitchen-garden, the frogs and cows and corn-stooks and church towers depicted on the cover.'[21] And so in his book, 'The combination of a real love for God's material world and a firmly christocentric approach frequently produces a marvellous blend of natural lore and theological insight in the best tradition of the early fathers'.[22] She cited a winning passage: 'Just as I contain traces of primordial stardust and the earth's humus in my being, so does Jesus "like unto us" in his complete humanity.'[23]

Echlin was a Catholic writer, and a former priest. Theokritoff also considered a more exalted author. She found the collected addresses of Bartholomew I on ecology well rooted in the theological tradition and the Church's liturgical life.[24] Themes included: 'the eucharistic and ascetic spirit, humans' responsibility for creation, and the necessity for sacrifice and for *metanoia*'.[25] But she thought eco-theologians would probably feel them unadventurous, and perhaps was relieved this was so.

Crina (otherwise 'Macrina') Gschwandiner wrote an unusual essay on ecology, taking her departure point from recent scholarly ruminations on the significance of the Sabbath in this perspective. The 'Sabbath rest extended to slaves, foreigners, animals and land, thus expressing a clear concern not just with people but also other creatures including the ground itself'.[26] In seventh and jubilee years this rest for the land was protracted to a year in length—and the jubilee year (the year after seven cycles of seven) pointed ahead to the Messianic era. The Sabbath is therefore the feast of creation looking forward to its eschatological climax.[27] Naturally, the seventh day Sabbath is more important for Jews than for Christians so she amplified her account by reference to Jewish writing in the hope, not least, of identifying 'certain structural parallels in the way in which time is experienced within Jewish Sabbath and festival liturgies and Christian Orthodox liturgy'.[28] Her hope was justified. 'In the Sabbath the past and the future are present in our own reality: it does not merely recall creation but practises it, it does not merely preview the Messianic age but really participates in it.'[29] Jewish scholars had noted how the Sabbath thus understood should increasingly spill its influence over the rest of the week. Likewise, for the Orthodox, Alexander Schmemann had considered that 'Sunday is not a "holy day" in opposition to the "profane" days of the rest of the week but rather it transforms time as a whole in eschatological fashion'.[30] This, the eschatological dimension, had also been the key to Schmemann's understanding of the Liturgy and of liturgical feasts, and more recently it had been echoed in the Catholic writer David Faberberg, a pupil of Schmemann as well as of the Benedictine Aidan Kavanagh, in an audacious work which put the Liturgy at the head of all theology, *Theologia prima*.[31] But to have an impact on believers' lives the Liturgy must be 'reinforced by homiletic and catechetical practices that foster a Christian (ascetic) lifestyle'.[32]

In her own study, *Living in God's Creation*, Elisabeth Theokritoff had an unusual take on the subject of blessing.[33] Since Christ, the creation has become secretly sacramental. It has become redeemed and sanctified in him, so that in consecrating a place or object what we are doing is to lift the veil of that secrecy. Theokritoff's book was glowingly reviewed in the succeeding issue of *Sobornost* by Gschwandiner herself, not least for the author's stress on the proper use of things and the counsel to live 'lightly' on this planet.[34] But whether the Orthodox could give a lead in this was a moot point. It suggests a move to my final chapter, 'Looking Ahead'.

→ 8 ←

Looking Ahead

Concern with ecology, even if qualified by the need to place it in a proper doctrinal context, was already an example of 'looking ahead'—for the good of man in the cosmos. But there were other ways of envisaging the future which focused more sharply on the condition of the Churches.

The menace of secularism

In 1987, in the course of a review of *The Study of Spirituality*, a newly published handbook with an ecumenical range, Norman Russell commended Alexander Schmemann's honesty in analysing a malaise of Orthodoxy in the West.[1] The sickness in question was caused by secularism. A 'specifically Western phenomenon, a Western "heresy" with roots in the Western spiritual and intellectual development',[2] secularism invited the adjustment of faith, liturgy and spirituality to itself—with disastrous results. Schmemann called instead for a return to the Byzantine spiritual tradition backed up by witness against the 'false values and pseudo-eschatology of secularism'.[3] Eric Mascall, now retired and living at St Mary's, Bourne Street, in London's West End as perpetual curate, had reviewed when it appeared half a dozen years earlier Schmemann's *Church, World, Mission*, a collection of articles for which a crisis in Orthodox consciousness was the common theme.[4] Secularism had infected Western Christianity and Orthodoxy, undergoing Westernization, had caught the disease. The Orthodox Diaspora in the USA were especially guilty as charged, not only in a 'capitulation to the ethos of secular democracy' but also for a 'failure to grasp the real nature of the Church and its life, as evidenced by their complacency with the existence of eighteen nationally based overlapping Orthodox jurisdictions'.[5]

In sharp contrast, judging by other entries in the 'spirituality' manual, Catholics, Anglicans and Protestants were satisfied with the condition of things in their own communities. Russell was sceptical about this. He was especially sceptical about the view of a Jesuit contributor that the losses in devotional life in Roman Catholicism since Vatican II were more than compensated for by the emergence of study circles, social action groups, Secular Institutes and the Charismatic Renewal. Donald Allchin, another contributor, admitted Anglican spirituality went into crisis in the 1960s. But now, he said, it was more or less healthy again, thanks to its capacity to assimilate. Gordon Wakefield, a Methodist, exemplified the spirit of assimilation when he wrote of how the best twentieth-century Protestant teaching on prayer originated in Catholic sources. This set of reactions, said Russell, had one point in common. 'Anglicans and Protestants have similarly [i.e. like Catholics] lost confidence in their own traditions and are searching for sustenance from new sources.'[6] Russell was inclined to invoke the word 'dilettantism' here, or, worse, the influence of the secularism charted by Schmemann. Looking ahead, Orthodox problems could not be entirely disentangled from those of Catholics and others, partly because in the West the same causal factors were at work—and partly because the Orthodox might have to ready themselves for an influx of Western Christian refugees if the attempt to keep the Churches of the West to the traditional norms was ultimately abandoned as hopeless.

Orthodoxy and the future of the West

In 2001, a conference was organized on 'Orthodoxy and the Future of Europe' by the Cambridge Institute of Orthodox Christian Studies, with distinguished participants. It concluded that the Orthodox were culturally schizophrenic toward the West. They were hampered by the plural ethnic jurisdictions. Yet they were also faced with an opportunity, for Europe had lost its spiritual identity.

Seven years before, John Zizioulas had told the Orthodox in Western Europe that they certainly should not let Orthodoxy become 'an "exotic" religion, offering refuge to those seeking mystical and other extraordinary experiences analogous to those offered by different oriental religions and cults'. It was not even enough to convert Western Christians to Orthodoxy. Instead, like the great Fathers, the Orthodox in the West must 'address themselves to the challenges of the culture of their time'.[7] This was especially so when Western culture was becoming global culture anyway.

In Zizioulas's view, the main problem of that culture was the way its thought was built on individualism, rooted in Boethius on the person and Augustine on self-consciousness. Individualism cannot help but make one nervous of the 'other'. Here was a consequence of the Fall. Fear of otherness becomes dislike of any difference, and the identifying of difference with division. Then 'communion' becomes a fragile arrangement for co-existence. But this situation is hellish. Isolation from the other is eternal death. Ethics cannot solve this. We need a new birth. '[T]his leads us to ecclesiology,' wrote Zizioulas.[8] It would surely have been more usual to say, 'This leads us to soteriology'. That gives some idea of how high Zizioulas's expectations of the Church are (surely too high?), specifically in this perspective of communion and otherness.

> We need a model by which to measure our existence. And the higher the model the deeper the repentance. This is why we need a maximalistic ecclesiology and a maximalistic anthropology—and even cosmology—resulting from it. Orthodox ecclesiology, by stressing the holiness of the Church, does not and should not lead to triumphalism but to a deep sense of compassion and *metanoia*.[9]

The 'model' concerned can only be God the Holy Trinity, where otherness is constitutive of unity even though Father, Son and Spirit are 'absolutely different'.[10] Zizioulas then factored in Christology and Pneumatology by asserting that communion with the other, if it really reflects the Trinity in history, must work in the kenotic manner of the Cross of Christ. So working, 'communion' will not be 'determined in any way by the qualities that he or she [the 'other'] might possess'.[11] And as to the Holy Spirit: being the Spirit of *koinonia* and the Last Days, he creates 'not good individual Christians, individual "saints", but an event of communion, which transforms everything the Spirit touches into a relational being' where the other 'becomes... an ontological part of one's identity'.

It is on the basis of the other's future, not his or her present (or past) that he or she should be accepted, for every other is a 'potential saint'.[12] In Baptism, the past ceases to be defining for one becomes a member of the City to come. But it is in the Holy Eucharist that communion and otherness are fully realized. The Eucharist sanctifies both communion and otherness. Zizioulas pronounced himself against all celebrations that are for particular groups of people. But are not some necessarily excluded? If not, why does the deacon sing out, 'The doors, the doors!'? Zizioulas replied that only excluders are excluded. Excluders are those who distort the source of communion by heresy or deny it through schism. The Church needs a ministry of unity, to protect difference from becoming division. That is why it needs the bishop, who therefore can only be numerically one in any given place (defenders of plural ethnic jurisdictions, please note!).

A proper anthropology follows from all this: 'the person is otherness in communion and communion in otherness', in the image of the Trinity.[13] A person has the freedom of being other, but it is freedom *for* the other not *from* them. That means it is also at the same time love and creativity. And all of this can help ecologically, since 'all forms of true culture and art are ways of treating nature as otherness in communion'.[14] This—Ziziulianism—should be the message of Orthodoxy to the West.

A question for a new millennium

In the second issue of 2004 Bishop Kallistos published in amended form a lecture he had given to major institutions in the Ukraine and Greece (the Kiev Philosophical-Theological Society and the Volos Academy of Theological Studies) on 'Orthodox Theology in the New Millennium: What is the most important question?'. In the twentieth century, the major question for Orthodox theology had been that of the Church. Great gains had been made, especially in regard to eucharistic ecclesiology.

> [W]hereas the Slavophiles had taken as their model for organ unity the Russian peasant commune, Afanas'ev gave a greater clarity and cogency to their standpoint by affirming a model that was not sociological but mysterial. Mutual love, he insisted—in a way the Slavophiles had failed to do—is essentially eucharistic in character. The love that holds the Church together is not just an inner subjective feeling, but it has as its basis an objective act, the joint participation of Christians in Holy Communion.[15]

John Zizioulas had gone on to strengthen the reference of eucharistic ecclesiology to the Church universal. He had insisted on the need for the communion of one local Church with all others, such that, in the end—at any rate on Kallistos's interpretation—eucharistic and universal ecclesiologies turn out to be complementary. In Kallistos's view, the revival of the practice of frequent Communion was an essential rider to this. But what would be the major question of the twenty-first century be? Zizioulas's other main preoccupation, theological anthropology, was his answer.

Looking Ahead

The coming shift to anthropology was prompted, said Kallistos, by four crises: urbanization and globalization; machine domination; genetic engineering and the collapse of family morality; and the state of the environment. He foresaw the emergence of three theological themes in the study of man: *mystery*, for which an apophatic anthropology will be required; *iconicity*, for the human being, made in the image of 'Christ the Creator Logos' and thus of 'God the Holy Trinity', is essentially a relation to its archetype in God;[16] and *mediation*, for man as 'priest of the creation' is the 'cosmic liturgist',[17] which implies, in the Church, that human beings should also be eucharistic animals, and in a fallen world this will mean, moreover, ascetic animals, who live sacrificially and kenotically. To which trio of terms he added in a conclusion, the theme of *love*. In an adaptation of Descartes's *cogito ergo sum*, 'I love (or am loved), therefore I am'.

Despite the reference to 'family morality', there was not much here about the matters engaging Catholic moral theologians at the opening of the new century. Admittedly, through Father Columba Flegg, that redoubtable survivor of the 'Irvingites' (the 'Catholic Apostolic Church'), *Sobornost* had done some justice to bioethical issues.[18] But for a Fellowship which, in the 1930s and 1940s, had prided itself on the number of children attending conferences that also functioned as family holidays, the record of the journal on the question of child-bearing and the nurture of children, considered as a normal part of married life, was pretty dismal.[19]

The plurality of jurisdictions

In 2005 Gerald Bray had read on *Sobornost*'s behalf *The Orthodox Churches in a Pluralistic World*, a World Council of Churches publication edited by Emmanuel Clapsis.[20] The book openly admitted that 'ethnic identity and nationalism have played far more of a role in Orthodox circles than elsewhere in the Christian world, and that this difficulty must be overcome if the Orthodox witness is to be credible in a global universe'.[21] Not much had changed, then, in the quarter century since Olivier Clément's frank assessment 'The Orthodox Diaspora in Western Europe: Its Future and its Role'. In 1979 Clément had summed up the position in a few words: 'an unquestionable spiritual radiance, a deplorable ecclesiological situation'.[22]

According to Clément's analysis, 'ancient European cultures' of real spiritual originality underlie the ever more global modern Western civilization with its 'increasingly absurd' surrogates for fulfilment.[23]

One of his concerns was how the Orthodox must contribute to the preservation of these cultures—which will not be possible if, for instance, they seek entirely to displace the historic Churches in Western Europe. He specifically excluded America from his purview in these remarks—not that the problem of multiple jurisdictions was any less there, rather the contrary. In 1993 Elizabeth Theokritoff remarked of a new 'Directory' of Orthodox parishes and institutions in North America that its etiquettes were helpful for those who 'do not have a morbidly encyclopaedic knowledge of jurisdictions in the Orthodox diaspora'.[24] Yet Christianity in general was more robust in the United States than in the European West, where, said Clément, the Orthodox must strengthen whatever signs of movement towards the transcendent they can find.

This they had already sought to do in the first generation of Diaspora exiles thanks to the work of the Russian philosophers, the 'fathers' of the Russian religious renaissance. They have done it too, in the succeeding generation, the generation of 'the sons', via the work of their neo-patristic theologians. That work was carried out in conjunction with the great representatives of *ressourcement* in European Catholicism, with its 'massive study of biblical, patristic and liturgical sources'.[25] It would be a dereliction of duty for the Orthodox to turn their back on Western Christian bodies (here the Church of England would also, surely, be included) that had listened to the first and collaborated with the second.

> We cannot but see that the influence of the Gospel, of the Eucharist and of at least the first four Ecumenical Councils has never faded in the West, producing a sanctity perhaps the more acute and heroic because it lacks theological backing. We cannot but note also that today everything is in process of thaw and of movement, and that the moment has come to witness with the intelligence of love. It would, I believe, be a grave spiritual mistake to give oneself over to a utterly negative reading of the Christian West, and to wish to make it responsible for all the ills of contemporary civilization. It would also, I believe, be a spiritual mistake to seek to give a positive value in the destiny of the Christian West only to the first thousand years, as though the Christian West between then and now had never had its saints, named and un-named.[26]

Orthodoxy, witnessing to the fullness of primitive Tradition, is not over against others, but with them.

The ecclesiology that comes from this is beautiful. But, owing to various factors, the practice is chaotic. Clément mentioned here:

the brutal and unforeseen circumstances of the first Orthodox emigration, the secular weakening of eucharistic and conciliar ecclesiology in the Orthodox Church, the stress laid, since the nineteenth century, on a national, even a nationalistic conception of ecclesial allegiance, reactions to Communist revolution and the new status of the Russian Church and of other Orthodox Churches in the People's Democracies, the different interpretations given in the Diaspora to the respective roles of the Ecumenical throne and the different autocephalies.[27]

What are the drawbacks of the resultant fragmentation? The ethnic dimension is no longer transfigured by the Church. Instead, ethnicity becomes a mode of secularization with Orthodoxy an aspect of ethnic culture that is soon, by assimilation, sloughed off. Moreover, in this situation, resources cannot be shared. With multiple bishops in one place, the vision of Orthodox ecclesiology is turning into a 'myth' in the vulgar sense of that word.[28] Western converts are caught up in the resultant quarrels and treat them as of the essence, generating a sectarian attitude in so doing. Far more important than summoning a hypothetical 'Great and Holy Council' is the task of recreating conciliarity among the Orthodox episcopates. The pentarchy (the five patriarchates acting in tandem) though reduced to a 'petrarchy' by the schism with Rome, worked well enough as a synodical form, as when for instance in 1848 and 1872 it clarified Orthodox ecclesiology in the 'face of two opposing temptations: to juridical centralization on the model of state control on the one hand and confederal fragmentation on the other'. But with the multiplication of national Churches and the 'new conception of autocephaly' in the nineteenth century that system became 'jammed'.[29]

He did not live to see a defence of several bishops in one see by an Anglican–use Catholic with a distinguished career as a patrologist behind him. Allan Brent of King's College, London, and St Edmund's College, Cambridge, and a priest of the Ordinariate of our Lady of Walsingham, wrote on a topic relevant to both the Orthodox in Western Europe and the Ordinariate itself—the territoriality (or otherwise) of bishops. Brent argues that episcopal territoritality was a Cyprianic invention, based on an analogy with the geographically circumscribed authority of the Roman magistrate and originating in the need to find a reason why Novatian, an orthodox *sacerdos*, must be condemned as an interloper on the proper terrain of Pope Cornelius's see. 'It is here, therefore, in Cyprian that ecclesial order becomes for the first time structured within the matrix of pagan, Roman jurisprudence with its spatially located notions of legitimation and power.'[30] Byzantium would follow suit, of course. 'But the question that I would wish to pose is what ecclesial order might be like if one were to recover features distorted by the territorial mould into which Ignatian Church order has been poured. This is why I would like us to take a closer and fresher look at the Eastern idea of bishop, priest, and deacons representing an iconography of divine order, and with different cultural forms representing different cultures in the process of redemption.'[31] He explained that as a Catholic priest he was 'committed to a wider unity and confluence of such cultures in the process of redemption'—but this would not be 'in terms of treaty bonds between their supreme episcopal presidents, but in terms of a unity and an integrity fashioned by the Petrine ministry of the Holy Father, a pastoral ministry of securing unity in diversity of the whole, fostering *koinonia*'.[32]

For his part, Clément appealed to the sees of Constantinople and Moscow in particular in the request he now put forward for a 'semi-autonomous Church' in Western Europe and especially in France. He hoped that status would be 'granted to our Diaspora by all the Orthodox Churches acting in conciliarity'.[33] He envisaged it as a body under the exarch of the Ecumenical Throne but in a 'permanent state of [wider] conciliarity', embodied in a standing committee to guide the new entity representative of all the Orthodox Churches which had members in the West.[34] No doubt not all Orthodox in the West agreed with him. But those who did are still waiting.

Orthodoxy and the Catholicism of the West

A Catholic historian of *Sobornost* might wonder how the journal will prosecute in the future any continuing interest in the Catholicism of the West—notably in its Roman form, since the Anglican is so weakened,[35] which one can say while recognizing that the Latin tradition is not in great shape either. The advent of Pope Benedict XVI in 2005 was, at the time, a very positive sign. Richard Price, a Westminster priest, formerly an Oratorian, who had joined *Sobornost*'s editorial board, introduced the new pope on his election. He spoke of the pope's wish to 'see an enrichment of Catholic theology through a deeper immersion in the liturgy and in the Church Fathers of the early centuries'.[36] Contextualizing this claim, Price continued:

> This makes him a member of that group of French and German theologians, including de Lubac, Daniélou, Bouyer, and von Balthasar, who rediscovered the Fathers and the non-Thomist medievals in the 1940s, were regarded as dangerously subversive in the later years of Pope Pius XII, came into their own at Vatican II, and were then bitterly disillusioned by the anarchy and modernism that swept through the Church after the council. There was, let us note, much mutual influence between this group and the contemporaneous flowering of Orthodox theology in the west, as in Lossky and Meyendorff.[37]

There was much in Benedict's life and writing, Price suggested, to endear him to his counterparts in the Orthodox hierarchy. 'They share Benedict's conservatism, his stress on fidelity to the tradition, his dislike of innovation, his sense of the Liturgy as God-given, his hostility to liberalism and consumerism.'[38] Shrewdly, Price noted that where they might well differ is on Benedict's belief that the Church of the future will be numerically smaller, if also qualitatively greater. Their concept of the role of the Church for the *ethnos* would make this notion unappealing. But that emphasis is mitigated by the fact that Benedict was certainly not 'resigned to a dechristianized Europe'.[39] In Price's words, 'It is clear that Rome is now looking to Moscow and Constantinople as allies in her campaign against modern secularism and the principles of the French Revolution.'[40]

There were obvious obstacles to close collaboration: the situation in the Ukraine; Rome's acceptance of the modern secular Western stress on freedom of religion, and freedom of conscience; the unlikelihood that she will climb down over the Petrine claims, not least because any weakening of her authority will mean in the local Churches of the West a strengthening of the theological liberalism she opposes; the comparable unlikelihood that the Eastern Orthodox will accept the essential orthodoxy of Roman Catholicism and an effective, as distinct from honorary, primacy. Price predicted for the Roman Catholic Church 'a quieter conservatism that sticks to the status quo', as understood by one who 'does not agree that pre-conciliar Catholicism was seriously amiss'. The confidence that this would be Benedict's legacy would be rudely shaken by the advent of his iconoclastic successor Pope Francis. Doubtless there are particular elements in Francis's programme that might attract the Orthodox. The lessening of the historic rigour of the Latin Church in matters of marriage and divorce comes to mind, though the pope's manner of proceeding, which includes the toleration of concubinage, is problematic. But conferring a hegemony on pastoral pragmatism will never suit any genuinely traditional Christianity.

A conversation piece

The first issue of 2014 began with an ecumenical conversation started by a piece of Stratford Caldecott on the theme of his own debt, as a Catholic convert, to the witness of Eastern Orthodoxy. Sent to the journal not long before his untimely death from cancer, it was responded to, at the editor's request, by a variety of voices.

Though specific in its allusions to writers and friends, Caldecott's message was general. 'All I know is that both Catholics and Orthodox need to penetrate beyond the polemics that divide us, to search for the wisdom that unites.'[41] The iconographer Aidan Hart was one of the friends. He thought that 'my Orthodox Church needs to learn from our Catholic and Anglican brethren in their greater engagement in contemporary issues, such as poverty, ecology, and secularism', but for himself he remained Orthodox because the 'Orthodox Church's doctrines and emphases seem to me to possess the greatest continuity with the Gospels and the early Church. This is what converted me, along with its detailed maps of the inner life (such as the *Philokalia*), its emphasis on deification, and its affirmation of the material world.'[42] But he concluded, 'Without resorting to papal supremacy, we could do well to learn from the more unified voice presented by our Roman Catholic brethren'—and he wrote in this context of delegating to 'the Patriarch of Rome' responsibility for convening general councils.[43]

Hart was followed by the principal of Pusey House, George Westhaver, who, despite the 'Protestant character of the English Reformers and Divines', had 'found in Prayer Book Catholicism a way of reading and interacting with Orthodox and Catholic sources',[44] though he admitted this was not hugely popular in the present-day Church of England. At a time when he was largely lapsed from the Canadian Anglicanism of his childhood and youth, a visit to Athos had been life-changing in sowing new seeds of faith. But the 'sacramental' sense of the created world, of Scripture, and of the Christian life at large also existed in the Western tradition (Andrewes, Herbert, the Tractarians, C. S. Lewis, Rowan Williams, the Cambridge priest-poet Malcolm Guite, and Michael Ward, sometime dean of Peterhouse, Cambridge, and interpreter of Lewis). The adversarial relations, historically, between Rome and the Church of England, and the way Rome serves as a way out for Anglicans disillusioned by confusion or complexity, has moulded his attitude to the former, but he was steering by the star of Dr Pusey's refusal to condemn the secession of Newman. Westhaver had been inspired by the 'fathers' of the *ressourcement* movement, by the 'spiritual guidance emerging from the monasteries of the Counter-reformation, the works of the liberation theologians, and in the patristic sensibility of Pope Benedict's sermons and exegesis', as well as 'the capacity of a Church to articulate definite and nuanced statements on doctrine and morals', though he added this can also seem 'totalizing' without space for human messiness.[45]

John Baggley, parish priest of Corpus Christi, Headington (two of his icon books had been reviewed in *Sobornost*), had been an Anglican pastor caught up in the turmoil of the 1980s and 1990s about women's ordination, and he began to look to Rome in that context though he had also had experience of the Latin Church in France, and read a number of Catholic authors. At Kelham he had been exposed to Orthodoxy, which led to visits to Athos in 1964 and 1965 (George Every's teaching of patristics was also important). 'The icon, the Jesus Prayer and St Gregory [of Nyssa] became key elements in my spiritual life and have remained so ever since.'[46] He considered becoming Orthodox, and had some conversations to that end. But the 'process of discernment brought me to the simple realization that I am a Western Christian, rooted in Western liturgical and spiritual tradition'—he had been brought up in a Lincolnshire parish, and educated theologically at Durham. Received into the Catholic Church he had a surprise in finding so much meaning in 'being in communion with the successor of St Peter', while still cherishing much in Orthodox and Anglican patrimony.

Andrew Louth then spoke for himself. There 'must be reasons why I abandoned Anglicanism and reasons why I embraced Orthodoxy rather than Catholicism', but he felt to identify them rationally would give a very surface account.[47] Like Mascall he was trained as a mathematician but unlike Mascall he felt no desire to carry over rational formalization into theology, being inclined to think that reason can prove anything and therefore nothing. Other contributors had spoken of visiting Athos, he went too but had a very mixed experience of monastic churches there, being expelled on one occasion and refused entry on another (as a non-Orthodox) at the Liturgy. His life had been marked by the experience of not having experiences. Yet the Liturgy or being in liturgical spaces was crucial for him. 'I once read somewhere of someone who found they could only pray in Orthodox Churches because only there could he, or maybe she, feel "the heartbeat of the Church, the breathing of the saints: yes, that is exactly what I feel, though I could never have found those words myself."[48] So much in Western Churches is explanation, even prayers can read like news bulletins, informing God. 'It is at this level that we are most fundamentally divided.'[49]

John Behr, the dean of St Vladimir's, in New York, had a sophisticated approach to Church divisions. 'It may be ... that "Eucharistic ecclesiology" is best understood not as the retrieval of an authentic, yet long-forgotten past, always there, living in the depth of the Orthodox soul, waiting to be reclaimed, but rather as the fruit of the Slavophile idea of *sobornost'*, blossoming in the Diaspora where the Eucharist naturally became the focal point for Orthodox self-identification.' Then the question arises as to 'whether it is possible to see the contrast between universalist ecclesiology and Eucharistic conciliar ecclesiology not as much as two opposing approaches, between which the Church has wavered throughout history and which theological integrity would force us to choose one (the latter), but instead to see them as two sides of a polarization which occurred in the nineteenth century: one leading to infallibility and universal jurisdiction, and the other leading to individualism in churches, whether parochial, diocese or autocephalous units, which have no common mission'.[50] The way forward may be a 'fuller expression of conciliarity and communion—a consensus model, rather than a primacy-in-love model'.[51] Here he mentioned the manner in which Bartholomew I *with the consent of the other primates* had sought to convene a pan-Orthodox synod. Yet, appealing to Ignatius of Antioch on the 'silence' of the bishop, perhaps there is here a special role for the bishop of Rome after all. 'In this perspective, it would be the silent witness of the Church of Rome, as the first among equals, being the last point of reference in the process of reception (or appeal), that enables the body to hold together as the one Body of Christ. And, if this is the case, then it might be more accurate (for the Orthodox) to say that we are not able to have an ecumenical council today, not because we don't have an emperor to call it (it can be done consensually), but because we don't have a Pope who won't be there!'[52]

Rowan Williams was given the last word. In the late 1960s, he explained, he was very worried by the question of Church authority, and was attracted to Roman Catholicism as a result, for 'dispute could be settled by appeal to the apostolic credentials of Rome.'[53] But there were difficulties with the idea of a Petrine charism of infallibility, not least when reading Farrer and Mascall, and his interest in the East, soon to be clinched by the decision to write his doctoral thesis on Lossky, prevented him from seeing anything outside the Roman Communion as 'somehow isolated from the mainstream.'[54] Looking not only at Lossky but at Lossky's predecessors, notably Khomiakov, and successors—he may have Clément in mind, it led him to a different way of approaching the topic of authority. '[W]hat if it were some sort of category mistake to look for some element within the Church's life that could be abstracted from the rest of that life and deployed as a device to settle disputes?'[55] So Orthodoxy kept him an Anglican. His debt to Orthodoxy was 'essentially in [the] sense of the Church as itself life and truth, the community that in its enacting of the work of Christ in the sacraments tells us who and what Christ is, and so, *by being itself*, establishes the Trinitarian mystery—not as a human imitation of divine 'community' (a rather dubious version of classical doctrine, to put it mildly!), but as the community which is together brought by the Spirit into the place where the Son stands, mirroring the glory of the Father, and itself mirroring that glory in its human diversity.'[56]

'Juridical' accounts seem irrelevant in comparison. Yet in his conclusion some elements of what that adjective might denote or at least connote returned. 'Like some of the early leaders of the Fellowship of St Alban and St Sergius, I continue to believe that we as Anglicans need to be converted to an ecclesiology that is rooted in what animated the great Orthodox minds of the modern period. And in this conversion we continue the conversation with the Catholicism of a de Lubac, in the hope that we may together discover ways of being fully ecclesial Christians that will steer between Scylla and Charybdis, between a centralized and monarchical polity in the Church and a well-meaning but theologically impoverished focus on locality and diversity.'[57]

It is hard to find a better conclusion for this 'story of a journal' than that.

NOTES

Notes to Preface

1. Paul L. Gavrilyuk, *Georges Florovsky and the Russian Religious Renaissance* (New York and Oxford: Oxford University Press, 2013), p. 134.
2. Kenneth Hylson-Smith, *High Churchmanship in the Church of England. From the Sixteenth Century to the Late Twentieth Century* (Edinburgh: T. & T. Clark, 1993), p. 329.

PART I

Notes to Chapter 1

1. Kallistos Ware, 'Nicolas Zernov (1898–1980)', *Sobornost* 3/1 (1981), pp. 11–33.
2. A. M. Allchin, 'Militza Zernov (1899–1994)', *Sobornost* 16/2 (1994), pp. 34–8; Wendy Robinson, 'Militza Zernov (1899–1994)', *Sobornost* 16/2 (1994), pp. 38–47.
3. Nicolas and Militza Zernov, *The History of the Fellowship of St Alban and St Sergius. A Historical Memoir* (Oxford: Fellowship of St Alban and St Sergius, 1979), p. 1.
4. Nicolas Zernov, *The Russian Religious Renaissance of the Twentieth Century* (London: Darton, Longman & Todd, 1963).
5. For the claim that the 'appeal to the Fathers has been a seminal feature of the Anglican tradition since the sixteenth century' see Arthur Middleton, *Fathers and Anglicans. The Limits of Orthodoxy* (Leominster: Gracewing, 2001), and here at p. 6. Compare A. M. Ramsey, 'The Ancient Fathers and Modern Anglican Theology', *Sobornost* 4/6 (1962), pp. 289–94.
6. Quoted in Middleton, *Fathers and Anglicans*, p. 53. The appeal recurs in the Canons of 1603, which remained the only collection of Anglican canon law until the later twentieth century. Canon A5 as currently in vigour states 'The doctrine of the Church of England is grounded in the Holy Scriptures, and in such teachings of the ancient Fathers and Councils of the Church as are agreeable to the said Scriptures'.
7. W. B. Patterson, 'Cyril Lukaris, George Abbot, James VI and I, and the Beginning of Orthodox–Anglican Relations', in Peter M. Doll (ed.), *Anglicanism and Orthodoxy 300 Years after the 'Greek College' in Oxford* (Oxford: Peter Lang, 2006), pp. 39–56.

8. See Judith Pinnington, *Anglicans and Orthodox. Unity and Subversion, 1559–1725* (Leominster: Gracewing, 2003), pp. 19–40.
9. Ramsey, 'The Ancient Fathers and Modern Anglican Theology', p. 290.
10. Pinnington, *Anglicans and Orthodox*, pp. 51–155.
11. The Greek church of St Mary opened in Soho had to close when the bishop of London refused to allow icons or the veneration of saints, or to permit the omission of the Filioque in the Creed, and required any priests to sign a repudiation both of transubstantiation and of the recent (1672) Synod of Jerusalem which, among other things, had sanctioned that language as a description of the Eucharistic change, *ibid.*, p. 99. See also Christopher Knight, '"People so beset with saints": Anglican attitudes to Orthodoxy, 1555–1725', *Sobornost/ECR* 10/2 (1988), pp. 25–35.
12. E. D. Tappe, 'The Greek College at Oxford, 1699–1705', in Doll, *Anglicanism and Orthodoxy*, pp. 153–74.
13. Pinnington, *Anglicans and Orthodox*, pp. 156–97.
14. Middleton, *Fathers and Anglicans*, pp. 267–306.
15. William Palmer, *Notes of a Visit to the Russian Church in the Years 1840, 1841*, selected and arranged by Cardinal Newman (London: Kegan Paul Trench and Co., 1882); see also Katharine Ridley, 'A Pioneer in Reunion—William Palmer', *Sobornost* 19 (1939), pp. 9–18; and for a full biography Robin Wheeler, *Palmer's Pilgrimage. The Life of William Palmer of Magdalen* (Oxford and New York: Peter Lang, 2006).
16. Michael Chandler, *The Life and Work of Henry Parry Liddon* (Leominster: Gracewing, 2000), pp. 32–4; Morton N. Cohen, *Lewis Carroll. A Biography* (London: Macmillan, 1995), pp. 264–74.
17. George Williams (ed.), *The Orthodox Church of the East in the Eighteenth Century, being the Correspondence between the Eastern Patriarchs and the Nonjuring Bishops* (London: Rivingtons, 1868).
18. Henry R. T. Brandreth, OGS, 'Anglican Eastern Associations: A Sketch', *Sobornost* 31 (1945), pp. 10–12, and here at p. 10.
19. Cited Michael Chandler, *The Life and Work of John Mason Neale, 1818–1866* (Leominster: Gracewing, 1995), p. 150.
20. *Ibid.*
21. Michael Hughes, 'The English Slavophile: W. J. Birkbeck and Russia', *Slavonic and East European Review* 82/3 (2004), pp. 680–706; J. Bibbee, *Anglo-Catholicism and the Orthodox East: William Birkbeck and the Quest for Unity, 1888–1916* (London: Anglo-Catholic History Society, 2007); Michael Hughes, 'Picturesque Visions and Hopeful Dreams. W. J. Birkbeck, Stephen Graham and British Responses to Russian Orthodoxy on the Eve of Revolution', *Sobornost/ECR* 33/2 (2011), pp. 6–27.
22. Cited from personal notes in Ronald Jasper, *Arthur Cayley Headlam. Life and Letters of a Bishop* (London: Faith Press, 1960), p. 47.

23. Cited *ibid.*, p. 56.
24. A. J. Maclean, *The East Syrian Daily Offices* (London: Rivington, Percival and Co., 1894).
25. W. J. Birkbeck, *Russia and the English Church* (London: Rivington, Percival and Co., 1895).
26. H. T. F. Duckworth, *Greek Manuals of Church Doctrine* (London: Rivington, 1901).
27. A. C. Headlam, *History, Authority and Theology* (London: John Murray, 1909).
28. Jasper, *Arthur Cayley Headlam*, pp. 58–9.
29. *Ibid.*, p. 60.
30. *Ibid.*, p. 61.
31. A. T. John Salter, *The Anglican Papalist. Henry Joy Fynes-Clinton* (London: Anglo-Catholic History Society, 2012).
32. Alan Wilkinson, *The Community of the Resurrection. A Centenary History* (London: SCM, 1992), p. 145.
33. A. C. Headlam, *The Doctrine of the Church and Christian Reunion* (London: John Murray, 1920).
34. Jasper, *Arthur Cayley Headlam*, p. 161.
35. George K. A. Bell, *Randall Davidson, Archbishop of Canterbury* (London: Oxford University Press, 1935), II., p. 1105; see on these initiatives Bryn Geffert, *Eastern Orthodox and Anglicans. Diplomacy, Theology and the Politics of Interwar Ecumenism* (Notre Dame, IN: University of Notre Dame Press, 2010).
36. Jasper, *Arthur Cayley Headlam*, p. 165.
37. Cited *ibid.*
38. Cited *ibid.*, p. 163.
39. *Ibid.*, p. 286.
40. Alistair Mason, *SSM. History of the Society of the Sacred Mission* (Norwich: Canterbury Press, 1993), p. 97.
41. *Ibid.*, p. 95.
42. Nicolas Zernov, *Sunset Years. A Russian Pilgrim in the West* (London: Fellowship of St Alban and St Sergius, 1983), p. 14.
43. *Ibid.*, p. 30.
44. *Ibid.*, p. 15.
45. Zernov, *The History of the Fellowship of St Alban and St Sergius*, p. 4.
46. Zernov, *The Russian Religious Renaissance of the Twentieth Century*, pp. 226–9. These European Conferences continued at intervals until the Second World War despite the emergence of opposition to Protestant patronage on the part of conservative Russian hierarchs in exile: *ibid.*, pp. 229–41.

47. See Donald Lowrie, *St Sergius in Paris. The Orthodox Theological Institute* (London: SPCK, 1954); Alexis Kniazeff, *L'Institut Saint-Serge. De l'académie d'autrefois au rayonnement d'aujourd'hui* (Paris: Beauchesne, 1974).
48. Matthew L. Miller, *The American YMCA and Russian Culture: The Preservation and Expansion of Orthodox Christianity, 1900–1940* (Plymouth: Lexington Books, 2013).
49. Paul Anderson, 'The Fellowship's Origins: A Charter Member's Notes', *Sobornost* 7/7 (1978), pp. 612–13, and here at p. 612.
50. Mason, SSM. *History of the Society of the Sacred Mission*, p. 106.
51. Nicolas Zernov, 'Dr G. G. Kullmann', *Sobornost* 4/7 (1962), pp. 464–5.
52. *Ibid.*, p. 465.
53. *Ibid.*, p. 466.
54. Nicolas Zernov, 'A Page from the Past History of the Fellowship of St Alban and St Sergius', *Sobornost* 4/12 (1965), pp. 717–21.
55. *Ibid.*, p. 720.
56. Zernov, *Sunset Years*, p. 87.
57. Nicolas Zernov, 'Zoe Fairfield (April 23rd, 1878 – December 9th, 1936)', *Sobornost* 1/10 (1937), pp. 38–40 and here at p. 39.
58. Wilkinson, *The Community of the Resurrection*, p. 25.
59. Andrew Blane, 'A Sketch of the Life of Georges Florovsky', in his (ed.) *Georges Florovsky. Russian Intellectual, Orthodox Churchman* (Crestwood, NY: St Vladimir's Seminary Press, 1991), pp. 11–218, and here at p. 59.
60. *Ibid.*, p. 64, with a concluding oral quotation from Blane's conversations with Florovsky at Princeton.
61. Zernov, *The History of the Fellowship of St Alban and St Sergius*, p. 5.
62. *Ibid.*, pp. 6–7.
63. Nicolas Zernov, in C. S. Phillips *et al.*, *Walter Howard Frere. A Memoir* (London: Faber & Faber, 1947), pp. 187–8.
64. *Ibid.*, pp. 185–6. W. H. Frere, *English Church Ways* (London: John Murray, 1914); W. H. Frere, 'The Life of the Anglican Church' (in Russian) (Paris: YMCA Press, 1930).
65. Nicolas Zernov, in Phillips *et al.*, *Walter Howard Frere*, p. 190.
66. Alan Wilkinson, 'A Biographical Sketch', in Benjamin Gordon-Taylor and Nicolas Stebbingm CR (ed.), *Walter Frere. Scholar, Monk, Bishop* (Norwich: Canterbury Press, 2011), pp. 18–19, citing the *Church Times* for 19 June 1914. Frere wrote of the Orthodox East, 'The lex orandi is more wholly treated as the equivalent of the lex credenda here than elsewhere: partly because it is essentially a worshipping Church, and partly because it has never been forced to make confessions of faith', cited in Wilkinson, 'A Biographical Sketch', p. 27.
67. John S. Peart-Binns, *Ambrose Reeves* (London: Gollancz, 1973).

Notes to Part I, Chapter 2

68. On this figure, see E. L. Mascall, *Saraband. The Memoirs of E. L. Mascall* (Leominster: Gracewing, 1992), pp. 166–9; Mason, SSM. *Society of the Sacred Mission*, pp. 162–88.
69. Mascall, *Saraband*, p. 80.
70. *Ibid.*, p. 81.
71. Bell, *Randall Davidson, Archbishop of Canterbury*, II., p. 1113. Given his fierce reputation as an ultra-conservative, Khrapovitsky's presence was surprising; it is explained in Andrei V. Psarev, '"The soul and heart of a faithful Englishman is not limited by utilitarian goals and plans": The Relations of Metropolitan Anthony Khrapovitskii with the Anglican Church', *Sobornost/ECR* 33/2 (2011), pp. 28–53.
72. Mascall, *Saraband*, p. 82.
73. *Ibid.*, p. 97.
74. He commented, 'as I had never had any academic training in theology at all, all my equipment as a theologian really consists of what I was able to acquire for myself during my eight years in Lincoln', *ibid.*, p. 120. His Cambridge BD was awarded for his 1942 publication *He Who Is*. He ascribed to his consequent reputation as a Thomist his lack of ecclesiastical preferment, *ibid.*, pp. 125, 147.
75. For Mascall's comments on some leading figures of the Fellowship (Zernov, Ramsey, Frere, Gore, Bulgakov, Florovsky, Berdyaev (with mentions, in the context of an account of the Institu Saint-Serge, of Arseniev, Fedotov, Kartashev, Weidlé, Zander), see *ibid.*, pp. 82–4. A point that intellectual historians might overlook lies in the statement that the Fellowship 'played its part in providing many of the Anglican priests who belonged to it with Russian Orthodox wives', *ibid.*, p. 84.
76. *Ibid.*, p. 190.
77. Grevel Lindop, *Charles Williams. The Third Inkling* (Oxford University Press, 2015), p. 301.
78. Anderson to Zernov, 23 October 1935, Archives of the Fellowship of St Alban and St Sergius.
79. *Journal of the Fellowship of St Alban and St Sergius* 1 (1928), p. 3.
80. *Ibid.*, p. 3a.

Notes to Chapter 2

1. 'Editorial', *Journal of the Fellowship of St Alban and St Sergius* 14 (1931), p. 4.
2. Canon T. Tatlow, 'The Russian Student Christian Movement in Emigration', *ibid.* 13 (1931), pp. 11–13.
3. Editorial, *ibid.* 12 (1931), p. 1.
4. 'Bishop Gore', *ibid.* 15 (1932), pp. 6–8, and here at p. 7.
5. *Ibid.*
6. Zernov to Meletios, 27 July 1932, Archives of the Fellowship of St Alban and St Sergius.

7. 'Fellowship of St Alban and St Sergius, Statements of Aims and Basis', *Journal of the Fellowship of St Alban and St Sergius* 19 (1933), p. 35.
8. Editorial, *Sobornost* 1/1 (1935), p. 3.
9. V. Illiin, 'The Nature and the Meaning of the Term "Sobornost", *Sobornost* 1 (1935), pp. 5-7, and here at p. 6.
10. *Ibid.*, p. 7.
11. *Sobornost* 1/7 (1936), p. 40.
12. Rowan Williams, 'Theology and the Churches', in Robin Gill and Lorna Kendall (ed.), *Michael Ramsey as Theologian* (London: Darton, Longman & Todd, 1995), pp. 9-28, and here at p. 13. Williams was referring to Ramsey's single most influential work, *The Gospel and the Catholic Church* (London: Longmans, Green and Co., 1936).
13. Owen Chadwick, *Michael Ramsey. A Life* (Oxford: Clarendon Press, 1990), p. 288.
14. *Sobornost* 1/7 (1936), p. 41.
15. 'The Theological Task of the Fellowship', *Sobornost* 9 (1937), pp. 35-7, and here at p. 36.
16. *Ibid.*, p. 37.
17. Zernov, *The History of the Fellowship of St Alban and St Sergius*, p. 10.
18. Sergius Bulgakov, 'Hoc signo vinces', *Sobornost* 1/21 (1940), pp. 24-6, and here at p. 26.
19. *Ibid.*
20. Zernov, *The History of the Fellowship of St Alban and St Sergius*, p. 10.
21. *Ibid.*
22. *Sobornost* 21 (1940), p. 2.
23. Nicolas Zernov, 'The Eucharist of the Eastern Rite and the Anglican Church', *Sobornost* 1/23 (1941), pp. 20-3.
24. *Sobornost* 24 (1941), pp. 5-6.
25. 'Memorandum on the Report of Father Alexis on the Need for an Orthodox Centre in England', in *Sobornost* 1/25 (1942), pp. 23-4, and here at p. 23.
26. *Ibid.*
27. *Ibid.*, p. 24.
28. 1942 was the first year when the Fellowship held a retreat (corporate guided retreats were a novelty for the Orthodox, the practice derived from Latin Catholicism); they would continue, with alternating Orthodox and Anglican leaders, at the House of Retreat, Pleshey, near Chelmsford in Essex.
29. Irina Findlow, *Journey into Unity* (New York and London: New City, 1975), pp. 13-14.
30. A full obituary appeared in *Sobornost* 6/2 (1970), pp. 121-4.
31. Zernov, *The History of the Fellowship of St Alban and St Sergius*, p. 11.

32. Sergius Bulgakov, *Apokalipsis Ioanna: opyt dogmaticheskago istolkavaniia* (Paris: YMCA, 1948).
33. *Sobornost* 1/34 (1946), p. 2.
34. Lev Gillet, 'Metropolitan Evlogi', *Sobornost* 1/34 (1946), pp. 4–7, and here at p. 6.
35. For a characterization, see Wilkinson, *The Community of the Resurrection*, p. 189.
36. A. M. Allchin, 'Herbert Arthur Hodges', *Sobornost* 7/4 (1977), pp. 306–8.
37. Mascall, *Saraband*, p. 186.
38. See for this figure Edward Every, 'Derwas Chitty as an Ecumenist', in Doll (ed.), *Anglicanism and Orthodoxy*, pp. 355–64.
39. Derwas Chitty, *Orthodoxy and the Conversion of England* (n. p., n. d.), p. 2.
40. *Ibid.*, p. 5.
41. *Ibid.*, pp. 5–6.
42. *Ibid.*, p. 6.
43. *Ibid.*, p. 7.
44. *Ibid.*
45. *Ibid.*
46. *Ibid.*, p. 9.
47. *Ibid.*, p. 10.
48. *Ibid.*, p. 17.
49. 'Nikolai Berdyaev, 1874–1948', *Sobornost* 3/3 (1948), pp. 77–80, and here at p. 77.
50. Nicholas Berdiaev, *Dostoevsky* (Cleveland: World Publishing Company, 1957).
51. George Every, SSM, 'Background to Berdyaev', *Sobornost* 3/3 (1948), pp. 105–8, and here at p. 106.
52. *Ibid.*, p. 108.
53. Germanos of Thyateira, 'Dedication of St Basil's Chapel. Address by the Honorary Orthodox President of the Fellowship', *Sobornost* 3/6 (1949), pp. 225–7, and here at p. 226, with an internal citation of John 17:21.
54. *Ibid.*
55. Lev Gillet, 'Our Lady of Walsingham', *Sobornost* 3/6 (1949), pp. 240–4, and here at p. 243.
56. E. I. Watkin, *Catholic Art and Culture* (London: Hollis and Carter, 1947), pp. 177–8, cited Gillet, 'Our Lady of Walsingham', pp. 243–4.
57. Gillet, 'Our Lady of Walsingham', p. 244.
58. *Ibid.*
59. Nicolas Zernov, 'The Aims of the Fellowship', *Sobornost* 3/10 (1951), pp. 456–61, and here at p. 457.

60. *Ibid.*
61. Hugh McLeod, *The Religious Crisis of the 1960s* (Oxford: Oxford University Press, 2007), pp. 29–30.
62. Zernov, 'The Aims of the Fellowship', p. 457.
63. Various authors, *Catholicity. A Study in the Conflict of Christian Traditions in the West, being a Report Presented to his Grace the Archbishop of Canterbury* (London: Faith Press, 1947).
64. Zernov, 'The Aims of the Fellowship', p. 458.
65. Helle Giorgiadis, 'Secretary's Report', *Sobornost* 3/10 (1951), p. 479.
66. *Sobornost* 3/14 (1953), p. 58.
67. *Ibid.*, p. 59.
68. *Ibid.*
69. Raymond Raynes, CR, and others to the secretary, 9 January 1952, Archives of the Fellowship of St Alban and St Sergius.
70. Nicolas Zernov, 'Walter Frere and the Russian Church', in Phillips, *Walter Howard Frere*, ch. xi.
71. C. B. Moss, *What Do We Mean by Reunion? A Reply to 'Problems of Reunion' by the Bishop of Derby* (London: SPCK, 1953).
72. *Sobornost* 3/14 (1953), p. 90.
73. *Ibid.*, p. 100.
74. *Ibid.*, pp. 100–1.
75. Minutes of 10 May 1954, Archives of the Fellowship of St Alban and St Sergius.
76. Zernov to Mascall, 23 April 1955, Archives of the Fellowship of St Alban and St Sergius.
77. Mascall to Zernov, 27 March 1955, Archives of the Fellowship of St Alban and St Sergius.
78. Nicolas Zernov, 'The Ways of the Fellowship, 1928–1958', *Sobornost* 4/24 (1959), pp. 636–42, and here at p. 641.
79. Barnabas Lindars to Zernov, 18 September 1959, Archives of the Fellowship of St Alban and St Sergius.
80. Lawrence to Charles Wright, 12 May 1959, Archives of the Fellowship of St Alban and St Sergius.
81. *Sobornost* 4/3 (1960), p. 156.
82. *Ibid.* 4/2 (1960), p. 50.
83. Philip Sherrard, *The Greek East and the Latin West* (London: Oxford University Press, 1959).
84. *Sobornost* 4/3 (1960), p. 140.
85. Michael Ramsey, 'Holiness, Truth and Unity', *Sobornost* 4/4 (1961), pp. 159–65, and here at p. 161.

86. *Ibid.*, p. 162.
87. *Ibid.*
88. *Sobornost* 4/1 (1960), p. 95.
89. *Ibid.*
90. *Ibid.*
91. *Sobornost* 4/3 (1960), p. 156.
92. Zernov, *The History of the Fellowship of St Alban and St Sergius*, p. 16.
93. *Ibid.*
94. Andrew Louth, 'Biographical Sketch', in John Behr, Andrew Louth and Dimitri Conomos (ed.), *Abba. The Tradition of Orthodoxy in the West. Festschrift for Bishop Kallistos (Ware) of Diokleia* (Crestwood, NY: St Vladimir's Seminary Press, 2003), pp. 9–27. See also the bibliography of his writings, *ibid.*, pp. 363–76.
95. Nicolas and Militza Zernov, *The History of the Fellowship of St Alban and St Sergius*, p. 19.
96. *Ibid.*
97. *Sobornost* 5/4 (1966), p. 226.
98. Olivier Clément, 'Purification by Atheism', *ibid.* 5/4 (1966), pp. 232–48.
99. D. W. Allen, 'Orthodox and the New Reformation', *ibid.* 5/4 (1966), pp. 227–32, and here at p. 229.
100. *Ibid.* For Afanas'ev, see Aidan Nichols, OP, *Theology in the Russian Diaspora. Church, Fathers, Eucharist in Nikolai Afanas'ev, 1893–1966* (Cambridge: Cambridge University Press, 1989); on Schmemann, see John Meyendorff, 'A Life worth Living', in Thomas Fisch (ed.), *Liturgy and Tradition. Theological Reflections of Alexander Schmemann* (Crestwood, NY: St Vladimir's Seminary Press, 2003), pp. 145–54.
101. Nadejda Gorodetzky, *The Humiliated Christ in Modern Russian Thought* (London: SPCK, 1938).

Notes to Chapter 3

1. Nicolas Zernov, 'Professor George Fedotov', *Sobornost* 3/10 (1951), pp. 462–3, and here at p. 462.
2. *Ibid.*, p. 463.
3. George Fedotov, 'The Russian Church. A Short Historical Sketch. Part I. The Pre-Mongolian Period', *Sobornost* 1/1 (1935), pp. 23–9, and here at p. 27.
4. *Ibid.*, p. 23.
5. *Ibid.*, p. 26.
6. *Ibid.*, p. 28.

7. G. Fedotov, 'The Russian Church. II. The Mongolian and Moscovite Period', *Sobornost* 1/3 (1935), pp. 30–9, and here at p. 31. 'Eurasianism' has since interested Western historians of Russian intellectual history, as in Otto Böss, *Die Lehre der Eurasier. Ein Beitrag zur russichen Ideengeschichte des 20. Jahrhunderts* (Wiesbaden: Veröffentlichungen des Osteuropa Instituts München, 1961); Marlène Laruelle, *Russian Eurasianism: An Ideology of Empire* (Baltimore, MD: Johns Hopkins University Press, 2008) which includes an account of Neo-Eurasianism in Russia today.
8. Fedotov, 'The Russian Church. II. The Mongolian and Moscovite Period', p. 31.
9. *Ibid.*, p. 33.
10. *Ibid.*, p. 34.
11. *Ibid.*, p. 35.
12. *Ibid.*, p. 37.
13. *Ibid.*
14. *Ibid.*, p. 39.
15. G. Fedotov, 'The Russian Church (A Historical Sketch) The Synodical period—the Eighteenth and Nineteenth Centuries', *Sobornost* 1/4 (1935), pp. 16–23.
16. *Ibid.*, p. 22.
17. George Fedotov, 'The Russian Church (A Historical Sketch). IV. The Two Revolutions and the Great War', *Sobornost* 1/5 (1936), pp. 23–9, and here at p. 25.
18. *Ibid.*, p. 26.
19. *Ibid.*, p. 28.
20. Nicolas Zernov, 'The Russian Church Thirty Years Ago', *Sobornost* 1/4 (1935), pp. 7–16.
21. This would be the subject of James W. Cunningham, *A Vanquished Hope. The Movement for Church Renewal in Russia 1905–6* (Crestwood, NY: St Vladimir's Seminary Press, 1981).
22. A magisterial study appeared in the early twenty-first century, Hyacinthe Destivelle, *Le Concile de Moscou (1917–1918): La Création des institutions conciliares de l'Église orthodoxe russe* (Paris: Cerf, 2006).
23. The reality of those hardships is highlighted by recent historians: see Robert C. Williams, *Culture in Exile: Russian Emigrés in Germany, 1881–1941* (Ithaca, NY: Cornell University Press, 1972); Robert H. Johnston, *New Mecca, New Babylon: Paris and the Russian Exiles, 1920–1945* (Kingston and Montreal: McGill-Queen's University Press, 1988); Marc Raeff, *Russia Abroad. A Cultural History of the Russian Emigration, 1919–1939* (New York: Oxford University Press, 1990).
24. I. Lagovsky, 'World Godlessness', *Journal of the Fellowship of St Alban and St Sergius* 11 (1931), pp. 38–42, and here at p. 38.
25. George Fedotov, 'The Russian Church (A Historical Sketch) V. The Revolution and After', *Sobornost* 1/6 (1936), pp. 21–7, and here at p. 24.
26. *Ibid.*, p. 25.

27. Ibid., p. 27.
28. Leo Zander, 'Light of Suffering', *Sobornost* 1/12 (1937), pp. 18–20, and here at p. 18.
29. Ibid., p. 19.
30. Ibid., p. 20.
31. Paul B. Anderson, 'New Soviet Anti-Religious Legislation', *Sobornost* 1/12 (1937), pp. 33–7, and here at p. 36.
32. 'An Anglican Archbishop and Russia', *Sobornost* 1/20 (1939), pp. 39–40.
33. Metropolitan Visarion, 'The Christian Faith in the Soviet State', *Sobornost* 1/20 (1939), pp. 16–21.
34. 'The Truth about Religion in Russia' *Sobornost* 1/31 (1945), pp. 23–6, and here at p. 23.
35. Ibid., p. 24.
36. Nicolas Zernov, 'The Restoration of the Patriarchate in Moscow', *Sobornost* 1/28 (1943), pp. 7–10, and here at p. 8.
37. Rawlinson to Zernov, 17 September 1943, Archives of the Fellowship of St Alban and St Sergius.
38. Walter Kolarz, 'Russian Protestants and the Soviet Government', *Sobornost* 3/17 (1955), pp. 243–56, and here at p. 253.
39. Philippe Sabant, 'Intellectual Life of the Russian Church', *Sobornost* 5/2 (1966), pp. 107–15, and here at p. 113.
40. Richard Rutt, 'The Orthodox Church of Korea', *Sobornost* 3/21 (1957), pp. 480–90, and here at p. 487.
41. Maria Kullmann, 'My Meetings with the Holy Women of the Russian Diaspora. The Nuns of Khopovo Convent', *Sobornost* 5/8 (1969), pp. 580–5.
42. Maria Kullmann, 'Meetings in Serbia: Mother Diodora's Convent', *Sobornost* 6/1 (1970), pp. 43–8, and here at p. 48.
43. Paul Verghese, 'The Christology of the Non-Chalcedonian Churches', *Sobornost* 4/5 (1961), pp. 248–57.
44. Peter Hammond, *The Waters of Marah. The Present State of the Greek Church* (London: Rockcliff, 1956).
45. Peter Hammond, 'A Greek Festival', *Sobornost* 3/6 (1949), pp. 247–53, and here at p. 248.
46. Ibid., p. 252.
47. Ibid.
48. Peter Hammond, 'A Thessalian Thebaid', *Sobornost* 3/8 (1950), pp. 338–42, and here at p. 342.
49. Timothy Ware, 'Between Heaven and Earth: Some Notes on Contemporary Greek Monasticism', *Sobornost* 4/7 (1962), pp. 398–408, and here at p. 399.
50. Sister Theodora Hambaki, 'Orthodox Monasticism for Women', *Sobornost* 4/7 (1962), pp. 408–10.

Notes to Chapter 4

1. G. W. O. Addleshaw, 'Our Domestic Difficulties', *Sobornost* 1/11 (1937), pp. 22–31, and here at p. 23.
2. *Ibid.*
3. *Ibid.*, p. 25.
4. *Ibid.*
5. *Ibid.*
6. *Ibid.*, p. 28.
7. *Ibid.*, p. 30.
8. *Ibid.*, p. 29.
9. *Ibid.*, p. 31.
10. A. G. H. [Gabriel Hebert, S. S. M.], 'The Holy Eucharist', *Journal of the Fellowship of St Alban and St Sergius* 4 (1929), pp. 4–7.
11. *Ibid.*, p. 7.
12. G. A. C. Whatton, *The Priest's Companion. A Manual of Prayers and Instructions for Priests and Religious* (London: Knott, 1946).
13. G. A. C. Whatton, 'Anglican Ritual Variations—An Explanation', *Journal of the Fellowship of St Alban and St Sergius* 6 (1936), pp. 16–19, and here at p. 17.
14. *Ibid.*, p. 18.
15. *Ibid.* 7 (1936), pp. 36–7.
16. Basil Jellicoe, 'Knights of the Holy Table', *Journal of the Fellowship of St Alban and St Sergius* 4 (1929), pp. 18–21. For a brief characterization of Jellicoe, see Kenneth Hylson-Smith, *High Churchmanship in the Church of England. From the Sixteenth Century to the Late Twentieth Century* (Edinburgh: T. & T. Clark, 1993), p. 286.
17. Humphrey Green, 'The Eucharist in Anglican Controversy: Catholic and Evangelical', *Sobornost* 3/18 (1955), pp. 287–304, and here at p. 287.
18. *Ibid.*, p. 289.
19. C. W. Dugmore, *Eucharistic Doctrine in England from Hooker to Waterland* (London: SPCK, 1940).
20. Green, 'The Eucharist in Anglican Controversy', p. 289.
21. *Ibid.*, p. 290.
22. *Ibid.*, p. 292.
23. *Ibid.*, p. 296.
24. Gregory Dix, *The Shape of the Liturgy* (Westminster: Dacre Press, 1944).
25. Green, 'The Eucharist in Anglican Controversy', p. 303.
26. Herbert Kelly, SMM, 'The Resurrection', *Journal of the Fellowship of St Alban and St Sergius* 5, pp. 18–22, and here at p. 18.

Notes to Part I, Chapter 4

27. Ibid., p. 19.
28. Mason, *SSM. Society of the Sacred Mission*, pp. 54–5, 59.
29. Ibid., p. 73.
30. Ibid., pp. 78–85.
31. Owen Chadwick, *Hensley Henson. A Study in the Friction between Church and State* (Norwich: Canterbury Press, 1994 [1983]), pp. 204–5. Chadwick suggests fear of a Socialist prime minister (with control of major Church appointments) was a further cause, though such anxieties were confided to his private journal.
32. Ibid., p. 203.
33. Ibid., p. 218.
34. [Herbert Hensley Henson], 'The Church and the Modern State', *Journal of the Fellowship of St Alban and St Sergius* 11 (1931), pp. 6–14, and here at pp. 10–11.
35. Ibid., p. 11, with a reference to Isaiah 49:23.
36. Ibid., p. 13.
37. Ibid., p. 14.
38. See John S. Peart-Binns, *Maurice Reckitt. A Life* (Basingstoke: Bowerdean Press, 1988).
39. Maurice Reckitt, 'A Dual Allegiance', *Journal of the Fellowship of St Alban and St Sergius* 11 (1931), pp. 20–30, and here at p. 21.
40. Ibid., p. 22.
41. Ibid., p. 23.
42. Ibid.
43. William Temple, *Christianity and the State* (London: Macmillan, 1928), pp. 89–90.
44. Cited in Reckitt, 'A Dual Allegiance', pp. 25–6.
45. John Kent, *William Temple: Church, State and Society in Britain, 1880–1950* (Cambridge: Cambridge University Press, 1992), p. 115.
46. Ibid., p. 28.
47. Ibid., p. 29.
48. Barry Spurr, 'Anglo-Catholic in Religion'. *T. S. Eliot and Christianity* (Cambridge: Lutterworth Press, 2010), pp. 174–202.
49. H. L. Goudge, 'Authority and Freedom in the Church', *Journal of the Fellowship of St Alban and St Sergius* 12 (1931), pp. 32–43, and here at p. 37.
50. Ibid.
51. Ibid., p. 40.
52. Jasper, *Arthur Cayley Headlam*, pp. 222–4.
53. Mascall, *Saraband*, p. 89. His engaging account of the visit with the chaplain of St Catherine's College, Cambridge, Christopher Waddams occupies pp. 85–9; see also the version in *Sobornost* 1/12 (1937).

54. Jasper, *Arthur Cayley Headlam*, pp. 232–3.
55. Paul B. Anderson, *People, Church and State in Modern Russia* (London: SCM, 1944).
56. Cited *Sobornost* 1/29 (1944), p. 21.
57. Ivan Young, 'Brooke Foss Westcott (1825–1901)', *Sobornost* 1/6 (1936), pp. 34–41, and here at p. 35.
58. Cited *ibid.*, p. 37.
59. Cited *ibid.*, p. 39.
60. Cited *ibid.*, p. 40. For his thought, see Folke Oloffson, *Christus redemptor et consummator. A Study in the Theology of B. F. Westcott* (Uppsala: Studia Doctrinae Christianae Upsaliensis, 1979).
61. G. P. Fedotov, 'Meeting the English', *Sobornost* 1/12 (1937), pp. 11–16, and here at p. 12.
62. *Ibid.*
63. *Ibid.*, p. 13.
64. *Ibid.*, p. 14.
65. *Ibid.*, p. 15.
66. *Ibid.*
67. Cited in Kent, *William Temple*, p. 35.

Notes to Chapter 5

1. Metropolitan Evlogy, 'Christ is risen!', *Journal of the Fellowship of St Alban and St Sergius* 5 (1929), pp. 13–15.
2. *Ibid.*, p. 14.
3. *Ibid.*, p. 13.
4. 'Sermon Preached by Fr. Sergius Boulgakoff at the Anglo-Russian Conference', *Journal of the Fellowship of St Alban and St Sergius* 9 (1930), pp. 8–10.
5. George Florovsky, 'Abundance of Glory', *Journal of the Fellowship of St Alban and St Sergius* 9 (1930), pp. 10–15, and here at pp. 11–12.
6. Cited *ibid.*, p. 12.
7. *Ibid.*, pp. 13, 14.
8. *Ibid.*, p. 14.
9. *Ibid.*
10. *Ibid.*
11. Sergius Bulgakov, 'A Note on Pentecost', *Journal of the Fellowship of St Alban and St Sergius* 9 (1930) pp. 27–31 and here at pp. 27, 28.
12. *Ibid.*, p. 28.

Notes to Part I, Chapter 5

13. Ibid.
14. Ibid., pp. 28–9.
15. Ibid., p. 29.
16. Ibid.
17. Ibid., pp. 34, 34–5.
18. F. L. Cross, 'Repentance', *Journal of the Fellowship of St Alban and St Sergius* 8 (1930), pp. 7–8b, and here at p. 7.
19. Ibid., p. 8.
20. Metropolitan Benjamin, 'Repentance in the Orthodox Faith [Confession]', *Journal of the Fellowship of St Alban and St Sergius* 8 (1930), pp. 9–14, and here at p. 13.
21. L. Gage-Brown, 'The Importance of Sacramental Confession in the Christian Life', *Journal of the Fellowship of St Alban and St Sergius* 8 (1930), pp. 15–17, and here at p. 16.
22. Ibid., p. 17.
23. Ibid., p. 16.
24. Militza Zernova, 'The Sacrament of Confession', *Sobornost* 1/31 (1945), pp. 13–20, and here at p. 13.
25. Ibid., p. 19.
26. Ibid., p. 17.
27. Ibid., p. 18.
28. Lev Gillet, 'Redemption by Christ according to the Belief of the Orthodox Church', *Journal of the Fellowship of St Alban and St Sergius* 8 (1930), pp. 18–20, and here at p. 18.
29. Ibid.;
30. Ibid., p. 19.
31. Ibid.
32. Ibid.
33. Ibid., p. 20.
34. Archpriest Sergius Tchetverikoff, 'The Great Fast (Lent) in the Orthodox Church', *Journal of the Fellowship of St Alban and St Sergius* 8 (1930), pp. 26–9.
35. Ibid., p. 29.
36. George Florovsky, 'On the Prize of the High Calling', *Journal of the Fellowship of St Alban and St Sergius* 11 (1931), pp. 32–7, and here at p. 33.
37. Ibid., p. 34.
38. Ibid., p. 35.
39. Oscar Hardman, *The Ideals of Asceticism. An Essay in the Comparative Study of Religion* (London: SPCK, 1924); Oscar Hardman, *Psychology and the Church* (London: Macmillan, 1927).

40. Oscar Hardman, 'What is Asceticism?', *Journal of the Fellowship of St Alban and St Sergius* 14 (1931), pp. 14–16, and here at p. 14.
41. *Ibid.*
42. *Ibid.*, p. 15.
43. *Ibid.*, p. 16.
44. George Florovsky, 'Asceticism and Culture in the Later Eastern Church', *Journal of the Fellowship of St Alban and St Sergius* 15 (1932), pp. 8–13.
45. *Ibid.*, p. 10.
46. *Ibid.*
47. *Ibid.*, pp. 10–11.
48. *Ibid.*, p. 11.
49. *Ibid.*
50. *Ibid.*
51. *Ibid.*, p. 12.
52. *Ibid.*, p. 13.
53. G. Fedotov, 'Asceticism (Askesis) and Culture in Russian Orthodoxy', *Journal of the Fellowship of St Alban and St Sergius* 15 (1932), pp. 19–21, and here at p. 19.
54. *Ibid.*
55. *Ibid.*, p. 20.
56. *Ibid.*, p. 21.
57. H. J. Carpenter, 'Some Tendencies in Asceticism and Culture in the Reformation and Post-Reformation Period', *Journal of the Fellowship of St Alban and St Sergius* 15 (1932), pp. 14–18, and here at p. 15.
58. *Ibid.*
59. *Ibid.*, p. 16.
60. *Ibid.*
61. *Ibid.*, p. 18.
62. Bede Frost, OSB, 'Asceticism and Culture in Christian Life Today', *Journal of the Fellowship of St Alban and St Sergius* 15 (1932), pp. 22–5, and here at p. 23.
63. *Ibid.*, p. 25.
64. Lev Gillet, 'Contemplation', *Sobornost* 1/23 (1941), pp. 24–7.
65. See H. A. and V. Hodges, 'The Revd. Gilbert Shaw', *Sobornost* 5/6 (1968), pp. 451–4.
66. Gilbert Shaw, 'Simplicity in Prayer' in *Sobornost* 3/9 (1951), pp. 382–94, and here at p. 383.
67. *Ibid.*
68. *Ibid.*
69. *Ibid.*, p. 385.

70. *Ibid.*, p. 391.
71. *Ibid.*, p. 388.
72. *Ibid.*
73. *Ibid.*
74. *Ibid.*, p. 392.
75. *Ibid.*
76. *Ibid.*
77. *Ibid.*
78. *Ibid.*, p. 393.
79. Cited *ibid.*
80. See Vladimir Lossky and Nicolas Arseniev, *La Paternité spirituelle en Russie au XVIIIème et XIXème siècles* (Bellefontaine: Abbaye de Bellefontaine, 1977).
81. Sergius Tchetverikoff, 'The Hermitage of Optino and its Elders', *Journal of the Fellowship of St Alban and St Sergius* 5 (1929), pp. 29–41, and here at p. 29.
82. *Ibid.*, p. 39.
83. Austin Oakley, 'Orthodox Spirituality', *Sobornost* 3/20 (1956), pp. 412–15, and here at p. 413.
84. *Ibid.*, p. 414. On those novels see Glen Cavallero, *Charles Williams. Poet of Theology* (London and Basingstoke: Macmillan, 1983), pp. 54–96.
85. Oakley, 'Orthodox Spirituality', p. 415.
86. G. Fedotov, 'On the Sacraments', *Journal of the Fellowship of St Alban and St Sergius* 25 (1934), pp. 35–9.
87. *Ibid.*, p. 36.
88. *Ibid.*, p. 38.
89. *Ibid.*
90. *Ibid.*, p. 39.
91. *Ibid.*
92. Vladimir Lossky, *The Mystical Theology of the Eastern Church* (London: James Clarke, 1957), pp. 227–9.
93. Timothy Ware, 'The Transfiguration of the Body', *Sobornost* 4/8 (1963), pp. 420–34, and here at p. 432.
94. *Ibid.*
95. Boris Bobrinskoy, 'Nicholas Cabasilas and Hesychast Spirituality', *Sobornost* 5/7 (1968), pp. 483–510, and here at p. 501.
96. N. S. Arseniev, 'The Eucharist and the Unity of the Church', *Journal of the Fellowship of St Alban and St Sergius* 4 (1929), pp. 8–16, and here at p. 8.
97. *Ibid.*
98. *Ibid.*, p. 9.

99. N. V. Gogol, *Meditations on the Divine Liturgy of the Holy Eastern Orthodox Catholic and Apostolic Church* (New York: Holy Trinity Monastery, 1952).
100. Arseniev, 'The Eucharist and the Unity of the Church', p. 9.
101. Ibid., p. 11.
102. Ibid., p. 12.
103. Ibid., p. 13.
104. Ibid., p. 14.
105. Ibid.
106. Nicolas Arseniev, *Mysticism and the Eastern Church* (London: Mowbray, 1964 [1926]).
107. Nicolas Arseniev, *Holy Moscow* (London: SPCK, 1940); *Russian Piety* (London: Faith Press, 1964).
108. Nicolas Zernov, 'Nikolai Arseniev (1888–1977), *Sobornost* 7/7 (1978), p. 616.
109. Georges Florovsky, 'On the Veneration of the Saints', *Journal of the Fellowship of St Alban and St Sergius* 2 (1928), pp. 14–18.
110. Ibid., p. 14.
111. Ibid., p. 15.
112. Ibid.
113. Ibid.
114. Ibid.
115. Ibid., p. 16.
116. Ibid.
117. Ibid.
118. Ibid., p. 17.
119. V. Illiin, 'Introduction to the Life of St Seraphim of Saroff', *Journal of the Fellowship of St Alban and St Sergius* 13 (1931), pp. 14–16, and here at p. 16. Polymath and composer, disciple of Bulgakov, former Eurasian, Illiin rallied to the Third Reich and was shunned by émigré associations in post-War Paris. For a synopsis of his turbulent life, see Antoine Arjakovsky, *La Génération des penseurs religieux de l'émigration russe. La revue 'La Voie' (Put')*, 1925–1940 (Kiev and Paris: L'Ésprit et la Lettre, 2002), pp. 645–6. Illiin's life of St Seraphim, published in 1925, gained him his place in the teaching body of the Institut Saint-Serge.
120. W. M. Whitley, 'The Intercession of the Saints', *Journal of the Fellowship of St Alban and St Sergius* 13 (1931), pp. 17–22, and here at p. 19.
121. Ibid.
122. Ibid., p. 21.
123. Anon., 'On the Veneration of Saints and on Calling to them in Prayer', *Journal of the Fellowship of St Alban and St Sergius* 13 (1931), pp 22–5, and here at p. 23.

Notes to Part I, Chapter 6

124. Militza Zernov, 'The Mystery of Death', *Sobornost* 1/13 (1938), pp. 25–30, and here at p. 25.
125. *Ibid.*, p. 26.
126. *Ibid.*, p. 27.
127. *Ibid.*, p. 28.
128. *Ibid.*
129. *Ibid.*
130. *Ibid.*, p. 29.

Notes to Chapter 6

1. E. N. Trubetskoy, *Icons: Theology in Color* (Crestwood, NY: St Vladimir's Seminary Press, 1973).
2. E. N. Trubetskoy, 'The Kingdom of God and the Kingdom of the beast', *Sobornost* 1/9 (1937), pp. 27–35, and here at p. 29.
3. *Ibid.*, p. 31.
4. Eric Prehn, 'The Development of Icon-painting in Russia', *Sobornost* 1/22 (1940), pp. 21–4.
5. Léonide Ouspensky, *La Théologie de l'icône dans l'Église orthodoxe* (Paris: Cerf, 1980); see on this figure, Patrick Doolan (ed.), *Recovering the Icon: The Life and Work of Leonid Ouspensky* (Crestwood, NY: St Vladimir's Seminary Press, 2008); also Paul Evdokimov, *L'Art de l'icône. Théologie de la beauté* (Paris: Desclée de Brouwer, 1970), on which see Peter C. Phan, *Culture and Eschatology. The Iconographical Vision of Paul Evdokimov* (New York: Peter Lang, 1985), chapter XIV.
6. Prehn, 'The Development of Icon-painting in Russia', p. 24.
7. Militza Zernov, 'The History of Creation of the Chapel at St Basil's House', undated, Archives of the Fellowship of St Alban and St Sergius.
8. See further on her work Irina Yazykova, *Hidden and Triumphant. The Underground Struggle to save Russian Iconography* (Brewster, MA: Paraclete Press, 2010), pp. 72–7.
9. Vladimir Lossky and Leonid Ouspensky, *The Meaning of Icons* (Boston, MA: Boston Book and Art Shop, 1952).
10. N. V. Lossky, 'The Place of Icons in the Church', *Sobornost* 3/6 (1949), pp. 238–41, and here at p. 239.
11. *Ibid.*
12. *Ibid.*, p. 240.
13. Vladimir Weidlé, *The Dilemma of the Arts* (London: SCM, 1948). For more on this figure and his thought, see Aidan Nichols, OP, 'Poetics in the Russian Diaspora', in his *Redeeming Wonder. Essays on Liturgy and the Arts* (Farnham: Ashgate, 2011), pp. 149–76.

14. *Sobornost* 3/7 (1950), p. 300.
15. *Ibid.*, p. 301.
16. L. H. Grondijs, *L'iconographie byzantine du Crucifié mort sur la Croix* (Brussels: Bibliotheca Byzantina Brucellensis, I. 1941).
17. Lev Gillet, 'Looking unto the Crucified Lord', *Sobornost* 3/13 (1953), pp. 24–33, and here at p. 25.
18. Though Gillet was always canonically correct in his obedience to Orthodox hierarchs, his even-handedness between Orthodox and Catholic traditions in Christianity led some to consider him a Uniate in disguise. The claim is considered and dismissed in Elisabeth Behr-Sigel, *Lev Gillet. 'A Monk of the Eastern Church'* (Oxford: Fellowship of St Alban and St Sergius, 1999), especially pp. 342–6.
19. Lev Gillet, 'Looking unto the Crucified Lord', p. 28.
20. *Ibid.*, pp. 29–30.
21. *Ibid.*, p. 30, footnote 2.
22. *Ibid.*, p. 31.
23. Nikolaus Pevsner, *The Buildings of England: London except the Cities of London and Westminster* (Harmondsworth: Penguin, 1952).
24. Derek Bowen, 'An Appearance of Byzantium', *ibid.* 3/20 (1956), pp. 416–22, and here at p. 420. The title of the essay was borrowed from the poet, novelist and critic Charles Williams.
25. Philip Sherrard, 'The Art of the Icon', *ibid.* 4/6 (1962), pp. 294–303, and here at p. 295.
26. *Ibid.*, p. 296.
27. *Ibid.*, p. 299.
28. *Ibid.*, p. 301.
29. *Ibid.*, p. 302.
30. *Ibid.*, p. 303.
31. *Ibid.*
32. *Ibid.*, p. 306.
33. *Ibid.*, p. 308.
34. *Ibid.*, p. 316.
35. Daphne Pochin Mould, 'The Sign of the Cross. The Orthodox Faith and the Irish High Cross' in *ibid.* 5/3 (1966), pp. 187–94, and here at p. 188.
36. For example, Joseph Raftery, 'Ex Oriente', *Journal of the Royal Society of Antiquaries of Ireland* 95 (1965), pp. 193–204.
37. Dennis Hickley, 'Time and Architecture in the Early Church', *Sobornost* 5/6 (1968), pp. 406–21, and here at p. 415.
38. *Ibid.*, p. 422.

Notes to Chapter 7

1. Anderson to Zernov, undated, Archives of the Fellowship of St Alban and St Sergius.
2. Zernov, *The Russian Religious Renaissance of the Twentieth Century*, p. 285.
3. Alexis van der Mensbrugghe, *From Dyad to Triad. A Plea for Duality against Dualism and an Essay towards the Synthesis of Orthodoxy* (London: Faith Press, 1934).
4. 'Correspondence', in *Sobornost* 1/5 (1936), pp. 20–2, and here at p. 21.
5. *Ibid*. A Thomist would agree with this though for a different reason. 'To speak as though the infinite being, God, and finite beings can be added together to make more than infinite being, with the result that one ends in self-contradiction, is to speak as though God and creatures were members of a genus. In reality they are incommensurable.' Thus F. C. Copleston, *Aquinas* (Harmondsworth: Penguin, 1955), p. 141.
6. 'Correspondence', *Sobornost* 1/5 (1936), p. 22.
7. Editorial, *Sobornost* 1/6 (1936), p. 2.
8. Sergius Bulgakov, 'Freedom of Thought in the Orthodox Church', *Sobornost* 1/6 (1936), pp. 4–9, and here at p. 5.
9. *Ibid*.
10. *Ibid*., p. 6.
11. *Ibid*.
12. *Ibid*., p. 7.
13. *Ibid*.
14. Serge Boulgakoff, *L'Orthodoxie* (Paris: Alcan, 1932); Serge Boulgakoff, *The Orthodox Church* (London: Centenary Press, 1935).
15. E. L. Mascall, '*The Orthodox Church*, by Sergius Bulgakov', *Sobornost* 1/6 (1936), pp. 32–3.
16. Editorial, *Sobornost* 1/7 (1936), p. 2.
17. Ignatius Loyola, Preface, *Spiritual Exercises*.
18. Lev Zander, *Bog i mir: mirosozertsanie ottsa Sergiia Bulgakova* (Paris: YMCA Press, 1948, two volumes).
19. Lev Zander, 'A Philosophical Discipleship', *Sobornost* 1/7 (1936), pp. 20–5, and here at p. 22.
20. *Ibid*.
21. *Ibid*.
22. *Ibid*., p. 23.
23. *Ibid*.
24. *Ibid*., p. 24.

25. *Ibid.*
26. *Ibid.*, p. 25.
27. *Ibid.*
28. 'Proceedings of the Conference at Mirfield between Anglican and Russian Orthodox Theologians', *Sobornost* 1/7 (1936), pp. 42–4, and here at p. 44.
29. Sergei Bulgakov, *The Wisdom of God. A Short Summary of Sophiology* (New York and London: Williams and Norgate, 1937).
30. *Sobornost* 1/12 (1937), p. 24.
31. Georgii Florovskii, *Puti russkago bogosloviia* (Paris: YMCA Press, 1937).
32. *Sobornost* 1/12 (1937), p. 26.
33. *Ibid.*
34. *Ibid.*, p. 27.
35. W. R. Matthews, *God in Christian Thought and Experience* (London: Nisbet, 1939 [1930]).
36. Thomas Parker, 'God and the World in the Light of the Doctrine of Creation', *Sobornost* 1/13 (1938), pp. 14–23, and here at p. 16.
37. *Ibid.*, p. 19.
38. *Ibid.*, p. 36.
39. *Ibid.*, p. 38.
40. For an overview of Bulgakov's theology as a whole, see Aidan Nichols, OP, *Wisdom from Above. A Primer in the Theology of Father Sergei Bulgakov* (Leominster: Gracewing, 2005).
41. Nicholas Berdiaev, *Spirit and Reality* (London: Geoffrey Bles, 1939).
42. *Sobornost* 1/19 (1939), p. 41.
43. Nicolas Zernov, *St Sergius, Builder of Russia* (London: Fellowship of St Alban and St Sergius with SPCK, 1939).
44. *Sobornost* 1/21 (1940), p. 36.
45. *Sobornost* 30 (1944), p. 6.
46. *Ibid.*, p. 8.
47. *Ibid.*
48. Leo Zander, 'In Memory of Father Sergius Bulgakov', *Sobornost* 1/32 (1945), pp. 5–12.
49. *Ibid.*, p. 6.
50. *Ibid.*, p. 12.
51. *Ibid.*

Notes to Chapter 8

1. Eric L. Mascall, 'Worship and Reason', *Journal of the Fellowship of St Alban and St Sergius* 2 (1928), pp. 18–21, and here at p. 18.
2. *Ibid.*, pp. 18–19.
3. *Ibid.*, p. 19.
4. Bertrand Russell, *The Analysis of Matter* (London: Kegan Paul, 1927). This needs to be carefully distinguished from the Thomist epistemology whose concept of 'turning to the phantasms' is far more sophisticated than anything found in British empiricism.
5. Mascall, 'Worship and Reason', p. 19.
6. *Ibid.*, p. 21.
7. *Ibid.*, p. 20.
8. *Ibid.*
9. *Ibid.*
10. Henry Balmforth, 'Tradition', *Sobornost* 3/10 (1951), pp. 425–31, and here at p. 427.
11. *Ibid.*, p. 426.
12. *Ibid.*
13. *Ibid.*, p. 429.
14. *Ibid.*, p. 430.
15. *Ibid.*
16. *Ibid.*, p. 431.
17. Cited *ibid.*
18. For his background, see Lewis Shaw, 'John Meyendorff and the Heritage of the Russian Theological Tradition', in Bradley Nassif (ed.), *New Perspectives on Historical Theology. Essays in Memory of John Meyendorff* (Grand Rapids, MI: Eerdmans, 1996), pp. 10–44.
19. Jean Meyendorff, 'The Sacrament of the Word', *Sobornost* 3/9 (1951), pp. 395–400, and here at p. 398.
20. Jean Meyendorff, 'The Sacrament of the Word, II. The Bishop in his See', *Sobornost* 3/10 (1951), pp. 432–6, and here at p. 432.
21. *Ibid.*, p. 436.
22. *Ibid.*, p. 432.
23. *Ibid.*, p. 433.
24. E. Kovalevsky, 'What is Sin?', *Journal of the Fellowship of St Alban and St Sergius* 7 (1929), pp. 6–9, and here at p. 8.
25. Sergei Bulgakov, 'On Original Sin', *Journal of the Fellowship of St Alban and St Sergius* 7 (1929), pp. 15–26, and here at p. 15.
26. *Ibid.*, p. 16.

27. *Ibid.*, p. 16.
28. *Ibid.*
29. *Ibid.* Italics are original.
30. *Ibid.*
31. *Ibid.*, p. 18.
32. *Ibid.*, p. 19, with an internal citation of Genesis 3:5.
33. *Ibid.*, p. 20.
34. *Ibid.*, p. 21.
35. *Ibid.*
36. *Ibid.*
37. *Ibid.*, p. 22.
38. *Ibid.*, p. 24.
39. *Ibid.*
40. Sergius Bulgakov, *The Burning Bush. On the Orthodox Veneration of the Mother of God* (Grand Rapids, MI: Eerdmans, 2009).
41. R. C. Langdon-Davies, 'Sin and Man's Freedom', *ibid.* 7 (1929), pp. 26–30, and here at p. 26.
42. *Ibid.*, p. 27.
43. *Ibid.*, p. 28.
44. Ralph Foster, 'The Conflict between Good and Evil in the Personal Life', *Journal of the Fellowship of St Alban and St Sergius* 7 (1929), pp. 30–3, and here at p. 31.
45. *Ibid.*
46. *Ibid.*
47. Sergius Tchetverikoff [Četverikov], 'Asceticism in the Lives of the Saints', *Journal of the Fellowship of St Alban and St Sergius* 10 (1930), pp. 12–16, and here at p. 13.
48. E. R. Morgan, 'Notes on the Place of Asceticism in the Christian Life', *Journal of the Fellowship of St Alban and St Sergius* 10 (1930), pp. 17–23, and here at p. 18.
49. *Ibid.*, p. 20.
50. *Ibid.*, p. 22.
51. *Ibid.*, p. 23.
52. Edward Every, 'Jerusalem and a Desert Monastery', *Journal of the Fellowship of St Alban and St Sergius* 10 (1930), pp. 23–6, and here at p. 26.
53. Arjakovsky, *La Génération des penseurs religieux de l'émigration russe*. This study has no fewer than seventy-seventy entries for Nicolas Zernov in its index. *Put'* was linked, through Berdyaev, its founder, more to Paris's 'Religious-Philosophical Academy' than to Bulgakov's Institut Saint-Serge, but Zernov was equally at home with both.
54. B. Visheslavzev, 'The Ethics of Sublimation as a Means for Overcoming Moralism',

Journal of the Fellowship of St Alban and St Sergius 10 (1930), pp. 27–43, and here at p. 27.

55. Ibid., p. 28.
56. Ibid., p. 32.
57. Ibid., p. 34.
58. Ibid., p. 35.
59. Ibid., p. 37.
60. Ibid.
61. Ibid., pp. 39–40.
62. Ibid., p. 40.
63. Ibid., p. 41.
64. There is here a remarkable anticipation of the argument of Francesca Aran Murphy's *Christ the Form of Beauty. A Study of Theology and Literature* (Edinburgh: T. & T. Clark, 1995).
65. L. S. Thornton, CR, 'The Revelation of the Trinity with Special Reference to the Procession of the Holy Spirit', *Sobornost* 3/20 (1956), pp. 398–404, and here at p. 404.
66. Ibid., p. 403, with an internal citation of Romans 8:15.
67. Ibid., pp. 403–4.
68. Ibid. p. 429.
69. Ibid., p. 430.
70. Basil Krivocheine, 'The Holy Trinity in Greek Patristic Theology', *Sobornost* 3/21 (1957), pp. 462–9, and here at p. 465.
71. Ibid., p. 463.
72. Ibid., pp. 467, 468.
73. Maximus Confessor, *Capita theologica et economica* I. 39, cited in B. Krivocheine, 'The Holy Trinity in Greek Mystical Theology, II', *Sobornost* 3/22 (1957), pp. 529–37, and here at p. 530.
74. Hans Urs von Balthasar, *Die gnostische Centurien des Maximus Confessor* (Freiburg: Herder, 1941), p. 138.
75. Sergius Bulgakov, 'One, Holy, Catholic and Apostolic Church', *Journal of the Fellowship of St Alban and St Sergius* 12 (1931), pp. 17–31, and here at p. 18.
76. Ibid.
77. Ibid., p. 19.
78. Ibid., p. 20.
79. Ibid., pp. 20–1.
80. Ibid.
81. Ibid., p. 22.

82. *Ibid.*
83. *Ibid.*, p. 23.
84. *Ibid.*
85. *Ibid.*, pp. 23-4.
86. *Ibid.*, p. 25.
87. *Ibid.*, p. 26.
88. *Ibid.*, p. 27.
89. *Ibid.*, p. 29.
90. *Ibid.*, p. 30.
91. *Ibid.*, p. 31.
92. *Ibid.*
93. The former is laid out neatly in George H. Williams, 'The Neo-Patristic Synthesis of Georges Florovsky', in Blane, *Georges Florovsky*, pp. 289–339; the latter is more the object of Paul L. Gavrilyuk, *Georges Florovsky and the Russian Religious Renaissance* (Oxford: Oxford University Press, 2013).
94. George Florovsky, 'The Work of the Holy Spirit in Revelation', *Journal of the Fellowship of St Alban and St Sergius* 17 (1932), pp. 5–16, and here at p. 5.
95. *Ibid.*, p. 6.
96. *Ibid.*
97. *Ibid.*, p. 8.
98. *Ibid.*, p. 9.
99. *Ibid.*
100. *Ibid.*, p. 11.
101. *Ibid.*
102. *Ibid.*, p. 12.
103. *Ibid.*
104. *Ibid.*, p. 13.
105. *Ibid.*
106. *Ibid.*
107. *Ibid.*
108. *Ibid.*, p. 14.
109. *Ibid.*
110. *Ibid.* Compare the discussion of Florovsky's negative attitude to the notion of doctrinal development in Gavrilyuk, *Georges Florovsky and the Russian Religious Renaissance*, p. 94–5.
111. Sergius Bulgakov, 'The Question of the Veneration of the Virgin Mary, at the Edinburgh Conference', *Sobornost* 1/12 (1937), pp. 28–9, and here at p. 28.
112. Cited *ibid.*, p. 29.

113. Nicolas Zernov, 'The Eastern Churches and the Ecumenical Movement in the Twentieth Century', in Ruth Rouse and Stephen C. Neill (ed.), *A History of the Ecumenical Movement, 1517–1948* (London: SPCK, 1954), pp. 645–76, and here at pp. 656–7.
114. Sergius Bulgakov, 'A Brief Statement of the Place of the Virgin Mary in the Thought and Worship of the Orthodox Church', *Sobornost* 1/12 (1937), pp. 29–31, and here at p. 29.
115. *Ibid.*, p. 30.
116. *Ibid.*
117. *Ibid.*
118. *Ibid.*
119. *Ibid.*, p. 31.
120. *Ibid.*
121. Stella Aldwinckle, 'The Unity of Theological Experience', *Sobornost* 1/29 (1944), pp. 4–7, and here at p. 5.
122. *Ibid.*
123. *Ibid.*
124. *Ibid.*, p. 6.
125. For an overview of his theological thought, see Cavallero, *Charles Williams*, pp. 126–57.
126. Aldwinckle, 'The Unity of Theological Experience', p. 6.
127. *Ibid.*
128. *Ibid.*, p. 7.
129. H. A. Hodges, 'The Integration of Heathenism and Unbelief into the Life of the Christian Church', *Sobornost* 1/29 (1944), pp. 7–9, and here at p. 7.
130. *Ibid.*, p. 8.
131. *Ibid.*
132. E. L. Mascall, *He Who Is. A Study in Traditional Theism* (London: Longmans, Green and Co., 1943).
133. *Sobornost* 1/29 (1944), p. 13.
134. *Ibid.*, p. 14.
135. *Ibid.*
136. *Ibid.*
137. *Ibid.*, p. 15.
138. Mascall, *Saraband*, p. 186.
139. *Ibid.* The poem was printed as 'Ecumenism Exemplified. Reminiscences of an Anglo-Orthodox Summer-School', in E. L. Mascall, *Pi in the High* (London: Faith Press, 1959), pp. 42–6.

140. E. L. Mascall, *Christ, the Christian and the Church. A Study of the Incarnation and its Consequences* (London: Longmans, Green and Co., 1946).
141. *Sobornost* 3/1 (1947), pp. 26–7.
142. *Ibid.*, p. 27.
143. Lev Gillet, *Communion in the Messiah. Studies in the Relationship between Judaism and Christianity* (London and Redhill: Lutterworth Press, 1942).
144. *Sobornost*. 3: 1 (1947), p. 28.
145. *Ibid.*, p. 29.
146. Vladimir Lossky, *Essai sur la théologie mystique de l'Église d'Orient* (Paris: Aubier, 1944).
147. *Sobornost* 3/2 (1947), p. 67.
148. For an overview of Lossky's theology see Aidan Nichols, OP, *Mystical Theologian. The Work of Vladimir Lossky* (Leominster: Gracewing, 2017).
149. Vladimir Lossky, *Théologie négative et connaissance de Dieu chez Maître Eckhart* (Paris: Vrin, 1960).
150. *Sobornost* 3/7 (1950), p. 295.
151. *Ibid.*
152. *Ibid.*, p. 296.
153. *Ibid.*
154. *Ibid.*, p. 297.
155. *Ibid.*
156. E. L. M[ascall]., 'Vladimir Lossky as a Theologian', *Sobornost* 3/23 (1958), pp. 568–9.
157. Mascall, *Saraband*, p. 187.
158. Irénée Chevalier, *Saint Augustin et la pensée grecque: les Relations trinitaires* (Fribourg: Librairie de l'Université, 1940).
159. Gerald Bonner, 'St Augustine's Doctrine of the Holy Spirit', *Sobornost* 4/1 (1960), pp. 51–65, and here at p. 53.
160. *Ibid.*, p. 59.
161. Augustine, *On the Faith and the Creed* IX. 19.
162. *Ibid.*, p. 65.
163. Jean Meyendorff, *Introduction à l'étude de Grégoire Palamas* (Paris: Patristica Sorbonensia, 1959).
164. *Sobornost* 4/3 (1960), p. 142.
165. *Ibid.*
166. George Florovsky, 'Saint Gregory Palamas and the Tradition of the Fathers', *Sobornost* 4/4 (1961), pp. 165–75, and here at pp. 165, 167.
167. Cited *ibid.*, p. 167.

168. Louis Bouyer, 'Le Renouveau des études patristiques', *La Vie intellectuelle* 15 (1947), p. 18.
169. Florovsky, 'Saint Gregory Palamas and the Tradition of the Fathers', p. 170.
170. *Ibid.*, p. 173.
171. *Ibid.*, p. 174.
172. *Ibid.*, p. 176.
173. A prolific writer, he was the author of the only full systematics in twentieth-century Orthodoxy. See Andrew Louth (a future editor of *Sobornost*), 'The Orthodox Dogmatic Theology of Dumitru Staniloae', *Modern Theology* 2 (1997), pp. 253–66.
174. Alexander Schmemann, *The World as Sacrament* (London: Darton, Longman & Todd, 1966).
175. Dumitru Staniloae, 'Some Characteristics of Orthodoxy', *Sobornost* 5/9 (1969), pp. 627–9, and here at p. 627.
176. *Ibid.*, p. 628.
177. *Ibid.*, p. 629.
178. *Ibid.*
179. Dumitru Staniloae, 'The Orthodox Conception of Tradition and the Development of Doctrine', *Sobornost* 5/9 (1969), pp. 652–62, and here at p. 653.
180. *Ibid.*, p. 655.
181. *Ibid.*, p. 659.
182. *Ibid.*, p. 658.
183. *Ibid.*, p. 659.
184. *Ibid.*, p. 661.
185. *Ibid.*
186. Dumitru Staniloae, 'The World as Gift and Sacrament of God's Love', *Sobornost* 5/9 (1969), pp. 662–73, and here at p. 664.
187. *Ibid.*, p. 665.
188. *Ibid.*, p. 667.
189. *Ibid.*, p. 668.
190. *Ibid.*
191. *Ibid.*, p. 670.
192. *Ibid.*
193. *Ibid.*, p. 671.
194. A. M. Allchin, 'Some New Tendencies in Greek Theology', *Sobornost* 4/8 (1963), pp. 455–63, and here at p. 460.
195. *Ibid.*, p. 462.
196. Savvas Agourides, 'What is Theology?', *Sobornost* 4/11 (1964), pp. 621–36, and here at p. 623.

197. *Ibid.*
198. *Ibid.*, p. 624.
199. *Ibid.*
200. *Ibid.*, p. 626.
201. *Ibid.*, p. 627.
202. *Ibid.*
203. *Ibid.*, p. 632.
204. *Ibid.*, p. 634.
205. *Ibid.*
206. For an introduction, see Sotiris Mitralexis, 'Person, Eros, Critical Ontology. An Attempt to Recapitulate Christos Yannaras's Philosophy', *Sobornost* 34/1 (2012), pp. 33–40.
207. Martin Heidegger, *Holzwege* (Frankfurt: Klostermann, 1950).
208. Christos Yannaras, 'An Orthodox Comment on the "Death of God"', *Sobornost* 5/4 (1966), pp. 249–57, and here at p. 250.
209. *Ibid.*, p. 253.
210. *Ibid.*, p. 255.
211. *Ibid.*
212. *Ibid.*
213. For his work, see Douglas Knight (ed.), *The Theology of John Zizioulas. Personhood and the Church* (Farnham: Ashgate, 2007).
214. John D. Zizioulas, 'Some Reflections on Baptism, Confirmation and Eucharist', *Sobornost* 5/9 (1969), pp. 644–52, and here at p. 646.
215. *Ibid.*, p. 652.
216. His thinking is well represented in Aristotle Papanikolaou, *Being with God. Trinity, Apophaticism and Divine–Human Communion* (Notre Dame, IN: University of Notre Dame Press, 2006).

Notes to Chapter 9

1. Eric Mascall, 'Worship and Reason', *Journal of the Fellowship of St Alban and St Sergius* 2 (1928), pp. 18–21, and here at p. 21.
2. Nicolas Zernov, 'Psychological Barriers to Reunion', *Journal of the Fellowship of St Alban and St Sergius* 2 (1928), pp. 22–5, and here at p. 23.
3. *Ibid.*
4. *Ibid.*, pp. 23–4.
5. *Ibid.*, p. 24.
6. *Ibid.*

7. H. Verrier Elwin, CSS, 'From the Closing Address of the Third Conference', *Journal of the Fellowship of St Alban and St Sergius* 5 (1929), pp. 6–8, and here at p. 7.
8. 'The Greeting of the Archbishop of Canterbury to the Anglo-Russian Conference', *Journal of the Fellowship of St Alban and St Sergius* 9 (1930), pp. 4–6, and here at p. 5.
9. Ibid.
10. Ibid., p. 6.
11. Ibid., p. 7.
12. Robert Beaken, *Cosmo Lang. Archbishop in War and Crisis* (London: Tauris, 2012), p. 45.
13. Cited *ibid*.
14. Ibid.
15. Ibid., p. 47.
16. Ibid., citing a diary entry of Lang's chaplain, Alan Campbell Don.
17. Nicolas Zernov, 'Notes on the 4th Anglo-Russian Conference', *Journal of the Fellowship of St Alban and St Sergius* 9 (1930), pp. 24–7, and here at p. 24.
18. Ibid.
19. Ibid., pp. 24–5.
20. Ibid., p. 25.
21. Ibid.
22. Ibid., p. 26.
23. J. A. Douglas, 'The Orthodox Delegation to the Lambeth Conference', *Journal of the Fellowship of St Alban and St Sergius* 10 (1930), pp. 5–11, and here at p. 5.
24. Ibid., p. 6.
25. Ibid.
26. Ibid., p. 12.
27. Ibid., p. 13.
28. Ibid.
29. Ibid., p. 14.
30. Ibid., p. 16.
31. Sergius Bulgakov, 'By Jacob's Well (On the Actual Unity of the Divided Church in Faith, Prayer and Sacraments', *Journal of the Fellowship of St Alban and St Sergius* 22 (1933), pp. 8–17, and here at p. 8.
32. Ibid., p. 16.
33. Ibid., p. 17.
34. Ibid. See, for an acute analysis, Anastassy Galaher, 'Bulgakov's Ecumenical Thought', *Sobornost* 24/1 (2002), pp. 24–55.

35. Dobbie-Bateman to Members of Executive, 10/10/1933, Archives of the Fellowship of St Alban and St Sergius.
36. Florovsky to Members of Executive, 16/10/1933, Archives of the Fellowship of St Alban and St Sergius.
37. Bede Frost OSB, 'Prayer and Reunion', *Journal of the Fellowship of St Alban and St Sergius* 23 (1934), pp. 5–10.
38. H. L. Goudge, 'Reunion and Intercommunion', *Journal of the Fellowship of St Alban and St Sergius* 25 (1934), pp. 4–6, and here at p. 5.
39. Ibid., p. 6.
40. A. Kartashev, 'The Paths towards the Reunion of the Churches', *Journal of the Fellowship of St Alban and St Sergius* 25 (1934), pp. 7–13, and here at p. 8.
41. Ibid.
42. Ibid., p. 9.
43. Ibid., pp. 9–10.
44. Ibid., p. 12.
45. Tissington Tatlow, 'The Church of England and the Movement towards Unity', *Journal of the Fellowship of St Alban and St Sergius* 26 (1934), pp. 13–18, and here at p. 13.
46. Cited *ibid.*, p. 15.
47. Ibid.
48. Ibid., p. 16.
49. Ibid.
50. David Davis, 'British Aid to Russian Churchmen, 1919–1939', *Sobornost/ECR* 2/1 (1980), pp. 42–56.
51. Tudor Pole to Fenn, 22 June 1934, Archives of the Fellowship of St Alban and St Sergius. Emphasis original.
52. Anderson to Fenn, 8 July 1935, Archives of the Fellowship of St Alban and St Sergius.
53. Anderson to Tudor Pole, 9 September 1935, Archives of the Fellowship of St Alban and St Sergius.
54. Spalding to Zernov, 26 July 1934, Archives of the Fellowship of St Alban and St Sergius.
55. Zernov to Spalding, 13 March 1935, Archives of the Fellowship of St Alban and St Sergius.
56. Memorandum of May 1933, Archives of the Fellowship of St Alban and St Sergius.
57. Eric Mascall (ed.), *The Church of God. An Anglo-Russian Symposium, by Members of the Fellowship of St Alban and St Sergius* (London: SPCK, 1934).
58. S. C. Carpenter, 'In Ecclesia Salus', *Sobornost* 1/1 (1935), pp. 20–2, and here at pp. 21, 22.

59. Sergius Bulgakov, 'From a World of Religious Contemplation', *Sobornost* 1/2 (1935), pp. 4–7, and here at p. 4.
60. Sergius Bulgakov, 'Ways to Church Union', *Sobornost* 1/2 (1935), pp. 7–15, and here at p. 10.
61. *Ibid.*, pp. 11–12.
62. See William Henn, OFM Cap., *The Hierarchy of Truths according to Yves Congar, OP* (Rome: Editrice Pontificia Università Gregoriana, 1987).
63. Bulgakov, 'Ways to Church Union', p. 12.
64. *Ibid.*, p. 14.
65. Michael Ramsey, 'Reunion and Intercommunion', *Sobornost* 1/2 (1935), pp. 15–17, and here at p. 15.
66. *Ibid.*
67. Gabriel Hebert, SSM, 'Intercommunion and Doctrinal Agreement', *Sobornost* 1/4 (1935), pp. 36–41, and here at p. 37.
68. *Ibid.*, p. 41.
69. A. M. Ramsey, 'The Significance of Anglo-Orthodox Relations', *Sobornost* 1/15 (1938), pp. 3–7, and here at p. 5.
70. *Ibid.*
71. *Ibid.*, p. 6.
72. *Ibid.*, p. 7.
73. Cited in Wilkinson, *The Community of the Resurrection*, p. 160.
74. A. F. Dobbie-Bateman, 'Kin', *Sobornost* 15 (1938), pp. 22–4.
75. G. W. H. Hewitt, '"Romanism" in the Church of England', *Sobornost* 15 (1938), pp. 25–9, and here at p. 25.
76. *Ibid.*, p. 29.
77. Thomas Parker, 'The Vision of Unity. The Future: Hopes and Fears', *Sobornost* 1/16 (1938), pp. 14–20, and here at p. 15.
78. *Ibid.*, p. 16.
79. *Ibid.*
80. *Ibid.*, p. 18.
81. *Ibid.*
82. *Ibid.*, p. 17.
83. *Ibid.*
84. Nicolas Zernov, 'Obstacles and Opportunities', *Sobornost* 1/18 (1939), pp. 11–16, and here at pp. 12, 13.
85. Editorial in *Sobornost* 1/19 (1939), p. 2.
86. Nicolas Zernov and Evgeny Lampert, 'The Fellowship and Anglican–Orthodox Intercommunion. A Restatement', *Sobornost* 1/20 (1940), pp. 9–16.

87. Evgeny Lampert, 'More about Intercommunion, II', *Sobornost* 1/23 (1941), pp. 28–33, and here at p. 30.
88. *Ibid.*, p. 32.
89. Henry R. T. Brandreth, 'Anglican–Presbyterian Reunion in America. The Second Phase', *Sobornost* 1/28 (1943), pp. 14–17, and here at p. 17.
90. George Florovsky, 'Ecumenical Aims and Doubts', *Sobornost* 3/4 (1948), pp. 126–32, and here at p. 128.
91. *Ibid.*, p. 129.
92. *Ibid.*, p. 132.
93. *Ibid.* The reference was to John Henry Newman's poem, later treated as a hymn, 'Lead, kindly Light'. See Thomas Fitzgerald, 'Florovsky at Amsterdam: His Ecumenical Aims and Doubts', *Sobornost/ECR* 21/1 (1999), pp. 37–51.
94. Meredith B. Handspicker, 'Faith and Order 1948–1965', in Harold E. Fey (ed.), *The Ecumenical Advance: A History of the Ecumenical Movement. Volume 2: 1948–1968* (London: SPCK, 1970), pp. 143–76, and here at p. 147.
95. Chadwick, *Michael Ramsey*, p. 66.
96. Nicolas Zernov, 'The First Assembly of the World Council of Churches', *Sobornost* 3/4 (1948), pp. 145–9, and here at p. 146.
97. *Ibid..*, p. 147.
98. Edward Every, 'The Moscow Conference, July, 1948', *Sobornost* 3/4 (1948), pp. 133–40, and here at p. 137.
99. *Ibid.*, p. 139.
100. Jack Newport, 'A Congregationalist in Orthodox Paris', *Sobornost* 3/6 (1949), pp. 253–6 and here at p. 255.
101. Eric Segelberg, 'The Whitby Conference', *Sobornost* 3/6 (1949), pp. 256–8.
102. Donald Allchin, 'Abingdon Conference, 1949', *Sobornost* 3/6 (1949), pp. 24–6, and here at p. 26.
103. *Ibid.* 3/6 (1949), p. 266.
104. Nicolas and Militza Zernov, 'A Visit to Greece', *Sobornost* 3/8 (1950), pp. 342–6, and here at p. 345.
105. *Ibid.*
106. *Ibid.*
107. *Sobornost* 3/8 (1950), p. 353.
108. *Ibid.*, p. 354.
109. *Ibid.*, p. 355.
110. A. E. J. Rawlinson, *The Problems of Reunion* (London: Eyre and Spottiswoode, 1950).
111. *Sobornost* 3/9 (1951), p. 374.
112. H. A. Hodges, 'Methodism: A Lost Anglican Doctrine of the Spiritual Life',

Sobornost 3/12 (1952), pp. 545-55.
113. Nicolas Zernov, 'The Third Faith and Order Conference at Lund', Sobornost 3/12 (1952), pp. 566-71, and here at p. 567.
114. Nicolas Zernov, *The Reintegration of the Church. A Study in Inter-Communion* (London: SCM, 1952).
115. Derwas Chitty, 'The Reintegration of the Church', Sobornost 3/13 (1953), pp. 33-44, and here at p. 33.
116. Ibid., p. 37.
117. Ibid., p. 41.
118. Nicolas Zernov, '*The Reintegration of the Church* and its Critics', Sobornost 3/15 (1954), pp. 199-203, and here at p. 203.
119. Ibid., p. 212.
120. Ibid.
121. Eric Hayman, 'Personal and Corporate Union. An Anglican Approach to Oecumenical Discussion', ibid. 3/17 (1955), pp. 225-42, and here at p. 225.
122. Ibid., p. 227.
123. Ibid., pp. 227-8.
124. See for instance, Hugh Ross Williamson, *The Walled Garden. An Autobiography* (London: Michael Joseph, 1956), pp. 170-83.
125. Sobornost 3/18 (1955), p. 274.
126. Ibid.
127. C. A. Abraham, 'Chalcedonian and Non-Chalcedonian Churches', Sobornost 3/19 (1956), pp. 372-4, and here at p. 373.
128. Ibid., p. 374.
129. Ibid., p. 375.
130. Cited in Nicolas Zernov, 'The Byzantine and Oriental Orthodox Churches: Suggested Terms for Reconciliation', Sobornost 3/21 (1957), pp. 473-80, and here at p. 474.
131. Ibid., p. 476.
132. Ibid., pp. 477, 478.
133. Ibid. 3/23 (1958), p. 564.
134. Patrick Rodger, 'Anglicans and Presbyterians', Sobornost 3/25 (1959), pp. and here at p. 611.
135. Sobornost 3/25 (1959), pp. 615-16.
136. Sobornost 4/2 (1960), p. 50.
137. William B. Green, 'The Anglican-Orthodox Dialogue and its Future', in Peter M. Doll (ed.), *Anglicanism and Orthodoxy 300 Years after the Greek College in Oxford* (Oxford: Peter Lang, 2006), pp. 380-93, and here at p. 379.
138. Marie-Jean Le Guillou, OP, *Mission et unité* (Paris: Cerf, 1960, 2 volumes).

139. A. M. A. [Donald Allchin], 'Mission and Unity', *Sobornost* 4/5 (1961), pp. 222–8, and here at p. 223.
140. *Ibid.*, p. 224.
141. *Sobornost* 4/6 (1962), pp. 286, 287.
142. *Ibid.*, p. 288.
143. A. M. Ramsey, 'The Ancient Fathers and Modern Anglican Theology', *Sobornost* 4/6 (1962), pp. 289–93, and here at p. 289.
144. *Ibid.*
145. *Ibid.*, p. 290.
146. Nikos Nissiotis, 'The Witness and the Service of Eastern Orthodoxy to the One Undivided Church', *Sobornost* 4/7 (1962), pp. 349–58, and here at p. 352.
147. *Ibid.*, p. 350.
148. *Ibid.*, p. 352.
149. *Ibid.*, p. 356.
150. Boris Bobrinskoy, 'Orthodoxy in the Ecumenical Movement', *Sobornost* 4/8 (1963), pp. 434–9, and here at p. 436.
151. *Ibid.*, p. 437.
152. *Ibid.*
153. *Ibid.*, p. 438.
154. *Ibid.*, p. 439.
155. Maximos IV Sayegh (ed.), *The Eastern Churches and Catholic Unity* (London: Nelson, 1963).
156. *Sobornost* 4/12 (1965), p. 691.
157. A. M. A. [Donald Allchin], 'Ecumenical Perspectives', *Sobornost* 4/12 (1965), pp. 694–702, and here at p. 699.
158. *Ibid.* p. 702.
159. Letter of 22 October 1965 from General Secretary of the Church of England Council on Foreign Relations to Minchin, Archives of the Fellowship of St Alban and St Sergius.
160. Undated Letter from Minchin to the General Secretary of the Church of England Council on Foreign Relations, Archives of the Fellowship of St Alban and St Sergius.
161. *Sobornost* 5/3 (1966), p. 156.
162. *Ibid.*
163. *Ibid.*, p. 157.
164. Kallistos Ware, 'Intercommunion. The Decisions of Vatican II and the Orthodox Standpoint', *Sobornost* 5/4 (1966), pp. 258–72, and here at p. 262.
165. *Orientalium ecclesiarum* 27.

166. *Unitatis redintegratio* 15; *Orientalium ecclesiarum* 26.
167. Ware, 'Intercommunion', p. 268.
168. *Ibid.*, p. 271.
169. *Ibid.*
170. Chadwick, *Michael Ramsey*, pp. 291–2.
171. Basil Minchin, 'A Very Special Ordinary Member', *Sobornost* 5/6 (1968), pp. 435-6, and here at p. 435.

PART II

Notes to Chapter 1

1. *Sobornost* 5/10 (1970), p. 704.
2. *Ibid.*, p. 705.
3. 'Pages from an Editor's Diary', *Sobornost* 5/10 (1970), pp. 753-64, and here at p. 755.
4. *Ibid.*
5. *Ibid.*, p. 756.
6. *Ibid.*, p. 758.
7. *Ibid.*
8. Marilyn Richardson, 'The Broadstairs Conference', *Sobornost* 5/10 (1970), pp. 777-9.
9. John Meyendorff, 'Orthodox Theology Today', *Sobornost* 6/1 (1970), pp. 11-25, and here at p. 14.
10. Nicolas Zernov, 'Patriarch Alexis', *Sobornost* 6/1 (1970), pp. 40-3.
11. Sophie Koulomzin, 'Encounter with Russia', *Sobornost* 6/3 (1971), pp. 191-6.
12. Philippe Sabant, 'The Weakness and Strength of the Russian Church', *Sobornost* 6/5 (1972), pp. 344-9, and here at p. 348.
13. *Sobornost* 6/1 (1970), p. 64.
14. A. M. Allchin, 'Celebration', *Sobornost* 6/5 (1972), pp. 307-16, and here at p. 308.
15. *Ibid.*
16. *Ibid.*, p. 310, with reference to Michael Novak's essay 'The New Relativism in American Theology', included in Donald R. Cutler (ed.), *The Religious Situation: 1968* (Boston, MA: Beacon, 1968). .
17. Allchin, 'Celebration', p. 316.
18. John Saward, *Perfect Fools: Folly for Christ's Sake in Catholic and Orthodox Spirituality* (Oxford: Oxford University Press, 1980).
19. John Saward, 'The Folly of Peter and Paul', *Sobornost* 6/6 (1972), pp. 373-6, and here at p. 375.

20. Donald Nicholl, 'Talking with Father Seraphim', *Sobornost* 6/6 (1972), pp. 376-86, and here at p. 377.
21. G. L. Fowden, 'Christian Communities in Jerusalem', *Sobornost* 6/6 (1972), pp. 430-4.
22. S. Parsons, 'A Visit to Lebanon and Syria', *Sobornost* 6/6 (1972), pp. 434-8.
23. Brian Frost, 'Living in Tension between East and West', *Sobornost* 6/7 (1973), pp. 486-90.
24. Nicolas Zernov, 'The One Holy Catholic and Apostolic Church and the Anglicans', *Sobornost* 6/8 (1973), pp. 529-33, and here at p. 529.
25. *Ibid.*, p. 530.
26. *Ibid.*, p. 531.
27. *Ibid.*, p. 532.
28. *Ibid.*, p. 533.
29. *Sobornost* 7/1 (1975), pp. 48-9.
30. *Sobornost* 7/1 (1975), p. 69.
31. Elisabeth Behr-Sigel, 'Western Orthodox seeking for Unity', *Sobornost* 7/1 (1975), pp. 49-52.
32. A Monk of the Eastern Church (Lev Gillet), 'Orthodox Spirituality. The New Appendix', *Sobornost* 7/1 (1975), pp. 41-7, and here at p. 41.
33. *Ibid.*, p. 46, note 3.
34. *Ibid.*, p. 42.
35. *Ibid.*, p. 43.
36. Nadejda Gorodetzky, *St Tikhon Zadonsky, Inspirer of Dostoevsky* (Crestwood, NY: St Vladimir's Seminary Press, 1976 [1951]).
37. Trevor Beeson, *Discretion and Valour. Religious Conditions in Russia and Eastern Europe* (London: Collins, 1974).
38. Barry Spurr, *'Anglo-Catholic in Religion': T. S. Eliot and Christianity* (Cambridge: Lutterworth, 2010), p. 247.
39. *Sobornost/ECR* 3/1 (1981), pp. 124-6.
40. *Sobornost* 7/5 (1977), p. 327.
41. *Ibid.*, p. 328.
42. E. R. Hardy, 'Background Notes on Anglican-Orthodox Fellowship in the United States', *Sobornost* 7/5 (1977), pp. 395-400, and here at p. 398; Frank Gavin, *Some Aspects of Contemporary Greek Orthodox Thought* (Milwaukee: Morehouse, 1923).
43. *Sobornost* 7/5 (1977), p. 406.
44. Philippe Sabant, 'On the Way to the Pan-Orthodox Council', *Sobornost* 7/5 (1977), pp. 409-13, and here at p. 409.
45. *Ibid.*

46. *Ibid.*, p. 410.
47. Elizabeth Behr-Sigel, 'The Participation of Women in the Life of the Church', *Sobornost* 7/6 (1978), pp. 480–92.
48. L. W. Barnard, *C. B. Moss (1888–1964). Defender of the Faith* (London: Mowbray, 1967).
49. Zernov, *The History of the Fellowship of St Alban and St Sergius*, p. 20.
50. Kallistos Ware, 'Church and Eucharist, Communion and Intercommunion', *Sobornost* 7/7 (1978), pp. 550–67, and here at p. 550.
51. *Ibid.*, pp. 550–1.
52. *Ibid.*, pp. 552–3.
53. *Ibid.*, p. 556.
54. *Ibid.*
55. *Ibid.*, p. 559.
56. *Ibid.*
57. *Sobornost/ECR* 2/1 (1980), p. 63.
58. *Ibid.*, p. 69
59. *Ibid.*, p. 70.
60. *Ibid.*, p. 72.
61. *Ibid.*, p. 74.
62. *Ibid.*, p. 107.
63. Vladimir Lossky, *Orthodox Theology. An Introduction* (Crestwood, NY: St Vladimir's Seminary Press, 1978).
64. *Sobornost/ECR* 2/1 (1980), p. 110.
65. Sister Thekla (ed.), *Mother Maria: Her Life in Letters* (London: Darton, Longman & Todd 1979).
66. Anne Borrowdale and Ann Loades, 'A Philosopher and his Faith: The Work of H. A. Hodges', *Sobornost/ECR* 2/2 (1980), pp. 50–6, and here at p. 53. A full bibliography was appended though his Gifford lectures, *God beyond Knowledge*, appeared too late to be included except in a footnote to the main text.
67. *Sobornost/ECR* 2/2 (1980), p. 83. The 'elsewhere' was in the pages of *Chrystostom*, the magazine of the Society of St John Chrysostom, in its eighth issue.
68. Undated note of 1982, Archives of the Fellowship of St Alban and St Sergius.
69. Cited in Elizabeth Behr-Sigel, 'The Concelebrant at Clamart: Lev Gillet in the year 1927–8', *Sobornost/ECR* 3/1 (1981), pp. 40–52, and here at p. 47.
70. *Ibid.*, p. 50.
71. David Balfour, 'Memories of Lev Gillet', *Sobornost/ECR* 4/2 (1982), pp. 203–11, and here at p. 207.
72. *Ibid.*, p. 211.

73. Ibid., p. 208.
74. Kallistos Ware, 'Nicolas Zernov (1898-1980)', *Sobornost/ECR* 3/1 (1981), pp. 11-33, and here at p. 11.
75. Ibid., p. 18.
76. Ibid., p. 27.
77. Ibid., p. 29.
78. Ibid.
79. *Sobornost/ECR* 5/2 (1983), p. 5.
80. *Sobornost/ECR* 6/1 (1984), p. 123.
81. Ibid.
82. Colin Davey, 'Anglicans and Eastern Christendom', *Sobornost/ECR* 7/2 (1985), pp. 6-17, and here at p. 16.
83. *Sobornost/ECR* 8/1 (1986), p. 51.
84. Ibid., pp. 55-8. See Paul B. Anderson, *No East or West* (Paris: YMCA, 1985).
85. Elizabeth Hill, 'Nadezhda Gorodetskaia: The Study and the Practice of Kenosis', *Sobornost/ECR* 8/2 (1986), pp. 51-61.
86. *Sobornost/ECR* 8/2 (1986), p. 86.
87. Ibid., p. 87.
88. E. C. Miller, author of *Towards a Fuller Vision: Orthodoxy and the Anglican Experience* (Wilton, CT: Morehouse Barlow, 1984).
89. *Sobornost/ECR* 8/2 (1986), p. 87.
90. Mary Cunningham and Elizabeth Theokritoff (ed.), *The Cambridge Companion to Orthodox Christian Theology* (Cambridge: Cambridge University Press, 2008).
91. *Sobornost/ECR* 9/2 (1987), p. 42.
92. Ibid., p. 43.
93. Arthur Michael Ramsey, *The Glory of God and the Transfiguration of Christ* (London: Longmans, Green and Co., 1949).
94. *Sobornost/ECR* 12/1 (1990), p. 111.
95. Ibid., p. 62.
96. Ibid., p. 71.
97. Ibid., p. 118.
98. One could consult E. J. B. Fry, 'Memoir of Dom Bede Winslow', in E. J. B. Fry and A. H. Armstrong (ed.), *Rediscovering Eastern Christendom. Essays in Commemoration of Dom Bede Winslow* (London: Darton, Longman & Todd, 1963), pp. 1-10.
99. Robert Murray, 'Symbiosis and *Sobornost*: the Eastern Churches Review Trust and the Fellowship of St Alban and St Sergius', *Sobornost/ECR* 13/2 (1991), pp. 6-16, and here at p. 8.

100. *Ibid.*, p. 8.
101. *Ibid.*, p. 9.
102. *Ibid.*, p. 12.
103. *Ibid.*, p. 13.
104. *Ibid.*
105. *Ibid.*, p. 14.
106. *Sobornost/ECR* 13/2 (1991), p. 101.
107. *Sobornost/ECR* 15/2 (1993), p. 90.
108. 'The Re-location of St Basil's Chapel, 52 Ladbroke Grove', undated document in the Archives of the Fellowship of St Alban and St Sergius, p. 9.
109. *Ibid.*
110. Cited in *Sobornost/ECR* 16/1 (1994), p. 98.
111. *Sobornost/ECR* 16/2 (1994), p. 108.
112. Hugh Wybrew, 'Anglican–Orthodox Dialogue: Its Past, its Present and its Future', *Sobornost/ECR* 15/1 (1993), pp. 7-19, and here at p. 18.
113. *Ibid.*
114. A monk of the Eastern Church, *On the Invocation of the Name of Jesus* (London: Fellowship of St Alban and St Sergius, 1950).
115. Kallistos of Diokleia, 'Father Lev and the Fellowship of St Alban and St Sergius', *Sobornost/ECR* 15/2 (1993), pp. 7-15, and here at p. 10.
116. Kallistos of Diokleia, 'The "Monk of the Eastern Church" and the Jesus Prayer', *Sobornost/ECR* 15/2 (1993), pp. 17-27, and here at p. 24.
117. Kallistos of Diokleia, 'Father Lev and the Fellowship of St Alban and St Sergius', pp. 10-11.
118. Cited in *Sobornost/ECR* 16/2 (1994), p. 99.
119. Kallistos of Diokleia, 'The Mystery of the Church according to Father Lev', *Sobornost/ECR* 27/2 (2005), pp. 27-35, and here at p. 31.
120. *Ibid.*, p. 32.
121. Cited *ibid.*, p. 33.
122. *Sobornost/ECR* 17/1 (1995), p. 114.
123. Kallistos of Diokleia, 'C. S. Lewis: An "Anonymous Orthodox"?', *Sobornost/ECR* 7/2 (1995), pp. 9-27.
124. St Athanasius, *On the Incarnation. The Treatise 'de Incarnatione Verbi'*, translated and edited by a religious of C. S. M. V., with an Introduction by C. S. Lewis (London: Centenary Press, 1944).
125. *Sobornost/ECR* 17/2 (1995), p. 45.
126. *Sobornost/ECR* 17/2 (1995), p. 47.
127. *Sobornost/ECR* 17/2 (1995), p. 54.

128. *Sobornost/ECR* 17/2 (1995), p. 54.
129. *Sobornost/ECR* 18/1 (1996), p. 109.
130. *Sobornost/ECR* 23/1 (2001), p. 5.
131. Andrew Walker, 'Intercommunion? An Orthodox Approach', *Sobornost/ECR* 25.1 (2003), pp. 9–24, and here at p. 21.
132. *Sobornost/ECR* 25/2 (2003), p. 86–7.
133. *Sobornost/ECR* 28/1 (2006), p. 59.
134. *Ibid.*, p. 60.
135. *Sobornost/ECR* 25/2 (2003), p. 135. See Paul Valliere, *Modern Russian Theology. Bukharev, Soloviev, Bulgakov: Orthodox Theology in a New Key* (Edinburgh: T. & T. Clark, 2000).
136. *Sobornost/ECR* 25/2 (2003), p. 137.
137. A. F. Dobbie-Bateman, *The Return of St Seraphim* (London: Fellowship of St Alban and St Sergius, 1970).
138. Letter to Florovsky of 27 November 1963, in the Florovsky Papers at Princeton, cited in Anastassy Brandon Galaher, 'Georges Florovsky on Reading the Life of St Seraphim', *Sobornost/ECR* 27/1 (2005), pp. 63–70, and here at p. 65.
139. *Ibid.*, p. 60. The closing citation in this passage is from Georges Florovsky, 'Patristics and Modern Theology', in *Diakonia* 4/3 (1969), p. 231.
140. Galaher, 'Georges Florovsky on Reading the Life of St Seraphim', p. 60.
141. *Ibid.*, p. 62.
142. Sergei Hackel, *A Pearl of Great Price: The Life of Mother Maria Skobtsova, 1891–1945* (London: Darton, Longman & Todd, 1981).
143. *Sobornost/ECR* 27/1 (2005), pp. 71–5.
144. *Sobornost/ECR* 27/2 (2005), p. 7.
145. *Sobornost/ECR* 28/1 (2006), p. 5.
146. *Sobornost/ECR* 29/1 (2007), p. 95.
147. *Sobornost/ECR* 30/1 (2008), pp. 83–4.
148. *Ibid.*, pp. 92–3.
149. Andrew Louth, *Greek East and Latin West. The Church AD 681–1071* (Crestwood, NY: Saint Vladimir's Seminary Press, 2007).
150. *Sobornost/ECR* 30/2 (2008), p. 108.
151. Hilarion Alfeyev, 'The Orthodox Understanding of Primacy and Catholicity', *Sobornost/ECR* 31/1 (2009), pp. 6–17, and here at p. 7.
152. *Ibid.*, p. 8.
153. *Ibid.*, p. 14.
154. *Ibid.*, p. 15.
155. *Ibid.*

156. *Ibid.*, p. 64.
157. *Ibid.*, p. 65.
158. *Ibid.*, p. 71.
159. *Sobornost/ECR* 31/2 (2009), 112–15.
160. A. M. Allchin, *The Silent Rebellion. Anglican Religious Communities, 1845–1900* (London: SCM, 1958).
161. *Sobornost/ECR* 33/1 (2011), p. 39.
162. *Ibid.*
163. *Ibid.*, p. 43.
164. Gerald Bonner, *St Augustine of Hippo. Life and Controversies* (London: SCM, 1963).
165. *Sobornost/ECR* 35/1-2 (2013), pp. 174–8.
166. *Sobornost./ECR* 37/1 (2015), p. 5.
167. Christopher K. W. Moore, 'Fostering Encounter: The Fellowship Trip to Moscow', *Sobornost/ECR* 36/2 (2014), pp. 83–7.

Notes to Chapter 2

1. Nicolas Zernov, 'Dostoevsky and Solzhenitsyn. Their Similarity and Contrast', *Sobornost* 6/5 (1972), pp. 323–30, and here at p. 328.
2. *Ibid.*, p. 330.
3. Avril Pyman, *Pavel Florensky. A Quiet Genius* (London and New York: Continuum, 2010); Avril Pyman, *Metropolitan Antony of Sourozh. A Life* (Cambridge: Lutterworth Press, 2016).
4. Avril Pyman, 'Sin and the weakness of God in the novels of Fedor Dostoyevsky', *Sobornost/ECR* 31/2 (2009), pp.7–18, and here at p. 16.
5. *Ibid.*
6. *Ibid.*, p. 18.
7. Michel d'Herbigny, *Vladimir Soloviev. A Russian Newman, 1853–1900* (London: Washbourne, 1918).
8. Mark Everitt, 'Vladimir Solov'ev: A Russian Newman?', *Sobornost/ECR* 1/1 (1979), pp. 23–38, and here at p. 29.
9. *Ibid.*, p. 30.
10. Cited *ibid.*, p. 34.
11. Cited *ibid.*
12. Vladimir Solovieff, *La Russie et l'Église universelle* (Paris: Albert Savine, 1889).
13. Vladimir Solovieff, *L'Idée russe* (Paris: Perrin, 1888).
14. Everitt, 'Vladimir Solov'ev: A Russian Newman?', p. 31.

15. R. D. Williams, 'The Spirit of the Age to Come', *Sobornost* 6/9 (1974), pp. 613-25, and here at p. 614.
16. Sergei Bulgakov, 'The Spirit of Prophecy', *Sobornost* 1/19 (1939), pp. 3-7.
17. Williams, 'The Spirit of the Age to Come', p. 615.
18. Alexander Schmemann (ed.), *Ultimate Questions: an Anthology of Modern Russian Religious Thought* (London: Mowbray, 1977).
19. Williams, 'The Spirit of the Age to Come', p. 621.
20. *Ibid.*
21. *Ibid.*, p. 622.
22. Rowan Williams, *A Margin of Silence. The Holy Spirit in Russian Orthodox Theology* (Quebec: Éditions de Lys Vert, 2008).
23. Robert Runcie, 'Millennium Greetings', *Sobornost/ECR* 10/2 (1988), pp. 6-8, and here at p. 6.
24. Kirill Golovin, 'Same Homeland, Different Future', *Sobornost/ECR* 10/2 (1988), pp. 12-24, and here at p. 13.
25. *Ibid.*, p. 15.
26. *Ibid.*
27. *Ibid.*, p. 16.
28. *Ibid.*
29. *Ibid.*, p. 23.
30. *Sobornost/ECR* 10/2 (1988), pp. 69-72.
31. Robert Runcie, 'Reflections on the Millenium of the Baptism of Kievan Rus', *Sobornost/ECR* 11/1-2 (1989), pp. 7-16, and here at p. 10.
32. *Ibid.*, p. 12.
33. Sergei Hackel, 'Post-Holocaust Theology and Orthodox thought', *Sobornost/ECR* 20/1 (1998), pp. 7-25, and here at p. 12.
34. Lida Havriljukova, 'Fr Aleksandr Men (1935-1990): Perceptions of him as a Spiritual Elder', *Sobornost/ECR* 32/1 (2010), pp. 36-52, and here at p. 37.
35. Cited in Sergei Hackel, 'Managerial Patterns in a Patriarchal Church', *Sobornost/ECR* 23/2 (2001), pp. 7-22, and here at p. 7.
36. *Ibid.*, p. 14.
37. *Ibid.*, p. 19.
38. Philip Walters, 'Pluralism versus Community: Religious Challenges in Russia', *Sobornost/ECR* 24/2 (2002), pp. 49-67, and here at p. 50.
39. *Ibid.*, p. 51.
40. *Ibid.*, p. 61.
41. *Ibid.*, p. 64.
42. Anthony Koumantos, 'An Outline of the Present Theological Situation in Greece', *Sobornost* 6/9 (1974), pp. 663-70, and here at p. 669.

43. *Sobornost* 6/4 (1972), p. 278.
44. *Ibid.*
45. Paul McPartlan, *The Eucharist makes the Church. Henri de Lubac and John Zizioulas in Dialogue* (Edinburgh: T. & T. Clark, 1993).
46. *Sobornost/ECR* 17/1 (1995), p. 70.
47. *Ibid.*
48. *Ibid.*
49. Christos Yannaras, 'La Métaphysique du Corps. Étude sur S. Jean Climaque' (Paris: 1970, unpublished doctoral thesis).
50. Christos Yannaras, *De l'absence et de l'inconnaissance de Dieu d'après les écrits aréopagitiques* (Paris: Cerf, 1971).
51. *Sobornost* 6/4 (1972), pp. 286–7.
52. Rowan D. Williams, 'The Theology of Personhood. A Study of the Thought of Christos Yannaras', *Sobornost* 6/6 (1972), pp. 415–30, and here at p. 428.
53. *Ibid.*, p. 416.
54. *Ibid.*, p. 417.
55. *Ibid.*
56. *Ibid.*, p. 419.
57. *Ibid.*
58. *Ibid.*, p. 420.
59. *Ibid.*
60. *Ibid.*, p. 422.
61. He thought an essay by the Scots Presbyterian divine Thomas Torrance, 'The Epistemological Relevance of the Spirit', in the collection *God and Rationality*, would have helped had Yannaras known of it, for one might regard the Spirit as he 'through Whom "analogical" participation in God, participation in the Divine energies, becomes a reality here and now', *ibid.*, p. 426.
62. *Ibid.*, pp. 427–8.
63. Christos Yannaras, *Orthodoxia kai Dyse: he theologia sten Hellada semera* (Athens: Ekdoseis Athena, 1972).
64. Garth Fowden, 'Mount Athos', *Sobornost* 6/8 (1973), pp. 558–62.
65. Garth Fowden, 'The Revival of Monasticism on Athos', *Sobornost* 7/2 (1975), pp. 321–6.
66. Fr Basil, Abbot of Stavronikita, 'Dying and Behold We Live', *Sobornost* 7/1 (1975), pp. 22–31, and here at p. 25.
67. Sebastian Brock, 'World and Sacrament in the Writings of the Syrian Fathers', *Sobornost* 6/10 (1974), pp. 685–96, and here at p. 691.
68. Sebastian Brock, 'The Poet as Theologian', *Sobornost* 7/4 (1977), pp. 243–50, and here at p. 248.

69. Cited Sebastian Brock, 'The Mysteries Hidden in the Side of Christ', *Sobornost* 7/6 (1978), pp. 462–72, and here at p. 462.
70. *Ibid.*
71. Cited *ibid.*, p. 465.
72. *Ibid.*, p. 466.
73. Cited *ibid.*, p. 468.
74. *Ibid.*, p. 470.
75. Robert Murray, SJ, 'A Hymn of St Ephrem to Christ', *Sobornost/ECR* 1/1 (1979), pp. 39–50.
76. Cited Sebastian Brock, 'Mary and the Eucharist: An Oriental Perspective', *Sobornost/ECR* 1.2 (1979), pp. 50–9, and here at p. 51.
77. Cited *ibid.*, p. 57.
78. *Ibid.*, p. 59.
79. Robert Murray, 'St Ephrem's Dialogue of Reason and Love', *Sobornost/ECR* 2/2 (1980), pp. 26–40, and here at p. 26.
80. *Ibid.*
81. *Ibid.*, p. 27.
82. *Ibid.*, p. 29.
83. Cited in Sebastan Brock, 'Jacob of Serugh and the Veil of Mercy', *Sobornost/ECR* 3/1 (1981), pp. 70–85, and here at p. 74.
84. Sebastian Brock, 'Dialogue Hymns of the Syriac Churches', *Sobornost/ECR* 5/2 (1983), pp. 35–45, and here at p. 36.
85. *Ibid.*, p. 41.
86. Cited *ibid.*
87. *Ibid.*, p. 44.
88. *Ibid.*, p. 42.
89. *Ibid.*, p. 41. See too for Sebastian Brock's contributions on the Syriac poets, 'Three Syriac Fathers on Reading the Bible', *Sobornost* 33/1 (2011), pp. 6–21, though here one of the figures chosen was the Nestorian, Isaac of Nineveh.
90. Stephen Griffith, 'Tur Abdin: A Time of Change', *Sobornost/ECR* 22/2 (2000), pp. 44–54.
91. Antonie Plamadeala, 'Monastic Renewal in Romania', *Sobornost* 5/10 (1970), pp. 764-
92. *Ibid.*, p. 766.
93. *Ibid.*, p. 771.
94. *Ibid.*, p. 774.
95. Dumitru Staniloae, 'The Cross on the Gift of the World,' *Sobornost* 6/2 (1970), pp. 96–110, and here at p. 107.

96. *Ibid.*, p. 109.
97. Ion Bria, 'A Look at Contemporary Romanian Dogmatic Theology', *Sobornost* 6/5 (1972), pp. 330–6, and here at p. 331.
98. *Ibid.*, p. 334.
99. *Ibid.*, p. 335.
100. Dumitru Staniloae, 'The Cross in Orthodox Theology and Worship', *Sobornost* 7/4 (1977), pp. 233–43, and here at p. 234.
101. *Ibid.*, p. 237.
102. Dumitru Staniloae, 'The Holy Spirit in the Theology and Life of the Orthodox Church', *Sobornost* 7/1 (1975), pp. 4–21, and here at p. 4.
103. *Ibid.*, p. 5.
104. *Ibid.*, p. 7.
105. *Ibid.*, p. 8.
106. *Ibid.*, p. 15.
107. *Ibid.*, p. 16.
108. *Ibid.*, p. 17.
109. *Ibid.*
110. *Sobornost/ECR* 38/2 (2016), p. 79.
111. *Ibid.*, p. 81.
112. *Ibid.*
113. *Ibid.*, p. 83.

Notes to Chapter 3

1. A. M. Allchin, *The Spirit and the Word* (London: Faith Press, 1963).
2. Allchin, *The Silent Rebellion*.
3. *Sobornost* 5/10 (1970), p. 706.
4. H. L. Mansel, *The Limits of Religious Thought* (London: John Murray, 1858).
5. Gregory Dix, *Jew and Greek. A Study in the Primitive Church* (Westminster: Dacre Press, 1953).
6. Michael Paternoster, 'Against the Agnostics', *Sobornost* 5/10 (1970), pp. 709–20, and here at p. 713.
7. *Ibid.*, p. 718.
8. *Ibid.*, p. 719.
9. Nicolas Lossky, 'An Orthodox Approach to Anglicanism', *Sobornost* 6/2 (1970), pp. 78–88, and here at p. 85.
10. *Ibid.*, p. 88. The passage occurs at p. 107 of Vladimir Lossky's *À l'image et à la ressemblance de Dieu* (Paris: Aubier, 1967). Readers of *Sobornost* with long

memories might have recalled its English dress from its appearance in the journal in 1947.

11. Nicolas Lossky, *Lancelot Andrewes le prédicateur (1555–1626). La théologie mystique de l'Église d'Angleterre* (Paris: Cerf, 1986).
12. A. M. Allchin, 'The Nature of Theology. A Study of R. M. Benson', *Sobornost* 6/2 (1970), pp. 89–96, and here at p. 89.
13. Cited *ibid.*, p. 90, from W. H. Longridge (ed.), *Further Letters of Richard Meux Benson* (London and Oxford: A. R. Mowbray, 1920), p. 213.
14. R. M. Benson, *Followers of the Lamb* (London: Longmans, Green & Co., 1900), p.10, cited in Allchin, 'The Nature of Theology', p. 92.
15. A. M. Allchin, 'Monastic Life and Unity in Christ', *Sobornost* 6/9 (1974), pp. 654–63, and here at p. 657.
16. A. M. Allchin, 'Trinity and Incarnation in Anglican Theology from the Sixteenth Century till Today', *Sobornost* 7/5 (1977), pp. 363–76, and here at p. 364.
17. *Ibid.*, p. 365.
18. *Ibid.*, p. 367.
19. *Ibid.*, p. 368.
20. *Ibid.*
21. *Ibid.*, p. 369.
22. *Ibid.*, p. 370.
23. *Ibid.*, p. 369.
24. *Ibid.*, p. 375.
25. *Ibid.*, p. 376.
26. Andrew Louth, 'The Hermeneutical Question approached through the Fathers', *Sobornost* 7/7 (1978), pp. 541–9, and here at p. 544.
27. *Ibid.*, p. 543.
28. *Ibid.*, p. 544.
29. *Ibid.*, p. 545.
30. *Ibid.*, p. 546.
31. *Ibid.*, p. 547.
32. *Ibid.*, p. 548.
33. Andrew Louth, 'The Oxford Movement, the Fathers and the Bible', *Sobornost* 6.1 (1984), pp. 30–45, and here at p. 30.
34. Cited *ibid.*
35. *Ibid.*, p. 36.
36. *Ibid.*, p. 39.
37. *Ibid.*, p. 41
38. *Ibid.*, p. 42.

Notes to Part II, Chapter 3

39. D. J. Chitty, 'The Spirit of Orthodox Christianity', *Sobornost* 6/3 (1971), pp. 147-54, and here at p. 148.
40. *Ibid.*, p. 147.
41. *Ibid.*, p. 153.
42. Edward Every, 'Derwas James Chitty, 1901-1971', *Sobornost* 6/3 (1971), pp. 178-9, and here at p. 179.
43. A. M. Allchin, 'Derwas Chitty: A Tribute', *Sobornost* 6/3 (1971), pp. 179-81, and here at p. 180.
44. Philip Sherrard, 'Christian Theology and the Eclipse of Man', *Sobornost* 7/3 (1976), pp. 166-79, and here at p. 166.
45. *Ibid.*, p. 171.
46. E. L. Mascall, *The Openness of Being. Natural Theology Today* (London: Darton, Longman & Todd, 1971).
47. *Sobornost* 6.5 (1972), p. 359.
48. *Ibid.*
49. *Sobornost/ECR* 18/2 (1996), p. 84.
50. Philip Sherrard, 'Christian Theology and the Eclipse of Man', p. 173.
51. *Ibid.*
52. *Ibid.*
53. E. L. Mascall, *Saraband. The Memoirs of E. L. Mascall* (Leominster: Gracewing, 1992), p. 187.
54. Philip Sherrard, 'The Christian Understanding of Man', *Sobornost* 7/5 (1977), pp. 329-43, and here at p. 329.
55. *Ibid.*, p. 331.
56. *Ibid.*, p. 330.
57. *Ibid.*, p. 333.
58. *Ibid.*
59. *Ibid.*, p. 335.
60. *Ibid.*, p. 338.
61. *Ibid.*
62. *Ibid.*, p. 339.
63. *Ibid.*, p. 340.
64. *Ibid.*
65. *Ibid.*, p. 341.
66. *Ibid.*
67. *Ibid.* 6/5 (1972), pp. 362-3.
68. Ernest Michael Beaumont, 'Man's Creative Spirit and the Holy Spirit', *Sobornost* 6/7 (1973), pp. 471-85, and here at p. 473.

69. Ibid., p. 474.
70. Ibid.
71. Ibid., p. 479.
72. Ibid., p. 480.
73. Gerald Bonner, 'Anglo-Saxon Culture and Spirituality', *Sobornost* 6/8 (1973), pp. 533-50, and here at p. 534.
74. Ibid., p. 536.
75. Ibid.
76. Ibid., p. 539.
77. Ibid., p. 541.
78. Ibid., p. 544.
79. Ibid., p. 545.
80. Gerald Bonner, 'The Saints of Durham', *Sobornost/ECR* 8/1 (1986), pp. 34-46, and here at p. 34.
81. Ibid., p. 35.
82. Gerald Bonner, 'The Church and the Eucharist in the Theology of St Augustine', *Sobornost* 7/6 (1978), pp. 448-61, and here at p. 457.
83. Augustine, *The City of God*, 10/20.
84. Bonner, 'The Church and the Eucharist in the Theology of St Augustine', p. 458. Cf. Augustine, *The City of God*, X.22.
85. Gerald Bonner, 'The Spirituality of St Augustine and its Influence on Western Mysticism', *Sobornost/ECR* 4/2 (1982), pp. 143-62, and here at p. 143.
86. Ibid., p. 145.
87. Ibid.
88. Ibid., p. 151.
89. Augustine Casiday, 'St Augustine on Deification: His Homily on Psalm 81', *Sobornost /ECR*. 23/1 (2001), pp. 23-44, and here at p. 25.
90. *Sobornost /ECR* 36/1 (2014), p. 102.
91. Ibid.
92. Ibid., p. 193.
93. John Eudes Bamberger, 'Thomas Merton and the Christian East', *Sobornost* 6/8 (1973), pp. 550-8, and here at p. 551.
94. Thomas Merton, *Conjectures of a Guilty Bystander* (London: Burns & Oates, 1968).
95. Étienne Gilson, *The Mystical Theology of St Bernard* (London: Sheed & Ward, 1940).
96. Thomas Merton, *The Climate of Monastic Prayer* (Shannon: Irish University Press, 1969).

97. Thomas Merton, *Disputed Questions* (London: Hollis & Carter, 1961), pp. 83–93.
98. Bamberger, 'Thomas Merton and the Christian East', p. 557.
99. *Ibid.*
100. Cited A. M. Allchin, 'The Worship of the Whole Creation: Merton and the Eastern Fathers', *Sobornost /ECR* 18/2 (1996), pp. 28–43, and here at p. 33.
101. Cited *ibid.*, p. 34.
102. *Ibid.*, pp. 34–5.
103. Cited *ibid.*, p. 33.
104. *Ibid.*, p. 41.
105. Neville Clark, 'The Jesus Prayer. Its History and Meaning', *Sobornost* 7/3 (1976), pp. 148–65, and here at p. 155.
106. *Ibid.*, p. 156.
107. *Ibid.*, p. 163.
108. *Ibid.*
109. Kallistos Ware, 'The Holy Name of Jesus in East and West: the Hesychasts and Richard Rolle', *Sobornost/ECR* 4/2 (1982), pp. 163–84, and here at p. 169.
110. *Ibid.*, p. 175.
111. *Ibid.*, p. 178.
112. *Ibid.*, p. 183.
113. *Ibid.*, p. 184.
114. Irénée Hausherr, *The Name of Jesus* (Kalamazoo, MI: Cistercian Publications, 1978).
115. *Sobornost/ECR* 2/2 (1980), p. 87.
116. Brant Pelphrey, '"Uncreated Charity": The Trinity in Julian of Norwich', *Sobornost* 7/7 (1978), pp. 527–35, and here at p. 527.
117. *Ibid.*, pp. 530–1.
118. Kallistos of Diokleia, 'A Russian Translation of Julian of Norwich', *Sobornost/ECR* 29/1 (2006), pp. 83–6.
119. Gerald Bonner, 'The Holy Spirit Within. St Cuthbert as a Western Orthodox Saint', *Sobornost/ECR* 1/1 (1979), pp. 7–22, and here at p. 14.
120. *Ibid.*, p. 20.
121. Andrew Louth, 'The Influence of Denys the Areopagite on Eastern and Western Spirituality in the Fourteenth Century', *Sobornost/ECR* 4/2 (1982), pp. and here at p. 186.
122. *Ibid.*, p. 188.
123. *Ibid.*, p. 195.
124. Jean-Claude Larchet, *Maxime le Confesseur, médiateur entre l'Orient et l'Occident* (Paris: Cerf, 1998).

125. *Sobornost/ECR* 21/2 (1999), p/ 73.
126. Jean-Claude Larchet, 'Ancestral Sin according to St Maximus the Confessor: A Bridge between Eastern and Western Conceptions', *Sobornost/ECR* 20.1 (1998), pp. 26–48. A mistake in the wording of the title was rectified in the following issue.
127. Marcus Plested, *The Macarian Legacy. The Place of Macarius-Symeon in the Eastern Christian Tradition* (Oxford: Oxford University Press, 2004).
128. Marcus Plested, '"East and East and West is West"?: The Theology of Grace in the Macarian Writings and in St Augustine', *Sobornost/ECR* 26/2 (2004), pp. 24–38, and here at p. 28. The citation is of Olivier Clément, *The Roots of Christian Mysticism* (London: New City, 1993), p. 312.
129. Plested, '"East and East and West is West"?', p. 31.
130. *Ibid.*
131. *Ibid.*, p. 32.
132. Cited *ibid*, p. 36.
133. Jean-Miguel Garrigues, *L'Ésprit qui dit 'Père'. L'Ésprit-Saint dans la vie trinitaire et le problème du Filioque* (Paris: Téqui, 1981).
134. Edward Every, 'The Filioque Question', *Sobornost/ECR* 1/2 (1979), pp. 42–9, and here at p. 44.
135. Philip Sherrard, *Church, Papacy and Schism: A Theological Enquiry* (London: SPCK, 1978).
136. *Sobornost/ECR* 1/1 (1979), p. 85.
137. *Ibid.*
138. Norman Russell, 'Anselm of Haverberg and the Union of the Churches. I. The Problem of the Filioque', *Sobornost/ECR* 1/2 (1979), pp. 19–41, and here at p. 22.
139. *Ibid.*, p. 40.
140. *Ibid.*, p. 41.
141. North American Orthodox–Catholic Theological Consultation, 'The Filioque: A Church-dividing Issue?', *Sobornost /ECR* 26/1 (2004), pp. 27–60, and here at p. 55–6.
142. *Ibid.*, p. 56.
143. *Ibid.*, p. 59.
144. Jouko Martikainen, 'Man's Salvation: Deification or Justification? Observations on Key-Words in the Orthodox and the Lutheran Tradition', *Sobornost* 7/3 (1976), pp. 180–92, and here at p. 190.
145. Veli-Matti Kärkkäinnen, 'The Doctrine of Theosis and its Ecumenical Potential', *Sobornost/ECR* 23/2 (2001), pp. 45–77, and here at p. 46.
146. *Ibid.*, p. 57.
147. *Ibid.*, p. 58.

148. Ibid., p. 68.
149. Norman Russell, *The Doctrine of Deification in the Greek Patristic Tradition* (Oxford: Oxford University Press, 2004).
150. Norman Russell, 'Why does Theosis Fascinate Western Christians?', *Sobornost /ECR* 34/1 (2012), pp. 5–15, and here at p. 13.
151. Ibid.
152. Ibid., p. 14.
153. Ibid., p. 15.

Notes to Chapter 4

1. A. M. Allchin, 'Portrait of a Patriarch', *Sobornost* 6/1 (1970), pp. 5–10. The book under discussion was Olivier Clément, *Dialogues avec le patriarche Athénagoras* (Paris: Fayard, 1969).
2. Richard Hanson, 'Orthodox Dogma and Anglican Vagueness', *Sobornost* 6/4 (1972), pp. 221–7, and here at p. 222.
3. Ibid., p. 223.
4. Ibid., p. 225.
5. Ibid., p. 226.
6. Michael Ramsey, 'Three Phases of the Ecumenical Movement', *Sobornost* 6/5 (1972), pp. 292–6, and here at p. 292.
7. Ibid.
8. Ibid.
9. Ibid., p. 293.
10. Ibid.
11. Ibid., p. 294.
12. Ibid., p. 295.
13. Ibid., p. 296.
14. A. M. Allchin, 'Anglican–Orthodox Relations, 1972', *Sobornost* 6/7 (1973), pp. 491–8, and here at p. 493.
15. Ibid., p. 495.
16. Archbishop Basil [Krivocheine], 'Christ's Redemptive Work on the Cross and in the Resurrection', *Sobornost* 6/7 (1973), pp. 446–58, and here at p. 447.
17. Ibid.
18. Cited *ibid.*, p. 450.
19. Ibid., p. 451.
20. Ibid., p. 452.
21. Ibid., p. 454.

22. Ibid., p. 455.
23. Ibid.
24. Ibid.
25. Metropolitan Stylianos of Miletoupolis, 'The Holy Spirit as Interpreter of the Gospel and Giver of Life in the Church Today', *Sobornost* 6/3 (1973), pp. 459–71, and here at p. 459.
26. Ibid., p. 460.
27. Ibid., p. 464.
28. Basil the Great, *On the Holy Spirit*, 16/38.
29. Metropolitan Stylianos of Miletoupolis, 'The Holy Spirit as Interpreter of the Gospel and Giver of Life in the Church Today', p. 468.
30. A. M. Allchin, 'The Hertford College Meeting, July 1973', *Sobornost* 6/8 (1973), pp. 587–90.
31. Frank Weston, 'Theosis or Philanthropy? Orthodox Critiques of Western Ecumenism', *Sobornost* 6/10 (1974), pp. 720–30, and here at p. 724.
32. Mark Santer, 'Scripture and the Councils', *Sobornost* 7/2 (1975), pp. 99–111, and here at p. 100.
33. Ibid., p. 103.
34. Richard Field, *Of the Church*, IV. 14, cited in Santer, 'Scripture and the Councils', p. 103.
35. Field, *Of the Church*, V, 51, cited in Santer, 'Scripture and the Councils', p. 105.
36. Cited *ibid*.
37. Ibid., p. 108.
38. Ibid.
39. Ibid., p. 109.
40. Ibid.
41. Ibid., p. 110.
42. Constantine Scouteris, 'Holy Scripture and Councils', *Sobornost* 7/2 (1975), pp. 111–16, and here at p. 111.
43. Ibid., p. 112.
44. Ibid., p. 113.
45. Ibid.
46. Ibid.
47. Ibid., p. 114.
48. Ibid.
49. John Meyendorff, 'Orthodox and Anglicans', *Sobornost* 7/3 (1976), pp. 201–3, and here at p. 202.
50. Kallistos Ware and Colin Davey (ed.), *Anglican–Orthodox Dialogue* (London: SPCK, 1977).

Notes to Part II, Chapter 4

51. *Christian Believing. The Nature of the Christian Faith and its Expression in Holy Scripture and Creeds* (London: SPCK, 1976).
52. David Jenkins, *The Contradiction of Christianity* (London: SCM, 1976).
53. Elisabeth Behr-Sigel, 'The Participation of Women in the Life of the Church', *Sobornost* 7/6 (1978), pp. 480–92, and here at p. 482.
54. *Ibid.*, p. 483.
55. *Ibid.*, p. 484.
56. *Ibid.*, p. 485.
57. *Ibid.*, p. 486.
58. *Ibid.*, p. 487.
59. *Ibid.*
60. Elisabeth Behr-Sigel, 'Mary and Women', *Sobornost* 23/1 (2001), pp. 23–39, and here at p. 23.
61. *Ibid.*, p. 33.
62. *Ibid.*, p. 35.
63. Behr-Sigel, 'The Participation of Women in the Life of the Church', p. 488.
64. *Ibid.*, p. 489.
65. *Ibid.*, p. 490.
66. For an analysis of her attitudes, see Sarah Hinlicky Wilson, 'Elisabeth Behr-Sigel—Feminist, Protestant, Orthodox? Part I. Feminism and Protestantism', *Sobornost/ECR* 32/1 (2010), pp. 53–74; Sarah Hinlicky Wilson, 'Elisabeth Behr-Sigel—Feminist, Protestant, Orthodox? Part II. Which School of Orthodox Theology?', *Sobornost* 32, 2 (2010), pp. 37–55.
67. Kallistos Ware, 'Orthodoxy and the World Council of Churches', *Sobornost/ECR* 1/1 (1979), pp. 74–83.
68. Norman Russell, 'Catholic–Orthodox Dialogue: Patmos and Rhodes', *Sobornost/ECR* 3/1 (1981), pp. 86–92, and here at p. 86.
69. *Ibid.*, p. 89.
70. *Ibid.*, p. 90.
71. *Ibid.*, p. 91.
72. *Sobornost/ECR* 3/2 (1981), p. 159.
73. Kallistos Ware, 'Anglican–Orthodox Dialogue 1982: A Second Spring?', *Sobornost/ECR* 4/2 (1982), pp. 219–22.
74. Eamon Duffy, *The Stripping of the Altars. Traditional Religion in England, c. 1400 – c. 1580* (New Haven and London: Yale University Press, 1992).
75. E. R. Hardy, 'The Blessed Dead in Anglican Piety', *Sobornost/ECR* 3/2 (1981), pp. 160–78 and here at p. 161.
76. Cited *ibid.*, p. 162.
77. Cited in *ibid.*, p. 165.

78. Cited in *ibid.*, p. 164.
79. *Ibid.*
80. Cited *ibid.*, p. 176.
81. *Ibid.*, p. 177.
82. Kallistos Ware, '"One Body in Christ". Death and the Communion of Saints', *Sobornost/ECR* 3/2 (1981), pp. 179–91, and here at p. 181.
83. *Ibid.*, p. 182.
84. *Ibid.*, p. 183.
85. *Ibid.*
86. Charles Williams, *All Hallows Eve* (London: Faber & Faber, 1948).
87. George Every, 'Toll Gates on the Air-Way', *Eastern Churches Review* 8/2 (1976), pp. 139–51.
88. Kallistos Ware, '"One Body in Christ"', p. 182.
89. Robert Ombres, OP, *The Theology of Purgatory* (Dublin: Mercier Press, 1978).
90. Kallistos Ware, '"One Body in Christ"', p. 188.
91. *Ibid.*, p. 190.
92. Michael Ramsey, 'The Communion of Saints', *Sobornost/ECR* 3/2 (1981), pp. 192–6, and here at p. 192.
93. *Ibid.*, p. 193.
94. *Ibid.*, p. 194.
95. *Ibid.*, p. 195.
96. *Sobornost/ECR* 4/1 (1982), p. 81.
97. *Sobornost/ECR* 4/2 (1982), p. 219.
98. *The Anglican-Orthodox Dialogue: The Dublin Agreed Statement 1984* (London: SPCK, 1985).
99. Hugh Wybrew, 'The Mystery of the Church in the Dublin Agreed Statement', *Sobornost/ECR* 8/1 (1986), pp. 15–22.
100. Militza Zernov, 'Unity and Disunity Today' *Sobornost/ECR* 8/1 (1986), pp. 23–7.
101. Philippe Sabant, 'The Panorthodox Preconciliar Conference of 1986', *Sobornost/ECR* 9/1 (1987), pp. 62–6.
102. John Zizioulas, 'Ecumenism and the Need for Vision', *Sobornost/ECR* 10/2 (1988), pp. 36–43, and here at p. 38.
103. *Ibid.*
104. *Ibid.* 12/1 (1990), p. 79.
105. *Ibid.*, p. 80.
106. *Ibid.* 38/2 (2016), p. 5.
107. Gregor Sneddon, 'Cornerstone Rejected? St Maximus the Confessor and Dyothelite Christology', *Sobornost/ECR* 38/2 (2016), pp. 40–60, and here at p. 60.

108. Hugh Wybrew, 'Anglican–Orthodox Dialogue', 13/1 (1991), pp. 63–5.
109. It would have its issue in the 'Cyprus Agreed Statement': see *Anglican–Orthodox Dialogue: The Church of the Triune God* (London: General Synod of the Church of England, 2008).
110. Hugh Wybrew, 'The Eastern Catholic Churches and Ecumenism', *Sobornost/ECR* 13/2 (1991), pp. 46–9.
111. Serge Keleher, 'A Comment on the Joint Report', *Sobornost/ECR* 13/2 (1991), pp. 55–64. In the body of the journal this article is entitled 'Reflections on Uniatism as a Method of Union'.
112. *Sobornost/ECR* 15/1 (1993), pp. 45–7. The book, ed. Paul McPartlan, was the optimistically titled *One in 2000? Towards Catholic–Orthodox Unity. Agreed Statements and Parish Papers* (Slough: St Paul's Publications, 1993).
113. Boris Bobrinskoy, 'Catholic–Orthodox Relations: the need for love as well as knowledge', in *Sobornost/ECR* 15/2 (1993), pp. 28–38, and here at pp. 35–6.
114. *Ibid.*, p. 37.
115. *Ibid.*, p. 36.
116. *Ibid.*, p. 37.
117. *Ibid.*, p. 31.
118. *Ibid.*, p. 33.
119. *Sobornost/ECR* 16/2 (1994), p. 61.
120. *Ibid.*, p. 62.
121. *Sobornost/ECR* 17/1 (1995), p. 52.
122. *Ibid.*, p. 53.
123. *Sobornost/ECR* 19/1 (1997), p. 79.
124. Cited in *Sobornost/ECR* 19/1 (1997), p. 79, with Brock's additions in square brackets.
125. Cited *ibid.*, p. 80.
126. *Ibid.*, p. 84.
127. Christopher J. Ellis, *Together on the Way: A Theology of Ecumenism* (London: British Council of Churches, 1991).
128. *Sobornost/ECR* 13/1 (1991), p. 75.
129. *Sobornost/ECR* 13/2 (1991), p. 81.
130. *Ibid.*, p. 82.
131. D. Preman Niles, *Resisting the Threats to Life: Covenanting for Justice, Peace and the Integrity of Creation* (Geneva: WCC Publications, 1989).
132. *Sobornost/ECR* 13/2 (1991), p. 89.
133. Colin Davey, 'Problems of Mission: A Colloquium at Chevetogne', *Sobornost/ECR* 17/1 (1995), pp. 41–5.
134. *Ibid.*, p. 44.

135. *Ibid.*, p. 45.
136. Colin Davey, 'The Successors of Peter and Paul. Three Documents and a Visit', *Sobornost/ECR* 18/1 (1996), pp. 52–66, and here at p. 52.
137. Kallistos of Diokleia, 'The Estonian Crisis: A Salutary Warning?', *Sobornost/ECR* 18/2 (1996), pp. 59–68, and here at p. 6.7
138. *Sobornost/ECR* 18/2 (1996), p. 71.
139. *Sobornost/ECR* 19/2 (1997), p. 62.
140. Hugh Wybrew, 'Anglican–Orthodox Dialogue, 1998', *Sobornost/ECR* 20/2 (1998), pp. 59–61.
141. Colin Davey, 'Orthodox–Roman Catholic Dialogue: The Ravenna Agreed Statement', *Sobornost/ECR* 30/2 (2008), pp. 7–36.
142. Cited *ibid.*, p. 28.
143. Adam DeVille, *The Orthodox and the Papacy . 'Ut unum sint' and the Prospects of East–West Unity* (Notre Dame, IN: University of Notre Dame Press, 2011).
144. *Sobornost/ECR* 37/2 (2015), p. 73.
145. George E. Demacopoulos, *The Invention of Peter: Apostolic Discourse and Papal Authority in Late Antiquity* (Philadelphia, PA: University of Philadelphia Press, 2013).
146. *Sobornost/ECR* 37/2 (2015), p. 75.

Notes to Chapter 5

1. Igumen Chariton, *The Art of Prayer: An Orthodox Anthology* (London: Faber, 1966), p. 63.
2. Kallistos Ware, 'The Theology of Worship', *Sobornost* 5/10 (1970), pp. 729–37, and here at p. 731.
3. *Ibid.*, p. 732.
4. *Ibid.*, p. 733.
5. *Ibid.*, p. 732.
6. *Ibid.*, p. 733.
7. *Ibid.*
8. *Ibid.*
9. Alexander Schmemann, *The World as Sacrament* (London: Darton, Longman & Todd, 1966), p. 34.
10. Kallistos of Diokleia, '"It is time for the Lord to act: The Divine Liturgy as Heaven on Earth', *Sobornost /ECR* 23/1 (2001), pp. 7–22, and here at p. 7.
11. *Ibid.*, p. 19.
12. Mother Mary and Archimandrite Kallistos Ware (tr.), *The Festal Menaion* (London: Faber & Faber, 1969).

13. *Sobornost* 6/3 (1971), p. 208.
14. Mother Mary and Archimandrite Kallistos Ware (tr.), *The Lenten Triodion* (London: Faber & Faber, 1978).
15. Nigel Gotteri, 'The Language of Orthodoxy: Pidgin or Pentecost?', *Sobornost* 7/4 (1977), pp. 251–61, and here at p. 255.
16. *Ibid.*, p. 256.
17. *Ibid.*
18. Nigel Gotteri, 'Tradition and Translation', *Sobornost/ECR* 2.2 (1980), pp. 41–49, and here at p. 49.
19. *The Orthodox Liturgy* (Oxford: Oxford University Press, 1982).
20. David Balfour, 'Translating the Liturgy', *Sobornost /ECR*. 6/1 (1984), pp. 84–96, and here at p. 86.
21. Robert F. Taft, SJ, *The Great Entrance* (Rome: Pontificum Institutum Studiorum Orientalium, 1975).
22. *Sobornost* 7/7 (1978), p. 626.
23. Catherine Pickstock, *After Writing. On the Liturgical Consummation of Philosophy* (Oxford: Blackwell, 1998).
24. E. R. Hardy, 'The Transfiguration in Western Liturgical Usage', *Sobornost* 6/9 (1974), pp. 626–41, and here at p. 626.
25. *Ibid.*
26. *Ibid.*, p. 626.
27. *Ibid.*, p. 631.
28. Michael Paternoster, 'Infrequent Communion', *Sobornost* 7/7 (1978), pp. 568–70; Hugh Wybrew, 'Infrequent Communion: A Comment', *Sobornost* 7/7 (1978), pp. 571–5.
29. R. C. D. Jasper's *The Development of the Anglican Liturgy 1662–1980* (London: SPCK, 1989).
30. *Sobornost/ECR* 12/2 (1990), p. 188.
31. Alexander Schmemann, *The Eucharist: Sacrament of the Kingdom* (Crestwood, NY: Saint Vladimir's Seminary Press, 1988).
32. *Sobornost /ECR* 12/1 (1990), p. 97.
33. *Ibid.*, p. 98.
34. *Ibid.*, pp. 101–2. See Hugh Wybrew, *The Orthodox Liturgy* (London: SPCK, 1989).
35. Thomas Pott OSB, *La Réforme liturgique byzantine. Étude du phénomène de l'évolution non-spontanée de la liturgie byzantine* (Rome: CLV-Edizioni Liturgiche, 2000).
36. *Sobornost/ECR* 24/1 (2002), p. 96.
37. Dominic White, 'Dance in Christianity: An Essay in Ressourcement?', *Sobornost/ECR* 35/1–2 (2013), pp. 81–122, and here at p. 121.

38. Andrew Louth, 'A New Funeral Service for the Orthodox?', *Sobornost/ECR* 35/2 (2013), pp. 123–35; cf. Andre Louth, 'A Revised Orthodox Ceremony of Marriage?', *Sobornost/ECR* 29/2 (2007), pp. 57–74.
39. Sotiris Mitralexis, 'Liturgical Originality in the Orthodox Church. A Case Study', *Sobornost/ECR* 39/1 (2017), pp. 73–88.

Notes to Chapter 6

1. Militza Zernov, 'The Icon of the Holy Trinity of Rublev', *Sobornost* 6/6 (1972), pp. 387–94, and here at p. 388.
2. *Ibid.*, p. 390.
3. *Ibid.*, p. 393.
4. Charles Lock, 'The Space of Hospitality: On an Icon of the Trinity ascribed to Andrei Rublev', *Sobornost/ECR* 30/1 (2008), pp. 21–53, and here at p. 27.
5. Gervase Mathew, *Byzantine Aesthetics* (London: John Murray, 1963), p. 168, note 2.
6. Gabriel Bunge, *The Rublev Trinity* (Crestwood, NY: St Vladimir's Seminary Press, 2007).
7. Vrej Nersessian, *Treasures from the Ark. 1700 Years of Armenian Christian Art* (London: British Library, 2001).
8. Lock, 'The Space of Hospitality', p. 51.
9. Joseph P. Frary, 'The Logic of Icons', *Sobornost* 6/6 (1972), pp. 395–404, and here at p. 396.
10. *Ibid.*, p. 399.
11. *Ibid.*, p. 401.
12. Bede, *Historia ecclesiastica* I. 25.
13. Ian Wilson, *The Shroud of Turin: The Burial Cloth of Jesus Christ?* (Garden City, NY: Doubleday, 1978).
14. Cited in A. M Allchin, 'Anglicans and the Decisions of the Seventh Ecumenical Council', *Sobornost* 7/7 (1978), pp. 588–94, and here at p. 590.
15. *Ibid.*, p. 593.
16. Constantine Scouteris, 'Never as Gods: Icons and their Veneration', *Sobornost/ECR* 6/1 (1984), pp. 6–18, and here at p. 10.
17. *Ibid.*, p. 12.
18. Cited *ibid.*, p. 16.
19. *Ibid.*
20. Christopher Walter, 'The Icon and the Image of Christ: The Second Council of Nicaea and Byzantine Tradition', *Sobornost/ECR* 10/1 (1988), pp. 23–33, and here at p. 33.

21. *Ibid.*
22. *Ibid.*, p. 31.
23. *Ibid.*, p. 33.
24. Sirapie der Nersessian, *Armenian Art* (London: Thames & Hudson 1979).
25. *Sobornost/ECR* 2/1 (1980), p. 114.
26. *Sobornost/ECR* 4/2 (1982), p. 245.
27. Christopher Walter, *Art and Ritual of the Byzantine Church* (London: Variorum 1982).
28. *Sobornost/ECR* 6/2 (1984), p. 76.
29. Otto Demus, *The Mosaics of S Marco in Venice* (Chicago and London: University of Chicago Press 1984, 4 vols.).
30. *Sobornost/ECR* 8/2 (1986), p. 83.
31. *Ibid.*
32. Eugène Troubetzkoi, *Trois études sur l'icône* (Paris: YMCA and OEIL, 1986).
33. John Baggley, *Doors of Perception. Icons and their Spiritual Significance* (London and Oxford: Mowbray, 1987).
34. *Sobornost/ECR* 11/1-2 (1989), p. 122.
35. Gennadios Limouris (ed.), *Icons: Windows on Eternity. Theology and Spirituality in Colour* (Geneva: WCC Publications, 1990).
36. *Sobornost/ECR* 12/2 (1990), p. 175.
37. *Ibid.*, p. 179.
38. *Ibid.*, p. 180.
39. Jill Storer, 'Byzantium: Treasures of Byzantine Art and Culture from British Collections', *Sobornost/ECR* 17/2 (1995), pp. 38-44, and here at p. 41.
40. Sophocles Sophocleos, *Icons of Cyprus, 7th-20th century* (Nicosia: Museum Publications, 1994).
41. *Sobornost/ECR* 19/2 (1997), p. 81.
42. Kallistos of Diokleia, 'Beauty will Save the World', *Sobornost/ECR* 30/1 (2008), pp. 7-20, and here at p. 8.
43. *Ibid.*, p. 17.
44. *Ibid.*, p. 19.
45. Jean-Claude Larchet, *L'Iconographe et l'artiste* (Paris: Cerf, 2008).
46. *Sobornost/ECR* 32/2 (2010), p. 91.
47. I may be allowed to draw attention to my own account in Aidan Nichols, OP, *In Search of the Sacred Image* (Leominster: Gracewing, forthcoming), ch. 5.
48. Andrew Louth, 'The Recovery of the Icon', *Sobornost/ECR* 39/1 (2017), pp. 7-35, and here at p. 12.
49. *Ibid.*, p. 23.

50. Léonide Ouspensky, *Essai sur la théologie de l'icône dans l'Église orthodoxe* (Paris: Editions de l'Exarchat patriarchal russe en Europe Occidentale, 1960).
51. Vladimir Lossky and Leonid Ouspensky, *Der Sinn der Ikonen* (Bern-Olten: Urs Graf Verlag, 1952); Vladimir Lossky and Leonid Ouspensky, *The Meaning of Icons* (Crestwood, NY: St Vladimir's Seminary Press, 1994).
52. Louth, 'The Recovery of the Icon', art, cit., p. 27.
53. *Ibid.*, p. 29.
54. *Ibid.*, p. 33.
55. Paul Ladouceur, 'The Saint as Artist: The Art of Saint Maria of Paris (Mother Maria Skobtsova). The Making of a Poet-Artist', *Sobornost/ECR* 36/1 (2014), pp. 48–70, and here at p. 59.
56. *Ibid.*, p. 70.

Notes to Chapter 7

1. Kallistos Ware, 'The Value of the Material Creation', *Sobornost* 6/3 (1971), pp. 154–65, and here at p. 156.
2. *Ibid.*
3. *Ibid.*
4. *Ibid.*, p. 159.
5. *Ibid.*, p. 163.
6. *Sobornost/ECR* 10/1 (1988), p. 59. See Philip Sherrard, *The Rape of Man and Nature* (Ipswich: Golgonooza Press, 1987).
7. *Sobornost/ECR* 15/2 (1993), p. 79. See Philip Sherrard, *Human Image: World Image. The Death and Resurrection of Sacred Cosmology* (Ipswich: Golgonooza Press, 1992).
8. Sebastian Brock, 'Humanity and the Natural World in the Syriac Tradition', *Sobornost/ECR* 12/2 (1990), pp. 131–42, and here at p. 140.
9. David Gosling, *New Earth: Covenanting for Justice, Peace and the Integrity of Creation*, by (London: CCBI, 1992); D. Preman Niles (ed.), *Between the Flood and the Rainbow: Interpreting the Conciliar Process (Covenant) to Justice, Peace and the Integrity of Creation* (Geneva: WCC Publications, 1992).
10. *Sobornost/ECR* 16/1 (1994), p. 72.
11. *Ibid.*, p. 74.
12. *Sobornost/ECR* 17/1 (1995), p. 51.
13. John Chryssavgis, 'Religion, Science and Environment', *Sobornost/ECR* 22/1 (2000), pp. 56–7.
14. John Chryssavgis, *Beyond the Shattered Image* (Minneapolis, MN: Light and Life, 1999).
15. *Sobornost/ECR* 22/1 (2000), p. 71.

16. Charles Birch and Lukas Vischer, *Living with the Animals: The Community of God's Creatures* (Geneva: WCC Publications, 1997).
17. *Sobornost/ECR* 22/1 (2000), p. 73.
18. Larry Rasmussen, *Earth Community, Earth Ethics* (Geneva: WCC Publications, 1996).
19. *Sobornost/ECR* 22/1 (2000), p. 75.
20. Edward Echlin, *Earth Spirituality. Jesus at the Centre* (New Alresford: Arthur James, 1999).
21. *Sobornost/ECR* 23/2 (2001), p. 99.
22. *Ibid.*, p. 100.
23. Cited *ibid.*
24. John Chryssavgis, *Cosmic Grace, Humble Prayer: The Ecological Vision of the Green Patriarch Bartholomew I* (Grand Rapids, MI, and Cambridge: Eerdmans, 2003).
25. *Sobornost/ECR* 27/1 (2005), p. 125.
26. Crina Gschwandiner, 'Sabbath and Eighth Day: On the Messianic Dimensions of Ecological Practice', *Sobornost/ECR* 33/2 (2011), pp 54–92, and here at p. 55.
27. Compare Jürgen Moltmann, *God in Creation: An Ecological Doctrine of Creation* (London: SCM 1985), which she cites.
28. Gschwandiner, 'Sabbath and Eighth Day', p. 63.
29. *Ibid.*, p. 70
30. *Ibid.*, p. 77.
31. David Faberberg, *Theologia Prima. What is Liturgical Theology? A Study in Methodology* (Chicago: Hillenbrand, 2004).
32. Gschwandiner, 'Sabbath and Eighth Day', p. 85.
33. Elisabeth Theokritoff, *Living in God's Creation. The Ecological Vision of Orthodox Christianity* (Crestwood, NY: St Vladimir's Seminary Press, 2009).
34. *Sobornost/ECR* 33/2 (2011), pp. 110–12.

Notes to Chapter 8

1. Cheslyn Jones, Geoffrey Wainwright, Edward Yarnold, SJ (ed.), *The Study of Spirituality* (London: SPCK, 1986).
2. Cited in *Sobornost/ECR* 9/1 (1987), p. 73.
3. Cited *ibid.*
4. Alexander Schmemann, *Church, World, Mission. Reflections on Orthodoxy in the West* (Crestwood, NY: St Vladimir's Seminary Press, 1979).
5. *Sobornost/ECR* 2/2 (1980), p. 108.
6. *Sobornost/ECR* 9/1 (1987), p. 73.

7. Metropolitan John (Zizioulas) of Pergamon, 'Communion and Otherness', *Sobornost/ECR* 16/1 (1994), pp. 7-19, and here at p. 8.
8. *Ibid.*, p. 11.
9. *Ibid.*, p. 12.
10. *Ibid.*
11. *Ibid.*, p. 14.
12. *Ibid.*
13. *Ibid.*, p. 17.
14. *Ibid.*, p. 18.
15. Kallistos Ware, 'Orthodox Theology in the New Millennium. What is the most important question?', *Sobornost/ECR* 26/1 (2004), pp. 7-23, and here at p. 9. See also Kallistos Ware, 'The Human Person as an Icon of the Trinity', *Sobornost/ECR* 8/2 (1986), pp. 6-23.
16. Kallistos Ware, 'Orthodox Theology in the New Millennium', p. 17.
17. *Ibid.*, p. 18.
18. In a ten-page assessment of John Breck, *The Sacred Gift of Life* (Crestwood, NY: Saint Vladimir's Seminary Press, 1998), *Sobornost/ECR* 23/1 (2001), pp. 86-96.
19. Philip Sherrard had a quartet of articles lambasting the 'stud farm': 'Bodily Thoughts upon Athos', *Sobornost* 5/3 (1966), pp. 181-7; 'Humanae Vitae. Notes on the Encyclical Letter of Pope Paul VI', *Sobornost* 5/8 (1969), pp. 570-80; 'An Approach to the Sacrament of Marriage', *Sobornost* 6/6 (1972), pp. 404-15; 'The Meaning of Sexual Love in the Work of Three Russian Writers', *Sobornost* 6/8 (1973), pp. 566-80. But he was not alone: see also John Behr, 'Marriage and Asceticism', *Sobornost/ECR* 29/2 (2007), pp. 24-50.
20. Emmanuel Clapsis (ed.), *The Orthodox Churches in a Pluralistic World. An Ecumenical Conversation* (Geneva: WCC Publications, and Brookline, MA: Holy Cross Orthodox Press, 2004).
21. *Sobornost/ECR* 27/2 (2005), p. 102.
22. Olivier Clément, 'The Orthodox Diaspora in Western Europe: Its Future and its Role', *Sobornost* 7/7 (1979), pp. 576-87, and here at p. 576.
23. *Ibid.*
24. *Sobornost/ECR* 15/1 (1993), p. 84.
25. Clément, 'The Orthodox Diaspora in Western Europe', p. 577.
26. *Ibid.*, p. 584.
27. *Ibid.*, pp. 577-8.
28. *Ibid.*, p. 578.
29. *Ibid.*, p. 579.
30. Allan Brent, 'Culture and Mission in Eastern and Western Catholicism: Can bishops represent cultures rather than territories?', *Sobornost/ECR* 34/2 (2013), pp. 17-33, and here at p. 33.

31. *Ibid.*
32. *Ibid.*
33. Clément, 'The Orthodox Diaspora in Western Europe', p. 582.
34. *Ibid.*, p. 583.
35. Francis Penhale, *The Anglican Church. Catholics in Crisis* (London: Mowbray, 1986).
36. Richard Price, 'Benedict XVI and Catholic–Orthodox Relations', *Sobornost/ECR* 27/2 (2005), pp. 8–26, and here at p. 10.
37. *Ibid.*
38. *Ibid.*, p. 23.
39. *Ibid.*, p. 19.
40. *Ibid.*, p. 23.
41. Various authors, 'Unity among Christians: A Conversation', *Sobornost/ECR* 36/1 (2014), pp. 7–34, and here at p. 9.
42. *Ibid.*, p. 10.
43. *Ibid.*, p. 14.
44. *Ibid.*, p. 16.
45. *Ibid.*, p. 17.
46. *Ibid.*, p. 20.
47. *Ibid.*, p. 21.
48. *Ibid.*, p. 23.
49. *Ibid.*, p. 24.
50. *Ibid.*, p. 28.
51. *Ibid.*, p. 29.
52. *Ibid.*, p. 31.
53. *Ibid.*, p. 32.
54. *Ibid.*
55. *Ibid.*
56. *Ibid.*, p. 33.
57. *Ibid.*, p. 34.

SELECT BIBLIOGRAPHY

Anderson, Paul B., *People, Church and State in Modern Russia* (London: SCM, 1944)

Arjakovsky, Antoine, *La Génération des penseurs religieux de l'Emigration russe. La revue 'La Voie' (Put'), 1925–1940* (Kiev and Paris: L'Ésprit et la Lettre, 2002)

Beaken, Robert, *Cosmo Lang. Archbishop in War and Crisis* (London: Tauris, 2012)

Behr, John, Andrew Louth and Dimitri Conomos (eds.), *Abba. The Tradition of Orthodoxy in the West. Festschrift for Bishop Kallistos (Ware) of Diokleia* (Crestwood, NY: St Vladimir's Seminary Press, 2003)

Behr-Sigel, Elisabeth, *Lev Gillet. 'A Monk of the Eastern Church'* (Oxford: Fellowship of St Alban and St Sergius, 1999)

Bibbee, J., *Anglo-Catholicism and the Orthodox East: William Birkbeck and the Quest for Unity, 1888–1916* (London: Anglo-Catholic History Society, 2007)

Böss, Otto, *Die Lehre der Eurasier. Ein Beitrag zur russischen Ideengeschichte des 20. Jahrhunderts* (Wiesbaden: Veröffentlichungen des Osteuropa Instituts München, 1961)

Blane, Andrew (ed.), *Georges Florovsky. Russian Intellectual, Orthodox Churchman* (Crestwood, NY: St Vladimir's Seminary Press, 1991)

Briggs, John, Mercy Amba Oduhoye, Georges Tsetsis (ed.), *A History of the Ecumenical Movement. Volume 3: 1968–2000* (Geneva: World Council of Churches, 2004)

Bulgakov, Sergei, *The Wisdom of God. A Short Summary of Sophiology* (New York and London: Williams & Norgate, 1937)

Chadwick, Owen, *Hensley Henson. A Study in the Friction between Church and State* (Norwich: Canterbury Press, 1994 [1983])

—— *Michael Ramsey. A Life* (Oxford: Clarendon Press, 1990)

Chandler, Michael, *The Life and Work of Henry Parry Liddon* (Leominster: Gracewing, 2000)

—— *The Life and Work of John Mason Neale, 1818–1866* (Leominster: Gracewing, 1995)

Cunningham, James W., *A Vanquished Hope. The Movement for Church Renewal in Russia 1905–6* (Crestwood, NY: St Vladimir's Seminary Press, 1981)

Cunningham, Mary, and Elizabeth Theokritoff (ed.), *The Cambridge Companion to Orthodox Christian Theology* (Cambridge: Cambridge University Press, 2008)

Destivelle, Hyacinthe, *Le Concile de Moscou (1917–1918): La Création des institutions conciliares de l'Église orthodoxe russe* (Paris: Cerf, 2006).

Doll, Peter M. (ed.), *Anglicanism and Orthodoxy 300 Years after the 'Greek College' in Oxford* (Oxford: Peter Lang, 2006)

Doolan, Patrick (ed.), *Recovering the Icon: The Life and Work of Leonid Ouspensky* (Crestwood, NY: St Vladimir's Seminary Press, 2008)

Evdokimov, Paul, *L'Art de l'icône. Théologie de la beauté* (Paris: Desclée de Brouwer, 1970)

Fey, Harold E. (ed.), *The Ecumenical Advance. A History of the Ecumenical Movement. Volume 2: 1948–1968* (London: SPCK, 1970)

Findlow, Irina, *Journey into Unity* (New York and London: New City, 1975)

Fisch, Thomas (ed.), *Liturgy and Tradition. Theological Reflections of Alexander Schmemann* (Crestwood, NY: St Vladimir's Seminary Press, 2003)

Gavrilyuk, Paul L., *Georges Florovsky and the Russian Religious Renaissance* (New York and Oxford: Oxford University Press, 2013)

Geffert, Bryn, Eastern Orthodox and Anglicans. Diplomacy, Theology and the Politics of Interwar Ecumenism (Notre Dame, IN: University of Notre Dame Press, 2010).

Gill, Robin, and Lorna Kendall (ed.), *Michael Ramsey as Theologian* (London: Darton, Longman and Todd, 1995)

Gordon-Taylor, Benjamin, and Nicolas Stebbing CR (ed.), *Walter Frere. Scholar, Monk, Bishop* (Norwich: Canterbury Press, 2011)

Gorodetzky, Nadejda, *The Humiliated Christ in Modern Russian Thought* (London: SPCK, 1938)

Hylson-Smith, Kenneth, *High Churchmanship in the Church of England. From the Sixteenth Century to the Late Twentieth Century* (Edinburgh: T. & T. Clark, 1993)

Jasper, Ronald, *Arthur Cayley Headlam. Life and Letters of a Bishop* (London: Faith Press, 1960)

Johnston, Robert H., *New Mecca, New Babylon: Paris and the Russian Exiles, 1920–1945* (Kingston and Montreal: McGill-Queen's University Press, 1988)

Kent, John, *William Temple: Church, State and Society in Britain, 1880–1950* (Cambridge: Cambridge University Press, 1992)

Kniazeff, Alexis, *L'Institut Saint-Serge. De l'académie d'autrefois au rayonnement*

d'aujourd'hui (Paris: Beauchesne, 1974)
Knight, Douglas (ed.), *The Theology of John Zizioulas. Personhood and the Church* (Farnham: Ashgate, 2007)
Laruelle, Marlène, *Russian Eurasianism: An Ideology of Empire* (Baltimore, MD: Johns Hopkins University Press, 2008)
Lossky, Vladimir, *Essai sur la théologie mystique de l'Église d'Orient* (Paris: Aubier, 1944).
—— and Leonid Ouspensky, *The Meaning of Icons* (Boston, MA: Boston Book and Art Shop, 1952)
Louth, Andrew, *Modern Orthodox Thinkers: from the Philokalia to the Present* (London: SPCK, 2015)
Lowrie, Donald, *St Sergius in Paris. The Orthodox Theological Institute* (London: SPCK, 1954)
McLeod, Hugh, *The Religious Crisis of the 1960s* (Oxford: Oxford University Press, 2007)
Mascall, E. L., *Christ, the Christian and the Church. A Study of the Incarnation and its Consequences* (London: Longmans, Green and Co., 1946)
—— *Saraband. The Memoirs of E. L. Mascall* (Leominster: Gracewing, 1992)
Mason, Alistair, SSM. *History of the Society of the Sacred Mission* (Norwich: Canterbury Press, 1993)
van der Mensbrugghe, Alexis, *From Dyad to Triad. A Plea for Duality against Dualism and an Essay towards the Synthesis of Orthodoxy* (London: Faith Press, 1934)
Middleton, Arthur, *Fathers and Anglicans. The Limits of Orthodoxy* (Leominster: Gracewing, 2001)
Miller, Matthew L., *The American YMCA and Russian Culture: The Preservation and Expansion of Orthodox Christianity, 1900–1940* (Plymouth: Lexington Books, 2013)
Nichols, Aidan, OP, *Mystical Theologian. The Work of Vladimir Lossky* (Leominster: Gracewing, 2017)
—— *In Search of the Sacred Image* (Leominster: Gracewing, forthcoming)
—— *Theology in the Russian Diaspora. Church, Fathers, Eucharist in Nikolai Afanas'ev, 1893–1966* (Cambridge: Cambridge University Press, 1989)
—— *Wisdom from Above. A Primer in the Theology of Father Sergei Bulgakov* (Leominster: Gracewing, 2005)
Ouspensky, Léonide, *Essai sur la théologie de l'icône dans l'Église orthodoxe* (Paris: Éditions de l'Exarchat patriarchal russe en Europe Occidentale, 1960), republished as *La Théologie de l'icône dans l'Église orthodoxe* (Paris: Cerf, 1980)

Papanikolaou, Aristotle, *Being with God. Trinity, Apophaticism and Divine-Human Communion* (Notre Dame, IN: University of Notre Dame Press, 2006)

Peart-Binns, John S., *Ambrose Reeves* (London: Gollancz, 1973)

—— *Maurice Reckitt. A Life* (Basingstoke: Bowerdean Press, 1988).

Phan, Peter C., *Culture and Eschatology. The Iconographical Vision of Paul Evdokimov* (New York: Peter Lang, 1985)

Phillips, C. S., et al., *Walter Howard Frere. A Memoir* (London: Faber & Faber, 1947)

Pinnington, Judith, *Anglicans and Orthodox. Unity and Subversion, 1559–1725* (Leominster: Gracewing, 2003)

Raeff, Marc, *Russia Abroad. A Cultural History of the Russian Emigration, 1919–1939* (New York: Oxford University Press, 1990)

Rouse, Ruth, and Stephen C. Neill (ed.), *A History of the Ecumenical Movement, 1517–1948* (London: SPCK, 1954)

Salter, A. T. John, *The Anglican Papalist. Henry Joy Fynes-Clinton* (London: Anglo-Catholic History Society, 2012)

Spurr, Barry, *'Anglo-Catholic in Religion'. T. S. Eliot and Christianity* (Cambridge: Lutterworth Press, 2010)

Trubetskoy, E. N., *Icons: Theology in Color* (Crestwood, NY: St Vladimir's Seminary Press, 1973)

Wheeler, Robin, *Palmer's Pilgrimage. The Life of William Palmer of Magdalen* (Oxford and New York: Peter Lang, 2006)

Wilkinson, Alan, *The Community of the Resurrection* (London: SCM, 1992)

Williams, Robert C., *Culture in Exile: Russian Emigrés in Germany, 1881–1941* (Ithaca, NY: Cornell University Press, 1972)

Yazykova, Irina, *Hidden and Triumphant. The Underground Struggle to Save Russian Iconography* (Brewster, MA: Paraclete Press, 2010)

Zernov, Nicolas, *The Russian Religious Renaissance of the Twentieth Century* (London: Darton, Longman and Todd, 1963)

—— *Sunset Years. A Russian Pilgrim in the West* (London: Fellowship of St Alban and St Sergius, 1983)

—— and Militza Zernov, *The History of the Fellowship of St Alban and St Sergius. A Historical Memoir* (Oxford: Fellowship of St Alban and St Sergius, 1979)

www.ingramcontent.com/pod-product-compliance
Lightning Source LLC
Chambersburg PA
CBHW030329240426
43661CB00052B/1574